To my father and in memory of my mother

REPRESENTING REVOLUTION IN MILTON AND HIS CONTEMPORARIES

Religion, Politics, and Polemics in Radical Puritanism

DAVID LOEWENSTEIN

Department of English,
University of Wisconsin-Madison

CAMBRIDGE
UNIVERSITY PRESS

PUBLISHED BY THE PRESS SYNDICATE OF THE UNIVERSITY OF CAMBRIDGE
The Pitt Building, Trumpington Street, Cambridge, United Kingdom

CAMBRIDGE UNIVERSITY PRESS
The Edinburgh Building, Cambridge CB2 2RU, UK
40 West 20th Street, New York, NY 10011–4211, USA
10 Stamford Road, Oakleigh, Melbourne 3166, Australia
Ruiz de Alarcón 13, 28014 Madrid, Spain
Dock House, The Waterfront, Cape Town 8001, South Africa

http://www.cambridge.org

First published 2001

Printed in the United Kingdom at the University Press, Cambridge

Typeface Monotype Baskerville 11/12.5 pt   *System* QuarkXPress™   [SE]

A catalogue record for this book is available from the British Library

Library of Congress Cataloguing in Publication data

ISBN 0 521 77032 7 hardback

Contents

vii

Contents

Acknowledgements

My research and writing were supported by the generosity of the John Simon Guggenheim Memorial Foundation, the University of Wisconsin-Madison Graduate School, the University of Wisconsin Institute for Research in the Humanities, the American Philosophical Society, and the National Endowment for the Humanities.

I wish to thank numerous friends and colleagues who offered advice, encouragement, or shared materials as this book developed: Sharon Achinstein, Norman Burns, Thomas Corns, Robin Grey, Christopher Hill, Laura Lunger Knoppers, Michael Lieb, Janel Mueller, David Norbrook, Joad Raymond, Regina Schwartz, Nigel Smith, and James Grantham Turner. On many stimulating occasions, Norman Burns shared with me his extensive knowledge of radical spiritualism and writing in seventeenth-century England. At a crucial point, Regina Schwartz helped me to rethink the book's structure. Thomas Corns and Stephen Fallon offered trenchant critiques of a number of the book's chapters. At the University of Wisconsin-Madison, I benefited from the advice of and discussions with a number of colleagues: Heather Dubrow, Howard Weinbrot, and Andrew Weiner. I am grateful as well to several diligent research assistants: Paul Acosta, David Ainsworth, Jean Merrill, and Susannah Brietz Monta. Two anonymous readers for Cambridge University Press provided helpful, detailed reports on the manuscript which prompted me to sharpen a number of key points and arguments. I also wish to thank Josie Dixon, Ray Ryan, and Rachel De Wachter of Cambridge University Press for their expert editorial advice and assistance. For copy-editing the book with efficiency and care, I am grateful to Philippa Youngman. I completed the final revisions of the book while I was an Overseas Fellow of Churchill College, Cambridge: I thank Matthew Kramer, as well as the Master and Fellows, for providing a particularly congenial and stimulating academic home-away-from-home. Finally, my wife Jennifer made numerous valuable comments on matters of style and content; her good judgment and lively sense of humor usually prevented my "black cloud," as she is fond of calling it, from growing too large.

I also want to thank the librarians and staff of the Cambridge University Library, the Bodleian Library, the Worcester College Library (Oxford), the Library of the Society of Friends (London), the British Library, the Newberry Library, the Huntington Library, and the Memorial Library of the University of Wisconsin-Madison.

Parts of the book have been published in earlier and different forms. Material from Chapter 2 was published in *English Renaissance Prose: History, Language, and Politics*, ed. Neil Rhodes (Tempe, AZ, 1997), pp. 227–46. An earlier version of Chapter 4 was published as "The War of the Lamb: George Fox and the Apocalyptic Discourse of Revolutionary Quakerism," *Prose Studies: History, Theory, Criticism*, 17, 3 (1994), 25–41. Material from "'An Ambiguous Monster': Representing Rebellion in Milton's Polemics and *Paradise Lost*," *Huntington Library Quarterly*, 55 (1992), 295–315, has been reworked and used in Chapters 6 and 7. An earlier version of Chapter 8 was published as "The Kingdom Within: Radical Religious Culture and the Politics of *Paradise Regained*," *Literature and History*, 3rd series, 3, 2 (1994), 63–89. An earlier version of Chapter 9 was published as "The Revenge of the Saint: Radical Religion and Politics in *Samson Agonistes*," *Milton Studies* 33: *The Miltonic Samson*, ed. Albert C. Labriola and Michael Lieb (Pittsburgh, 1996), pp. 159–80. I am grateful for permission to draw upon these materials here.

Note on abbreviations and citations

I use the following abbreviations and editions throughout this book. Milton's poetry is quoted from *John Milton: Complete Poetry and Major Prose*, ed. Merritt Y. Hughes (New York, 1957). Marvell's poetry is quoted from *The Poems and Letters of Andrew Marvell*, ed. H. M. Margoliouth, 3rd edn., rev. Pierre Legious with E. E. Duncan-Jones, 2 vols. (Oxford, 1971). Where a work is named and discussed at length in the text, page or line references are given parenthetically in the text. Biblical citations are from the Authorized (King James) Version.

I have modernized i/j and u/v in titles and quotations, but have left the original spelling and punctuation unchanged; in the case of a few Lilburne texts, however, I have quietly modified awkward punctuation. Dates are given old style, but with the year taken to begin on 1 January.

Acts and Ordinances	*Acts and Ordinances of the Interregnum, 1642–1660*, ed. C. H. Firth and R. S. Rait, 3 vols. (London, 1911)
CJ	*The Journals of the House of Commons*
Clarendon, *History*	Edward Hyde, Earl of Clarendon, *History of the Rebellion and Civil Wars in England*, ed. W. D. Macray, 6 vols. (Oxford, 1888)
Constitutional Documents	*The Constitutional Documents of the Puritan Revolution*, ed. S. R. Gardiner, 3rd edn. (Oxford, 1906)
Corns, *Uncloistered Virtue*	Thomas N. Corns, *Uncloistered Virtue: English Political Literature, 1640–1660* (Oxford, 1992)
CPW	*The Complete Prose Works of John Milton*, Don M. Wolfe et al., 8 vols. (New Haven, 1953–82)

Cromwell, *Writings and Speeches*	*The Writings and Speeches of Oliver Cromwell*, ed. W. C. Abbott, 4 vols. (Cambridge, MA, 1937–47)
EHR	*English Historical Review*
ELH	*English Literary History*
ELR	*English Literary Renaissance*
Fox, *Journal*	*Journal of George Fox*, ed. John L. Nickalls (1952; repr. London, 1975)
Hill, *WTUD*	Christopher Hill, *The World Turned Upside Down: Radical Ideas during the English Revolution* (Harmondsworth, 1975 [1972])
HJ	*The Historical Journal*
HLQ	*Huntington Library Quarterly*
JBS	*Journal of British Studies*
JEH	*Journal of Ecclesiastical History*
JFHS	*Journal of the Friends Historical Society*
JHI	*Journal of the History of Ideas*
JRH	*Journal of Religious History*
Life Records	*The Life Records of John Milton*, ed. J. Milton French, 5 vols. (New Brunswick, 1949–58)
MQ	*Milton Quarterly*
MS	*Milton Studies*
Norbrook, *English Republic*	David Norbrook, *Writing the English Republic: Poetry, Rhetoric, and Politics, 1627–1660* (Cambridge, 1999)
P&P	*Past and Present*
Pride's Purge	David Underdown, *Pride's Purge: Politics in the Puritan Revolution* (Oxford, 1971)
Puritanism and Liberty	*Puritanism and Liberty: Being the Army Debates (1647–49) from the Clarke Manuscripts*, ed. A. S. P. Woodhouse, 3rd edn. (London, 1986)
Radical Religion	J. F. McGregor and B. Reay (eds.), *Radical Religion in the English Revolution* (Oxford, 1984)
Ranter Writings	*A Collection of Ranter Writings from the*

	17th Century, ed. Nigel Smith (London, 1983)
SC	*The Seventeenth Century*
SEL	*Studies in English Literature, 1500–1900*
Smith, *Perfection Proclaimed*	Nigel Smith, *Perfection Proclaimed: Language and Literature in English Radical Religion, 1640–1660* (Oxford, 1989)
Stuart Constitution	*The Stuart Constitution, 1603–1688: Documents and Commentary*, ed. J. P. Kenyon, 2nd edn. (Cambridge, 1986)
Tracts on Liberty	*Tracts on Liberty in the Puritan Revolution, 1638–1647*, ed. William Haller, 3 vols. (New York, 1934)
Walwyn	*The Writings of William Walwyn*, ed. Jack R. McMichael and Barbara Taft (Athens, GA, 1989)
Winstanley, *Works*	*The Works of Gerrard Winstanley*, ed. George H. Sabine (Ithaca, NY, 1941)
Woolrych, *Commonwealth*	Austin Woolrych, *Commonwealth to Protectorate* (Oxford, 1982)
Worden, *Rump Parliament*	Blair Worden, *The Rump Parliament, 1648–1653* (Cambridge, 1974)

Introduction

In the spring of 1649, a month after the monarchy was abolished, Gerrard Winstanley and the Diggers could describe "the old World . . . running up like parchment in the fire, and wearing away."[1] The exhilaration expressed by that vivid image of an old order rapidly consumed and expiring was also sharply qualified in their visionary writings by a darker sense of the English Revolution's unresolved contradictions as they perceived new forms of menacing power and vested interests in the Republic. This book examines the ways canonical and noncanonical writers of mid-seventeenth-century England attempted to represent the unsettling, dramatic processes of political, religious, and social revolution. It considers how their literary representations of revolution and rebellion attempted to probe or promote religious ideologies, shape political perceptions, purify and purge the nation, challenge the power of worldly regimes, and contest institutionalized ecclesiastical authorities. And it examines how a wide range of revolutionary and radical Puritan writers struggled with the crises, contradictions, and ambiguities of the English Revolution.

This cross-disciplinary study therefore explores the interactions of literature, polemics, and religious politics in the Revolution and its diverse culture of radical Puritanism. Part I examines polemical and visionary writings by some of Milton's most notable radical Puritan contemporaries, beginning with John Lilburne and Gerrard Winstanley; as these writers vigorously challenged the authority of the political regimes and the religious and economic institutions of the 1640s and 1650s, they acutely analyzed the ambiguities and contradictions of the English Revolution, including its conservative and counter-revolutionary trends. The studies in Part I often portray a dark, faction-riven, and violent seventeenth-century revolutionary culture whose unresolved religious and political tensions Marvell would attempt to address during the Protectorate (see Chapter 5). In Part II, I turn to Milton's polemical responses during the crises of 1649 as he confronted (along with William Dell, John Goodwin, and other godly republicans) the faction-riven, counter-revolutionary politics of the Presbyterians, as well as the ambiguous politics of the Irish Rebellion, one of the most troubling religious conflicts of the revolutionary years. The book's final three chapters build on previous ones to highlight interconnections between politics and radical Puritan polemics in Milton's great poems. The concluding two chapters thus reconsider the double-edged way in which Milton's political and religious radicalism expressed itself after the Interregnum and during the Restoration. By provocatively juxtaposing his austere spiritual epic, *Paradise Regained*, with his drama of holy revenge, *Samson Agonistes*, Milton was able to present in one poetic volume divergent representations of radical sainthood. The three chapters on Milton's great poems all emphasize intersections between radical Puritan politics and spirituality during both the Revolution and the Restoration, thereby suggesting greater continuities between pre- and post-1660 radical Puritan politics, polemics, and poetry.

The study of writing in the English Revolution has become an increasingly lively and significant field, complicating and enriching our understanding of the politics of literature in early modern England. Valuable recent scholarship is helping to "politicize and historicize" the literature of the English revolutionary period, and "to return to [its] texts the political potency they once possessed."[2] Such work is particularly welcome because literary historians have continued to devote much more critical attention to reexamining the relations between politics, literary culture, and symbolic representation in the Elizabethan and early Stuart periods. Unlike scholars in the field of history, literary historians are only now beginning to consider many of the political texts of the English Revolution, especially those produced during the Republic and Protectorate, and to find fresh ways of evaluating the interconnections between their aesthetics and politics.[3] Nevertheless, we still require more integrated studies which address, rather than ignore, powerful religious ideologies and beliefs in relation to the political literature of the Revolution. More than most recent accounts of politics and aesthetics in the period, this book emphasizes the religious politics of revolutionary radicalism and the remarkable writings it generated. I explore the ways in which these writings represented the Revolution's intense ideological and religious conflicts and the ways in which their authors struggled with its contradictions and inconsistencies.[4]

Regrettably the newer historical criticism has not always adequately addressed the complex interactions between religion and politics in early modern England. It has, until recently, too often ignored religion as a major ideological and cultural force; or it has viewed it primarily as a front for power in the public and political spheres.[5] My study of literature, revolution, and radical Puritan politics stresses the crucial roles of religious discourses and beliefs, especially heterodox ones which alarmed the orthodox godly. Milton the polemicist himself perceived that religious and civil liberty were "two things God hath inseparably knit together" (*CPW* 1:923–24); conversely he observed, in sinister language resembling Winstanley's, how "the very dark roots" of "Tyranny and fals Religion . . . twine and interweave one another in the Earth" (3:509). After the shattering of the Church, the destruction of the monarchy, and the abolition of the House of Lords – the dramatic overthrow of ungodly forces – Winstanley grimly perceived how clergy and kingly powers, as he called them, were still darkly intertwined in the new Commonwealth and perpetuating sharp class conflicts. This book examines the polemical literary responses of radical Puritan writers to the interactions between religious institutions and civil power during the convulsions of the Revolution.

Because religion was so deeply interwoven with politics, some recent historians have suggested that the mid-seventeenth-century crisis was nothing less than "England's Wars of Religion."[6] In an age when a good religious cause was rarely able to "sustaine it selfe upon a temperate dispute" (to quote Sir Thomas Browne), cultural conflicts over ceremonial issues were intense, and we now have a substantial account of their literary implications.[7] Moreover, there is little doubt that religious contention and the urge for more godly reformation fueled revolution during the 1640s and 1650s. Religion itself was an inflammatory ideological force that helped to impel events in a radical direction: so contemporary commentators as diverse as Baxter, Hobbes, Clarendon, and Hugh Peter recognized.[8] Explaining the forces which corrupted the people during the 1640s and 1650s in terms of various "seducers," Hobbes himself deplored radical religious ferment, including the new freedom to interpret scriptural texts, as inciters of revolution: "this license of interpreting the Scripture," one of the interlocutors famously observed in *Behemoth*, "was the cause of so many sects, as have lain hid till the beginning of the late King's reign, and did then appear to the disturbance of the commonwealth."[9] As Peter the New Model Army chaplain observed at the finest Whitehall debate about freedom of conscience, "you will find that [religion is the cause of] those contests that have been in the kingdom"; it had, in the words of another radical preacher, "kindle[d] . . . such unnatural heats, as are now stirring almost every where."[10] The crisis in Puritan culture and politics during the mid-seventeenth-century in England may have caused separatists and radical sectarians to "subdivide and mince themselves almost into Atomes," as the conservative Browne observed with playful mockery.[11] But it also stimulated some of the period's richest radical religious writings, and this book studies, especially in Part I, how their visionary and polemical authors fomented revolution, escalated political and religious tensions, and probed the ambiguities of the period's regimes.

Exciting recent work on mid-seventeenth-century republican literary culture and aesthetics has also reassessed the interconnections between literature and politics.[12] Nevertheless, this important work offers a largely secular account of the period's literature, including Milton's anti-monarchical politics and writings, by reconsidering them principally in the context of the classical republican tradition – the sort of intellectual political discourse that would have appealed to a cultured radical like Milton. The aim of the present book is not to dispute the major contributions in this area, for they confirm more thoroughly than ever Aubrey's observation that Milton's antimonarchicalism was sharpened by his "being so conversant in Livy and the Roman authors and the greatnes he saw done by the Roman commonwealth."[13] Still, we now need to look for ways to bring together the republican and radical spiritual dimensions of Milton's writings. The emphasis of this book therefore differs crucially from studies focused primarily on the secular republicanism of Milton and his contemporaries.[14] It considers instead (particularly in the last three chapters) how the religious politics of his great poems contribute to their polemical edge. It also highlights the role of powerful spiritual beliefs and religious ideologies in the polemical struggles of Milton's radical Puritan contemporaries during the crises of the revolutionary years and their aftermath.

Radical political and religious groups preoccupied Milton's contemporaries and have often preoccupied historians of early modern England; nevertheless, literary scholars are only now beginning to analyze the texture of their writings in the kind of detail and with the sustained attention traditionally conferred on more canonical literary works.[15] There are, for example, relatively few literary studies concerned with the vast numbers of revolutionary Quaker texts and I have therefore chosen to examine, in a sustained fashion, some of the most powerful millenarian writings by George Fox (see Chapter 4). Remarkably prolific writers from the time they emerged as a charismatic sect in the early 1650s, Fox and early Quaker prophets vigorously reinterpreted the apocalyptic myth of the Lamb's War as an allegory of the Revolution's political, religious, and social conflicts. I likewise provide a sustained discussion of the radical religious politics of Winstanley's writings and their figurative qualities (ranging from his early pre-communist works to his final utopian tract, *The Law of Freedom*): their striking, idiosyncratic revisions of scriptural myths represent in vigorous prose the unresolved contradictions of the Commonwealth which failed to ease the grievances of the poor while enabling darker kingly powers to flourish. Radical perspectives on religious toleration, political freedom, and economic and social reform were thus vividly expressed by writers articulating the often unrecorded beliefs and aspirations of ordinary men and women – voices (including the "middling sort") normally outside the political nation and not part of the dominant culture.[16] Hence I devote considerable attention in Part I to the polemical language, rhetorical density, and powerful myths of the dramatic, intensely disputatious revolutionary writings by radical sectarian authors.

Radical religion and sectarianism were closely linked by orthodox contemporaries and conservative Puritans with political and social revolution, especially as the authority of church and Scripture were replaced by the authority of the inner light or impulses of the Spirit, and as freedom of individual conscience became a major issue (particularly during the Interregnum). The subversive religious, political, and social implications of "submitting unto that light which is lighted in us by [God's] Spirit" is the subject of a number of this book's chapters.[17] Many radical Puritans believed that the age of the Spirit was at hand: the powers of Antichrist would imminently fall and King Jesus would reign. Part I therefore considers compelling examples of the literature of the "Spirit within," when some men and women chose to follow their own individual consciences rather than the dictates of churches and ministers; and when some exalted the light of the indwelling God above the written word of Scripture itself. Hence I emphasize the radical spiritualism infusing Winstanley's communist agrarian writings, the fierce millenarianism of early Quaker discourse and its ideology of the light within, and the radical spiritual visions of Ranter and Fifth Monarchist prophets who sharply challenged political conservatism and religious orthodoxies during the Republic and Protectorate. Moreover, later in the book, I examine how profoundly the radical religious politics of the Spirit inform Milton's 1671 poems through the spiritual inwardness and sharp

polemical responses of Jesus in the wilderness and through the holy violence and militant apocalypticism of Samson in the temple of Dagon.

The religious politics of the Spirit alarmed the orthodox godly, fueling
their polemical war against the growth of sectarianism. Deeply anxious
about religious division, the frenetic heresiographer Thomas Edwards
passionately upheld social and constitutional conservatism, envisioning
radical sectarianism as a massive gangrene plaguing the body politic. In
the third part of *Gangraena* (December 1646) he specifically linked sectarianism with political revolution as he warned of the anarchic dangers of
sectarian writing and preaching, including the emergence of Leveller
politics and books, in an unstable age that was witnessing the frightening disintegration of Puritanism and the Church of England:

> The Reader shall find in this Booke the Sectaries Designe and Practise, not to
> be only corrupting Religion . . . but to be against Magistracy and Civill
> Government, their designe of opposing settled Goverment, and bringing an
> Anarchy and confusion into Church and State . . . they have *in Terminis* in divers
> Pamphlets and some Sermons declared against Monarchie and Aristocracie,
> and for Democracie they have expressed themselves in such a manner concern-
> ing that, that they make it noe other then an Anarchie, making all alike, con-
> founding of all rancks and order, reducing all to Adams time and condition.[18]

Revolution was thus stimulated by sectarian ferment and was additionally fueled by the radical development of Protestant eschatology during
the 1640s and 1650s, when millenarian enthusiasm, including popular
manifestations, was especially widespread in the writings and beliefs of
the age.[19] Religion in the form of zealous Protestantism not only incited
civil war due to fears of popish innovations, counter-reforming policies,
and the menacing Irish Rebellion: in its more radical manifestations, it
stimulated the deposition and execution of the king, as well as the belief
that he would be succeeded by King Jesus and the rule of the saints on
earth. Sectarian excesses and millenarian fervor fed increasing anxieties
about religious division; thus the moderate Puritan minister Richard
Baxter yearned for the day when religious factions would "be swallowed
up in Unity."[20] Even Cromwell, a man often torn between conservative
social and radical Puritan impulses, was anxious about the "many" in
the Interregnum who had "apostatized" and justified themselves "under
the notion of Liberty," and "instead of contending for the Faith, . . . con-
tended against Magistracy, against *Ministery*, against *Scriptures*, and
against *Ordinances*."[21]

Anxiety about rebellion was acute in these unsettled decades; godliness, particularly if it smacked of sectarianism, was often seen as "a

Cloak for Rebellion, and Religion a pretence for Treason."[22] Milton's contemporaries, after all, were constantly reminded of the importance of obedience and social hierarchy since they had been sanctioned by nature and God, custom and tradition. In making their case against resistance (even against bad kings) and the disruption of order and sub-ordination, orthodox writers regularly cited scriptural texts such as Romans 13:1–2 and I Peter 2:13, and echoed well-known Tudor homilies on *Obedience* (1547) and *Rebellion* (1571), while Anglican catechisms likewise stressed the importance of obedience and reminded subjects that rebel-lion was the worst of all sins and the epitome of all evils.[23] Even William Prynne, viciously punished by Laudian authorities for seditious writing against the king, queen, and Arminian clergy, would later defend the rights of the king, the Lords, and the Presbyterian church by citing and elaborating upon Paul's serious admonition, "Let every soul be subject to the higher powers. For there is no power but of God: the powers that be are ordained of God. Whosoever therefore resisteth . . . the power, resisteth (oppugneth, abolisheth) THE ORDINANCE OF GOD: and they that resist . . . shall receive to themselves DAMNATION."[24] Such crucial biblical texts became the subject of intense hermeneutic debate in the period, so that Milton himself would carefully scrutinize these scriptural supports for political submission in *The Tenure* and else-where, stressing instead (regarding I Peter 2) that the "Kingdom and Magistracy, whether supreme or subordinat, is . . . call'd *a human ordi-nance*" which we are to submit to "*as free men*" (*CPW* 3:209–10; echoing I Peter 2:16).[25] In Milton's view, it was a matter of "every kind of human ordinance which can legitimately be obeyed," so that "we are freed from the judgments of men, and especially from coercion and legislation in religious matters" (*De Doctrina Christiana, CPW* 6:800, 537–38). Since "any civil power unaccountable" was no more than "an Ordinance of man," then "how can we submit," Milton wondered in *The Tenure*, "as free men?" With little faith in human ordinances, this radical Puritan's aim was to shake the authority of orthodox political and religious interpre-tations of such frequently cited scriptural texts.

Despite the profound fears of rebellion and subversion in the culture of early modern England and the yearning to maintain social order, many well-known institutions and landmarks of the old order collapsed during the revolutionary decades, stimulating the fragmentation of zealous Protestant culture and the proliferation of radical sects and movements. In less than a decade there occurred the breakdown of the traditional bulwarks of church and state, including the hated prerogative institutions that supported their power: the Star Chamber, the Court of High Commission, the Councils of Wales and the North were abolished before the end of 1641; episcopacy and ecclesiastical courts were abolished in 1646; the House of Lords was abolished three years later; the Earl of Strafford (1641) and Archbishop Laud (1645) were impeached, tried, and executed; the king was tried and executed in 1649 and the monarchy abolished, so that many people believed that these were the upheavals prophesied in Scripture to herald the world's transformation or end. The battle for a comprehensive (though reformed) national church was lost; and the vision of an ordered, unified, godly community was challenged by sectarian and radical groups who generated fears of moral chaos and confusion. Indeed, Puritanism itself harbored contradictory impulses: its tendencies towards liberty of conscience and towards discipline, towards spiritual individualism and towards building a godly community.[26] During the upheavals of the English Revolution, radical Puritanism, social hierarchy, and moderate constitutionalism often proved incompatible, fueling dangerous political and religious tensions expressed in the polemical writings of the age (one of the themes of Chapter 5).

During the Interregnum, radical religious writings poured forth from the presses and continued to threaten social hierarchies, order, and customs, while also challenging the authority of its experimental regimes that governed for, but not necessarily by the will of, the people.[27] Some of the most radical writers (e.g. Lilburne and Winstanley) acutely perceived an unresolved conflict between political and social revolution after the coup d'etat of 1648–49 resulted in "a Commonwealth and Free State" (May 1649) dedicated to the notion that all just power derives from the people and was to be exercised by their chosen representatives.[28] This book examines how radical visionary writers exposed ambivalent trends within the Revolution, including tensions between political conservatism and religious radicalism, and between radical social change and a society organized along traditional lines. Such tensions stimulated their literary creativity as they produced their daring polemical and religious writings. The discussion of Marvell, immediately following the chapters on radical religious writers in Part I, examines how this most skillful of polemical poets attempted to confront the fierce sectarian challenges during the Protectorate when radical saints gave apocalyptic discourse a dangerously militant edge by contesting the authority of an experimental regime uneasily combining godly rule with a quasi-regal style. I thus consider how Marvell attempts to negotiate the unresolved tension between radical millenarian Puritanism and moderate godly reform.

During the "confusions and revolutions" of the mid-seventeenth century,[29] moreover, Milton's radical Puritan contemporaries were beginning to register a more modern political sense of revolution as a dramatic, violent break in historical continuity. The term "revolution" was poised between older and newer meanings: it could refer to the original astronomical sense of a circular movement in space or time, but it was acquiring the more modern sense of a radical alteration and unidirectional political change involving a "revolt" against an established order, regime, or the social structure.[30] Preaching before the House of Commons in October 1648, just before the Revolution's most traumatic events, Matthew Barker spoke of "the great *revolutions* of States and Kingdoms" as "but Answers to the prayers of Saints" and then observed "the Lord knows what revolutions and changes we may see before your next monthly Fast."[31] The Fifth Monarchist Christopher Feake recalled the older sense, while gesturing toward the new, when he told saintly readers of Mary Cary's *The Little Horns Doom* (1651), a rich apocalyptic account of the upheavals, that they "shalt in due time, behold, with a mixture of joy and wonder, those other grand Mutations, and extraordinary Revolutions, which are even at the door, and ready to break in upon the *Princes* and upon the *People* of the whole earth."[32] Cromwell himself brought together the old and new senses when, in his fiery millenarian speech to the Nominated Parliament (4 July 1653), he referred to Pride's Purge, the downfall of the king and the Lords, and the establishment of the Commonwealth as "this revolution of affairs."[33] In language that equated revolution with a traumatic political overturning and a vital transformation of society, the Quaker prophet Edward Burrough could write that "many memorable revolutions hath come to pass in this last age, even in cutting down one power and authority of oppressions after another, till many great mountains [are] removed, and the Nations levelled."[34] Indeed, contemporaries could use intensely dramatic language to express their sense of living through an age of unprecedented upheaval, as well as the exultation and fears it produced: people were now witnessing "great and mighty *Changes*" wrought by God; this was an age of "dreadfull *providentiall alterations*" in which the coming of Christ would be attended "with the most astonishing . . . desolations," so that nations which had "given their power to the *Dragon* and the Beast" would be "broken, translated, and turned off their old foundations"; these were "*shaking and trying times*" in which the godly would need to be "firme and resolved" or they would "scarce be able to stand."[35] A number of chapters in this book explore how such dramatic language was reinvigorated in the apocalyptic revolutionary writings of Milton's radical Puritan contemporaries, and how it then found particularly powerful, disturbing literary expression in the dreadful holy destruction dramatized in *Samson Agonistes*.

In attempting to illuminate the variety and literary complexity of revolutionary Puritan writers, this study emphasizes their distinctive polemical voices as they struggled with the unresolved conflicts of the mid-seventeenth century.[36] Thus, for example, Winstanley's social and spiritual radicalism clearly differs in important ways from Lilburne's (who, unlike the Digger, links "liberty and propriety"), and this has significant implications for their differing literary responses to the ambiguities of the Revolution and the Republic. Yet for all their differences, some of the writers considered in this book do share notable connections or perspectives through radical religious culture: Milton himself was closely connected with the Quakers in the early Restoration (though he never joined a gathered church); Lilburne converted to Quakerism at the end of his career; the communist visionary Winstanley, whose prophecies of social levelling are prompted by the Spirit, also probably converted to Quakerism in the Restoration; the Ranter Coppe distinguished his ecstatic levelling rhetoric from "digging-levelling" (and, conversely, the Digger writer rejected the antinomian excesses of Ranterism), yet his daring communist social vision is at times close to Winstanley's. Milton was obviously not a social radical in the sense that Winstanley, Coppe, or Fox were; moreover, the exceptional range of his learning and literary references clearly distinguishes him from them and accounts for the recent tendency to situate his politics after the early 1640s in the context of classical republican thought.[37] Still, his spiritual radicalism, I will argue, deserves comparison with these and other religious radical writers and helps to explain the daring partisan and polemical dimensions of his great poems.

Yet while his connections with the Quakers are indisputable and deserve more thorough consideration (an issue addressed in Chapter 8), Milton, at moments of acute political and religious tension, tends not to mention by name radical groups and sectarians and invoke them as authorities in his writings – a strategy whereby he maintains his own polemical authority and independence as a writer.[38] To be sure, there are exceptions to this observation: in the antiprelatical prose he deplores the "mist of names" applied to the proliferating sects and, in a provocative statement that could hardly have pleased his Presbyterian allies, urges the English people to "look quite through this fraudulent aspersion of a disgracefull name into the things themselves: knowing that the Primitive Christians in their times were accounted such as are now call'd Familists and Adamites, or worse" (*The Reason of Church-Government, CPW* 1:788). Yet had Milton, during the crisis of 1649, cited the Levellers favorably and by name in *The Tenure*, where his arguments are often close to theirs (e.g. that the power of kings and magistrates are derived from the people in whom it remains fundamentally), he might well have never been invited to serve a regime which immediately ordered him (in late March) to refute Lilburne's seditious writings against the new Republic and then notoriously suppressed this radical movement less than two months later at Burford.[39] Instead, Milton remained silent – refusing to use his pen against the agitating Levellers at a moment when more radical and con-servative forces were clashing and defining the Revolution's limitations. (Conversely, Lilburne, we shall see in Chapter 1, did not hesitate to cite Milton the republican author as a polemical ally when he wished to expose the Republic's ambiguities.) Or, to take a later example, we might note how closely Milton's radical spiritual concerns in his twinned texts, *A Treatise of Civil Power* and *The Likeliest Means to Remove Hirelings* (February and August 1659), resemble Quaker ones: his attack on compulsory tithes, his emphasis on the inward persuasive motions of the Spirit, and his deep mistrust of institutional political and ecclesiastical authorities in relation to spiritual matters, including his fierce opposition to any public provision for a preaching ministry. Yet Milton never invokes the Quakers, who were pugnacious and militant during 1659, as polemical allies. His radical religious politics often resemble those of radical groups and sectarians; yet at times he insists upon his polemical and authorial independence from them.[40]

Consequently, we need not agree with Christopher Hill that Milton was always in direct dialogue with sectarian contemporaries and fringe groups in order to illuminate connections between the poet's radical spiritual convictions and theirs. To be sure, one cannot imagine that the highly cultured Milton, immersed in the classical republican tradition, would have sympathized with Fox's coarse, humorless prophetic railing against academic learning and the universities (despite Jesus's sweeping critique of Athenian culture and learning in *Paradise Regained*). Nevertheless, Fox's fierce anticlericalism (including his hatred of a uni-versity-educated ministry),[41] his emphasis on the power and impulses of the Spirit, his anti-Trinitarianism, and his longing for the Good Old

Cause remind us that there are also similarities between these two visionary writers, however significantly they differ in temperament, education,
and literary achievements. As we shall see, Fox's terrifying God of wrath
bears comparison with the dreadful God of wrath and holy vengeance
in *Samson Agonistes*. Moreover, a revolutionary sect like the Quakers illustrates that we should in any case be wary about insisting upon firm divisions between popular and elite culture in this period. Many Quakers
came from the middling and lower ranks of society, but two of the early
Quakers with whom Milton developed close connections – his student
Thomas Ellwood and Isaac Penington the younger – were well educated
(the latter at Cambridge University) and cultured gentlemen. Milton
himself may not have had direct contact with such fiery Quaker prophets and charismatic leaders as George Fox, Edward Burrough, or James
Nayler; yet Ellwood and Penington certainly did.[42]

Written from the perspective of a literary historian, this book focuses
on aesthetic and symbolic expressions of religious politics in revolutionary texts. It often analyzes contemporary discourses assumed by scholars to be less literary or aesthetic – political pamphlets and manifestoes,
parliamentary sermons and speeches, radical religious tracts, historical
narratives of the Revolution, and (in a few cases) manuscript sources by
or concerning sectarians. Its critical/historical readings consequently
push beyond a history-of-ideas approach. In *The Experience of Defeat*,
Christopher Hill has given us a moving account of the ways in which
radical intellectuals and writers struggled with the failure of the
Revolution, but unlike my more literary-oriented study, "[his] book deals
with ideas."[43] Indeed, I aim to illuminate the literary texture of revolutionary political and religious writings as their visionary authors
responded polemically to the crises and ambiguities of the 1640s and
1650s and their aftermath. Focusing on the literature of revolution and
radical Puritan politics, I pay close attention to its vigorous language, its
figurative and rhetorical features, and its arresting reinvigoration of
visionary scriptural texts.

My study has been stimulated by the recent historicist emphasis on
the dynamic interactions between literary texts and sociopolitical contexts in early modern England. Yet my work also challenges the newer
historical view (originally influenced by the work of Foucault or Louis
Althusser) that in Renaissance and seventeenth-century England individual human identity, agency, and political actions – even oppositional
ones – were often controlled, formed, and constrained by impersonal
historical forces, as well as by social institutions and authorities.[44] In the

English Revolution heterodox and radical voices were not always easily contained, and masses of people outside the normal political sphere became actively involved in politics and religious controversy. Writers, including new kinds of radical authors, did not passively articulate revolutionary discourses, but gave them fresh political and polemical expression: writing in "a Nation so pliant" (*CPW* 2:554) as revolutionary England (as Milton put it in *Areopagitica*) meant interrogating and refashioning political and religious discourses – not merely reflecting them.[45] Indeed, the extraordinary volume of printed works produced between 1640 and 1660 – as books, polemical pamphlets, sermons, weekly newsbooks, petitions, broadsides poured out from the presses – ensured that a remarkable range of political and religious voices found expression. George Thomason's massive collection of over 22,000 printed works remains a testament to the remarkable vitality of textual production in this wordy Revolution, when politics and religion were interconnected and intensely debated.[46] To be sure, we have notable examples of state and ecclesiastical authorities attempting to suppress subversive pieces of imaginative writing and introduce new censorship.[47] In 1650 the Rump Parliament ordered the burning of the pamphlets of the notorious Ranter Coppe, whose extravagant language and blasphemous texts proclaiming the end of sin and transgression fiercely admonished all earthly powers and assaulted Puritan theological conservatism (see Chapter 3). Yet even in his public recantations Coppe, who suffered imprisonment as a result of his inflammatory writing, never renounced the radical communal vision underpinning his alarming levelling rhetoric. The Levellers, closely connected with the sectarian community, were also decisively defeated by the Army and Rump after the traumatic political events of 1648–49; and yet, though committed to the Tower, their leaders still smuggled out their pamphlets fueling tensions and the war of words in the fragile new Republic. During the Protectorate, the flamboyant visionary Anna Trapnel (also discussed in Chapter 3) was imprisoned for several months for her subversive prophecies made while traveling in the West of England; yet in Whitehall, the very center of power, the Fifth Monarchist delivered in a trance millenarian commentaries and ecstatic verses challenging the new regime of Cromwell while large inquisitive audiences, including members of the aristocracy and prominent politicians, gathered to hear her visionary utterances.

Recent historians of the English Revolution, including David Underdown, Blair Worden, G. E. Aylmer, John Morrill, and Austin

Woolrych, have done much to reassess its achievements and shortcomings, especially during the years when the experimental Republic retreated from its revolutionary origins and when political revolution was not followed by radical social and religious reform.[48] My study, however, examines how acutely radical Puritan writers themselves probed ambivalent trends within the faction-riven Revolution, as they promoted their own daring ideological programs and unorthodox religious beliefs. And it explores, especially in Part I, their fervent polemical responses to the experimental Republic's troubling contradictions (an issue which recent work on the period's classical republicanism has yet to address adequately). Milton's contemporaries could express wonder at the unprecedented events of the Revolution: "was there in any Man's Memory such Changes in Government, and marvellous Transactions in them, as in these our Days?" John Reeve asked.[49] Yet other radical Puritan writers kept confronting the limits of the Revolution as they struggled with the ambiguities of its political institutions and regimes which had promised greater freedoms, fewer delusions, and the demystification of kingly power. "Have you shoke this Nation like an Earthquake," the Leveller writer Richard Overton pugnaciously demanded of the House of Commons in 1646, "to produce no more then this for us: Is it for this, that ye have . . . been so bold with our Persons & Estates?"[50] Radical and heterodox writers in this period of "free writing and free speaking" (as Milton put it in *Areopagitica*, *CPW* 2:559) struggled over what a recent commentator on early modern revolutions has observed: "Revolutions . . . create great debates about freedom but often shrink from establishing it."[51] These writers registered the anxieties, doubts, and fluctuation of hopes generated by unsettling political transformations and religious conflicts when it indeed seemed as though "the old World . . . [was] running up like parchment in the fire."

PART I

Radical Puritanism and polemical responses

CHAPTER ONE

Lilburne, Leveller polemic, and the ambiguities of the Revolution

Among Milton's radical contemporaries perhaps no writer expressed greater conflict with the Revolution and its evolution in the 1640s and 1650s than did the flamboyant and fiery John Lilburne, leader of the Levellers during the Civil War and the Interregnum. Throughout his turbulent career as a writer, from the late 1630s to the mid-1650s, the charismatic and immensely popular radical daringly challenged successive regimes and lamented the uneven course of the Revolution, and was in turn represented by political authorities as seditious, treasonous, and scandalous: he was perceived as an anarchist and leveller of social hierarchies, the state, and the legal system.[1] In an age full of preaching and writing against rebellion and popular tumult – when there was intense fear of "factious, seditious, rebellious disturbers of the publike peace, destroyers of all civill relation, and subordinations" – Lilburne came to symbolize the dangers of seditious behavior and writing against the state, including the Republic, whose dissimulating arts and political rule his polemical works vigorously probed and attempted to expose.[2] Judging from his unsystematic, undisciplined, and often prolix tracts, we may hesitate to regard him as the most gifted or skillful of the Leveller writers, despite his considerable linguistic energy (the urbane and less zealous William Walwyn, for example, is capable of more literary variety, nuance, and wit);[3] nevertheless, he was the central figure in this highly politicized but short-lived popular radical movement, and thus he deserves attention in a book that examines how Milton and his radical Puritan contemporaries responded to the crises and contradictions of the Revolution.

This chapter explores the ways in which Lilburne's polemical writing, to which he often makes self-conscious references, became his means of probing the ambiguous workings of power during the Revolution and proved an essential expression of his restless agency in the midst of its crises. Constituting the left wing of the parliamentary forces in the

English Civil War,[4] the Leveller movement which Lilburne led emerged during a period of political and economic distress caused by the dislocations of war (1646–49), a period, moreover, when there was intense concern over attempts to pursue a political settlement with the king, over the imposition of an oppressive religious system, and over issues of popular sovereignty and executive power. The act of writing became especially crucial to Lilburne's relentless, often dramatic struggles against monarchy, the aristocracy, the Lords, the state church, the tyranny of the legal system, the unchecked monopolies of mercantile powers, and a series of changing regimes. As an advocate of revolution, Lilburne turned out to be one of the Revolution's sharpest, most potent critics. Every regime he lived under became the target of his criticisms and polemics; however impolitic or idealistic we may judge his uncompromising behavior to be, his contentious writings show that he acutely perceived that politics is about power. This chapter thus particularly considers the ways in which his polemical writings addressed the darker ambiguities of a revolution and Commonwealth which had promised yet painfully failed (so it seemed to Lilburne and the Levellers) to make the people themselves the supreme authority and "the original of all just Powers."[5]

"A TURBULENT SPIRIT": WRITING, REBELLION, AND AGENCY

Presenting himself as a tireless campaigner for his country's liberties and "a free-man of England,"[6] Lilburne would nevertheless find himself imprisoned by the Long Parliament, the Republic, and Cromwell's Protectorate. As a fiery young writer and radical, he had already been tried and sentenced by the Court of Star Chamber for printing in Holland and distributing in England seditious pamphlets against the bishops (he was accused of being "one of the notoriousest disperser[s] of Libellous *bookes* that is in the Kingdome"), and, after refusing to take the *ex officio* oath (employed in the prerogative courts to compel Puritan objectors to indict themselves), he consequently suffered savage whipping, the pillory, gagging, and imprisonment.[7] "Free-born John," as he was nicknamed, had thus begun his career as a contentious separatist writer in 1638 when, at the age of twenty-three, he fearlessly attacked the power of the prelates. Inspired as a young writer and political martyr not only by John Foxe's famous book, but also by the militant symbolism and language of the Book of Revelation which explained "the mistery of iniquitie," he determined to "put on couragious resolution like valiant souldiers of *Jesus Christ*, and fight manfullie in this his spirituall battell, in which battell some of his souldiers have already lost part of their blood."[8] Like the zealous Milton and like God, this writer of the Revolution could not "of all things . . . indure *Lukewarmenes*,"[9] and he would go on to produce combative pamphlets written in vigorous defence of himself and his cherished ideals of civil and religious liberty, while attacking what he perceived as treacherous forms of unchecked power in the Civil War and Interregnum regimes.

Lilburne's persecution under the Laudian bishops and during subsequent periods only fueled his combativeness (he was imprisoned seven times altogether): he was captured by the royalists, tried for high treason, and suffered imprisonment at Oxford Castle during 1643; he was arrested no less than three times in 1645 for offenses related to unlicensed printing and then imprisoned for nearly four months; from mid-1646 to late 1647 he was imprisoned in the Tower of London by the House of Lords for libeling the Earl of Manchester; he was then imprisoned in the Tower by the Commons in 1648 for his Leveller activities; in March 1649 the Rump's Council of State incarcerated him and other Leveller leaders for the publication of seditious writing and for suspicion of high treason; and in October 1649 he stood indicted for high treason and underwent a highly dramatic trial in which he challenged the authority of the court, appealed to his jury of fellow citizens, and was finally acquitted. In 1652 he was exiled by an Act of Parliament, though after the Rump's dissolution he returned to England in defiance of that act and brilliantly defended himself so that he was again acquitted of charges of treason to great public acclamation in London.[10] Cromwell's Protectorate, however, could not afford to let this fiery critic and rebel go, and so he spent his final years in prison in Jersey and Dover (1653–57) where he converted to Quakerism when that sect was emerging as an alarming revolutionary movement. Since he himself suffered religious and political persecution, economic disaster, and legal oppression during his career, Lilburne quickly developed a knack for making his personal crises symbolic of a larger political crisis in the English Commonwealth perpetuated by changing regimes, the orthodox clergy, the legal system, monopolizing merchants, and other institutions of power and human authority: "as I am an individual," he asserted in *An Impeachment of High Treason against Oliver Cromwell* (1649), "I am a part of the whole Nation, and if it perish in the eye of reason, I and mine must perish with it."[11]

The persecuted Lilburne often attempted, for polemical reasons, to present himself publicly as "a man of peace and quietnesse,"[12] but his fiercely contentious works hardly confirm this self-representation and tend to confirm instead Lucy Hutchinson's description of him as "a turbulent spirited man that never was quiet in aniething."[13] During his career as a combative writer and personality, he was in any case represented by state and church authorities as "a man of a turbulent spirit," a "denier of God and the Scripture," and one of those "rooters up of Parliaments and disturbers of States and Commonwelthes."[14] However much he and other Levellers resisted the idea that they were levellers of social hierarchies, their opponents feared that they were in fact out to "Levell all mens estates" and "would have no distinction of Orders and Dignities amongst men," thereby leading to "Popular confusion" and "a Chaos."[15] That frenetic Presbyterian defender of social and constitutional conservatism, Thomas Edwards, was especially anxious about religious heterodoxy and considered Lilburne "the great darling of the Sectaries." Like other arch-sectaries plaguing the health of the body politic, Lilburne exhibited "insolent loose ungodly practices" and, by the third part of his massive *Gangraena* (December 1646), Edwards was mounting a vigorous, sustained assault on Leveller books and radical politics, including notions of popular representation and the denial of the existing laws and constitution as among Lilburne's "Anarchicall Principles, destructive to all Civill Government whatsoever."[16] While Lilburne himself recognized that his criticism of the existing social order was never as radical as that of the communist Diggers (the son of a family of gentry, he defended private property), he nevertheless appeared to orthodox Puritans to represent what was most threatening about radical political and religious forces of the Revolution. He seemed like a despiser of government, the aristocracy, and established authorities – one who used his writing as a daring weapon to incite insurrection and the "utter subversion of the said Government."[17]

Although Milton's combative prose writings, written in their "rougher accent," can convey the shrillness of revolutionary polemic, Lilburne's writings are surely among the most contentious produced during this age of upheaval; as his contemporaries noted, his texts often resort to uncompromisingly "harsh language" to make polemical points.[18] Lilburne relished polemical confrontation and his voluminous writings indeed record his many battles with public authorities and institutions. In these confrontations he vigorously asserted his own agency: over the course of his career, he wrote heated polemics attacking the bishops, the Presbyterians and their state church, the mystique of kingship and Charles I, the New Model Army command, both houses of the Long

Parliament and their committees, the House of Commons Speaker, the government of the City of London, and the English legal system. After the Revolution of 1648–49, he vehemently opposed the ambiguous political authority of the new Republic and attempted to expose the dissimulating politics of its leaders and Army officers. His works record his contempt for the judicial power and privilege of the peers in the Long Parliament who attempted to control his agency by making him kneel at their bar – that symbolic act of deference "would be no act of mine" he would insist[19] – or by preventing him from having access to essential writing materials. His writings also record his confrontations with the jailers of England and their prisons, which symbolically represent (as in Digger works) the worst political oppression of a state whose tribunals practice arbitrary methods of trial and punishment and whose penal system remains unreformed; and they vividly record his dramatic confrontation with the Commonwealth's Attorney General and his cunning power.[20] In addition, they record his sharp encounters with the Grandees (as opponents disparagingly called the senior Army officers), notably Cromwell and Henry Ireton, both of whom he represents after the mid-1640s as Satanic, serpentine, and dissimulating, and his angry confrontations with other prominent public figures such as the fiery near-Presbyterian William Prynne, the Earl of Manchester, and the parliamentarian Sir Arthur Haselrig. As Walwyn observed of his highly combative friend, he had dared to oppose himself "against so mighty a streame or torrent of worldly power."[21] Indeed, this sense of defining himself and his polemical role in terms of a series of powerful oppositions was summed up by Lilburne's own condensed description of himself and the Levellers as "Anti-Grandees, Anti-Imposters, Anti-Monopolists, Anti-Apostates, Anti-Arbitrarians, and Anti-[economic] Levellers."[22]

Lilburne's energetic productiveness as a polemical writer was itself evidence of his unrestrained subversiveness and "seditious wayes."[23] As the most popular Leveller leader and propagandist, he would prove to be the highly prolific author of eighty pamphlets, while co-authoring others – works which fueled ideological debate over the nature and uneven course of the Revolution. His contemporaries were struck by his breathless productivity. One complained about the rapid proliferation of Lilburne's quarrelsome works by referring to his "multitude of licentious and abusive Pamphlets" which seemed "continually [to] fly abroad like Atomes in the Air"; and another prominent adversary observed to the tireless Leveller that "without doubt you scarce sleep for studying and writing of books, doe you?"[24] The pugnacious Lilburne, indeed, resolved "never to sit still, so long as he hath a tongue to speake, or a hand to write."[25] Contemporary authorities thus believed that this restless, subversive Leveller was expressing his "wicked and devilish mind and imagination . . . by writing and imprinting" so many scandalous, traitorous, and poisonous books.[26]

Lilburne's writings and verbal combativeness, moreover, were never easily contained by political, judicial, and clerical authorities, as his many self-conscious references to his verbal assertiveness suggest. From the time of his earliest works he calls attention to "the boldness and courage in [his] speech"; and in one text, where he attacks the powerful Presbyterian influence in the Long Parliament, he asserts that "nor by the power of heaven shall my tongue be silent, or my Penne be slack, for the cause of God and this miserable Land."[27] His flair for striking dramatic gestures in the midst of persecution likewise provided the occasion for him to express his sense of the power of writing and reading. During his speech in the pillory in 1638, the young Lilburne not only fearlessly condemned the prelates, but pulled out of his pocket books by the Puritan martyr Bastwick "and threw them among the people" and said, before the authorities gagged him, "There is part of the bookes for which I suffer, take them among you, and read them, and see if you finde any thing in them, against the Law of God, the Law of the Land, the glory of God, the honour of the King or state."[28] Attempts by the Lords in Parliament to constrain Lilburne's verbal expressiveness during the 1640s, moreover, only fueled his vehemence, prompting him to assert himself more fiercely in *An Anatomy of the Lords Tyranny*: "therefore tell them, I will whether they will or no, talk with any man that will talk with me, till they out-strip the Bishops (who gagged me for speaking) in cruelty, by cutting out my tongue, or sowing up my lips."[29] Lilburne's adversaries themselves acknowledged that sedition against the state could operate at a dangerous verbal level, and accused him of employing in his contentious books "scandalous, treacherous, tumultuous and traiterous clauses and words."[30] The newer historical model of subversion and containment in early modern England thus could hardly apply well to a highly contentious revolutionary writer like Lilburne, despite the state's repeated attempts to contain his rebellious gestures and combative works. For Lilburne, who spent much of his active life imprisoned in London, writing, speaking, and symbolic gestures of self-assertion became thoroughly inseparable in his career as Leveller agitator. As a hothouse for the growth of radical ideas, London was the center of ideological debate during the Revolution, as well as the center of Leveller support and literary culture. And so however much successive regimes attempted to silence him, Lilburne continued his controversial activities, while his linguistic energy and powers continued to fuel the intensity of that debate and, in Milton's words, the "hoars disputes" of these years (*CPW* 1:821).

Committed to fashioning a revolutionary literary culture and readership, the Levellers were famous for exploiting techniques of agitation promoted by petition, pamphlet, journalism, party organization, and public demonstration. All these methods, including the Levellers' pioneering use of the unlicensed press, were vigorous ways of asserting political agency and of shaping public discourse, debate, and political perceptions. Writing and print were so crucial to that dynamic process that the Leveller movement was ultimately united around what amounted to the first written constitution or social contract based on inalienable natural rights and emanating from the people who were the supreme power. Striking at the roots of traditional notions of political authority and attempting to restrict the power of Parliament and magistrates, their new revolutionary manifesto for England, *An Agreement of the People*, went through three printed versions (November 1647, December 1648, May 1649), though the cautious Rump Parliament refused to do any more than listen to its preamble.[31] Eager to extend active political rights beyond the elite and financially powerful to the politically dispossessed, Lilburne and his fellow Levellers were thus engaged in issuing a vast outpouring of manifestoes, petitions, pamphlets, and other forms of printed polemic aimed at effecting their bold revolutionary campaign. "By printing and publishing of bookes," Lilburne and the Levellers were helping to create an empowered and informed political readership and attempting "to open the understandings of men, and stirring them up to a timely prevention of that intolerable bondage . . . coming fast upon them."[32] Indeed, women themselves would become a crucial part of that informed political readership as well as Leveller authorship, particularly at moments of great urgency: unable "to keep in [their] compass, to be bounded in the custom of [their] sex," they were thus stirred in late April and early May 1649 to produce their own sharply worded petitions addressed to Parliament as they agitated vigorously on behalf of the imprisoned Lilburne and other Leveller leaders, protested against "the exercise of an arbitrary power," and challenged the limits of the Revolution itself.[33]

Lilburne of course could hardly imagine himself not engaged in

writing, even under the most difficult circumstances; as the imprisoned
Leveller observed in *An Anatomy of the Lords Tyranny*, "it is impossible in a
manner, to keep a man from writing, where he hath light, who by one
meanes or other, will come by Pen, Ink, and Paper."[34] And so the more
Lilburne was attacked for his turbulent spirit, the more insistent he
became in asserting his restless agency through potent verbal means: "is
it not more then high time to speak and stirre, when our just and lawfull
Petitions are not onely rejected, but infamously burned as seditious[?]"[35]
Polemical writing itself thus became one of the most essential forms of
rebellion for "Free-born John" and other leading Levellers. When
attacked by the parliamentarian establishment because of one of his
seditious texts, Lilburne would cling to the printed work as though it
were his very lifeblood: "avowedly I tell you," he characteristically
asserted, "I invented, compiled and writ that booke, and caused it to be
printed and dispersed, and every word in it I will own and avouch to the
death."[36] Confronted by the Republic's Attorney General when imprisoned in the Tower, Lilburne defiantly identified himself with his books,
refusing to retract any of them: "I scorn to deny any Book that ever I
made in my life."[37] Richard Overton likewise sensed the intimate connection between writing and rebellion and was no less protective about
his books: when abusive soldiers came to arrest him in March 1649, he
narrates how he immediately threw his seditious works that lay upon the
table into the beds between the sheets, "the better to shelter the books."[38]
Both Overton and Lilburne sensed that writing was a crucial weapon of
response to the treacheries of unlimited political and judicial power in a
revolution that had gone awry: "If you dally with us, and befoole our
expectations too long," Overton warned the Army in 1647, "we shall
turne our pens, our hearts, and our hands against you."[39] And so when
Lilburne wishes to get back at a parliamentarian adversary, writing is
again the primary means of assault: since "I cannot meddle either with
his body or goods, I will by Gods assistance (seeing I have no other
remedy) pay him with my pen."[40]

Because writing was so important to Lilburne's sense of combative
agency, the deprivation of writing materials could generate a sense of
urgency in the persecuted Leveller. This accounts for his constant insistence on his basic right and privilege to possess "pen, inke, and paper"
(which cannot "justly be denied to the greatest Traytor in *England*") so
that Lilburne can continue his revolutionary campaign through polemical writing and "declare the truth of his cause to the world."[41] Indeed,
as Overton suggested in 1647, both reading and writing were themselves

part of a suppressed birthright of "the free men of England" and crucial to their ability to combat excessive power and encourage its decentralization.[42] Even under the most trying circumstances, Lilburne would exploit that birthright and resist its suppression. The execution of a parliamentary order against him in 1646 is particularly "barbarous and tyrannicall" not only because it separates him from his wife Elizabeth and debars him of his friends, but because it debars him of the liberty of "pen, inke, or paper" for three weeks.[43] Like Milton, who addressed the Lords and Commons of England, insisting that in a revolutionary city and nation there must be "much arguing, much writing, many opinions" (*Areopagitica*, *CPW* 2:554) to promote ideological confrontation, Lilburne senses the vital role of argumentative written discourse as weaponry in fighting the wars of truth to protect the sovereign people's rights, civil liberties, and power – even if that means employing his pen to expose the encroaching treacheries of oligarchical power in the Long Parliament and the Commonwealth of Cromwell.

Lilburne repeatedly presents himself as a daring, godly revolutionary who continues to struggle against new forms of oppression in the same spirit that he had once responded to the call to arms and conducted himself in the Civil War: he defines himself as "a freeman of *England*, who has freely hazarded all, for the recovery of the common Liberty," and he has defended his country's freedom "against all Tyrants in the Kingdome" "by his Words, Deeds and Sufferings."[44] Writing thus became for Lilburne an act of gallantry that replaced the act of fighting on the battlefield, which had made him, during 1642–45, into a lieutenant-colonel of Dragoons in the parliamentary forces (he served under the pro-separatist Puritan Lord Brooke admired by Milton, but left the Army because he would not subscribe to the Solemn League and Covenant). In the past he had fearlessly ventured his life in the field against the king and his party, as Lilburne proudly recalls for his readers;[45] now, with no less urgency and sense of chivalric honour, he responds to the call to write as he ventures his life as a combative polemicist against Parliament itself – this time as "a Valiant and Faithfull Souldier for his Countreys *Liberties*."[46] Significantly, Lilburne retains this military title – lieutenant-colonel – on the title-pages of those works in which he challenges the regimes of the 1640s and 1650s. As Lilburne told both Houses of Parliament in 1646 while imprisoned in the Tower: "I will venture my life and heart-blood against you to oppose you, with as much zeale and courage as ever I did any of the Kings party."[47] And later, when he addresses *As You Were* to Lord General Cromwell, Lilburne

the chivalric combatant likewise self-consciously calls attention to the potency of his barbed writing which sets him against the powers of the English Republic, even more formidable and treacherous than those of the Laudian regime: "You know, I have a quick & sharpe pen (*My Lord*) and therefore give me not cause to *challenge you*, or any of your Champions . . . all that evill that in your owne thoughts you can colourably imagine the *Byshops, Starr-chamber, Counsell-table, High-commission*, or any persons therein were *guilty* of . . . [I] aver that you outstrip them all."[48] The crisis of the Republic, which dangerously threatens the supremacy of the people themselves, can prompt a reluctant yet self-consciously dramatic Lilburne to engage his polemical pen yet once more, as the following reference to himself in theatrical terms suggests: as he concludes his address to Cromwell, he writes, "But MY LORD you have forced me when I was quiet, to come upon the stage againe much against my will and studious indeavours."[49]

The difference of course between Milton and Lilburne is that the rebellious Leveller mostly fought his wars of truth behind the walls and bars of a prison: more than four-fifths of his writings were issued while he was incarcerated. One anecdote illustrates just how crucial the medium of writing remained to the embattled Leveller as an ongoing form of agency in his propaganda war. When Lilburne was intensely involved in petitioning and conducting meetings as Leveller leader during 1647–48, he found himself and John Wildman betrayed by a hostile Presbyterian minister and informer named George Masterson; both he and Wildman were called to the bar of the House of Commons and then were ordered to prison for treasonable and seditious practices. Unsuccessful in defending himself and challenging the authority of Parliament by drawing (as he was so fond of doing) upon the works on the common law by the great seventeenth-century lawyer Sir Edward Coke, the impetuous free-born John prepared to fight with his sword, only to find himself dragged off to the Tower by soldiers. But this would not be the end of the matter, as the newsbook *Mercurius Pragmaticus* observed; published discourse was essential to the expression, sustaining, and shaping of his ongoing rebellion: "Now, the next time that John comes abroad," it reported, "it will be in Print, I warrant you, to wire-draw the whole Story of the businesse."[50]

Writing in what he considered "the present . . . tyrannizing, oppressing, and invassalizing times," Lilburne nevertheless managed to produce his tracts and get them printed and circulated, and to maintain his contacts, even when he was imprisoned in the Tower and supposedly did not possess writing materials.[51] Indeed, imprisonment by such authorities as Cromwell and Ireton tended to fuel rather than restrain his feverish resolve to publish his pugnacious works; as the anonymous author of *Englands Weeping Spectacle* (1648) observed, the imprisoned Lilburne "ceases not day and night to make this injustice and cruelty known to the deceived world, [and] still writes, prints, and publishes both his own just cause, and their malicious and cruell dealings, so plainly, so power-fully, and couragiously."[52] His revealing comparisons of himself to Samson, who commits acts of vengeance and destruction against the Philistines both when he is imprisoned and when he is not, suggest that the Leveller would never remain quiet, but would rather use his writing as a form of polemical assault to provoke his opponents. In one text Lilburne resolves to sell his life to his adversaries "as ever *Sampson* did his to the *Philistines*: of whom it is said, he did them more mischiefe at his death, then he did them in all his life, *Judg.* 16"; and elsewhere Lilburne relishes the thought that he would vex his adversaries "as Sampson did the Philistines, and prove as fatall to [their] decaying, tottering spirituall, Babilonian, Anti-Christian Kingdome, as his Foxes with fire brands at their tayles, were to the Philistines corne."[53] Even after Cromwell crushed the Leveller-inspired mutiny at Burford in Oxfordshire (May 1649), an event that eclipsed their effectiveness as a unified political movement and revealed the limits of the Revolution, the restless Lilburne dared to continue publishing his fiery pamphlets and manifes-toes, thereby fueling the war of words against the fragile republican regime and first Protectorate, and defending himself and his unortho-dox political causes.

Lilburne, however, was always alert to the adverse effects of his highly contentious writing; the price of proclaiming "the testimony of Truth" against the prevailing regimes of his age was that he would be met by nearly universal reproach, while his sharp writing would only fuel the rage of his adversaries. In *Londons Liberty in Chains discovered*, he observes that "*a whole sea of indignation* [may] arise against [him]" and he knows that he is sure "to meet with the revilings, and reproaches of the barking curs of the times." He presents himself there as a prophetic and embat-tled Jeremiah: "Thy word was in my heart as a burning fire shut up in my Bones, and I was weary with forbearing, and I could not stay" (Jer. 20:9).[54] Here one may compare him with the polemical Milton, who both early and late in his revolutionary career, presented himself as a sad Jeremiah figure speaking sharp but saving words to the nation (*CPW* 1:803–4; 7:462–63). But while he could defy the authority of the Rump

Parliament (for example, when he licensed the so-called blasphemous Racovian Catechism in 1652) and while he dared to warn the Protectorate of its potential royalist excesses, Milton never got into serious trouble with those cautious regimes; nor was he, despite his concerns about the politics of arbitrary and rash censorship, ever in danger of being deprived of pen, ink, and paper. As he pours out his polemical writings, Lilburne reveals that he is acutely aware of both the power and precariousness of his sharp but undisciplined words, for his own words may be used to ensnare him so that he suffers further persecution; writing of the Lords who have imprisoned him, he observes that they attempt "to provoke him to let some words fall, or do some actions to ensnare himselfe, that so they might have some colour for their future proceedings with him."[55]

The interconnections between writing and rebellion, moreover, are underscored by Lilburne's reading and self-conscious use of other written authorities, including legal, historical, and scriptural ones, in order to sustain his campaign of polemical warfare. In *The Legall Fundamental Liberties* he discusses the formative reading that helped to shape his combative Protestant polemic (including Foxe's *Book of Martyrs*, Luther, Calvin, Beza, Perkins, among other Protestant authorities and separatist writers); his immersion in such apocalyptic books of the Bible as Isaiah, Jeremiah, Daniel, and Revelation especially incited his polemical radicalism and his sense that he was "accompanied with Divine strength and power, through the Lord Almighty, to grapple, and incounter with" many worldly adversaries.[56] In his works beginning in 1645 he regularly challenges the Long Parliament by citing verbatim from and analyzing its own large official collection of remonstrances, orders, and declarations, the *Book of Declarations* ("a definition of Law by the Parliament in the days of their primitive puritie," published in 1643). Lilburne's fierce struggles with Parliament's authority thus often operate at the level of texts and citations. He regularly defends his controversial positions by citing from the legal authority of the *Institutes* of Sir Edward Coke ("that great Oracle of the Laws of ENGLAND" who emphasized the immutability of common law) and from Magna Carta ("that little Remainder of Light") and the "excellent" Petition of Right.[57] In *Regall Tyranny Discovered*, where he deflates the mystique of earthly kingship, he not only draws extensively upon the Bible but makes a polemical appeal to history by drawing upon Speed's *Historie of Great Britaine* and Daniel's *History of England* to define the oppression and tyranny of all monarchs from the time of William the Conqueror, and to consider the encroachments of the House of Lords, the rapaciousness of lawyers, and the attractiveness of representative institutions in Anglo-Saxon England. Lilburne's historical investigations reveal that even the esteemed Magna Carta fell short of Edward the Confessor's laws, evidence of English liberties obscured by Norman practices.[58] Lilburne therefore makes highly self-conscious polemical use of English history and the legal texts which protect the civil liberties and rights of free-born Englishmen. He uses textual authorities as polemical weapons in the fierce ideological battles he wages against magistrates, legal authorities, and other institutions of the state. Even when he finds himself heatedly engaged in debate with a notable radical chaplain like Hugh Peter, who continued to support Cromwell, the Army, and Parliament during the Republic, Lilburne resorts polemically to the works of Coke and to the Petition of Right.[59] In addition, the textual nature of Lilburne's writing is further heightened by the fact that he frequently cites as authorities – often with specific page references – his own contentious printed works in the texts and margins of his subsequent revolutionary works, thereby reminding readers of his ongoing written struggles against omnipresent forms of tyranny and treacherous power.[60]

Because Lilburne's pugnacious rhetoric, symbolic gestures, and contempt of social conventions tend to be uncompromising, they anticipate the fiery rhetoric and shocking symbolic behavior of the early Quakers (see Chapter 4). Lilburne won't bow or kneel before political authorities, including before the Lord's bar, and he repeatedly shows contempt and scorn for the parliamentarian establishment. *A Pearle in a Dounghill* (1646), an anonymous work by Overton or Walwyn, describes how Lilburne infuriated the House of Lords by not showing them proper symbolic deference (so that they seemed to thirst after this just man's life more than Cain did after Abel's), and *A Whip for the Present House of Lords* describes how his constant refusal to kneel before them landed him in Newgate prison.[61] In *An Anatomy of the Lords Tyranny* he describes himself resorting to the sort of defiant symbolic gestures repudiating social deference that characterized continental Anabaptist behavior and that would make the Quakers so distressing to state authorities: there Lilburne writes that he will come to the bar of the House of Lords only by "a forcible compulsion, and . . . come in with my hat upon my head, and . . . stop my eares when they read my Charge, in detestation, and bearing witnesse against their usurpations and injustice."[62] Members of Parliament, after all, wore their hats in the chamber to symbolize that they alone were the ultimate authority there. Lilburne thus behaves in an unflinching manner towards established political authorities and refuses to do hat honor to his supposed masters, much like the revolutionary Quakers. And so, however we explain Lilburne's shift away from orthodox Calvinism (which he seemed to subscribe to until 1645 or 1646) to more antinomian and Arminian doctrinal views (the influence of Walwyn can be detected here),[63] it makes sense that during his final imprisonment he chose to convert to Quakerism, that most radical of religious movements which was then rapidly spreading and alarming mainstream Puritans. As Lilburne puts it in *Strength out of Weakness*, he is able "in any ground in England" to say something of himself and his persecutions "without dauntednesse or amazement of Spirit in the least."[64] The display of worldly power and authority will not move Lilburne, as it could not move the Quakers or the unaltered Jesus who faces trials, temptations, and worldly allurements in *Paradise Regained*: "I am not daunted at the multi-tude of my Judges," Lilburne asserts when put on trial in October 1649, "neither at the glittering of your scarlet Robes, nor the Majesty of your presence and harsh, austere deportment towards me, I bless my good God for it, who gives me courage and boldnesse."[65] Like a fearless Quaker prophet facing persecution and great tribulations, Lilburne could write that "it is the work of the Saints to incounter with difficul-ties in the Cause and Quarrel of their Lord and Master, and not to be afraid of bonds nor imprisonments."[66]

Although Lilburne was neither a consistent nor full-fledged millenar-ian in his revolutionary writings – in the sense that the visionary Winstanley or the early Quakers were[67] – his attraction to apocalyptic and prophetic scriptural discourse nevertheless contributed to his politi-cal radicalism and pugnacious rhetoric. Early in his career, when he already depicted himself as one of the Lord's "chosen ones," his restless agency as writer and combative martyr had been inspired by the mili-tant symbolism of Revelation, later an inspiration for religious radicals of the Revolution, including the Quakers who politicized the powerful myth of the Lamb's War: "you shall see," Lilburne observed of that scriptural book in 1638, "what great spirituall battels have beene fought betwixt the Lambe & his Servants, and the *Dragon* (the *Devill*) and his vassals, and some are yet to fight."[68] As a fiery young separatist, then, Lilburne envisioned himself embattled in an eschatological drama with the popish Church of England as a manifestation of the Beast and a limb of Antichrist. Like some bellicose Quaker lambasting the Antichristian clergy by calling them "greedy dogges" (see Isaiah 56:11–12), a prophetic Lilburne concluded *Englands Birth-Right Justified* (1645), a text where he clashes with Parliament, by citing Isaiah 10:1–6 with its warning of divine woe to tyrants: "what will ye doe in the day of Visitation; and in the desolation which shall come from farre?"[69] The greatest of princes and states, he envisioned in the same year, would taste a cup of trembling and drink the dregs of God's fury and wrath.[70] In the polemics Lilburne produced during the Republic, we also find passages of fiery prophetic discourse intended to unsettle his adversaries: in *An Impeachment of High Treason against Oliver Cromwell*, for example, he describes how he approached the bar of the House of Commons and then he fixed his mind "very seriously upon the Lord Jehovah, my old experienced refuge, strength and support . . . so I might speak freely and boldly, in his might and power (if it were possible) to the amazement and terrour of his enemies."[71] And later in *As You Were* (1652), where he continued to challenge the authority of Cromwell and the Army Grandees, the visionary Lilburne resorted at length to the threatening apocalyptic language of Isaiah (e.g. 2:11–15; 13:6, 11; 23:9; 26:5) about the mighty Lord of the Hosts bringing down the proud and lofty, as well as the cedars of Lebanon and the oaks of Bashan. Such heady scriptural passages, we shall see in Chapter 4, were just beginning to be invoked in the apocalyptic discourse of revolutionary Quakerism, which challenged widely accepted assumptions of social hierarchy, refused to recognize titles, and threatened Interregnum magistrates, parliaments, and ministers.[72]

Lilburne's *Strength out of Weaknesse* (September 1649) is a good example of a pugnacious polemic written when he was imprisoned in the Tower for high treason during the first year of the Republic and several months after the Leveller defeat at Burford. Even in prison Lilburne's rebellious agency – expressed through seditious writing, symbolic gestures, and the record of his confrontational verbal exchanges – could not be contained as he dared to write and speak "against the present Ruling Power sitting at Westminster" (title page). The tract illustrates the dramatic impulse so prominent in Lilburne's writing and self-presentation, as well as his formidable powers as a debater who finds himself energized by verbally sparring with his adversaries. The work mostly consists of a narrative and vivid record of Lilburne's tense and dramatic confrontation with the Rump's Attorney General Edmund Prideaux that occurred on 14 September 1649. Despite the posture of civility adopted at first by both participants during the interview (Prideaux is described "as a gentleman of some note"), Lilburne remained deeply suspicious of his antagonist – aware of the Attorney General's civility while noting that he was "otherwise smoothly cunning in his pretended Examining of [him]." It is thus hard to miss the undercurrent of tension throughout Lilburne's account. His work shows that he is self-conscious about his own defiant symbolic gestures contesting the authority of the state official interrogating him (Lilburne insists on addressing the Attorney General merely "as a private man") and providing the occasion for him to flaunt his recent polemical publications. When Prideaux puts on his hat, Lilburne puts on his and then pulls out a book from his glove attacking the powerful parliamentarian Sir Arthur Haselrig: "I said with an audible voice . . . there is a new booke with my name to it, which is my owne writing, every line which . . . I will owne and seale with my blood."[73] When Prideaux defends the Commonwealth as the people's representative government, Lilburne confronts him with the contradictions and inconsistencies of a regime never based (as the Levellers urged it should be and the Commons had originally declared) on the will of the people and their right to choose those who represent them; rather, the purged Parliament had unilaterally assumed sole legislative and most executive power: "the People chuse you, and yet you are absolute, I pray Sir reconcile me these contrarities." When Prideaux contrasts the Commonwealth to the kingdom under Charles, Lilburne shows only greater contempt for the treacherous power under that unicameral sovereign body, the Rump Parliament, and its rule of "arbitrary will." The authority of the new regime was not founded (as the Levellers hoped) on the principle of genuine consent which the people themselves had a right to withdraw if its power exceeded just bounds and limitations: "I tell you Sir, the same principle that led me to hate [Arbitrary and Tyrannical] Will in the King, leads me a thousand times more to hate Will in you, seeing you have promised better things, ye absolute freedom, and yet perform nothing, but do worse then ever he did."[74] Ultimately, Lilburne's fierce attack on the Commonwealth and its claim to legal authority derives from his sense that its power was a kind of "mock Power" – a fiction based upon practices of political dissimulation threatening the liberties of the nation and revealing both the limits and contradictions of the proclaimed "Free State" of 1649–53.[75]

LEVELLER POLEMIC AND THE NEW ARTS OF POLITICAL DISSIMULATION

Lilburne often uses his highly polemical texts to expose interconnections between new forms of tyranny and political dissimulation as he responds to the contradictions of the Revolution. Distrustful of Leveller egalitarianism, the Army leaders symbolize all that has become equivocal about the new Commonwealth. Lilburne employs the language of dissimulation to convey the treachery of Antichristian politics and power practiced under the guise of revolution and liberty; and to emphasize the continuity of political tyranny and repression from the time of the Laudian bishops to the Revolution itself, when Civil War and Interregnum regimes seemed to "practice nothing but playing at Hocus Pocus."[76] Tyranny in the 1640s and 1650s, Lilburne believed, had taken on more ominous forms.[77] "Arbitrary Usurpation" has assumed new locations in the Houses of Parliament, in the Presbyterian clergy, in the political behavior of Cromwell, Ireton, and the Grandees, in the practices of professional lawyers and judges, as well as in the Merchant Adventurers' trading monopoly: all these institutions and leaders seemed to Lilburne to imperil the rising popular movement for revolution.[78] Indeed, Lilburne's writings convey a sense of omnipresent tyranny that infects the whole kingdom, as the image of the sick and distressed nation in the preamble to *Englands Birth-right* suggests.[79]

In *Londons Liberty in Chains discovered* (1646) he had hoped that God would "raise up heroical Instruments, to unvaile and unmask" the oppressing forms of power and those who practice them with their "jugling, and machivel-like endeavours":[80] Lilburne himself attempted to assume the role of such a godly instrument during the Revolution. Like Winstanley he perceived the dissimulation associated with new forms of power. But Winstanley differs from Lilburne (as we shall see later) by freely revising scriptural myths to evoke a sense of urgent crisis and to expose the politics of contemporary class conflict; though Lilburne often inserts biblical references into his works, he, more than the Digger, resorts to justifications of himself to wage his polemics. Nevertheless, like Winstanley, Lilburne attempts to expose "the Power and delusion of the *Clergy*" who use "faire speeches and glosing pretences" to keep the people in darkness.[81] Indeed, the Levellers, like the Diggers, perceived a network of oppressive Antichristian powers – political, judicial, ecclesiastical, and economic – operating throughout the realm to create an ominous new state of tyranny: in Overton's *An Alarum to the House of Lords* the Peers, clergymen, judges, professional lawyers, and monopoly capitalists are all characterized as the people's "deadly adversaries." Sometimes Lilburne's prose will swell with the names of professions which have spread oppression throughout the central city and realm, thereby creating an omnipresent network of oligarchical power: "the rest of the whole Nation is become unto Lawyers, Attornies, Clerks, Solicitors, and cruell Jaylors, and such instruments of contentions, by whom the peace and flourishing State of this Kingdome is quite devoured."[82] Lilburne recognized during the 1640s that London could play a crucial role in the kingdom's political transformation, but not while "Prerogative men of London" and "great and mighty *Nimrods* of the world" constrain the lawful rights of the godly people in both the city and nation at large.[83] His perception that one form of unchecked power has replaced another resembles Winstanley's, except that the Digger focuses on the crisis of the Republic which has failed to act as a revolutionary "free state" and eradicate the system of private property; Lilburne would consistently link "liberty and propriety."[84]

Because of his years of suffering and martyrdom, Lilburne acutely perceives tyranny's continuity, as well as its new locations.[85] Tyranny, however, not only appears in different guises; it has increased under the Long Parliament, as his pungent colloquial writing can assert: "King *Charles* his seventeen years mis-government before this Parliament . . . was *but a flea-biting, or as a mouldhill to a mountain, in comparison of what this everlasting Parliament* already is, and will be to the whole Kingdome."[86] Like Winstanley, Lilburne exposes forms of kingly power that have manifested themselves in the practices of both the state and clergy: "Nay yee your selves exercise the Kingly office; yee, I say it againe, yee yourselves exercise the Kingly office," he proclaims in *Plaine Truth without Feare or Flattery* (1647), where he attacks the Presbyterian establishment and their conservative influence in the Long Parliament. The specter of Charles I itself becomes a potent polemical weapon in Lilburne's assaults on other ecclesiastical and political powers in the 1640s and 1650s: as he puts it in *Jonahs Cry out of the Whales belly*, "Parliament tyrannizeth ten times more over us then ever the King did."[87]

Like the Digger, Lilburne associates usurping authorities with subtle practices that cloak the pursuit of covetous ends. In *Plaine Truth*, where he sharply criticizes Parliament and its Machiavellian members, he especially assails the double-dealing politics of the Presbyterian majority: "this destroying Party in both Houses . . . these cunning contrivers of our intended Vassalage and thraldome frame a . . . confederacy by covenant with the Scots, and by power and subtilty surprize and ensnare therein the whole Parliament and Kingdom."[88] Devilish, they resemble the nation's Lucifer-like leaders: he portrays them as a "serpentine brood (like the old Serpent)" sending forth "wrath and revenge, reproaches, [and] curses."[89] His sense of their equivocal behavior and pretended support of reformation in terms of their "turnings and windings," moreover, anticipates Milton's impassioned analysis of their contradictory political allegiances in *The Tenure of Kings and Magistrates* (see Chapter 6): "At first they were against the King; then while he was with them, they speak and write highly for him, and now they have made the most they can of him, they are again become adversaries to him."[90] Later, in 1649, the author of *Eikonoklastes* would expose the Circean arts of the Stuart King whose deceptive powers he symbolized by the cup of servitude; in *Regall Tyranny Discovered*, published in the same year as *Plaine Truth*, Lilburne addresses the Commons of England, exhorting them to be wary of the Circean arts practiced not by the king but by "usurping" apostate Lords in Parliament who have especially come under the powerful Presbyterian influence: "Oh, ye *Commons* of *England* . . . take speciall heede that by their charmes and Syren-like songs, you be not divided . . . into factions to your own destruction."[91]

In Lilburne's writings there is often an overwhelming sense of municipal, state, military, ecclesiastical, and legal authorities engaged in "juggling" practices. Tyrannical powers in the clergy and state equivocate in their behavior and words: they practice "double dealings . . . in every businesse they transact or negotiate with us." So do the professional lawyers who "juggle, and put false glosses upon the *Law* (meerly) for their own ends"; written in a foreign tongue – Latin or law French – the law is rendered so obscure and complex to the common people that the lawyers in Lilburne's day differ little from the "State Clergy" who "in the daies of old," before the Scripture was translated into the vernacular, "could easily make the poor people beleeve the Popes unwritten verities were as binding as Scripture Rules."[92] In *Regall Tyranny Discovered*, he complains of ongoing Norman laws in Westminster Hall "by reason of their tediousnesse, ambiguities, uncertainties, the entries in Latine, which is not our own Tongue":[93] the product of a legal system created by William the Conqueror, such laws (as opposed to natural law favored by the Levellers) are thus especially susceptible to ambiguous interpretations. Indeed, when he was tried by the Rump in October 1649, Lilburne was concerned that he himself might be ensnared by the unreformed legal system; accusing those who put him on trial as acting like "the Scribes and Pharisees, & Pilate . . . who by questions went about to insnare [Jesus]," the self-consciously dramatic Leveller managed to represent himself as a Christ figure who speaks "openly to the world" as he engages sharply with the Pharisees of his day.[94] Furthermore, in the *Charters of London*, the text where he makes the memorable Leveller claim that "the poorest that lives hath as true a right to give a vote, as well as the richest and greatest," he sharply warns those who abuse power in

London's government by resorting to the arts of juggling which he hopes "to anatomize to [his] fellow-citizens": "Look to it you Lord Major and Aldermen, *brethren in evill*: for I professe there is the most notorious jugling and cheating amongst you, that is amongst any generation of men in *England*."[95] And in *Englands Birth-Right Justified*, he cites verses by the prophetic George Wither (from *Vox Pacifica*) in order to highlight the need for vigilance – particularly in the House of Commons – against mercenary lawyers who resort to prevarication and subtleties in the making and execution of laws, thereby increasing oppression in "this mournfull Land." Those who possess political power in the city and realm thus too often resort to deluding arts and sophistry: the Commons of England have been "jugled with, by some of those they have reposed their greatest trust in."[96]

In *A Remonstrance of Many Thousand Citizens* (1646), the republican Overton (with Walwyn) analyzes the origins of enslavement, cruelty, and unlimited power in the nation in terms of Norman tyranny and the softening "delusive Arts" of kingship, including those of King Charles.[97] Lilburne's polemical writings, however, are even more concerned with exposing evasive political behavior operating in the Commonwealth. References to dissimulation in his works convey the treachery of equivocal politics practiced in the name of revolution and religious reformation. Both Levellers remain committed to the notion that powerful state institutions which claim to represent the people (such as the House of Commons) should "forsake, and utterly renounce all craftie and subtill intentions."[98] Lilburne often writes as though dissimulation, along with ambiguous words and jealousies (one manifestation of Satanic evil in *Paradise Lost*), are widespread in the behavior and language of the nation's political, religious, legal, and economic institutions and leaders. In *The Just Defence* (August 1653), a vigorous late apology for his political life, he voices his concern with "the appearance of things, the gloss and outside . . . made by politicians, the Arts-men and Craftsmen of the world, for the maintenance of their corrupt interests." They use "art and sophistry" and "by changing themselves into the shape of Angels of light, deceive (were it possible) the very elect"; and so Lilburne recalls in this tract how he set out to prove the Army Grandees' "pretences of joyning in an Agreement of the People to be but delusion, and that they neither broke the Parliament in pieces, nor put the King to death, in order to the restauration of the Fundamental Laws of the Nation . . . but to advance themselves."[99] Lilburne's caustic analysis is close to the visionary tracts of Winstanley, who also perceives that treacherous forms of power and artifice remained interconnected after the traumatic events of 1648–49.

The issue of verbal dissimulation likewise emerges at moments when Lilburne considers his role as a writer and the politics of communication in the Revolution. He claims to speak plainly and directly, thereby avoiding the ambiguous words he detects in the discourse of state and ecclesiastical authorities: "[his] words," he self-consciously writes to Cromwell in one text, "are the cleare demonstrations of the cordiall affections of a reall, plaine and single hearted friend of yours, who you very well know was never skilfull in the wicked art of flattery, colloging, or dissimulation."[100] The Leveller leaders were therefore anxious to eschew subtle artifice in their discourse: the principles they promote, they wrote from the Tower in April 1649, are "not moulded nor contrived by the subtill or politick Principles of the World, but plainly produced and nakedly sent, without any insinuating arts."[101] Indeed, Lilburne's concern that the press remain "open," and not regulated by rules of state and church censorship (which, like Milton, he likened to Antichristian practices of the Inquisition), grows out of his concern about the flourishing of political dissimulation in the realm, including the Commonwealth, where its uses seem more perfidious and darker than in the days of Charles I. Thus the most urgent reason for maintaining an open popular press, he told the Republic's House of Commons in *Englands New Chains Discovered*, is that "all trecherous and tyranical designes may be the easier discovered, and so prevented, which is a liberty of greatest concernment to the Commonwealth."[102]

In his own attempts to discover treacherous political designs, Lilburne assaults Cromwell, Ireton, and the Grandees for their equivocal practices and their "base and indirect means"[103] – political behavior signaling their pursuit of unchecked power and monopoly in government, and the corruption of their position in the late 1640s by royal favor. Indeed, Lilburne was subjecting Cromwell, once his friend and Puritan ally, to intense pressure well before other radical writers were doing so. The first text in which he publicly attacks Cromwell for juggling and dissembling is *Jonahs Cry out of the Whale's Belly* (July 1647), soon followed by similar accusations in *The Juglers Discovered* (September 1647), and his later texts return to this theme, connecting it more thoroughly with political treachery and equivocation.[104] Lilburne responds acutely to what he perceives as Cromwell's prevarications and Machiavellian hypocrisies, stressing in *The Grand Plea* (also written in 1647) how they have stimulated his pugnacious verbal responses: "my pen and tongue hath been very free since in discovering L. G. *Cromwells Hocus Pocus* dealing with mee and the Kingdome, who appeares to be one of the notablest Juglers."[105] His urge to expose political dissimulation, moreover, can lead to radical pro- phetic warning, as in *An Impeachment of High Treason against Oliver Cromwell, and his Son in Law Henry Ireton* (1649); alluding to one of the woes expos- ing the failings of the Pharisees and warning of hidden graves in Luke 11:44, Lilburne attacks "the pretended false Saint Oliver" and the Grandees who had courted and juggled with the king after the Parliamentary victories and who seemed to prevaricate over the ques- tion of decentralizing power and authority in the new order: "therefore woe unto them hypocrites and painted Sepulchers, who for all their fair pretences hate the Liberties of England more then they do the Devil."[106] In *As You Were* (May 1652), written after his banishment from the Commonwealth, Lilburne attempts to display for Cromwell and the Grandees – "as in a glass" – "the *faces of their Soules*, spotted with *Apostacy*," and he blasts them for their "hocus-pocus-*juggleing* with the honest *Soldiers*, and the rest of the *Free-people of England*," whose common rights and freedoms they have claimed to uphold without calling new, annual Parliaments. The Grandees are "seeming deliverers" who assume a specious religious appearance by means of their cunning words: "Behold these your great commanders and *seemingly Religious* Friends thus cloathed with the glorious garment of their owne Declarations."[107]

But then Satanic dissimulation, as Milton dramatizes in *Paradise Lost*, may easily beguile the sharpest-sighted observer who may not immedi- ately recognize a cunning apostate when he sees one, since "neither Man nor Angel can discern / Hypocrisy," as the poet observes in response to "the false dissembler unperceiv'd" (3.681–83). So Lilburne himself sug- gests in a series of rhetorical questions that powerfully convey a sense of shock and betrayal with regard to the apostate Grandees – their brutal ambition barely cloaked by verbal dissembling – and the failures of a regime never truly founded upon the principle of popular sovereignty:

And what Eagle-eye could at first discerne that this glorious cloathing, *was but painted paper?*, what jealous heart could have imagined, that these promising Patriots, *were only sweet mouthed dissemblers?* Who could have harboured the least suspition that these seeming visible starrs of heaven, *were but blazing Comets* that would quickly *turne their backs* as they have perfectly done upon all these glorious promises and declarations, and prove the *vilest apostates* that ever the earth bore?[108]

Significantly it is in this text about the politics of dissimulation, and just after the passage cited above, that Lilburne introduces as one of his literary and polemical allies Milton himself, the daring republican author of the recent *Defence of the People of England* (1651).

Presenting himself "as a man that intirely loves [his] native Countrey," Lilburne quotes at considerable length – and in English – from the conclusion of Milton's Latin polemic, a passage in which, as the Leveller rightly notes, Milton warns his countrymen and the Rump to remain vigilant against self-seeking forces that could undermine the glorious achievements of the Revolution.[109] In the Leveller's text, the republican Milton becomes a kind of Lilburne-style hero and writer: assertive and bold towards both his enemies and his leading countrymen, while also presenting himself as patriotic and chivalric.[110] The Leveller praises the eloquent way that the "valiant and learned Champion MR. MILTON" routed "the forces of SALMASIUS" and then notes how Milton advised his own Commonwealth masters "with much *faithfullness* and Freedome" to conquer ambition and avarice lest in time of peace they "prove base and unworthy" and bring God's wrath upon themselves – a divine hatred even greater than that manifested against their royalist enemies. Milton's "excellent and faithfull advice" to his countrymen thus becomes a means of buttressing Lilburne's own polemical authority as a contentious, undaunted writer in exile continuing to challenge the legitimacy of the Republic. Lilburne has taken Milton's republican writing and turned it directly against the Commonwealth; indeed, more sharply than Milton's *Defence*, his Leveller text associates the failures of the Revolution and Cromwell as earthly redeemer with the new political arts of dissembling.[111] In effect, Lilburne condemns his "grand adversary" Cromwell, the leader who had once promised to call a newly elected Parliament (the Levellers insisted upon fresh elections), of being as guilty as the former king of "tamperings, juggleings & machiavilian devices."[112]

In a series of devastating pamphlets, the republican Levellers confronted the hypocrisy of the worldly rule of the Rump and that government's power of oligarchy based on military force, thereby subjecting the Grandees, especially in late February and during March 1649, to one of the most serious internal threats they faced. One of the most searching of these texts, *The Hunting of the Foxes from New-Market and Triploe-Heaths to Whitehall* (21 March 1649), was written by five pro-Leveller cavalry troopers "late of the Armie," and presented a particularly caustic attack on the new tyranny of Cromwell, Ireton, and the Grandees; it is likely that Lilburne or Overton contributed to this text.[113] In a work permeated with theatrical language, the issue of dissimulation is repeatedly addressed as the authors condemn the Army officers and their new order: as the title page itself boldly announces, "THE GRANDIE-DECEIVERS [are] Unmasked (that you may know them)" before "the Free-People of England." The authors' use of the fox to describe members of the executive power who have perverted basic principles of freedom, while appearing to be godly, highlights a sense of dangerous political and religious cunning in terms that sound almost Miltonic: "they are Wolves in Sheeps clothing, Foxes in the habit of Saints."[114] The potent language of sorcery and theatrical illusion heightens the sense of treacherous practices by the Army officers. The author of *Eikonoklastes* would soon employ similar language to expose the equivocal politics and language of the martyred Stuart king; and Winstanley would use it to expose the crafty behavior of the professional clergy who bewitch the common people and keep them powerless (see Chapter 2). The authors of this daring Leveller text, however, use it to expose the powerful leaders of the Army and to generate a sense of urgency about such artfulness operating in revolutionary England: the pamphlet refers to "their fair speeches and fawning dissimulations" with which "they courted the Souldiery and honest party of the Common-wealth into a strong delusion, even to believe their lyes, their enchantments, and sorceries . . . *Pharaohs* Egyptian Sorcerers were short of their Art."[115]

The aim of these Leveller authors resembles that of the discerning poet of *Paradise Lost* who at crucial moments intervenes to unmask the arch-apostate's seductive theatrical language and posturing which conceals "deep malice": that "Artificer of fraud . . . was the first / That practis'd falsehood under saintly show" (4.121–23). Likewise, the Levellers highlight the way in which the public discourse of godliness may easily conceal insidious political designs, serpentine behavior, and ruthless ambition: when the Grandees underhandedly negotiated with the king to enhance their power, "this was drest out in such . . . Saint-like language, as the religious people might best be surprised, not suspecting any venemous thing to be lurking under the leaf of their holy and sacred pretences."[116] The memorable portrait of Cromwell, with his smooth godly behavior masking his viciousness, vividly highlights the equivocal politics of saintly show operating in the Commonwealth – a Leveller view of contemporary Satanic dissimulation:

Was there ever a generation of men so Apostate so false and so perjur'd as these? did ever men pretend an higher degree of Holinesse, Religion, and Zeal to God and their Country than these? these preach, these fast, these pray, these have nothing more frequent then the sentences of sacred Scripture, the Name of

God and of Christ in their mouthes: You shall scarce speak to *Cromwell* about any thing, but he will lay his hand on his breast, elevate his eyes, and call God to record, he will weep, howl and repent, even while he doth smite you under the first rib.[117]

During the same month that *The Hunting of the Foxes* appeared, Lilburne, no less sensitive to the ways in which men in power could exploit the cloak of religion for treacherous political ends, himself bitterly expressed such sentiments against the Rump and its Army leaders in *The Second Part of Englands New-Chaines*: they "saw a possibility of making progress to their designs, which course of theirs they ever termed a waiting upon providence, that with colour of Religion they might deceive the more securely."[118] Like Milton, Lilburne and the Levellers perceived that "Tyranny and fals Religion" have "very dark roots" which "twine and interweave one another" (*Eikonoklastes*, *CPW* 3:509). At the end of *Paradise Lost*, Milton's solemn prophetic angel bitterly laments those sad postlapsarian political ages characterized by men who pursue forms of "Secular power, though feigning still to act / By spiritual" (12.517–19); in the eyes of the Levellers, the new Republic itself was such a dark period in human history.

The *Hunting of the Foxes* also suggests that power in the Republic manifests itself in terms of renewed regal practices, an accusation later frequently made by radical sectarian critics of the Protectorate (see Chapters 3 and 5), but also one made by Lilburne in *The Legall Fundamentall Liberties* about Cromwell and the Grandees and their new power. "These Court-Officers are now a moulding . . . a *New Regality*," warn the Leveller authors, invoking the grim specter of Charles I and other English monarchs with their supporting prerogative institutions: "their Conclave of Officers at White Hall hath suckt into it the venome of all former corrupt Courts . . . we shall shew you how the Court of the High Commission, the Star-chamber, the House of Lords, the King and his Privie Councel are all still alive in that Court, called the General Councel of the Army."[119] Such forms of theatrical political behavior and regal-style power are dangerously subversive, so that the alarming language of political levelling regularly used against Levellers and sectarians is now applied to the destabilizing politics practiced by the Grandees who threaten to level the laws and liberties of the people: "by their *Machiavilian* pretences . . . they are become masters and usurpers of the name of the Army, and of the name of the Parliament; under which Visors they have levell'd and destroyed all the Authority of this Nation."[120] At times, moreover, the Leveller authors sound close to Winstanley in their sharp condemnation of the Commonwealth and its newer forms of centralized kingly power, now ominously increased after the traumatic political events of 1648–49: "We have not the change of a Kingdom to a Commonwealth; We are onely under the old cheat, the transmutation of Names, but with the addition of New Tyranies to the old."[121]

A hostile response to the politics of dissimulation likewise fuels Lilburne's impassioned attacks on the Republic's leaders, its military origins and rule, and its fictitious claims to political legitimacy. On the title page of *The Legall Fundamentall Liberties of the People* (June 1649), one of his longest works, the disenchanted Leveller boldly condemns Pride's Purge which forcibly dissolved the Parliament in December 1648 and reduced it to ninety MPs in January 1649, even though that military event had purged supporters of Presbyterianism. Because it seemed based on the assertion of raw political power (without wide popular support) and another instance in history of rule dangerously maintained by the sword, the Rump, in Lilburne's eyes, has become the new "pretended mock-Parliament": and so he grimly proclaims 1649 "the grand yeer of hypocriticall and abominable dissimulation." He then examines the treachery of such "a MOCK-POWER" based on a purged Parliament pretending – that is, operating with the fiction or shadow of magistrates – to serve as the people's representatives and try the king, yet with no legal authority to do so.[122] Lilburne thus felt compelled to use his writings to expose the "*fictionated Power*" of the Rump which, as he tells its Attorney General, he considers it his "duty (and to render [him] self faithfull and upright in [his] generation) to discover to [his] friends and Countrey-men."[123]

Lilburne, moreover, can convey a sense of republican England in crisis by modulating between writing that is intensely introspective and spiritual and writing that is more politically topical. In *An Impeachment of High Treason against Oliver Cromwell* (August 1649) he inserts a striking prayer to God, interrupting a narrative of his arrest in January 1648 and appearance before the House of Commons:

But O thou Just, Righteous, Powerful and Compassionate God; that sensibly hath been my God and guide about these twise seven years: that hast often refreshed my soul with those . . . soul satisfying refreshments, that hath made my heart sing and be merry, in the midest of many deaths; and which hast made me lightly esteeme the cruel malice of all my fierce, and murdering Enemies: O thou glorious God, that hath taken me by the arme when I have been ready to fall, and by whose power alone, I have been kept upright before thee, in the midst of so many soul piercing temptations.[124]

The emotional charge of this passionate address is heightened by accounts of Lilburne's persecution and imprisonment in the pages before and after the prayer itself. In the first year of the Commonwealth, Lilburne prays to God as he feels himself fallen on evil days, with dangers compassed round, and living in a cold political climate, not unlike the isolated Restoration poet of *Paradise Lost* or the Miltonic Samson "enclos'd . . . round" by "many evils": the godly Leveller is a "servant in the midst of all adversity, afflictions, trials, and sorrows (that never more in all my life incompassed me round about then now)."[125]

Yet Lilburne's prayer of intense spiritual yearning quickly becomes more topical as he considers Cromwell's power in the new regime: "protect and deliver me *from the cruell and bloudy rage, of thy once SEEMING servant, CROMWEL*, who if my soul is now able to judge, is visibly become a FALNESTAR, an *Apostate* from thee, an ENEMY to thee." In Lilburne's text, Cromwell becomes a dark, raging Satanic power with almost Miltonic qualities. A fallen Lucifer, Lilburne's Cromwell is "furious" in his "drivings to destroy Righteousnesse, Truth, and Justice," and dangerous in his political deception and dissimulation. The prayer acquires an urgent apocalyptic tone as Lilburne highlights the Satanic powers of his enemies in the new Republic and echoes Christ's warnings about counterfeit deliverers (Matt. 24:24): "O discover him . . . and his wicked oppressing and tyrannical accomplices, to be what they are . . . the SONS OF SATHAN AND WICKEDNESSE, THE PER-VERTERS OF TRUTH, JUSTICE, AND ALL KIND OF RIGHTEOUSNESSE; THE DECEIVERS AND SEDUC-ERS THAT THOU HAST DECLARED SHOULD COME INTO THE WORLD IN THESE LAST DAIES, TO DECEIVE, IF IT WERE POSSIBLE, THE VERY ELECT." In August 1649, after Cromwell had broken the Levellers in pieces at Burford,[126] it seemed as if he, not a Stuart king, was the mighty Nimrod or eastern despot ruling a newer regime based on military force and central-ized power: "this great and mighty (apostatizing) hunting *Nimrod*, CROM-WELL," Lilburne adds, possesses an "absolute commanding power . . . over an over-awing, mercinary, Turkish Army."[127] Even while writing under the most hostile, treacherous political circumstances and in the face of persecution, the contentious Lilburne would not let up on his polemi-cal onslaught and revealed that his radical reformist voice, like Milton's in the Restoration, would remain "unchang'd / To hoarse or mute."[128]

Lilburne's anxieties about fictional power and political dissimulation turned out to be no less central to his two most notorious texts from 1649, both of which sharply expose "the uncertainty of our government" at a moment in the infant Republic when tensions between more radical and more conservative forces in the Revolution were escalating.[129] In the late winter, anxious that the country was fast slipping under military rule, Lilburne renewed his vigorous political activity and produced, with several of his colleagues, *Englands New Chains Discovered*, a daring petition addressed (and presented in person) to the Commons on 26 February. This polemic contains passionate writing confronting the "shew and pretense" of the Commonwealth, its Rump Parliament, and the Army leadership after the Levellers felt that the new regime had betrayed their *Agreement* of December 1648 and while the people were "flattered with notions of being the Original of all just power." A realm governed by the politically conservative Rump, "where . . . liberty [is] so much pretended, so deerly purchased," only confirms for Lilburne the alarming disjunction between a vision of hard-won revolutionary freedom achieved with great difficulty by the people and the reality of a new age of centralized, military power cunningly masked by the public discourse of liberty. Lilburne builds emotional pressure in his polemical text as he uses rhetorical repetition – his successive statements prefaced by the word "notwithstanding" – to express this painful point about the Commonwealth whose freedoms were created out of suffering, economic deprivation, and the dislocations of war as well as remarkable providential triumphs (such as the New Model Army's military victories):

Insomuch that we are even agast and astonished to see that notwithstanding the productions of the highest notions of freedom that ever this Nation, or any people in the world, have brought to light, notwithstanding the vast expence of blood and treasure that hath been made to purchase those freedoms, notwithstanding the many eminent and even miraculous Victories God hath been pleased to honour our just Cause withall . . . When we consider what rackings and tortures the People in general have suffered through decay of Trade, and deernesse of food . . . That yet after all these things have bin done and suffered . . . Behold! in the close of all, we hear and see what gives us a fresh and pregnant cause to believe that the contrary is really intended, and that all those specious pretences, and high Notions of Liberty . . . appear to us to have bin done and directed by some secret powerful influences, the more securely and unsuspectedly to attain an absolute domination over the Common-wealth.[130]

Similarly, in the same text he accuses the Rumpers of exploiting "fair promises of good, and dissembled repentance," as he would soon do at length in the subsequent manifesto *The Second Part of Englands New-Chaines*

Discovered (24 March). That work of timely warning, addressed to the purged Parliament, expresses a sense of urgency about the new kinds of political duplicity operating in the Republic under its Council of Officers and endangering the sovereignty of the people: on the title page, Lilburne proclaims his work a "sad Representation of the uncertain and dangerous condition of the COMMON-WEALTH."[131]

As tensions between Leveller agitators and more conservative forces in the Revolution were becoming particularly acute, Parliament declared *The Second Part of Englands New- Chaines* "a very dangerous Book" and "highly seditious, and destructive to the present Government" (its publication promptly led to the arrest of the four Leveller leaders for high treason).[132] Lilburne's text reinterprets the recent events of the Revolution from a Leveller perspective that underscores patterns of treachery, delusion, and betrayal: Lilburne's narrative considers how Cromwell, Ireton, and the Grandees played "fast and loose with the King and his party," how they courted and deceived the Leveller leaders, how they apparently helped to contrive and cover up the murder of the Army Leveller Colonel Thomas Rainsborough (who passionately espoused the cause of manhood suffrage in the Putney Debates), how they artfully "moulded and qualified the Army to their own bent" and designs, how they attempted "to new-mould the City, and make it theirs," and how, indeed, after "all their glorious flattery of the King and his Party" vanished, "their notorious dissimulation appeared."[133] The events of the Revolution of 1648–49, whose traumatic character Lilburne acknowledges, have become the occasion for these new political masters to assume their position of power, which they have concentrated in a few hands so that they practice "a new way of breaking the spirits of the English, which Strafford and Canterbury never dreampt of." "The Removing the King, the taking away the House of Lords, the overawing the House, the reducing it to that passe, that it is become but the Channell, through which is conveyed all the Decrees and Determinations of a private Counsell of some few Officers, the erecting of their Court of Justice, and their Counsell of State, The Voting of the People the Supreme Power" – all these remarkable and unsettling political events have become a "sole conducement to their ends, and Intents, either by removing such as stood in the way between them and the Power, wealth, or command of the Common-Wealth."[134] And so it was, Lilburne ruefully observes about the recent history of a revolution badly gone awry, that "the most hopefull opportunity that ever England had for recovery of our Freedome, was spent and consumed."[135]

Lilburne's text thus remains one of his most haunting accounts of the Revolution and the evil days of its new Republic. The Leveller's concern with the politics of dissimulation in the Commonwealth, which he felt compelled to discover to his contemporaries, enabled him to express forcefully his suspicion of the dangers of oligarchical power and his acute sense of the Revolution's most disturbing ambiguities: "By these Arts," he observed of the Republic's leaders and Grandees, "are they new fastened in their Power."[136] Or as Marvell so memorably put it at the end of the "Horatian Ode," "The same *Arts* that did *gain* / A *Pow'r* must it *maintain*" (lines 119–20): less nuanced than Marvell's lines, Lilburne's observation about the arts of power in the new Republic conveys a much grimmer resonance.[137] In his radical visionary writings, we shall see in the next chapter, Winstanley the Digger would likewise address that sense of crisis over the powers of darkness that continued to flourish in the Revolution and the Republic it had created.

CHAPTER TWO

Gerrard Winstanley and the crisis of the Revolution

One of the most gifted radical religious writers of seventeenth-century England, Winstanley the Digger (1609–76) produced nearly all his remarkable visionary works during the republican revolution which overthrew the monarchy and the House of Lords and established the new Commonwealth under the worldly rule of the Rump regime.[1] Between 1648 and 1652, in the midst of the mid-century crisis, he published more than twenty pamphlets, letters and broadsides, including his major utopian text, *The Law of Freedom in a Platform*.[2] In effect, Winstanley believed that even after the Civil Wars, Pride's Purge, and the dramatic republican revolution, "kingly power," as he called it, continued to exist in various Antichristian forms in the newly erected and free Commonwealth: the professional clergy, state rulers, the Army, lawyers, and landlords were all contributing to an elaborate system of institutional powers which oppress the poor of the earth and keep England under a curse of kingly power. The great danger, Winstanley perceived, was that one form of tyranny was merely replacing another, as it assumed new shapes; this condition would perpetuate the sharp class conflicts that had troubled England under the legacy of Norman power reinforced by the reign of Charles I. As he put it in *Fire in the Bush*, "as yet the power and dominion of the Prince of darknesse rules every where" and "the Dragon is not yet cast out"; and as he complained to Cromwell in his last work, "Kingly power remains in power still in the hands of those who have no more right to the Earth then our selves."[3] The majority of Winstanley's texts thus provide an acute analysis of the complex network of kingly power and class oppression which he believed was operating in subtle and menacing forms in England's Republic.

While writing many of his visionary works he was the leader, along with William Everard, of the remarkable protest movement of poor laborers which began, with about twenty or thirty followers, at St.

George's Hill in Surrey on 1 April 1649, and which finally collapsed (having later moved to Cobham common), after harassment and physical violence by local landlords and freeholders, a year later in April 1650. The 1640s, when he was struggling with poverty and beginning to write, was a period of severe economic depression, political uncertainty, and social dislocation for the lower classes. Disastrous harvests from 1646 to 1649 accentuated the social and economic crisis immediately following the Civil War by causing high food prices, near famine, heavy taxation, and escalating poverty – a sense of turmoil frequently expressed in Winstanley's writings.[4] While working as a hired farm laborer in the Surrey countryside, Winstanley converted to communism during the unsettled period of December 1648 to January 1649, an experience that profoundly affected his subsequent writings and political activities. Digging the Surrey commons and cultivating the undeveloped waste lands were in one sense practical georgic and communal activities; yet they were also highly provocative political and symbolic acts challenging the powers of the earth and their subtle Antichristian practices:[5] digging was a means of "declaring freedome to the Creation" and of uprooting "Tythes . . . Lawyers Fees . . . Prisons, and all that Art and Trade of darknesse" (pp. 316, 335). It was related to Winstanley's prophetic vision of the rising of God's Spirit within all sons and daughters which would establish a new agrarian commonwealth on earth, as well as the kingdom of heaven within believers.

Righteous acting on the land was thus essential to bring about Winstanley's revolutionary vision, since it served to advance the Kingdom of Christ on earth and within every man and woman. Writing, he concluded, could not simply become an end in itself; alone, it was not an adequate response to the profound political/religious crisis of the Revolution. "Action is the life of all," Winstanley therefore proclaimed in his Digger writings, "and if thou dost not act, thou dost nothing" (p. 315), for he acutely perceived that in this period of turmoil "every one talks of freedome, but there are but few that act for freedome" (p. 317).[6] In his career as communist visionary writer and Digger, prophetic words and symbolic actions would interact since "words and action going together are the declaration of a sincere heart" (p. 138). Commanded by the voice of the Spirit within, he would declare his message of visionary revelation, his new law of righteousness as he called it, both "by [his] pen" and "in [his] action" (p. 194).[7]

Committed to a program of righteous action as a means of freeing the Creation from the curse and regaining its paradisal state, the Diggers became the unique movement of the poor during the Revolution, establishing ten communities in 1649–50; these agrarian communist experiments spread as widely as Buckinghamshire, Middlesex, Bedfordshire, Leicestershire, Kent, Northamptonshire, and Gloucestershire, among other counties.[8] The Digger colonies attempted to eradicate the tyranny of particular interest and private property and to make "the earth a common treasury" (as it had been at the beginning), a theme that first emerges in Winstanley's *New Law of Righteousnes* (January 1649) and which is pervasive in his writings until his *Law of Freedom* (February 1652). By calling themselves the "True Levellers," the Diggers were distinguishing themselves from their socially less radical brethren, the Levellers, whose political program never advocated redistributing property. In Digger writings, the notion that the poor and the meek would inherit the earth was indeed a daring revolutionary vision that deeply challenged orthodox assumptions about class, hierarchy, property, and power in seventeenth-century England.[9]

Yet despite their visionary utopianism, the Diggers, like the early Quakers, found themselves rejected by the larger culture as they encountered intense hostility and mob violence: they were physically assaulted, arrested, and imprisoned; their crops were spoiled, their farm tools destroyed, and their houses pulled down or burned.[10] On one occasion Diggers were savagely beaten by men in women's apparel led by two local freeholders: the beating by "women" was symbolic of the reversal of the natural order in which the Diggers themselves were unsettling the conventions of society.[11] In the dramatic apocalyptic terms Winstanley himself invoked, such was the sharp persecution that the patient Diggers, meek in spirit, endured "FROM THE GREAT RED DRAGONS POWER SINCE APRIL 1. 1649" (p. 392). It should hardly surprise us that the ultra-radical Digger writer may well have turned to Quakerism at the end of his life.[12]

While it is certainly tempting to see the communist visionary as a major precursor of Marx and Engels, his daring social ideas, agrarian communism, and radical theology are so deeply interconnected – especially in his works beginning in early 1649 and thereafter – that such comparisons can also blur historical differences.[13] To be sure, the intensity of his religious enthusiasm differs from text to text; but even in his final work, *The Law of Freedom*, his communism and radical religious vision remain fused as he responds to the continuing presence of treacherous Antichristian powers in his age.[14] As I will stress in this chapter, his social and spiritual radicalism are also closely integrated with the mythopoeic and figurative dimensions of his writing, including his apocalyptic myth-making stimulated by the crises of the Revolution.

Winstanley's perception that political, spiritual, and individual freedom must begin with economic freedom and common ownership of the land has received valuable attention from historians studying the Digger in relation to his radical sociopolitical milieu and its ferment of ideas.[15] Often more concerned with social, political, or religious ideas, such historical work rarely considers in any detail the rich mythopoeic, figurative, and verbal dimensions of Winstanley's texts. Consequently I consider how these literary features intersect with his distinct revolutionary vision and his scrutiny of Antichristian power in its multiple manifestations. Winstanley, for example, acutely perceives that the politics of class oppression, exploitation, and religious orthodoxy are interconnected with issues of language and artfulness; this dimension of his vision has received little attention from commentators.[16] Like Milton and Lilburne, he was sensitive to the uses of verbal and artful equivocation in an age of revolution, particularly when practiced by political and ecclesiastical authorities which had opposed kingly power during the upheavals of the 1640s.

At the same time, Winstanley's visionary prose is often intensely poetic. He recreates biblical myths to represent and analyze contemporary spiritual and sociopolitical crises: his fantastic recreation of Daniel's vision of the four beasts in *Fire in the Bush* (March 1650) will serve as a striking illustration later in this chapter. But Winstanley, who does not read scriptural texts and history literally, also gives fresh allegorical interpretations to other potent myths such as Cain versus Abel, Jacob versus Esau, Michael versus the Dragon, as well as the myths of Exodus and Eden. Winstanley believed that "al this great change, or seting up of this new law of right-eousnesse, ruling in every one" could be construed as "the fulfilling of Prophesies, and Visions, and Reports of the Scriptures" (p. 206). And yet the radical religious writer moved by the Spirit more than the letter of the Bible is free to reinterpret those texts and myths, since "whether there was any such outward things or no, it matters not much, if thou seest all within" (p. 462). Winstanley thus reinvests biblical myths with urgent new religious and political symbolic meaning, as he interrogates multiple forms of Antichristian power in his age, and as he represents his apocalyptic expectations for a radical transformation of the existing social order. He envisions a new age of universal salvation for all to be established by the spreading of the power and spirit of righteousness, as Christ begins to rise up in his sons and daughters, the saints and True Levellers, and as Abel (symbolic of the exploited) triumphs over Cain, Jacob over Esau, and Michael over the Dragon. Like many other radical Puritan writers, Winstanley draws heavily upon the prophecies of Daniel and Revelation in his apocalyptic visions and speculations about the second coming and Christ's kingdom within.[17] Yet he also gives apocalyptic and millenarian discourse his own original mythopoeic expression. As a radical religious writer, he is keenly sensitive to the abuses of the fleshly imagination, yet the power of his visionary writing is enriched by its revolutionary mythmaking and the figurative texture of his prose.

From his earliest tracts, then, Winstanley depicted himself as "drawn forth by the Spirit to write" (p. 101; cf. pp. 194, 199) his visionary works, a claim that would soon become characteristic of Quaker writers who were likewise led by the Spirit within, while sharply engaging the world without (see Chapters 4 and 8). His texts are "Written in the Light of inward experience," as the title page of *Several Pieces Gathered into one Volume* (1649) announces, and so he follows above all authorities the impulses of "the Spirits inward workings,"[18] freely declaring the Law of Righteousness within, as well as his visionary communist message. The power of the indwelling Spirit can indeed operate as a subversive force, prompting Winstanley to challenge the religious and social orthodoxies of his age with polemical fervor. His visionary works are therefore not texts generated second-hand from books or any form of human learning and external religious authority.[19] The radical religious writer eschews the "enticing words of man's wisdom," preferring, like St. Paul himself, to speak to his age "in demonstration of the Spirit and of power" (1 Cor. 2:4).[20]

The allegorical writer inspired by the Spirit thus freely transforms biblical myths and apocalyptic language to express his distinctive socioeconomic vision of the Fall, social change and power relations during England's mid-seventeenth-century crisis. His visionary mythmaking conveys with urgency his acute analysis of the Revolution, including its contradictions and darker dimensions, during the years of the Republic whose regime did little to alleviate "the crie of the poore" (p. 472).[21] While addressing the sociopolitical dimensions of Winstanley's revolutionary vision, as well as his vigorous metaphorical language, this chapter explores the convergence of aesthetic, religious, and political issues in the substantial works he produced between 1649 and 1652. But first I consider those lesser known texts by Winstanley which immediately preceded but led up to the remarkable works by the communist visionary.

THE PRE-DIGGER VISIONARY

Though stimulated by the widespread apocalypticism and enthusiasm at the height of the Revolution, the intensely millennial writings of Winstanley's pre-Digger career may seem at first less politically engaged than the works he produced just before and while he was leader of his communist agrarian movement. Yet their visionary prose can express with powerful urgency Winstanley's perception of spiritual strife and renewal in his age of religious and political crisis. Indeed, their fierce apocalypticism and anticlericalism would later become thoroughly interconnected with Winstanley's sociopolitical and economic concerns – as they do in *Fire in the Bush*, the most mythopoeic of his Digger works. His early apocalyptic writings, the first four tracts which appeared in 1648–49, already reveal his emerging radicalism – his challenges to orthodox systems of theological belief and social order – and his striking originality as a visionary mythopoeic writer.[22]

The pre-Digger texts begin to develop Winstanley's distinctive rendering and critical analysis of spiritual conflicts and forces – especially Christ's struggle against the menacing institutions of Antichrist – which would soon take on more explicit sociopolitical significance in his writings. *The Mysterie of God, Concerning the whole Creation, Mankinde* (1648), addressed to his "Beloved Countrymen, of the Countie of Lancaster" (sig. A2r),[23] presents an apocalyptic vision of history which he would subsequently revise to accommodate his original socioeconomic view of the Fall in terms of the dark effects of capitalism which make the earth a form of merchandise. In his early text, Winstanley envisions seven great dispensations spanning the age of Adam to the Day of Judgment, all of which humankind must pass through before God will subdue the dark powers of the Serpent. Thus Winstanley's apocalyptic account describes how, during the sixth dispensation, God sends angels "to poure out viols of wrath upon all the glory of the beast" (alluding to Revelation 16), as the fury of the Serpent increases because his time grows short – "his violence, wrath, reproach, oppression, provocations . . . against the Saints are multiplied, and times grow very bad, for now iniquity abounds" (pp. 44–45). While his apocalyptic vision usually operates on a generalized level, at moments his writing assumes more specific historical urgency: "the great bitternesse, envy, reproachfull language, and expressions of malicious wrath in, and among men and women in these dayes, against others whom they brand Sectaries by severall names" (pp. 45–46) all manifest the raging spirit of the Serpent operating in the contemporary world. Alluding to such apocalyptic scriptural passages as Daniel 8:24 and Revelation 19:20, Winstanley's historical vision culminates in a passage reminding his saintly readers that God has been judging the warfaring Serpent, in his various appearances, throughout the ages:

As by the pouring out of the seven viols and the sounding of the seven trumpets, declares how God hath been subduing the Beast, the Whore, and the false Prophet, which hath been the severall appearances of the Serpent under those names, by which he hath made war with Christ and his Saints, so that God hath been about this worke of judging the Serpent long before this day of Judgement came. (p. 64)

Such intensely apocalyptic prose not only highlights Winstanley's sense of the saints embattled in his tumultuous age, it also suggests that the forces of redemption are themselves simultaneously working in history – that the great power of the Spirit will ultimately overcome and destroy the formidable power of the Serpent and his seed, the "mysterie of iniquity." Winstanley's earliest visionary prose conveys a keen sense of apocalyptic anticipation as he yearns for a future when the saints will be freed from the insecurities of their age.

No less intensely apocalyptic is the second-longest tract in his oeuvre, *The Breaking of the Day of God* (its address is dated 20 May 1648), a work that, along with his other early texts, was printed for the radical bookseller Giles Calvert. Its mystical and numerological dimensions (Winstanley extensively explicates, among other biblical numbers, the prophetic meaning of the 1260 days of Revelation 11:3 and 12:6) can make the work seem like one of his more abstruse millenarian texts.[24] But its apocalyptic urgency also anticipates the visionary qualities of his Digger writings, including their more politicized and anticlerical dimensions. Addressed to the unorthodox godly – "The despised Sons and Daughters of Zion, scattered up and down the Kingdome of England" who are "counted the troublers of Kingdoms and Parishes where [they] dwell" (sig. A2r-v) – and highlighting the bitterness of the Beast's reign, the title page nevertheless announces that "Christs dominion over the Nations of the world" is "near the approach." At points Winstanley's text is infused by a sense of heightened expectation for the coming millennium: referring to Revelation 20:6, Winstanley writes "Then Christ, or the Anointing, who is King of righteousnesse and King of peace, shall reign in the Kingdomes and Magistracy of the world, for a . . . thousand years as the scripture speakes"; the visionary writer thus rejoices "in expectation of that universall glorie which God will reveale to his Saints" (pp. 89, 88), including, as his Digger works would soon emphasize more provocatively, "the poorest members that [live] alone among the scoffing sons of bondage" (p. 11).

More keenly than his other tracts of 1648, this text conveys a sense of "these great nationall divisions" and the stormy "cloud of Nationall troubles" (sigs. A4v, A5v) which the bright Son of righteousness, who comes in spirit, will disperse, leading to a period of renewal and redemption – "the Breaking of the Day of God." Yet the breaking of the day of God must occur not only outwardly but also inwardly, in the hearts of the saints themselves: thus Winstanley describes the "inward refreshments" of God in him and the breaking of the Serpent's head within (p. 65). Indeed, Winstanley acutely perceives here that inner division and strife are themselves the origin of external human warfare and restlessness, for "if there were not an inward root of bitternesse in every mans heart against truth, there would not be such strivings and warres amongst men as there is" (p. 73).

Winstanley's poetic prose vividly expresses both his hopes for a period of renewal in England and his anxieties about the overwhelming power of Antichristian darkness in "the age of the Beast" (p. 101). At one moment he blends natural and scriptural imagery, revealing that his natural images, closely connected with the English landscape, are never purely metaphorical; thus he draws upon Canticles 2:10 and 11:12 to express his sense of the process of inward and outward renewal:

now the winter is neer past, the somer is come, the flowers [appear] in the earth: that is, the glorious workings of the Anointing, in the Spirit of Saints, The time of the singing of Birds is come, that is, all the Saints begin to sing *Halelujah*, for the Lord God omnipotent reigneth within; and begins to reigne in the world, And the voice of the Turtle is heard in our land, that is, the voice of the Lord Christ. (p. 62)

At other moments, however, he draws upon another potent biblical image – that of the river Euphrates – to convey the overpowering forces of spiritual darkness in his age: the "spirit of the Beast or serpent is called Euphrates, because as the River Euphrates in the History, overflowed a great part of the Earth, So this spirit of darknesse overflowes man kind" (p. 90). Indeed, it is an image Winstanley returns to at the very end of his visionary tract, as he urges his godly readers to "Wait patiently upon the Lord, let every man that loves God, endeavour, by the spirit of wisdom, meeknesse, and love to drie up *Euphrates*, even this spirit of bitternesse, that like a great River hath over-flowed the earth of man-kinde" (p. 126). Winstanley alludes here to the drying up of the great river Euphrates, after an angel pours God's bowl of wrath into it, described in Revelation

16:12: its drying up, brought on by the efforts of the godly saints in Winstanley's age, is a prelude to Babylon's eventual doom, as the prophet Jeremiah had suggested (see Jer. 50:38).

Fiercely antimonarchical, Winstanley begins to reveal his perception that ecclesiastical and kingly powers remain intimately connected in his troublesome times, a perception more thoroughly informing his Digger tracts where he analyzes proliferating forms of Antichristian powers endangering the Republic. The menacing ecclesiastical power, with all its fleshly forms and customs, is thus "a power which the crafty flesh hath got from the Kings of the Earth" (p. 77); it is "got in fornication" with earthly kings (p. 81) who have given their power to the persecuting Beast, an interpretation consistent with the anonymous but intensely antimonarchical and apocalyptic *Light Shining in Buckinghamshire* (December 1648), which likewise linked earthly kings to the Beast and devil.[25] "When the Kings of the earth give their Authority and power to it," Winstanley writes, then the flesh or the Beast "puts all politike Laws and Ecclesiasticall constitutions into execution to kill the appearances of truth every where" (p. 79). This persecuting power forces orthodox religious beliefs and operates through their established forms, rather than through the teachings of the Spirit, "the indwelling of the holy breathings of Almighty God" (p. 111).

The Breaking of the Day of God also begins to envision Antichristian powers in more theatrical and aesthetic terms, a feature that would characterize the Digger's analysis of state and ecclesiastical institutions: the powers of the flesh and Serpent can assume different menacing "Antichristian shapes" (p. 69) and are "Masters of Art" (p. 120). In one respect, Winstanley's antitheatrical prejudice owes much to an intense radical Puritan suspicion of all outward forms of worship and ritual – "false shewes and formes of Gods worship" (p. 62)[26] – for therein lies the worship of the Beast: Winstanley, after all, follows the antinomian impulses of the Spirit, as did Ranters, Quakers, Seekers, and other religious radicals. He characterizes the "power . . . of the flesh" in terms of its "invensions, actings and appearances" (p. 41); yet when Christ "comes in his brightnes," he reassures his godly readers, "Then will this Beast or wisdom of the flesh be distroyed, in all her shapes and disguises" (p. 57). Winstanley envisions times of sweeping iconoclastic reform (alluding to Haggai 2:7) when God unsettles all social and political institutions and "will yet shake Kings, Parliaments, Armies, Counties, Kingdoms, Universities, [and] humane learnings," as he "shakes down all false shews, forms and customs of pretended divine worship" so that he may "be the only teacher of truths in the heart of his Saints" (p. 115). Only such a mighty divine force can counter the great shape-shifting powers of Antichrist which persecute the saints, compel common men and women to religious conformity, and oppose the establishment of the kingdom of Christ within.[27]

The Saints Paradise: Or, The Fathers Teaching the only satisfaction to waiting Souls (summer 1648)[28] further internalizes the intense spiritual agon between the kingly power of the flesh and the kingly power of the Holy Spirit, a mighty conflict which generates internal restlessness and which would take on notable sociopolitical implications in Winstanley's subsequent writings: "The power of my unrighteous flesh strives to maintain the kingly power in me, and the righteous Law, or the pure spirit strives to maintain his owne righteous and kingly power in me, by tredding the other under foot" (pp. 34–35). In this early work, too, Winstanley's religious radicalism, especially in terms of the way he conceives of his prophetic authority, emerges more intensely. In the past all he knew was what was received "by tradition from the mouths and pen of others," including the teachings, "words or writings of other men," as he looked for a God without: yet that was an unsettled condition when he lived in "the dark, being blinded" by the fleshly imagination. Now, modelling himself on the biblical prophets and apostles, the visionary writer is guided only by "the King of righteousnesse . . . within" (sig. A2r-v), a mighty spiritual power which potentially dwells in all sons and daughters.

The prophetic Winstanley writes in "these troublesome times" when the saints or "the sincere hearted ones" often find themselves under siege: anticipating his more thorough analysis of the menacing system of power operating in the Republic, Winstanley depicts the embattled and martyred saints "in the middest of these stormes" persecuted by "High Commission Courts, Sessions, Canon Laws, Whips, Prisons, and death" (pp. 20, 25–26, 21), as he evokes the earlier savagery of Laudian prerogative courts. Like the radical Protestant poet of the invocations to *Paradise Lost*, who, alluding to Psalm 17:9, finds himself "with dangers compast round" (7.27) in the Restoration, Winstanley, writing during the turmoil of the late 1640s ("all this hurly-burly"), observes that "in these dayes, we see and feel great troubles and temptations do compasse men round" (p. 42). And yet he assures his godly readers that the Father, who allows his faithful saints to endure Job-like afflictions, "will not suffer a finall rooting out of his Saints" and that their "oppressions and sufferings will bring glory to him" (pp. 23, 26) if the saints bear them patiently, demonstrating the power of the Spirit. The spiritual struggle is keen:

"the mysterie of iniquity, Beast, whorish spirit, or flesh . . . strives might and maine to root out all the appearance of God out of mankinde." Nevertheless, while subtle hypocrisy and fleshly power may indeed reign for a period in his age, the prophetic writer envisions the mighty forces of holy wrath at work: "But alas poor Serpent . . . Gods time is neer expired that he gave thee, and he is rooting thee out of mankinde, and consuming in the fire of his wrath" (p. 27).

Furthermore, Winstanley expresses in *The Saints Paradise* an intense yearning for a regained spiritual unity with the Father, whose powerful, dynamic Spirit burns up sin and consumes the curse of the flesh within (as it would later in *Fire in the Bush*): "now the Spirit, the Law of love, this quickens, and unites the Father and his creature again, and makes them one: This Spirit doth burn up, and cast away the flesh" (p. 55). Winstanley's desire for a state of mystical oneness with the Father is combined with his desire for a state of perfection regained, in which the Spirit reigns within, expressed by his references to the paradisal state of Eden whose mythic garden a fallen Adam might eventually reinhabit: God is "beginning to work a great mysterie, and that is, to pull *Adam* out of selfish flesh again, and to plant him into the pure spirit, and so to bring him into the most fruitfull garden of *Eden*" (p. 46). The impulse towards oneness, moreover, has urgent national implications, expressed here through the discourse of alchemy; the process of fiery trials and spiritual purging, with God or the Spirit acting as alchemist, is a process of transmutation taking place both within individuals and in the distressed nation as a whole:[29]

this wrath, bitternesse, discontent that appears generally in mens spirits in *England*, one against another, upon the breakings forth of the truths of God, doth whisper in my spirit, that the Father hath cast *England* into the fire, and is purging the drosse from the gold, that liberty is not far off, and that the plentifull pouring out of the Anoynting, even the spirit of love, truth, and onenesse is near at hand. (pp. 62–63)

Winstanley's yearning for the oneness created by the mighty Son of righteousness healing the earth and "treading down the powers of the flesh" (p. 121) anticipates his later revolutionary tracts: but there it is a oneness – a regaining of Edenic perfection through making the earth a common treasury for all – achieved by overcoming the powers of capitalism, as well the interdependent kingly and clerical powers which have survived the 1648–49 Revolution, proliferating during its ambiguous aftermath.

At moments in *The Saints Paradise*, however, there emerges a more sinister vision of the ensnaring spirit of human selfishness; it manifests itself in a range of social classes, imperils the Revolution, and keeps the saints in bondage:

The national peace and liberty is pretended (that is, the outward shew of love to God) but secretly most men, both of high and low degree, intend either to inrich themselves with the kingdomes monies & ruins, or else by their secret underhand working, endeavour to vent their malice upon the kingdomes friends, even the Saints. (p. 28)

Winstanley's sense of "pretended" national liberty and the appearance of "love to God" (an "outward shew") recalls his perception of the theatrical forms of Antichristian power. Commitments to godly reform, he implies, are often superficial at best and, in the case of most people, simply driven by "self-love, subtile imagination, and the like" (pp. 28, 73), which he associates with the Serpent within, as well as with all specious forms of worship, religious customs, and imaginary inventions. Like Bunyan, moreover, he can at moments represent the spiritual crisis of an age given over to fleshly pursuits in terms of an allegorized interior landscape: instead of running up "the hill of self denial," "these earthly minded men run lower and lower from God, who is called *Sions* hill; in hunting after covetousnesse, self-love, temporal glory, fleshly imaginations, and thoughts," they "run downwards, further and further from the life of the spirit" (p. 97). Winstanley's darker analysis can trigger his prophetic exhortation, as he warns great earthly powers (and not only monarchs) of the mighty power of the Spirit, as he would later do more sharply in his politically engaged Digger writings: "Assure your selves, you Kingly, Parliamentarie, and Army power, and know this, that all unrighteous powers and actings must be destroyed; the father is about his work, and his hand will not slack" (p. 81).

At the beginning of *The Saints Paradise*, Winstanley suggests that the world where the king of righteousness is ultimately the "mighty governour" ruling within and where the Spirit is spreading in sons and daughters would indeed be a world turned upside down: "wise men in the flesh are made fools, fools are made wise, scholars are declared to be ignorant, the ignorant ones in mens learning, become abundantly learned in the experimentall knowledge of Christ" (sigs. A3v-A4r). But as Winstanley observes in his *Breaking of the Day of God*, the saints are now despised and "such as the world counts fools" (p. 21).[30] Learned himself in "the experimentall knowledge of Christ" and writing from the Spirit's testimony, the visionary writer who rejects established theological doctrine and who would soon produce a radical reconception of the social order might indeed be regarded as a blasphemous fool in the eyes of orthodox ecclesiastical authorities who could now easily appeal, for political support, to Parliament's recent ordinance against blasphemies and heresies (May 1648): as the heretical Winstanley complains to the clerical elite in his next major tract, he, as well as William Everard, have been slandered by parish ministers and "branded . . . guilty of horrid *blasphemy*" (*Works*, p. 101).[31]

That work of vindication entitled *Truth Lifting Up Its Head Above Scandals* (1649), which includes an opening epistle addressed to the scholars of Oxford and Cambridge (dated October 1648), develops radical themes anticipated in Winstanley's earlier apocalyptic writings, while looking forward to his Digger works. Winstanley expresses his persistent hatred of religious orthodoxies and forms in vigorous homely metaphors as he attacks the professional ministers – "yee proud Priests" possessing "fleshly learning" – who claim "to teach the People the mystery of the Spirit": they "leade the People like horses by the noses; & ride upon them at [their] pleasure from one forme and custome to another, and so quite from the Spirit" (pp. 145, 99, 100). This, indeed, is the first text in which he accuses the professional ministry of reinforcing orthodox theological beliefs (including the otherness of God) by means of linguistic and hermeneutic practices: by "moulding those Scriptures into their own language . . . [and] by holding forth God and Christ to be at a distance from men" (p. 104). Highly sensitive to alienating uses of orthodox theological language by the institutional clergy, the heterodox Winstanley now provocatively chooses the word Reason to mean God or the Spirit;[32] as he observes regarding the name God and its oppressive uses by learned ministers, "I have been held under darknesse by that word, as I see many people are" (p. 105). Winstanley's spirit of Reason is that dynamic power that purges the dark self-oriented powers of the flesh and human imagination, while creating the kingdom of God within the hearts of all men and women and, like a pantheistic force, infusing the Creation with new life: "Reason is that living power of light that is in all things . . . it is the fire that burns up drosse, and so restores what is corrupted; and preserves what is pure; he is the Lord our righteousnesse" (p. 104). Furthermore, *Truth Lifting Up Its Head* begins to depict the inward operations of the mighty Spirit Reason, which controls the unruly powers of the flesh, in sociopolitical language that Winstanley's writings were about to redefine in visionary communist terms: "the spirituall power that governes in thee, hath a community in thee with the whole globe; and thou art made subject to that spirit of righteousnesse" (p. 108).

Most of Winstanley's text consists of a lengthy series of questions and responses aimed at justifying his heterodox vision of the Creation permeated and ruled by the mighty Spirit Reason. Indeed, his last response, which begins by addressing the use of words in prayer (inspired by the power of the inward Spirit), quickly develops into an extensive passage vindicating the heretical Winstanley, whose practices follow "the light of pure Reason," and inveighing against "the Ministers of England" with their "customary way of performances" and ritualistic practices (e.g., maintaining compulsory Sabbath and the ritual of infant baptism), all of which "mightily deceive the people" (pp. 139–45). Linking back to Winstanley's opening addresses to the professional ministers and to the "gentle reader," his concluding answer to *Truth Lifting Up Its Head* highlights the crafty powers of the paid ministry – the way their practices, constructions upon Scripture, and "fleshly learning" have enabled them to keep the common people in "slavish bondage." Such vehemence in response to the subtle practices and rituals of the educated clergy would eventually culminate in the dramatic, original apocalyptic mythmaking of his most visionary communist text, *Fire in the Bush*, as we shall see later.

THE SPIRIT OF RIGHTEOUSNESS IN A NEW AGE OF BONDAGE

Published right in the midst of the political crisis of 1648–49, Winstanley's next major tract elaborated a new law of righteousness and its relation to the spreading power of the Spirit within. *The New Law of Righteousnes budding forth, in restoring the whole creation from the bondage of the curse* (26 January 1648/49) evolves from his earlier visionary writings, but in character with his subsequent Digger works, it transforms the mighty spiritual conflicts of his unsettled age by giving them a more urgent socioeconomic interpretation, while simultaneously analyzing their interior origins. Here Winstanley first develops his central radical socioeconomic vision of the whole earth becoming again "a common treasury" for all (rather than a particular treasury from some), as it had been at the beginning of the Creation. And here Winstanley – having heard a voice within telling him "*Worke together. Eat bread together*; declare this all abroad" (p. 190) – first records his visionary trance at the end of 1648 that resulted in his conversion to communism, that crucial event in his career coinciding with the climactic events of the Revolution. Not until April 1649, however, would he "act materially this Law of Righteousnesse" (p. 195) which he found himself boldly proclaiming in his visionary writing at the beginning of 1649. This substantial tract, itself "a true declaration of the Spirit" (p. 194), is thus crucial in developing the heterodox religious and radical political emphases of his later writings, so that this text can indeed be regarded as a major transitional work in his oeuvre. Here too Winstanley manifests his gift for original revolutionary mythmaking based loosely upon the Scriptures. He freely reworks biblical myths to represent contemporary political and class conflicts, as well as the conflict between the power of darkness and the Spirit raging within the heart of each restless individual groaning under the curse; the story of the younger brother Jacob and the oppressing Lord Esau appears, with an urgent potency, for the first time in his visionary prose: "he is hated, persecuted and despised in you, he is Jacob in you, that is and hath been a servant to Esau a long time; but though this Jacob be very low, yet his time is now come, ... and he will rise up in you that are trod under foot like dust of the earth" (p. 149).

Winstanley published his *New Law of Righteousnes* in the midst of the momentous events which gave birth to the Republic – its preface is dated 26 January, one day after Charles I was sentenced and four days before he was executed. Winstanley indeed had every reason to hope that the cataclysmic Revolution followed by a republican regime would finally effect social revolution and radical godly reform. This was a historical moment when the saints, inspired with millenarian fervor, could expect great things, now that Parliament had recently been purged and kingly power seemed cast out of the realm for once and for all: "the powers of this world shall be given into the hands of the Lord and his Saints," observed the Fifth Monarchist Thomas Harrison in the recent Whitehall Debates, "this is the day, God's own day, wherein he is coming forth in glory in the world."[33] This was an apocalyptic revolution in which all earthly kings would be destroyed, along with Antichrist, and Christ's kingdom would be set up in England. The Diggers too could exult: "the old World . . . is running up like parchment in the fire" (p. 252). The destruction and demystification of monarchy and the establishment of the English Republic seemed to herald the New Jerusalem.

But the sense of euphoria generated by the traumatic events of December 1648 to February 1649 was qualified – even in early 1649 – for some radicals by a keen sense of disappointment. The Rump, during whose regime Winstanley produced most of his theological and political works, was hardly a zealously radical governing body or a gathering of saints, as recent historians have noted; indeed, it was a cautious assembly with little revolutionary fervor and was no more radical about

religious than about social reform: few of its members shared the godly
zeal of a Henry Vane or even a Milton.[34] The Levellers had no illusions
at all about the new Republic which they accused of menacing dissimulation (as we saw in Chapter 1). Thus the first part of Lilburne's
England's New Chains Discovered (February 1648/49), published a month
after Winstanley's *New Law of Righteousnes*, revealed, in language suggesting the perversion of a potentially fruitful political age, precisely how
defiantly embittered radical writers could become with the shortcomings
of a regime which failed to enact God's work: "after these fair blossoms
of hopefull liberty, breaks forth this bitter fruit, of the vilest and basest
bondage that ever English men groan'd under."[35] Using another metaphor nearly a year later, Isaac Penington the younger (the son of the
radical London alderman) likened the purged Parliament to a doctor
tending to a "very sick" nation, but then perceived that "now most men
are grown sick both of the Phisitian and the cure."[36]

How, then, would Winstanley's new law of inward righteousness, a
revolutionary law of equity and reason, spread itself among all men and
women in England in a volatile age when its regime – at first envisioned
by radicals as a means of transforming the social order and freeing the
Creation from "the curse it groans under" (p. 149) – was beginning to
show little evidence of godly progress in religious and social reform?
Winstanley thus finds himself, from 1649 on, struggling with the ambiguities of a republic and revolution which failed to effect radical social
change and set up the inward rule of Christ on earth. Having contained
and overthrown the Norman kingly power, it boldly professed in early
January 1649 that "all just power" originates from the people,[37] yet its
regime was supported by a narrow base and was hardly likely to abolish
private property or make the earth a common treasury for all (especially
the poor). Even in the midst of the dramatic republican revolution, when
he published *The New Law*, Winstanley complained to "the despised ones
of the world," to whom his text is addressed, that the curse "hath been
rather multiplied from year to year," a "thick darknesse" overspreads the
corrupt earth, and "misery breaks forth upon man-kind." The oppressive powers of the flesh and covetousness, Winstanley laments, rule
everywhere in the nation: "a man can go into no place, but he shall see
the curse and enmity is that power that rules the creatures" (pp. 149, 152).
"Heavy oppressions" lie upon the poor of England in an age when the
buying and selling of land, which Winstanley associated with the Beast
of Revelation 13:17, upholds "this particular propriety of *Mine* and
Thine" (p. 159), a social condition which destroys the Creation and fuels

class conflicts as the rich and the gentry harden their hearts against the commoners, "treading them like mire in the street" (p. 208).

Acutely sensitive to the politics of economic enthrallment, class division, and ecclesiastical bondage, Winstanley looks within in order to analyze the Antichristian darkness and curse he finds without. His *New Law* depicts the great cosmic conflicts of his age allegorically as two powers which continue to struggle within humankind, the site of the most intense combat between flesh and Spirit: "For these two powers are the two *Adams* in mankind; they are *Jacob* and *Esau*, striving who shall rule in the Kingdom, the flesh first" (p. 173). The first Adam, unrighteous and a bringer of woe, does indeed govern within every man and woman, so that the Christ within, the "second man . . . which is the righteous power, doth cast the other man (which is the unrighteous power) out of the house, even the heart, and makes it a temple for himself to dwell in" (p. 177). The present crisis of Winstanley's revolutionary age, then, is not to be explained historically by appealing, in the usual manner of orthodox preachers, to the first Adam's fall or by looking at "things that were done 1649 years agoe" (p. 212); it cannot be explained ultimately by looking at external historical events themselves, since "all that which you call the history . . . is all to be seen and felt within you" (p. 215). The conflicts between the old and new Adams and between the oppressive Lord Esau and the meek Jacob are all within us and occurring in the present: the second Adam "doth kill and crucifie the first *Adam* daily" (p. 173). And so the workings of the living Spirit must likewise take place within believers:

Because that which a man seeks for, whereby he might have peace, is within the heart, not without. The word of life, Christ the restoring spirit, is to be found within you . . . *The Kingdome of heaven* (which is) Christ *is within you,* and disobedient *Adam* is within you; for this is *Esau* that strives with *Jacob* in the womb of your heart to come forth first. (p. 213)

Like the Milton of *Paradise Regained*, whose inward-oriented Jesus rejects all temporal kingdoms and powers, Winstanley envisions a kingdom of righteousness reigning within the self – ruled by the authority of the Spirit and subverting the kingdom of the flesh.

But whereas Milton's intensely inward spiritual poem concerns itself with a historical Jesus, Winstanley's visionary text never does at all. In *The New Law* biblical history, representing the great spiritual and social conflicts unsettling Winstanley's age, is altogether relocated inwardly: "*Cain* and *Abel* is to be seen within," as are Abraham, Isaac, and Moses; "The *Canaanites, Amalekites, Philistines* . . . are to be seen within you, making war with Israel, Christ within you"; and "*Judas*, a treacherous self-loving and covetous spirit . . . is to be seen within you" (p. 215). Heaven and hell, light and darkness, and good and bad angels in Winstanley's heterodox vision likewise are within the self. One does not need , then, to "go to *Rome*, nor hell below ground, as some talke, to find the Pope, Devil, Beast or Power of darknesse";[38] nor does one need "to go up into heaven above the skies to find Christ the word of life" (p. 176). Christ likewise lies within, as the revolutionary Quakers themselves believed, while the "outward heaven" of orthodox religion is, in Winstanley's heterodox account, nothing more than "a fancy which . . . false Teachers put into your heads to please you with, while they pick your purses . . . and hold *Jacob* under to be a servant still to Lord *Esau*" (pp. 226–27). Even the whole Creation, before man sought satisfaction in outward objects, "was in man, one within" (p. 155). Thus the new law of righteousness, essential to the fulfillment of Winstanley's materialist theology and communist vision, would itself be completely internalized – "plainly writ in every ones heart" (p. 183) – and rule within the self, a vision Winstanley shares with the antinomian Ranter Jacob Bauthumley.[39]

Indeed, it is the curse within that generates great restlessness among the people in Winstanley's age, prompting them to run "from one form and custome to another, meeting with confusion . . . every where" (p. 230). Winstanley depicts such inner torment as acute, characterized by a sense of intense sinfulness, vexation, and fear. It recalls the guilt and despair of inwardly tormented Calvinist Puritans anxious about election or damnation, a harsh predestinarianism this radical religious writer rejects (as did Ranters, Quakers, General Baptists, and other radical spiritualists). Winstanley's homely metaphors remind us of Bunyan, but his analysis of inner bondage and shame differs significantly: "poor Creatures" who "are in bondage within . . . are filled with sighings and secret mournings, to see themselves in confusion and losse, to stick in the mire, but cannot come out: This is inward slaverie" (p. 230). In an age when devout Englishmen and women often felt themselves possessed, pursued, and tormented by demons,[40] the heterodox Winstanley depicts the "hell-torment" (p. 223) within, a state of Antichristian tyranny, as an unsettled condition we have created by enthralling ourselves to Lord Esau, the power of the proud flesh and self-interest: "if . . . a man be tormented by visible bodies of fury, and ugly shapes . . . they be all the creatures of his own making, and rods which the flesh hath made to whip and punish himself withall" (p. 218).

Winstanley associates his new law of righteousness only with the "inward testimony" and experience of the living Spirit (much as Milton himself did), and with no other ecclesiastical power or external form.[41] In this sense, the radical religious emphasis of his *New Law of Righteousnes* resembles the georgic radicalism and spiritual inwardness of *Paradise Regained*, though Winstanley's materialist theology is unique to him. Like Milton, who presents an inward, lowly Jesus guided by the Spirit in his messianic calling, Winstanley highlights those humble people who have been moved by the Spirit to act and speak righteously – those "Fishermen, Shepherds, Husbandmen, and the Carpenters son, who spake and writ as the Spirit gave them utterance, from an inward testimony" (p. 238). That inward testimony, and the new law inspired by it, is found more often in the hearts of the lowest classes and will spring up out of the earth: "the declaration of the righteous law shal spring up from the poor, the base and despised ones, and fools of the world" (p. 205). Throughout his revolutionary tract, Winstanley contrasts this inward authority with the subtle practices of the public preachers whose formal learning, when it comes to spiritual matters, he despises as much as Milton would in his passionate attack on the pretences of the hireling Antichristian ministry:[42] they "draw people under a new bondage" and "darken knowledge by their words" as they substitute "words and histories for spirit" (pp. 239, 241, 214). At the end of *The New Law*, he recalls his earlier days of orthodox belief when he, then spiritually weak and enslaved, was "a blind Professour and a strict goer to Church, as they call it, and a hearer of Sermons, and never questioned what they spake, but believed as the learned Clergy (the Church) believed"; but now, though called "a blasphemer, and a man of errors," the heretical Winstanley speaks and writes only "from an inward light and power of life within" (p. 243; cf. p. 224), as his unorthodox theological discourse questions the system of fashionable religious belief maintained by those who preach for hire. Like the controversialist Milton who defends his "sharp, but saving words," Winstanley acknowledges that his righteous polemical "words" in *The New Law* "may seem sharp to some," though he does "not write them out of any envy to any man, but out of love to all" (p. 244), particularly the poor and weak.

Using richly metaphorical prose in *The New Law*, Winstanley draws upon vivid tropes taken from the natural world, as well as Scripture, and reworks them allegorically in order to convey his urgent sense of social and spiritual conflicts, including the two powers striving for government within humankind. By fusing natural and biblical tropes, he enriches, while giving distinctive expression to, his analysis of the formidable powers which nourish and oppress the Creation. Thus, for example, he associates the light and power of "the day-vine within" with Christ (recalling John 15:1, "I am the true vine") who, like a spreading tree, fills the Creation with himself. This is the spreading, flourishing law of righteousness within: those "in whom Christ is spread . . . make up but one vine, knit together by that one spirit, into one body; whether they be poor or rich; learned or unlearned" (pp. 237, 236). "A night-vine," however, is Lord Esau, the power of darkness and the fleshly government which has likewise branched forth, thereby keeping Jacob, the spirit of meekness, under and hindering Christ from rising and filling the earth with himself: "And every man and woman that is guided by this selfish power of darknesse, are but branches of the night-vine." Based partly on his immediate experience of working the land, Winstanley's metaphor assumes a potent social and spiritual resonance as he suggests how the Spirit has been treacherously betrayed: "Now this night-vine (but rather Thorn-bush) is the branchings forth of the wisdom and power of selfish flesh: every bud from it, is a sharp prickle: treacherous & covetous *Judas*, is one branch from that root, and he hath risen up to a mighty great tree; for every treacherous and covetous heart, is but the buddings forth of *Judas*" (p. 237). Judas, Demas, Simon Magus, and the learned Pharisees, Winstanley suggests, all exist in newer manifestations in the present age and "have covered the earth with their branches" (p. 238): they are those "zealous Preachers and Professours of other mens words and writings, and upholders of forms . . . that still pursue Christ in enmity." Because of their oppressive power, "the night-Vine, or branches of the Thorn-bush, are so mighty great and thick" that they block out "the light and heat of the Sun of Righteousnesse" (p. 240) – that spreading power of Christ able to remove the curse inwardly, as well as outwardly from the burdened Creation.

The first Digger manifesto, *The True Levellers Standard Advanced* (20 April 1649), further reinforces the radical vision and analysis of Winstanley's *New Law*, including its revolutionary mythmaking. Published just as Winstanley and Everard were meeting with Fairfax at Whitehall to defend their radical activities,[43] that text justifies to the world the righteous work of the Diggers on St. George's Hill as they were beginning to enact the law of righteousness within them. Although a collaborative work (Winstanley's name appears on the title page along with fourteen others), this text clearly shows the mark of Winstanley's own creative vision as it opens by revising, in terms of Digger communism and language, the myth of Genesis itself: "In the beginning of Time, the great Creator Reason, made the Earth to be a Common Treasury, to preserve, Beasts, Birds, Fishes, and Man . . . not one word was spoken in the beginning, That one branch of mankind should rule over another" (p. 251).[44] Even more stridently than *The New Law*, this Digger work polemically confronts the contradictions of the so-called free Commonwealth (formally declared by the Rump the next month) as it addresses the "Powers of *England*" (p. 255) and blames them for having brought heavier hardships upon the already distressed common people, thereby preventing the earth from becoming "a Common Treasury of relief for all" (p. 252):[45]

Thou hast made many promises and protestations to make the Land a Free Nation: And yet at this very day, the same people, to whom thou hast made such Protestations of Liberty, are oppressed by thy Courts, Sizes, Sessions, by thy Justices and Clarks of the Peace, so called, Bayliffs, Committees, are imprisoned, and forced to spend that bread, that should save their lives from Famine. (p. 256)

The private landlords, especially, have assumed the role of Lord Esau, the man of flesh, and thereby epitomize the failure of the Revolution to free the Creation from bondage: using their "subtile wit and power" (p. 258) to abuse and deceive the plain-hearted people, they enrich themselves while impoverishing others; and by rising up to become justices and rulers, they perpetuate a social system which only reinforces the misery of the poor.

Employed for the first time by Winstanley and the Diggers, the powerful myth of the Norman Conquest, blended with the scriptural myths of Jacob and Esau and Babylon, enables them to represent English history in terms of the continuity of terrible class oppression which has beaten down the poor and meek in spirit throughout the ages:

If you cast your eye a little backward, you shall see, That this outward Teaching and Ruling power, is the Babylonish yoke laid upon Israel of old, under *Nebuchadnezzar*; and so Successively from that time, the Conquering Enemy, have still laid these yokes upon Israel to keep *Jacob* down: And the last enslaving Conquest which the Enemy got over Israel, was the *Norman* over *England*; and from that time, Kings, Lords, Judges, Justices, Bayliffs, and the violent bitter people that are Free-holders, are and have been Successively: The *Norman* Bastard *William* himself, his Colonels, Captains, inferiour Officers, and Common Souldiers, who still are from that time to this day in pursuite of that victory, Imprisoning, Robbing, and killing the poor enslaved *English* Israelites. (p. 259)

Charles I had been the successor to William the Conqueror who had originally deprived the English people of their rights and liberties in 1066 and who had divided up the land among his followers: in Winstanley's writings, the anti-Norman legend becomes a myth of the Fall of humankind itself.[46] Despite the recent victory over Charles, Norman power has never ended. Warning England of her peril, the prophetic Winstanley would reinforce that point in *A Watch-Word to the City of London* (August 1649), where he employs a military trope to convey the ominous expansion of Norman oppression in his age: the "chief Captain *Charles*" may be gone, Winstanley observes, but his colonels (the lords of manors), his counsellors (the lawyers and priests), and his officers and soldiers (the rich freeholders, gentry, and landlords) constitute such a numerous body or camp that England is now more vulnerable than ever (pp. 330–31, 334, 337). *The True Levellers Standard* drives home the Diggers' point about the oppressiveness of laws upheld since the Norman Conquest by using another ominous metaphor: they evoke the harshness of contemporary prison conditions by characterizing the laws as "the Cords, Bands, Manacles, and Yokes that the enslaved *English*, like *Newgate* Prisoners, wears [sic] upon their hands and legs as they walk the streets" (p. 259). Yet the brutal imprisonment of the poor is not confined to a particular place – Newgate prison – but finds reinforcement in the larger culture with its uncompromising system of laws, judges, courts, and so on. All of England itself "is a Prison," Winstanley urgently reiterated to Parliament and the Army the next year, and "the varieties of subtilties in the Laws preserved by the Sword, are bolts, bars, and doors of the prison; the Lawyers are the Jaylors, and poor men are the prisoners" (*A New-Yeers Gift*, p. 361). The powers of England in the age of the new Commonwealth thus live in "mighty Delusion" as they "pretend to throw down that *Norman* yoke, and *Babylonish* power" (p. 259): the reality, the Diggers suggest, is much grimmer. The claim that the poor commoners have finally been freed from Norman oppression is no more than an illusion perpetuated and exploited by the great landlords and new rulers of England.

The tone of *The True Levellers Standard* is often sharp, anticipating the pugnacious sectarian challenge to the dominant social order that would emerge even more strongly in the early 1650s.[47] The visionary Diggers warn not only the unrighteous, hard-hearted powers of England – "you that are the great Ones of the Earth" (p. 266)[48] – but also the laborers themselves who, working for hire, help to perpetuate a cycle of tyranny and poverty. The visionary Diggers thus record another voice "heard in a Trance" warning of God's judgment and intervention: "*Whosoever labours the Earth for any Person or Persons, that are lifted up to rule over others, and doth not look upon themselves, as Equal to others in the Creation: The hand of the Lord shall be upon that Laborer: I the Lord have spoke it, and I will do it*" (p. 262). The present age of Norman slavery recalls the Old Testament bondage of Israel under Egyptian taskmasters; but while echoing the language of Exodus – "*Let Israel go Free*" – and assuming the warning voice of the Lord, the prophetic Digger writers radically redefine social and political oppression in terms of a system of capitalism that must be shattered before a new age of righteousness can truly begin: "break in pieces quickly the Band of particular Propriety, dis-own this oppressing Murder, Oppression and Thievery of Buying and Selling of Land" (p. 264).

In *A New-Yeers Gift Sent to the Parliament and Armie* (January 1650), Winstanley analyzes even more extensively the spiritual and social implications of a dark kingly power which operates contrary to the new law of righteousness and power of universal love, and which upholds the Norman Conquest in the Republic. Though he supported the controversial Engagement, the government's new loyalty oath, as symbolic of a new age of righteous freedom for all classes,[49] his view of the Commonwealth remains deeply ambivalent: its rulers have provided the occasion for radical social and spiritual renewal, while having also made England fertile ground for the spread of kingly power. His vigorous colloquial prose, written as he was digging the commons, conveys the expansiveness and deep-rootedness of kingly power after the regicide and the Act of Parliament abolishing kingship (17 March 1649): "that top-bow is lopped off the tree of Tyrannie, and Kingly power in that one particular is cast out; but alas oppression is a great tree still, and keeps off the sun of freedome from the poor Commons still, he hath many branches and great roots which must be grub'd up, before everyone can sing Sions songs." Developing his metaphor of the great tree, Winstanley registers how kingly power has manifested itself in other branches of oppressive power which darken the Creation and entangle the earth: "Now there are Three Branches more of Kinglie power greater then the former that oppresses this Land wonderfully" – "the power of the Tithing Priests," "the power of Lords of Mannors," and "the intolerable oppression" of "bad Laws" and "bad Judges." Indeed, by letting "the other Branches and root stand," the great tree of kingly power will only "recover fresher strength" (pp. 357, 353), as it has since the beginning of the Republic. Its "several limbs and members must be cast out" before

"Kingly power," which has become widely spread in the nation, "can be pulled up root and branch" (p. 372): as his trope suggests, Winstanley's figurative language is frequently rooted in the natural world, but it gains potency by fusing allegorical and biblical meanings (in Malachi 4:1 the Lord shall leave the proud "neither root nor branch"), along with historical ones (the phrase "root and branch" had had political resonance since the popular petition of December 1640 calling for radical reform and the abolition of a Romish episcopacy "with all its dependencies, roots and branches").[50]

In *A New-Yeers Gift*, moreover, Winstanley expresses his sense of class division by displaying a keen sense of Civil War history. Addressing the Parliament and the Army Grandees, presented more as dissembling powers of the earth than as true liberators,[51] Winstanley explains that during the Civil War years the poorer people and the gentry were united by a common cause – to make England a free Commonwealth – as they struggled together against the Norman power and prerogative represented by Charles I: "by the joynt assistance of Parliament and People, the King was beaten in the field, his head taken off, and his Kingly power voted down; and we the Commons thereby virtually have recovered our selves from the Norman Conquest" (p. 370). Indeed, the common people, Winstanley stresses, played a particularly active role in that momentous struggle and "bore the greatest heat of the day in casting out the oppressor" (p. 371), a claim a powerless Winstanley would later reiterate to Cromwell in *The Law of Freedom*. But since casting out that Norman power and cutting off the top bow of the tree of tyranny, the gentry have turned against the poor commoners – the very people who helped them win the Civil Wars and resist the Norman yoke. This argument, supported by his vivid evocation of Norman oppression, is Winstanley's strategy for allying the Digger cause with that of the Republic's rulers ("My Advice to you Gentlemen is this, Hereafter to . . . cherish the Diggers," p. 362), and for generating a sense of urgency that might reconcile the regime with its suffering people and the promising words of Parliament – their proclaiming England "a Commonwealth and Free State" in May 1649 – with righteous actions.[52] But at this historical juncture, "Justice is pretended" (p. 387) and the contradictions of the Commonwealth remain acute.

Winstanley's most visionary representation of the dark powers of the world proliferating in the Commonwealth, however, occurs in the major apocalyptic tract which appeared several months after *A New-Yeers Gift*: *Fire in the Bush*. There Winstanley's analysis of "a confederacie between the Clergy and the great red Dragon," between ecclesiastical and kingly powers (p. 387), with all their interconnected forms and subtle manifestations, reaches its most complex articulation. There too his revolutionary mythmaking, generated by his response to the urgent social and spiritual crises of his unsettled age, achieves its most memorable expression.

THE POWERS OF THE BEAST

In *Fire in the Bush* the Digger uses a terrifying image of evil based upon the great red Dragon of Revelation 12 to represent ecclesiastical power: a form of kingly power, "clergy power," Winstanley writes, "makes a man a sinner for a word, and so he sweeps the Stars of Heaven downe with his tayle, he darkens Heaven and Earth, and defiles body and mind" (p. 469). This striking image conveys the frightening character of the professional clergy in his age; indeed, his prose frequently depicts that ecclesiastical institution as a monstrous, Antichristian iniquity. Winstanley's passage suggests, moreover, that language and interpretation themselves are exploited by ecclesiastical authorities as dark instruments of power which restrain "the liberty of the inward man" (p. 469). This oppressive use of language (in addition to outward forms of worship) is a manifestation of the great spiritual battles of his age between the powers of darkness and light, flesh and Spirit, bondage and righteousness, and property and community.

To illuminate further the Digger's original apocalyptic mythmaking, I want to look in a moment at one of the most potent symbolic passages in *Fire in the Bush*, a work addressed to the churches "IN THE PRES-BYTERIAN, INDEPENDENT, OR ANY OTHER FORME OF PROFESSION" (p. 445) – by which Winstanley means the university-trained professional clergy.[53] This work appeared in March 1650, more than a year after his conversion to communism.[54] In this text, where his materialist theology and social radicalism remain fused, he assumes a fiercely prophetic stance, often admonishing earthly powers as he and the Diggers had done in *The True Levellers Standard*: his impulse to write this prophetic text is a "free gift . . . from the Father himselfe . . . the voyce was in my very heart and mouth, ready to come forth; goe send it to the Churches" (p. 445). In his mythopoeic writing, moreover, Winstanley recreates Biblical images and language – from Genesis and especially from the Books of Daniel and Revelation – as a means of giving dramatic urgency to his polemical attacks on political and ecclesiastical institutions and their established beliefs; and to express his intense vision of the heated battle between the Spirit and flesh, the Lamb and the Dragon raging within the self and "within the garden mankinde" (p. 460). Here Winstanley makes arresting, idiosyncratic uses of scriptural myths and language, along with their figurative qualities, to represent his socioeconomic vision of the Fall and the multiple shapes of Antichristian power in his age. Biblical and eschatological metaphors take on fresh potency as they assume contemporary sociopolitical significance, suggesting the interdependence of the political, literary, and theological dimensions of his visionary Digger writing.[55]

Repudiating the doctrine of original sin, Winstanley's heretical theology does not interpret the Fall as an event to be blamed on Adam who died thousands of years ago. Rather, it is a historical process unfolding within us all, just as the Serpent itself lies within us. Moreover, as *Fire in the Bush* highlights, it is directly linked to the human creation of private property, which results in enclosures (i.e. the "dividing of the Earth into parcells" and hedging the weak out of the earth (p. 490)), as well as the artful craft of buying and selling the land, and which then leads to discontent, divisions, and wars – a kind of vicious, competitive Hobbesian state of nature. Driven out of the Garden by the Serpent "blinde Imagination," this self-alienated mankind "is like the Beasts of the field, who live upon objects without them," while being filled "with feares, doubts, troubles, evill surmisings and grudges" (p. 452). Similarly, the fierce apocalyptic battle between the powers of Michael and the Dragon will take place not at some distant point in the future, but indeed is taking place at this very moment – within the souls and hearts of each individual, as well as within the culture at large.[56] Its internal character is highlighted in the subtitle of Winstanley's visionary text: *The spirit burning, not consuming, but purging mankinde. Or, The great battell of God Almighty, between Michaell the seed of life, and the great red dragon, the curse fought within the spirit of man* (p. 72).

One of the most vivid symbolic passages in *Fire in the Bush* provides a striking illustration of the way in which Winstanley combines political representation and creative apocalyptic mythmaking with an almost Blakean prophetic imagination. He recalls and expands the Book of Daniel's vision of the four great beasts or world empires rising out of the chaos of the great sea (see Daniel 7:2–12), a favorite passage in this revolutionary age for millenarian speculation and interpretation.[57] In order to convey the potency and texture of his visionary writing, it is worth examining crucial details of that allegorical prophecy – and the distinctive sociopolitical interpretation Winstanley gives it – at some length:

These foure powers are the foure Beasts, which *Daniel* saw rise up out of the Sea . . . And this Sea is the bulke and body of mankinde, which is that Sea, and waters, upon which the Spirit of God is said sometimes to move; for out of Mankinde arises all that darknesse and Tyranny that oppresses it selfe; And though these Beasts appeare divers, one from another, yet they are all one in their power; for Imaginary-selfe ruling in mans heart, is the Father that created and bred them all.

Although all the beasts are different from each other, as the Book of Daniel indicates, Winstanley stresses that they are really "all one in their power," and he proceeds to give the symbolic creatures a contemporary significance that expresses his urgent sociopolitical concerns and vision of the rule of the Serpent in its fourfold external power. In Winstanley's mythic version, all the fantastic beasts are indeed human creations rising "up out of the deceived heart of mankinde" (p. 464); kingly power, the institutional church, the law, and private property are thus all visible manifestations of the Serpent or Dragon within humankind. External tyranny, according to Winstanley, whatever shapes it assumes or power it manifests, always derives from an internal origin: as he puts it in *The New Law*, "Our own works are our tormenting devils" (p. 220). The first beast of his vision, like a lion with eagle wings (representing Babylon in the Bible), is symbolic of the conquering "Kingly Power": dividing the Creation with the sword, it gives "the Earth to some, denying the Earth to others"; and his eagle wings are symbolic of the swiftness with which this power conquers and divides what it takes. The second beast, appearing like a bear and commanded to devour flesh in Daniel's vision, represents the power of the predatory and "selfish Lawes, which is full of covetousnesse" (p. 465), as it devours the fearful and helpless poor: the three ribs in this beast's mouth represent in Winstanley's allegorical vision a series of hellish torments including the power of prisons, the power of whipping and banishment, and the power of hanging and burning.[58]

Indeed, Winstanley's terrifying allegory becomes increasingly elaborate – symbolic of a great cosmic drama and the "fruitfull generation" (p. 468) and branching forth of the interconnected powers of Antichrist in his age – as he continues to expand upon Daniel's vision (while also recalling the worldly and tyrannical beast rising from the sea in Revelation 13). Thus the third beast resembles "a Leopard, spotty" (that it is "spotty" is symbolic of its impurity),[59] and this becomes in

Winstanley's vision "the thieving Art of buying and selling the Earth
with her fruits one to another," while its four wings represent "Policy,
Hypocrisie, Self-Love, and hardnesse of Heart; for this Beast is a true
self-Lover, to get the Earth to himselfe, to lock it up in Chests and
barnes, though others starve for want." Furthermore, its four heads,
supporting the beast's tyranny and enslaving others to it, become in
Winstanley's interpretation "the power of the sword," "the power of
the Law," "the power of the covetous Imaginary Clergie," and the
power of "a blinde deceived Heart, over-awed with feare of men"
(pp. 465–66). In effect, Winstanley is engaging in his own highly original mythmaking as he radically revises a prophetic scriptural text to represent his perception of the acute social crisis, economic oppression and
class conflict dividing his age.

But the grimmest beast of all is the fourth – "the Imaginary Clergy-
Power . . . more terrible and dreadful then the rest" (p. 466) – since he,
"the Father" of them all, has begotten the other three devouring beasts
out of himself: "the other Beasts," Winstanley observes, "are this Beasts
sons, he bred them" and they have "their strength and succour from
him" (pp. 467, 468).[60] In that sense he resembles the Satan of *Paradise Lost*
who has begotten out of himself his own monstrous allegorical progeny
who are self-generating – "he knows / His end with mine involv'd" (*PL*
2.806–7) observes Sin of her son, the grim devouring Death. The "little
horne" arising out of the ten horns of Winstanley's dreadful clergy beast
– and which, in Daniel, wages war against the saints and persecutes
them (Dan. 7:21–22, 25) – becomes "Ecclesiasticall power" (p. 469) in
Winstanley's historical myth, the dominion and rule of church establishment supported by the might of kingly power.[61] This, then, is
Winstanley's potent way of expressing the interconnections which exist
in his age between political and institutional ecclesiastical powers. The
learned clerical beast is more menacing too, we shall see, because he
cunningly employs the tyrannizing power of language itself. All these
Antichristian beasts, "with all their heads and hornes," reign in power
"while propriety" – the cursed institution of private ownership and
material advantage in Winstanley's vision – "rules as King" (p. 466); and
all "oppresse, burden, and destroy universall Love . . . who is the Sonne
of righteousnesse" (p. 467). Thus Winstanley's eschatological representation of the various powers of the world, as he creatively revises scriptural prophecy and myths and invests them with fresh potency, assumes
a distinctive sociohistorical interpretation. It expresses with great
poetic vividness Winstanley's response to the social and religious order,

as well as the economic and legal system, which continues, in the Commonwealth, to oppress the poor of the earth and control their common lands[62] – not only by means of physical force, but also by means of verbal and artful practices.

Like Milton in his antiprelatical and antimonarchical tracts, Winstanley in his visionary discourse is passionately concerned with exposing the multiple shapes and images of "Clergy power" and "Kingly power," along with the other two Antichristian powers he saw operating and proliferating in his age: "All these Beasts," as he calls them in *Fire in the Bush,* may "differ in shape, and yet they agree all in one oppressing power, supporting one another; one cannot live without another . . . These foure Beasts are all very fruitfull; for from them, as from foure Fountaines, or Monarchs, springs up divers heads and hornes; that is, severall spreadings forth, of selfish tyrannicall Power, whereby the Creation is opprest" (p. 466). Using dramatic language, the Independent divine John Owen commented to the House of Commons in April 1649 about the manifestations and web of Antichristian power: "The opening, unravelling, and revealing the Antichristian interest, interwoven, and coupled together in civill and spirituall things, into a State opposite to the kingdom of the Lord Jesus, is the great discovery of these dayes."[63] Engaged himself in unravelling the complex network of Antichristian powers in the new Commonwealth, Winstanley would add that the "Antichristian interest" is no less interwoven in "economic things" or "propriety." Indeed, Winstanley finds that these interconnected forms of worldly power, oppression, and institutional authority regularly manifest themselves not only through the power of the sword, but through craft, cunning, artfulness, and subtle uses of language: "these [Beasts] rise up by craft," he observes, "supported by the kingly power" (p. 467). Even "buying and selling" the earth, that great cause of inequality, is an "Imaginary" and "crafty Art" (pp. 374, 382, 464, 531, 532), as he calls it in his tracts, "the neat art of thieving and suppressing fellow-creatures" (p. 188) and cheating the poor commoners out of their rightful land. This is the subtle art and power of Cain and Lord Esau operating in his age. As Winstanley puts it in his final tract, such subtle forms of *"the Power and Government of the Beast"* manifest "the cunning Machavilian spirit" which fills "the heart of Mankind with enmity and ignorance, pride and vain-glory"; and that "subtle spirit of darkness" is prompted in the present economic system by the covetous agents of kingly and clergy power (pp. 531–32).

Moreover, like Milton, the Digger acutely perceives in his own way the

equivocal art of tyranny that makes use of verbal ambiguity. The institutional power of the Beast becomes particularly treacherous not only
when it is maintained by the power of the sword, but when it operates
at a subtle verbal level – in the cunning and dark uses of "speaking
words" (p. 475). Addressing his "brethren" of the churches at the
opening of *Fire in the Bush*, Winstanley notes how their "verball profession" reveals them serving "the government of darknesse" (pp. 445, 447),
and in his pamphlet he ominously characterizes the clerical beast as
"understanding dark sayings . . . [for] he shall by craft deceive many" (p.
467). Winstanley's visionary writing offers an acute analysis of "that
spirit which in words [the Churches] *seeme* to professe" (p. 445; emphasis added) as they practice their "teaching Art" (pp. 467–68).

He thus begins this prophetic tract by attacking the "verball profession" of the clergy and (what he calls elsewhere) their "close dissimulation" (p. 171): "you acknowledge Christ in your words, and the Dragon
in your actions" (pp. 447–48) – actions like imposing tithes on the poor
of the earth, which Winstanley and other religious radicals regarded as
"the greatest sin of oppression" (p. 238) and behind which might be
detected the power of the Beast itself.[64] (Compulsory tithes, a controversial issue the Rump failed to settle, seemed oppressive because they
maintained an Antichristian state church while becoming a severe economic burden for the poor.) The learned clergy not only invent "much
shew of holinesse" and "pretend to be saviours of the people" (pp. 446,
472), suggesting the theatricalism of Antichristian powers and recalling
his analysis in *The Breaking of the Day of God*;[65] their crafty covetousness is
also manifested by linguistic practices as they use their subtle, "insinuating words" (p. 387) as an instrument of power to ensnare the poor and
"to bewitch [them] to conforme" (p. 470). Thus, Winstanley observes
throughout his works, they use a "multitude of words" (pp. 219, 291, 365,
563) and engage in formal "preaching by arguments and expositions" (p.
223) to delude the simple or common people, making them more dependent upon clerical authority and interpretation. A power of divinity
which uses words to deceive the simple is, as he puts it in *The Law of
Freedom*, "a monster who is all tongue and no hand" (p. 567). Winstanley
is profoundly suspicious of the artifice of "verbal worship" (p. 185) and
"the language of Pulpits" practiced by a pharisaical professional ministry – "blinde guides," "painted sepulchers," and "enemies to the
Gospel" (p. 214) and the inner promptings of the Holy Spirit itself.
Indeed, in *The New Law* he had recalled how at one time, when he
himself succumbed to "strong delusions, and powers of darknesse," "the

words" the learned clergy spoke to him "were like a pleasant song" (p. 243), a comparison that underscores the artifice of their verbal performance and recalls Paul's warning that the faithful should be wary of the "enticing words of man's wisdom" (1 Cor. 2:4). Like William Dell, Winstanley perceives that Antichrist cunningly "builds up *his Church* by the *Word* without the *Spirit.*"[66]

Moreover, he is acutely sensitive to the way scriptural hermeneutics practiced by professional preachers has become an instrument of power and social control – a subtle means of reinforcing the orthodoxies of the clerical elite, as well as economic exploitation and exclusion. It is thus an art of what he calls "black interpretation" which draws "a veyle over the truth" of the Scriptures; in *Fire in the Bush* he observes that they

were written by the experimentall hand of Shepherds, Husbandmen, Fishermen, and such inferiour men of the world; And the Universitie learned ones have got these mens writings; and flourishes their plaine language over with their darke interpretation, and glosses, as if it were too hard for ordinary men now to understand them; and thereby they deceive the simple, and makes a prey of the poore, and cosens them of the Earth, and of the tenth of their labors" (pp. 474–75).[67]

As cunning artificers "new moulding . . . Scriptures into their own language" (pp. 103–4), the ministers of the gospel practice "their own inventions" without the authority of the Spirit, thereby turning the Scriptures "into a lie" (p. 140). Like the Leveller Walwyn, Winstanley was anxious about those clergy who make "Marchandize of the blessed Word of Truth" and therefore "dress it up in what shape their Art or Rhetorick can devise."[68] Especially vulnerable to such verbal and interpretative arts are the plain-hearted, common people who have "no guile" or "know'st not the wiles of the tempter," for their state, Winstanley observes in *Fire in the Bush*, is "a state like wax, flexible and easie to take any impression" (pp. 479–80). As he perceived, the poor and downtrodden, more likely to be illiterate and awed by learned scriptural interpretation, could too easily be shaped and exploited by such subtle Antichristian practices.[69]

Winstanley, then, considers the orthodox clergy no less ambiguous in their political and religious allegiances than Milton does in *The Tenure of Kings and Magistrates* (see Chapter 6). In Winstanley's words, these equivocal ministers "will serve on any side" and "under any Government": "They will serve the Papists, they will serve the Protestants, they will serve the King, they will serve the States" (*A New-Yeers Gift*, p. 358). Furthermore, like Milton who draws upon the myth of Circe to depict the bewitching effects of Stuart power and representation (in *Eikonoklastes* he describes the people as easily "stupifi'd and bewitch'd" and the divines as "wizzards"), Winstanley perceives that both clergy and kingly powers bewitch the common people; and he links these sinister forms of bewitching power with the Beast "in all her shapes and disguises."[70] The learned clergy, he had observed in *The New Law*, do "bewitch & delude man-kinde in spiritual things, yet it is that great Dragon that hath deceived all the world, for it draws men from knowing the Spirit" (p. 214). Kingly power, as well as other guileful forms, he writes in *Fire in the Bush*, "depend upon the Clergy, to bewitch the people to conforme" (p. 470), for the "Kingly Clergy," supported by tithes, as he notes in *The Law of Freedom*, most effectively preserve their authority "among a charmed, befooled and besotted people" (p. 544; cf. p. 569), a perception that Winstanley shared with the antinomian radical John Saltmarsh.[71] Since the "Image of the Beast" reigns within, as well as without, Winstanley envisions that a great "overturning" and social revolution in his age of institutional craft and "bewitching knavery" (pp. 472, 470) must involve not the restless seeking of an external kingdom but the regaining of a new "Kingdome within" (pp. 445, 458, 494) – a "new law of righteousnesse" set up within "every man and woman" (p. 206), as he had announced in his first communist tract. "This Seed or Christ then is to be seen within, to save you from the curse within," he writes at the end of *Fire in the Bush*, and "therefore your publicke Ministers bewitches you," he warns his godly readers, "by telling you of a Saviour at a distance" (p. 496). Such a bewitching clergy power manifests the sorcery and subtlety of the power of Antichrist himself.

In Winstanley's prophetic discourse, then, the Kingdom of Darkness, with its sorcery, oppression, and multiple Norman powers, is reinforced by the deadening and ensnaring uses of language, artfulness, and the fleshly imagination: when we live in a "dark time" associated with the Dragon or Beast, he writes in *A New-Yeers Gift*, we lie under "Ceremonies, Forms, Customes, Ordinances, and heaps of waste words, under which the Spirit of Truth [lies] buried" (p. 377). In *The New Law* Winstanley had accused the public divines of using "fine language" yet "words without life" (p. 242), in contrast to the living law of righteousness within the hearts of those whom they despise.[72] One response to the many kinds of bondage in his age was popular and symbolic political action in the form of that "pure righteous action" (p. 445) of digging. Another response was his own fiery prophetic writing with its verbal purging power, an expression of "the burning flame" and "the fire of pure Light" (p. 471, alluding to Dan. 7:11) and the power of the Spirit itself: as he wrote in the subtitle to *Fire in the Bush*, "The Spirit [is] burning, not consuming, but purging Mankinde" (p. 451).[73]

Thus moved in his prose "by Vision, Voyce, and Revelation" (p. 257), Winstanley could respond to the subtle manifestations of worldly power not only by provocative communal action, but also through his sharp but saving prophetic writing, which at times is no less fiery and fiercely polemical than the apocalyptic prose of some of his radical religious contemporaries. And so, in *Fire in the Bush* he appropriates the forceful, unsettling prophetic language of Haggai 2:6–7, applying it to the contemporary historical moment: "The Imaginary Kingly power" "must be shaken to pieces," the Digger prophet proclaims; Christ who "is coming now once more" to destroy the power of the four great beasts, to deliver the Creation from the kingly curse, and to set all men free, will "shake terribly the Nations, not *England* only, but all Nations" (pp. 445, 463–64), for this is the age of the world when the apocalyptic battle between Michael and the Dragon "growes hotter and sharper then formerly" (p. 457). Though Winstanley himself may fight with "the sword of Love" (p. 471), the iconoclastic and embattled revolutionary writer, whose "Armour," he tells us in *Fire in the Bush*, "is tryed," would become a mighty leveller too and use his inspired prose to "batter to pieces all the old Lawes" (pp. 446, 331) of Antichristian powers who have made England "a blinded and a snared generation" (*The Law of Freedom*, p. 591). Like other visionary writers in the early years of the Republic – the Ranter Coppe in *A Fiery Flying Roll* (1649), inspired by the prophecies of Ezekiel, or the millenarian George Foster in *The Sounding of the Last Trumpet* (1650) – Winstanley depicts the God of apocalyptic shakings and the radical religious writer both as mighty levellers of economic and social hierarchies at a time when the lower orders continued to be oppressed and their plight ignored. Echoing the unsettling prophetic language of Ezekiel 21:27 in *Fire in the Bush*, Winstanley warns the great "oppressing powers of the world" that their "overturning, overturning, overturning, is come on to you" (p. 472). So, too, Foster wrote in 1650 that the work of a mighty God and the visionary writer "is now to breake in peeces all things, and to make all things become new: which change is to restore the whole creation from bondage and slaverie"; and Coppe, responding in his extravagant apocalyptic prose (discussed further in Chapter 3) to the crisis of the Revolution and the oppression of the poor, envisioned the Lord and himself as great levellers of "the Great Ones" of the earth – both are "now RISEN to shake terribly the Earth," for

"The Eternall God, the mighty Leveller is comming, yea come, even at the doore."[74]

In the impassioned prose of *Fire in the Bush*, moreover, the prophetic Digger assumes the visionary warning voice of St. John of Patmos (see Revelation 8:13, 12:12), as he directs his admonitions to those great powers of the earth that have opposed the coming of the kingdom of Christ, as well as a new age of equality, communism, freedom, and spiritual inwardness: "Therefore woe, woe, woe, to the Inhabitants of the Earth; when Christ rises in power, and begins to come in the glory with his Saints" (pp. 470–71); "then woe, woe, woe, to the imaginary power, that rules the world, he shall be shaken with terror, and fall, and burst asunder" (p. 463). In Winstanley's visionary writing, Jesus Christ himself is "the greatest, first, and truest Leveller" "tearing to pieces . . . all rule, power, and Authority"; he is an unsettling spiritual force who will make smooth "the rough wayes" and "levell mountaines and valleys" (pp. 386, 455, 448), potent biblical symbols of class hierarchy and division in Winstanley's age.[75] Meanwhile, Winstanley's own revolutionary prose, with its striking uses of prophetic language and original recreations of scriptural myths, becomes an urgent means of envisioning the coming millennium, as well as the destruction of monstrous kingly and clerical powers. In his final utopian text, he would nevertheless continue to struggle with the ambivalent trends within the English Revolution.

THE LAW OF FREEDOM AND THE CRISIS OF THE COMMONWEALTH

In early 1652 Winstanley published his longest, most ambitious revolutionary tract, which he dedicated to Oliver Cromwell as Lord General (the epistle is dated 5 November 1651); intended for the Commonwealth leader more than two years before this, "the disorder of the Times caused [Winstanley] to lay it aside, with a thought never to bring it to light" (p. 509).[76] Yet hearing a voice saying "*Thou shalt not bury thy talent in the earth*" (the gifted writer Winstanley, like Milton, could be obsessed by the Parable of Talents),[77] he resurrected his rough-hewn work, first conceived during his Digger years and hastily assembled from his "scattered papers" (p. 510). To be sure, *The Law of Freedom in a Platform or True Magistracy Restored* sometimes lacks the intense visionary and poetic qualities of Winstanley's earlier works. Still, Winstanley's last major piece of writing, beginning with its lengthy epistle addressed to Cromwell (pp. 501–14), conveys an ongoing sense of urgency about "the disorder of the

Times"; despite its apparent commitments to righteous freedom and reformation, the English Commonwealth remains in a state of spiritual
and social crisis. It is Winstanley's perception and representation of that
crisis in *The Law of Freedom* that I want to highlight here. The powers of
the Beast still operate in the state: "the great Antichrist," kingly power
with all its subtleties and artifice, "makes War with Christ and his Saints
under pretence of owning him" (p. 530), Winstanley observes, reminding his readers that a treacherous Antichrist has assumed new shape. His
sober utopian tract thus responds to the troubling ambiguities of the historical moment in England and fuels his passionate appeal to the nation
at large: "O *England, England,* wouldst thou have thy Government sound
and healthful?" (p. 533). The fragile Digger experiment had collapsed in
the spring of 1650 and, since assuming power in late 1648, the republican regime, whose intention was never to make dramatic social changes,
had produced few results in terms of radical reform of the law, taxation,
the Church and the clergy. The tension between radical godly reformation and a society organized according to traditional social hierarchies
remained embodied within Cromwell himself.

   Winstanley's political realism is marked by the fact that he addresses
his last work to Cromwell, the godly Puritan leader and the most powerful man in England: "I have no power" (p. 510), the defeated Digger
plainly confesses, with which to remove the "very great" "confusion and
thick darkness that hath over-spread our Brethren" and which
Winstanley deeply "lament[s]" (p. 509). Like Milton and Marvell in the
early 1650s, Winstanley represents Cromwell as "a successful
Instrument" of God's providence in recent political history: he is one of
those "men of publick spirits, as *Moses* was" (p. 589), whose achievements
in resisting Egyptian subjection, in leading God's chosen people through
the Red Sea of civil war, and in casting out "an Oppressing *Pharaoh*" (p.
501) parallel those of Moses as a revolutionary deliverer. Religious radicals especially highlighted this mythmaking comparison which had, after
all, found support in the recent past.[78] In September 1651, two months
before the date of the epistle to *The Law of Freedom,* Cromwell had won
the battle of Worcester, a "marvellous salvation" which ended the royalist threat to the Commonwealth and enhanced his stature in the eyes
of millenarian radicals; Milton would soon remember the occasion in
his sonnet to "our chief of men" (May 1652).[79] Indeed, Cromwell continued, during the Commonwealth years, to believe in a sense of providential mission and the godly cause, and his religious convictions,
including his millenarianism, accounted for his support in the Army and

the religious sects. As the radical preacher William Dell told the leader in the same year Winstanley published his *Law of Freedom*, "the Lord hath done *great* things *by* you, and *great* things *for* you, and hath made you a *Name* like the *Name* of the *great men* of the *Earth*."[80] So, too, Winstanley senses that in this age, Cromwell the man of action is the only hope for genuine social and spiritual reform and for a new godly order. The Puritan leader remained committed to godly reformation during the years of the Rump and thereafter, despite his instinctive conservative constitutional and social impulses which seemed to contradict his religious enthusiasm.[81] Thus in a famous letter written in September 1650, following his dramatic victory at Dunbar, Cromwell had exhorted Parliament to relieve the oppressed and "to reform the abuses of all professions": "if there be anyone that makes many poor to make a few rich, that suits not a Commonwealth," he asserted.[82] And yet he remained England's most powerful country gentleman; his concern that the poor not be oppressed was by no means a call to turn the world upside down or to alter, in a decisive way, the existing social order, including property ownership.[83] Responding acutely to a godly Commonwealth in crisis, Winstanley's spiritual vision in his last work was indeed such a call.

Winstanley suggests that the Puritan leader, who now possesses "place and power" (p. 503), including the power over the land, may well have acted in the past as a providential instrument, but he was crucially aided in his Civil War victories by the commoners who have remain enslaved in the Commonwealth. Like the prophetic Milton, George Wither, or Anna Trapnel in the 1650s, Winstanley modulates his praise by warning Cromwell, as well as those "in power" with him, of the danger of being "found walking in the Kings steps" and following the powers of the earth: this could well lead to a dramatic "overturn" (p. 502).[84] Warning of the dangers of regal forms and practices in the Republic, the prophetic Winstanley thus differs in his bold discourse from those who "in these dayes . . . dare not speak against the minds of those men who are the chief in power" (p. 586). The defeated Digger writer may lack real political power: not only have his "health and estate . . . decayed" (p. 575), he observes in a more personal moment, but the language of his rough-hewn platform, he suggests in a self-conscious and self-deprecating passage, may seem unpolished and "clownish," his text being "like a poor man that comes cloathed to your door in a torn country garment" (p. 510). Still, the powerless Winstanley maintains his vigilant stance. Cromwell has yet to prove that his ways are "more righteous then the Kings" (p. 502) and to perform decisive actions that will eliminate subtle forms of kingly and clergy power in the so-called free Commonwealth.

Unfortunately, even by late 1651 little has changed, in Winstanley's eyes, except for the outward regime: the poor remain as poor as they were under the old monarchy, he tells Cromwell, but now are burdened with "new Task-masters" (p. 507). Despite complaints from the poor about hardships caused by enclosure and about the destruction of common rights by acquisitive landlords, the Rump had done little to relieve their burdens and oppression and had shown themselves more protective of the powerful.[85] The troubling ambiguities of the Commonwealth remain, Winstanley dares to remind the godly leader. "A man must either be a free and true Commonwealthsman, or a Monarchial tyrannical Royalist," Winstanley observes, yet since the beginning of the Republic its gentry and political leaders have too often taken an ambiguous "middle path between these two" positions (p. 513).[86]

Here too we find Winstanley revising scriptural texts in striking ways, giving them a distinctive contemporary sociohistorical interpretation that underscores both the urgency and challenge of his appeal to the leader of the troubled Commonwealth. Indeed, Winstanley's creative use of scriptural texts confirms that his social radicalism still includes, at the end of his career as a communist writer, an important religious component. Thus in one notable instance he takes the story of Jonah and the gourd (see Jonah 4:5–11), which tells of God's dramatic challenge to the prophet, and recreates the scriptural parable in allegorical political terms. The parable of the gourd, which shelters the prophet from the fierce heat of the sun but is destroyed by a worm sent by God, becomes in Winstanley's text "a remembrancer to men in high places" (p. 502) like Cromwell. In the Bible, we recall, the parable is a means of highlighting the unrighteousness of Jonah who becomes angry over the perished gourd but who shows no sympathy for the ignorant people of Nineveh. Winstanley dramatizes unrighteousness in the English Commonwealth through his unique rendering of the Old Testament parable. The earth in Winstanley's revision of the allegory is where the gourd grows – that is the commoners of England – and the gourd itself is the power that covers Cromwell himself: it "will be established to you by giving the People their true Freedoms, and not otherwise," the Digger writer tells the leader. Moreover, the root of the gourd is the heart of the people, still groaning under kingly bondage. The worm in the earth gnawing at the root of the gourd in Winstanley's scriptural allegory represents

"Discontents" (p. 503), because promises made to the oppressed commoners by those in power have not been kept: popery, presbytery, and
tyranny still thrive in the Republic. The established clergy, sympathetic
to monarchy and supported by tithes, continue to make those who challenge their orthodox authority "sinners for a word" (p. 504). The worm
itself in Winstanley's allegorical account has three heads: the first two
represent spirits which are self-interested, including one which "pretends
fair" to Cromwell, reminding us of Winstanley's suspicion of theatricalism and power; only the third is a spirit which is genuinely "faithful" and
"plain-dealing" – much like the writer Winstanley himself who speaks
"truth plainly" to Cromwell – but this spirit is many times "cashiered,
imprisoned, and crushed," as the Diggers had been. If Cromwell wants
his gourd to stand forever and to act righteously, he must, in the terms
of Winstanley's allegory, "cherish the root in the Earth" or the commoners of England. Only "performance of professions, words, and promises" will kill the worm (p. 503), Winstanley suggests, conveying through
his allegorical prose his urgent, oft-repeated plea that righteous "action
is the life of all" in a free commonwealth.

Elaborating more systematically than ever before his vision of social
reform and true righteousness in a communist state, Winstanley's
utopian platform nevertheless expresses his anxiety about the spirit of
darkness overspreading the land and his sense that lordly oppression,
operating in subtle ways, can easily invade a commonwealth. Thus, for
example, having just appropriated the prophetic words of Isaiah 60:2
("*Darkness hath covered the Earth, and thick darkness the people, for the Leaders of
the people have caused them to err*"), Winstanley highlights the need to choose
each year new public officers (the same arrangement later applies to
overseers) in his ideal commonwealth, recognizing that "the heart of
man is so subject to be overspred with the clouds of covetousness, pride,
and vain-glory" (p. 540). Unlike Milton, who nearer the Restoration
would oppose an annually rotating governing body because such a
"watery situation" provides no firm basis to a commonwealth,[87]
Winstanley uses images of stagnant versus fresh water to drive home his
point: "Nature tells, *That if water stand long, it corrupts*; whereas running
water keeps sweet, and is fit for common use" (p. 540). The choosing of
new officers, individuals whose spirits are humble and free from covetousness, prevents the evils of pride and blindness from developing
inwardly, thereby preventing the ensuing fall which might occur –
"witness the Fall of oppressing Kings, Bishops, and other State-
Officers." Furthermore, such regular change prevents "the creeping in

of Oppression into the Commonwealth again" – precisely as had occurred during the three years of the Republic, where forms of kingly power were flourishing. Another homely natural metaphor vividly expresses the danger of creating conditions in a commonwealth which allow the growth of oppression and which prevent England from becoming "the Lilly among the Nations of the Earth": "if Burthens and Oppressions should grow up in our Laws and in our Officers for want of removing, as Moss and Weeds grow in some Land for want of stirring, surely it will be a foundation of misery" (p. 541).

Winstanley never stopped yearning for the kind of dramatic social change which would restore the earth as a common treasury and release the people from the Norman hardships they suffer under – an ongoing kingly oppression created by "the Clergy, Lawyers, and Law; for all the Complaints of the Land are wrapped up within them three, not in the person of a King" (p. 505). His urgent desire in *The Law of Freedom* to reform and simplify the system of intricate laws in England expresses his frustration, shared by many radicals (including the Levellers), with the abuses of professional lawyers whose pharisaical laws seemed to maintain not just the ruling power of landlords and the gentry but the spirit of Antichrist itself.[88] The profession of the law was, at the time *The Law of Freedom* appeared, a powerful symbol of social slavery in the Commonwealth, since the Rump had failed to reform the legal system with its archaic language and severe penalties.[89] The "course" of "the Law and Lawyers hath been a meer snare to entrap the people" and to get their estates from them "by craft" (p. 590), Winstanley writes; lawyers, in his analysis, thus uphold the Norman Conqueror's interests and reinforce class oppression. His response to the profession of the law conveys his particular sense that kingly power is still maintained by treacherous artfulness; indeed, Winstanley's platform itself includes a brief but revealing section entitled "Laws against Treachery" (p. 597). The kingly system of laws, in Winstanley's eyes, especially symbolizes the equivocal nature of that protean power which has easily adapted itself and survived into the Commonwealth, as one of his tropes suggests: these old kingly laws "have indeed served many masters, Popish and Protestant: they are like old souldiers, that will but change their name, and turn about" (p. 585). Exemplifying godly simplicity, short, pithy laws resembling the few laws of Israel's commonwealth would eliminate some of the treacherous evils which darken this age of frustrated reform.[90]

The Law of Freedom, however, is by no means a uniform piece of writing

or a straightforward platform for a new commonwealth. Rather, it alter-
nates between practical recommendations for governing Winstanley's
model commonwealth and more visionary, dramatic passages of writing
expressing his sense of spiritual and social crisis. Thus, for example, in
his section analyzing divinity, Winstanley considers the socioeconomic
consequences of orthodox religion in a commonwealth, especially the
way this Antichristian power terrorizes the simple and poor with frightening theological doctrines about hell after death, thereby keeping them
in a state of anxious submission so that they will not raise disturbances.
Winstanley reinforces his perception of a treacherous orthodox divinity
by employing the myth of the two warring brothers – the subtle elder
brother and the younger simpler one – which he had been using in his
writings since early 1649. Having highlighted the sense of spiritual
despair and torment which the doctrines of orthodox Puritanism can
generate, Winstanley introduces an unsettling dramatic dialogue
between the two brothers:

> For saith the elder Brother, *The Earth is mine, and not yours, Brother; and you must not
> work upon it, unless you will hire it of me: and you must not take the fruits of it, unless you
> will buy them of me, by that which I pay you for your Labor: for if you should do otherwise,
> God will not love you, and you shall not go to Heaven when you dye, but the Devil will have
> you, and you must be damned in Hell.*

If the younger brother replies that "*The Earth is my Birth-Right, as well as
yours, and God who made us both, is no Respecter of persons,*" then the subtle
elder brother, drawing upon the frightening doctrines of Calvinist orthodoxy, crushes him by responding: "*You must not trust to your own Reason and
Understanding, but you must beleeve what is written and which is told you; and if you
will not beleeve, your Damnation will be the greater*" (pp. 568–69). And so the
younger brother, "being weak in spirit" and succumbing to fears of damnation in hell, while hoping to go to heaven, gives up his right to the
earth. This dramatic dialogue thus closely links orthodox religion and its
Antichristian doctrines with class exploitation; it gives Winstanley's
writing immediacy as he explores interconnections between the spiritual
and socioeconomic crises. The lament of the powers of the earth over
the doomed mercantile city of Babylon from Revelation 18:10, which
Winstanley quotes at the very end of this section, does, however, suggest
an intense yearning for apocalyptic retribution; the mighty Babylon in
England becomes a potent symbol of the power of divinity and its
sorcery which has spread in his Antichristian age, while recalling an
earlier apocalyptic identification of kingly government with the "City

Babylon, full of confusion": "*Alas, alas, that great City Babylon, that mighty City Divinity, which hath filled the whole Earth with her sorcery, and deceived all people, so that the whole world wondered after this Beast; how is it faln, and how is her Judgment come upon her in one hour?*" (pp. 529, 570).

As if to respond to the disorder of his unsettled times, Winstanley's *Law of Freedom* does feature his revolutionary vision of a dynamic, informed citizenry; if righteous action is to be the life of all, it must involve the productive rechannelling of potentially unruly, anarchic impulses. Hence he devotes particular attention to education, which the cautious regime of the Republic itself had done little to reform,[91] as a means of mastering and overcoming "the dangerous events of idleness" (p. 577), as well as regulating "unrational" (p. 583) and beastly impulses, for "Mankinde in the days of his youth" resembles "a young Colt, wanton and foolish" (p. 576) until he be broken by education and correction, Winstanley observes in a vigorous analogy. He had particularly associated the danger of idleness and of wild, immoderate behavior with the extravagant practices of Ranterism,[92] a form of antinomian freedom highlighting the life of the senses from which he hoped to dissociate the Diggers. Though himself a spiritual antinomian, Winstanley offers a model commonwealth where the rebellious fleshly practices of Ranterism, which deeply shocked his orthodox Puritan contemporaries, would never flourish and where the monogamous family, under paternal authority and instruction, would thrive.[93] Self-governance, Winstanley perceives, makes for good commonwealthsmen and women: so after children have learned "civil and humble behavior" and are bought up in schools, they should "be set to . . . Trades, Arts and Sciences." Like Milton's *Of Education* eight years earlier, Winstanley's text emphasizes the dynamic activity necessary to the making of a productive revolutionary citizenry (though Milton's social vision is more elitist). But for Winstanley (unlike Milton) the practical learning of various trades, crafts, and skills teaches the revolutionary citizens, above all else, "how to govern the Earth in right order" and in a spirit of communal cooperation; education is thus essential to his larger vision of agrarian social reform which involves liberating "the Secrets of Creation" from the kingly and clergy powers which continue to live off the labors of others. In Winstanley's platform the scriptural Parable of Talents can possess a symbolic significance very different from that in Milton's writing (where it always has personal vocational implications): one employs one's "Talent in some bodily action, for the encrease of fruitfulness, freedom, and peace in the Earth" – otherwise one is "an unprofitable son." Milton, moreover, had imagined the revolutionary saints of his godly nation in *Areopagitica* energetically reforming and building the great temple of the Lord; Winstanley, in contrast, imagines the active citizens of his godly commonwealth engaged in the free and "right ordering of Land." The emphasis of his georgic vision,[94] no less dynamic than Milton's vision of reform, is on the energetic activity needed to create a fruitful agrarian society – a strenuous process of "planting, digging, dunging, liming, burning, grubbing" (pp. 576–80).

Nevertheless, the harsher features of Winstanley's platform for a new commonwealth have sometimes disturbed commentators, prompting them to suggest that this final work expresses the hardened views of a disillusioned man.[95] Winstanley's emphasis on restraining idle behavior, on the state sharply punishing those who are disruptive and who have broken the laws,[96] and on patriarchal authority and government (though here it is the paternal government of a Parliament not a Stuart king) can at times suggest an urge to regulate his commonwealth in ways that seem to clash with his radical social vision of class equality, liberation, and free use of the earth. Yet given Winstanley's anxieties about the extravagant, theatrical behavior of Ranterism (which he criticized for focusing excessively on outward objects) and given that his platform is addressed to Cromwell, that urge is partly explainable.[97] The darker tone of his utopian platform does indeed suggest a writer who has endured the disappointments of Digger defeat, while nevertheless refusing to give up his daring vision of a righteous commonwealth liberated from the power of the professional clergy, the institution of private property, and the Antichristian art of buying and selling. Winstanley is attempting to mold that revolutionary vision to suit an English Commonwealth whose contradictions he has acutely perceived and whose godly leader, Cromwell, was himself divided between radical Puritan impulses and conservative social ones. Moreover, highly sensitive to the subtle manifestations of Antichristian powers operating in the present – including their linguistic, artful manifestations – Winstanley responds to their threat and treacherous proliferation in ways that may sometimes strike us as stern.[98] The inconsistencies of his platform for a free commonwealth may partly reflect that his text was hastily assembled; they also reflect the difficulties of shaping his radical vision to confront the frustrating political, social, and economic realities of his age which he so keenly perceived. In a way, the Digger visionary at the very end of his writing career is not unlike the saintly officers he imagines – "men of courage" who "have suffered under Kingly Oppression" and "who are

not afraid to speak the Truth" (p. 543) – as Winstanley is moved to
address the unresolved contradictions of the Revolution and its troubled
Commonwealth, whose public professions of freedom had clashed with
the sober realities of vested interests.

The title page of Winstanley's *Law of Freedom* itself registers the pro-
visional nature of the radical visionary's ambitious project. It refers the
readers of his sociopolitical platform to two resonant scriptural texts –
Revelation 11:15 and Daniel 7:27 – which remind the godly Cromwell, as
well as all Englishmen who are Winstanley's "brethren," of the millennial reign itself, another indication of the radical religious dimension of
this late text: "The kingdoms of this world are become the kingdoms of
our Lord, and of his Christ; and he shall reign for ever and ever"; "And
the kingdom and dominion, and the greatness of the kingdom under the
whole heaven, shall be given to the people of the saints of the most High,
whose kingdom is an everlasting kingdom, and all dominions shall serve
and obey him." But the title page also includes verses by Winstanley
written in the conditional mode, while signaling the inward law of righteousness and equity:

> In thee, O England, is the Law arising up to shine,
>   If thou receive and practise it, the crown it wil be thine.
> If thou reject, and stil remain a froward Son to be,
>   Another Land wil it receive, and take the crown from thee.[99]

Under the oppressive influence of kingly and other subtle Antichristian
powers, that "thick darkness" still overspreading Winstanley's brethren,
England had indeed continued, three years after the Republic's traumatic founding, to remain "a froward Son." Profoundly aware of the
ambiguities of the Revolution and its Commonwealth, the former
Digger thus began his final work by registering a sense of political uncertainty and unease about the future restoration of true magistracy, even
as he dared to press ahead, one last time, with his arresting new vision
of society.

As I have tried to show, Winstanley's visionary writings, including his
Law of Freedom, offer a compelling illustration of the way political, religious, aesthetic, and linguistic concerns intersect in the discourse of revolutionary England. Winstanley's unorthodox and poetic prose, his
revolutionary mythmaking, his allegorical imagination, his sensitivity to
the subtle uses of language, scriptural interpretation, and artfulness by
kingly and clergy powers: all these features suggest a radical religious

writer whose prophetic and political discourse cannot be divorced from the textual domain. One reason why the Diggers matter, Ronald Hutton has recently stressed, is "because of their contribution to the history of ideas,"[100] a remark certainly confirmed by Winstanley's revolutionary views of an egalitarian economic and social order. But his visionary writing cannot simply be confined to the history of ideas, however striking his social radicalism may be. His prose matters because its contribution is also aesthetic: his mythopoeic writing was stimulated by his creative responses to the upheavals of the 1648–49 Revolution and its ambiguous aftermath. No other literary figure of the age responded so acutely to the contradictions of the Commonwealth whose leaders had professed a new age of freedom and reformation. His visionary tracts are creative works interrogating political ideology and religious orthodoxies in an age of revolution, as well as the world of state power and social injustice, including their sinister verbal manifestations. Like the anonymous author of *Tyranipocrit, Discovered* (1649), Winstanley understood that tyrannical power in his age had by no means disappeared with the Revolution and the new Republic, but could too easily be established "in other formes and fashions" which deceive men and women: "wee have no need of tyranny in a new fashion," observed that author in 1649, "but of a changing of manners and customes, which are evill and prejudiciall to the common-wealth."[101] Like Milton, Winstanley perceived that the power of darkness and hypocrisy "turns himself into divers shapes; yea, sometimes into an Angel of light" (p. 174) who practices "falsehood under saintly show" (*Paradise Lost* 4.122): so we shall see later in this study how Milton's mercurial Satan, who assumes diverse shapes, manipulates contradictory kinds of political discourse and postures from the revolutionary years. This was an age of revolution, after all, when kingly power – "the great Antichrist, and Mystery of Iniquity, that makes War with Christ and his Saints under pretence of owning him" (p. 530) – had been cast out in one tyrannizing form only to reappear afterwards in other subtle "shapes and disguises."

The visionary and mythopoeic writings of Gerrard Winstanley, then, should be of particular interest at this moment in critical history when sociohistorical work in early modern studies has been prompting scholars to reexamine the complex interactions between the aesthetic and the political, the linguistic and the social. But the heterodox works of the Digger writer should prompt us as well to examine the interaction of aesthetic, social, and religious concerns in less traditional kinds of literary discourses produced during his turbulent age of civil war and revolution. Unorthodox writers in this age, as Winstanley's remarkable visionary works illustrate, registered acutely the anxieties and doubts generated by a period of political and religious crisis, as they engaged in searching explorations of its cultural and historical ambiguities.

CHAPTER THREE

Ranter and Fifth Monarchist prophecies: The revolutionary visions of Abiezer Coppe and Anna Trapnel

Although Gerrard Winstanley produced some of the most acute contemporary responses to the contradictions of the Revolution, other radical apocalyptic writers were no less imaginative as they struggled with the sense of crisis intensified by the convulsions of 1648–49 and the ambiguities of their aftermath. Radical religious unrest, as we saw in the last chapter, not only generated some of the most novel political and social ideas of the Revolution, but stimulated some of its most vigorous and original writing. The present chapter examines writings by two flamboyant visionaries based in London, whose powerful and distinctive prophetic responses to the Revolution's limitations and darker sides continued to challenge social, political, and religious orthodoxies in mid-seventeenth-century England. In their own highly dramatic ways, Abiezer Coppe and Anna Trapnel illustrate how two of the most radical apocalyptic writers in the Interregnum attempted to reinterpret, by means of startling symbolic gestures and arresting prophetic language, the processes of social and political revolution. Coppe, the notorious Ranter prophet, fiercely denounced the great ones of the earth, using his ecstatic writing, blasphemous behavior, and strange symbolic actions to alarm his contemporaries in the new Republic. Trapnel, the prominent Fifth Monarchist prophetess and poet, engaged in her own form of political protest against the retreat from revolution during the Commonwealth and Protectorate years: her ecstatic prophecies and popular millenarian visions delivered in public at Whitehall were deeply stimulated by this unsettled period and by radical religious beliefs. Her visionary trances, like those of Winstanley and the Diggers during the Republic, became the occasion to take part actively in political controversy as she responded dramatically to the crises of the new Protectorate.

RANTING, WRITING, AND REVOLUTION: THE BLASPHEMOUS
VISIONS OF ABIEZER COPPE

When visionary passages of the flamboyant apocalyptic work entitled *A Fiery Flying Roll* by the Ranter writer Abiezer Coppe (1619–1672) were read before the House of Commons in February 1649/50, it was immediately resolved that this book "composed by one *Coppe*, doth contain in it many horrid Blasphemies, and damnable and detestable Opinions, to be abhorred by all good and godly People." It was then ordered that all printed copies of the book should be "burnt by the Hand of the Hangman," that a diligent search be made of all places where the inflammatory book was or might be suspected, and that "all Mayors, Sheriffs, and Justices of the Peace, in the several Counties, Cities, and Towns, within this Commonwealth, be required to seize all the said Books in all Places where they shall be found" so that these too could be burned.[1] To members of the new Commonwealth's Parliament, the fiery writing of the radical visionary Coppe seemed alarming and subversive, especially with its powerful apocalyptic rhetoric of overturning and levelling all forms of social hierarchy, and with its fierce prophetic warnings aimed at earthly powers and rulers.

Indeed, in an age when religion and politics intersected, and when the purged Parliament considered it "their duty, by all good ways and means to propagate the Gospel in this Commonwealth, to advance Religion in all Sincerity, Godliness, and Honesty,"[2] such provocative heretical writing itself could stimulate fears of social and religious disorder. To the more mainstream godly, Coppe's blasphemous text boldly proclaiming that "Sin and Transgression is finished and ended," like the Ranter Laurence Clarkson's text asserting that "sin hath its conception only in the imagination," seemed to countenance amoral behavior and social anarchy as it unsettled and overturned customary notions of good and evil, sin and holiness, the moral law, and the Protestant ethic itself.[3] As Coppe himself well knew, blasphemy was considered by his contemporaries as nothing less than a crime against both the state and God – a highly dangerous form of treason and sedition.[4] Thus, according to one contemporary tract, the Ranters, who presented themselves as exempt from the moral law and who represented an extreme form of heterodoxy, were both "Church and State Levellers, mortall enemies to an Orthodox, Learned, Godly, Protestant Ministry, and no better friends to a Consciencious, Religious, Righteous, Protestant Magistracy."[5] Eager to promote moral reform, Parliament consequently decided to hold a fast day to contemplate the "sins, hideous blasphemies, and unheard of abominations" practiced "under pretence of liberty, and greater measure of light."[6] On 9 August 1650, moreover, the Rump cracked down decisively on Coppe and Ranter antinomianism by issuing a strict act "against several Atheistical, Blasphemous and Execrable Opinions": this blasted "divers men and women who have lately discovered themselves to be most monstrous in their Opinions, and loose in all wicked and abominable Practices . . . not onely to the notorious corrupting and disordering, but even to the dissolution of all Humane Society, who rejecting the use of any Gospel Ordinances, do deny the necessity of Civil and Moral Righteousness among men."[7] Punishment for such execrable or blasphemous opinions and unrestrained enthusiasm included six months in prison or a house of correction without bail. "Numbered amongst Transgressors,"[8] Coppe himself had already been arrested and imprisoned at Warwick and Coventry in January 1649/50 before being transferred to Newgate in March; conducting himself with "wild deportment," refusing to remove his hat, and feigning madness before a parliamentary committee in October 1650, he was promptly returned to prison.[9]

The Ranter writers and prophets emerged as a threat to public order, morality, and the Puritan establishment between 1649 and 1651. They first appeared during a tense period when more conservative and radical forces in the Revolution were clashing: following the Army purge, the regicide, the abolition of kingship and the House of Lords, and during the same month England was declared a "Free State" (May 1649), there also occurred the military suppression of the troublesome Levellers, a crisis to which Coppe prophetically refers at several points, as we shall see. Yet except for the fiery Quakers, who emerged a few years later in the 1650s and alarmed the orthodox godly (see Chapter 4), no radical group more than the Ranters seemed so profoundly subversive of the social, ecclesiastical, and moral order.[10] To be sure, the Ranter prophets, of whom Coppe was the most notorious, never constituted a particularly coherent movement or an organized sect with a recognizable membership.[11] Nevertheless, in an age when the godly were particularly anxious about escalating religious divisions, the Puritan minister Richard Baxter could warn that the example of Coppe's blasphemous behavior, ideas, and writing "fresh in our memory . . . should be heard with trembling, as one of Gods most fearfull Judgments."[12] Nor is it likely that the Ranter threat, while no doubt exaggerated in this unsettled period by hostile observers, was merely the propaganda fabrication of a paranoid regime or of the scurrilous press projecting Civil War stereotypes.[13]

Moreover, between 1649 and 1651, as we have seen, Winstanley was producing his probing analyses of the Revolution's ambiguities and was profoundly challenging orthodox Puritan beliefs. There are, we shall see, some striking ideological affinities between the revolutionary writings and social concerns of Winstanley and those of Coppe.[14] Both writers, after all, were spiritual antinomians reacting against Puritan theological conservatism: the Ranters claimed to be inspired by the Spirit within (it "alone is the incorruptible Key," Coppe observed),[15] as Winstanley and the Diggers themselves were. Through vigorous prose, both writers expressed a sense of the unity of all creation, emphasized that God dwelled in all men, and stressed a biblical communal ethic, thereby denying outward economic and social distinction. Nevertheless, Winstanley, as we saw, could respond to extreme Ranter antinomianism with intense hostility and anxiety as he rejected their theatrical excesses (with which the Diggers had been slandered) in at least two of his works. "That immoderate ranting practise of the Sences," he asserted, brings no peace at all and may even distemper whole nations; Ranterism – "the outward enjoyment of drink, pleasures, and women" – was, from Winstanley's agrarian communist perspective, a wasteful "spending of the Treasures of the Earth." The excessive behavior of the licentious Ranters, including their alleged sexual promiscuity or "community of women," manifested the power of the Beast itself: "the Ranting power," Winstanley believed, was a "devouring Beast."[16] Even the radical Puritan Milton, though he never specifically mentions Ranter prophets, praised Parliament in 1659 for the Blasphemy Act of 1650, aimed at curbing their transgressions at a moment when the new Republic was attempting to assert its political authority and legitimacy.[17]

Indeed, the Blasphemy Act, a direct response to Coppe and the antinomian Ranters, was only the most notable in a series of repressive Acts aimed at restraining sectarian excesses and dangerous religious enthusiasm, as well as challenges to Calvinist orthodoxy in the aftermath of the traumatic Revolution of 1648–49. The Commonwealth regime, which punished Coppe for his blasphemous opinions and flamboyant writing, was especially preoccupied with political and social stability and wished to enforce a godly Puritan code of morality and discipline – even above sanctioning religious liberty and expression in the free state of England.[18] Other severe measures passed by Parliament during the spring and summer of 1650 marked a trend towards a state-imposed

religious orthodoxy: these included a law strictly enforcing proper obser-
vance of the Lord's Day, a measure imposing the death penalty for "the
abominable" sin of adultery, and an Act against "prophane Swearing
and Cursing," behavior especially associated with Ranterism.[19] As
Coppe himself observed, "The two Acts of May 10. [against swearing]
and Aug. 9. 1650 [against blasphemy] were put out because of me."[20]
When it came to religious toleration, the new regime, under which
Coppe wrote and published his shocking works, was conservative and
clearly set itself against the radical sects; it became even more determined to crack down on sectarian license and to establish a legislative
program of moral reform after confronting the antinomian excesses and
writings of the Ranters. Yet, as we have also seen, the blasphemous
behavior and social excesses of the Ranters disturbed Puritans of very
diverse religious and political persuasions – not only Presbyterians and
Independents, but also such radical writers as Winstanley and George
Fox, the latter strenuously disputing with "very rude" Ranters, including, quite possibly, Coppe. When in prison at Coventry in 1649, Fox
encountered Ranters who began to "to rant . . . and blaspheme" and say
"they were God"; he tested and confounded them and then "reproved
them for their blasphemous expressions."[21]

An expression of blasphemous enthusiasm and antinomianism
infused with chiliastic fervor, Coppe's visionary prose is characterized by
linguistic virtuosity and literary inventiveness, as well as rhetorical intensity and vehemence. His extravagant writing in *A Fiery Flying Roll* and *A
Second Fiery Flying Roule*, published together at the very beginning of 1650,
illustrates how the crisis of the Revolution could generate works which
fuse linguistic, social, and radical religious concerns in highly arresting
ways. In the previous chapter we considered how religious radicalism,
mythopoeic writing, and revolutionary politics intersected in
Winstanley's works. In the case of Coppe, extravagant spiritual writing
becomes a form of aggressive rebellion against social privilege and the
tyranny of Puritan ideology (especially its notions of sin, guilt, and
moral restraint), as well as a powerful means of expressing the release of
the Spirit within the flesh. Coppe's colorful writing deserves to be considered alongside Winstanley's and that of the early Quakers: he produced some the most striking and original visionary responses to the
social and spiritual limitations of a revolution which continued to stag-
nate after the traumatic political events of 1649.[22]

I thus concentrate on Coppe's most startling pieces of revolutionary
writing, his two *Fiery Flying Rolls*, focusing on the ways their flamboyant

language, prophetic rhetoric, dramatic qualities, and poetic vision express their author's religious extremism and radical social doctrines. These remarkable texts, which disturbed state and ecclesiastical authorities, enabled Coppe to respond imaginatively and vigorously to the sense of social crisis and uncertainty in the early Republic. Nor is it insignificant that his apocalyptic sense of crisis prompted the Ranter to warn and advise London in particular: his two *Fiery Flying Rolls* are based upon shocking sermons he preached to "all the Great Ones of the Earth" in the streets of the city that had been so vital to the Revolution itself.[23] Indeed, his visionary works often represent a vivid urban landscape – one of extreme contrasts – inhabited by the poor and wretched, as well as by Cavaliers and gentry. Like Winstanley's visionary texts, Coppe's provide a deeply challenging commentary on the social and spiritual conditions of the new Commonwealth, which did little indeed to satisfy revolutionary hopes of genuine reform and freedom and to create a new state of righteousness on earth.[24] And like the Digger writings or the apocalyptic Quaker texts considered in the next chapter, Coppe's flamboyant prophetic writing crystallizes, from its own ecstatic religious perspective, an acute sense of the social and spiritual crisis which was threatening to undermine the Revolution itself.

Like Winstanley, Coppe underwent a conversion that would shape his subsequent spiritual and social vision. During the revolutionary period of 1648–49, he experienced a highly dramatic spiritual crisis recounted in the preface to his first *Fiery Flying Roll*. Both intensely introspective and engaged with the outward world, his visionary writing conveys the sense of personal crisis which led to his conversion to a messianic revolutionary writer addressing "the great ones" of his age. In his earlier life, well before Ranterism existed, Coppe had felt oppressed by a sense of sin and a horror of damnation: "with grief of soul, sighs and groans," he constantly confessed his sins, while keeping a daily register of them and setting them down in a book. The Puritan repressiveness of his adolescence is a marked contrast to the highly flamboyant Ranter behavior described in the two *Rolls*. The younger Coppe's sober existence was characterized by "Zeal, devotion, and exceeding strictness of life and conversation"; often fasting, "Tears were [his] drink: dust and ashes [his] meat."[25] Having later left Oxford without taking a degree, Coppe then began a spiritual journey that took him from Presbyterianism to Anabaptism; indeed it was as an Anabaptist that he developed his skills and achieved success as an itinerant preacher with a considerable following.[26] A period in prison followed, and then the spiritual crisis that resulted in Coppe's conversion to Ranterism. In highly dramatic terms he evokes the personal calamities and acute sense of sin that character- ized his life before he experienced the visions of God and was trans- formed into a Ranter prophet called upon to reprove the city of London for its abominations: "First, all my strength, my forces were utterly routed, my house I dwelt in fired; my father and mother forsook me, the wife of my bosome loathed me, mine old name was rotted, perished; and I was utterly plagued, consumed, damned, rammed, and sunke into nothing" (p. 82). Coppe tells us he was reborn after experiencing several terrifying thunderclaps, seeing a light as great and bright as the Sun and as red as fire – "whereupon with exceeding trembling and amazement on the flesh, and with unspeakable joy in the spirit, I clapt my hands, and cryed out, *Amen, Halelujah, Halelujah, Amen*" (p. 82). He describes his dra- matic spiritual conversion as a mystical experience "beyond expression." Both the visionary Coppe and the prophet Ezekiel, upon whom the Ranter closely models himself, are concerned with the inner experience and the renewal of the spirit: "A new heart also will I give you, and a new spirit will I put within you" (Ezek. 36:26) says the Lord to his prophet. Coppe now himself assumes "a new name, with me, upon me, within me" and, before receiving his commission, he experienced (like Ezekiel) the "visions and revelations of God": they were "stretched out upon me, within me, for the space of foure dayes and nights, without intermission" (p. 83). Coppe, moreover, had an intense vision of unity and universal- ity, and this has been "[his] song many times since," suggesting the poetic texture of his writing. At times it becomes an ecstatic prose poem – the subject of his visionary "song" or extravagant hymn is the "unity, uni- versality . . . [and] Eternall Majesty" (p. 82) he yearns for.

Coppe's highly provocative uses of biblical texts and prophetic lan- guage are therefore apparent from the beginning of his first *Fiery Flying Roll.* Unlike Winstanley he tends not to elaborate scriptural myths with new revolutionary meanings. Rather, the flamboyant Ranter dramatizes himself and his calling by presenting himself as a latter-day Ezekiel prophesying in the midst of revolutionary England at a moment of social and spiritual crisis. Having received a divine summons to go to London to "preach and print" during 1649, Coppe links radical proph- ecy and the power of writing as, in the manner of Ezekiel, he prepares to proclaim God's righteous judgment against the "Great Ones" of the earth: "Go up to *London*, to *London*, that great City, write, write, write" (p. 83). Internalizing the visions and revelations of God, Coppe consumes the "word of the Lord" (Ezek. 1:3), so that it does indeed dwell within the Lord's chosen one, before he proclaims it to the Commonwealth and its great metropolis:

And behold I writ, and lo a hand was sent to me, and a roll of a book was therein, which this fleshly hand would have put wings to, before the time. Whereupon it was snatcht out of my hand, & the Roll thrust into my mouth; and I eat it up, and filled my bowels with it (*Eze.*2.8. &c. *cha.* 3.1,2,3.) where it was as bitter as worm-wood; and it lay broiling, and burning in my stomack, till I brought it forth in this forme. (p. 83)

On one level, Coppe presents himself as an amanuensis taking down the prophetic discourse communicated to him: "the Word of the Lord came expressly to me, saying, write, write, write, write . . . And ONE stood by me, and pronounced all these words to me with his mouth, and I wrote them with ink in this paper." The roll itself is therefore the sacred receptacle of the Lord's powerful Word and message; it is not to be defiled or dismembered in any way, as the Lord's curse (recalling the curse at the very end of Revelation) forcefully suggests: "tear it not. . . . Read it through, and laugh not at it; if thou dost I'l destroy thee, and laugh at thy destruction" (p. 99). At the same time, Coppe's text dramatizes the agency of the visionary writer whose aggressive apocalyptic rhetoric and shocking language have the power to unsettle his contemporaries. Like Ezekiel to whom the word of the Lord came saying "Son of man, cause Jerusalem to know her abominations" (Ezek. 16:2), the prophetic Coppe will warn London of hers. Like Ezekiel's prophecy, Coppe's fiery text also contains "lamentations, and mourning, and woe" (Ezek. 2:10), though now for England in the midst of her present crisis. And as he warns his contemporaries of impending danger, he himself becomes, in his own way, a latter-day "watchman unto the house of Israel" (Ezek. 3:17) and, like the Old Testament prophet, an acute observer of political events.[27]

In Coppe's visionary writing, moreover, the threatening Word of the Lord and the prophet's sharp warning voice fuse: indeed, it is not always easy to distinguish in the two *Fiery Flying Rolls* between the mighty activism of the Lord and the mighty activism of his fiery prophet. The "Most Excellent MAJESTY" of the Lord is, after all, "dwelling in, and shining through" the fiery writer himself (p. 80), he announces on the title page of his first *Roll*, thereby enhancing his own authority and agency as God's terrifying warning voice at this critical historical moment. Like his mighty Lord, as the title page further suggests, the hugely active Coppe is no less engaged in informing, advising, warning, charging, judging and sentencing "all the Great Ones of the Earth."

Like the polemical and prophetic Milton, the visionary Coppe in his own way writes with "a sanctifi'd bitternesse against the enemies of truth";[28] in Coppe's case, these enemies are all the earthly powers and godly Puritans in the fleshly Israel that is Interregnum England. His fiery writing and strange actions may indeed make Coppe seem, in the eyes of his contemporaries, like an outrageous and ecstatic rebel. Nevertheless, he presents himself, much like Ezekiel, as a fearless prophet who is addressing the angry words of the Lord to "a rebellious house" and hard-hearted nation (Ezek. 2): in this case, the Puritan England of the Commonwealth, where, even after the Revolution of 1648–49, social relations, hierarchy, and power continue to be defined by propriety, nobility, and superfluity. Moreover, echoing the language of Ezekiel 21:9, Coppe presents his fiery roll as "an edg'd toole," "a sharp sword, sharpned, and also fourbished" (p. 86) – a prophetic weapon ready to smite the mighty ones of this world: "it is sharpened to make a sore slaughter; it is furbished that it may glitter" (Ezek. 21:9–10). His aggressive writing in the two parts of the *Fiery Flying Roll* is itself like "the *Sword* of the *Spirit*, which is quick and powerfull," as the visionary Ranter preaches "plaine and powerfull, quick and keene, short, and sweete Sermons."[29] Echoing as well the threatening and unsettling language of Ezekiel 21:27, Coppe has his mighty levelling Lord announce: "I inform you, that I overturn, overturn, overturn" (p. 86; cf. p. 106). The bishops, Lords, and king have had their cataclysmic turn in recent history; so the "surviving great ones" will have theirs next. Although Coppe never uses the phrase "kingly power" in his revolutionary writing, as Winstanley and John Warr do in theirs,[30] he clearly has something similar in mind as he addresses the "great ones" of the earth who have perpetuated privilege and inequity in the Commonwealth. The great powers in the Interregnum which he and his Lord threaten to overturn suddenly have more in common with the old order, defined by religious orthodoxies and social hierarchy, than with a new order of social and economic equality envisioned by radical spiritualists like himself and Winstanley.

In a way, this fiery Ranter is just as much of a visionary idealist as Winstanley who wishes to inaugurate a new age of righteousness in England: his God, much like Winstanley's, is also a God of "Universall Love" and equality who may "fill the Earth with universall love, universall peace, and perfect freedome; which can never be by humane sword or strength accomplished" (p. 89). And like Winstanley, Coppe hopes that "the pure spirit of universall love . . . can break the neck of tyranny,

oppression, abominable pride, and cruell murder" (p. 109) and inaugurate a state of everlasting righteousness, "the new *Hierusalem*" (p. 81) here
on earth.[31] To be sure, Coppe's Biblical rhetoric, like that of his Lord of
vengeance, often seems savage as he thunders against the earthly powers
of the Commonwealth. Yet Coppe's prophetic rhetoric is not only
violent but intensely sympathetic, ferocious as well as compassionate.
While fiercely condemning the rich and powerful in Interregnum
England, he is "also *most compassionately* informing, and *most lovingly and
pathetically* advising and warning *London*" (p. 80; emphasis added), as the
title page of his first *Fiery Flying Roll* announces. However unsettling this
Ezekiel-like prophet may be, his shocking rhetoric of social revolution
and mighty levelling is indeed provoked by his deepest pity stirred in this
time of spiritual and social crisis: "O *London, London*, my bowels are rolled
together (in me) for thee, and my compassions within me, are kindled
towards thee" (p. 95).[32]

Coppe's compassion for the oppressed poor and the underdog, like
Winstanley's, contributes to the vigor of his visionary prose with its
violent rhetoric aimed at alarming all earthly powers. Like Winstanley's
visionary prose, Coppe's ecstatic writing expresses an urgent sense of
ongoing crisis just after the traumatic upheaval of 1648–49. Indeed, his
extravagant writing suggests what early modern historians of England
themselves have been recently stressing:[33] in the Commonwealth social
revolution did not necessarily follow political revolution. Coppe conveys
a vivid sense of urban suffering during these years of instability caused
by class division and inequalities which, as Winstanley likewise
lamented, continued to plague the Commonwealth as yet another manifestation of tyranny never eradicated: "How long shall I heare the sighs
and groanes, and see the teares of poore widowes; and heare curses in
every corner; and all sorts of people crying out oppression, oppression,
tyranny, tyranny, the worst of tyranny, unheard of, unnaturall tyranny."
Coppe himself experiences the urban misery as a terrible burden and
oppressive weight which he feels acutely, not unlike Bunyan's Christian
with a great burden upon his back (though the Ranter of course spurns
a patriarchal Calvinist sense of guilt): "O my back, my shoulders. O
Tythes, Excize, Taxes, Pollings, &c. O Lord! O Lord God Almighty!"
The hyperbolic character of Coppe's prose, punctuated by frequent
exclamations as he and his Lord respond with compassion and threats
of vengeance to "the cries of *England*," reinforces the sense of socioeconomic crisis in the Commonwealth: "O the innumerable complaints and

groanes that pierce my heart (thorow and thorow) O astonishing complaints"; "O the abominable perfidiousnesse, falseheartednesse; self-
seeking, self-inriching, and Kingdome-depopulating, and devastating"
(p. 93). As David Underdown has observed about the early years of the
Commonwealth, "It is difficult to resist the conclusion that the Rump
was more protective of the rich and the powerful than of the poor and
oppressed."[34] That observation is confirmed again and again by Coppe's
impassioned prose and his "many strange Postures" (p. 104) in the streets
of Interregnum London. He dramatizes the sharp disparity between
"the Great Ones of the Earth" and those urban outcasts who suffer
oppression – beggars, rogues, gypsies, widows, and other poor, whose
voices or appearances are so striking in his visionary writing.

With its emphasis on a radical restructuring of society, his writing
conveys an acute sense of social injustice in a world where inequity has
been perpetuated in part by orthodox Protestant notions and clerical
authorities. Like Winstanley, Coppe attacks hypocritical holiness and
threatens "the Formalists" (p. 105) in religion. He rejects all church ordinances and any form of external ministry, as did Milton, Winstanley, the
Quakers, and other religious radicals who preferred to rely on the
inwardly persuasive teachings of the Spirit: "I'l scorn carnall
Ordinances, and walk in the Spirit" (p. 115), he proclaims; or as he puts
it elsewhere, "every *forme* is a persecutor."[35] Much like the Digger visionary, he represents ecclesiastical authorities – "The Ministers, fat parsons,
Vicars, Lecturers" – as the subtle Antichristian Beast manifesting outwardly a "fleshly holinesse": they use their power "to maintaine their
pride, and pompe, and to fill their owne paunches, and purses" as they
persecute the poor of the nation, while charming the great ones into
believing (contrary to Coppe's ominous prophecies) that the mighty will
not be unsettled from their seats (pp. 88, 92). In a description worthy of
Bunyan, Coppe personifies "the Man of Sin," a cunning version of
Antichrist, as "a brisk, spruce, neat, self-seeking, fine finiking fellow" who
"worketh with all deceivablenesse of unrighteousnesse" and who
opposes the work of the Spirit while indeed claiming to believe it (p. 111).
As Coppe observes elsewhere of the manipulative uses of religious
behavior, such "carnal mock holiness . . . is a cloak for all manner of
Villany" which provokes "the vengeance of God."[36] All churches and
ordinances will thus be destroyed in the apocalypse which Coppe envisions being near at hand. His attempt to confound orthodox notions of
sin, blasphemy, and transgression is an attempt to undermine clerical

authorities who have used such concepts, as well as worldly learning and doctrinal teaching, to keep the poor and needy powerless:

Be no longer so horridly, hellishly, impudently, arrogantly, wicked, as to judge what is sinne, what not, what evill, and what not, what blasphemy, and what not.

For thou and all thy reverend Divines, so called (who Divine for Tythes, hire, and money, and serve the Lord Jesus for their owne bellyes) are ignorant of this one thing.

That sinne and transgression is finisht, its a meere riddle, that they, with all their humane learning can never reade. (p. 91)

Like the prophetic Blake of *The Marriage of Heaven and Hell*, the visionary Ranter takes orthodox religious categories and turns them completely inside out (underscored by his chiastic prose) as he admonishes the great ones of his age: "you call Good Evill, and Evill Good, Light Darknesse, and Darknesse Light; Truth Blasphemy, and Blasphemy Truth" (p. 91). Coppe's levelling Lord demands that branding with the letter "B" – symbolic of blasphemy – be abolished once and for all. Moreover, as Coppe passionately challenges clerical powers, he envisions, like his Digger contemporary, a "pure spirit of universall love, who is the eternall God" (p. 85) able to subvert class tyranny and oppression, as well as orthodox Protestant moral codes and practices.

Like the Ranter Laurence Clarkson, Coppe was an experienced itinerate preacher,[37] as the exhortations and rhythms of his vigorous prophetic writing often suggest. In his *Fiery Flying Rolls* he addresses the mighty of the earth, warning them of the impending judgment and miseries to come and of an overturning time when "Kings, Princes, Lords, great ones, must bow to the poorest Peasants . . . or else they'l rue for it" (p. 109). With its frequent repetitions, its fierce admonitions to those in power, and its tone of apocalyptic exhortation, Coppe's prose conveys a sense of powerful urgency, as well as a sense of immense verbal energy: "Howl, howl, ye nobles, howl honourable, howl ye rich men for the miseries that are coming upon you" (p. 112) Coppe writes, echoing and intensifying the prophetic language of James 5:1. His frenetic prose itself enacts the process of social levelling and overturning it envisions.

In order to achieve a righteous state of universal love and perfect freedom, and to save England as the contemporary Zion, Coppe's Lord of Hosts operates as a powerful revolutionary force which shakes terribly "not the earth onely, but the heavens also" (like the God of Haggai 2:6–7 and Hebrews 12:26) and which symbolically levels social hierarchies and differences by his Spirit: "Behold, behold, behold, I the eternall God, the Lord of Hosts, who am that mighty Leveller, am comming (yea even at the doores) to Levell in good earnest, to Levell to some purpose, to Levell with a witnesse, to Levell the Hills with the Valleyes, and to lay the Mountaines low" (pp. 89, 87; cf. p. 94). These potent metaphors of levelling, suggesting the redistribution of power and wealth downward through the social order, were particularly reso- nant in radical religious writings produced during the late 1640s and early 1650s. They inform the millenarian visions of the near-Ranter George Foster who published his first work, *The Sounding of the Last Trumpet*, only a few months after Coppe's *Fiery Roll* appeared: in "his great and terrible work" the mighty God who avenges the poor and the oppressed does "levell and lay mountaines and hils low, and make plaines and vallies equall with them" as he "take[s] away that stumbling block of private interest";[38] such a great leveller as Foster's God embod- ies the acute social concerns of radical writers in this period of revolu- tionary upheaval. Though the Ranter Joseph Salmon does not employ these same exact tropes, he nevertheless envisions the Army in 1649 as a powerful social and apocalyptic leveller – the Lord's instrument car- rying out his unsettling work "fully, hotly, sharply": "in this Day of the Lords Wrath you strike thorow King, Gentry, and Nobility, they all fall before you: You have a Commission from the LORD to scourge ENGLAND'S Oppressors."[39] In Coppe little indeed is spared by the process of levelling and overturning. Thus his mighty God, acting with the power of the Lord of Isaiah and Ezekiel, levels all ecclesiastical structures, rituals, and authority:[40]

Ile overturne, overturne, overturne, I am now . . . bringing into contempt all the honourable of the earth . . . not only honourable persons . . . but honorable things, as Elderships, Pastorships, Fellowships, Churches, Ordinances, Prayers, &c. Holinesses, Righteousnesses, Religions of all sorts, of the highest strains. (p. 106)

Nevertheless, however much he shares the Digger vision of social level- ling which would usher in a new righteous age, he also distinguishes his powerful rhetoric from that of Winstanley and other radicals, including more militant ones (the recently martyred Levellers, for example): the principle of his mighty Lord is as far from "sword levelling" or "digging- levelling" as "the East is from the West, or the Heavens from the Earth" (p. 86).

There is a powerful iconoclastic dimension to Coppe's levelling vision of the Lord's mighty Spirit. His prophetic text was written, after all, at nearly the same moment of religious ferment as Milton's major idol-smashing polemic, *Eikonoklastes* (October 1649), which envisioned, at times with apocalyptic fervor, the Lord and his saints smashing to pieces and dissolving the "great power and Dominion" of "the Kings of this World."[41] Milton demolishes the idols of earthly kings, whereas Coppe demolishes the surviving idols of social privilege. The Ranter prophet confronts deep class divisions as he presents an ecstatic vision of social levelling inspired by the prophet Isaiah's unsettling vision of the Lord's terrible power and iconoclasm in the last catastrophic day (see Isa. 2:17–21):

And the LOFTINESSE of man shall be bowed down, and the haughtinesse of men shall be laid low. And the Lord ALONE shall be exalted in that day, and the Idols he shall utterly abolish.

And they shall go into the holes of the Rocks, and into the Caves of the Earth, for feare of the Lord, and for the glory of his Majesty, when he ariseth to shake terribly the earth.

In that day a man shall cast his Idols of Silver, and Idols of Gold – to the bats, and to the Moles. To go into the Clefts of the Rocks and into the tops of the ragged Rocks, for feare of the Lord, and for the glory of his Majesty. For the Lord is now RISEN to shake terribly the Earth. (p. 87)[42]

Like the communist Digger or the anonymous author of *Tyranipocrit, Discovered* (1649), Coppe and his levelling God are confounding honor, pomp, and greatness and bringing about a new utopian age of "parity, equality, [and] community" (pp. 88–89). Coppe perceives, as Winstanley does, that "this Honour, Nobility, Gentility, Propriety, Superfluity" have bred "hellish horrid pride, arrogance, haughtinesse, loftinesse, murder, malice, of all manner of wickednesse and impiety; yea the cause of all the blood that ever hath been shed, from the blood of righteous *Abell*, to the blood of the last Levellers that were shot to death" (p. 88). Like the Digger, Coppe draws upon the potent scriptural myth of Cain and Abel to attack private property, the class system, and social injustice; and he gives the myth poignant contemporary resonance by linking it with the ruthless suppression and execution by Cromwell and the Army leaders of the Leveller mutineers at Burford in May 1649, when the infant republican regime was facing its most serious internal challenge: "their blood cries vengeance, vengeance, in mine ears, saith the Lord" (p. 94).

There is, then, an urgent sense of apocalyptic doom and millenarian expectation in Coppe's writing, which emphasizes that the terrible yet glorious Day of the Lord is at hand – a dreadful day of judgment, vengeance, and revelation envisioned in this "last WARNING

PIECE" (p. 80). Like the visionary Winstanley, Coppe writes at that apocalyptic moment of conflict when the Lord's "mighty Angel" Michael "just now fights that terrible battell in heaven with the great Dragon" (p. 101). He also reports the scriptural warning from Daniel "MENE, MENE, TEKEL" (p. 95, echoing Dan. 5:25–7); here the handwriting on the wall becomes the divine sentence passed against all the great ones of the earth and is symbolic of the power of God: they have been weighed in the balances and found wanting, and God has numbered the days of their kingdom. Moreover, as the millenarian Coppe proclaims, "The Eternal God, the mighty Leveller is comming, yea come, even at the doore," much like Milton's ominous apocalyptic "two-handed engine at the door" ready to smite once and smite no more. Indeed, such apocalyptic levelling – "the substantiality of level-ling" – far exceeds in power that "very shadow of levelling, sword level-ling" and "man levelling" (p. 90). Coppe's mighty God of vengeance and wrath is the Lord of 1 Thessalonians 5:2 and 2 Peter 3:10 who comes "as a thief in the night," suddenly and unexpectedly, and with a sword drawn in his hand.[43] He is, moreover, vividly represented by Coppe as a highwayman, a divine folk hero stealing from the rich to give to the poor: "I say deliver your purse, deliver sirrah! deliver or I'l cut thy throat!"[44] Coppe's levelling deity is ferocious in his promise of vengeance against "the rich ones," should they refuse to deliver up their wealth to the wretched of the earth: "I will torment thee day and night, inwardly, or outwardly, or both waies, my little finger shall shortly be heavier on thee, especially on thee thou holy, righteous, religious *Appropriator*, then my loynes were on *Pharoah* and the Egyptians in time of old" (p. 100). Ready to pour forth his wrath upon the unreformed rich and great ones, Coppe's God will visit them with his judgments of dearth, pestilence, and the sword. Coppe's aim, like that of Ezekiel and the author of the Book of Revelation, is to convey the absolute dread of God's wrath.

The repetition of denunciation in Coppe's visionary prose (recalling that of Ezekiel), moreover, contributes to its fierce rhetorical power as a weapon of levelling, while conveying a keen sense of apocalyptic doom: "Repent, repent, repent, Bow down, bow down, or howle, resigne, or be damned; Bow downe, bow downe, you sturdy Oakes, and Cedars, bow downe" (p. 90), Coppe proclaims in his (and his Lord's) admonitions to great ones. Coppe's metaphorical and scriptural language, especially the bowing down of sturdy oaks and tall cedars, anticipates the threatening prophetic language of revolutionary Quakerism, which aimed at dra-matically assaulting the proud and lofty, as well as all outward power, authority, and rule, during the pamphlet warfare of the 1650s.[45] Recalling the unsettling language of Isaiah, Coppe himself prophesies the Day of the Lord in which the cedars of Lebanon and the oaks of Bashan shall be brought low (Isa. 2:13; cf. Ps. 29:5). Such prophetic passages, moreover, suggest the fusion of oral and print culture in the English Revolution:[46] one can hear the voice of the itinerant Coppe prophesying against the mighty of the earth as he preaches his shocking sermons and proclaims the great Day of the Lord "thorow the streets of the great City" London (p. 87), which he addresses directly in chapter 5 of his first *Fiery Roll*. At the same time, Coppe is disseminating God's terrible Word through his own visionary writing. The constant verbal repetition conveys the energy of his visionary prose, as well as its threatening power – "Behold, behold, behold, I the eternall God, the Lord of Hosts, who am the mighty Leveller, am comming" (p. 87). And so, when Coppe wants to highlight the unjustness of the great powers of the earth for having slain the Levellers at Burford, those righteous martyrs for truth whose blood cries out for vengeance, he again resorts to vigorous verbal repetition: "Ye have killed the just—Ye have killed, ye have killed, ye have killed the just," he proclaims, echoing the prophetic words of doom which James directs at the rich and powerful (James 5:6; p. 94). Intense verbal repetition would likewise soon characterize the style of Quaker writing, with its fierce reproofs, warnings, and apocalyptic exhortations. Indeed, like Coppe, the Quakers used such iterative prophetic rhetoric to alarm the proud and imperiled city of London itself.[47]

Furthermore, like Winstanley, who represents the internal dynamics of social processes and spiritual conflicts, Coppe depicts the process of levelling and destruction taking place within the self since "the Prime levelling, is laying low the Mountaines, and levelling the Hils in man": that is "the true and pure levelling" (pp. 88, 116). Levelling in that internal sense is a matter of unsettling conventional and misguided Protestant perceptions of behavior, morality, religion, and the social order – one aim of Coppe's shocking writing and strange acts. Encouraging levelling neither by the sword nor by digging up communal lands, Coppe's visionary writing promotes "*Bloud-Life-Spirit levelling*" (p. 116), as he puts it at the end of the second *Fiery Flying Roll* – a radical religious form of levelling that is spiritual and inward as well as external.

Completely overturning social conventions and illustrating the meaning of "*Bloud-Life-Spirit levelling*," Coppe preaching in the streets of London conveys the admonitions of the Lord who commands the great ones of the earth to fall down before each beggar they meet: "kisse

Beggers, Prisoners, warme them, feed them, cloathe them, money them, relieve them, take them into your houses." The verbs pile up as Coppe's vigorous prophetic prose increases in rhetorical force. So, too, Coppe's piling up of adjectives conveys the sharp edge of his aggressive prose in which the rules of social hierarchy, especially between master and servant, are thoroughly challenged and turned upside down: "Bow before those poore, nasty, lousie, ragged wretches, say to them, your humble servants, Sirs, . . . we let you go free, and serve you," commands his admonishing Lord (p. 90). Moreover, as Coppe himself performs in public his strange postures – shocking and dramatic actions – he himself becomes, like some of the theatrical Quakers in Interregnum England, "no small signe and wonder in fleshly *Israel*" as he expresses his compassion for the wretchedness of the poor:[48] thus he shocks the inhabitants of London as he falls "down flat at the feet of creeples, beggars, lazars, kissing their feet, and resigning up my money to them" (pp. 81, 96). Quoting Matthew 25:43 ("I was a Stranger, and ye tooke me not in" (p. 96)), Coppe dramatizes himself as a social outcast and outsider in an urban world full of misery and oppression. There is an urgent prophetic message behind his levelling commands and bewildering postures aimed at shattering social conventions, polarization, and hierarchies: the poorest beggar or rogue "is thy brother, thy fellow, flesh of thy flesh" (p. 90), he boldly proclaims to the great ones. In this new age of upheaval, pleading "priviledge and Prerogative from Scripture" will no longer do; in Coppe's radical social vision, "rich men must stoop to poor rogues" (p. 109). If they turn their eyes from their own flesh, Coppe warns them, then his wrathful God will "pull out thine eyes, and throw thee headlong into hell" (p. 90): this Lord who promotes universal love among his creatures is simultaneously punishing through his mighty levelling of the political order and class system.

Coppe's visionary prose, like his unconventional, riddling behavior recorded in it, is itself a means of choosing base things "to confound things that are" (p. 107) – to challenge and assault Puritan orthodox ideology. In his own eccentric and unorthodox way, Coppe aims, like the poet of *Paradise Lost*, to subvert the "worldly strong" "by things deem'd weak" (*PL* 12.566–67). Like his contemporary George Foster, Coppe himself shows how "the mighty Jehovah will do his strange worke by poor, weak, and dispised instruments; even by those that are as nothing in themselves."[49] Like the prophetic James, whose fierce admonitions and imagery Coppe often appropriates, the Ranter writer suggests that God has "chosen the poor of this world rich in faith" (James 2:5); as

Richard Coppin observed in his *Divine Teachings* (1649), a work introduced by Coppe, the Lord seemed to be leaving the great and learned and "exalt[ing] himself in the poor and ignorant."[50] Coppe's paradoxical utterances were stimulated by a revolutionary age when social radicalism often assumed unorthodox religious expression.

His lively prose dramatizes the social politics of his radical religious beliefs. And so, in the third chapter of his second *Roll*, Coppe invites the reader to hear a narration of one of his "various, strange, yet true stories" (p. 98): the story of his encountering in an open field a poor, ragged man on 30 September 1649. Coppe's dramatic account employs dialogue to explore the social and spiritual meanings of this memorable encounter with "a most strange deformed man, clad with patcht clouts" (p. 101). Coppe provides not only the dialogue between himself and the "poor wretch" – "How now friend, art thou poore? He answered, yea Master very poore" – but also between himself and the subtle harlot, "the mother of witchcrafts" (pp. 101–2, 99) who rises up within Coppe, tempting him to restrain his urge to be charitable. As he feels compassion for the beggar's plight, she responds in a tone of hypocritical morality: "It's a poor wretch, give him two-pence. . . . Besides (saith the holy Scripturian Whore) hee's worse then an Infidell that provides not for his own Family." The story thus dramatizes, on one level, a kind of psychomachia between the "EXCELLENCY and MAJESTY" within Coppe, the inner Spirit itself, and the whore within who "flattereth with her lips, . . . her words being smoother then oile" (a recollection of Proverbs 5:3). But moved by "the great God within," the divided Coppe is determined to resist the subtle language of the inner harlot, and to show the desperate man more generosity and justice. Yet when he offers him a shilling, Coppe discovers the poor man has no change to give him in return – "I have never a penny," says the wretch – to which Coppe responds: "I would fain have given thee something if thou couldst have changed my money" (p. 102). Having then received the poor man's blessing, Coppe finds it difficult to ride away (though he begins to do so) and leave the wretched man with nothing. As Coppe turns back to direct the poor wretch to call for six pence at a house in the next town, he himself experiences the very judgment predicted by the prophet James as he admonishes the rich ("Your gold and silver is cankered; and the rust of them shall be a witness against you, and shall eat your flesh as it were fire," James 5:3): "the rust of my silver did so rise up in judgement against me, and burnt my flesh like fire: and the 5 of *James* thundered such an alarm in mine ears, that I was fain to call all I had into the hands of him,

whose visage was more marr'd then any mans that ever I saw." Coppe
then throws his "rusty canker'd money into the poor wretches hands"
and rides away feeling "the sparkles of a great glory"; but prompted by
"that divine power" within to confront the poor man one last time,
Coppe puts off his hat, bows to him seven times and says: "because I am
a King, I have done this, but you need not tell any one" (p. 103).

The Ranter's strange story – "true in the history" as well as "in the
mystery" – illustrates dramatically his provocative spiritual vision and
radical social message. Even the most mundane of encounters, like
Coppe's with this poorest of wretches, can dramatize the greatest spiritual truths as powerfully as any text in the Bible. As Coppe urges his
readers, just before he presents his own strange story of giving his money
away, "give, give, give up, give up your houses, horses, goods, gold,
Lands, give up, account nothing your own, have ALL THINGS
common, or els the plague of God will rot and consume all that you
have" (p. 101). The ending of the strange story indeed illustrates an altogether radical revision of the spiritual and social meaning of "communion" and the Eucharist and of breaking one's bread "to the hungry": in
Coppe's utopian vision, which includes repudiating private property,
"The true Communion amongst men, is to have all things common, and
to call nothing one hath, ones own" (p. 114).[51] As Coppe tells his readers
before concluding his text:

But take this hint before I leave thee.
He that hath this worlds goods, and seeth his brother in want, and shutteth up
the the bowels of compassion from him, the love of God dwelleth not in him;
this mans Religion is in vain. (p. 115)

The compassion the unorthodox Coppe finally shows the poor wretch is
the same compassion he feels for the suffering city of London, even as
he fiercely admonishes her "great ones" and warns them of impending
destruction.

But in a text in which he radically redefines the meanings of communion between men and with God, Coppe shows that orthodox Puritan
notions of organized religion, morality, and communion have only been
reinforced by "the wel-favoured Harlot" herself, who is clearly a version
of the Whore of Babylon. Having "made the Nations of the earth
drunk, with the cup of [her] fornications" (see Rev. 14:8), the subtle
harlot has been opposing the Spirit's work internally as well as outwardly, as she urges her followers to be holy, righteous, and religious –
and to adhere to church ordinances:

Thou hast come to a poor irreligious wretch, and told him he must be of the same Religion as his neighbours, he must go to Church, hear the Minister, &c. and at least once a year put on his best cloaths, and receive the Communion – he must eat a bit of bread, and drink a sip of wine – and then he hath received, &c. he hath been at the Communion. (p. 113)

Coppe's bold communal ethic and practice – bowing down "to equality, or free community" (p. 96) – is one means by which he, who walks in the Spirit, can expose and conquer the Antichristian harlot and (to quote from another of his visionary texts) by which he "may be lifted up into pure Religion, and undefiled."[52] But in bringing his radical communal vision to fruition, Coppe must act as well as write. We recall Winstanley, for whom prophetic words required righteous actions, asserting in his address to the city of London that "Action is the life of all":[53] though the Ranter writer does not choose to take his action with a spade, Coppe nevertheless demonstrates the meaning of "Blood-life-spirit-commu-nion" (p. 112) and *"Bloud-Life-Spirit levelling"* through his own kinds of righteous deeds and communal gestures illustrated by the striking nar-rative of "A strange, yet most true story."

In the second *Fiery Flying Roll*, Coppe elaborates further on his con-nection with the eccentric behavior and visions of the prophet Ezekiel, who has inspired the Ranter's prophetic self-fashioning. Like the Old Testament prophet, Coppe uses fiery oratory as well as symbolic actions to warn and unsettle his contemporaries. Like Ezekiel, the transgressive Coppe is also "a sonne of *Buzi*" or "the son of contempt" in his own age. Coppe justifies his outrageous prophetic postures and symbolic "pranks" by referring to those of Ezekiel performed "in the midst of the streets of the great City Hierusalem":[54] "Amongst many of his pranks – this was one, he shaves all the hair off his head: and off his beard, then weighs them in a pair of scales; burns one part of them in the fire, another part he smites about with a knife, another part thereof he scatters in the wind, and a few he binds up in his skirts, &c." (p. 104). The prank to which Coppe refers, described in Ezekiel 5:1–4, has symbolic resonance in the Bible: it represents the destruction awaiting the inhabitants of Jerusalem who were to be burned, slain, and scattered (see Ezek. 5:2). This passage, like the others from Ezekiel to which Coppe then alludes (Ezek. 12:3 ff., 4:3, 24:3–27), concerns the Lord's righteous judgments on the iniquity of Judah and Jerusalem. Like the prophet Ezekiel, the antinomian and pro-phetic Ranter has himself been made "a sign and wonder" (cf. Ezek. 4–5; 12:3–16; 24:24, 27), and he acts "by that omnipotency dwelling in him" (p. 104) since he insists that he is one with God. Coppe himself is

self-conscious about the theatrical dimensions of his highly transgressive, Ezekiel-like behavior and its "various effects . . . upon the
Spectators" which generate such wonder (p. 103). Challenging hypocritical moral conventions and parodying social gestures through his strange
postures, Coppe has stimulated a great range of responses, from "the joy
and refreshment of some, both acquaintances and strangers, to the wonderment and amazement of others, to the terrour and affrightment
of others; and to the great torment of the chiefest of the Sects of
Professours" (p. 104). He is engaged in a bizarre and extreme form of
theatricalism meant to unsettle and to subvert social conventions, as well
as Puritan godliness practiced by those "who pretend most for God"
("The Contents," p. 84). His blasphemous and ecstatic rants have a per-
formative quality as does his flamboyant, experimental prose itself, with
its striking use of dramatic dialogue.[55] The symbolic gestures and dramatic performance of Coppe in his prose embodies the visionary spirit
of Ezekiel in an age of social unrest.

As he acts out his role as Ezekiel-like prophet, Coppe performs a series
of shocking gestures and verbal assaults meant to startle the great ones
of his age. Indeed, his behavior reminds us that imprecation remained
a formidable weapon in a culture that still believed in the power of the
curse to bring divine vengeance upon the rich and powerful and to strike
terror into the hearts of the guilty.[56] Such conduct could alarm the mainstream godly as well; Baxter recalled the following passage, describing
one of Coppe's transgressive postures in the streets of London and
Southwark, to illustrate why the Ranter's behavior and book, "in which
he blasphemously arrogates to himselfe the sacred Name and Titles of
God, and crys down Duties and godly Life," should indeed "be heard
with trembling":[57]

Wherefore waving my charging so many Coaches, so many hundreds of men
and women of the greater rank, in the open streets, with my hand stretched out,
my hat cock't up, staring on them as if I would look thorough them, gnashing
with my teeth at some of them, and day and night with a huge loud voice proclaiming the day of the Lord throughout London and Southwark . . . (p. 105)

Such subversive and inspired gestures, as Coppe acts out "strange and
great exploits" prompted by "the Eternall God," are aimed directly at
"men and women of the greater ranke," including "roystering roaring
Cavalliers (so called) and other wilde sparks of the Gentry" (p. 97).
Moreover, Coppe's lowly carriage and histrionic behavior towards the
poor wretches he encounters on the streets dramatize further the com-

munal ethic underpinning the strange narrative of his encounter with the beggar in the field. Thus Coppe describes another startling scene in which he is "hugging, imbracing, kissing a poore deformed wretch in London, who had no more nose on his face, then I have on the back of my hand. . . . and afterwards running back to him in a strange manner, with my money giving it to him, to the joy of some, to the afrightment and wonderment of other Spectators." In Coppe's theatrical world, where social conventions, especially gestures associated with social privilege and order, are inverted, the poorest wretches – "rogues, beggars, cripples," and gypsies – are greeted as though they were the greatest lords in England: Coppe describes himself "kissing the feet of many, rising up againe, and giving them money" (p. 105). His extravagant gestures, as he curses the great ones and bows down to the poor, parody those of a conventional stratified social world where the poor are spurned and the rich honored. Through his many strange postures, the inspired Coppe takes the subversive possibilities of imitation to an ecstatic extreme.[58]

Coppe's wild, eccentric behavior, as he assumes different scriptural roles, dramatizes his aim to subvert "plaguy holinesse" and righteousness by choosing base things to confound "things that ARE." This Ranter writer, after all, prefers the excessive behavior of a Nehemiah (coming in "like a mad-man, and pluck[ing] folkes hair off their heads" and cursing: see Neh. 13:25) to hearing "a zealous Presbyterian" or Independent "pray, preach, or exercise" (pp. 106–7, 92). And so in the second *Fiery Flying Roll* the theatrical Coppe presents himself as David leaping and dancing before the Lord, making an undignified public spectacle of himself (and becoming "base in [his] own sight," 2 Sam. 6:22), while shocking Michal, the daughter of Saul, who watches the shameless performance of the naked ecstatic: "I am confounding, plaguing, tormenting nice, barren *Mical*, with *Davids* unseemly carriage, by skipping, leaping, dancing, like one of the fools; vile, base fellowes, shamelessely, basely, and uncovered too before handmaids" (p. 106). Like the Ranter Joseph Salmon, Coppe plays the inspired fool in order to confound the world of conventional Protestant morality, religion, and conduct: "I am now a fool, I care not who knows it . . . but I am now carried out of my wits, a fool, a mad man, besides my self."[59] Behaving basely and extravagantly, Coppe hugs, fondles, and kisses gypsies and enjoys "concubines without number," while he imagines being reproached by the demure and shocked Michal. Through his strange, erotic acts he explodes Puritan notions of sinfulness and transgression as he paradoxically manages to remain untempted even in the midst of his provocative sexual behavior – "I abhorred the thought of Ladies, their beauty could not bewitch mine eyes . . . or intangle my hands in their bosomes" (p. 109, 107).[60] Through base acts and gestures, including swearing and cursing (later condemned by the Rump), Coppe confounds "stinking family duties" (p. 107), churches, gospel ordinances, and other apparent manifestations of holiness. In this way Coppe has indeed confounded "base things" by "base things." Fully aware of the paradoxes of his subversive words and actions, he represents himself as a riddling Samson: "Ther's my riddle, but . . . neither all the Lords of the Philistins, no nor my Delilah her self can read it." By acting out base things, the ecstatic Coppe transcends sin itself, as well as all the religious and social constraints of his culture: "I [have] been carried up into the arms of my love, which is invisible glory, eternall Majesty, purity it self, unspotted beauty" (p. 108).

As Blake observed, "The road of excess leads to the palace of wisdom": his famous Proverb of Hell could well be applied to the sensational revolutionary writing and ecstatic behavior of the Ranter Coppe.[61] His extravagant language and postures take the road of excess to challenge customary Protestant perceptions of social hierarchy, good and evil, and sin and transgression in Interregnum England. But only by taking the road of excess, which included writing with a particularly violent rhetoric of levelling, could Coppe hope – paradoxically – to bring about a "pure spirit of universall love" and thereby provide "An inlet into the Land of Promise, the new *Hierusalem*" itself (pp. 85, 81).

Coppe, however, later issued two recantations while in prison: *A Remonstrance of The sincere and Zealous Protestation of Abiezer Coppe* (January 1650/51) and *Copp's Return to the wayes of Truth* (July 1651). Both texts can be read as ambiguous responses to the punishment he received as a result of his flamboyant revolutionary writings and heretical doctrines. The first, a "Remonstrance, Vindication and Attestation," engages in "the clearing up of those mistakes, and the wiping away of those aspersions, which (through malice, weakness, ignorance, and mistake) have been cast upon [Coppe]."[62] The Ranter vindicates himself in the contexts of the Acts of May and August 1650 to suppress adultery and fornication and to suppress atheistical and blasphemous opinions: the innocence of this prophet's name has been "clouded with the name of *Transgression*" (p. 118). He protests "against all those blasphemous Opinions or Tenents" in the Blasphemy Act; similarly, he now proclaims that such social ills as swearing, blasphemy, drunkenness, adultery, and fornication are unholy and sinful. Contrary to his earlier radical spiritualism, he even seems to concede to Protestant orthodoxy when he asserts "That there is Heaven, and Hell, Salvation and Damnation," though he continues to insist on the indwelling God or Christ – that "God Christ is in the creature" (p. 121), the sort of claim that easily led to a rejection of external ordinances.[63] At the same time, Coppe, having endured long imprisonment and having been attacked in the anti-Ranter literature, can display the same fierceness that characterized his rhetoric in the two *Fiery Flying Rolls*: he lashes out against "All fleshly interests, carnall Gospellers, and pretenders to Religion," having already "faithfully and boldly declared against their hypocrisie, pride, covetousness, self-seeking, and villainy, covered under the cloak of fleshly holiness and religion" (p. 119, column). Furthermore, he has "thundered" against "*Idolatry, Superstition, and Idolatrous Formality*"; nor does he "repent" that the Almighty has made him "A SIGNE and a WONDER" – exactly as he had appeared on the streets of London performing his provocative strange postures, evoking the wonder of astonished spectators through base actions, and savagely denouncing the great ones of his age. Engaged in a kind of Pauline self-fashioning, Coppe adds that he was set "*as a stumbling stone, and ROCK of OFFENCE to both the Houses of Israel*" (p. 120; based on Romans 9:33): just as Israel had stumbled when it sought righteousness "not by faith, but as it were by the works of the law" (Romans 9:32), so the English Commonwealth has not appreciated that Coppe's prophetic words and wondrous actions represent a kind of righteousness-by-faith, separate from – and indeed above – the moral law. Coppe may protest against "all Sinful liberty" in this text of recantation, but he has not retreated from the radical communal vision underpinning his levelling rhetoric and eccentric acts in the *Fiery Flying Rolls*: "I either will or should call nothing I have mine own: if I have bread, it shall or should be his; else all my Religion is vain, I own for dealing bread to the hungry, for cloathing the naked, for the *breaking of every yoke*, for the *letting of the oppressed go free*" (p. 122). Such was the radical social lesson of the strange yet true story Coppe had narrated in his second *Roll*.

Coppe's ambiguous recantation of his Ranter beliefs and practices, moreover, was dramatized as soon as he was released from prison in September 1651. On a tour of Oxfordshire, one of the areas where he had made his reputation as a skillful itinerant preacher, he delivered a recantation sermon to the skeptical orthodox godly: "againe and againe with dreadfull curses" and "execrations" the Ranter proclaimed that he had indeed now truly reformed.[64]

THE "MIGHTY VISIONS" OF ANNA TRAPNEL: FIFTH
MONARCHIST PROPHECIES AT WHITEHALL

Like Abiezer Coppe, the flamboyant Fifth Monarchist Anna Trapnel (fl. 1642–1660) produced some of the more striking radical prophecies of the Interregnum as she vigorously addressed its political tensions and crises.[65] Only a few weeks after Cromwell was installed as Lord Protector, she delivered in a notorious public display at White-hall "*Revelations* touching his Highness . . . and the ARMY," as well as "her *Declaration* touching the State-Affairs of *Great-Brittain*; Even from the Death of the late King CHARLES, to the Dissolution of the last PARLIAMENT."[66] In a trance-like state she issued sensational political prophecies in a mixture of visionary prose and verses which attracted large, inquisitive and enthusiastic audiences, including not only the Fifth Monarchy firebrand Christopher Feake, but members of the aristocracy, recent members of the Barebone's Parliament, and other notable people – an indication of ongoing and widespread interest in popular millenarian visions.[67] Like some of the leading Fifth Monarchists, including Feake, John Simpson, and John Rogers, Trapnel possessed a great flair for self-dramatization and exhilarating prophecies. Like the Ezekiel-inspired Coppe, Trapnel and other Fifth Monarchist visionaries sensed that these were indeed "Overturning, Overturning, Overturning dayes";[68] their prophecies were fueled by the convulsions of the Revolution and the regicide, which they interpreted as the end of the fourth and last great earthly monarchy foretold in the apocalyptic visions of Daniel. The fifth monarchy envisioned in Daniel 7 – that of King Jesus and his saints – had begun and Cromwell himself as God's instrument seemed like a new Gideon or Moses righteously dissolving the unpopular Rump.[69] The reign of Christ on earth was imminent: it was their mission to bring it about by fulfilling Daniel's prophecy that the saints shall take the kingdom and possess it forever (Dan. 7:18). Yet with an ambivalent Cromwell assuming the novel title of Protector, an alarming opposition between Christ and Cromwell had become apparent, stimulating outraged Fifth Monarchist preachers to issue fiery, bitterly seditious public attacks on the apostate Protector as the little horn that was making war with the saints (Dan. 7:21).[70]

The daughter of a London shipwright and a member of the Allhallows congregation of John Simpson, Trapnel became as much of a colorful personality during the Interregnum as the Ranter Coppe, especially on those dramatic public occasions when she was "seized upon by the Lord" and "carried forth in a spirit of Prayer and Singing, from noon till night" (*Cry of a Stone*, p. 1).[71] Although she began having millenarian visions from 1647, she committed herself to Fifth Monarchism in 1652 and then denounced the new Protectorate in her millenarian prophecies produced between 1654 and 1658. In early January 1654, she accompanied the charismatic Fifth Monarchist preacher Vavasor Powell to his examination by the Council of State at Whitehall, since he had been accused of inflaming sedition against the government; there she experienced a twelve-day trance and delivered a series of "Mighty Visions" concerning the imminent coming of the Kingdom of Christ, the failings of the Lord Protector, and the plight of the poor.[72] Indeed, the "Strange and Wonderful Newes" of her public visionary seizure got the attention of the newsbooks and Cromwell himself, to whom Marchamont Nedham observed that the prophetess "does a world of mischief in London, and would do in the country."[73] Later in 1654, on a mission to Cornwall for Simpson's congregation, her radical activities aroused further controversy: fearing that she was a diabolically possessed madwoman encouraging subversion, the local clergy and government had her arrested and imprisoned for four months during the spring and summer. According to Trapnel, who published an account of her journey, clerical and state authorities had made her "the worlds wonder, and gazing stock" and represented her as "a dangerous seditious Person" attempting "to move, stir up, and raise discord, rebellion and insurrection among the good People of *England*."[74] She would later undertake a second mission west and experience another major trance, resulting in further ecstatic prophecies and an untitled thousand-page book of verse (now at the Bodleian Library) in which she continued her unrestrained attacks on the backsliding clergy and Protectorate, proclaiming "The Spirit and Voice hath made a league / Against *Cromwel* and his Council all," who could expect "Utter ruine and over-throw."[75] For our purposes, however, *The Cry of a Stone. Or a Relation of Something Spoken in Whitehall* (1654) illustrates vividly the ways in which her prophecies voiced daring political criticisms and a keen sense of spiritual crisis, as she challenged the Protectorate at its center of authority, while confronting all earthly powers – "the *Governors, Army, Churches, Ministry, Universities*: And the whole NATION" – in millenarian visions "uttered in Prayers and Spiritual Songs, by an Inspiration extraordinary, and full of wonder."[76] As an inspired woman, Trapnel would not only not keep her silence (as Pauline texts insisted), but she would break through traditional gender barriers to issue her daring prophecies at

Whitehall, the nation's symbolic and political locus of power.[77] With flamboyance, Trapnel the prophetess was asserting her right and authority to have a public voice and an active role in the great religious and political affairs of the nation.

The Cry of a Stone offers a highly dramatic narrative account of Trapnel's utterances "taken from her own mouth," including the "Visions and Revelations of things to come" which she had during her twelve-day trance as she lay in bed in a Whitehall lodging "with her eyes shut, her hands fixed, seldom seen to move . . . [and spoke] every day, sometimes two, three, four, and five hours together" (p. 2).[78] Moreover, during the first five days of this trance-like state she ate nothing and then very little after that. Many of the ecstatic prayers and spiritual songs which poured out of her were written down by a friend and recorded in *The Cry of a Stone*, a text intended to present "a true and faithful Relation of so much as for some 7 or 8 dayes could be taken from her" (sig. a2v). Her extraordinary visionary performance at Whitehall was not, however, a demonstration of wild Ranterism, as the account and her personal narrative try to make clear.[79] Trapnel begins by emphasizing that she is well known to Simpson's congregation and to numerous respected Baptist preachers; moreover, in order to establish that she is a credible visionary, she attributes her prophetic gifts to the dying words of her mother nine years earlier: "Lord! Double thy spirit upon my child; These words she uttered with much eagerness three times, and spoke no more" (p. 3). The passage recalls the Lord's promise in Joel 2:28–29, reiterated in Acts 2:17–18, that both sons and daughters would prophesy – powerful evidence in these times of millenarian expectations that the Bible authorized female as well as male prophecy – and that he would pour out his Spirit upon his servants and handmaids (Trapnel refers to herself as a "poor hand maid" sent by God to Whitehall: p. 70).[80] Trapnel thus believed herself to be an instrument of God so that she had been granted personal illumination and could act as a channel of divine revelation and a bearer of urgent political messages:[81] experiencing her first visions in 1647, while afflicted with an intense fever, she recalls the Lord telling her that "particular souls shall not only have benefit by [her], but the universality of Saints shall have discoveries of God through [her]" (p. 3). Indeed, the title *The Cry of a Stone* alerts readers to her prophetic authority by alluding to Habakkuk 2:11–12, where the Old Testament prophet, capable of hearing a cry imperceptible to others, has been delivering a series of judgment prophecies: "For the stone shall cry out of the wall . . . Woe to him that buildeth a town with blood, and stablisheth a city by iniquity!" Like the Book of Habakkuk, Trapnel's prophetic performance in the public political space of Whitehall combines vision and prayer, and concerns itself with the downfall of the unfaithful, as well as the coming of the kingdom of God and his new order of righteousness; like the Lord, whose "voice comes forth with much power," the prophetess too "speakest with a mighty alarum" to the nation (p. 63).

Indeed, the early part of Trapnel's *Cry of a Stone* vividly describes (in addition to the Bunyan-like assaults and temptations she experienced from Satan) the multiple revelations and political prophecies she had in the past, including a vision, while fasting for many days, of the defeat of the Scots at Dunbar six weeks before that major battle occurred in 1650: General Cromwell, not yet the Lord Protector denounced in her Fifth Monarchist prophecies, then appeared to her as a heroic Gideon "going before *Israel*, blowing the trumpet of courage and valour" (p. 6). In another she foresaw Cromwell's forceful expulsion of the Rump four days before it happened; and then on 3 September 1653, while in the company of Colonel John Bingham, one of the most respectable and moderate members of the Barebone's Parliament, she had a vision of its dissolution which revealed the Lord's rejection of Cromwell: she envisioned "the deadness of *Gideons* spirit toward the work of the Lord, shewing me that he was laid aside, as to any great matters, the Lord having finished the greatest business that he would employ him in" (p. 10).[82] Listening to the issue of Trapnel's trance-like state, Bingham called it a prophecy, saying he was in fact glad of it, "for he thought little good would be done by" that assembly (p. 11). Other politically symbolic visions included one of an ominous high tower with rooms resembling the council's apartments at Whitehall; this faced a gleaming white tower filled with many saints ("their eyes fixed toward Heaven"), which Cromwell's senior Army officers were attempting unsuccessfully to blow up (pp. 11–12). Trapnel also beheld, two nights before the Protectorate was established in December 1653, a great darkness covering the earth with "a marvellous dust" and "a great company of Cattel" with faces and heads like men, "having each of them a horn on either side of their heads." They raised a great shout in honor of their leader, whose countenance of course resembled that of Cromwell, upon whom they were fawning. When he charged with his horn Trapnel and "many precious Saints" who stood boldly in his way (the little horn of Daniel 7–8 was now regularly identified with Cromwell in Fifth Monarchist discourse), she and the saints were suddenly saved by a "great fury coming from the

Clouds" – a manifestation of apocalyptic judgment – so that all the cattle were scattered and destroyed and their horns broken, to the delight of the visionary who sang praises to the Lord (pp. 13–14).[83] By the time we get to the account of her ecstatic prophecies at Whitehall, then, we have indeed begun to see the extraordinary "effects of a spirit caught up in the Visions of God" (p. 14), as well as the ways in which Trapnel's visionary powers, dramatic performances, and fertile symbolic imagination were deeply stimulated by the political unrest and religious radicalism of the Interregnum and by the prophetic books of Scripture.[84]

Trapnel's performance of prayers and prophetic songs, often continuing for hours at a time as she lay in bed, was a memorable dramatic and linguistic occasion, arousing great wonder and admiration in those who witnessed it.[85] Reading through *The Cry of a Stone* one may be struck by the untutored nature of the ecstatic verses which poured out of her during her long trance-like state. Yet at least one contemporary newsbook account of her unusual performance stressed her impressive delivery and vigorous language, as well as the variety of her utterances (including spiritual songs, autobiography, exhortations, prayers, and mystical revelations) aimed at challenging "the *Governors, Army, Churches, Ministry, Universities*: And the whole Nation"; the sharp dictates of truth issuing from the mouth of this humble prophetess were, as Milton's Satan might have conceded, "pleasing to th' ear" (*Paradise Regained* 1.479). According to the newsbook, "Her prayers are in exceeding good method and order, good language, and such as indeed all that come doe much admire what they hear from her, excellent words, and well placed, such as are not ordinary."[86] The same account stressed that her visionary matter was "full of variety" aimed at warning the Lord Protector from pursuing "earthly pomp and pleasure" and following the "carnall Councels" of worldly-wise powers in the nation; and aimed as well at encouraging the millenarian saints who had kept faith and who might soon "rejoyce in the Lords goodness to them."[87]

The account of her trance and Whitehall performance in *The Cry of a Stone* contains ecstatic verses and extravagant language expressing Trapnel's passionate yearning for the coming of King Jesus ("Oh King Jesus thou art longed for, / Oh take thy power and raign, / And let thy children see thy face"), as well as her sense of apocalyptic overturning and excitement: she envisions the uprooting of Babylon without and within; the destruction of the great whore and Antichrist; the great powers cast off their thrones; Protectors lying in graves; and the fourth great monarchy cast out. "The Lord will reckon with them all," prophesies the visionary maid as she imagines the holy destruction which accompanies the social revolution hitherto deferred and unrealized after 1649, for "They have not brought forth Righteousness, / Nor relief to the poor." The Lord, Trapnel envisions, will "batter" the "great Powers," including those of Cromwell and his Army officers in his fragile Protectorate regime. Parliaments will thus be put down as well as kings. "Blustring Oaks" and cedars will fall, she threatens, using scriptural imagery exploited by Interregnum radicals, including the Ranter Coppe, as we saw earlier. In this age of apocalyptic convulsions, writing itself will become a means of proclaiming the uprooting of earthly powers and the fall of Babylon and Antichrist: "Write how that Protectors shall go, / . . . Let pens make known what is said, that, / They shall expire and die / O write also that Colonels / And Captains they shall down / . . . Pen down how all their Gallantry, / Shall crumble into dust" (pp. 19–20). And so prophesying in a tone of fiery millenarian exultation, Trapnel imagines the Lord in these last days of the world "gone forth mightily" and casting "out / The fourth great Monarchy," his enemies trembling and astonished as "Rulers shall flye" and the orthodox clergy "utterly shall fall" (p. 72). Other verses depict the saints as soldiers who can expect "Great Victories indeed" if they side not with "the earthly Kings below" but with the Lord, their colonel, general, king, and protector (pp. 25–27) – a mighty warrior not unlike the conquering Lord of the Book of Habakkuk. This was the warrior Lord who brought spectacular victories against the Scots and, most recently, the Dutch naval forces in the summer of 1653: "Oh he it was that broke their masts, / And humbled the great ships all." Trapnel envisions the popular Dutch War of 1652–54 (see pp. 27–28) in terms of a larger, world-wide millenarian crusade that was breaking down Antichristian earthly powers, since the Fifth Monarchists scorned the Dutch for their Presbyterianism and because, as apostates to Mammon, they seemed more interested in commerce than in God.[88] Indeed, Trapnel's militant yet homely prophetic verses also include touches of popular romance as she depicts the mighty Lord slaying "all Giants in the world" and making them "roll in their gore" (p. 27).

At points during her ecstatic prayers and songs Trapnel engages directly with the Protector, whom she depicts as "backsliden" from the arduous work of the Lord and no longer the valiant Gideon of old, now that he has shown himself to be impressed by "great pomp and revenue, whiles the poore are ready to starve" (p. 50). The prophetic Trapnel, it is worth recalling, was issuing her warnings in the same year that Milton, looking to the Protectorate with greater hope, would urge Cromwell to remain vigilant and not become susceptible to the alluring trappings of royalist excess and vanities, for they could easily undermine the precarious authority of the regime and the hard-won achievements of the revolutionary years: "thou art not to wallow in pleasures at home," she tells the Lord Protector, "but thou art to be labouring for the Lord . . . oh do not thou bring in that rubbish now, that thou hast cast out before; they have cryed down the King, the Court and such things" (p. 53).[89] Though merely a humble handmaid to Christ, the prophetess is conscious of her radical activism and of her potent language as a sharp verbal weapon capable of penetrating the very center of worldly power: as she boldly addresses Cromwell, "I have brought my word into thy place, thy very Pallace, and it shall enter the very walls and hangings thereof against thee" (p. 70).

Her representation of the Protector in terms of the biblical deliverer and general Gideon intensifies the controversial political issues at the heart of her visionary prayers and songs. Gideon's humility and religiosity, we recall, were exemplified by his refusal to accept the power of human kingship and his insistence that there was only one permanent king: "I will not rule over you," says Gideon, "the Lord shall rule over you" (Judg. 8:23).[90] Passionately wishing that she might celebrate in verse the heroic achievements and work of Cromwell at this moment – "Oh Gideon would that I could sing / a triumph here for thee" – Trapnel remembers the godly commander of the New Model Army she praised in the past, a martial deliverer faithful to the righteous cause of the saints:

> Poore Gideon I did pray for thee,
>   when like Jacob so clean,
> Thou hast been valiant in the field,
>   and there thy foes hast slaine.
> Oh then! the flock of God lov'd thee
>   more than their earthly lives.   (pp. 53, 54)

But once this second Gideon came into the city of London with "the great ones there" with "their great Royalties of food," "these pleasures did him smother" and "did darken his spirit" (p. 55), prompting the prophetess to warn the Lord Protector of the dangers of being seduced by "great pomp and revenue," as well as other outward trappings of regal power, however much the godly ruler perceived a difference between his title and that of king.[91] Emboldened by the Fifth Monarchist dictum of "no king but Jesus," Trapnel reminds Cromwell of the danger of aspiring, as the antimonarchic Gideon did not, to such a title "As King, or Protector" – "Let him not imitate those Kings, / which knew nothing of God" (pp. 29, 54). He must, moreover, show much greater vigilance than Samson so "That no Delilahs so great & strange" can tempt him "with speeches fair and sweet" (p. 54).[92] Asserting conservative principles and assuming a quasi-regal style in "this great Pallace," Cromwell as Protector has forsaken the cause of the millenarian saints and betrayed the Revolution, thereby no longer deserving the name Gideon:[93] "where is thy Victory, thy Righteousness, thy Zeal, thy Love, thy Conquest now?" wonders the prophetic maid, "Will not the Lord shut thee out, thou that goest about to shut out the Saints?" (p. 68). Later that year, in his anxious opening speech to the first Protectorate Parliament (4 September 1654), Cromwell would indeed "shut out the Saints," despite his own millenarianism, as he turned against those advocating "the mistaken notion of the Fifth Monarchy," as well as other radical groups seeking to abolish the established ministry and threatening anarchy in the nation by means of "Levelling principles."[94]

While sharply challenging earthly powers ("All you Great Ones," p. 65), especially those in danger of mutating into regal forms during the Protectorate, Trapnel's millenarian prophecies of a world dramatically transformed and ruled by the saints for the saints never, however, project an egalitarian or communist order without property rights, as do the revolutionary writings of Coppe and Winstanley. Rather, Trapnel envisions that King Jesus, who in "apparel [is] rich," will elevate his "poor Flocks" or saints – including presumably poor and obscure handmaidens – by making them, paradoxically, "Earls" and "Potentates" (p. 40), a social and spiritual elite among the ungodly.[95] In Trapnel's Fifth Monarchist millenarian vision, there would indeed be, with the establishment of the kingdom of Christ, a new aristocracy of the saints.

Moreover, in her stream of divinely inspired verses, she longs fervently and, at moments, lyrically for the coming of the reign of King Jesus whose "lovely looks will be so bright" (p. 19). The prophetess foresees days beyond the great uprooting of Babylon and Antichrist and the destruction of earthly kings and powers – a time when the embattled and weary saints of Interregnum England might finally enjoy abundance, glory, and eternal rest. During one such ecstatic vision, according to the account, Trapnel "seemed to have over-flowings of joy and delight in spirit, and poured out her heart in a Song" (p. 48), which concluded with the following verses:

Unto his Saints, and he onely
shall draw the quintesence out
Of all things they shall draw the sap,
that runneth from the root,
And get up into the high tree,
where none shall go and pluck.
No, none shall be above to see
thine, when th'are in thy nest;
For they are closed in so round,
they lodge within that breast,
That none can fear, nor them afflict;
no musquet shot can come:
There is not any can draw their spears
or at all shoot their Canon.
Though nests in trees may shaken be,
yet thine shall e'r remaine;
They rest and nest in Jesus Christ,
his hand shall them sustain.   (p. 49)

Expressed in homely metaphors and language, Trapnel's popular millenarian vision of eternal rest is one in which the saints, "closed in so round,"
are sheltered from worldly assaults, afflictions, and uncertainties as they
are sustained by King Jesus himself. Christ thus becomes the natural and
only true Protector, the supreme nourisher of the saints in a prophetic text
consisting of visionary prayers and songs which have boldly contested –
in the symbolic center of earthly power – Cromwell's authority to assume
his semi-regal role as Lord Protector. Indeed, unlike the "great Pallace"
of Whitehall which, as Trapnel tells Cromwell, "the Lord will rent from
thee" (p. 68), Christ's "nest" in her millennial vision will never be shaken.
The Book of Revelation had prophesied not only great wars and desolation, but also a millennial age in which all things were made new and the
saints reigned, freed from the insecurities, fears, and disappointments
generated by England's mid-seventeenth-century crisis: "there shall be
no more death, neither sorrow, nor crying, neither shall there be any more
pain: for the former things are passed away" (Rev. 21:4). Like those of
other radical visionaries of her age, Trapnel's sensational prophecies and
millennial dreams were equally stimulated by the overturning days of the
1640s and 1650s. Distressed by spiritual apostasies and political conservatism during the Interregnum, this poor but inspired handmaid confronted the Revolution's ambiguities through her "Mighty Visions" at
Whitehall, while singing ecstatically of the glories of King Jesus and the
New Jerusalem, and truly arousing the wonder of her contemporaries.

CHAPTER FOUR

The War of the Lamb: the revolutionary discourse of George Fox and early Quakerism

During Interregnum England, the terrifying Quakers waged war against the world, fighting with the weapons of the Spirit as their prophets "alarum'd the Nation." In the folio collection of his works, *Gospel-Truth Demonstrated* (1706), the posthumous testimonies presented George Fox as a "Valiant Warriour of the Lamb, by whom the Lord wrought wonderful things, who never turned his Back in the Day of his Spiritual Warfare":[1] the allusion is to the Lamb's War from Revelation 17:14 – "These shall make war with the Lamb, and the Lamb shall overcome them" – an apocalyptic text that had great mythic potency during this revolutionary period when Quaker writing and prophecy were emerging.[2] Indeed, the Lamb who battles earthly kings not only fueled a sense of early Quaker persecution, but, as an agent of apocalyptic victory, it inspired the sense of intense human agency interwoven with divine forces which characterizes the fierce Quaker engagement with worldly institutions and Antichristian powers. Both a symbol of meekness and of apocalyptic triumph, the Lamb had an ambiguous, provocative resonance in early Quaker writing.[3] My concern in this chapter is with its apocalyptic resonance in relation to Fox's verbal and prophetic powers and with the texture of his revolutionary writings. Fox himself radicalizes the myth of the Lamb's War in his revolutionary works, giving it new, energized meaning and fresh urgency during the turbulent years of the Interregnum, when the Quakers were rapidly emerging as a formidable and troublesome sect.

In the case of the early Quakers, the ideology of the inner light produced extraordinary effects in the 1650s, when they became the most dynamic of all sects in the English Revolution, reaching every county in England and Wales with about 40,000 active members by the Restoration.[4] The early Quakers, led by such charismatic prophets as Fox, James Nayler, and Edward Burrough, differed strikingly from their more respectable successors. They were particularly radical and pugnacious during the Interregnum. They demonstrated the mighty power of the Lord and his Word to shake the foundations of ordered society as they created a martyrology out of their persecutions, represented themselves as fearless warriors of the Lamb, confronted temporal and ecclesiastical authorities, and appealed to the indwelling light above all else. Their unorthodox sense of inward power, which caused orthodox contemporaries to consider them rebellious and fanatical, found expression in linguistic and aesthetic ways: the plainness of their discourse (their insistence on using "thee" and "thou") and the general plainness of their culture, including architecture, dress, and so on. Their interruptions of church services, refusal to pay tithes, and rejection of oaths and hat honor only contributed to the perception that they were deeply subversive of order and established religion. The early Quaker notion of inward spiritual power was aggressively political, affecting every aspect of their culture and behavior.

Among the radical sects which flourished during the tumultuous years of the English Revolution, the early Quakers were particularly aware of the power of the written word to promote their prophetic visions, unorthodox religious doctrines, and subversive social ideas. From their beginnings in the Interregnum, starting in 1652 when Fox and other itinerant preachers began moving through rural areas of northern England, they assumed an intensely activist role and attempted to define themselves as an emerging radical movement through their confrontational writings and polemical uses of the press.[5] Thus during the first years of their movement, as they spread aggressively throughout England, they produced hundreds of tracts which fiercely denounced temporal authorities, attacked orthodox godly ministers, rejected social hierarchies and etiquette, spurned set forms of worship, promoted the ideology of the Lamb's War, proclaimed the power of the light within, dramatized their persecution and suffering, and alarmed their contemporaries. In a text bearing witness to Fox as "one that speaks the Word of the Lord from his mouth," the Quaker prophet Edward Burrough proclaimed in 1654 that "all the holy men of God Write, and Declare": and so the early Quakers were themselves guided by the divine inner light "to Act, Speak, or Write" as they incited controversy and challenged the religious orthodoxies and social practices of their age.[6] Beginning in 1653, the charismatic Fox himself produced some of the most forceful and alarming of these Quaker revolutionary texts as he prophesied "with Dread, Power and Authority."[7] Yet their arresting combination of sublime and coarse language and their bold scriptural mythmaking have not been adequately examined by scholars of literature and radical religious culture in the Revolution.

ALARMING THE NATION: QUAKER IDEOLOGY AND FOX'S APOCALYPTICISM

The following discussion examines the politics of apocalyptic language and scriptural mythmaking in some of Fox's most polemical writings of this revolutionary period, when he himself was actively serving as the "Lamb's Officer."[8] It considers how his millenarian texts, which announced that the dreadful day of the Lord was coming, engaged with religious and political authorities as Fox attempted to "be bold . . . in the power of truth, triumphing over the world"; and how their militant apocalyptic rhetoric promoted the myth of the warfaring Lamb during this crucial period of emergent Quakerism when the sectarian challenge was dominating the printing press.[9] Fox's fiery prophetic texts appeared at a moment in English culture when politics, radical religion, and writing were deeply interconnected; in early Quaker discourse, religion was indeed politicized and radicalism took a religious form.[10] While Fox, like other Quakers, made the power of the light within (inspired by such texts as John 1:9 and Ephesians 5:8) his supreme spiritual authority and the center of his radical religious ideology, he was thoroughly steeped in the Bible; he continuously adopted and reinvigorated violent scriptural language and vivid apocalyptic images to conduct his impassioned warfare of the Lamb against false churches, worldly rulers, and the social order.[11]

The revolutionary Quakers, after all, were by no means quietist or pacifists; indeed, their apocalyptic militancy cannot easily be reconciled with the image of their later respectability. A number of their leaders had served in the New Model Army which, in the early 1650s, was increasingly affected by the forces of religious heterodoxy.[12] Moreover, they frequently used their prophetic writings as aggressive verbal weapons during the Interregnum years, when they engaged in heated political and religious protest. Their verbal aggressiveness and missionary zeal only fueled widespread fear that their light within was a great leveller of church, state, and hierarchical order.[13] In their writings and preaching, prophetic language became a sublime weapon of the Spirit in its uncompromising war against the world: the early Quaker visionaries were conducting their holy warfare by verbal means. Richard Baxter, far from sympathetic to the Quaker prophets, was alarmed at how these extreme enthusiasts could promote the spirituality of the inner light while "they go up and down preaching with great zeal and violence" and using "reviling words" and "railing language" – those sharp weapons of the tongue.[14] Even an admirer, William Penn, noted that Fox's expression in preaching "might sound uncouth and unfashionable to nice ears," though his message was spiritually deep and emotionally intense.[15] Fox's powerful language in his polemical writings of the 1650s is indeed often coarse, plain, and colloquial; and it is often violently apocalyptic. In this chapter, my aim is to examine, more distinctly than commentators on Quaker culture have usually done, the verbal and scriptural texture of Fox's vehement apocalyptic writing during the Interregnum years, when he and other Quaker prophets thought that they were living "in the last times."[16] Often highly combative in their prophetic rhetoric, his visionary texts during this period were a potent force in defining the revolutionary language of early Quaker radical spirituality and politics.

Unlike his more famous *Journal*, which often suppresses his violent millenarian language,[17] Fox's early pamphlets use fiery apocalyptic rhetoric and bellicose language as they challenge established beliefs and threaten to subvert the social, religious, and political order. He draws repeatedly upon the fiercest language of prophecy in the Old and New Testaments, employing that violent language and imagery as his own weapons to hew down and hammer away at the powers of the earth. Thus in *To all that would know the Way to the Kingdom* (1654), a text urging readers to turn their minds within and wait upon the Lord and dwell in the light, Fox emphasizes the power of the Word which "cuts asunder" and burns as fire;[18] the coming of Christ and his kingdom will be accompanied by great apocalyptic forces that will unsettle all the religious, social, and political institutions and forms of the present age. Fox's writing conveys in physical terms the terror of that imminent apocalyptic judgment:

before him the Hills shall move and the mountains shall melt, and the rocks shall cleave . . . great Earth-quakes shall be, the terrible day of the Lord draws neer, the Beast shall be taken, and the false Prophet, into the fire they must go. . . . Now the Lord is coming to sit as Judge, and reign as King. . . . now is the Sword drawn, which glitters & is furbished, the Sword of the Almighty, to hew down *Baals* Priests, corrupt Judges, corrupt Justices, corrupt Lawyers, fruitless trees which cumber the ground.[19]

Evoking a series of catastrophic devastations from Scripture, including the great eschatological earthquakes prophesied in Revelation (see 6:12,

11:13, 16:18; cf. Isa. 2:19), the foundations of hills moved and shaken (as in Ps. 18:7; cf. Rev. 6:14), the cleaving of rocks (Matt. 27:51), the melting of mountains before the powerful and indignant Lord (see e.g. Ps. 97:5, Isa. 34:3, Nahum 1:5, Micah 1:4), Fox presents an avenging force that cannot be withstood.[20] Fox likewise evokes the glittering sword of Ezekiel, an eschatological weapon and instrument of God's wrath ready not only to cut down "fruitless trees" (a reference to Luke 13:6–9), but to smite the mighty ones of this world, including false prophets like those of Baal slaughtered by Elijah (1 Kings 18:40): "it is sharpened to make a sore slaughter; it is furbished that it may glitter" (Ezek. 21:9–10).[21] Fox sees himself as a prophetic agent of the Lord, full of the Spirit and illuminated by the light within (as were Jeremiah, Isaiah, Ezekiel, and the apostles),[22] while engaged in a great millenarian conflict against all false prophets, priests, and sorcerers, who despise the power of the light. If there is to be a new heaven and a new earth, as Revelation prophesies, there will also be terrible devastations and wars: in Quaker discourse of the Interregnum the gospel of the indwelling light and power of Christ produced a dynamic ideology of spiritual regeneration, yet this involved a vision of violently uprooting all worldly powers. The militant rhetoric of revolutionary Quaker discourse – promoted by Fox himself as one of "the true Prophets of God" who "spoke forth freely" to the earthly powers of his generation – was contributing to that radical apocalyptic process.[23]

Later in the same apocalyptic text, Fox conveys his intense feelings of social justice by appropriating the vigorous language of the prophetic James to express his violent hostility towards the powers of the earth – to curse them (as the Ranter Coppe had done) and to announce their doom and retribution:

Oh ye great men, and rich men of the earth! weep and howl, for your misery is coming, who heaps up treasures for the last day, your gold and silver shall eat you up as the rust and the canker; the fire is kindled, the day of the Lord is appearing, a day of howling will be amongst your fat Bulls of *Bashan*, that all the tall Cedars and strong Oaks must be hewen down, and all the loftiness of men must be laid low, then shall the Lord alone be exalted.[24]

Fox uses the same language of apocalyptic prophecy and exhortation, based on James 5:1–3, that the flamboyant Coppe had employed a few years earlier in *A Fiery Flying Roll* (1649) to warn the great ones of the earth of "the dreadfull day of JUDGEMENT" and mighty levelling soon to come (see Chapter 3).[25] To this Fox adds the unsettling language of Isaiah, as he prophesies the Day of the Lord in which the cedars of

Lebanon and the oaks of Bashan shall be brought low (Isa. 2:13; cf. Ps. 29:5), scriptural imagery frequently invoked in revolutionary Quaker discourse to assault the lofty and powerful of the world; and in his scriptural allusion to the "bulls of Bashan" (Ps. 22:12; Ezek. 39:18) he likewise evokes an unrighteous world that shall be destroyed. Prompted by the inward Spirit and light, Fox uses scriptural prophecy and language as devastating verbal weapons in his holy war against worldly agencies, social corruption, and religious forms.

One of his most significant and powerful early prophetic tracts is *Newes Coming up out of the North, Sounding towards the South*, printed for the radical bookseller Giles Calvert (who published many Quaker writings) and dated 21 December 1653. This substantial text of forty-six pages exemplifies the militant and millenarian themes of early Quaker prophecy, when Quakerism was emerging as a revolutionary force about to spread rapidly from northern England, where it originally flourished, to the south during 1654 and 1655, thereby making the feared movement one of widespread national protest:[26] "The Army is coming up out of the North against you terrible ones," Fox's title page boldly proclaims. His prophetic text is itself "A Blast out of the North . . . into the South" intended to alarm the nation, as it announces the eschatological "trumpet sounding abroad throughout the whole world."[27] The tone and language of Fox's text is often fiercely apocalyptic as he addresses the contemporary generation of Cain and warns all England and the world that the mighty day of the Lord is coming, bringing woe and misery (one of the refrains of this text): the dreadful day of vengeance is near at hand, as Fox, Nayler, and other Quaker prophets were beginning to warn, when "all your hearts must be ript up and laid naked and open before the mighty God, before him where nothing can be hid."[28] This millenarian tract illustrates the sheer exhortative force of Fox the inspired writer who, in the words of the Oxfordshire Friends Testimony to him, "shook the sandy Foundations of many, and overthrew the Babylonish Buildings" as he performed "with Dread, Power and Authority, which he was attended with from God, which made the Hearts of many to fear and tremble."[29]

Expecting the imminent coming of the Lord and the destruction of the Antichristian Beast, Fox here highlights the myth of the War of the Lamb in order to give special urgency to his prophecy: "Rejoyce, O all you Prophets and righteous ones, the Beast which made war with the Lamb and the Saints, the Lamb hath gotten the victory, and hath gotten victory over the Beast, and the ten horns which pusheth at him."[30] Fox's eschatological passage alludes directly to Revelation 18:20, while also echoing Revelation 15:2 and 17:14 – scriptural passages announcing the victory of the Lamb and expressing Fox's sense of millenarian expectation.[31] Later in the text, Fox again draws upon the myth of the Lamb's War, having just placed himself in the visionary line of Isaiah, Jeremiah, Ezekiel, and Micah; fusing his prophetic voice with that of the "Lord God of powers," he utters his thundering words against teachers of the world now in England: "be valiant for the Lord, bow not to the deceit: tremble all Nations before the Lord, and before his Army, his Host. Sound the Trumpet, sound an Alarm, call up to the battell, gather together for the destruction, draw the sword . . . hew down all the powers of the earth . . . a day of slaughter is coming to you who have made war against the Lamb and against the Saints."[32] Here the sublime Quaker visionary blends the language of Revelation with the militant language of the prophet Joel ("Blow ye the trumpet in Zion, and sound an alarm in my holy mountain . . . for the day of the Lord cometh," Joel 2:1) and the language of Psalm 114:7, while also evoking a prophetic day of slaughter (as in Jeremiah 12:3). Fox's fiery prophecies, in this and other passages, convey a sense of mighty spiritual forces engaged in a great apocalyptic conflict – one involving a God of all-consuming vengeance, saints guided by the inward light, and the fleshly powers of Antichrist.

Fox's text, moreover, includes provocative political commentary that is colored by powerful apocalyptic language and images. Thus, for example, in the third section of *Newes Coming up out of the North* the Quaker prophet warns not only the present heads of the nation under the new Protectorate but "all who are under the Dominion of the earthly Powers, Nations and Kingdoms every where in all the world." His strident prophetic writing aimed at worldly rulers is a conflation of scriptural texts reinforced by vigorous verbal repetition: "Tremble all before the Lord, O earthly Powers, tremble before the Lord God Almighty; to you the Lord is uttering his thunders, to you the Lord is uttering his voyce, to you the Lord is sounding his trumpet, to you the warning piece is gone out."[33] Here Fox's thundering prophecy has fused such scriptural passages as Psalms 99:1 and 114:7 with Joel 2:1. Fox adopts other potent scriptural images to continue his assault on worldly powers. Having stressed, much like Gerrard Winstanley, that laws and justice will be established inwardly and set in people's hearts, Fox first evokes the great tree of Daniel 4:10–12, which in his *Newes Coming up out of the North* becomes a fruitless tree whose branches are symbolic of the spread of injustice; then he invokes the messianic stone of Daniel 2:34–35, which will dash to pieces the image and kingdom of unjust rulers and justices. Then returning to the theme of nations trembling before the Almighty's power (this time by evoking Ezekiel 26:16 and 32:10), Fox proclaims the Lord's kingdom "whose dominion is a dominion for ever" and fiercely chastises England: "Oh England, England, thou hast forsaken thy visitation, thou hast not minded thy visitation. . . . The god of the world doth blind your eye." His verbal chastisement continues and gains further specificity and immediacy as he warns the Protectorate now in power: "you must be cut down with the same power that cut down the King who reigned over the Nation, in whose family was a Nurse for Papists and for Bishops." God may have given England victories over the Antichristian papists, but Antichristian powers still operate in the land under its newest political regime which has retreated from revolution: "the Beast and the false Prophet is standing still, which held up these [papist] things, and they keep their places: so another Parliament grew, and God hath cut down that. Beware of yourselves, for the Lord will pluck down you."[34]

Fox's political analysis and apocalyptic prophecy resemble Winstanley's several years earlier, when the Digger prophet was challenging the interconnected clerical, legal, and state powers of the newly formed Republic (see Chapter 2). As both Fox and Winstanley warn, the powers of the Beast continue to operate in the nation: they were by no means eradicated by the dramatic Revolution of 1648–49, nor were they eradicated during the early years of the Republic when the Rump Parliament was in power. Like Winstanley and other religious radicals who were keenly aware of the disparity between promise and performance during the Republic,[35] Fox highlights the disparity between promise and achievement: "you have promised many fair promises to the Nation, but little you have performed." Drawing upon the language of Habakkuk 2, with its oracles of woe, and challenging worldly powers with a series of "woes" common in early Quaker prophetic discourse, Fox stresses the continuity of the powers of the Beast which shall be destroyed: "Woe, woe is coming upon you all, the same Teachers are standing that were in the time of the King, and the same that were in the time of the Bishops, and many of these are and have been your Counsellers, and the same that held up the Rails, Crosses and Pictures, are standing still." Fox evokes the hated Laudian clergy and practices as he addresses orthodox Puritans who were promoting a well-paid clergy and a compulsory national church. During the Interregnum, the nation was especially suffering under the curse of tithes, which were maintaining a privileged worldly ministry and fueling class divisions by creating a terrible burden for the poor; Quakers like Fox believed the Revolution had been thwarted because Cromwell had betrayed his promises to abolish them.[36] Nevertheless, in these turbulent and iconoclastic times, Fox could proclaim that the God of power is pouring forth his Spirit (as prophesied in Joel 2:28) so that "his Sons and his Daughters shall prophesie, and thousands of them do prophesie," though "thousands of them have been mocked, some stoned, prisoned, whipped and beaten."[37] Indeed, despite persecution, Fox and the revolutionary Quaker prophets, moved by the inward Spirit and speaking from the inner light, were now poised to proclaim the day of the Lord from the north to the south of England as they dared to warn the Protectorate and other worldly rulers, as well as all "dissembling hypocrites" in this generation of Cain, that the religious and political institutions of Antichrist would soon perish when the Lord Jesus comes "to rule all Nations with a rod of Iron" (as in Rev. 19:15).[38]

In *Newes Coming up out of the North* and his other fiery apocalyptic tracts of the Interregnum, Fox repeatedly represents God as a dreadful and mighty power – shaking and levelling mountains, making "the Earth reele to and fro" and cleaving it "asunder," bringing down low all who are exalted, and throwing down the worldly kingdoms as he prepares to reign within his saints.[39] Fox's Lord is a God of fury, vengeance, and overturning: he is "the terrible One," as Fox calls him in *Newes Coming up out of the North*, recalling that the day of the Lord will indeed be "very terrible" (as it is described in the eschatological passages of Joel 2:11 and 2:31): echoing Isaiah 2:19–21, Fox prophesies that he is "coming with his power, to shake terribly the earth; and the glory of the Lord is arising, and all the Idols of gold must be cast out, and all the honours must be cut down and cast out, and the high-places puld down, . . . and the powers of the earth are shaking."[40] In Fox's apocalyptic writings, the awesome "power of God is endless": when he overthrows the Romish church, he overthrows "root and branch" and "overturns all the foundation" of "churches and dominions," and with his "Arm and Power" he "layes down the Mountaines with the Valleys, and layes down the sturdiest Oak."[41] He is a powerful whirlwind gone forth in fury to scatter the ungodly as chaff.[42] He is truly a God of sublime hatred who pours his wrath upon his enemies and the adversaries of righteousness. "Thou art hated of God eternally, hated for ever," writes Fox, expressing through his own vehement prose that fierce divine hatred as he blasts the profane children of Esau in his generation; as the prophesy of Malachi had proclaimed, against Esau and his heirs "the Lord hath indignation for ever" (1:2–4). Thus they will feel the terrible, burning power of the *odium Dei* and "shalt be a wilderness barren" and burnt up "as stubble" (alluding to Isaiah 47:14 and Malachi 4:1): in his fervent prophecies, Fox envisions that "the Lord Jesus Christ is coming in flames to render vengeance upon all [the] ungodly ones."[43] In "the day of the Lords Wrath," all the ungodly who have not repented will feel "sudden Judgements and Plagues come upon" them.[44] Such, then, is the power and "the wrath of the Lamb" (Rev. 6:16–17).

Compared to the God of Fox's fiery revolutionary tracts, the omnipotent God of *Paradise Lost*, who promises mercy and grace to fallen humans who choose to accept grace (Book 3.131–34), seems mild, though he is certainly capable of pouring "indignation on [the] Godless" (6.811). Rather, Fox's God, in his response to all worldly authorities, false prophets, and Antichrists who hate the light, resembles the dreadful Lord of *Samson Agonistes* (as we shall see in Chapter 9), a mighty Lord who brings swift destruction upon the ungodly and idolatrous "Fall'n into wrath divine" (line 1683); or in the words of the prophetic Fox (alluding to Rev. 16:1–17, as well as 22:18), "all the plagues of God are to be poured out upon them, the vials of the wrath of the Almighty."[45] In the day of the Lord's vengeance, such plagues are "to be poured out without mixture" (an echo of Rev. 14:10) on the blind priests of Fox's generation.[46] Fox's wrathful God is a terrifying, unconquerable force who is rising and overturning temporal magistrates and authorities: this ferocious vision no doubt reinforced the sense of Quaker fearlessness and resolve which the prophetic Fox exemplified in his righteous and often bellicose defiance of hostile worldly powers. It reinforced, moreover, the perception that the revolutionary Quaker prophets – those warriors of the Lamb – were themselves terrifying and alarming.

Fox's *The Vials of the Wrath of God, Poured forth upon the Seat of the Man of Sin* (1654)[47] offers another striking example of the kind of revolutionary rhetoric he exploited early in his prophetic career when he was at war with the world and proclaiming that the day of the Lord would shortly come. His prophetic discourse, addressed like the fiery writing of Abiezer Coppe to "Great men, and Rich men," derives its potency by employing both vigorous verbal repetition and a mosaic of scriptural allusions to characterize graphically the wilderness of England in an unrighteous age:

Tremble and be astonished you heathen that knows not God; for you are all heathens that know not God, and the land is full of crooked waies, the land is full of rough places, the land is full of hills and mountains, the land is full of bryers and thorns, dogs and swine, fighting and barking, snarling and biting one another, for the husks, and for the earthly creatures.[48]

Here Fox has woven together phrases from a variety of scriptural passages including Proverbs 2:15 ("crooked waies"; cf. Lam. 3:9, Ps. 125:5), Isaiah 40:4 and 42:15 (the land "full of rough places" and hills and mountains which shall be laid low), and Isaiah 7:24 (the land full of "bryers and thorns"). Fox's vision of the land full of dogs and swine fighting for the husks evokes Revelation 22:15, which describes those outside the kingdom of God as "dogs, and sorcerers, and whoremongers, and murderers, and idolaters, and whosoever loveth and maketh a lie," an apocalyptic passage Fox cites in *Newes Coming up out of the North*;[49] and it seems to recall as well "the husks that the swine did eat" in Luke 15:16. But Fox's powerful image of the dogs and swine fighting, barking, snarling, and biting gives the ungodly of the world a particularly vicious and bestial character.[50] Fox's hostile ungodly world is indeed one of scorners, dissemblers, "quarrellers, fighters, stoners, wrathful malicious ones," and other vicious haters of the light within.[51] Fox relegates them all to the level of subhuman beasts in an vigorous catalogue of epithets: "ye goats, ye wolves, ye dogs, ye swine, ye serpents, ye vulterous ones, ye beasts, ye lyons, ye strong hourses neighing up and down, walking after your lusts." Such fierce "Scripture-language," as Fox calls it in *The Vials of the Wrath of God* (he insists "this is not railing"),[52] contributes to the coarse, raw texture of his highly confrontational writing, augmenting its prophetic authority and violent denunciation of a hostile world.

Scriptural allusions and phrases have an immediate potency for Fox, who reinvigorates them as he uses them to combat the ungodly world in its multiple manifestations. Thus, for example, working from the passage in Luke 13:6–9, which concerns the fruitless tree which cumbers the ground, Fox in *The Vials* powerfully exploits the repetition of a key phrase along with its variation as his prophetic writing increases in its emotional vehemence:

Cumber not the ground ye fruitless trees; ye proud ones, ye scorners, cumber not the ground; ye drunkards, ye cumber the ground; ye cumber the ground, ye lyers, cheaters and cozeners, ye cumber the ground, who use deceit; ye mockers and lustful ones, which devours the creation, ye are the fruitless trees that cumber the ground; you fair outside professors and teachers, you cumber the ground, who lives in high swelling words . . . and you are the trees that bear leaves, but no fruit; so ye are they that cumber the ground.

The scriptural "fruitless trees" become, in Fox's visionary writing, all the many worldly or fleshly powers in his age which "cumber the ground"

and which, as Winstanley himself might have put it, "devour the creation."[53] Then, piling up epithets and again employing verbal repetition
based on the same scriptural text, Fox continues his prophetic assault:
"Drunkard, swearer, cursed speaker, thou art this corrupt evil tree,
whoremonger, envious one, fighter, quarrellers, malicious ones, scorner,
mocker, reproacher, thou art this corrupt tree, that cannot bring forth
good fruit. . . ." A page later Fox reiterates and varies his prophecy by
inserting a series of "woes": "Woe unto you drunkards, ye cumber the
ground; woe unto you hypocrites, ye cumber the ground; woe unto you
lyers, ye cumber the ground. . . ." The prophetic Fox, who reviles any
form of secular play and festive culture, can likewise convey his stern
condemnation through a vigorous list of activities associated with an
ungodly and ensnaring world; thus he blasts the lustful ones who follow
"pleasure, rioting, feasting, sporting, drunkenness, gluttony, hawking,
hunting, *Esau*-like, ye cumber the ground." The symbolic reference to
Esau at the end of Fox's list places the whole condemnation in a larger
scriptural-historical context: this is the current generation of Esau, as
well as Cain, that the prophetic Fox is lambasting. Such passages, with
their energetic verbal repetition, convey the coarseness of Fox's visionary prose as well as its undeniable rhetorical power. The frequent use of
verbal repetition, a notable feature of Fox's prophetic tracts, underscores
a sense of urgency, as well as a sense of impending judgment as Fox envisions his apocalyptic Lord "coming in power to sweep the land of evil
doers, and to hew down you fruitless trees which cumber the ground."[54]

Published during the same year, Fox's fiery text, *The Trumpet of the Lord
Sounded, And his Sword drawn* (1654), proclaims that the Lord's apocalyptic
sword will now separate "the Precious and the Vile," much as Fox, the
spiritual visionary, attempts to discern between the two. The prophecy
is issued by those "who have come thorow great tribulation, whose garments have been washed in the blood of the LAMB," a reference to
Revelation 7:14 and to Quaker martyrdom and purity in an age full of
spiritual dissimulation and Antichristian sorcery.[55] The tract highlights,
among its principal themes, the treachery of dissimulation in relation to
orthodox religion: one can "make a profession of God and Christ, and
make a fair shew to the world, and yet be an hypocrite," especially at a
moment when "the well-favoured harlot . . . is painted with the Saints
words, and with Christs." Like Abiezer Coppe, Fox makes the
Antichristian harlot a symbol of the subtlety of formal, external religion
(as opposed to the religion of the Spirit within) engaged in "deceiving
the simple, and ensnaring them."[56] Fox depicts the theatricalism of the

clerical establishment whose priests have made a trade of the spiritual words of the prophets and apostles. The minister who preaches Christ without is "like a Stage-player, which acts a Stage-play aloft, with Points, and Reasons, . . . and Authors, and old Fathers, and Tryals, and Mattens . . . and where they will not give him money, he will not act his Play there."[57] Resorting to the kind of verbal repetition he often employs so energetically, the prophetic Fox conveys a sense of a world full of deceitful practices and conjuring as he foresees the consequences of the day of the Lord "coming in power": "all secret pride, and secret envie, and secret malice, and secret revenge, and secret subtilty, and secret hypocrisie, and secret dissimulation, shall be laid open, and made manifest."[58] The tract concludes with passages of visionary warning which proclaim woe "to all the Priests of *England*" and announce that the "Lord God of power" is thundering against all "Powers of Witchcraft, Charmers, and Inchanters": "For the day of the Lords wrath is come among you; a day of Vengeance: the fire is kindling. . . . now is the hand of the Lord of hosts upon you all, and his Army is gathering, and his Sword is drawn, which hath two edges, that before him none should escape." At such moments of violent apocalypticism, the active Quaker visionary blends his voice with that of the militant Lord's. His scorching words and the Word have become one: "The Lord hath spoken it. To you all, this is the word of the Lord."[59]

Later during this revolutionary decade Fox produced two notable apocalyptic works: *The Great Mistery of the Great Whore Unfolded: and Antichrists Kingdom Revealed unto Destruction* (1659), containing a lengthy prefatory epistle by the Quaker prophet Edward Burrough, and *The Lambs Officer* (1659). Drawing extensively upon the myth of the Lamb's War in a powerful account of Quaker spiritual ideology, suffering, and savage persecution during the preceding seven years, Burrough proclaims that in fighting their righteous wars of truth with the sword of Revelation ("the sword that goes out of his mouth"), "the followers of the Lamb" have become "an Army dreadful and terrible before whom the wicked do fear and tremble," so that "they that follow the Lamb shall overcome, and get the victory over the beast, and over the Dragon."[60] Moreover, in the massive main text of *The Great Mistery*, Fox reinvigorates the violent language of Revelation as he vehemently responds to countless Quaker detractors. Thus he wages his verbal warfare on behalf of the saints, and highlights a sense of mighty eschatological forces engaged in fierce spiritual conflict at this very moment as he evokes a series of apocalyptic images, including not only the armies of the Beast and the kings of the earth (see Rev. 19:19), but the vials of the wrath of God, the seven angelic trumpets sounding (see Rev. 8, 9, and 11:15), the seven last plagues (filled up with the wrath of God: Rev. 15:1), and divine thunderings: "*now* is the vials, and thunders, and plagues and trumpets sounding and going forth . . . And *now* are the Kings of the Earth, and the Beast, and the false Prophets, and Antichrists . . . gathering together, with the old deceiver the Devil, to battle against the Lamb, and the Saints of the Lamb" (emphasis added). And so while the godly Quaker soldiers strengthen themselves with the light within, "all those false Prophets, Beasts, Antichrists, and mother of Harlots, great Whore, and Kings of the Earth, and the Devill, are making War against the *Lamb* and the Saints. . . . Now are all the *Antichrists* appearing, and are in armes, and rising against Christ and his *light*." That dramatic sense of the Interregnum Quakers besieged and at war with "the whole world . . . standing against the light, and against the Saints" was constantly expressed in such vigorous bellicose language and fervent apocalyptic images.[61]

THE POWER OF THE LAMB

Fox's apocalyptic fervor and rhetorical power as a prophetic writer are particularly evident in *The Lambs Officer*, the last of his visionary texts I want to consider. This unusually forceful apocalyptic text appeared during 1659, at a moment of radical exhilaration during which occurred a wave of Quaker pamphleteering fueled partly by the collapse of the Cromwellian regime in April and the restoration of the Rump Parliament in early May – both a result of revolutionary pressure from the Army.[62] This was a year of particularly vigorous radical pamphleteering, and Quaker preachers proved to be active, proselytizing in the Army throughout 1659.[63] Radical pamphleteers, including sectarians, were again pressuring the restored Rump to abolish tithes and to humble covetous lawyers and sweep away the whole clerical establishment.[64] During the summer of 1659, the terrifying Quakers were raising the specter of social and religious revolution, thereby increasing fears of radical sectarianism.[65] Indeed, there was widespread panic that thousands of millenarian Quakers and sectarians were in arms, and Fox's *Lambs Officer* needs to be seen in the context of this heightened sense of aggressive Quaker militancy which threatened to destroy the godly ministry and religion itself.[66] The pro-royalist Presbyterian rising of Sir

George Booth later that summer, however easily put down by John Lambert, was clearly directed against the recalled Rump (though hardly a radical Puritan regime interested in further reform) and the sectarian threat, especially from "this fanatick Quakeisme."[67] Fox's fiery text of 1659, displaying his rhetorical powers at their zenith, registers the heightening of radical expectations about the revival of the Good Old Cause, though they would soon be dashed by deep political instabilities ahead.

While *The Lambs Officer* does not refer explicitly to the unsettling political events of that year of crisis, it nevertheless belongs to this historical moment when the Quakers seemed particularly subversive and threatening: it conveys a sense of apocalyptic expectation as it proclaims the warring Lamb's victory over "the false prophets, Beast and Dragon" now that the "Lord Jesus Christ has come to reign, and his Everlasting Kingdom and Scepter is set up."[68] This fiercely anticlerical and millenarian text becomes the occasion for Fox to pour out his sweeping condemnation of church and state authorities in a long series of provocative rhetorical questions rich in apocalyptic references. Asserting his own prophetic agency, Fox assumes a militant posture as the "Officer" of the Lamb entrusted by God to issue forth the "Lambs Message . . . in this his day which is come."[69] An impassioned monologue and a work of sustained apocalypticism, Fox's visionary work achieves its exhortative force, however, through a kind of repetition different from that which he usually employs in his earlier revolutionary tracts. He punctuates his flood of rhetorical questions and apocalyptic themes in *The Lambs Officer* by his constant refrain of "Guilty, or not guilty?" – a provocative question he poses to priests, magistrates, earthly kings, as well as other Antichristian powers, as he imagines them all being brought, not before the courts of the nation, but before the "Judgement Bar" of the Lamb itself and compelled to drink "the cup of the indignation of the Almighty" (see Rev. 14:10). Altogether Fox repeats this accusatory question, or a variation upon it, more than fifty times throughout this tract of twenty-two pages; and sometimes he repeats the question as many as five times per page. Frequent, too, is Fox's refrain that these worldly powers have all drunk the great whore's cup – "do you not drink it daily?" he asks[70] – and given themselves up to the power of the Beast and Dragon. Such insistent repetition of accusatory questions creates the emotional concentration of Fox's prophetic tract and heightens its dramatic forcefulness.

After narrating for a page and a half, at the beginning of his text, a history of Antichristian power – an account of the Dragon giving his power to the Beast, the Beast making war with the saints, the earthly kings drinking the great whore's wine, and the whore as the persecuting power then drinking the blood of the prophets, martyrs, and saints – the visionary Fox launches into his lengthy series of thundering rhetorical questions. These denounce the professional, university-trained ministers of his age and link them with the flourishing powers of Antichrist and a world wholly given over to whorish spirituality: "And did not you stand in the day of the Beasts power, when he killed the Saints, and made War with them, the true Ministers?. . . . And did you not shelter under the Beasts power, and the whores, when the Martyrs, and the Prophets, and the Saints blood was drunk? did not you turn from the Dragon to the Beast, after the Beast, to the whore? and had not the Beast power over the Tongues, Orthodox men, and the Original? Come, *Guilty, or not Guilty?*"[71] Fox continues this powerful monologue for another twenty pages – his threatening rhetorical questions, themselves potent verbal weapons, are saturated in the language and metaphors of the Book of Revelation interspersed with concrete details evoking Quaker persecution. He reviles the hireling priests for persecuting the saints in stocks, prisons, and houses of correction ("doth not the blood of many lye upon you, as in *York*-Goal, *Lancaster*-Goal, *Glouster*-Goal, &c.") and for knocking them down in "Steeplehouses," the Quaker's deflationary term for idolatrous churches: the Lamb's officer commands the ministers and kings of the earth to face the judgment of the Lamb – "Come, answer me before the Lambs Power, Throne, and Dominion." And so he hammers away, page after page in *The Lambs Officer*, with his fierce, unrelenting questions connecting the established religious powers – "the wolves in the sheeps clothing, the inwardly raveners" – and their titles with the Antichristian church of Rome and its treacherous legacy in England. Such church powers, with their tithes and ritual celebrations ("*Michaelmas, Christmas,* and *Candlemas,* and *Lammas*"), are far removed from the inward spirit of apostolic religion after which, as *Paradise Lost* depicts, "Wolves shall succeed for teachers, grievous Wolves" (12.508): "But come Priests, did not the whore of *Rome* give you the name of Vicars and Clerks, and Parsons, and Curates, and Batchelors of Art, and Batchelors of Divinity ? . . . for, where was there any such names among the Apostles? are you guilty, or not guilty?"[72]

At several moments in the midst of his powerful monologue, Fox interrupts his relentless series of questions to proclaim that the apocalyptic War of the Lamb will culminate in the long-persecuted saints triumphing over the formidable powers of Antichrist:

but now the Man-child, the Lamb is come to reign, who makes war in righteousness, and rides on the white Horse conquering, and to conquer, and the Lamb and the bride his wife is witnessed, who will rule all Nations with a rod of iron . . . and the Lamb, and the Saints shall have victory over the Beast, over the false prophet, over this Whore, who will kill with his Sword, and slay with his Sword, which are the words of his mouth, and blessing and honour will be given to the King of kings, and the Lord of lords, who is Lord Omnipotent and Everlasting.[73]

Once again Fox, the prophetic Lamb's officer, has drawn imaginatively upon the potent imagery and language of the Book of Revelation: evoking the rider on the white horse of Revelation 6:2 who "went forth conquering, and to conquer" (the first of John's four horsemen), his visionary passage highlights the theme of the warfaring Lamb and its mighty spiritual power while evoking too the righteous rider of Revelation 19:11–16 – Christ – who descends from heaven to earth mounted on a white horse followed by his conquering angelic armies mounted in a similar fashion. Indeed, Fox's passage combines the two apocalyptic horsemen of Revelation 6:2 and 19:11, since the first is armed with a bow (not mentioned by Fox) and the other with a sword which issues out of his mouth.

Fox's powerful vision of the victorious scene at the end of time evokes not only the messianic wedding of the Lamb (in Rev. 19:7), symbolic here of the union between the Lamb and the faithful saints (the godly consort and true church), but also the militant apocalyptic passage which envisions the warrior Lamb vanquishing the Beast, the false prophet, the kings of the earth, as well as other forces of Antichrist: "And the remnant were slain with the sword of him that sat upon the horse, which *sword* proceeded out of his mouth" (Rev. 19:21). As "the King of kings, and the Lord of lords" (see Rev. 19:16; cf. 1:5), the conquering Lamb will have sovereignty over all earthly rulers and clerical authorities – "for now," Fox announces to them at the end of his apocalyptic monologue, "is your time and day of judgement."[74] Such eschatological passages of writing, infused with the rhetoric of the Lamb's War inspired by Revelation and reinvigorated by a prophet of the Spirit, gives Fox's revolutionary prose its sense of exhilaration and urgent expectation voiced during a year when Quaker agitation was particularly intense and threatening.

One could of course highlight numerous other rich passages of sublime apocalyptic writing from the many revolutionary pamphlets of Fox's Interregnum years. A pressing sense of living "in the last times," as he actively proclaimed that the terrible day of the Lord's wrath was imminent, clearly stimulated the verbal and rhetorical powers of this Lamb's prophetic officer who had many times "gone forth with the Lambs Message." As he poured out his fiery apocalyptic tracts during these emerging years of Quaker writing, Fox managed to revitalize prophetic scriptural language, metaphors, and myths so that they indeed acquired fresh eschatological meanings and became potent weapons with which to alarm the nation and wage the unsettling War of the Lamb.

As we shall see in the next chapter, the fiery apocalyptic discourse of revolutionary Quakerism, Fifth Monarchism, and other radical religious movements of the Interregnum became one of Andrew Marvell's acutest concerns in his representation of Cromwell's experimental Protectorate and its precarious authority, as that poet imaginatively attempted to confront the unresolved tension between political conservatism and religious radicalism in the Revolution. The fiery writings of radical religious culture, especially the revolutionary Quakers, would also spill over into the Restoration, even after the Lamb's War itself had been lost: the relation of such writings to the radical religious politics of *Samson Agonistes* will be the subject of this book's final chapter.

CHAPTER FIVE

Marvell, the saints, and the Protectorate

In previous chapters we have considered the polemical ways in which a range of radical visionary writers in Milton's age confronted the conflicting trends within the English Revolution and struggled with the ambiguities of its regimes. Strident sectarian challenges during the 1650s, expressed in the visionary and flamboyant apocalyptic works we have examined, aggravated during the revolutionary decades an ongoing tension between radical millenarian fervor and moderate godly constitutionalism.[1] Andrew Marvell's major poem on the Protectorate vividly illustrates that tension during the Interregnum.

This chapter thus considers Marvell's creative response to the crises of the Protectorate and, in particular, considers how he attempted to negotiate the unresolved tension between political conservatism and religious radicalism in his public verses written to commemorate the experimental regime, *The First Anniversary of the Government under His Highness the Lord Protector*. Marvell's Protectorate verses were themselves a sophisticated work of polemical propaganda: published anonymously as a quarto pamphlet in January 1655, they were printed by the government printer and advertised in the government-controlled newsbook, *Mercurius Politicus*, the same week that Thomason dated his copy (17 January).[2] Like John Hall and Marchamont Nedham, who offered major vindications of the Protectorate, Marvell chose to respond directly to the challenge of radical religious ferment while depicting the arduous process of "pulling down" and "erecting New" (line 247) the edifice of the state under Cromwell, its political architect. Marvell's poem vigorously attacks earthly kings, exposing the failures of "their earthy Projects" (line 19) at the same moment that the radical millenarian saints, disaffected with the Protectorate, were aggressively demanding "No king but Jesus." And yet he defends the new settlement with its power exercised by a single-person executive restrained by a council and periodic parliaments; the regime thus attempted – uneasily and ambiguously – to combine godly rule with a quasi-regal leader, the Lord Protector. Marvell is acutely sensitive to the precarious and unsettled political and religious tensions which Cromwell himself personified and which threatened the stability of his fragile regime. The apocalyptic vision and providential language of *The First Anniversary* express Marvell's imaginative attempt to negotiate these deep-rooted tensions and ambivalent trends within the Revolution.

First, however, it is crucial to examine the radical political and religious pressures that were so intensely exerted just before and at the time he published his skillful apologia, thereby enabling us to situate his polemical poem within the tensions of its historical moment. Those tensions had only escalated as a result of the disintegration of Puritan unity during the 1640s and early 1650s and the strident sectarianism which consequently emerged. To be sure, the Protectorate came under criticism from many sides – from royalists and religious Presbyterians to disillusioned Independents, republicans, and sectarians.[3] But at the end of 1653 and throughout 1654, radical religious protest was especially sharp and unsettling. Marvell produced a highly imaginative response to the profound religious/political crisis of the Protectoral years.[4]

MARVELL'S "FRANTIQUE ARMY"

This was an age, Nedham observed in his major vindication of the Protectorate, "wherein men are very apt to be rooting and striking at Fundamentals."[5] Yet although at times driven by millenarian fervor and a zeal for godly reformation – "I do think something is at the door: we are at the threshold," Cromwell had excitedly told the Barebone's Assembly – the Protector had no desire to tear down "the ranks and orders of men" or to subvert "propriety and interest."[6] The more conservative social impulses which vied in his breast with radical millenarian ones can be discerned in Cromwell's speeches and writings of the 1650s. Indeed, as Protector he deeply wished to reunite the godly in the face of strident religious radicalism and division and to avert political and social breakdown. In March 1654 he anxiously declared a day of prayer and fasting in order to end faction and promote "Brotherly Love, and a Healing Spirit."[7] And in his tense opening speech to the first Protectorate Parliament in September 1654, he lamented "the nation rent and torn in spirit and principle from one end to another" as he yearned for a period of "healing and settling" – his paramount concern – after "so many changes and turnings which this nation hath laboured under." The recent experiment in radical godly rule under the Barebone's Assembly, dissolved in December 1653, had brought little political and religious stability – only millenarian saints lamented its fall.

The socially conservative Cromwell thus deplored "men of Levelling principles" (Lilburne, his old friend and now enemy, was again imprisoned), as well as an age of such "prodigious blasphemies; contempt of God and Christ, denying of him, contempt of him and his ordinances and of the Scriptures." And he expressed alarm at the apocalyptic rhetoric of "overturning" which had recently found renewed expression in the flamboyant writings and millenarian visions of the Ranters, Fifth Monarchists, and Quakers, thereby encouraging "men of discontent spirits" to "justify unpeaceable practices," promote "divisions and distractions," and threaten the existing social order.[8] Although the Instrument of Government (16 December 1653) had included a provision expressing tolerance towards those "differing in judgment from the doctrine, worship or discipline publicly held forth," the new constitution (while refusing to tolerate "Popery or Prelacy") had also expressed concern about antinomians and sectarians who abuse religious "liberty . . . to the actual disturbance of the public peace."[9] In late 1653 and throughout 1654 such radical Puritan disturbances – as the Protectorate was being virulently attacked in press and pulpit – were tearing apart the religious fabric of the nation. They were endangering its political stability and preventing the "healing and settling" Cromwell envisioned and to which Marvell alludes in *The First Anniversary*, where he depicts the godly Protector as "the *Angel* of our Commonweal" who, after the troubling of the waters, "yearly mak'st them Heal" (lines 401–2; echoing John 5:4).[10]

During 1654 the menacing Quakers, following the authority of the inner light, were especially pugnacious in their apocalyptic exhortations and missionary zeal, as their heretical books seemed to spread like a gangrene infecting the nation, alarming the mainstream godly who complained to Cromwell; in the autumn of that year the Quakers made a dramatic appearance in London, exacerbating fears of religious divisions within the capital itself.[11] Quaker prophets proclaimed that the Lord had "set up his standard to gather his men of war together";[12] indeed, the month after the Protectorate was established, William Dewsbury's *True Prophecy of the Mighty Day of the Lord* announced that Jesus Christ had raised up "his Army . . . in the North of *England*, and is marching South in mighty Power to cut down high and low . . . and all the Powers of the Land" (title page). The "frantique Army" of the

Quakers was thus aggressively on the move in 1654–55. Nor did the rapidly growing sect "want for Men" (*First Anniversary*, line 299) to voice their radical prophecies about God's impending judgments, as Dewsbury, Fox, Nayler, and other bellicose Quaker prophets threatened clerical and political powers with the Lord's language from Ezekiel 21:27: "I will overturn, overturn, overturn."[13] "The Lord Protector of Heaven and Earth is above all Highnesses," Fox fiercely admonished Cromwell: that Protector "alone" would be exalted; all other forms of human loftiness would be swiftly cut down.[14]

Indeed, for the first time since the defeat of the Levellers, polemical agitation against Cromwell exploded and reached a new fury – a sense of radical sectarian "rage" Marvell was to respond to in his Protectorate verses. The most extreme millenarian saints, believing that Cromwell was usurping the role of King Jesus, were inflamed by the Protectorate and posed a considerable threat to the new regime. Immediately after Cromwell accepted the title of Lord Protector in December 1653, two of the fieriest Fifth Monarchists – Christopher Feake and John Simpson, singled out by Marvell for satirical treatment (line 305) – were waging a sustained, well-orchestrated campaign against the regime for betraying the Revolution. It had established the rule of "one single person," thereby creating a monstrous Antichristian state contrary to the Army's Declaration of 14 June 1647 against complying with an absolute or arbitrary power.[15] The fact that the regime aimed to achieve a balance between executive, legislative, and judicial powers, and subjected the Protector's personal authority to close conciliar control, made no impression on leaders of this "frantique Army" who were suspicious of new and exorbitant powers given to the Protector.[16] There was, furthermore, a contradiction between the Fifth Monarchist vision of government by the saints for the saints and Cromwell's belief in civil liberties which distinguished between the spheres of nature and of grace so that mere natural men might exercise their right in choosing temporal legislators.[17] Such a radical religious ideology stipulated that before the kingdom of Christ could be established, Parliaments as well as kings would need to be put down. Full of "seditious expressions" and "bitter language," the fiery preaching of the saints at Christ Church and Blackfriars was reported in detail so that Feake and Simpson were arrested and examined by the Council of State where they were told that such inflammatory behavior "has given confidence to our enemies abroad and home." (As we shall see, Marvell's depiction of a foreign monarch paying tribute to the Protector can be seen as the poet's imaginative polemical response to concerns about how fierce internal dissension might encourage enemies abroad.) Once hailed as a second Moses leading the saints from the Rump's bondage, Cromwell was now openly called "the man of sin, the old dragon, and many other scripture ill names," as well as identified, as King Charles had formerly been, with the little horn making war with the saints (Dan. 7:8, 21). The Protector had quickly become in Fifth Monarchist eyes "the dissembleingst perjured villaine in the world," as Vavasor Powell and Christopher Feake proclaimed him in Christ Church only two days after the Protector was installed: his "raigne was but short."[18]

Indeed, Cromwell's new regime was now presented as a more menacing Antichristian power than the unpopular "apostate" Rump, whose dissolution these radical saints considered a crucial step towards the inauguration of the kingdom of Christ.[19] Fifth Monarchist propaganda aimed to stir up deep-seated popular fears of new popery: Cromwell's supreme power was as popish as the former king's – "This popery and the old monarchie are one and the same," preached a vehement Feake at Allhallows.[20] On 19 December 1653 Nedham himself attended a fiery Fifth Monarchist meeting at Blackfriars in which Powell, after suggesting that "a vile person" would "obtain the kingdom by flatteries" (as Dan. 11:21 prophesied), seditiously demanded in the midst of his venomous rhetoric: "say Lord wilt Thou have Oliver Cromwell or Jesus Christ to reign over us?"[21] Simpson himself was soon to have millenarian visions of "the downfall of great O" in which he was seen running towards a crown, sitting in the chair of state, sprouting horns, and finally being destroyed – only the final vision had yet to come to pass.[22]

Fiercely opposed to a national church, the Fifth Monarchists were additionally enraged by Cromwell's attempt to encourage settling within the Protectorate by means of the ecclesiastical order of Triers and Ejectors introduced in March and August 1654, a system they variously likened to the Bishops' Court of High Commission, the image of the Beast in Revelation 13:15, a limb of Antichrist, and a manifestation of Babylon itself.[23] This means of testing and ensuring an effective, established ministry (thereby building a broad yet doctrinally orthodox church) was also intended to control radical preaching and political disaffection, and was thus perceived by the saints as a treacherous encroachment of human authority on religious matters.[24] At the moment of the Protectorate's first anniversary, a month before Marvell's poem was advertised and published, the fiery saints Feake and Simpson were crying out against the Protector as "The Father of Lyes." The

Antichristian fourth monarchy, formerly discerned in Charles I and associated with the "exceedingly dreadful" fourth Beast (Dan. 7:19), was yet to be destroyed: "the spirit of the fourth Beast," Feake dared to write from prison after being charged with sedition, "is yet living and acting its part in England."[25] Thus the Fifth Monarchists, who had ingeniously related the monsters and beasts of scriptural prophecies to the reign and destruction of King Charles, were now daring to relate them to the living Protector and his regime. Such discourse, moreover, was inflaming a "frantique Army" of their saints: Feake urged the faithful, who had not bowed "either to the Beast or to his Image," to come together "to make a standing Army for the King of Saints, in the time appointed of the Father."[26] Though imprisoned, Feake would nevertheless "throw ope his windowes like the gates of Janus" and preach seditiously as he and other leading saints continued to declare war against the Protectorate.[27]

Early defenders of the regime were therefore acutely aware of the dangerous implications of sectarian threats, factionalism, and the inflammatory rhetoric of its various seditious groups, which frequently stressed a vision of destructive vengeance more than one of a new millennial age. On the same day that Thomason dated Dewsbury's *True Prophecy of the Mighty Day of the Lord*, he also dated *Confusion Confounded*, the official apologia by the radical pamphleteer, republican, poet, and educational reformer, John Hall. Anxious "That every *Civil* debate shall be turned into a *Religious*" and that "Religion shall perish by her own Divisions,"[28] Hall confronted the challenge of radical groups and sectarians. The Fifth Monarchists especially exemplified the worrisome problem of "drawing all *Politick* debates into matter of *Conscience* . . . for they will tell you he is only fit to judge or *rule* that hath the Spirit, and they will judge him to have the Spirit, who is a sure *Assertor* of their *Faction*," at the same time that they, and other radical religious groups, are engaged by their "discourses at *Black Fryers*" in the "pulling down of *Antichrist, Forms, Orders, Ordinances* of *Man*" and "the plucking up of all *Ecclesiastical* and *Civil* policy."[29] As we shall see, Marvell would respond skillfully to this heady apocalyptic discourse of "pulling down" earthly powers by envisioning a Cromwell who both pulls down and erects "a firm State" anew and whose "sober Spirit" counters the raging one of the "frantique Army" of saints (lines 247–48, 230, 299).

In *A True State of the Case of the Commonwealth* (February 1654), published anonymously a few weeks after Hall's text, Nedham likewise expressed concern about the recent radicalization of religious politics in the infant Protectorate and about aggressive millenarian saints who were endangering "the more sober and equitable way" offered by Cromwell's new regime – "That sober Liberty" (line 289) to which Marvell refers.[30] Nedham expressed his anxiety about the spreading abroad of blasphemous, heretical opinions under the banner of religion in defiance of the Scriptures, and of God the Father, Son, and Holy Spirit; and he was alarmed about "the licentious subverting of all Order and Government" by religious extremists, especially the Fifth Monarchists, whose inciteful preaching at Blackfriars he had witnessed and reported to Cromwell.[31] Great obstructors of the work of reformation, settlement, and political stability, "the hot men at *Black Fryers*" (as Nedham dubbed them) "assumed to themselves only the name of Saints, from which Title they excluded all others that were not of their Judgment and opinion" as they blasted "both the Governors and Government, as *Babylonish* and Antichristian" and set out "to war with all other Powers, and break them in peeces."[32] Cromwell would soon draw upon and commend Nedham's book in his speeches justifying the Protectorate against bitter attacks from its enemies, including radical sectarians.[33]

Indeed, as Cromwell himself attacked "the mistaken notion of the Fifth Monarchy" in his speech of 4 September, he warned – much like Hall and Nedham – of a dangerous radical religious politics in which men "entitle themselves, upon this principle, that they are the only men to rule kingdoms, govern nations, and give laws to people; to determine of property and liberty and everything else, upon such a pretence as this is: truly, they had need give clear manifestations of God's presence with them, before wise men will receive or submit to their conclusions."[34] To be sure, Cromwell considered liberty of conscience a "natural right," but the recent divisive politics of sectarianism had dangerously narrowed its implications, making the cry for liberty a gesture fraught with ambiguity and a threat to his cherished vision of a stable nation united in godliness: as Cromwell told Parliament, "Every sect saith, Oh! Give me liberty. But give him it, and to his power he will not yield it to anybody else."[35] The tension between political conservatism and religious radicalism was aggravated by the ambiguous character of the new Protectorate, by ambivalent impulses within Cromwell himself, and by sharp sectarian challenges.

Marvell's *First Anniversary* therefore attempts to confront what is arguably the dominant issue of 1650s pamphleteering and a crucial concern of the Protectorate's apologists: the challenge of menacing sectaries and radical groups with their millennial fervor now turned against the experimental government with its commitment to moderate godly reform. In some cases polemical sectarian challenges were clearly carefully orchestrated. Just days before Cromwell's meeting with the new Parliament, the London Fifth Monarchists published their manifesto lamenting that the cause of Jesus was "so much disowned . . . in these times of *Apostacie*" when the government is "so fully gorged with the flesh of King, Captains, and Nobles . . . so as to . . . comply with Antichrist"; and this attack was immediately preceded by John Spittlehouse publishing a tract accusing Cromwell of high treason by enslaving the Commonwealth to "the Government of one single person."[36] Moreover, the publication of Cromwell's first two speeches to the Protectorate Parliament, in which he responded tensely to the dangers of the sectarian threat, occurred as other polemicists were publishing their tracts in response to the rebellious groups, an indication of the paranoia that could be fueled by radical sectarianism and its writings. Thomason dated 26 September 1654 *His Highness the Lord Protector's Speeches to the Parliament*, only the day after he dated a text by William Prynne blasting "a strange monstrous Generation of New TYRANNICAL STATE-HERETICKS sprung up among us," including leading Levellers and Fifth Monarchists (e.g. John Lilburne, John Canne, and John Rogers), who had employed "words, writing, Counsels and overt Acts to subvert . . . Liberties, Customes, Parliaments, and Government."[37] And on the same day that he dated Cromwell's speeches, Thomason dated a more sympathetic text concerning the suffering and persecution of the rapidly emerging Quakers: *The Immediate Call to the Ministry of the Gospel*. Nor were fears about a "frantique Army" of radical sectaries and their gathering strength assuaged in the more immediate context of the writing and publication of Marvell's poem. In two texts addressed to Parliament in December 1654, a conservative Puritan lamented that England had become a "seditious and divided Nation, wherein . . . such multitudes of Anabaptists, Quakers, and other Hereticks, that are enemies to all Government, are lately crept up to a considerable strength."[38]

In "An Horatian Ode," Michael Wilding has argued, Marvell deliberately excluded Leveller opposition to the Army Grandees and the "restless" Cromwell's rise to power (*HO*, line 9); and in *Upon Appleton House* he had satirically glanced at the egalitarian agrarian and social practices of the True Levellers or Diggers, as well as the levelling principles of other radicals, in his depiction of a meadow as a common for grazing (st. 57).[39] But in *The First Anniversary* the sharp challenges and sustained propaganda campaign mounted by millenarian saints and radical groups could not easily be shut out or simply be addressed in passing. Cromwell, we have seen, was troubled with the "contempt by men of Levelling principles," and Marvell recognized the need to address recalcitrant saints and radicals who would have "quickly Levell'd every Cedar's top" (line 262) in a political poem attempting to sustain the vision of a new regime that hoped to create an ordered, godly nation in the face of deep divisions.[40] Nevertheless, Cromwell could not hopefully urge this regime, as he had the Barebone's Assembly, to "have respect unto all [saints], though of different judgments. . . . have a care of the whole flock!"[41] His patience towards those who had strayed had been sorely tried, though he would persist in his strenuous dialogues with sectarian opponents and firebrands, including Feake and Simpson (in December 1654) and the fearless George Fox.[42] The "unity of Spirit" (*CPW* 2:565), which the Milton of *Areopagitica* once envisioned might include many schisms and sects in a revolutionary nation of prophets, now seemed a shattered ideal. Indeed, contrary to Marvell's vision, it seemed as though the "crossest Spirits," "whose Nature leads them to divide," had become too recalcitrant to "take their part" in building the godly Commonwealth (lines 89, 91). In 1654–55, the vociferous sects needed to be contained and their extravagant apocalyptic rhetoric rechanneled. Not until his writings after the Restoration would Marvell show greater sympathy for radical sectaries.[43]

Yet Marvell's own political proclivities at this moment in the Interregnum remain complex and ambivalent, combining and negotiating tendencies from both the Revolution's conservative and radical trends. He is no simple apologist for the Protectorate, but a writer who skillfully attempts to bridge key tensions in the Revolution. Thus, in line with the antimonarchical fervor of more apocalyptic revolutionaries, who envisioned shaking the monarchies of the earth, his poem repeatedly questions and diminishes the authority and achievements of earthly kings: Marvell characterizes them as "Unhappy Princes, ignorantly bred, / By Malice some, by Errour more misled" as they "adore" the Great Whore of Babylon, and he promises "with graver Accents [to] shake" their "Regal sloth"; the godly, visionary magistrate, moreover, is unlike those "heavy Monarchs" who "neither build the Temple in their dayes, / Nor Matter for succeeding Founders raise; / Nor sacred Prophecies consult within" (lines 117–18, 113–14, 121–22, 15, 33–35). As an alternative to monarchy, then, the Protectorate did not simply offer hope to political reactionaries.[44] Radical Puritan writers, including Milton and Wither, supported the Protector's experimental regime, even as they did not hesitate to issue advice and keen warnings about the abuses of power.[45] Marvell, however, is also acutely sensitive to Cromwell's wish to steer the Commonwealth, especially at this moment of religious/political instability, between extremes of unbounded rule, including the radical saints' strident claim to rule as a result of a direct call from Christ; just days after Marvell published his poem, Cromwell observed the need "to avoid the extremes of monarchy on the one hand, and democracy on the other, and yet not to found *dominium in gratia*" (i.e. a Fifth Monarchist regime in which an elected few ruled until the return of Jesus).[46] So Marvell's Cromwell is truly an artful steersman – in contrast to the careless one the poet depicts – as he saves the ship of state and its "giddy" passengers from "threat'ning Rocks" (see lines 265–78) and avoids steering the Commonwealth into radical seas. The "sober liberty" Marvell envisions avoids the dangerous extremes that Cromwell believed had recently threatened the stability of the Commonwealth: " 'Tis not a Freedome, that where All command; / Nor Tyranny, where One does them withstand: / But who of both the Bounders knows to lay / Him as their Father must the State obey" (lines 279–82).

At the same time, Marvell's lengthy depiction of radical groups as a "frantique Army" (lines 289–324) stimulates his satirical imagination and can be associated with the more conservative tone of the Protectorate and its polemical apologists, including sympathetic newsbooks combating challenges from "factious firebrands" who "pretend Revelations to raise Rebellions" so that "Government can never be safe and settled which is infested with seditious Sectaries."[47] Political fears about sectarian excesses were acute in the weeks before Marvell's poem appeared: in December Parliament fiercely condemned the blasphemous publications of the extremist Socinian John Biddle, who questioned Christ's divinity and the existence of the Holy Spirit.[48] Though Marvell's rhetoric is less frenetic and alarmist than that of contemporary anti-sectarians and heresiographers, his sneering at the "frantique Army" nevertheless recalls, at moments, their cruder assaults as well; the fifth and expanded edition of Ephraim Pagitt's *Heresiography* had just appeared in 1654, with new and extensive sections on the Quakers and Ranters as radical groups illustrating the dangers of social and moral anarchy.

There is an edginess to Marvell's treatment as he depicts these venomous, incensed groups, particularly the Fifth Monarchists, as rebellious sons who plague the nation (much as heresiographers, Presbyterians, and Cromwell all characterized the alarming sects) and whose millenarian excitement is stirred when Cromwell seems most vulnerable.[49] And so he was when his foot was caught in the reins of a horse as he was

violently pulled from his coach in the course of a serious accident on 29
September when he narrowly escaped death:[50]

> Yet such a *Chammish* issue still does rage,
> The Shame and Plague both of the land and Age,
> Who watch'd thy halting, and thy Fall deride,
> Rejoycing when thy Foot had slipt aside;
> That their new King might the fifth Scepter shake
> And make the World, by his Example, Quake:
> Whose frantique Army should they want for Men
> Might muster Heresies, so one were ten.   (lines 293–300)

Having just evoked Cromwell's sobriety and georgic role by way of comparison with the drunken Noah in Genesis 9:20–27 (see lines 283–88),
Marvell characterizes the recalcitrant radical groups, "a *Chammish*
issue," by alluding to the curse on Ham and his descendants as a result
of his disrespect towards his naked father. Augustine had claimed that
Ham, whose name means "Hot," signified himself "the hot breed of
heretics . . . [who] are wont to be fired not by the spirit of wisdom, but
by that of impatience, and thus disturb the peace of the saints."[51]
Marvell's depiction of the inflamed sectarians and radical groups as
"Chammish issue" conveys a similar sense of hot-headedness and rage,
while suggesting they are cursed. The term "Chamite" was in any case
one of obloquy in the mid-seventeenth century; it had been used,
according to Pagitt, by the sectarian group called the Brownists, "Bitter
raylers" against the Church of England who characterized her as
Antichristian and her followers as "Idolaters, *yea Sodomites, Canaanites,
Balamites, Chamites, Cainites*."[52] Marvell, however, has appropriated the
reproachful term, applying it to the Fifth Monarchists and other sectarians who were venting their rage against the Protectorate. Indeed, the
end-rhyme of lines 298–99 – shake/quake – reinforces Marvell's satirical depiction, which tends to blend together the Fifth Monarchists and
the Quakers (also called "Shakers" by hostile contemporaries),[53] the two
radical groups whose challenges to Cromwell's regime had most sorely
tried his patience. The term "frantique Army" picks up the theme of
"rage" in line 293 as it conveys those militant millenarians who are "violently or ragingly mad" (OED, s.v. "frantic")[54] – wild and ungovernable
with excitement and rage, and mustering heresies (as heresiographies
were warning), so that the size of their army swells, with one heresy
counting as ten men.

Marvell now exploits the more stereotypical seventeenth-century representation of Muhammad as a false prophet and imposter who could
rise again in this new and fertile age of apostasy:[55]

> Oh *Mahomet*! now couldst thou rise again,
> Thy Falling-sickness should have made thee Reign,
> While *Feake* and *Simpson* would in many a Tome,
> Have writ the Comments of thy sacred Foame:
> For soon thou mightst have passed among their Rant
> Wer't but for thine unmoved Tulipant;
> As thou must needs have own'd them of thy band
> For prophecies fit to be *Alcorand*.   (lines 303–10)

The radical Protestant Henry Stubbe would powerfully challenge
Christian accounts of the prophet, casting doubt on the story of his epi-
leptic fits (that "he was troubled with the falling sickness, and took advantage from thence to pretend to raptures");[56] but the polemical poet
chooses to retain the story as he links the religious radicals and their wild,
distracted prophecies with the early prophet and his ("thou must needs
have own'd them of thy band") contained in the Koran, first translated
into English in 1649. Marvell sarcastically imagines the enthusiastic Fifth
Monarchists writing the revelations of the prophet's "sacred foam" in
their inspired books, having just suggested a link between the "frantique" religious radicals, their calling upon the Spirit, and falling sickness ("their Religion only is to Fall," line 302). That he imagines the
"rant" of the leading Fifth Monarchists or refers to the "unmoved
Tulipant" of the Muslims, clearly alluding to the Quaker practice of
refusing to remove their hats before social superiors (including
Cromwell), reveals how Marvell blends together the religious radicals
and their different forms of extravagant, socially iconoclastic behavior.[57]

Marvell's language becomes more splenetic, closer to the language of
heresiographies and other hostile commentators, as he satirically cata-
logues the swarm of sectarians further:

> Accursed Locusts, whom your King does spit
> Out of the Center of th'unbottom'd Pit;
> Wand'rers, Adult'rers, Lyers, *Munser's* rest,
> Sorcerers, Atheists, Jesuites, Possest;
> You who the Scriptures and the Laws deface
> With the same liberty as Points and Lace.   (lines 311–16)

Anti-sectarians were equating the multiplying sects and heresies in the
age with the terrifying locusts emerging from the bottomless pit in
Revelation 9:2–3, 11, a new onslaught from the forces of destruction
spreading over the nation: "*Behold suddenly a numerous company of other*
Hereticks *stole in upon us like the Locusts*, Revel. 9."[58] Marvell employs the
same ominous apocalyptic image: his locusts are presided over by "the

angel of the bottomless pit" – Abaddon or the Destroyer – as they pour out and take on a multitude of forms. In a compressed fashion, his catalogue evokes a wide range of popular fears and exaggerated representations of the radical sectaries. Thus the early Quakers were sometimes depicted as Jesuits in disguise; they were also associated with sorcery and witchcraft – their extravagant tremblings and shakings seemed like testimony of demonic possession.[59] Indeed, Jesuits "Possest" were themselves included in accounts of devilish sectarians endangering the state. Pagitt had written about their heavenly visions and revelations, and considered them of "all Sects most pernicious and dangerous"; and Cromwell himself lamented that "the emissaries of the Jesuits never came in these swarms, as they have done since [these divisions and distractions] were set on foot."[60] The blasphemous Ranters, moreover, were especially associated with adultery.[61] In addition, Ranters, Seekers, and Quakers, as well as other radical religious groups and individuals, were regularly perceived as defacing the Scriptures.[62] This issue was dramatically illustrated at the end of 1654: Parliament imprisoned the eccentric millenarian Thomas Tany (alias Theaurau John) for assaulting its members with his sword, burning the Bible, and declaring it was not the Word of God.[63]

Marvell's compressed catalogue evokes other popular fears and perceptions. Sectarians were accused of lying as well as atheistical doctrines; one apology for the Protectorate praised Cromwell for cleansing away the latter, while in December 1654 Parliament voted to restrain "Atheism" and "damnable Heresies."[64] Furthermore, the "frantick zeale and giddy Revelations" of radical millenarians linked them, in hostile eyes, with the original Munster Anabaptists; the saints seemed to breathe "nothing but fire and sword" as they looked "upon their country-men with such an eye as the *Anabaptists* cast upon *Munster* when they came first to it."[65] In its own way, Marvell's satirical catalogue reminds us that Cromwell's priority in the unsettled Commonwealth was unity among the godly rather than toleration or religious diversity: he remained largely unsympathetic to Quakers, Ranters, Fifth Monarchists, and Socinians, as well as to Roman Catholics and Anglicans.[66]

Indeed, fears that sectarians were defacing the Scriptures as well as subverting "known laws" or trying to replace the English common law tradition with a severe Mosaic code, as Fifth Monarchists demanded, were acute during the Protectorate. The new regime aimed to guarantee the rule of law to avert political as well as religious breakdown: Cromwell feared that these "perilous times" when "men forget all rules of law and nature" were worse than the Antichristian state described by St. Paul in 2 Timothy 3.[67] Marvell's mockery of the radical groups who deface the Scriptures and the laws "with the same liberty as Points and Lace" cannot conceal his sharp impatience, which breaks through as he considers their godlier-than-thou zeal – "Oh Race most hypocritically strict!" (line 317).[68] So Cromwell considered the recalcitrant sects in their vociferous demands for more liberty.[69] And as Marvell ridicules the pretenses of the so-called Adamites and the Quakers who went naked as a sign – "Well may you act the *Adam* and the *Eve*; / Ay, and the Serpent too that did deceive" (lines 319–20) – he links the "Chammish issue" with diabolical ensnaring powers, much as theologically conservative Puritans did.[70]

Jotham's parable in Judges 9:7–15, to which Marvell alludes, likewise had acquired new polemical significance as radical saints were furiously assaulting the Protectorate:

> Though why should others all thy Labor spoil,
> And Brambles be anointed with thine Oyl,
> Whose climbing Flame, without a timely stop,
> Had quickly Levell'd every Cedar's top.
> Therefore first growing to thy self a Law
> Th'ambitious Shrubs thou in just time didst aw.   (lines 259–64)

In her visions at Whitehall, Nigel Smith notes, Trapnel the Fifth Monarchist prophetess had depicted the saints as "growing and thriving" yet "despised shrubs" saved from great oaks, including monarchs and Cromwell himself.[71] Indeed, in a text devoted to attacking Vavasor Powell for spreading disaffection in Wales, one godly minister considered the parable's contemporary application as he specifically connected brambles and "ambitious Shrubs":

The *Bramble* is a most fruitless, *tearing shrub*; fit for nothing, but the *stopping* of *Gaps*, and afterwards to be burned: And by the Parable of this *Bramble, Jotham* meant, proud and *ambitious men*, base in *birth*, wicked in *life*, barren in *goodness*, and cruel in *nature*; If you examine your *heart*, you will find the true *Mythologie* and moral of this Parable *couched* in your own *breast*.[72]

Furthermore, Cromwell himself bitterly complained, only a few days after Marvell's poem appeared, that "weeds and nettles, briers and thorns" had thrived under the shadow of the first Protectorate Parliament as discontent and division multiplied, threatening "more desperate and dangerous confusion than England ever yet saw."[73] In Marvell's passage, the "climbing flame" of the brambles evokes the inflammatory behavior of "the hot men at *Black Fryers*" (to recall Nedham's words), including Feake and Powell, whose apocalyptic levelling rhetoric Cromwell had anxiously confronted in his first Protectorate speech; associated with the fury of usurping Abimelech, Gideon's bastard son and half-brother to Jotham, they are inferior brothers to Cromwell to whom they had clung ("first growing to thy self a Law"), as in the Barebone's Assembly. The "ambitious Shrubs" evoke, as the commentary above suggests, those rebellious, obdurate saints who then wished to destroy the "labour" of Cromwell – his new regime – as they attempt to usurp his "oil" and set up an exclusive rule of the saints. Much as he did "awe" the Levellers, Cromwell "in just time didst aw[e]" the fiery saints, imprisoning their leaders and shutting them out of power in the Protectorate; yet, as we have seen, their unbridled rhetoric had not been silenced nor their spirit broken.

To be sure, Marvell the poet is more skillful in his polemical assaults, his sarcastic tone is more controlled, and he is infinitely more capable of urbane compressed expression than the cruder, more prolix antisectarians and heresiographers. And his political position is more complex and less consistently conservative than theirs as he attempts to negotiate the tension between political conservatism and religious radicalism which had become acute during the crisis of the Protectorate. His mockery deflates the religious radicals and is a rhetorical means of diminishing their threat; yet his sharpness keeps breaking through, reminding us of the powerful anxieties which the "frantique Army" of jarring sects and radical saints were capable of arousing as they challenged, in fiery apocalyptic language, Cromwell's vision of godly union and a godly regime.

Furthermore, Marvell's poem counters the hostile radical millenarian image of Cromwell as a ruler through whom "the Mystery of Iniquity" was "hard at work" – a double-dealing apostate with a ruthless craving for personal power who, just as the Levellers had depicted him, "knows how to suit his words to the several parties and things which he speaks unto" as he covers over "abominable Treachery, Apostacy, and Backsliding."[74] So Marvell's Cromwell, reared by a "Saint-like Mother," is an upright, godly man with a "Heart from Evil still unstain'd" who "always hast [his] Tongue from fraud refrain'd."[75] Indeed, by assuming the onerous leadership over the Commonwealth, with its seemingly intractable constituents, the leader who would have preferred "his private Gardens" ("Horatian Ode," line 29) has had to resign his "Privacy so dear, / To turn the headstrong Peoples Charioteer."[76] He has, moreover, borne "securely [his] undaunted Head" as he has weathered "ponyarding Conspiracies / Drawn from the Sheath of lying Prophecies" (lines 161, 167–68, 223–24, 170–72) – the venomous prophecies of seditious groups like the Fifth Monarchists, as well as the recent threat of royalist conspiracy.[77] Cromwell's coaching accident, when unruly horses pulled him from his seat, came dangerously close to fulfilling such grim prophecies and satisfying the "men of discontented spirits" in whose "hearts and minds," as Cromwell had recently put it to the first Protectorate Parliament, there was nothing "but overturning, overturning, overturning":[78] "How near they fail'd, and in thy sudden Fall / At once assay'd to overturn us all" (lines 175–76).

Marvell nevertheless imagines Cromwell's triumphant death as, like the prophet Elijah in 2 Kings 2:11, he ascends to "the Kingdom blest of Peace and Love" in a chariot of fire with fiery horses; yet as he leaves behind "the low World" of "thankless Men" who "grumble discontent" (lines 217–18, 277), there is no Elisha to take up his mantle and authority. Marvell, indeed, employs the extravagant language of pathetic fallacy ("And all about was heard a Panique groan, / As if that Natures self were overthrown") to imagine the shattering impact of Cromwell's fall and mortality ("It seem'd the Earth did from the Center tear; / It seem'd the Sun was faln out of the Sphere"), thereby highlighting the immense loss in a nation itself left "rent and torn in spirit and principle" and bereft of the one forward pressing man who might heal its deep divisions: "We only mourn'd our selves, in thine Ascent, / Whom thou hadst left behind with Mantle rent" (lines 203–6, 219–20). Cromwell had publicly lamented the "sad and . . . deplorable condition" of the nation when he accepted the role of Protector;[79] and so while Marvell imagines him triumphantly released from governing "thankless Men," the poet's emphasis on mourning, as well as his powerful vision of nature "overthrown," poignantly convey how much sadder and more deplorable might the spiritual and political state of the nation be without its godly Protector.

RADICAL MILLENARIANISM AND MARVELL'S VISION OF APOCALYPSE

The fiery apocalyptic language and symbolism used by radical saints to assault the Protectorate needed to be contested, and Marvell's visionary poem takes up that polemical challenge. Yet Cromwell himself personified ambivalent trends within the Revolution: while socially conservative elements in his temperament drew him towards more cautious godly reform, his religious convictions had drawn him towards apocalyptic revolutionaries like Major-General Thomas Harrison, his close associate in the Army. Cromwell, after all, had shared the millenarian enthusiasm of the religious radicals and, like them, looked forward to the kingdom of Christ, though he envisioned it less literally than some;[80] but he also became alarmed with them as they urged more radical social, legal, and religious reforms. As Marvell addresses the tensions of the Protectorate and engages with radical opposition to the regime, he appropriates and transforms the saints' millenarian language, giving it a new potency; as we have seen, such language had been given an alarmingly militant edge by saints vigorously contesting the Protector's authority as though it were a new and more menacing form of Antichristian treachery.

"Neither do I think that the liberty we now enjoy," observed a fierce critic of the Protectorate, "is all that which the Lord would have us to expect . . . or in answer to those glorious prophecies and promises which are to be fulfill'd in the latter dayes."[81] Marvell's poem addresses such criticisms from radical saints who were disparaging the sobriety and liberty this new providential leader had brought: such is "That sober Liberty which men may have, / That they enjoy, but more they vainly crave" (289–90). Marvell skillfully transmutes the explosive, colorful apocalyptic language of extreme millenarianism, using the same potent language to legitimatize the new regime's power and Cromwell's apocalyptic role. Thus he envisions in Cromwell "a Captain" who alone might "raise / The great Designes kept for the latter Dayes" (lines 109–110) – the Fifth Monarchy and the reigning of the saints prophesied by Daniel (Dan. 7:18, 27 and 10:14) – in an age full of "thankless Men" who have dangerously misinterpreted apocalyptic discourse, misrepresenting Cromwell himself as the agent of Antichrist.[82]

In his exuberant moments, Cromwell himself was gripped by fervent millenarianism and drew upon its language in his public discourse. If he felt the need to restrain radical millenarian rhetoric as Protector, he had also helped to unleash it. He had notably emulated Fifth Monarchist rhetoric in the opening speech to the Barebone's Parliament, an expectant assembly designed to hasten the imminent rule of the saints and uproot all corrupt institutions: "I confess I never looked to see such a day as this . . . when Jesus Christ should be so owned as He is, at this day, and in this work. . . . I say, you are called with a high call." In early July 1653, the ecstatic Cromwell, whose prophetic language drew upon the Books of Daniel and Revelation, seemed allied with the millenarians (including a dozen Fifth Monarchists and other radicals in the audience) who believed themselves chosen by God to exercise power: "you are called to be faithful with the Saints, who have been somewhat instrumental to your call." Cromwell thus shared the language and some of the dreams of the militant, radical godly ("We know who they are that shall war with the lamb, against his enemies; they shall be a people called, and chosen and faithful"; echoing Rev. 17:14) and in the Barebone's Assembly had been the patron of the religious sectaries.[83] Nor would the saints, when attacking him for betraying the Revolution, let Cromwell forget how he had employed their ardent millenarian language.[84] Indeed, the fact that his famous millenarian speech was later published as a pamphlet without printer or official authority (Thomason dated his copy 13 October 1654) only highlighted further the sharp contrast between Cromwell's unguarded millenarian language addressed to the saints and his recent denunciation of them as Protector.[85] Nevertheless, while Cromwell had shared their urgency for moral reformation, he showed no desire to undermine social structures or traditionally organized religion in the process of erecting the new godly order.[86] Nor did his religious enthusiasm, expressed so strongly to the Parliament of Saints, ever fuel his belief in the exclusive rule of the saints. Indeed, his zealous rhetoric was qualified, unlike Fifth Monarchist discourse, by his more tentative language: "But I may appear to be beyond my line; these things are dark."[87] His exuberant religious zeal and his antiformalism, which he shared with the sects, were offset by a desire to maintain religious unity; and his desire to unite the godly – by which he largely meant Presbyterians, Independents, and Baptists but excluded Anglicans and Roman Catholics – meant that he abhorred sectarian factionalism.[88] Such were the ambivalent trends within Cromwell himself, ambiguities inherent within the Revolution. In his visionary representation of the Protectorate, Marvell perceived these tensions as he skillfully modified extreme millenarian rhetoric, which Cromwell had recently shared, at least up to a point, with the radical godly.

Exploiting the same kind of apocalyptic language and symbolism which animated radical millenarian discourse, Marvell reinvigorates such visionary language as he criticizes earthly princes and envisions the Protectorate whose rule signals the potential for the fulfillment of a millennial future. Not only does Marvell suggest that the "Footsteps" of princes are "numbred" like the "numbered" days of Belshazzar's kingdom in Daniel 5:26, but he wishes that they would follow Cromwell's example (lines 105–6) and suggests that he and his regime provide "The path where holy Oracles do lead" – those "great Designes kept for the latter Dayes" (lines 108, 110).[89] Instead, such ignorant princes of the earth "sing Hosanna to the Whore" of Revelation 17 (line 113) rather than contribute to her fall, in contrast to the saints who "had not worshipped the beast" and would therefore reign with Christ for a thousand years (Rev. 20:4). Nor do earthly kings contribute to the gathering in of the gentiles and nations, especially the conversion and restoration of the Jews, which the saints themselves considered a crucial sign that the millennium was nearing: thus "Indians, whom they should convert," they "subdue; / Nor teach, but traffique with, or burn the Jew" (lines 115–16).[90] For Cromwell the conversion of the Jews, whose readmission to England he would soon seek, was not only a precondition of the millennium; it was also an essential step to establishing the unity of the godly people.[91] In contrast to earthly kings and princes, it is "Angelique *Cromwell*" (line 126) who is engaged in a lonely crusade against the forces of Antichrist as he pursues the destruction of the Great Whore, her teeth gory with the blood of the saints (as in Rev. 17:6). Leading Fifth Monarchist firebrands might continue to preach that Cromwell's regime was "A Limbe of the Whore and of the Beast" or warn the Protector "how near it is to the end of the Beast's dominion."[92] But here Marvell envisions that it is Cromwell who

> outwings the wind;
> And in dark Nights, and in cold Dayes alone
> Pursues the Monster thorough every Throne:
> Which shrinking to her *Roman* Den impure,
> Gnashes her Goary teeth; nor there secure.   (lines 126–30)

By envisioning Cromwell in his solitary pursuit of the Antichristian Beast, Marvell's poem thus counters the recent tendency among millenarian opponents to identify Cromwell himself with the beasts and monsters of the scriptural prophecies in Daniel and Revelation. Hostile saints were warning that now "many worship the beast and his image";[93] but in the apocalyptic vision of Marvell's poem, such worshippers are earthly monarchs, not Cromwell who vigorously pursues its destruction.

Marvell's Cromwell is a godly Puritan warrior girded and standing ready "to fight" and who "in his Age has always forward prest" (line 146), especially in his pursuit of godly reformation (including liberty of conscience). Marvell echoes a major theme of Cromwell's first Protectoral speech, where Cromwell had urged Parliament itself to be forward moving ("therefore I wish that you may go forward, and not backward"), despite the English lingering many years in the wilderness and despite resistance from men with stubborn minds, including the recalcitrant sects, who were especially guilty of "unbelief, murmuring, repining, and other temptations and sins."[94] The stubbornness or unworthiness of such men, unable to rise above their narrower self-interests ("Men alas, as if they nothing car'd, / Look on, all unconcern'd, or unprepar'd" (lines 149–50)) to share Cromwell's faith that God had glorious dispensations in store for England,[95] could have dire consequences, delaying rather than hastening the millennium itself. Without Cromwell to combat the dark powers of the great dragon of Revelation 12:3–4, they remain unchecked and as ominous as ever: "And Stars still fall, and still the Dragons Tail / Swinges the Volumes of its horrid Flail" (lines 151–52). Cromwell's first two Protectoral speeches had forcefully linked the issues of spiritual disunity and sin; and so does Marvell.[96] In such an age, the prospect of a coming millennium could not be certain as the fiery Fifth Monarchists were so stridently insisting:

> For the great Justice that did first suspend
> The World by Sin, does by the same extend.
> Hence that blest Day still counterpoysed wastes,
> The Ill delaying, what th'Elected hastes.   (lines 153–56)

Alluding to Daniel 2:44 ("and the kingdom shall not be left to other people"), Cromwell himself, in an enthusiastic mood, had once told the Parliament of Saints, "you are at the edge of the promises and prophecies."[97] Envisioning Cromwell as a providential instrument in an unfolding millennial drama, Marvell for a moment allows himself to imagine how "the mysterious work, where none withstand, / Would forthwith finish under such a Hand." But the poet's millennial vision also remains tentative, his language qualified by the conditional tense:[98]

> Hence oft I think, if in some happy Hour
> High Grace should meeting in one with highest Pow'r,
> And then a seasonable People still
> Should bend to his, as he to Heavens will,
> What we might hope, what wonderful Effect
> From such a wish'd Conjuncture might reflect.   (lines 131–38)

Now, in an age of Puritan divisiveness and spiritual crisis, the fulfillment of "the promises and prophecies" seemed dim indeed, the future more cloudy than certain (see lines 141–44).

"THE NATION RENT AND TORN IN SPIRIT": HEALING CONTRADICTIONS

Marvell offers a visionary poetic response to the acute political/spiritual crisis of the Protectorate in his mythic vision of Cromwell's harmonious spirit, conveyed by the elaborate comparison to the divinely inspired

Amphion (lines 49–66) who "with his gentle hand, / The rougher Stones, unto his Measures hew'd," thereby creating with "his sacred Lute" a "harmonious City" – a place of "wondrous Order and Consent" (line 67). Indeed, this and other passages in the poem echo, and imaginatively rework, the language of Nedham, Hall, and Cromwell with regard to building a new godly state based on a settled, more harmonious foundation. "Scattering, division, and confusion": these were, in Cromwell's eyes, "the greatest plagues" which could rack a nation and prevent its healing and settling.[99] The jarring sects, who lacked what Cromwell called "that spirit of kindness," were particularly associated in his mind with scatterings.[100] Fusing the language of music and architecture, Marvell's brilliant conceit of Cromwell as "our Amphion," whose music imitates the cosmic harmony and who works "with gentle hand" to create wondrous "consent" as he "tune[s] the ruling Instrument," not only alludes to the Protector's passion for music; it responds as well to his more conservative anxieties about healing and settling the common "carnal divisions and contentions among Christians" in a "nation rent and torn in spirit . . . from one end to another." Royalist verses, published in the summer of 1654, had invoked the "sweet . . . tones" of Amphion to accentuate more sharply a sense of royalist grief ("For whereas he could move but woods or Stones / I shall move men").[101] In Marvell's verses the invocation of the mythic builder and musician takes on fresh potency as he responds to the unsettled state of the Protectorate. England was still an unreformed nation where there seemed to be too little evidence of consent, where there seemed to be rancorous, "noisome opinions," and "where every stone is turned to bring confusion."[102] And so Marvell recreates, through its own imaginative conceits, Nedham's vision (subsequently reiterated by Cromwell) of the Protectorate as a government applying "a healing hand" and with the ability to erect a godly state on a more firm foundation: "it is high time for our Government to lay a healing hand to these mortal wounds and breaches, by holding forth the Truths of Christ to the Nation in some solid Establishment."[103]

At a time when the radical saints and sects were intent on "rending and tearing" the church and state,[104] the language of building a new, harmonious foundation was thus itself polemically charged. Nedham was concerned about clamorous millenarian saints whose vision and "principles led them to a pulling down all, and establishing nothing," while John Hall recalled, in alarmist language addressed to those fearful for the national institutions of orderly life, that during the previous regime there had been much more pulling down than erecting: "The

Law was looked on as a noisome ruinous building, not capable of repair or alteration, but fit to be pulled down to the very ground"; "*Propriety* was struck at" and "the *Ministry* was to be demolished."[105] By the end of 1653, it looked to millenarian saints as if Cromwell himself was simply protecting "the Towers of Babylon" which must be thrown down with violence (so John Rogers warned in a broadsheet of "humble Cautionary Proposals"): and these "must fall (and with fury too) upon the Heads of their Protectors."[106] Indeed, Anna Trapnel soon lamented that the backsliding, quasi-regal Protector had "come to rear up the pillars, the stones which are laid aside."[107] The commissions of Triers and Ejectors themselves "[stood] upon an Antichristian foundation": so one hostile millenarian would later claim in a text which raised doubts about the answers to such as questions as "Are not we upon a good foundation? have not we the Liberty of our Consciences? . . . hath not [the Protector] been very instrumental formerly for good to the Nation, and the people of God? and doth not he promise to be so for the future?"[108] And at the end of 1654, the imprisoned Christopher Feake warned that, notwithstanding "all these Earthquakes" which had recently shaken the nation, there was still "*Antichristian morter . . .* yet remaining in these *States and Kingdoms*."[109] Feake, moreover, was so convinced that there was "a great deal of work to be done about new moulding of churches," that he would deliver a fiery oration on the very "subject of renting and tearing of churches" in which he promised that he would "never leave renting" them "in pieces."[110]

Apologists for the Protectorate were quick to counter this worrisome language of "dividing and renting." While the Lord had "been shaking and moving foundations," Nedham's defence observed, he had been doing so in 1653–54 "not to overturn" – as extreme millenarians threatened – "but to establish this Commonwealth upon a better and more sure *Basis* of Government," not "the foundation of a new platform, which was to go under the name of a *Fifth Monarchy*."[111] Marvell's poem about the arduous process of building a state based on "sober liberty" deftly captures, in his poetic language and elaborate analogies, Nedham's vision of building a "more sure *Basis* of Government," especially his concern that after many "Rents of civil Divisions, and Contestings for Liberty, as [are] here now in *England*," it was crucial "to prevent a razing of those Foundations of Freedom that have been but newly laid."[112]

And so the restless, active Cromwell whose iconoclastic energy Marvell captured in "An Horatian Ode" – the leader who "Pallaces and

Temples rent" and who could "ruine the great Work of Time" (lines 22, 34) – is now depicted as not only "pulling down" but arduously and meticulously reconstructing the body politic upon a stable foundation. It becomes a wondrous edifice that could settle and endure the deep rifts Cromwell had lamented in his first Protectoral speech as he deplored the saints' vision of a state "where every stone is turned to bring confusion." Indeed, still believing then that the "entrances and doors of hope" were open to the distracted nation, a visionary Cromwell urged the new Protectorate Parliament "to put the top-stone to this work, and make the nation happy."[113] Marvell develops such metaphorical language as he presents Cromwell creatively shaping the new political structure,

> Choosing each Stone, and poysing every weight,
> Trying the Measures of the Bredth and Height;
> Here pulling down, and there erecting New,
> Founding a firm State by Proportions true. (lines 245–48)

The poet's precise language and depiction of Cromwell respond to publicly voiced fears of political, religious, and social anarchy. Here is a godly magistrate who erects anew after pulling down, who is a skillful architect of the state, and who possesses mythic powers enabling him to create harmony and proportion in a discordant body politic – the "heap of confusions . . . upon thee poor nations!" as the Protector had deplored.[114] Nedham especially had envisioned "a just and probable foundation . . . laid for extinguishing all animosities . . . and divisions contracted by Civil War" so that "the people may be harmoniously disposed to a lasting peace and settlement." He thus had warned of the danger of spoiling "the harmony of Government" and observed the challenge of a new government which, after a period of darkness and near-anarchy, was attempting to "create a little World out of *Chaos*, and bring Form out of Confusion."[115] Cromwell was not simply restoring: he was creating anew. So Marvell has imagined Cromwell's Commonwealth as the "harmonious City" of "wondrous Order" created "from the Quarreys rude"; in such a Commonwealth "all [are] compos'd by his attractive Song" and enter "the willing Frame" (lines 66–67, 52, 85, 76).[116] In composing the body politic, Cromwell was, moreover, responding to "a conviction that now only he could save the Commonwealth from impending anarchy" – from further "divisions, and animosities, and scatterings."[117] Marvell puts it more positively in *The First Anniversary* as he conveys how the man of action who has energized and "Fore-shortned Time" speeds godly reformation and settlement: set apart from other earthly rulers, the "indefatigable *Cromwell*" "cuts his way still nearer to the Skyes," as he "alone doth with new Lustre spring" and "the force of scatter'd Time contracts, / And in one Year the work of Ages acts" (lines 139, 45–46, 11, 13–14).

Marvell envisions England as a godly nation forged by Cromwell, who harnesses its sharp political and religious tensions, and whose capital, an alternative to the radical saints' New Jerusalem, becomes an "Animated City" (line 86) symbolic of dynamic godly reform (like Milton's vision of a dynamic London in *Areopagitica*). The poet's language is particularly artful as he highlights the stresses and strains in the building of the new godly state and its mixed constitutional edifice based on a balance between the legislative, executive, and judicial powers. He gives elegant figurative expression to the vision of order, stability, and constitutional respectability which the Protectorate regime yearned to provide on the basis of "a free Parliament":[118]

> The Common-wealth does through their Centers all
> Draw the Circumf'rence of the publique Wall;
> The crossest Spirits here do take their part,
> Fast'ning the Contignation which they thwart;
> And they, whose Nature leads them to divide,
> Uphold, this one, and that the other Side;
> But the most Equal still sustein the Height,
> And they as Pillars keep the Work upright;
> While the resistance of opposed Minds,
> The Fabrick as with Arches stronger binds,
> Which on the Basis of a Senate free,
> Knit by the Roofs Protecting weight agree.   (lines 87–98)

Marvell's sophisticated passage of *concordia discors* captures essential tensions of the Revolution which, in the new body politic, are kept in a state of equilibrium despite "the Minds of stubborn Men" who refuse to accept Cromwell's framing of the new constitution and who are compared to "a Stone so hardly wrought" (lines 78–79). Indeed, even the "crossest Spirits" and those "whose Nature leads them to divide" contribute, under Cromwell's shaping and artful leadership, to the elaborate structure as "the resistance of opposed minds" binds together the new edifice of the state more firmly.[119] The splintering of Protestant unity feared by Cromwell has now been imaginatively addressed by Marvell in this potent vision of a Commonwealth united, the fabric of its wondrous edifice strengthened by the powerful tensions which had seemed to threaten its very stability.

In recalling the spiritual architecture Milton had envisioned ten years earlier, the Temple of the Lord with its "many schisms" (*CPW* 2:555), an image of "the unity of Spirit," Marvell has given it a different inflection. Milton, in any case, had dismissed the "fantastic terrors of sect and schism" (*CPW* 2:554) and celebrated the combative, exhilarating energy generated by the new sectarianism. Marvell has included divisive sectarians and schismatics who now seemed to threaten the consensual basis of "a firm State" and, hardened in their convictions, refused to enter "in the willing Frame" (line 76); yet the poet's satirical rhetoric and image of swarming sectarians elsewhere in the poem, as we saw earlier, convey less visionary optimism. Moreover, Marvell's attractive vision of "wondrous order and consent" in a balanced polity was a vision of "healing and settling" whose realization was already unlikely by the end of 1654: about a hundred MPs, including doctrinaire republicans, were forced to withdraw from the "senate free" for refusing to sign a loyalty oath to the government as it was settled in a single person and a parliament. Nevertheless, Parliament still failed to validate the Instrument by statute and spent much of its session revising the constitution in a way that threatened both religious liberty and the regime's security.[120] In addition, the "crossest Spirits" – including implacable radical opponents of the Protector who continued to rage – were not helping to fasten "the Contignation."

GODLY RULE: PARADOXES AND AMBIGUITIES

Marvell's portrait of Cromwell in *The First Anniversary* deftly captures the novelty of the Protectorate itself, with its uneasy combination of godly rule and a semi-monarchical idea of the Protector. His comparison of Cromwell to the valiant but humble Gideon is itself an attempt to address the ambiguities of the Lord Protector by drawing upon a scriptural story of national deliverance with antimonarchic implications.[121] We have seen in Chapter 3 how Anna Trapnel, in visions delivered at Whitehall, contentiously invoked the warrior figure of Gideon, who refused to be king, to challenge Cromwell's Protectoral power which had shut out the saints. The analogy became increasingly contested during the political/religious crisis of the mid-1650s. A fierce Fifth Monarchist petition denouncing the Protectorate used the biblical military hero and other rulers of old as models with which to contrast the backsliding Cromwell for betraying the Good Old Cause and millenarian ideals; published in late 1655 with over 300 signatures, it was read out at a mass meeting in Allhallows by John Simpson and another saint.[122] But at the same time Puritan apologists for the Protectorate, including George Smith and John Moore, were also resorting to such scriptural mythmaking for their own polemical ends as they considered Cromwell a Gideon-like instrument of God's providence stirred up to be a deliverer of his people – "an higher Force," in Marvell's words, pushing him "Still from behind" (lines 239–40).[123] Cromwell, whose own models were biblical, admired the zeal of Phineas and had come to see himself as Gideon *redidivus* in 1648, envisioning his own godly military struggles and victories – "breaking the rod of the oppressor, as in the day of Midian" – in terms of the struggle of Israel, skillfully led by Yahweh's man and his small force, against impossible odds, the huge Midianite army and its kings, Zebah and Zalmunna.[124]

The comparison thus assumed greater urgency during the crisis of the Protectorate when depictions of Cromwell as a second Gideon could differ sharply:

> When *Gideon* so did from the War retreat,
> Yet by the Conquest of two Kings grown great,
> He on the Peace extends a Warlike power,
> And *Is'rel* silent saw him rase the Tow'r;
> And how he *Succoths* Elders durst suppress,
> With Thorns and Briars of the Wilderness.
> No King might ever such a Force have done;
> Yet would not he be Lord, nor yet his Son.   (lines 249–56)

Marvell envisions a Gideon-like Cromwell who as Lord General had overcome two kings – Charles I and II – and who had recently awed England as Israel with his own "Warlike power." The analogy conveys a more punitive side to the militant godly leader as well: not only had he broken two Parliaments, but, Marvell reminds his readers, this second, no less decisive Gideon would not flinch from taking vengeance on those who betray him, just as the biblical Gideon did on the men of Succoth and Penuel who refused to help his campaign against the Midianites (Judg. 8: 3–17). But Cromwell likewise resembles the modest, wise Gideon in his refusal to be King Oliver and therefore Marvell exploits here (as he does throughout the poem) the paradoxes of a wondrous and singular Lord Protector whose power exceeds that of a king and yet would not "be Lord." And by adding "nor yet his Son," Marvell deftly recalls that the office of the Protector was not to be hereditary, just as the popular hero Gideon showed humility by refusing to inaugurate a hereditary monarchy, but who, after subduing the Midianites, still brought his country forty years of quietness and rest (Judg. 8:22–23, 28).[125] Cromwell

indeed distinguished between his title and that of king, and was probably instinctively against accepting the crown in December 1653; the
extended analogy with Gideon likewise enables Marvell to counter the
view of hostile millenarians and republicans who suggested that the
apostate Protector, practicing a form of military despotism, was treacherously and brazenly hypocritical: "Thou with the same strength, and
an Heart as plain, / Didst . . . still refuse to Reign" (lines 257–58).[126]

Marvell has boldly transferred to Cromwell regal symbolism, thereby
heightening the sense of the Protector's paradoxes: he is "Sun-like" (line
8), setting a "Pattern" for kings to follow (105–6), and yet he is more vigorous than monarchs, whose "earthy Projects" and hereditary kingship
(lines 19–22) the poet attacks. By placing praise of Cromwell in the
mouth of a hostile prince, Marvell at the end is able to avoid the charge
of flattery as he encourages the poem's readers to wonder one last time
at Cromwell's paradoxical achievements and godly office:

> He seems a King by long Succession born,
> And yet the same to be a King does scorn.
> Abroad a King he seems, and something more,
> At Home a Subject on the equal Floor.   (lines 387–90)

Though regularly addressed as "Your Highness" and as ceremonious as
European monarchs, the Protector, a "great Prince" (line 395), nevertheless is no king, however he may appear abroad.[127] And by presenting him
as an English "Subject on the equal Floor" – despite the fact that his
regime and constitution were never the result of a direct popular mandate
or a Leveller-style agreement – the poet also glances at the fears of radical
critics of the Protectorate who continued to proclaim against an arbitrary,
brutal power: "the Government of one single person" who enforced his
position "by reason of the power of the sword, which is over us."[128]

The imaginary speech of the foreign prince, moreover, is a skillful
polemical passage which enables Marvell to counter the claim of radical
millenarians that a divided nation under the new Antichristian, quasi-
regal Protector would encourage enemies abroad to reproach England
for backsliding and weakness.[129] One of the most trenchant and sustained millenarian attacks on the Protectorate and its apostasy, *The
Protector (so called) in Part Unvailed*, voiced precisely this concern:

Now the divisions of the people of God, being upon this account, and the glory
which formerly was upon *England* being departed, which made the Nations
begin to fear, and tremble; instead of doing so now, they speak reproachfully of
us and count us, as a perfidious people: . . . Because they hear a Protector is set
up as King in the room of the late King, after we declared and engaged so much
against it.[130]

The foreign observer in Marvell's poem, however, confesses that he is struck with wonder at England's remarkable progress under its new godly ruler, especially after having gone through a civil war as well as the Dutch War (1652–54); the recent conclusion of the latter war only fueled the radical millenarian saints' belief that the apostate Cromwell had betrayed their cause by renouncing an apocalyptic foreign policy (as we noted in Chapter 3):

> Is this, saith one, the Nation that we read
> Spent with both Wars, under a Captain dead?
> Yet rig a Navy while we dress us late;
> And ere we Dine, rase and rebuild their State.
> What Oaken Forrests, and what golden Mines!
> What Mints of Men, what Union of Designes!   (lines 349–54)

"Reproach and scorn" is not the response of this representative of European monarchy towards the new regime, as hostile saints were predicting,[131] but awe at the astonishing and rapid achievements of Cromwell, a sense of esteem mixed with surprise and puzzlement: "Where did he learn those Arts that cost us dear? / Where below the Earth, or where above the Sphere?" (lines 385–86). Responding to the dangers of religious and political divisions in a nation "dissettled at home," Cromwell himself observed to the Protectorate Parliament that "nothing so much gratified our enemies as to see us at odds, so, I persuade myself, nothing is of more terror nor trouble to them, than to see us thus reconciled."[132] With the praise of the Protector and the wondrous achievements of his godly reformation carefully placed in the mouth of a skeptical foreign power, Marvell could give fresh – and indeed dramatic and polemical – expression to such a conviction.

Marvell's major celebratory poem, with its paradoxical portrait of the godly Protector steering the Commonwealth between monarchy and republic, could not of course resolve the ongoing tension between radical millenarianism and moderate Puritan reform or settlement. These ambivalent tendencies ran too deep in the political and religious culture of Interregnum England – and in the "restless" Cromwell himself – and were never to be resolved. In *The First Anniversary*, however, Marvell offered the most aesthetically skillful attempt we have to address them. Frustrated and impatient with increased "dissettlement and division," Cromwell dissolved Parliament impulsively in January 1655; as he observed then: "you might have had opportunity to have settled peace and quietness amongst all professing Godliness, and might have been instrumental, if not to have healed the breaches, yet to have kept the godly of all judgments from running upon another."[133] The godly nation was not to be healed or settled in "peace and quietness." There had been troubling rumors of plots involving the Levellers, republicans, royalists, and Fifth Monarchists; and within the month after Cromwell dissolved the first Protectorate Parliament, the ex-Leveller John Wildman was arrested, as were Harrison and other millenarian saints, including the recalcitrant Feake and Rogers, who remained imprisoned throughout much of 1655 (and beyond). Simpson continued his hostility towards the Protectorate, while royalist risings and republican plots, though they would go awry, were soon to trouble the regime as well, further reminders of actual and potential discontent.[134] The Quaker menace likewise troubled the Protectorate prompting Cromwell to issue a proclamation aimed at restraining "*Quakers, Ranters,* and others, who do daily reproach and disturb" the mainstream godly.[135] Neither Parliament nor its Protector could therefore heal "the breaches," as Cromwell and Nedham had hoped. Yet despite such inauspicious signs for "healing and settling," Marvell was able to envision a godly regime in which the Revolution's deeply conflicting strands – religious radicalism and political conservatism – might be creatively harnessed and, indeed, energized in the "sober spirit" of Cromwell.

PART II

Milton: radical Puritan politics, polemics, and poetry

CHAPTER SIX

Milton, Antichristian revolts, and the English Revolution

This book examines the religious politics of revolutionary literature during the turbulent decades of the mid-seventeenth century, when political tensions were fueled as Puritanism was fragmenting into different sects and movements. Thus this study has also considered the ways in which radical Puritan writers confronted more ambiguous forms of political and religious revolt as well as conservative reaction, and the ways they struggled with the Revolution's contradictions and limitations. The following chapter considers Milton's polemical responses to the political and religious ambiguities of the explosive Irish Rebellion (which broke out in October 1641) and to Presbyterian equivocation when the orthodox Puritan clergy wished to restore the king to power. No less alarming to Milton was the shifty behavior of a Stuart king engaged in treacherous negotiations with Irish Catholic rebels. Indeed, in 1649 we find Milton deeply troubled by various manifestations of equivocal political behavior and verbal ambiguity. He is struggling with the counter-revolution of the Presbyterians; and he is obsessed with the king's own equivocal behavior and language: the Irish Rebellion only made that perception more alarming. These forms of political and religious sedition were closely linked in Milton's eyes, and his creative polemical responses to them are part of the complex story of his engagement with the Revolution's crises. Later, in Chapter 7, where I turn more fully to *Paradise Lost*, I reconsider how the equivocal language and politics of revolt there are indebted to Milton's experiences engaging polemically with a diversity of revolts and seditions in the 1640s and 1650s, including Presbyterian and Irish ones.

THE AMBIGUOUS LANGUAGE AND FORMS OF REBELLION

The idea of rebellion in Milton's age, with its association of violent resistance to an established ruler or government, and with its implications of

usurpation, treason, and disobedience to orthodox ecclesiastical authorities, could fuel great rage and anxiety on opposing political sides – royalists who defended the king and abhorred the levelling tendencies of his
opponents, as well as parliamentarians who revolted against his authority. In a period when politics interacted with religion, the terms "rebel"
and "revolter" evoked fears of lawless anarchy, political subversion, and
religious radicalism, as well as Antichristian popery, a society of master-
less men, and "turning States upside downe, and bringing all to confusion."[1] No doubt Milton's contemporaries were deeply anxious about
political rebellion because it suggested that such fundamental principles
as social hierarchy and habits of deference were being violently
assaulted, and because it confirmed their fears of an irrational hatred of
authority. Using inflammatory rhetoric, Griffith Williams, a royalist
apologist of the 1640s, described the horror of rebellion this way:

> I am here in this Treatise to shew unto you a *Monster*, more hideous & monstrous
> then any of those that are described either by the *Greek* or *Latine* poets; and more
> noysome and destructive to humane kinde, then any of those that the hottest
> regions of *Africa* have ever bred, though this be now most frequently produced
> in these colder Clymates: The name of it is *Rebellion*, an ugly beast of *many*
> heads, of *loathsome* aspect . . . and . . . great vivacity; for the whole world could
> not subdue it to this very day.[2]

The reality of political and religious rebellion in this age of sedition and
civil war is even more terrifying than any fictional version that the most
venerable ancient poets could represent; Hydra-like, it keeps proliferating and reproducing with such energy that it has become a nearly inex-
pressible horror – "'tis *monstrum horrendum*," another commentator
anxiously observed to the fiery Puritan minister Stephen Marshall, and
"the ruine of *Religion*, Church and Common-wealth, of States, families,
and men."[3] Rebels were indeed represented – by writers of both royalist and parliamentarian persuasion – as monstrous and demonic: barbarous and bloody cannibals, a bastard brood, strange children and
accursed devils in the shape of men, hellhounds and Hydra-like monsters.[4]

   The revolutionary Milton could represent the horror of Antichristian
rebellion and its proliferating power by using images of the monstrous
and unnatural in his prose and poetry. In his early tracts he expressed
rage at the prelates throughout the ages, as well as under the recent
Laudian regime, by calling them "a continuall *Hydra* of mischiefe [to the
state] . . . the forge of discord and Rebellion" (*CPW* 1:603), breeders of
"that *Viper* of *Sedition*" which eats "through the entrals of . . . *Peace*" (614),

and (in the language of Spenserian epic) that "mighty sailewing'd monster that menaces to swallow up the Land" (857). His 1648 sonnet commemorating Fairfax's military victories characterized the monstrousness of royalist revolts which had broken out in the provinces, as well as the new Scottish and Presbyterian support for King Charles, in terms of the proliferating "new rebellions" of the second Civil War which "raise / Thir Hydra heads" (lines 6–7). And in *Paradise Lost* he associates the rebel Satan, his "revolted Rout" (10.534), and his offspring with the monstrous: Satan, after all, gives painful birth to Sin in the midst of his "bold conspiracy" (2.751) against the king of Heaven; the depiction of Sin's hideous progeny – including the "abhorr'd" hellhounds and "yelling Monsters" gnawing at her entrails (2.659, 790–802)[5] – owes something to these tumultuous times when writers regularly configured, in horrifying images of the monstrous, political rebellion, which continues to renew itself with great energy or vivacity. But for Milton monstrous rebellion could be equivocal and many-headed in the sense that it readily assumed many forms and operated through language and artifice, as well as in political action. Like the tyranny Milton describes in *An Apology against a Pamphlet*, rebellion itself was easily "growne an ambiguous monster," "strong and suttle," a monster capable of taking on new life and assuming new "shapes," especially when "guarded with superstition which has no small power to captivate the minds of men" (*CPW* 1:924). This ambiguity of rebellion was manifested not only in political and religious practices, but also in verbal and aesthetic ones. The "Artificer of fraud" in *Paradise Lost*, who can assume the posture of "saintly show," speaks "Ambiguous words and jealousies" as he, revolting in Heaven against the Father and Messiah, generates the first and greatest of all rebellions (4.121–22, 5.703). The nature of Satan's mythic political rebellion, we shall see later in Chapter 7, owes much to the ambiguous forms of rebellion and sedition that Milton confronted during the crises of the Revolution.

It is the conjunction of political and religious representation with linguistic and aesthetic issues that I wish to stress here as I explore from a sociohistorical perspective the ambiguous revolts against the state with which Milton engaged in his controversial writings, especially those produced before and during the Revolution of 1648–49. Yet in addressing this subject, I want to avoid oversimplifying Milton's varied polemical responses to rebellion and the language associated with it: Milton experienced and wrote about diverse and contradictory forms of political revolt in his age – republican, royalist, Presbyterian, and Irish forms.

Though a fierce supporter of the regicide and the republican revolution, he was also deeply anxious about Antichristian forms of revolt threatening the stability of the English Commonwealth and endangering the Revolution itself. Milton's godly republican engagement with the crisis of the Irish Rebellion, for example, is an unsettling episode still not adequately examined by scholars addressing interconnections between politics and religion in his works.[6] That frightening Antichristian rebellion and its connections with the king's equivocal politics, I suggest here and in the next chapter, contributed to his representation of the first great rebellion in *Paradise Lost*, including its depiction of Satan's ambiguous political discourses. No less significant was Milton's intense engagement with the equivocal politics and language of the influential Presbyterian clergy, who in this factious age had become "the most pragmatical Sidesmen of every popular tumult and Sedition" (*CPW* 3:241) as they attempted to thwart the Revolution's radical religious and political directions. Like Hobbes, he saw the Presbyterian ministers as among the greatest "seducers" who disturbed the state and incited the people with seditious preaching and artifice, though he analyzed their equivocal behavior in much different terms.[7]

The political language of rebellion during these decades, however, was far from stable, as Milton the polemicist came to realize during the religious and political crises of the 1640s. He was especially sensitive to the slippery, equivocal ways in which the political parties of his time could employ the language of rebellion and sedition in their discourse. We recall that startling moment in *Paradise Lost* when Satan, in the midst of his rebellion in Heaven, sharply accuses Abdiel, the lone faithful witness, of being "seditious" and speaking with a "tongue / Inspir'd with contradiction" (6.152, 154–55) for revolting against his authority: as we shall see in Chapter 7, Satan's accusation acquires greater resonance when we consider the aspersions used by orthodox Puritans and ecclesiastical authorities to revile nonconformists and religious radicals. Moreover, those lines in which Michael associates the usurping Nimrod explicitly with rebellion – "And from Rebellion shall derive his name, / Though of Rebellion others he accuse" (12.36–37) – assume a greater resonance when we recognize this reversibility of polemical language in Milton's age, especially how readily the inflammatory language of rebellion and sedition was exploited by both political sides during the upheavals of the 1640s and 1650s. This age of rebellion and overturning could stimulate alarming linguistic innovations and reversals, so that political language and names themselves became dangerously malleable and unstable: in the caustic words of one royalist observer, "these are *new times*, and many . . . things have *new names*; Loyalty is called Treason, and Treason Loyalty; Obedience Rebellion, and Rebellion Obedience."[8] The antimetabole of this observer's discourse conveys the shocking reversibility of political labels and their conventional meanings.

One of Milton's "particular Friends," the versatile Marchamont Nedham, registered this instability in his ballad-style *History of the English Rebellion*.[9] A fellow apologist for the regimes of the Interregnum with extensive experience writing for both sides, he commented on the ambiguity associated with the word "Rebel," the opprobrious name applied to both political parties, especially in an unstable age when the locus of authority itself continually keeps shifting: "Rebellion makes our nation bleed / . . . But yet it is not well agreed / Who must the Rebel be." "The Round-head first the Rebel was," Nedham adds, yet "The thriving Cause with high disdain, / . . . Throws Rebel in the face again / Of King and Cavalier."[10] A rebel could refer to a Puritan revolutionary like "the Diabolical Rebel Milton," as well as to dangerous and subversive autocrats, innovators, and usurpers such as Strafford, Laud, and the king and his popish supporters; or, as we shall see in the next section, it could refer to counter-revolutionary Puritans like the Presbyterian clergy who reversed their political allegiances in the later 1640s.[11] The paradoxical portrait of Satan as both raging tyrant and defiant political rebel, whose political vocabulary is unstable and contradictory (see Chapter 7), owes something to this tendency in Milton's age, on the part of revolutionaries and counter-revolutionaries alike, to appropriate and manipulate with appalling ease the inflammatory language of rebellion.

By the late 1640s, Milton found himself vehemently justifying political rebellion, while simultaneously scrutinizing and combating numerous other kinds taking shape both inside and outside the state: the alarming rebellion in Ireland against the authority of Protestant England and the fragile new Republic, the seditious practices and rhetoric of the English as well as Ulster Presbyterians, and the power of a Stuart king who would subvert Parliaments and cunningly enslave his people by putting his "Tyranny into an Art" (*Eikonoklastes, CPW* 3:344). These experiences with treacherous forms of rebellion reinforced Milton's sense that this political and religious phenomenon was indeed often equivocal and many-headed. Like Lilburne and Winstanley, he saw that its locations and forms could easily shift, especially in the case of the Presbyterian clergy, agents of Antichrist, who had once used their fiery pulpits and incendiary pamphlets to fuel godly resistance to the king. Milton linked all of these forms of subversion, with their many "monstrous shapes" (*PL* 1.479), and throughout his prose explored their aesthetic and verbal dimensions. He was a writer who gained considerable experience in analyzing and interpreting forms of rebellion, which he saw as both a political and a discursive monster threatening the state, and this sharpened his sense of *Realpolitik*. We may recall that he even served as a kind of anti-insurgency reporter for the Cromwellian government: in 1649 and 1650, the Rump Parliament ordered him to report on the rebellious Irish affairs, as well as to procure and peruse information about the dangerous Royalist insurrections in Kent and Essex.[12] Furthermore, in June 1650 he was ordered "dilligently to search for all writeings, letters or other papers" by William Prynne in his rooms at Lincoln's Inn; Milton had recently attacked the conservative Puritan in *The Tenure of Kings and Magistrates*, and Parliament was looking for further evidence of his "seditious writieings and practices against the Commonwealth."[13] Milton's polemical engagement with Presbyterian religious politics and allegiances (which Prynne supported) especially confirmed his sense of the more ambiguous forms and language of sedition endangering the state and the Revolution of 1648–49.

REVOLUTION AND COUNTER-REVOLUTION: RADICAL PURITAN
POLITICS IN MILTON'S *TENURE OF KINGS AND MAGISTRATES*

In his controversial writings Milton often associates ambiguous forms of rebellion with verbal and political equivocation – as he does in his heated engagement with the shifty political allegiances of the Presbyterian party, as well as the shifty political behavior of the king. This is true even in his boldest, most theoretical defense of revolution, *The Tenure of Kings and Magistrates*, first published on 13 February 1649 (the date of Thomason's copy) and mostly written during the period of the king's trial and when he was under sentence. Milton's work promotes the violent process of revolution which entails "the alteration of Lawes, [the] change of Goverment, [the] downfal of Princes with thir families," and the subversion of monarchy itself, while its author bluntly defends the state of liberty by employing the language of natural rights: no one "can be so stupid to deny that all men naturally were borne free" (*CPW* 3:192, 198). Milton's daring text, cited with approval by such republican writers as George Wither and the radical Independent minister John Goodwin,[14] was an attempt to justify in godly terms the traumatic revolution of the winter of 1648–49 in which the Rumpers violently assaulted the authority and iconicity of the Stuart monarchy. Writers like Milton and Goodwin, who tended to valorize active citizenship, characterized these "great actions, above the form of Law or Custom" (*CPW* 3:194) in heroic terms – "how unaccustomed the present Age is to bear the weight of such Heroique transactions," observed the latter writer – as they urged that "the people are the makers of Kings, and Kings their creatures" by appealing to theories of natural right and natural law.[15]

Nonetheless, Milton's vehement writing is aimed not only at idolatrous kings who prove themselves "such Rebels against God and oppressors of thir Country" (*CPW* 3:251) by assuming a kind of unaccountable prerogative.[16] He often writes in the spirit of the fiery Protestant John Knox, the original Presbyterian defender of regicide whose authority he skillfully employs against the shifting politics and language of the present-day clergy.[17] Once having vigorously promoted war against Charles – they were "no mean incendiaries of the Warr against him" (*CPW* 3:193), Milton observes – they have become monstrous in their habits of "prevaricating" (3:232) over the king, and imperil the precarious course of the Revolution. To be sure, much of *The Tenure* considers the right of free-born citizens to change their government and execute God's judgments by deposing or putting to death an unbridled tyrant or potentate who has abused his exorbitant will and who would turn upside down whole kingdoms; to bolster his case – and to demonstrate that as polemicist he can perform as skillfully as any Presbyterian propagandist – Milton draws upon and analyzes ample scriptural and classical references, as well as an impressive array of Protestant authorities and witnesses. But Milton's most passionate writing in *The Tenure*, including his most colorful and pungent polemical prose, is fueled by his responses to equivocal Presbyterian party politics in relation to the unprecedented events of the Revolution of 1648–49. And that keen perception of verbal and political equivocation would later contribute to the mythic depiction of ambiguous political revolt in *Paradise Lost*.

Although Milton had found religious Presbyterianism attractive during 1641–42, he had hated the Presbyterians since the Westminster Assembly had sharply denounced him in Parliament during the summer of 1644 as a heretic for writing his divorce tracts. Yet in the early days of the Civil War it would be a mistake to present the Presbyterians as deeply conservative or even neo-royalist; from the early 1640s until the parliamentarian victory over the royalists at Naseby (June 1645), Presbyterians and Independents had both promoted ecclesiastical reform and had engaged in an active prosecution of the war, a "common effort" that, as

Valerie Pearl observes, "contraverts a simplistic political division into radicals and conservatives."[18] Nevertheless, by 1646–47 the Presbyterian establishment was a conservative Puritan one reacting against radical developments and the violence caused by civil war, and attempting to check revolutionary forces that they themselves had helped to unleash. The Presbyterians feared popular sectarian revolution and enthusiasm, as well as radical politics, including those of the Levellers; as we saw in Chapter 1, the power of the Presbyterian establishment in London stimulated the polemical response of the fiery Lilburne, who was already responding, several years before Milton's *Tenure*, to the "turnings and windings" of their political allegiances and discourse.[19] Preferring a compulsory national church, the Presbyterians were particularly anxious about the sectarian menace and the spread of frightening heterodox opinions, including some of those to which the radical spiritual Milton would subscribe: in *The Tenure* Milton notices "all the Sects and Heresies they exclaim against" in their pulpits and pamphlets (*CPW* 3:196).[20] Recent historians have thus studied the vocal Presbyterians in relation to the forces of "counter-revolution" in the late 1640s.[21]

True, militant Presbyterians had promoted war against Charles I, their ministers employing aggressive apocalyptic rhetoric in their pulpits; yet they deeply distrusted the New Model Army, which had become politicized by 1647, and they had no wish to destroy the king or his whole system of government or to devest him of regal authority.[22] In the eyes of radical Puritan writers, the Presbyterian desire to negotiate with the king after waging war against him for seven years and their retreat from revolution – they recoiled from Pride's Purge, the king's trial and execution, and the new Republic – seemed dangerously equivocal (even though as late as December 1648 about three-fifths of MPs were prepared to keep trying for a constitutional and religious settlement with Charles).[23] Milton's biting rhetorical questions in *The Tenure* barely contain his fury as he reviews their convoluted history and exposes their contradictory politics in relation to the Revolution: "Have they not hunted and pursu'd him round about the Kingdom with sword and fire? Have they not formerly deny'd to Treat with him, and thir now recanting Ministers preach'd against him, as a reprobate incurable, an enemy to God and his Church markt for destruction, and therfore not to be treated with?" (*CPW* 3:231). Two years later Milton would recapitulate for an European audience his heated response to the inconstancy of the ministers and their party by referring to "the swelling revolt of the Presbyterians": they had revolted against the Revolution itself when "with strange ficklessness, if not actual treachery, they decreed that this deep-dyed foe, who was king in name alone, should, without giving any real satisfaction or guarantees, be . . . reinstated in the full dignity and power of office as though he had done great things for the state" (*A Defence*, *CPW* 4:510). The "judgement of Divines" at this critical juncture in history seemed to Milton "so various and inconstant to it self" (*CPW* 3:257) – in contrast to the poet's subsequent portrait of Abdiel, that faithful Protestant angel who, confronted in Heaven with dangerous political faction, inflammatory rhetoric, and faithless rebels, would not "change his constant mind" (*Paradise Lost* 5.902).

During the same year Milton published his *Tenure*, the radical spiritual writer, former Army chaplain, and Independent spokesman William Dell likewise attacked the Presbyterian clergy by calling attention to their politics of prevarication. In order to highlight this point, Dell's *City-Ministers unmasked* recalls, as does Milton's *Tenure*, their most famous blood-thirsty sermon, *Meroz Cursed* (1641) by Stephen Marshall, the foremost preacher of the Civil War. Preached more than sixty times, this militant apocalyptic text inspired by the Song of Deborah – the first of many incendiary sermons by Puritan divines – had exhorted the Long Parliament and the godly to fight the battles of the Lord against the mighty of the world, including ungodly kings: "you may soone perceive how grosly and odiously you have prevaricated in this matter, and how you have turned *backward* and *forward* for your advantage," Dell addresses the Presbyterians, "first preaching *Curse ye Meroz, because they went not forth to help the Lord against the mighty*, & after, *curse Israel, because they did goe forth to help the Lord against the mighty*."[24] Because of their prevaricating politics and allegiances, including their practice of shifting their consciences with the times, Dell represented the orthodox clergy as "glorious pretenders to conscience" who attempted to further "*Antichristian* designs"; Dell, Goodwin, and Milton were all alarmed by what they perceived as the Presbyterians' "most notorious prevarications."[25] In *The Tenure*, and then later in *A Defence*, Milton likewise recalls the famous theme of Marshall's incendiary parliamentarian sermon, as well as "almost . . . all the Sermons, prayers, and Fulminations that have bin utterd this sev'n yeares by those clov'n tongues of falshood and dissention": he stresses how the Presbyterian divines, in the spirit of militant Puritanism, had from their fiery pulpits exploited bloodthirsty Old Testament rhetoric (e.g. the language of Judges 5:23) as they tried "with exhortation to curse all those in the name of God that made not Warr against [the king], as bitterly as *Meroz* was to be curs'd, that went not out against a Canaanitish

King" (*CPW* 3:234–35).[26] Milton, moreover, concluded the first edition of *The Tenure* by taking the powerful curse of Meroz and turning this polemical weapon against the prevaricating divines themselves. His own ferocious rhetoric there, like that of a revolutionary preacher haranguing an assembly, recalls the fiery pulpit language they themselves had once exploited so effectively (and that Milton himself had vigorously employed in the apocalyptic ending to *Of Reformation*): "to vindicate his own glory and Religion, [God] will uncover thir hypocrisie to the op'n world; and visit upon thir own heads that *curse ye Meroz*, the very *Motto* of thir Pulpits, wherwith so frequently, not as *Meroz*, but more like Atheists they have blasphem'd the vengeance of God, and [traduc'd] the zeale of his people" (*CPW* 3:242).[27]

Indeed, opposed to the Rump's politics and claims to legality, the Presbyterian ministers were, at the end of the tumultuous decade, using their pulpits to conduct an aggressive campaign to prevent moves to bring Charles to justice, to protest against his death, and to discredit the infant Commonwealth.[28] Milton's more radical Puritan contemporaries were alarmed by the polemical ingenuity of the London preachers and polemicists. To further their counter-revolution, the Presbyterians appealed to the authority of the Solemn League and Covenant (1643) as a kind of loyalty oath obligating its adherents to uphold the reformed religion and preserve the king's person and authority; the regicide, in their view, was thus a horrid violation of the Covenant which urged "the discovery of all such as have been or shall be incendiaries, malignants or evil instruments, by hindering the reformation of religion, dividing the King from his people, or one of the kingdoms from another, or making any faction or parties amongst the people."[29] Radical Puritan writers, however, saw treacherous equivocation in Presbyterian appeals to the Covenant and their complaints about its breach by the Army and Parliament. Milton commented on the "ridling Covenant" "so cavillously . . . urg'd against us" by the Presbyterians (*CPW* 3:232, 307), while Goodwin called the Covenant "a sword wherewith they can strike both ways . . . a sword which they can turn every way"; meanwhile John Price, a leading figure in Goodwin's gathered church, observed that "it serves you at every turne . . . using it as you doe the holy Scriptures themselves" and "making it looke East and West, North and South, as your interest works with King, Parliament, or Army, or against them all."[30] Milton was no less alert to their equivocal uses of pulpit rhetoric: "an enemie to God and Saints, lad'n with all the innocent blood spilt in three Kingdoms," the king had become in recent Presbyterian discourse, "the

Lords anointed," "though nothing penitent or alter'd from his first principles" (*CPW* 3:197). Like Goodwin, who drew upon his revolutionary writings, Milton assails the Presbyterians for their seditious discourse in relation to the king whose authority and person they are so anxious to preserve:

Ministers of sedition, not of the Gospel, who while they saw it manifestly tend to civil Warr and blood shed, never ceasd exasperating the people against him; and now that they see it likely to breed new commotion, cease not to incite others against the people that have sav'd them from him, as if sedition were thir onely aime, whether against him or for him.[31] (*CPW* 3:236)

Milton highlights their shift in allegiances during the Civil War years in order to undermine their political legitimacy and their rhetoric of dissent issued from the pulpit, "the strong hold and fortress of thir sedition and rebellion" from which they continue to "stirr up tumult" (*CPW* 3:258, 242).[32] Throughout *The Tenure* and in subsequent political writings, Milton stresses the mercurial language and politics of the orthodox clergy: "restless for power" like the equivocal arch-rebel of *Paradise Lost*, they "never cease their seditious attacks against the present government as formerly against the king" (*A Defence, CPW* 4:335).[33]

The treacheries of sedition, then, are practiced not by "those Worthies" (*CPW* 3:192) Milton addresses – the purged Parliament and Military Council – who have been carrying out a godly republican revolution and establishing a new order (they "doe what they doe without precedent" (3:237), he observes); rather, dangerous sedition has been fomented by those "mutinous Ministers" (3:257) who have cried out against political revolution by warning that such a process will "subvert . . . the whole frame and fundamentall constitution of the Government of the Kingdome."[34] *The Tenure* portrays the purged Parliament and Military Council in valiant godly terms: Milton refers to "the glorious way wherin Justice and Victory hath set them" and reminds his readers that the Greeks and Romans would have considered the regicide nothing less than "a glorious and Heroic deed" (*CPW* 3:194, 212), as he identifies these institutions with the power of the people, while representing the malevolent Presbyterians as treacherously equivocal in their religious politics.[35] In this sense Milton resembled and yet differed crucially from Lilburne: while reacting vehemently to their prevaricating politics, the Leveller writer also vehemently resisted identifying the oligarchical regime of the new Republic and its senior Army officers with the will and sovereign power of the people – such an identification seemed fraught with disturbing contradictions (see Chapter 1). Like "free-born" John and other Levellers, the author of *The Tenure* passionately believes that "the power of Kings and Magistrates . . . was and is originally the peoples" (*CPW* 3:211).[36] But for Milton the unique political events of 1648–49 can be configured as a heroic story of "strenuous liberty" (*Samson Agonistes*, line 271) achieved by the Herculean "Worthies" in the Army and Parliament who have "swett and labour'd out" the "enter-prize" of republican revolution "amidst the throng and noises of Vulgar and irrational men" (*CPW* 3:192). And so, as he wholeheartedly supported the Purge and subsequent events which generated the infant Republic ("exemplary" and "matchless deeds" he calls them: *CPW* 3:237),[37] Milton the controversialist sidestepped the political ambiguities of identifying the authority of the Rump, despite its revolutionary origins, with the just and supreme power of the people and "a free Nation" (3:236, 237). Revolutionary writers like the Levellers and Winstanley would confront the Rump's ambiguous authority, including its dangerous isolation from the population, more directly and publicly; Milton at this moment chose to speak with its authority and back its political power, though privately he would soon voice reservations.[38]

While the republican Milton would not acknowledge this point in his political writings of 1649, the regime of this "reformed Common-wealth" (*CPW* 3:236) was less radical than the extraordinary circum-stances that brought it into being; political revolution, effected in this case by a military coup, was not followed by social revolution, nor was it necessarily driven by fervent republican ideology.[39] Moreover, most Rumpers were appalled by the outburst of radical religious enthusiasm that accompanied the political events of 1648–49. More radical than the regime he chose to support in early 1649, Milton also chose in his polem-ical writings published that year not to examine its contradictions and potential limitations; instead, his fiercest criticisms in *The Tenure* were aimed at exposing the ambiguous politics and verbal contradictions of the orthodox Puritan clergy in terms of their relation to the Civil War years and the most traumatic events of the Revolution.

In *The Tenure*, moreover, Milton gives seditious Presbyterian political behavior, language, and printed discourse during the 1640s a particularly alarming character by evoking the rich equivocations and ambiguous linguistic constructions that haunt *Macbeth*: "And be these juggling fiends no more believ'd, / That palter with us in a double sense; / That keep the word of promise to our ear, / And break it to our hope" (5.8.19–22).[40] At the beginning of his text, Milton alludes to this passage when he describes how the Presbyterian "Ministers of sedition," who once seemed like zealous promoters of revolution and war against the king, were recently willing to reinstate him and have therefore paltered "in a double sense" just like the "juggling fiends" in Shakespeare's tragedy:

after they have juggl'd and palter'd with the world, bandied and born armes against thir King, devested him, disannointed him, nay curs'd him all over in thir Pulpits and thir Pamphlets . . . beyond what is possible or honest to retreat from, not only turne revolters from those principles, which only could at first move them, but lay the staine of disloyaltie, and worse, on those proceedings, which are the necessary consequences of thir own former actions. (*CPW* 3:191)

Milton, moreover, echoes the language of apologetical Presbyterian discourse, while also alluding to Lady Macbeth's blood guilt and famous sleepwalking scene (and her own "staine of disloyaltie"). He conveys the guilt of the Presbyterians who have equivocated in their political behavior and language over the king and who have therefore proven themselves seditious in the most treacherous sense, since during the past seven years of civil war Charles Stuart, "that Man of Blood" (as he was called by radicals and Army leaders), had been responsible for "so great a deluge of innocent blood" of God's chosen people, "polluting with [his subjects'] slaughterd carcasses all the Land over" (*CPW* 3:197, 214; cf. 3:376); as Goodwin observed, the king was "the Supreme Actour . . . in the tragedie of bloud, which hath been lately acted upon the stage of this Nation."[41] Milton therefore aligns equivocal Presbyterian politics and language with the king's blood guilt. During the violent revolution of 1648–49, the Presbyterians were indeed anxious, as one of their apologies put it, to "wipe off that foul *blot* and scandalous *stain* that will (otherwise) inevitably fall upon *Religion*, by this most horrid *breach* of [their] *Covenant*, especially in relation to [their] King"; and they hoped that they might "wash [their] hands and clear [their] *innocencie* in the sight of God and the whole Christian world."[42] Yet like the guilt-ridden and inwardly diseased Lady Macbeth, the equivocal ministers, Milton suggests, will never clear their consciences nor clean their hands of their own horrid, "unnatural deeds" committed in this bloody age of civil war when they themselves have "unking'd the King" (*CPW* 3:230) and broken the Oaths of Allegiance and Supremacy: "the Presbyterians, who now so much condemn deposing, were the men themselves that deposd the King, and cannot with all thir shifting and relapsing, wash off the guiltiness from thir own hands. For they themselves, by these thir late doings have made it guiltiness, and turn'd thir own warrantable actions into Rebellion" (*CPW* 3:227).[43]

As Milton responds to "the fast and loos" discourse of the "prevari-cating Divines" (*CPW* 3:232), he therefore often focuses on aesthetic, verbal, and hermeneutic issues. Just before he launches into his attack on the juggling Presbyterians, he comments on the treacherous manipula-tion of political names, observing that "consequentlie neither doe bad men hate Tyrants, but have been alwayes readiest with the falsifi'd names of *Loyalty*, and *Obedience*, to colour over thir base compliances"; and several paragraphs later he highlights the equivocal politics of scriptural hermeneutics as he observes how the clergy "come with Scripture in thir mouthes, gloss'd and fitted for thir turnes with a double contradictory sense, transforming the sacred verity of God, to an Idol with two Faces, looking at once two several ways; and with the same quotations to charge others, which in the same case they made serve to justifie themselves" (*CPW* 3:190–91, 195–96).[44] Further highlighting their proclivity to her-meneutic and verbal ambiguities, Milton notes that these "doubling Divines . . . ready to calumniat" (*CPW* 3:198) operate politically "under such a latitude and shelter of ambiguous interpretation" and speak "with a ridling Covnant in thir mouths, seeming to sweare counter almost in the same breath Allegeance and no Allegeance" (*CPW* 3:232).[45] Indeed, Milton's emphasis on their verbal equivocation, as well as mental reservation, would probably have evoked the popular Protestant association of equivocation with the Jesuits: that was precisely the con-nection Marchamont Nedham himself made as he characterized the Presbyterians during the early years of the Republic.[46] The rebellious Presbyterians depicted in *The Tenure* consequently resemble not only the equivocal "juggling fiends" in *Macbeth*, who palter in a "double sense" and issue "fals prophecies" (*CPW* 3:236); they also possess the same mer-curial characteristics as the mutinous Satan, the original verbal and political equivocator, who speaks with "Ambiguous words" and "calum-nious Art" (*Paradise Lost* 5.703, 770–71; cf. *De Doctrina Christiana, CPW* 6:350), and whose political language is unstable and contradictory. The calumniating responses of the "doubling Divines" likewise anticipate those "answers" and interpretations of Milton's Satan in *Paradise Regained* which the polemical Jesus sharply challenges: the responses of the Presbyterians are also "dark / Ambiguous and with double sense deluding" (1.434–35).

Moreover, in *The Tenure* and subsequent tracts, Milton associates the maneuvering behavior of the Presbyterians with treacherous artifice. Like the poet of *Paradise Lost*, he aims to unmask such artificers and expose their calumnious art, much as his early polemical prose had sought to present "the Prelates . . . thus unvisarded" (*Animadversions, CPW* 1:668). He refers scornfully in *The Tenure* "to all the acted zeale that for these many yeares hath filld thir bellies" and to their "painted freedom" and "own art" (*CPW* 3:236, 257); likewise, in the Digression to his *History of Britain*, probably written soon after *The Tenure*, he assails the politics of the Presbyterian divines, commenting on "the affected zele of thir pulpits" (*CPW* 5:449) and suggesting that they exemplify, to use the poet's words in *Paradise Lost*, "close ambition varnisht o'er with zeal" (2.485).[47] Having "beene fiercest against thir Prince," the artful divines suddenly appear "in a new garbe of Allegiance," plead for the king, "pity him, extoll him, [and] protest against those that talk of bringing him to the tryal of Justice."[48] Milton depicts them and their apologists as guileful in their political actions, language, and "pretended counsel" (*CPW* 3:193, 195; cf. 258); indeed, the zealous Puritan pamphleteer Prynne, who by 1648 was defending the rights of the king and the state-controlled Presbyterian Church, is among the "new Apostate Scarcrowes, who under show of giving counsel, send out their barking monitories and *memento's*, empty of ought else but the spleene of a frustrated Faction" (*CPW* 3:194–95).[49] William Dell chose to associate the alarming political shifts of the orthodox clergy with a treacherous theatricalism identified with "the third disguise of Antichrist" (the papacy and the prelacy being the other two): "Antichrist having this policy, that when he is discovered in one guise, presently he goes off the stage, and puts on another, and being discovered in that, he withdraws again, and puts on another."[50] Harpy-like in their rapaciousness (*CPW* 3:252), Milton adds, they use their "clov'n tongues of falshood and dissention" and "a dissembl'd and seditious pity, fain'd of industry to begett new [political] discord" (*CPW* 3:235, 193) by acquitting an impenitent king (3:197).[51] Indeed, by referring here to the Presbyterians' verbal powers in terms of "cloven tongues," Milton ironically transforms the gift of Pentecost in Acts 2:3–4 – that gift of the Spirit "to speak with other tongues" – into a linguistic, Antichristian monster which has become serpentine, loathsome, and dissimulating.

One of *The Tenure*'s most striking passages concerning the counter-revolutionary clergy illustrates especially well the texture and sardonic wit of Milton's anticlerical writing during this period of political crisis and transition. After having cited from an earlier generation of "true Protestant Divines of *England*" – Marian exiles who had suffered "stormes and persecutions" (*CPW* 3:251) and written against ungodly rulers – Milton sums up the equivocal politics and ingenuity of the present generation of orthodox clergy by developing an elaborate military trope. At the end of *The Tenure* he describes them as "nimble motionists," London militiamen who easily shift ground with "cunning and dexterity" for their own political advantage-taking (as Dell likewise suggested in *City-Ministers unmasked*); they invoke Providence, as godly preachers and soldiers regularly did in the Civil War years, though in this case to justify equivocal means and covetous ends:

For Divines, if ye observe them, have thir postures, and thir motions no less expertly, and with no less variety then they that practice feats in the Artillery-ground. Sometimes they seem furiously to march on, and presently march counter; by and by they stand, and then retreat; or if need be can face about, or wheele in a whole body, with that cunning and dexterity as is almost unperceavable; to winde themselves by shifting ground into places of more advantage. And Providence onely must be the drumm, Providence the word of command, that calls them from above, but always to som larger Benefice, or acts them into such or such figures, and promotions. At thir turnes and doublings no men readier; to the right, or to the left; for it is thir turnes which they serve cheifly . . . that with them there is no certain hand right or left; but as thir own commodity thinks best to call it. (*CPW* 3:255)

This rich passage highlighting their "turnes and doublings" recalls in its pungent sarcasm Milton's earlier description of the prevaricating Presbyterians who, exploiting scriptural hermeneutics ambiguously, "come with Scripture in thir mouthes, gloss'd and fitted for thir turnes with a double contradictory sense." Like the equivocal mythic revolter in *Paradise Lost*, their cunning maneuvers and contradictory "postures" are at times "almost unperceavable." The military trope vividly captures the doubleness of their political behavior throughout the turbulent years of the Civil Wars as Milton characterizes these guileful, serpentine clergymen who "winde themselves" into different positions. In their hollow theatrical postures they recall the "meer artificiall *Adam*" of *Areopagitica* operating "in the motions" (*CPW* 2:527). Their former revolutionary zeal and militancy, just like their other various postures, were no less calculated. Having energetically prosecuted the war against the king by maximizing the fiery rhetoric of militant Puritanism in their sermons and polemics, these dexterous "Pulpit-firebrands" (*CPW* 3:243) had retreated from that position later in the decade, as if they were a disciplined regiment of soldiers "furiously" marching one way and then marching "counter."

REPRESENTING THE IRISH REVOLT: MILITANT PROTESTANTISM
AND GODLY REPUBLICAN POLEMIC

Milton's acute perception of political, verbal, and aesthetic ambiguities associated with sedition was sharpened not only by engaging with Presbyterian politics but by shattering Charles I's symbolic representation in *Eikonoklastes*, as he links the king with treacherous Antichristian forms of revolt, including its alarming Irish manifestation. There Milton exposes the disjunction between seductive image and dangerous reality, between the king's "fair spok'n words" and "his own farr differing deeds" (*CPW* 3:346–47);[52] under his mask of martyrdom and behind his "cunning words" (3:600), the guileful Stuart king of *Eikon Basilike* (1649), like the theatrical, self-enclosed Satan of *Paradise Lost*, was willful, revengeful, unrepentant, guilty of prevaricating, full of rage and malice, imperious and violent, and monstrous. In effect, the reversibility of polemical language itself operates in Milton's own discourse, as Charles comes to represent in *Eikonoklastes* the treacherous rebelliousness of all royalist powers. In *Eikon Basilike* the king himself had warned the Prince of Wales, in a moment of almost Blakean insight, that "*That the Devil of Rebellion doth most commonly turn himself into an Angel of Reformation*" (*CPW* 3:573). But Milton scornfully cites this passage to show that the angel of martyrdom there – the king alluringly dressed up as martyr in one of those "shrewd books, with dangerous Frontispices" (*CPW* 2:524) – is really a devil of rebellion in disguise, since this king has proved himself thoroughly "disobedient and rebellious to that Law by which he raign'd" (*CPW* 3:529). Indeed, Charles had represented rebellion as a monstrous thing, describing Parliament as a "*many headed hydra of Government*" and "*a monstrositie*," provoking Milton to throw that trope of rebellion back in the face of the rebel king, as he wonders in *Eikonoklastes*: "which be now the greater Monstrosities?" (*CPW* 3:455).[53] That fear of an Antichristian monstrosity threatening the Protestant state was particularly fueled by the suspicion that both Strafford, the deputy of Ireland, and his king were playing the dangerous game of seeking the support of Irish rebels "cunningly rais'd" in order "to reduce *England*" (*CPW* 3:369). Yet both the king and his book have managed to conceal the monstrous power of royalist subversion by fashioning its politics "into an Art" with "Stagework" and "Sorcery" that beguiles the unwary people (*CPW* 3:344, 530, 601).[54]

    Indeed, in Milton's mind, the duplicitous Charles, a Satanic contriver of "suttle and unpeaceable designes" (*CPW* 3:523) against Parliament, was thoroughly implicated in the most nightmarish of all Antichristian revolts – the Irish Rebellion – "which in words onely he detested, but under hand favour'd and promoted" (*CPW* 3:477). The crisis in Ireland epitomized for Milton the cunning exploitation of ambiguous words and behavior in relation to the politics of revolt. He would thus devote a whole section of *Eikonoklastes* to the question of a devious king and the Irish Rebellion (*CPW* 3:470–85), and he would make numerous passing references to that crisis in his other controversial works. Furthermore, in May 1649 he would publish the English Republic's chilling ideological manifesto that would serve to justify, in providential and apocalyptic terms, Cromwell's reconquest of a rebellious Ireland later that year.

If any political or religious crisis confirmed Milton's sense of monstrousness and devilishness interwoven with the politics of verbal and artful equivocation, it was the Irish revolt against England that broke out in October 1641 and the war against the Irish rebels that continued until 1649. We know that Milton had read the 1633 published version of Spenser's *A View of the Present State of Ireland* (in his Commonplace Book he notes its authority on "the wicked policies of divers deputies & governours in Ireland"), so that his polemical response to the Irish and their menacing popish threat during the 1640s can be partly placed in the context of that radical Protestant and imperialist tradition, since Spenser himself had urged the Protestant English to uproot Irish traditions and customs.[55] But Milton's ongoing responses to the Irish revolt and its subversive implications cannot be understood only in relation to his reading of Spenser's treatise. Erupting after over thirty years of peace under English and Protestant authority, the Irish Rebellion seemed unusually alarming to Milton and his Protestant contemporaries, who saw their world and its conflicts in fiercely eschatological terms.[56] In their eyes, this was no war of national liberation or resistance, but a monstrous Antichristian threat and a great Popish design that seemed more terrifying, subversive, and potentially uncontainable than any other form of rebellion that they had witnessed in their age. "Intending the utter extirpation of the reformed Religion," this ongoing revolt was "beyond all paralell of former ages," as one influential account addressed to the House of Commons put it; Bulstrode Whitelocke, whom Milton would praise in the *Second Defence*, agreed, adding that the present revolt "goes to the extirpation of our Nation" as well.[57]

With all its unsettling religious and political implications, the Irish revolt was, moreover, no isolated crisis: it was closely linked in Milton's mind with the prevaricating politics of the king and the Presbyterians.

Thus in the midst of attacking the Presbyterians' equivocating pulpit rhetoric in relation to Charles, Milton alludes to the frightening Irish revolt, noting that "whole massachers have been committed on [the king's] faithfull Subjects" and that the king attempted to buy off the Irish rebels by offering his provinces "to pawn or alienation" (*The Tenure, CPW* 3:197). And his attack on the popish Irish rebels would soon include a ferocious attack on the Scottish Presbyterian clergy of Belfast who, fearing the blasphemous practices of sectaries in England and the "lawlesse Anarchie" of a violent republican revolution, were manifesting the "worse guilt of rebellion" by supporting in their *Necessary Representation* (February 1649) and "thir seditious practises . . . those bloudy [Irish] Rebels and Papists in the South" (*CPW* 3:334, 325), the Catholic Confederates.[58] Ultimately Milton's engagement with the Irish revolt culminated in what may seem to us his most disturbing prose work – a text that challenges us to confront the depth, limits, and contradictions of his revolutionary political and religious toleration. Though less read now than his more famous revolutionary works, that polemical text would fuse political and aesthetic representation in its godly republican response to the Irish crisis.[59]

His first official piece of writing on behalf of the Republic, Milton's vituperative *Observations upon the Articles of Peace with the Irish Rebels* was written at the request of the Rump in response to a treaty of January 1649 between the king's lord lieutenant, James Butler, the Earl of Ormond, and the Confederate Catholics of Ireland, an agreement or "Articles of Peace" which posed a military threat to the new regime and which Milton, with caustic irony, refers to "as one of [the king's] last Masterpieces" made "with those inhuman Rebels and Papists of *Ireland*" (*CPW* 3:301).[60] On 28 March 1649 Milton was thus instructed by Parliament "to make some observations upon the Complicac[i]on of interest wch is now amongst the severall designers against the peace of the Comonwealth . . . that it be made ready to be printed wth the papers out of Ireland wch the House hath ordered to be printed."[61] In these "observations" – his grim republican polemic – Milton mounts an ideological argument that would justify, rather than challenge or question (as readers today no doubt wish he had done), Cromwell's vigorous suppression of Irish resistance following the purging of Parliament and the king's execution: namely, the New Model Army's infamous campaign in the late summer to crush "those bloudy Rebels" (*Observations, CPW* 3:301), destroy Antichrist, and reconquer Ireland, which remained unsubdued and largely under the control of the Catholic Confederates

or the royalist Protestants.[62] That campaign, executed with ruthless efficiency, would result in the dreadful providential victories at Drogheda
and Wexford in September and October, for that indeed is precisely how
Cromwell, the godly regime's instrument of divine retribution, envisioned them.[63]

In considering Milton's zealous republican text, it is important to
recall that the Irish Rebellion of 1641, whose blood guilt Cromwell eventually avenged, had greatly intensified, in the minds of fervent parliamentary sympathizers, anxieties about a satanic popish conspiracy
aimed at overthrowing godly Protestantism and the Puritan Parliament
of England and thereby subverting English liberties. Evoking irrational
fears of Antichristian treachery, the Irish revolt seemed like nothing less
than a "Monstrous Rebellion."[64] Thus Henry Parker, the parliamentary
pamphleteer and later secretary to Cromwell's army in Ireland, depicted
the revolt as a nightmarish and "infernall plot" linked with terrifying
popery.[65] Nothing "blew the Coals" of civil war, the moderate Puritan
Baxter would recall, more than "the terrible Massacre" and rebellion in
Ireland and the perceived threat that the Antichristian rebels would
imminently invade England. Generating a national mood of anxiety, the
rebellion and the "monstrous Cruelties" of the rebels "filled all *England*
with a Fear both of the *Irish*, and of the Papists at home."[66] Cromwell
himself expressed the view of the majority of his Protestant countrymen
when, in 1649, he called the horrid rebellion the "most barbarous massacre . . . that ever the sun beheld"; aiming his bloodthirsty tirade at the
Irish clergy, he issued a ferocious blast: "You are a part of Antichrist,
whose Kingdom the Scripture so expressly speaks should be laid in
blood; yea in the blood of the Saints."[67]

The alleged savagery of the revolt was often wildly exaggerated with
lurid tales of Irish atrocities and, fueled by anti-papist paranoia, reached
mythic proportions, including the large numbers of Protestants apparently killed; indeed, a quarter of the pamphlets collected by the London
bookseller George Thomason during November and December 1641
concerned the Irish Rebellion and fed the English Protestant craving for
sensational news of the crisis.[68] That craving had hardly died out by the
time of the Interregnum when a main threat to the fragile new English
Commonwealth was believed to emanate from Ireland and when an
army could finally be raised to suppress the uprising. In January 1650,
while Cromwell continued his military campaign in Ireland, Milton
himself was ordered by the Council of State to arrange "the speedy
printing" of Thomas Waring's *Brief Narration of . . . that Execrable Rebellion*

and Butcherie in Ireland (March 1650), a text "Published by special Authority" (like Milton's *Observations*) and full of grisly descriptions of the tortures and killings of innocent Protestants by the monstrous and diabolical Irish rebels whose "design" was "so divellish."[69] Though produced well after the outbreak of the Irish Rebellion, Milton's own godly republican writings, with their fluctuating and wildly exaggerated numbers of English Protestants murdered, contributed to these mythic accounts of the terrifying Antichristian revolt and therefore helped to sustain, justify, and shape the militant Protestant response under Cromwell. In *Eikonoklastes* Milton gives a figure of 154,000 slaughtered in Ulster alone in the "horrid massacher" and then suggests, in the 1650 edition, that the total sum murdered amounted to "in all likelyhood fowr times as great" (*CPW* 3:470); in his *Observations* he gives a figure of over 200,000 of the king's subjects "assassinated and cut in pieces by those *Irish* Barbarians" (*CPW* 3:308); and in *A Defence of the English People*, his figures change again as he addresses a wider European audience and suggests that no less than "some five hundred thousand English" were "slaughtered with every refinement of cruelty" (*CPW* 4:522–23).[70] Milton's polemical writings written on behalf of the Republic thus helped to perpetuate the legend of the 1641 massacre and rebellion – both in England and abroad – at a time when appearances were indeed often more potent than reality.

Besides horrifying English Protestants deeply imbued with the Foxean tradition,[71] the Irish revolt irreparably damaged Charles; militant Protestant writers responded to the crisis by highlighting his duplicitous religious politics in relation to the rebellion. Charles's captured correspondence, published by Parliament as *The King's Cabinet Opened* (1645) and well known to Milton, revealed his treacherous negotiations with the Irish rebels, as well as other foreign powers, and contributed decisively to the perception of his untrustworthiness: he was covering "acts of hostility . . . over with deeper and darker secrecy."[72] His earlier efforts to negotiate with the Confederate Catholics likewise fueled acute suspicions about his complicity in the Irish Rebellion; as Milton noted in *Eikonoklastes*, Charles had already spurned the advice of Parliament and made concessions to the Irish Catholics as early as 1628, and later had "ingag'd the Irish Papists in a Warr against the Scotch Protestants" (*CPW* 3:473).[73] During the 1640s the king was accused of secretly condoning the rebellion since, in Milton's words, "the King was ever friendly to the Irish Papists" whom he "call'd . . . good and Catholic Subjects" (*CPW* 3:473, 526; cf. 483) – a point about his equivocation stressed as well by such radical writers as John Cook and William Lilly, the latter of whom admired "the learned Milton" for his vigorous response to *Eikon Basilike*.[74] In her retrospective account of the Revolution, Lucy Hutchinson would also recall that "the cursed rebellion in Ireland" received countenance from a devious Charles and she stressed the king's "falsehood and favour of the Irish rebels, with whom he had . . . employ'd Ormond to treat and conclude a peace."[75] Indeed, in response to the inflammatory charge that the king himself had secretly fomented this monstrous revolt, *Eikon Basilike* included a chapter "Upon the Rebellion and Troubles in Ireland" which addressed the image of Charles as a savage ruler: "I might be represented . . . to the world the more inhuman and barbarous; like some Cyclopic monster, whom nothing will serve to eat and drink but the flesh and blood of [his] own subjects."[76] In the meantime, during the 1640s Charles was calling the English themselves "Rebels" (*CPW* 3:526), and London especially "he would often say . . . was the *Nursery* of the present Rebellion."[77] Like the shifty Presbyterians, the king could palter in a "double sense" – especially when it came to the Irish revolt – since he proved guilty of "incorporating with the murdrous Irish, formerly by himself declar'd against, for *wicked and detestable Rebells*" (*CPW* 3:580). Such royalist alignment with "an accursed race," for that is how Milton represented the rebellious Irish, seemed like "criminal madness" (*A Defence, CPW* 4:323). In the eyes of English Protestant writers, including Thomas Waring and more radical ones such as Milton and Cook, nothing symbolized the treacherous equivocations of an untrustworthy king more arrestingly than his involvement in the monstrous Irish revolt: "he and the Irish Rebels had but one aime, one and the same drift," Milton caustically observes, "and would have forthwith joyn'd in one body against us" (*CPW* 3:482).[78]

The Irish Rebellion and the war which followed – with their associations of royalist conspiracy, secret treachery, and political equivocation – haunted Milton's imagination from the time of his early revolutionary prose until the very eve of the Restoration, when he was working on *Paradise Lost* and when he published the second edition of *The Readie and Easie Way* (April 1660). In *An Apology*, where he observes that "rebellion rages in our Irish Province" (*CPW* 1:927), he gives his attack against his polemical adversary a particular intensity when he characterizes the language of the Remonstrant "and his accomplices" as "seditious and Butcherly Speech," a phrase meant explicitly to evoke the savagery of the Irish rebels and to suggest that the Protestant Milton has been verbally attacked with a similar viciousness, since "as the rebels have done in *Ireland* to the Protestants, they would do in *England* the same to them that would no Prelats" (*CPW* 1:896).[79] Within a few months the zealous Protestant writer would contribute not only sharp but saving words, but also, it seems, money to help relieve suffering Irish Protestants.[80] In his much later tract, produced as he was working on his epic about the ambiguous genesis of rebellion, Milton is still vividly recalling the king's "occasioning, if not complotting, as was after discoverd, the *Irish* massacre, his fomenting and arming the rebellion, his covert leaguing with the rebels against us" (*CPW* 7:410).

Milton's anxiety about papist and royalist rebellion breeding in Ireland was fueled especially by his fears of verbal equivocation, covert machinations, and ambiguous authorship. Charles I's famous and alleged assertion to Henry Ireton that "I shall play my game as well as I can," does not go unnoticed by Milton in the *Observations*: he wonders about "the rare game likely to ensue from such a cast of his Cards," as "these Articles of peace [made] with the [Irish] Rebells" (*CPW* 3:332). In Milton's mind, the horrid conspiracy of the Irish rebels – both Catholics as well as the Ulster Presbyterians – is linked to the king's "tyrannicall designes in *England*" (*CPW* 3:308), particularly the wily game and Satanic machinations he manifested in "his secret intercours with the cheif Rebels" with whom he demonstrated his own proclivity, like that of the English Presbyterians, to "equivocat or collogue" (*CPW* 3:480–81). Like the radical lawyer John Cook or Lilburne the Leveller, Milton sensed "that the King had a finger in the Irish Rebellion: for all his many solemn protestations to the contrary: and that at the very beginning."[81] This charge concerning the king's treacherous secrecy runs throughout the *Observations* and *Eikonoklastes* and recurs in *A Defence*.[82] Like the staunch godly republican Edmund Ludlow, Milton believed that Charles's political "treachery as well as blood-guiltyness" was evident from the time of the Irish massacre and rebellion which he seemed to countenance and favor.[83] Even when Charles was finally in custody, and Parliament's supporters "expected his repentance, [and] his remorse at last," he engaged in "contriving and fomenting new plots," including plans to encourage Irish rebels (*CPW* 3:332). So too the mythic arch-rebel of *Paradise Lost* shows no repentance or remorse as he continues to contrive new plots: he works his political schemes through calculated indirection (in the great consult of Book 2) as well as secrecy (as he begins his great rebellion in Heaven in Book 5). Indeed, Milton's sense that the most treacherous, darkest kind of political rebellion is one fomented "in secret" (*PL* 5.672; cf. 6.521–23) and with ambiguous words – since that is precisely how his poem presents its Satanic genesis – may well have been have been stimulated by his intense scrutiny and recollection, even as late as April 1660, of Charles's "covert leaguing" with Irish rebel leaders whom the king had called "good" subjects. Like the contradictory Presbyterians, the untrustworthy king was guilty of fomenting sedition in secret: their negotiations with Charles had "joyn'd them secretly with men sentenc'd so oft for Reprobats in thir own mouthes" (*CPW* 3:233).

In exploring the genesis of this monstrous rebellion – for as polemicist as well as mythmaking poet he was preoccupied with origins, causes, and beginnings – Milton links the political with the vocabulary of authorship. Like Satan, "the Author of all ill" in *Paradise Lost* (2.381; cf. 6.262) and the very first author and progenitor of Antichristian rebellion, King Charles turns out to be the perverse creator of the English Civil War, "the impenitent author of all our miseries" (*CPW* 3:328): he is the prime "*Author or Instigator* of that Rebellion" in Ireland (3:477; see also 3:472) which escalated divisions within England itself, making him "the first beginner of these civil Warrs" (*CPW* 3:451) and their "chief author" (7:419), as Milton continued to recall in *The Readie and Easie Way*.[84] Rather than sectarians or violent republicans, Charles himself has now become associated with that "first author and founder of rebellion," Lucifer, condemned in the orthodox and frequently reprinted *Homilie against Disobedience and Wilfull Rebellion*.[85]

In his republican polemics of 1649, Milton's vituperative portrait of the Irish rebels as demonic is itself a representation which blurs the boundary between the imagined and the political, conveying the exigencies of polemical propaganda, which attempted to link the royalist party and the Irish resistance with popery, Antichristian tyranny, savagery, and monstrous rebellion.[86] During the years of the Civil War and Interregnum, only a few radical writers – the republican Henry Marten, the Leveller William Walwyn, and the author of *Tyranipocrit* – resisted or challenged such a popular representation, suggesting (in the case of Marten) that the Irish rebels should be left alone to practice their popery and that Parliament should in any case make peace with them.[87] Godly republican writers like Milton and George Wither, however, were swept up in the apocalyptic fervor and indeed contributed actively to it. Their polemics and poetry helped to create a hostile representation of Irish rebelliousness during the Commonwealth and served to vindicate the thirst for vengeance and reconquest. Like Cromwell, they would have seen the harsh suppression of these agents of Antichrist in 1649 as "a marvellous great mercy" and "a righteous judgment of God": the blood guilt of 1641, after all, was finally being revenged.[88] As Milton would later cry out in response to another famous massacre of Protestants: "Avenge, O Lord, thy slaughter'd Saints." In his *British Appeals* (1651), the poet Wither not only emphasized the hundreds of thousands slaughtered in the Irish Rebellion, "the late Inhumane *Massacre*"; he also associated the Irish with the ten horns of the Beast of Revelation and suggested, like Milton and Thomas Waring, that the Antichristian Charles had "first contriv'd" the horrid massacre while "he did palliate, and look thereon / Without Compassion, when the *Deed* was done." In terms that Milton would concur with, Wither thus claimed that the revolt had been righteously avenged by Cromwell's godly military victories: "How swiftly he hath prosecuted there, / *Avengements* for the bloody *Massacre*, / Of our dear *Brethren*; and what fair hopes, *he* / Vouchsafes, that fully it aveng'd will be."[89] Reviewing the course of the Revolution and the Good Old Cause in 1659, Christopher Feake, the fiery Fifth Monarchist, would likewise recall the vengeance and justice done by Cromwell at Drogheda and Wexford, as would Milton in *A Defence*, where he justified to a European audience that the war in Ireland against the rebels there was executed "in full accordance with the will of God" and gave the brave leader Cromwell "many victories" during 1649–50.[90]

In the *Second Defence* Milton continued to admire Cromwell's severe response to the Irish revolt as among the "greatest events" of his career – an illustration of the ruthless efficiency with which he carried out the will of God.[91] Even in "An Horatian Ode upon Cromwel's Return from Ireland" (written about a year after Milton's *Observations* appeared), that most nuanced of political poets, Andrew Marvell, would reinforce the view that the republican military campaign to conquer the Irish rebels once and for all – a manifestation of Cromwell acting as "The force of angry Heavens flame" (line 26) – was indeed justified and confirmed by recent providential history. With grim irony, Marvell depicts the recently rebellious Irish praising the man whose New Model Army had just reconquered them with holy ruthlessness and terror, thereby reestablishing nominal English authority over much of Ireland:[92]

> And now the *Irish* are asham'd
> To see themselves in one Year tam'd:
> So much can one Man do,
> That does both act and know.
> They can affirm his Praises best,
> And have, though overcome, confest
> How good he is, how just,
> And fit for highest Trust.   (lines 73–80)[93]

Indeed, the savagery of Milton's own godly response to the Irish revolt could be linked to the holy revenge and terror envisioned later in his drama about an Old Testament saint who slaughters the heathens and thereby manifests the dreadful providences of God (see Chapter 9). But while helping to create such an ideologically charged representation during the unsettled years of the Commonwealth, Milton's perception of the demonic Irish rebels who, along with Charles, practice the treacherous politics of dissimulation, would also eventually contribute to a richer, more nuanced representation of ambiguous political rebellion in *Paradise Lost*. Nevertheless, we may never easily reconcile his militant, nationalistic Protestant responses to the Irish crisis to our sense of Milton as a towering author of courageous, often fierce intellectual independence, a fervent defender of religious freedom and civil liberty, a writer who dared (in *Comus*, *Areopagitica*, the *Second Defence*, and elsewhere) to challenge, test, or question political ideologies and regimes even when he praised them. His fierce polemical engagement in the politics of the Irish crisis reminds us that such unsettling inconsistencies are themselves part of his disturbing complexity as a godly revolutionary writer.

In Milton's case there were clearly limits to his sympathy for certain kinds of political revolts, and his polemical writings helped to shape social perceptions and promote republican ideology by representing the Irish rebels in terms of an alien Antichristian power and an irredeemable otherness. In his *Observations* he emphasizes their bloody treachery and fiendish malice, their blind rage and monstrous cruelty, "their endlesse treasons and revolts" against "all subjection" and "all true fealty and obedience to the Common-wealth of *England*" (*CPW* 3:303, 305). Their frightening otherness and dangerous sedition can manifest itself by means of verbal assault – "injurious words" and linguistic "virulence" – as in the case of the Belfast Presbyterians who, in their "seditious" work *A Necessary Representation*, "presume to op'n their mouths not *in the spirit of meeknesse*, as like dissemblers they pretend, but with as much devillish malice, impudence and falshood as any Irish Rebell could have utter'd"; thus denouncing the new regime they "dare send such defiance to the sovran Magistracy of *England*" (*CPW* 3:300, 321, 327, 333), much as the rebel angels of *Paradise Lost* hurl "defiance toward the Vault of Heav'n" (*PL* 1.669).[94] Indeed, when Milton describes the rebellion of the Irish and the late king in terms of an "utter alienating" of Ireland from the Protestant Commonwealth (*CPW* 3:305; cf. 3:307), we may note a resemblance to the rebel angels who become "alienate[s] from God" (*PL* 5.877) when they deny their own "true fealty and obedience." The fervency of

Abdiel's response to Satan's blasphemous discourse and political revolt carries an emotional charge similar to Milton's scorn against the Antichristian rebels and their Articles of Peace in his *Observations*. Much like Charles and Satan, the arch-rebel of *Paradise Lost*, the Irish "arch Rebels" – as Milton calls them – act with "obdurate wilfulnesse" (*CPW* 3:304) and steadfast hatred, though the Stuart king and Satan prove more subtle and secretive in their rebellious behavior and manipulation of political language.

Furthermore, in order to highlight the monstrousness of the Irish Rebellion – in all its political, religious, and aesthetic dimensions – and to situate its frightening power in a more cosmic historical perspective, Milton, in a visionary moment, not only links it with papist idolatry, but with its most terrifying shape and symbolic representation, that great and many-headed eschatological monster of Revelation 13:5–6. This was the Antichristian beast with which Milton, like the Fifth Monarchists during the Interregnum, had aligned Charles's own unaccountable powers and those of worldly monarchs in *The Tenure of Kings and Magistrates*: "for in the thirteenth of the *Revelation* wee read how the Dragon gave to the beast *his power, his seate, and great autority:* which beast so autoriz'd most expound to be the tyrannical powers and Kingdoms of the earth" (*CPW* 3:210). Believing in the *Observations* that there is "not a more immediate and killing Subverter of all true Religion then Antichrist" (*CPW* 3:309), the apocalyptic Milton depicts the northern rebels of Ireland – including "their Ringleader," the Earl of Ormond himself – as blasphemous papists "plung'd into Idolatrous and Ceremoniall Superstition, the very death of all true Religion; figur'd to us by the Scripture it selfe in the shape of that Beast, *full of the names of Blasphemy*" (*CPW* 3:316; cf. 3:320). This beast "whose names are not written in the book of life" possesses, as Revelation tells us, power over tongues as well as nations (Rev. 13:7–8): in the Irish crisis it had taken on a new and more menacing shape, becoming a political and linguistic monster with an unprecedented apocalyptic power.

CHAPTER SEVEN

Radical puritan politics and Satan's revolution in Paradise Lost

Decades of political upheaval and uncertainties, as well as spiritual trials in the wilderness of the world, taught radical Puritan saints hard lessons about Antichristian powers, particularly regarding their subtle uses of appearances and linguistic resourcefulness. Milton's friend, the radical spiritual writer Sir Henry Vane, wrote in 1656 that recent years had especially shown that "Antichristian Tyranny . . . will be alwayes apt to renew . . . afresh, under some new forme or refined appearances, *as by late years experience we have been taught*" (emphasis added).[1] Vane the political observer was struck by the plasticity of form that characterized Antichristian treachery and politics in his age. His phrase "refined appearances" suggests that, in its reappearance, such tyranny may indeed become even more nuanced and precise in its ability to simulate.

Radical religious writers therefore frequently warned the saints that Antichrist could take on diverse appearances or "so many cunning resemblances" (to borrow a phrase from *Areopagitica*: *CPW* 2:514), including contradictory and unforeseen ones. In *Antichrists Government Justly Detected* (1661), the Quaker leader Edward Burrough alerted the saints, "Encompass'd round with foes" (*PL* 5.876), to the formidable powers of Antichrist, observing that he may appear "in the World as a Zealous Church-Member, as a Saint, as a Promoter of Righteousness, and a Destroyer of the contrary." Burrough added that Antichrist was "so Deceivable" that "he hath not always dwelt in one kind of Form . . . but he hath dwelt in many . . . and removed out of one false Form into another, according to his Opportunity and Advantage." Indeed, the saints had to be especially vigilant because "*Antichrist* doth not generally deceive men in his works and appearance as he is in his own Proper Nature; but in his appearance and works transformed and changed into another likeness, even unto the likeness of Truth and Righteousness."[2] Thus during one dark year of the Restoration – 1670, the time of the new and severe Conventicle Act – Milton's Quaker student and friend,

Thomas Ellwood, was alarmed to discover persons of "deep dissimulation" sent among the sectaries to effect their ruin: "Proteous-like [the pliant dissemblers] change their shapes, and transform themselves from one religious appearance to another as occasion should require," even assuming "the counterfeit appearance[s]" of Quakers and Baptists.[3] In *Paradise Lost* the protean Satan can give that "likeness of Truth and Righteousness" an especially provocative political form: fashioning himself as political revolutionary and alluring legions of angels with "Ambiguous words" (5.703), he assumes the likeness of a defiant radical voicing the rousing language of freedom and spurning the politics of submission to Heaven's kingly power and rituals.

SATAN'S REVOLUTION: "CUNNING RESEMBLANCES"

The relation between the politics of Satan's revolt in *Paradise Lost* and Milton's religious politics in the Revolution and its immediate aftermath, however, is neither straightforward nor unidirectional. Unlike other commentators who have attempted to treat Milton's poem as an historical allegory, I see no need to align the mercurial Satan and the politics of his revolt exclusively or consistently with one political figure or group of Milton's age, whether that be with a duplicitous and impenitent Charles I, divisive Laudian prelates, Cromwell and his supposed political hypocrisy, ambitious Army leaders of the Revolution, a prevaricating Presbyterian clergy, or the Irish Catholic rebels of the 1640s.[4] Some of these historical persons and groups make more sense than others in terms of discerning the polemical meanings of Milton's radical Protestant poem. Nevertheless, *Paradise Lost* does not ask its readers to make literal equations between its mythic characters and major historical figures from the revolutionary years.[5] Rather, it constantly challenges its engaged readers by showing them how to discern the treacherous ambiguities and contradictions of political rhetoric and behavior, including their more revolutionary manifestations.[6] And in that sense the poem remains polemically alive in the adverse milieu of Restoration England, thereby encouraging its "fit audience . . . though few" – by which Milton very probably means dissenting readers – to remain especially vigilant about endangered spiritual and political liberties, without Milton having to burden the epic with extensive and overt references to recent political events. His imaginative portrayal of the rebel archangel indeed owes much to Milton's polemical representations of the seditious Presbyterian party, the treacherous Irish rebels as "the enemies of God

and mankind" (*CPW* 1:798), or even royalist rebels like Charles I and his "evil councillors" perceived by means of their plots and secret designs to subvert the state, its laws, and reformed Protestant religion; this can only be expected, since a significant part of Milton's career as controversialist was spent observing and engaging polemically with cunning, Antichristian agents threatening the Revolution and godly reformation. But the character and significance of Satan's revolt never need to be confined by any one of these historical identifications.

The protean Satan of Milton's poem voices various and contradictory kinds of political rhetoric as he incites revolt and creates divisions among the angels in Heaven. In this sense, if his shifty language and political behavior display the characteristics of any ambiguous political or religious group during the Revolution, it would most probably (though, again, not exclusively) be Milton's representation of the mercurial Presbyterian party, especially its "mutinous Ministers" and "disturbers of the civil affairs," who in "thir turnes" spoke political discourse and interpreted Scripture "with a double contradictory sense" as they treacherously generated their "swelling revolt" – just as Satan often speaks in a "double contradictory sense" and shows "the spleene of a frustrated Faction" (*CPW* 3:257, 240, 195; 4:510) as he inflames rebellion against the powers of Heaven. Milton compares the aggressive, cunning Presbyterians, agents of Antichrist, to "rav'nous Wolves" (*CPW* 3:241), as he does Satan, who surreptitiously violates Eden; so Milton in the revolutionary decades had on many occasions observed with alarm how "lewd Hirelings" (like Satan) had easily invaded God's "Church" (*PL* 4.183–87, 193), using cunning as well as "acted zeale" (*CPW* 3:236). If I often invoke Milton's polemical responses to the ambiguous discourse and religious politics of the Presbyterian party, it is not, however, to claim a simple identification between Satan's political behavior and theirs, but to provide a compelling and neglected context from Milton's controversial writings and the Puritan politics of the Revolution for the poem's representations of ambiguous, treacherous revolt.

What is disconcerting about Satan's political discourse is that he easily manipulates opposing kinds of political rhetoric, sometimes within the very same speech. His self-presentation and "potent tongue" (6.135) are especially compelling precisely because, capable of assuming new shapes and using different political discourses, he himself readily appropriates, in addition to aggressive martial rhetoric, the language and gestures of seventeenth-century revolutionary politics and resistance. Satan exploits verbal equivocation in the name of revolution against the law

and power of God. He of course does not present himself as a vengeful, manipulative tyrant with a "boundless and exorbitant" will and great
desire for power, as Milton characterizes the raging tyrant and Stuart
sower of discord in *The Tenure of Kings and Magistrates* (*CPW* 3:212, 239).
Rather, he presents himself to his legions as an active revolutionary, bold
political liberator, and "Patron of liberty" (4.958) and the public good,
whose hatred of submission, oppression, and idolatrous adoration of
God and the Messiah prompts him and them to conspire to free themselves from "servitude inglorious" in Heaven (9.141), as Satan provocatively calls it, and the "Bondage" (1.658) of their dismal Hell. "For who
can think Submission?" (1.661) he demands of his fellow citizens exiled
from Heaven; during the celestial war itself he is addressed as their
"Deliverer from new Lords" (6.451), as though his fearless leadership has
delivered his angels from new forms of oppression and ceremonial
worship. Indeed, his rhetoric of active political resistance against regal
tyranny at times resembles in startling ways the aggressive polemical
rhetoric of Milton's controversial writings or even the dramatic rhetoric
of a contentious, charismatic revolutionary hero like John Lilburne, who
continually cried out against new forms of oppression, injustice, and
enslaving laws, and who complained about cruel punishments imposed
upon him, while refusing to bend his knee as a gesture of deference
before arbitrary tribunals.

At one moment Satan may sound like an antimonarchical revolutionary or heretic who rejects the laws of God, but at another like a royalist
apologist or conservative Puritan like William Prynne. We need to be
alert to the mercurial qualities of Satan's political language. In a recent
stimulating study, "Milton's Republicanism and the Tyranny of
Heaven," Blair Worden has considered the ways in which Satan's language echoes the rousing discourse of republicanism; thus the poem,
Worden concludes, expresses Milton's sense that the language of republicanism, like that of political resistance, "has become unfitting."[7]
Satan's political language, however, is considerably more volatile than
Worden suggests, and this has important implications for how we construe the poem's political and polemical meanings – and how we read it
historically.

In Hell Satan speaks "bold words" as he assaults what he calls "the
Tyranny of Heav'n" (1.82, 124), scorning much like the fiercely antimonarchical Milton the very idea of assuming the idolatrous posture of an
obsequious, sycophantic courtier who must "bow and sue for grace /
With suppliant knee" and "deify" the "power" (1.111–12) of a king whose

reign he and his followers disdain. And in his speech that finally rallies the "Groveling" fallen angels (1.280), a defiant, sarcastic Satan asks: "in this abject posture have ye sworn / To adore the Conqueror?" (1.322–23). This forceful language does indeed seem alarmingly close to Milton's just weeks before the Restoration; flaunting his godly republican convictions and showing his own dauntless "courage never to submit or yield" (1.108) to the bondage of a regal power he scorned, Milton did not hesitate to spurn "the base necessitie of court flatteries and prostrations" and "the perpetual bowings and cringings of an abject people . . . deifying and adoring" a new Stuart king (*The Readie and Easie Way*, 2nd edn., *CPW* 7:428, 426), as many of his servile countrymen had done before the seductive image of the king projected in *Eikon Basilike*. An uncompromising Lilburne (as we saw in Chapter 1) had also responded contemptuously to the notion of paying knee tribute to magistrates, judges, or political representatives – especially those in the House of Lords – and his dramatic symbolic acts of defiance against powers he believed to be usurping his liberties landed him in prison or resulted in his exile. Moreover, Satan's hatred of "new Laws . . . impos'd; / New Laws from him who reigns" (5.679–80) may indeed remind us of Milton urging Cromwell to propose "fewer new laws" (*Second Defence*, *CPW* 4:678; cf. 7:459), or even Milton scorning "gibrish Lawes" (*The Tenure*, *CPW* 3:193), much as other Puritan radicals of his age were keen to reduce and simplify the ambiguous Norman laws of England.[8] Satan's depiction of God as a vengeful tyrant who acts with "impetuous rage" (1.175) and seeks idolatrous adoration, and whose "Regal State" is "upheld by old repute" and "custom" (1.639–40), seems remarkably close to Milton's hostile representation of King Charles as a raging absolutist monarch whose arbitrary power and authority are sustained by the tyranny "of Custom" and the idols of tradition (*The Tenure*, *CPW* 3:190; cf. 3:401) from which the English people must break free. At moments Satan's stirring language and gestures, as he "sdein[s] subjection" (4.50) in Heaven and Hell, evoke the radical ideology and politics produced during the Revolution and daringly promoted by Milton's own polemical writings.

Yet the poem's political discourse associated with Satan and his great rebellion is never so consistent or stable; indeed, the poem prompts its dissenting "fit" readers themselves to keep "strictest watch" (9.363), to borrow Adam's warning words to Eve, and observe carefully the ambiguous, slippery uses of political rhetoric, including the uses of provocative republican discourse itself. The urgency of such watchfulness was stressed as well by Milton's radical Puritan contemporaries, who sensed Antichristian powers constantly at work to seduce the saints. The "great work of a Saint," the Independent minister Peter Sterry told Parliament during the Commonwealth (as he warned them of "Rigid Presbytery"), was not only "to watch the Spirit of CHRIST," but "to watch the spirit of Antichrist, as that also shifts its forms."[9] "Do but never so little watch them," the Leveller William Walwyn warned his readers about artful politicians "in these warping times"; he considered them "Satan's chief agents" and begetters of all discord "made up of Contradictions. . . . In a word, observe them well, and you shall see Christ and Belial, God and Mammon in one and the same person."[10] Walwyn's warning captures essential qualities of Milton's Satan: his contradictions, unsettling to the reader of Milton's poem, are no less evident in his uses of political vocabulary and his ambiguous behavior. During his revolt in Heaven Satan lashes out against the seraph Abdiel for his "tongue / Inspir'd with contradiction" (6.154–55) because the single angel has dared to oppose the rebel legions with fierce godly zeal. But these words – "Inspir'd with contradiction" – could apply equally well to Satan's own inconsistent political discourses in *Paradise Lost*.

Milton the controversialist, after all, was acutely aware that the enemies of God could also "usurp and imitate [the] words" of God's "best servants," appropriating "to themselves those properties which belong onely to the good and righteous" (*CPW* 3:528). "A deep dissembler" might therefore easily counterfeit the discourse of religion (*CPW* 3:362), so that as the anonymous author of *Tyranipocrit* observed in 1649, the evasive white devil seeks to cloak Antichristian tyranny "with a simulated sanctity."[11] In *Eikonoklastes*, where Milton was particularly sensitive to the ways "Tyranny and fals Religion" may "twine and interweave one another," he recalled the account of one cruel Byzantine tyrant, Andronicus Comnenus, who "by continual study" of St. Paul's epistles "had so incorporated the phrase & stile of that transcendent Apostle into all his familiar Letters, that the imitation seem'd to vie with the Original" (*CPW* 3:509, 361). Might not then that most cunning of dissemblers, the original "Artificer of fraud" (*PL* 4.121), whose dissembling can sometimes go "unperceiv'd" (3.681) by his sharpest-sighted observers, likewise usurp and imitate the rousing discourse of militant republicanism, as well as the language and arguments of Milton's polemics, so that the imitation seems "to vie with the Original"? Indeed, Milton had closely watched the volatile Presbyterians during the 1640s as they had paltered "in a double contradictory sense" and turned "revolters" from their original principles, employing the inflammatory language of militant revolution and religious zeal – or "acted zeale," as Milton characterizes it (*CPW* 3:191, 236; cf. 5:443, 447, 449) – when such discourse suited their political interests. The sharp-sighted poet of *Paradise Lost* can unmask a cunning adversary who "under covert of hypocritical zeal insinuate[s] basest" (to quote from the Digression in the *History of Britain, CPW* 5:445), just as he and William Dell had unmasked the Presbyterians and their equivocal language as they engaged in the politics of counter-revolution. But as Milton's poem suggests, other readers and observers may find themselves misled by "cunning resemblances hardly to be discern'd" (*CPW* 2:514): "For neither Man nor Angel can discern / Hypocrisy, the only evil that walks / Invisible, except to God alone, / ... through Heav'n and Earth" (3.682–85).

At the same time, royalist apologists in Milton's age were anxious to highlight how easily godliness had become a cloak for political and religious rebellion during the revolutionary decades and their aftermath. Thus one Restoration commentator on the lives, speeches, and writings of the regicides (including Thomas Harrison, John Cook, and Hugh Peter) had observed that "the last Legacy they leave . . . is Rebellion, cloaking it under the Fair Pretence of Conscience and Religion."[12] Stimulated by violent radical insurrections in London during January 1661, Thomas Marriot was anxious about the uses of religion to further rebellious designs, and his aim was therefore to unmask the treachery underneath the cloak: "hath not our own time showed us beyond all Contradiction what hath crept in under *this Maske*, and what hath been introduced under *this cloke*?"[13] In a sense Milton's poem is concerned with the origins of such practice, since Satan "was the first / That practis'd falsehood under saintly show, / Deep malice to conceal" (4.121–23). But placed in its more immediate historical context – the Interregnum and Restoration – Milton's mythic poem also prompts its dissenting readers to reconsider the implications of royalist accusations that pretended reformation was nothing more than treacherous rebellion against the established church and state. By dramatizing the ambiguities and contradictions of Satan's rebellion against Heaven, it undermines the simple identification of such deep dissembling with truly radical political behavior and convictions.

As we saw in Chapter 1, for Leveller writers it was Cromwell – "the pretended false Saint Oliver"[14] – along with his fellow military Grandees, who most alarmingly possessed this notorious ability to simulate a godly discourse masking underneath conservative convictions,

Machiavellian designs, and ruthless ambition. Perhaps no piece of political polemic conveyed the image of the double-dealing Cromwell underneath a guise of pious principles more vividly than did *The Hunting of the Foxes. . . or the GRANDIE-DECEIVERS Unmasked*, whose Leveller authors wondered whether "there [was] ever a generation of men so Apostate . . . as these": "You shall scarce speak to *Cromwell* about any thing, but he will lay his hand on his breast, elevate his eyes, and call God to record, he will weep, howl and repent, even while he doth smite you under the first rib."[15] Lucy Hutchinson, whose plain-dealing republican husband was particularly intimate with the Levellers, was no less alarmed by what she and the godly Colonel perceived as Cromwell's dissembling designs, his cunning behavior and uses of "smooth insinuations" during the Revolution and Interregnum as he surrounded himself, in the manner of an oriental despot, with major-generals who were "like Bashaws."[16] This biting depiction of a dissimulating, Satanic Cromwell who has, under the guise of godliness, brutally usurped power does indeed possess the sinister qualities that may remind us of the cunning apostate of *Paradise Lost*, who uses "saintly show" to conceal "deep malice" and whose politics are driven by that malice which he instills into his associates "once upright / And faithful, now prov'd false" (6.270–71). Yet Milton himself never represented the ambiguities of Cromwell's character and religious politics in such Satanic and opportunistic terms; despite his godly republican ideals and his likely disappointment with the Protectorate, there is not a shred of evidence that Milton came to envision Cromwell himself as a "false dissembler" (3.681).[17] Rather, like the radical preacher William Dell (see Chapter 6), he tended to reserve such biting, satirically pointed language for those "doubling Divines" whose treacherous counter-revolutionary tendencies and "acted zeale" he repeatedly attempted to unmask in his political tracts, right up until the second edition of *The Readie and Easie Way* (*CPW* 3:198; cf. 7:451, 453–54).

The poet of *Paradise Lost* underscores that the malleable Satan can feign "so well" (3.639), and Raphael's narrative of Satan's political intrigues relates that, while promoting his revolution in Heaven among his legions, he was "Affecting all equality with God, / In imitation of that Mount whereon / *Messiah* was declar'd in sight of Heav'n" (5.763–65; cf. 2.511). Even Satan's language at the moment when he publicly declares revolution at first closely imitates God's (cf. 5.772 and 5.601). Such skillful feigning therefore might well include usurping contradictory political discourses and ideologies, both republican and royalist, radical and conservative. Indeed, just before his last guileful speech tempting

Eve – a rhetorical tour de force – Satan is compared to "some Orator renown'd / In *Athens* or free *Rome*." Here the theatrically artful tempter, with his own "show of Zeal," simulates the impressive rhetorical skills of a Demosthenes or a Pericles addressing a democratic Athens, or an orator and statesman from republican Rome (9.665–71) – for example, Cicero, one of the orators Milton modelled himself upon in his political tracts, especially the *Defences*.[18]

During the revolt in Heaven, we witness Satan's skill in appropriating words and properties that belong to the righteous and godly. Political and religious vocabulary are interwoven in his provocative discourse, a reminder that issues of political and religious liberty were closely interconnected in the English Revolution.[19] Satan's scorn towards the newly anointed Son imitates that of the militant, antimonarchical Puritan who hates court rituals and ceremony, and whose resistance to his king has been stiffened by godly zeal and his abhorrence of image-worshipping. Addressing a third of Heaven's angels, he depicts the Son himself, though explicitly exalted "by right of merit" (6.43; cf. 3.309), as a royal usurper who "hath to himself ingross't / All Power," and who will demand "Knee-tribute" and "prostration vile" "to his image now proclaim'd" (5.775–76, 782, 784); in pronouncing the Son "Anointed universal King" and "Head Supreme," the Father had observed that "All knees to thee shall bow, of them that bide / In Heaven, or Earth, or under Earth in Hell" (3.317, 319, 321–22; cf. 5.605–8). Later, in Hell, the fallen angels, sounding like Puritan separatists alarmed by Laudian ritualized worship, will complain about the ceremonialism of Heaven in terms of religious conformity as they balk at the thought that they, under "Strict Laws impos'd," might have "to celebrate [God's] Throne / With warbl'd Hymns, and to his Godhead sing / Forc't Halleluiahs"; this would indeed be "wearisome" – an "Eternity so spent in worship paid / To whom we hate" (2.241–43, 247–49).

Moreover, when Lucifer offers his assembled compatriots rebellious counsel by appealing to equality and freedom and by urging them, through his "better counsels," to "cast off this Yoke" – "Will ye submit your necks, and choose to bend / The supple knee?" (5.785–88) – his defiant political rhetoric seems for a moment close to that of a revolutionary pamphleteer like Richard Overton warning against oppressive government: calling his contemporaries "the men of the present age," Overton insisted that they "ought to be absolutely free from all kindes of exorbitancies . . . or *Arbitrary Power*," as he invoked the myth most closely associated with the radical ideology of the Revolution and urged English citizens to free themselves from "the *Norman* yoke of an *unlawfull Power*."[20] In *The Readie and Easie Way to Establish a Free Commonwealth* the godly republican Milton himself had, like his Satan, employed provocative rhetorical questions, as he sarcastically wondered how his countrymen could face the prospect of new kingship and expiring liberty: "Is it such an unspeakable joy to serve, such felicitie to wear a yoke? to clink our shackles lockt on by pretended law of subjection . . . ?" (*CPW* 7:448). There are striking moments, then, when Satan's political language and rhetorical formulations *simulate* the discourse of radical politics and zealous Puritan resistance. Indeed, Satan cunningly embeds explosive resistance language in his rhetorical questions and then, answering one of them, cleverly appeals to his compatriots as he raises the issue of their compliance with the political rituals of deference which, he suggests, they will naturally reject: "ye will not, if I trust / To know ye right, or if ye know yourselves / Natives and Sons of Heav'n possest before / By none" (5.788–91).

Satan's reckless claim that he and his newly assembled compatriots are "self-begot" and "self-rais'd / By [their] own quick'ning power" (5.860–61) – and therefore that he and his fellow rebels have no obligation to a higher power, a constraining authority, or a prior creator – can be seen as a provocative though distorted version of bold statements by English revolutionaries who asserted that they were free-born as well as self-governed, and that their daring political actions were not constrained by historical precedent. Milton himself had made this last point as he defended the valorous role of the Rump and the Army during the momentous and violent events of 1648–49.[21] Furthermore, English republican ideology had recently linked political liberty with military power: thus Marchamont Nedham's lively editorials in *Mercurius Politicus*, the government newsbook under the general oversight of Milton, had specifically argued (following Machiavelli and Aristotle's *Politics*) that a free republic was best sustained by a vigorous, active people in arms.[22] "Our puissance is our own" (5.864), Satan brashly asserts to Abdiel, and so it had been in the case of the new Commonwealth, whose regime had begun with the military coup d'etat of Pride's Purge and was sustained by a show of force, as were successive political regimes of the Interregnum. On the battlefield, moreover, the rebel archangel praises his comrades in arms for their "Vigor Divine" and love of liberty rather than sloth and servility (6.158, 164–70). The Republic's conquering of England, Ireland, and Scotland, as well as its humbling of the mightiest naval power in Europe (the Dutch), all within a period of four years, had heightened a sense of its glorious military achievement and prowess. However short and turbulent the Republic's life, the Commonwealth's military might was still being recalled by the godly republican Algernon Sidney in his Restoration *Court Maxims* (1664–65) as a particularly positive example of how recent commonwealths employ better than kings their power in war.[23] The rebel angels' appeals to military might – "since by strength / They measure all" (6.820–21; cf. 5.864–66) – as they reject God's new laws and edict and attempt to establish their own self-created political authority in the name of liberty could thus be seen as a kind of perversion of that recent republican equation of political liberty with military power.

But as Milton had observed in the apocalyptic climax to *Eikonoklastes*, those Antichristian powers and European monarchs who rebel against the King of Kings and derive their power from the eschatological Beast of Revelation (as in Rev. 17), shall be "doubtfull and ambiguous in all thir doings" (*CPW* 3:598–99), which included, as Milton learned during years of polemical engagement, their many subtle, equivocal uses of language, artifice, and dissimulation. The controversialist was acutely aware that "the artificialest peece of fineness" could be used "to perswade men into slavery" (*CPW* 3:392). As Milton wrote when he engaged polemically with the Remonstrant's verbal ambiguities, he is "purposely bent to delude the *Parliament* with equivocall Sophistry, scattering among his periods ambiguous words, whose interpretation he will afterwards dispence according to his pleasure" (*Animadversions*, *CPW* 1:694). This description of "equivocall Sophistry" could well apply to the politics of Satan's own "ambiguous words" and interpretations as he addresses his compatriots and defies the polity and laws of Heaven. As the republican Nedham observed, the interest of absolute monarchy, while "often disguised by *Sophisters* in *Policie*," could be "discoverd under the artificiall Covers of every *Form*, in the various Revolutions of Government."[24] In his intense concern to expose the treacheries of artful equivocation and palliation in a revolutionary age, Milton resembles writers like Lilburne and Winstanley, as well as the one writer on the Irish Rebellion whose work Milton was ordered by the Rump to see printed: "it is a custome amongst the Disciples of Sathan (no lesse frequent than subtile) never to act any thing of high concernment, and especially to put nothing in execution, without knowing first how to palliate . . . it."[25] Furthermore, however much the "Interests & tenets" of Hobbes and Milton may have run "counter to each other," Milton understood from his polemical experiences how the "end" of "ambiguous words," including those issuing from seditious pulpits in the 1640s and 1650s, could be "contention, and sedition, or contempt."[26] Ambiguous in all his doings, Satan is a master of verbal and political equivocation himself, as he usurps and manipulates the rhetoric and ideology of political resistance and skillfully impersonates the role of radical revolutionary. If, as John Toland suggested, "the chief design" of *Paradise Lost* is "to display the different Effects of Liberty and Tyranny," then Milton's poem dramatizes how malicious and tyrannical designs manifest themselves through artifice, as well as through subtle forms of verbal and political equivocation.[27]

Radical Puritan writers during the Revolution had become acutely sensitive to the shifting and contradictory forms of Antichristian power in their age, and in their own way the political behavior and language of the mythic Satan in *Paradise Lost* illustrate that awareness more compellingly than any other work of Milton's age. Lilburne, who vigorously opposed successive regimes during the 1640s and 1650s, was continually anxious about new guises of tyranny and was therefore determined in his polemical writings to expose "all Arbitrary Usurpation, whether REGALL or PARLIAMENTARY, or under what Vizor soever."[28] Furthermore, in its war against the saints, the Beast employed dissimulation so that he might seem to strive against Babylon while simultaneously working for the kingdom of Antichrist: during the Interregnum the Fifth Monarchist John Canne warned the saints that the Beast "make[s] war with one part of *Babylon* . . . pretending therein to be *without the great City*, . . . and yet at the same time to be *of it*, and *for it*, in making Leagues and Covenants, Offensive and Defensive, with others of the same Antichristian kingdome."[29] Working by cunning and indirection, Milton's Lucifer engages at first in his own form of "Pretending" (see 5.768) as he assembles his angels and yet begins to make "Leagues and Covenants" that lead to the creation of his own "Antichristian kingdome."

Milton recognized that political discourse could itself be precarious and malleable, that the rhetoric of liberty and reformation could be pretended, and that even the fiery language of revolution could be used and then abandoned by the same party.[30] He had observed the politicized Presbyterian clergy "erewhile" call Charles "a cursed Tyrant, an enemie to God and Saints," thereby revealing themselves to be "no mean incendiaries of the Warr against him," and then "on a suddain and in a new garbe of Allegiance," turn around and voice the rhetoric of counter-revolution by calling him "the Lords anointed" (*CPW* 3:197, 193; cf. *Second Defence, CPW* 4:640). Satan's unstable political rhetoric reveals similar fluctuations, equivocations, and contradictions. But in his case, the ambiguities are often registered within the very same speech. The instability of Satan's political discourse is made apparent to the reader early on in the poem, for example when the exiled archangel discusses the unhappy plight of the rebel legions fallen from Heaven after their civil war. As their leader, he begins by styling this new realm of Hell a free state from God's regal tyranny:

> Here at least
> We shall be free; th' Almighty hath not built
> Here for his envy, will not drive us hence:
> Here we may reign secure, and in my choice
> To reign is worth ambition though in Hell:
> Better to reign in Hell, than serve in Heav'n.   (1.258–63)

The political language of Hell's forceful rhetorician and revolutionary patron of liberty subtly shifts as he begins by proclaiming the freedom of his compatriots – "our faithful friends" (264) he calls them a few lines later – and then addresses the issue of reigning in their new realm. As Satan's pronouns switch from "we may reign secure" to "in my choice / To reign is worth ambition," the reader begins to sense a menacing instability in Satan's political discourse: here is a leader who modulates quickly from voicing the interest and common good of his subjects – the community of exiles at large concerned about their political security – to expressing the self-interest of kingly power and personal rule as he substitutes his own will for the will of the body politic.[31] The more we observe Satan's postures and his slippery political vocabulary, and the more we witness his cunning, the more we may recall Milton's responses to the alarming tactics and "postures" of the Presbyterian party, "nimble motionists" during the revolutionary years who, "with that cunning and dexterity *as is almost unperceavable*," were unusually adept at "shifting ground into places of more advantage" (*The Tenure, CPW* 3:255; emphasis added).[32] Such slippery political discourse, indeed, illustrates "the cunning drift of a factious and defeated Party" (*Eikonoklastes, CPW* 3:338) – both in Milton's polemical prose and his great poem.

Later in the poem, as Satan first fuels his revolt against the powers of Heaven, we hear more of his ambiguous words, which register contradictory political signals. The bold oration in Heaven in which he begins to sound most radical in his political rebelliousness – as he employs verbal artifice to urge his compatriots to cast off their new yoke – is also the speech which begins and ends by his valorizing their "magnific" and "Imperial Titles." Such titles, he insists to his legions from his newly created "Royal seat" (5.756), should not remain "merely titular" or symbolic; rather, titles "assert / [Their] being ordain'd to govern, not to serve" (5.774, 801–2). This is the political leader who, once in exile, appeals during the parliament in Hell to "the fixt Laws of Heav'n" which made him their leader, and then rouses his fallen legions, potentates, and princes to "return / To claim [their] just inheritance of old" (2.18, 37–38). In urging them to reclaim their titles and old "inheritance," as he will likewise do in his victory speech delivered upon returning to Hell (10.460–62), "thir great Potentate" (5.706) appropriates the kind of argument and authority – the idea that inherited titles of honor mean the very right to power – that a royalist apologist or Presbyterian spokesman might well appeal to; but Milton, the Levellers, and godly republicans like Edmund Ludlow and John Hutchinson all spurned the "seeking or delighting in emptie titles" in an age that was particularly conscious of such symbols of rank and status.[33]

Thus, when the contentious Lilburne attacked the House of Lords in the 1640s for usurping power, his Leveller defender Richard Overton scornfully designated members of the House "arrogaters of Titles of Honour" and produced a sharply worded tract arguing that hereditary or ancient titles had little to do with natural rights and freedoms. Milton agreed: referring his readers to Isaiah 26:13 and Tertullian, he observed in *The Tenure of Kings and Magistrates* that "the Titles of Sov'ran Lord, natural Lord, and the like, are either arrogancies, or flatteries, not admitted by Emperours and Kings of best note, and dislikt by the Church both of Jews . . . and ancient Christians."[34] Moreover, in the *Second Defence*, as he praised Cromwell's political and military achievements, he scorned "the popular favor of titles" which "seem so great in the opinion of the mob" (*CPW* 4:672).[35] In the last book of *Paradise Lost* the pursuit of titles and secular power by clerical authorities characterizes the darkest moments of human history and religious persecution; the grimmest passage in the poem's concluding historical narratives, one marking a long period of error and superstition after the age of the apostles, criticizes those who shall

> seek to avail themselves of names,
> Places and titles, and with these to join
> Secular power, though feigning still to act
> By spiritual.   (12.515–18)

After hearing the narrative of the aspiring rebel Nimrod, the first kingly oppressor in human history, and a type of Satan and Antichrist linked by Milton with Stuart monarchy,[36] Adam voices an instinctive republican response in which he too suspects the authority of titles in relation to human politics and monarchy: "Man over men / [God] made not Lord; such title to himself / Reserving" (12.69–71). The old Puritan martyr William Prynne, a fierce adversary of Lilburne and target of Milton's polemical criticism, took a different view of the controversial subject of high titles: during the period when the Presbyterians were urging negotiations with Charles I, this orthodox Puritan polemicist, who zealously defended the rights of kings and the Presbyterian Church, attempted to vindicate the House of Lords against the "Sectaries, Levellers and Lilburnists" by insisting that "*Titles* of Honour and Nobility (as *Kings, Princes, Dukes, Lords, &c.*) are as ancient almost, as the world itselfe" and honored "with special *privileges.*"[37] Satan's own insistence on the "special privileges" of the rebel angels' imperial titles, at the moment that he first vigorously promotes revolt against the Father and the Messiah, thus exposes the ambiguity of his incendiary rhetoric.

Moreover, the poet's reference to Satan's calumny, just before he launches into his first public speech of revolt, is itself revealing about his political inclinations: "with calumnious Art / Of counterfeited truth" he holds the "ears" of his legions (5.770–71). The issue of calumny had been addressed during the Interregnum by Nedham in the pages of *Mercurius Politicus*, where he had discussed the advantages of a free state: "know that *Calumniation* (which signifies a malicious slandering of men by whisperings, reports, or false Accusations) was never allowed or approved in this form of Government." Satan practices what Nedham would therefore call "the crooked way of *Calumniation,*" much like Milton's "doubling Divines," the Presbyterian faction, who were "ready to calumniat" (*The Tenure, CPW* 3:198) in their opposition to the religious politics of revolution in 1648–49, or the Laudian prelates who had earlier shown "the worst of [their] unreasonablenesse in calumny and false report" (*Reason of Church-Government, CPW* 1:788). The archangel's secretive collusion with Beelzebub and his "false" (5.809) accusations against the Father and the newly exalted Son, as his rhetoric instills his "malice into thousands" (6.270), are thus associated with calumny arising from "those emulations, jealousies, and suspitions, which usually abound with furie in men's mindes, when they see such persons seated so far above."[38]

Fueling Satan's "Ambiguous words and jealousies" (5.703), as he orchestrates rebellion against the divine polity, is a desire furthermore for power and a keen sense of competition and rivalry. In Satan's eyes the Son "hath to himself ingross't / All Power, and us eclipst under the name / Of King," and the archangel already "great in Power" and "preeminence" – for "high was his degree in Heav'n" – therefore becomes "fraught / With envy" (5.775–77, 660–61, 707, 661–62) he can barely control and that will impel his vengeful campaign against Adam and Eve (see 1.35). We of course witness the mighty power of the Son during the holy war in Heaven as he defeats the rebel angels in his visionary "Chariot of Paternal Deity" (6.750), a dramatic event of eschatological significance.[39] But in Satan's first speech to his assembled legions, the sense of power and enmity expressed are much closer to the Hobbesian vision of ruthless energy and "a perpetuall and restless desire of Power after power" – that "Competition of Riches, Honour, Command, or other power" described in *Leviathan* that "enclineth to Contention, Enmity, and War."[40] Instead of "Liberty alone," which Satan later defines in terms of "too mean pretense," what the rebel angels really aspire to or "affect" is "Honor, Dominion, Glory, and renown" (6.420–22), so that their fierce competition reveals their mixture of Hobbesian and Homeric values. Even when Satan lashes back at Abdiel for his dissenting behavior, the archangel distorts the godly seraph's motives, accusing him of being driven by competition for honor – "But well thou com'st / Before thy fellows, ambitious to win / From me some Plume, that thy success may show / Destruction to the rest" (6.159–62). Unbridled ambition, Nedham observed, was more characteristic of kingly power and a good recommendation for a free commonwealth in which "the People are the best *Keepers of Liberty*" precisely "because they are not ambitious; They never think of usurping over other mens rights."[41] Satan's "restless desire of Power after Power," as he attempts to equal God in power, suggests the vacuousness of his simulated radical republican discourse which he uses to fashion himself as a patron of political liberty. And it recalls Milton's ongoing engagement with those so "restless for power" during the unsettled Republic: the embittered Presbyterian faction, "disturbers of the civil affairs" who were "accustomed to incite riot and to hate peace," and therefore never ceasing "their seditious attacks against the present government" (*CPW* 3:240, 4:335), schismatics, and sectaries. As Michael's troubling prophecy foretells later in *Paradise Lost*, after Babylonian captivity, it will be "first among the Priests" – those who "should most / Endeavor Peace" – that "dissension springs" among the Israelites (12.353–55).

Milton's Satan is therefore hardly consistent in his political discourse – even within the same speech – and so at one moment he can use his "potent tongue" (6.135) to speak like a radical or militant Puritan who abhors the constraint of a political yoke and at another to speak like a royalist or a defender of Lords who would justify the ancient authority of magnific titles and powers. Like the prevaricating Presbyterians whose counter-revolutionary language Milton had exposed in *The Tenure*, Satan gives his own discourse of political rebellion "a double contradictory sense," to recall Milton's allusion there to the language of equivocation in *Macbeth* (see Chapter 6). And like the verbally duplicitous Charles of Milton's *Eikonoklastes*, "the *malitious Author*" of the rebellion in Ireland and "the first beginner" of the Civil Wars, Satan's authorship "of evil" (6.262) is expressed by means of his equivocal linguistic powers, since he too can "knit contradictions as close as words can lye together" as he employs "words which admitt of various sense" (*CPW* 3:472, 451, 372–73, 342).[42] Satan's potent but equivocal tongue resembles the cunning politician of Walwyn's *Fountain of Slaunder Discovered* (1649) and his "calumnious Art"; operating as one of "Satan's chief agents, by whom all discords and dissentions . . . are begot and nourished,"

the Politicians chief Agent is his tongue, wherewith in an evil sense, and to an evil end, he speaks to every man in his own language . . . by it he becomes all things to all men, that by all means he might deceive some.

In Walwyn's eyes, such verbally resourceful politicians who try to "hide their double dealing" were "Monsters."[43] Satan's potent tongue, which sows political discord in Heaven (followed by the horrid "discord" of war: 6.210, 897), recalls as well the serpentine Presbyterian clergy of *The Tenure*, who "stirr up tumult" and "begett new discord" against the state with their "clov'n tongues of falshood and dissention" as they plot and contrive "opportunities to trouble all again" "under such a latitude and shelter of ambiguous interpretation" (*CPW* 3:242, 193, 235, 232).[44] The ambiguity and monstrousness of political rebellion – Milton's poem (like his political prose) suggests – can indeed manifest itself in various discursive practices, including equivocal acts of speaking, writing, and interpreting.

Satan's initial incendiary oration, stirring up "tumults" (5.737) and "new discord" in Heaven itself, exploits "a latitude and shelter of ambiguous interpretation" as he further prepares his legions to engage in violent revolution. Here again a rhetorically skillful, charismatic Satan appropriates the defiant language of republicanism to persuade his compatriots, whose emotions he plays upon, that their ancient liberties (since the angels have been "Equally free") are endangered by the new monarchical rule of the Son. Such liberties, Satan provocatively urges, must be defended against an encroaching power and its binding "new Laws" and "new commands" (5.792, 679–80, 691):

> Who can in reason then or right assume
> Monarchy over us as live by right
> His equals, if in power and splendor less,
> In freedom equal? or can introduce
> Law and Edict on us, who without law
> Err not? much less for this to be our Lord,
> And look for adoration . . .   (5.794–800)

Placed in the context of the mid-seventeenth-century crisis, Satan's political discourse resonates deeply. The outbreak of the English Civil War was partly triggered by a need to protect parliamentary liberties against the highly unpopular regime of an arbitrary and inflexible king who stressed absolute obedience and wished to enhance royal authority.[45] Satan's bold rhetorical questions attempt to present the new rulership of the Son as an arbitrary, unjust imposition upon himself and his followers as he appeals to the notion of equal freedom and the preservation of their natural rights. To be sure, Satan's simulated radicalism in these lines is not as socially daring as that of some of Milton's most radical contemporaries (e.g. Winstanley or Coppe) who believed, unlike Cromwell, that the overthrow of kings prefigured the end of traditional social hierarchies. "Orders and Degrees / Jar not with liberty, but well consist," the archangel asserts (5.792–93), even as he voices his disdain for the newly appointed king and new laws. Yet as the ambiguities of his political oration suggest, Satan is not simply an aristocratic revolutionary crying out for freedom from the politics of regal adoration, while defending social distinction and rank. As soon as he scorns the idea of the Son as their new Lord and appeals to the authority of "Imperial Titles," his aristocratic disdain surfaces again, reminding us that he himself insists upon superior elevation and is speaking about endangered liberty from a throne on a mountaintop, a "place . . . so high above [his] Peers" (5.812).

Behind Satan's potent political rhetoric lies a distorted interpretation of the Son's advancement and rule "by right of merit" and the significance of his God-given power. Indeed, because the anointed Son's new "great Vice-gerent Reign" (5.609) is specifically based on merit rather than hereditary power (he becomes "heir" of all God's might by virtue of his being "worthiest" (6:177, 707–8, 888)), it strikingly revises the orthodox Stuart conception of kings as viceregents of God on earth and the Lord's anointed who expected to be adored, a vision underpinning their doctrine of royal absolutism which insisted they were accountable to none but God.[46] One recent historian commenting on the poem has observed that "in the civil war in heaven the rebel Milton had to be a royalist";[47] but the ambiguities and contradictions of Satan's political rhetoric, as well as Heaven's unorthodox version of kingly politics and advancement based on "Merit more than Birthright" (3.309) – since Milton's Son, after all, grows in power – suggest the inadequacy of this formulation. As we shall see later, divine politics and kingship cannot in any case simply be equated with temporal politics, power, and rituals.[48]

Satan's great rebellion and civil war, in fact, are ultimately instigated not by a need to effect more godly reformation and godly discipline in the kingdom – as was the case for most parliamentarian activists in the Civil War[49] – but by his prideful envy and "Deep malice" because he "thought himself impair'd" (5.665–66) in his heavenly status. Here is a warning to the poem's vigilant readers that Satan's forceful political language, when he publicly declares a revolution, cannot be taken at face value and that what lies behind it is "secret hatred," to use Hobbes's apt phrase, that turns Satan's obligation (in this case to God) into hateful "thraldome" (*Leviathan*, Part 1, chap. 11).[50] Beyond that, Milton is wary about entertaining "long-term causes" as he tells the story of the first great rebellion breaking out and disrupting the harmonious realm of Heaven, where "all seem'd well pleas'd" with the Almighty's words and recent decree (5.617).[51] By the early 1640s, just before civil war erupted, an authoritarian and aloof Stuart king, who expected political and religious conformity, had alienated a great majority of his subjects, weakening his hold on their affections, including subjects who had daily contact with him.[52] The situation in the courtly realm of Milton's Heaven at the beginning of that mythic first rebellion and civil war, however, is distinctly different, if we judge by Raphael's account. There most of God's subjects are engaging, to the delight of "th' all bounteous King" himself, in a great celestial celebration with "song and dance about the sacred Hill" and much feasting; and so they often do (see 6.92–95), but this time it is to mark the special occasion of the Son's exaltation (5.618–41). It is Lucifer by himself who begins a furtive, devious campaign to incite revolt, using Beelzebub as his instrument to assemble their legions under the pretence of preparing "Fit entertainment to receive our King / The great *Messiah*" (5.690–91).

As Satan begins to apply cunning words to foment rebellion, Milton's God, "whose sight discerns / Abstrusest thoughts," discourses with the

Son, who "with calm aspect" answers the Father by indicating that the biblical laughter of Psalm 2:4 is the appropriate divine response: "Mighty Father, thou thy foes / Justly hast in derision, and secure / Laugh'st at thir vain designs" (5.711–12, 733, 735–37). This scriptural passage of sacred scorn was a resonant one during the recent years of national upheaval. Thus the fear of verbal equivocation in relation to political and sectarian rebellion against earthly kings, and the urge to control its monstrous proliferation, prompted one high church commentator on its horrors to recall the scriptural passage by stressing that "hee that dwelleth in the Heavens *shall laugh it to scorne*; when with such *equivocation* men shall thinke to justifie their *rebellion*."[53] Rebellion initiated by verbal equivocation in Milton's Heaven likewise arouses sacred scorn. But in calling attention to the divine response to Satan's justification by means of equivocation, Milton's poem does not attempt, like a conservative apology, to remind readers of the dangers of resisting earthly kings. Not only does it begin to place the emerging plot of Satan and his rebel angels in divine perspective, since the Father himself is not particularly anxious but "smiling" as he addresses his Son about the "defense" of their holy "Sanctuary" and "high place" (5.718, 731–32); it also prompts its watchful readers to discern carefully how verbal equivocation can fire revolt and allure multitudes "with lies" (5.709).

This scriptural passage clearly had particular resonance for Milton, who translated Psalm 2 during the Interregnum (in August 1653) soon after English saints had bound earthly kings, "ambiguous in all thir doings," with chains: "the Kings of th'earth upstand / With power, and Princes in their Congregations / Lay deep their plots together through each Land / Against the Lord and his Messiah dear," but "he who in Heaven doth dwell / Shall laugh, the Lord shall scoff them" (lines 2–5, 8–9). In *Paradise Lost* it is the seditious "plots" of Satan and his powers, furthered by their ambiguous words, which recall rebellious earthly kings and "Princes in their Congregation." Indeed, Satan's provocative rhetoric, urging his legions "to cast off this Yoke" of the Lord and his Messiah, echoes not only the stirring radical discourse of the Revolution, but also the defiant language of earthly kings against the Lord and his anointed in Milton's version of Psalm 2: "Let us break off, say they, by strength of hand / Their bonds, and cast from us, no more to wear / Their twisted cords" (lines 6–8). Edmund Ludlow, the fierce godly regicide, would recall the very same verses in the mid-1660s, evidence that such scriptural passages continued to have great resonance for the embattled saints who refused to accept defeat quiescently:

But God will not be mocked. For though as David prophecied, Psal. 2.2, 3, The kings of the earth sett themselves, and the rulers take counsell together against the Lord, and against his annoynted, saying, Let us breake their bands assunder, and cast away their cordes from us, Yet saith the prophet, vers. 4, 5, 6, He that sits in the heavens shall laugh, the Lord shall have them in derission. Then shall he speake unto them in his wrath, and vexe them in his sore displeasure.[54]

In *Paradise Lost*, this scriptural recollection of earthly kings rebelling and the Lord scoffing at them complicates our response to Satan's cunning rhetoric, highlighting further the ambiguities of his simulated revolutionary discourse and preparing the poem's readers to distinguish God's rule and indignation from that of temporal powers.

The ambiguity of Satan's rebellion is dramatized no less through his protean political behavior and ideology as he engages in what Lilburne had called, in reference to treacherous Presbyterian behavior, "various double dealings, turnings and windings," while actually aiming, as the Presbyterian parliamentarians did in the late 1640s, "to drive on their own premeditated design of dominion and sovereignty" and "erect a government after their owne inventions."[55] Pursuing his "design of dominion and sovereignty," he is the subtle rebel always able to assume "some new forme or refined appearances," to use Henry Vane's words, as he simulates contradictory political roles. At one moment Lucifer himself played the most sycophantic courtier in Heaven, the very kind he himself seems to revile, as he, more than any other angel, "Once fawn'd, and cring'd, and serviley ador'd / Heav'n's awful Monarch . . . but in hope / To dispossess him" (4.959–61); and yet at another point, the angel Gabriel observes, after shrewdly exposing Satan's equivocation (4.917–23), he "wouldst *seem* / Patron of Liberty," who despises the politics and rituals of regal adoration as he scoffs at those in Heaven who "practis'd distances to cringe, not fight" (4.957–58, 945; emphasis added).[56] There is thus an unsettling incongruity generated by Satan's guileful ability to fashion himself in one political guise – by using the vehement language of radical revolution which captivates the minds of his legions – while he acts in another, like a royalist rebel creating through covert politics and verbal equivocation his own resistance movement and conspiracy in Heaven.[57] Satan acts, moreover, like the Presbyterians, who in their swelling revolt against the state had "made a secret alliance, which ill befitted their former words and acts" (*A Defence, CPW* 4:511).

Milton highlights the secrecy of Satan's operation at its early stages. His secretive collusion with Beelzebub, as Satan foments rebellion in Heaven, does indeed recall the treacherous behavior of that "deep dissembler" Gloucester in *Richard III*, whom Milton had discussed in *Eikonoklastes* in conjunction with the counterfeiting Byzantine tyrant Andronicus Comnenus mentioned above.[58] "More in this place / To utter is not safe" (5.682–83) he whispers to his confederate, thereby creating an ambience of dark intrigue as he slyly suggests that Heaven is a tyrannical realm where inciteful language would be regarded as treasonous. Furthermore, the genesis of Satan's revolt in secrecy and his subsequent war illustrate, to use Edward Burrough's words, that "the Kingdom of the Son of God hath been warred against . . . and the Lamb, and his Army and Followers have been opposed by open and secret Rebellion."[59] On an apocalyptic level, the poem itself dramatizes that the forces of Antichrist operate through secrecy as well as more open forms of rebellion; indeed, the rebel angels continue to resort to secrecy during their celestial war, as when "With silent circumspection unespi'd" they develop horrific engines of destruction and then "hide the fraud" of their "devilish Enginry" by means of their military formations while they prepare a new assault on God's armed saints (6.523, 552–55). The embattled saints, both in the poem as well as in Milton's England, must therefore continually be vigilant in order to combat both "open and secret Rebellion" against the kingdom of the Son of God.

As we began to see in Chapter 6, Satan's campaign of intrigue and "covert guile" (2.41), which begins "in secret" (5.672) as he feeds suspicions about the newly elevated Son, recalls as well Milton's repeated attacks on Charles I's "secret intercours" and "covert leaguing" with Antichristian Irish rebels and other foreign powers. "His fomenting and arming the rebellion" intensified parliamentary mistrust of the king, fueled the flames of civil war, and was a charge Milton stressed in *Eikonoklastes* and maintained until the second edition of *The Readie and Easie Way* (*CPW* 3:481, 7:410), when he was working on *Paradise Lost*. The devious king was himself discovered working "in close design, by fraud or guile" (1.646), to use Satan's words. As he defended the king's trial and execution to a European audience, Milton observed that he was involved in dark plots secretly stirred up against Parliament while he was pretending otherwise:

Though he had assured the Parliament by repeated promises, pronouncements, and sworn oaths that he had no hostile intentions towards the state, he was at that very time assembling drafts of papists in Ireland or sending secret emissaries to the king of Denmark to request arms, horses, and reinforcements expressly against Parliament, or attempting to hire at a price an army whether of Englishmen or Scots. (*A Defence, CPW* 4:522)

Such was the "deeper and darker secrecy" that had been discovered about the furtive king, after the battle of Naseby had yielded his captured correspondence and Parliament had published *The Kings Cabinet Opened*.[60] Moreover, even when he was in custody, "where wee expected his repentance, [and] his remorse at last," Milton stressed elsewhere, the intransigent king carried on his "contriving and fomenting new plots against us" (*CPW* 3:332), much like Satan in *Paradise Lost*; thus the apostate will never "repent or change, / Though chang'd in outward luster" (1.96–97), and continues, after suffering his major military defeat, to contrive his own "new plots." Similarly, Milton was alarmed at "the fast and loos" behavior of the "prevaricating Divines" who, after the king's defeat and during the crisis of 1648–49, had "been plotting and contriving new opportunities to trouble all again" (*The Tenure, CPW* 3:232; cf. 4:335) in the English Republic. Milton's polemical engagement with Presbyterian plotting against the state and with the treacherous politics of the Irish crisis had sharpened his sense of *Realpolitik*; he perceived more keenly than ever the genesis and nature of ambiguous forms of rebellion, including uses of secretive political discourse and behavior.

Indeed, as Satan erects "his Royal seat / High on a Hill" in "The Quarters of the North," in order to foment rebellion in the "ears" of his compatriots (5.756–57, 689, 771) and infuse them with his Antichristian malice, his calumnious rhetoric and actions recall the equivocal and defiant Ulster Presbyterian divines whom Milton had scorned in his *Observations* for their "devillish malice": those "accomplices . . . to the abhorred *Irish* Rebels," characterized by "their calumnies, their hatred," and their "defiance to the sovran Magistry of *England*," "imagin themselves to be marvellously high set and exalted in the chaire of *Belfast*" from where they "sow sedition in the Eares of all men. . . . at the very time when with thir lips they disclaim'd all sowing of sedition" (*CPW* 3:327, 300, 333, 322).[61] Even as he simulates the gestures and language of a Protestant revolutionary who would scorn the very idea of worshipping an image and adoring a new king, the aspiring Satan appears "exalted as a God" on "his gorgeous Throne" and becomes an "Idol of Majesty Divine" (6.99–103), and later, in exile, continues to be "adore[d] . . . on the Throne of Hell" by the idolatrous legions whom he "seduc'd" (4.89, 83), much like the tyrant-rebel of Milton's political prose who "must be ador'd like a Demigod, with a dissolute and haughtie court about him" (*The Readie and Easie Way, CPW* 7:425).[62] In his political role-playing, the mercurial Satan has therefore made himself into "an Idol with two Faces, looking at once two several ways" (*CPW* 3:195), to borrow words Milton uses in *The Tenure* to characterize the equivocal practices of the English Presbyterians. So it is, to use the words of Vane, that Satan in his "Counter-work to the . . . government of Christ" "puts himself into all formes" – including political ones, as *Paradise Lost* shows – "in order to make his opposition the more universal and formidable" and "gaine thereby Proselytes to himself in all ages."[63]

And yet even though Satan's scorn and incendiary public rhetoric may simulate that of a righteous revolutionary who despises court rituals and regal images, his dramatic rebellion, in the end, differs markedly from the violent revolution of 1648–49, which had abolished monarchy and (in Marvell's words) "cast the Kingdome old / Into another Mold," a period of acute civil tension when radical Puritans had also attempted to effect great changes in the structure of their society and government as they envisioned a new regime, a "Commonwealth and Free State," without king and Lords. In such an unprecedented age of civil war and upheaval, one participant in the Putney Debates observed, "The greatest powers in the kingdom [had] been shaken."[64] In *Paradise Lost*, Heaven is disturbed by Satan's rebellion and cataclysmic civil war lasting three days, its landscape is torn up in the midst of the "ruinous assault" and "horrid confusion" (6.216, 668), its faithful angels are humiliated and derided by the rebel host, and "the steadfast Empyrean" sphere is shaken "throughout" (6.833) as the mighty conflict assumes apocalyptic proportions. The great "tumult" (6.674) created by Satan and his rebel saints threatens to turn Heaven upside down as millions of angels fight on either side. Yet God's throne and power are never truly shaken as a result of "the fierce contention," despite the exiled archangel's boastful claim to the contrary (see 1.100–5; cf. 6.834).

His violent revolt in Heaven, indeed, turns out to be much closer to one of the kinds defined by Aristotle in *The Politics*, a text Milton cited often in his political tracts because he considered that author to be "one of the best interpreters of nature and morality" (*The Tenure, CPW* 3:204). Satan's revolution "is not in regard to the established constitution" or an attempt to change "to democracy from oligarchy"; rather he resembles the "promoters [of revolution who] desire the same form of government, for instance oligarchy or monarchy, but wish it to be in their own control."[65] The rebel archangel can at moments skillfully impersonate the stance, gestures, and language of radical revolutionaries and Puritan reformers, but he cannot genuinely conceive of casting the kingdom into another mold, including a republican one or any other kind of new, just, and accountable government. In that sense, he remains politically conservative in Milton's unorthodox Heaven where "Merit more than Birthright" and hereditary power is valued as the principal basis for authority and rule in accordance with Milton's convictions in *The Readie and Easie Way* and elsewhere.[66] Satan's right-wing revolution is not one which results in a decisive break – at least in terms of its model of government – with the past social order and political structures, such as republicans, regicides, and religious radicals in Milton's age had imagined and attempted to effect (even if sweeping legal, social, and religious changes did not always follow). Self-enclosed, the royalist or conservative rebel in Satan cannot imagine genuine historical change.

ABDIEL'S GODLY RESISTANCE: HEAVENLY KINGSHIP AND
EARTHLY POLITICS

Just as the mercurial Satan, skilled at counterfeit appearances and political discourses, partakes of the distinctive characteristics of seventeenth-century rebels (albeit in ways that conflate opposing political categories, as I have argued), so too the character of Abdiel captures the spirit of seventeenth-century resistance writing and its radical Protestant roots, while he stimulates debate in Heaven about the nature of its politics and laws. As John Goodwin warned in *Anti-Cavalierisme* (1642), his vehement defense of godly resistance, one of the royalists' designs is "to put *Lucifer* againe into heaven, I meane, to advance the tyrannicall Thrones of the Hierarchie to their former height, or higher."[67] But as that original Presbyterian reformer John Knox himself had asserted, in a text admired by Milton in *The Tenure*, the raging "Satan will not be expelled from the possession of his usurped kingdome without resistance";[68] and through his own "sharpe or vehement" polemic, Knox urged elsewhere that, despite the danger of being called "a sower of sedition," every servant of God should demonstrate godly duty by boldly resisting "to the uttermost of [his] power" the rage, tyranny, and blasphemous acts of a prince or king who rebels against God.[69] In his attempt "to resist that high hand of iniquity," to use Goodwin's words again, the righteous saint does "not feare to look the enemy in the face,"[70] unlike those countrymen in the midst of political upheavals who, to quote from Milton's *Tenure*, "begin to swerve, and almost shiver at the Majesty and grandeur of som noble deed . . . when the Common-wealth nigh perishes for want of deeds in substance, don with just and faithfull expedition" (*CPW* 3:194). Abdiel, however, "unmov'd, / Unshak'n, unseduc'd, unterrifi'd," will not "swerve from truth, or change his constant mind" (5.898–99, 902) in the midst of Heaven's political commotions. His own revolt against Satan's more ambiguous kind embodies the spirit of such radical writings, giving dramatic and elocutionary force to the notion that the godly witness rebels with greatest vehemence in perilous times, and maintains a fierce constancy of mind, when such political responses and acts of dissent may be judged "as out of season" and greeted by "hostile scorn" (5.850, 904) – as they were in the case of the unflinching Quakers in Interregnum and Restoration England or in the case of Colonel Hutchinson "too constant to be wrought upon to serve" new forms of state tyranny, including (in his view) Cromwell's.[71]

Abdiel reacts swiftly and with verbal sharpness to the ambiguous rhetorical power of Satan's "bold discourse": "O argument blasphemous, false and proud! / Words which no ear ever to hear in Heav'n / Expected" (5.803, 809–11). Satan, with his own "tongue blasphemous" (6.360), is like the Antichristian Beast of Revelation 13:5–6, with its "mouth speaking great things and blasphemies," including "blasphemy against God . . . and them that dwell in heaven";[72] and that apocalyptic Beast and his power Milton had associated in *The Tenure* with "the tyrannical powers and Kingdoms of the earth" (*CPW* 3:210). Satan's rebellion, as he speaks with "impious obloquy" condemning "the just Decree of God" (5.813–14), thus begins as a kind of linguistic monstrousness, though concealed by artifice and couched in ambiguity. Without any check, such as Abdiel's verbal resistance at this tense dramatic moment, it would renew itself, in the narrator's words, "without control" (5.803). The Satan whose bold rhetoric fuels division and stirs up his followers to rebellion against the laws and rule of the Father and Son, moreover, resembles the incendiary Presbyterian ministers of Milton's age, whose calumnious rhetoric and malicious zeal justifying "rebellion, treason, mutinies, [and] insurrections against the Parliament and Army," as well as the Republic, had provoked such sharp polemical responses from Milton and other radical contemporaries.[73] Lucy Hutchinson would remember well how at the very founding of the Commonwealth the treacherous and "angrie Presbiterians spitt fire out of their pulpitts and endeavour'd to blow up the people against the Parliament."[74] In response to the factious and bitter rhetoric of Presbyterian firebrands, one separatist contemporary observed that "God put enmity between Satan and Saints, but Satan puts enmity between Saints and Saints" – and so Satan indeed does in *Paradise Lost* as his "impious rage" (5.845) and blasphemous words, like the alarming pulpit rhetoric of the Presbyterian party, are calculated to heighten "divisions, differences, and distempers" among the "saints" in Milton's Heaven.[75]

As John Morrill has observed, the shock of revolution in England assaulted external religious and political structures so that "men were freed to think hitherto unthinkable thoughts."[76] In Milton's Heaven, where vigorous debate, theological questioning, and liberty of conscience are permitted and pursued, even between the Son and the Father (as their dramatic colloquy in Book 3 shows), the restless Satan is certainly free to think his own "unthinkable thoughts" and to voice them in "bold discourse" to his regent powers as he builds momentum for his revolt. But he also must be held accountable for them as Abdiel's sharp but saving words suggest: his responses question Satan's ambiguous interpretations by opening them up to the test of dialogue or, as Abdiel puts it, a "debate of Truth" (6.122), as well as a contest of arms. Abdiel's swift intervention is therefore crucial because it provides the occasion for the poem's readers, as well as the assembled angels listening to Satan's powerful and seductive rhetoric, to scrutinize critically his version of republican discourse and make discriminating choices: will those who have followed Satan and become his credulous audience continue to be allured with ambiguous words, which can simulate radical political discourse, as they perform his commands and obey his signals? Or will they fence their ears against his potent rhetoric? Satan's rebellious actions and language have begun to challenge the just nature of kingly politics, rituals, and laws in Heaven, depicting them as oppressive, as if God's laws were the same as enslaving monarchical ones which radical preachers and pamphleteers had been so keen to criticize and reform during the Interregnum. Abdiel's fiery responses therefore enable us to reconsider the nature of Heaven's laws and politics. They also give Satan and the rebel angels a crucial opportunity to reform their dangerous political course, which has thus far been shaped by ambiguous rhetoric: "Cease then this impious rage, / And tempt not these; but hast'n to appease / Th' incensed Father, and th' incensed Son, / While Pardon may be found in time besought" (5.845–48).

Most importantly, while Raphael has raised the tantalizing possibility that earth and Heaven may be more alike than Adam and Eve ever thought (5.574–76; cf. 7.160–61) – and indeed often measures "things in Heav'n by things on Earth" (6.893) – the angel's account of divine politics also invites the poem's readers to discriminate between these two realms. By means of Abdiel's dramatic intervention, Milton suggests that political "things in Heav'n" cannot simply be equated with the earthly forms, rituals, and decrees of kingly power and those who adore them. Infernal and earthly politics, the poem reveals, are more truly alike, as numerous recent commentators have noted.[77] In any case, it is one thing to rebel against an earthly monarch – as English saints had done in the revolution of 1648–49 – and another to resist "Heav'n's matchless King" (4.41). As the commonwealthsman in the *Court Maxims* of the godly republican Algernon Sidney put it, echoing Acts 5:29–30, "order requires . . . that we obey God rather than men"; and the sentiment had likewise been forcefully expressed – with specific reference to Protestant saints obeying God before earthly kings and magistrates – in the militant resistance treatise *Vindiciae contra Tyrannos* (1579), which Milton had approvingly cited in his *Defensio Secunda*.[78] Furthermore, the "service" demanded by the "matchless King" was by no means "hard," as Satan himself admits from his own experience, in his first highly revealing soliloquy. Thus, to use Milton's words elsewhere, the rituals of Heaven truly exemplify a "milde *Monarchy*" (*Of Reformation, CPW* 1:616) rather than the constraining power of religious conformity, which the devils complain about when exiled to Hell: "he deserv'd no such return / From me," Satan confesses, and "with his good / Upbraided none"; "What could be less than to afford him praise," Satan adds, "The easiest recompense, and pay him thanks, / How due!" (4.41–48). As Satan's own words reveal here, the politics of Milton's Heaven hardly possess what one commentator has recently called "a Tiberian character."[79] To be sure, Satan's public discourse suggests otherwise: but that discourse exploits rhetorical simulation and ambiguous words, plays upon its audience's emotions, and is fraught with contradictions.

Abdiel's vehement words therefore confront the potentially radical implications of Satan's explosive rhetoric, open up his ambiguous and audacious interpretations of divine politics and power to sharp debate and questioning, and remind the poem's godly readers that the courtly rituals and dynamics of Milton's Heaven operate differently from the rituals of earthly kingship and temporal politics familiar from Stuart theory and practice:[80]

> Canst thou with impious obloquy condemn
> The just Decree of God, pronounc't and sworn,
> That to his only Son by right endu'd
> With Regal Sceptre, every Soul in Heav'n
> Shall bend the knee, and in that honor due
> Confess him rightful King? (5.813–18)

Abdiel's trenchant responses begin to reveal the ways in which Satan's simulated revolutionary rhetoric has perverted "The just decree of God," and remind the poem's watchful readers that the divine polity, including its laws and its rituals, must be evaluated on its own terms – not the fallen terms of earthly kingship, power, and symbolism. The people of England, as Milton reminded one royalist sympathizer in April 1660, had been "put to warre with thir King for his misgovernment" (*CPW* 7:481) and for misusing his powers;[81] Abdiel therefore confronts directly Satan's provocative insinuations that divine misgovernment threatens freedom among equals in Heaven's polity, where binding laws are not needed. This, however, turns out to be more than just a passionate debate that invokes the discourse of political theory.

No less importantly, the godly witness Abdiel invokes the lessons of common political "experience" (as had Vane in his observations about Antichristian tyranny) to make his case against Satan's bold argument about God's constraining new laws and recent decree:

> Yet *by experience taught* we know how good,
> And of our good, and of our dignity
> How provident he is, how far from thought
> To make us less, bent rather to exalt
> Our happy state under one Head more near
> United.   (5.826–31; emphasis added)

Likewise Abdiel's reference to the "indulgent Laws" of God's polity (5.883) draws upon "experience" rather than merely a political theory of divine rule. Indeed, Satan's own experience under God's rule, as his first soliloquy reveals, was not altogether different. Abdiel's word "good" echoes Satan's soliloquy where the word is likewise applied to God and the politics of service in Heaven: Satan too had experienced that goodness, though as he confesses, "all his good prov'd ill in me" (4.48). Furthermore, the seraph's critical response to Satan's scornful interpretation of "the name / Of *Servitude*" (6.174–75) defines issues of service and rule by the worthy (see 6.174–82) in a way that recalls Raphael's discourse on the paradoxes of service in the divine polity (God requires "voluntary service" not "our necessitated" (5.529ff.) and so "freely we serve," the angel explains to Adam). Raphael's discourse thereby anticipates and confirms Abdiel's account of the nature of Heaven's laws and politics, better enabling the poem's fit readers – including watchful dissenting ones – to discern the contradictions in Satan's political actions and his cunning manipulations of revolutionary political vocabulary. There is, moreover, much irony in the fact that as soon as the godly seraph finishes responding sternly to Satan's ambiguous charges about servility, he brings to his knees (see 6.193–95) the mighty rebel angel who, like a revolutionary spurning the ritual gestures of social and political deference, had so scornfully refused to pay knee tribute to his almighty Lord and the newly anointed Son.

Abdiel's sharp engagement with Satan – ambiguous in all his words and doings as he revolts against God and the Messiah – may remind Milton's fit audience in the Restoration of what that godly republican Algernon Sidney pointedly observed in the mid-1660s: "The kings of the earth that for a long time have gathered together against the Lord and his anointed, have the same master still, Satan, and have not changed their design."[82] Moreover, while the poem encourages its readers to discriminate between the politics of earthly and heavenly kingship, it also, in eschatological terms, envisions a time when its newly appointed king, the Son, will no longer rule by means of a regal scepter. When the Almighty proclaims the Son and then offers a millennial vision of "New Heav'n and Earth, wherein the just shall dwell, / And after all thir tribulations long, / See golden days," he concludes by underscoring this point:

> Then thou thy regal Sceptre shalt lay by,
> For regal Sceptre then no more shall need,
> God shall be All in All. (3.335–37, 339–41)

The politics of divine kingship, then, are not by any means equivalent to their temporal counterpart, as Abdiel's vehement exchanges with Satan have enabled the poem's dissenting readers in particular to appreciate; in addition, Milton's daring Puritan epic invites its readers to envision a future time when the metaphor of kingship and its potent symbols will not only be reformed but ultimately abandoned.

REBELLION IN HEAVEN AND THE POLITICS OF SCRIPTURAL ALLUSION

Milton's propensity for giving particular political and religious resonance to this great archetypal revolt in Heaven also operates complexly at the level of scriptural allusion. Thus at the end of Book 5, in the tense exchange between Abdiel and Satan, Milton significantly evokes the rebellion of Korah, Dathan, Abiram, and 250 leaders from the Israelite assembly against Moses and Aaron in Numbers 16:

> Well thou didst advise,
> Yet not for thy advice or threats I fly
> These wicked Tents devoted, lest the wrath
> Impendent, raging into sudden flame
> Distinguish not: for soon expect to feel
> His Thunder on thy head, devouring fire.   (5.888–93)

The revolt of Korah and his confederates, concerning the unique political and priestly roles of Moses and Aaron, was ended after the rebels
were tested before the tabernacle and swallowed up in an earthquake,
while their 250 followers were consumed by divine fire. This Old
Testament story of willful rebellion against divine authority was an
unusually resonant one for Milton and his contemporaries. It was one of
the biblical subjects he included among his outlines for tragedies (see
CPW 8:555) and is an instance of ungodly rebellion, as opposed to justified rebellion against unjust magistrates, cited in *De Doctrina Christiana*
and used to illustrate the principle of "divine justice" and "anathema"
(*CPW* 6:385, 736, 800).[83] In his tracts, including *The Tenure*, Milton associates the equivocal political behavior of the Presbyterian party and royalist sympathizers explicitly with the rebellion of Korah, Dathan, and
Abiram (see *CPW* 3:196–97, 7:485); and so indeed had William Dell in
his *City-Ministers unmasked* (1649), a polemical text we examined in conjunction with *The Tenure* in Chapter 6.[84]

    This was in fact a scriptural story of warning about sinful rebellion
and its dreadful judgments from God appropriated by royalist sympathizers, Presbyterian ministers, Independent radicals, republicans,
Levellers, and apologists for the Protectorate alike for polemical and
political ends during the revolutionary decades and their aftermath.[85]
Thus during the revolution of 1648–49, as they vociferously protested to
the Army about Pride's Purge, the trial of the king, the transformation
of Parliament, and the danger of "Heresies against the Truth of God,"
the Presbyterian ministers of London underscored the dangerous political situation by recalling the "severe threatenings and exemplary judgements from God" awaiting those now holding power: "You know the sad
examples of *Corah, Dathan*, and *Abiram* in their mutinous Rebellion, and
Levelling designe against Magistracy and Ministry, in the Persons of
Moses and *Aaron*."[86] Writing in the same year from his much different
polemical perspective, Lilburne invoked the biblical story to assault what
he believed to be the treacherous usurpation of power by Cromwell and
his Grandees.[87] A few years later, however, an author apprehensive
about seditious sectaries threatening the stability of Cromwell's new

Protectorate was highlighting the "rebellious *Corah*, and his company" as one of the most "memorable admonitions . . . of heavy Judgements to all the factious firebrands, and mutinous murmurers of these times."[88]

The scriptural story of Korah and his rebellious followers continued to have considerable polemical force in the Restoration. Thus, anxious about recent insurrections in London – particularly the violent Fifth Monarchist rising in January 1661 – Thomas Marriot delivered a hardline Anglican sermon entitled *Rebellion Unmasked* (1661), which repeatedly invoked the story to warn against the dangers of ongoing rebellion against the state and church, magistrates and ministers, represented in this case by "Gods Vicegerent" Moses and the priestly Aaron. Marriot stressed the relation between the scriptural story of rebellion and the political and religious upheavals of the revolutionary decades: "now these persons lay a Rebellious design, they gather together *and rise up against Moses and Aaron*, their *Magistrates and Ministers*, as our late Rebells against the *King* their lawful Magistrate, and against the *Ministry* and *Rulers of the Church*." His sermon highlighted, as the story of Satan's revolt and inflammatory rhetoric in *Paradise Lost* does in its own way (though for much different purposes), how quickly a dangerous rebellious design can spread like a "contagion" – the alarming image Abdiel himself invokes (5.880) – if not checked. There was indeed no "greater plague" striking "at the very life and *Vitals of Church and State.* . . . *How suddenly will seeds of sedition and Rebellion spring up?* How soon will a few Rebells increase, and cover a whole Nation: *one Corah with a Rebellious design soon draws in two hundred and fifty into his Rebellious Conspiracy.*" Moreover, just as Milton's Satan is "fraught / With envy against the Son of God" (5.661–62) on the occasion of his exaltation, so Korah and his followers "*Envyed*" Moses and Aaron "for that state of Superiority wherein God had set them, and hence their *Rebellious design and practises.*"[89]

During the Interregnum, religious radical writers like Dell, John Goodwin, John Canne, and Milton, however, were already challenging and revising the orthodox Protestant interpretation of this fearful scriptural story of mutinous rebellion and levelling as they engaged polemically with Presbyterian and royalist uses of it. A leading Independent preacher who drew upon the "Authority and Power" of Milton's pen in *The Tenure* to buttress revolutionary arguments in favor of regicide, Goodwin derided the Presbyterian party for "how ridiculously they intitle the Scriptures to their Opinion" and noted that the eminent men in the rebellion of Korah more truly resembled "the rebellious Insurrections in, and about the Citie of late years, both *Priests*, and others."[90] William Dell developed the scriptural analogy even more sharply, using it as a polemical weapon against the prevaricating London Presbyterians who "turned *backward* and *forward* to [their] advantage" and showed contempt for the authority of a godly Parliament. Dell's polemical writing is close to the biting spirit of Milton's *Tenure* and the dramatic allusion in *Paradise Lost* highlighting the revolted multitudes of Satan's confederacy:

> thus like *Corah*, you have gathered your selves together against the Lord, in his chosen and sanctified ones. There were two hundred and fifty *Princes* in that Rebellion against God, and there are nine and fifty *Priests* in and about the City of *London* in this, besides the rest of the same confedracie all the kingdom over: *they* then, and *you* now, rebell against God himself in his chosen instruments; and therefore let all good people *depart from the Congregations of these wicked Priests*, as the *Israelites* were commanded to *depart from the tents of those wicked Princes*, lest they be consumed in their sins.[91]

Milton's allusion to this story of ungodly revolt at the end of Book 5 of *Paradise Lost* therefore places it in a fresh dramatic and imaginative context. In the midst of Satan's mythic revolt against God and "his chosen and sanctified" Messiah, Milton recalls the sins of the biblical revolt of Korah and his assembly of princes, so that the great political rebellion in his poem takes on, simultaneously, particular and universal resonance. There it has become a scriptural type, a specific allusion to Milton's own polemical circumstances, and a trope for the treachery of ambiguous seventeenth-century rebellions and mutinies.

Associating Satan's host with Korah, Dathan, Abiram and their fellow rebels, the fearless Abdiel addresses Satan and his legions congregated in the North by assuming the voice of Moses, who warns the congregation of Israelites to "Depart . . . from the tents of these wicked men, and touch nothing of theirs, lest ye be consumed in all their sins" (Numb. 16:26) and provoke the Lord's fiery wrath. The divine punishment of Korah and his faithless men – swallowed up into the pit of earth – is clearly a type of the punishment suffered by the rebel angels who are cast down with the wrath of God into "the bottomless pit" (6.866).[92] It recalls furthermore details of Milton's Interregnum translation of Psalm 2: earthly kings, as well as "Princes in their Congregations," who "Lay deep their plots" against the Lord and his Messiah and are therefore warned of Heaven's "fierce ire" which will "take fire like fuel sere" (lines 3–4, 11, 27). As Milton had also envisioned in the threatening apocalyptic climax to *Eikonoklastes*, those Antichristian powers "ambiguous in all thir doings" and "*joyning thir Armies with the Beast* . . . shall perish with him by the *King of Kings* against whom they have rebell'd" (*CPW* 3:598–99). By alluding in *Paradise Lost* to the famous biblical rebellion from the Book of Numbers, Milton underscores the eschatological and the historically particular implications of the great rebellion of Satan and his host against "the King of Kings": this is the original version of the ambiguous seditious behavior writers like Milton and Dell had, in their own tumultuous times, confronted first-hand among the Presbyterian party, their incendiary orthodox preachers, and earthly monarchs.

Indeed, during the period he was working on *Paradise Lost*, the polemical Milton alluded to the biblical story of Korah's rebellion in his attack on royalist pulpit rhetoric. Published just weeks before the Restoration, Milton's *Brief Notes Upon a Late Sermon* (April 10–15, 1660) suggested that the fanatical royalist chaplain Matthew Griffith, who would "*blow the Trumpet of Sedition* from [his] Pulpit against the present Government," "might with much more reason have added [his] own name" to those "examples of seditious men" (including Korah, Dathan, and Abiram) whom Griffith had recently cited in his highly inflammatory sermon, *The Fear of God and the King* (preached March 1660). There Griffith, who railed against Quakers, schismatics, and other sectaries for crying down the king and the church, had assumed the role of Moses in Numbers 16 counselling the Israelites to depart from the tents of wicked, seditious men.[93] In *Paradise Lost* Milton thus incorporates into his narrative the scriptural text that had become a *locus classicus* about rebellion against ministers and magistrates for his contemporaries, as he portrays the highly charged confrontation between Satan and Abdiel. But as Milton imaginatively recreates his polemical encounters with ambiguous forms of sedition and revolt, his sacred poem transforms the orthodox implications of that biblical story of sinful rebellion and its terrifying consequences, giving fresh and dramatic expression to the typical early modern warning concerning "how dreadfully the wrath of GOD is kindled and inflamed against all rebels."[94]

ABDIEL, SATAN, AND THE POLEMICS OF SEVENTEENTH-CENTURY DISSENT

The sharp verbal exchange between Abdiel and Satan is further couched in the specific and volatile language of mid-seventeenth-century dissent and sectarianism. It again powerfully dramatizes the ambiguity of seditious behavior and the names and labels associated with it during the revolutionary decades. As a promoter of political rebellion, Satan is, indeed, the only character in the poem to apply that inflammatory epithet – "seditious" – to another character, in this case the fiery single saint in Heaven who defends "the Cause / Of Truth" against "revolted multitudes" and thus "for the Testimony of Truth hast borne / Universal reproach" (6.31–34). Satan therefore anticipates Nimrod and other equivocal authorities in human history who would persecute the saints who fight the godly wars of truth on earth: as Michael says of Nimrod, "from Rebellion shall derive his name, / Though of Rebellion others he accuse" (12.36–37). In 1663 the anonymous radical author of *Mene Tekel* urged readers "to be wise . . . and be not frightened . . . by those Traitors and Rebels, who would make you believe that it is Treason and Rebellion, to call them to account for the *Treason* and *Rebellion* they are guilty of."[95] This is precisely what Milton dramatizes in *Paradise Lost* as the dissenting Abdiel becomes, in the midst of the heavenly turmoil, a "seditious Angel" whose "tongue / Inspir'd with contradiction durst oppose / A third part of the Gods, in Synod met" (6.152, 154–56).

In the early modern period, sedition was especially associated with factionalism and became a political crime punishable by the Court of Star Chamber. Even after the Court had been abolished in 1641 by the Long Parliament, the doctrine of sedition remained useful to political authorities; by then it had already taken on a secondary meaning – the sense of inciting by words or writings disaffection towards the state or constituted authority, including the church.[96] As Richard Overton reminded the House of Lords during the Civil War, the provocative language of sedition had been employed by Laudian authorities in the late 1630s ("this being . . . *Canterburies* old language, to any that discovered their oppressions and corruptions") in an effort to silence Lilburne and other separatists.[97] "The late Prelats," the Leveller Walwyn observed, had regularly reviled the "faithfull Puritan under pretence of herisie, schisme, faction, sedition, and the like" – much as the "faithful" Abdiel in Milton's poem is reviled by Satan's slanderous tongue and judged perverse by his synod of gods.[98] As Lilburne himself complained in 1653 in his *Just Defence* (for he was acutely sensitive to this issue: see Chapter 1), it was easy to be labelled "factious and seditious . . . for no other cause, but for standing for the truth."[99]

Yet "Aspersions," Lilburne wrote elsewhere, were "the known marks of corrupt States-men, and usually working no other effect, but the discredit of the Aspersers"; and in any case, reproachful "appellations" were often "names both contradictory in themselves, and altogether

groundlesse in relation to the men so reputed."[100] Stung by such
reproachful names and slanders, Walwyn believed that he too had fallen
on "evil tongues" and, in words that may remind us of the conflict in
Milton's Heaven, he observed how the orthodox clergy, who themselves
"blew the coales of dissention," are ready to label separatists "a dangerous and factious people . . . and then like the crafty Politician cry out
upon them as the causers of division."[101] Walwyn was thus acutely aware
that "generally the asperser is really guilty of what he unjusty brands
another withall."[102] Indeed, on a more apocalyptic note, John Canne
warned the saints during the Interregnum that in its warfare against
them the Beast would resort to "reproachfull names" "as Blasphemy, . . .
Faction, Treason, [and] Sedition."[103] Moreover, as George Wither and
other radical Puritan writers recalled during both the Interregnum and
Restoration, Christ and his apostles, the servants of God, "were charged
with *sedition* . . . when they declared GOD's Judgements."[104] By the
Restoration, "Dissent is Sedition" had become a powerful political
slogan.[105]

In the context of the poem's tense Restoration milieu, when religion
remained a profoundly divisive issue, Abdiel embodies, in a forceful and
imaginative way, the fierce nonconformist who has endured the highly
charged slander of sedition by the potent tongues of political or ecclesiastical authorities and who chooses to fight back – much as Lilburne or
Walwyn had once done when represented as seditious by state authorities or Presbyterian clergy who met (as Satan puts it) "in Synod." The
term "synod" itself links Satan and his compatriots, whom he elevates
above angels by calling "Gods," with more orthodox clerical powers of
Milton's day, notably the Presbyterian Assembly of Divines, who
attempted to determine and reinforce spiritual laws and matters of religion (including the suppression of heresies and blasphemies) by their
synods, part of their system of jurisdiction or "classic Hierarchy" (see
"On the New Forcers of Conscience," line 7) that Milton could write
about with such biting satire.[106] In the parliament of Hell the rhetorically skillful Beelzebub likewise addresses the fallen angels as "Synod of
Gods" after their rigged political debate, an address meant to flatter
them once he has proposed the "bold design" of Satan against human-
ity and they, easily swayed, have shown their "full assent" (2.391, 386,
388). Like the Levellers Overton and Lilburne, Milton scorned the idea
of a national synod and its association with a national church and theological hegemony, observing in *Eikonoklastes* that "Synods from the first
times of Reformation," are "liable to the greatest fraud and packing" so

that they offer "no solution, or redress of evil, but an increase rather" (*CPW* 3:535; cf. 492).[107] Referring to the other godly angels, those loyal "Saints" (6.47), Abdiel speaks scornfully and ironically to his adversary on the battlefield, throwing the language of sectarianism back in the face of the rebel Satan:

> but thou seest
> All are not of thy Train; there be who Faith
> Prefer, and Piety to God, though then
> To thee not visible, when I alone
> Seem'd in thy World erroneous to dissent
> From all: my Sect thou seest, now learn too late
> How few sometimes may know, when thousands err.   (6.142–48)

Abdiel's polemical words fuse the discourse of radical religion and non-conformity with the tense political events of Milton's Heaven – a dramatic reminder that the political upheavals of the 1640s and 1650s, as well as the fierce backlash after 1660 against dissidents, had been fueled by religious ferment and acute fears of radical godly dissent and sectarianism. In the poem's mythic Heaven, where rebellion leading to "horrid confusion" is not generated by the faithful Puritan dissenter, as it were, Milton is also prompting his fit godly readers to reconsider the relations between political rebellion, sectarianism, and civil confusion which inflammatory heresiographers like Thomas Edwards and other orthodox authorities had been so keen to link in previous decades.[108]

In his polemical prose and verse, Milton was as sensitive as Lilburne or Walwyn to the political and ecclesiastical uses of invidious names to silence "with one word" anyone holding unconventional beliefs.[109] In *The Reason of Church-Government*, where his vigorous defense of religious sects could hardly have pleased his (former) Presbyterian allies, he challenged the "fraudulent aspersion of a disgracefull name" (*CPW* 1:788). And later, in "On the New Forcers of Conscience," he sharply observed how "Men whose Life, Learning, Faith and pure intent / Would have been held in high esteem with *Paul*, / Must now be nam'd and printed Heretics" by "shallow" Edwards and other fiercely prescriptive heresiographers (lines 9–12): so, indeed, were all those named who chose to follow the leadings of the inward Spirit during the 1640s and 1650s, when the professional clergy and orthodox Puritans feared left-wing Arminianism, anti-Trinitarianism, and the rejection of external ordinances, as well as other manifestations of religious radicalism. In *Eikonoklastes*, Milton complained that in the age of Charles I "all

Protestant Churches, not Prelaticall, and what they piously reform'd"
had been tainted "with the slander of rebellion, sacrilege, and hypocrisie," and defamed and "spit at with all the odious names of Schism
and Sectarism"; moreover, Milton added, "valor, justice, constancy, pru-
dence united and imbodied to defend Religion and our Liberties, both
by word and deed against tyranny, is counted Schism and faction" –
much as the Protestant angel Abdiel, with his "constant mind" (5.902),
is counted "seditious" during the political crisis in Heaven wherein he
has chosen "to stand upright and stedfast in his cause" (*CPW* 3:347–48).
In the last days of the Good Old Cause Milton was lashing out against
the preacher Matthew Griffith and his "Prelatical partie" in their
"guilded temples" for reviling Protestant nonconformists and saints "by
those names" of "schismatics and sectarians," labels, Milton believed,
"more truly" befitting the accuser than the accused (*CPW* 7:486).

Like the verbally equivocal Satan of *Paradise Lost*, Griffith had distorted and rashly employed the inflammatory term "sedition" in his
sermon, *The Fear of God and the King. Brief Notes Upon a Late Sermon* is a
fiercely polemical Miltonic text concerned, among other things, with the
dangerous and calumnious uses of the language of sedition.[110] Griffith
was a preacher – "this Antifanatic" Milton calls him – who, in Milton's
words, operated "cunningly," "covertly and like the tempter."[111] He had
urged his audience to "*fear God and the King, and meddle not with them that be
seditious, or desirous of change*," a passage in which he diverged from the
Authorized Version of Proverbs 24:21 ("meddle not with them that are
given to change") by inserting (as if following the Geneva version here)
the provocative word "seditious" (*CPW* 7:469–70, 471). Thus in Milton's
view, Griffith, who had accused rebellious sectaries of a deceitfulness
which "is ever producing *new Monsters*,"[112] was himself one of those
ambiguous ministers of sedition in Milton's factious age "who to thir
credulous audience dare thus jugle with Scripture" (*CPW* 7:477), just as
the Presbyterians had "juggl'd and palter'd with the world" in the late
1640s as they "gloss'd [Scripture] for their turns with a double contradictory sense" (3:191, 195). In the final days of the Commonwealth, he
was "preaching open sedition, while [he] would *seem* to preach against
it" (*CPW* 7:485; emphasis added). And so in his own way does Milton's
Satan, thus making the imagined scene in Heaven particularly pointed
in the context of the 1660s. As the ambiguous arch-rebel reviles the
godly witness for acting as a disloyal and seditious sectary because he has
demonstrated unusual "constancy of mind" and "stedfastnesse of faith"

(so Lucy Hutchinson described another unshaken servant of God in the Restoration), Milton's poem poignantly dramatizes yet again how "th'unjust tribunals," to use language from *Samson Agonistes*, may indeed continue "under change of times" (line 695).[113]

Paradise Lost, then, continues to challenge commentators who wish to decode its polemical meanings. Its religious politics remain extremely resonant; yet the poem also resists contextual readings that insist on simple historical identifications or reflections (e.g. that Satan is a dramatic study in Cromwellian hypocrisy, that he represents the egocentric revolutionaries of Milton's time, or that he embodies the ways the Good Old Cause had gone wrong, and so on). Still, despite its pointed evocations of the cold political climate of the Restoration, in which Milton's defiant voice remains "unchang'd / To hoarse or mute" (7.24–25), some commentators have also seen his great spiritual poem as ultimately disengaged from the polemical world of radical Puritan politics, its poet seeking solace in a personal, quietistic faith: it strives to represent "eternal verities" during years when Milton "withdraws from politics into faith," Worden concludes; its "universal spiritual values" are untainted by "partisan ideologies," asserts another scholar.[114] No doubt Marvell's calculated observation of 1673 in *The Rehearsal Transpros'd* (most probably made to protect his friend) has helped to reinforce this view: having lived "in a tumultuous time" and "writ *Flagrante bello* certain dangerous Treatises. . . . At His Majesties happy Return, *J. M.* did partake . . . of his regal Clemency and has ever since expiated himself in a retired silence."[115] Nevertheless, if one of the "chief social value[s]" of poetic works, as Jerome McGann suggests, "is that they are conceptual forms which [can] operate at a high level of generality, on the one hand, and at an equally high level of particularity on the other,"[116] then *Paradise Lost* is a poem whose radical Puritan author skillfully negotiates both levels of meaning. In giving historical particulars mythic resonance, a daring poem like *Paradise Lost* does not simply remove itself from them – the religious, verbal, and aesthetic ambiguities of rebellion scrutinized in Milton's controversial writings, as well as the specific texture of seventeenth-century Antichristian revolts themselves. Rather, it draws freely upon such historical particulars, reconceiving them in a highly dramatic and imaginative way, so that the poem may indeed remain polemically alive at a time when the godly cause of radical dissidents was fiercely embattled as "Worlds / Judg'd [them] perverse" (6.36–37) and they needed to remain more watchful than ever. Fueled "with calumnious

Art," the revolution of Satan and his factious party in *Paradise Lost* reveals – as powerfully as any poetic fiction – that the ambiguous politics of Antichristian treachery, in the words of Henry Vane, will always be apt to renew themselves "afresh, under some new forme . . . as by late years experience we have been taught."

CHAPTER EIGHT

The kingdom within: radical religion and politics in Paradise Regained

"Christ hath a government of his own," Milton wrote in 1659, "it governs not by outward force . . . it deals only with the inward man and his actions . . . [it shows us] the divine excellence of his spiritual kingdom, able without worldly force to subdue all the powers and kingdoms of this world."[1] And a year later, the Quaker leader and prophet Edward Burrough urged the saints that "in the *Day* of *Temptations* and *Tryals*," in order that they "may not be *overcome* of the *wicked*," they should "put on *strength*, that [they] may *stand*, and never *be moved* from the *hope* of *Eternal Life*, and *feel* the *renewing* of [their] *inward man*."[2] These two passages, written close to the Restoration, capture essential qualities dramatized in Milton's last spiritual epic: its striking revision of external forms of politics and kingship; its emphasis on the mighty power of a spiritual kingdom within; and its depiction of Jesus as a pious and inward saint, armed with the power of the Lord and unmoved in the midst of the greatest worldly temptations.

Yet despite recent attempts to address the political implications of *Paradise Regained*, no critical consensus has emerged.[3] Does this spiritually inward poem repudiate politics after Milton's disappointments in the Restoration?[4] Does it espouse political quietism and a withdrawal from politics into faith or suggest that Milton himself, towards the end of his life, assumes a more pacifist outlook?[5] Early modern historians have themselves sometimes noted the political inactivity and quietist resignation of religious radicals after 1660; and yet recent scholarship has begun to reveal greater continuities between pre- and post-1660 radical Puritan dissent, religious beliefs, and writing than we have previously recognized.[6] Religion, including its more radical forms, indeed remained an important cause of political and social instability after 1660. This recent historical perspective may challenge us to rethink our understanding of the religious politics of Milton's great poems and their polemical dimensions. Arguments claiming that *Paradise Regained* espouses pacifism and passivity, for example, would distinguish it from the militant apocalypticism characterizing some of Milton's earlier revolutionary works; and they would also distinguish it from its companion poem dramatizing Samson's spectacular and vengeful destruction of Dagon's power. How, then, can we consider this inward-looking spiritual epic as a polemically engaged and highly imaginative response to the worldly trials, temptations, and politics of Restoration England?

One way is to consider the contemporary cultural milieu in which *Paradise Regained* is deeply embedded: the radical religious world of mid-seventeenth-century England which helped to shape Milton's poem and whose unorthodox spiritual beliefs it expresses and represents. In this age of unprecedented social and religious ferment, when politics and religion were closely connected (as we have seen throughout this book), radical spiritual convictions found expression in political discourse.[7] By emphasizing this rich religious and sociopolitical matrix – a cultural context still not adequately examined in relation to *Paradise Regained*[8] – we can illuminate its intense inwardness, its apocalyptic subversiveness in relation to temporal powers and kingdoms, as well as the political and verbal engagement manifested by Jesus in his firm, often contentious responses to Satan's smooth rhetoric and spectacular temptations in the wilderness.

This chapter thus connects *Paradise Regained* with important aspects of Quaker writings on politics and religion from the 1650s and 1660s, though it draws upon additional contemporary radical religious texts as well – works by Gerrard Winstanley, George Wither, and others.[9] But the early Quakers, who represented the largest and most dynamic movement of social, political and religious protest in the period's revolutionary culture, as we saw in Chapter 4, deserve special emphasis because of Milton's close connection with them in the 1660s, when one of their major strongholds was London and its surrounding counties. Although he never refers specifically to them and their religious heterodoxies in his late pre-Restoration prose works, Milton nevertheless became closer to the Quakers than to any other major group of religious radicals. Besides his significant contact with Thomas Ellwood, his Quaker friend and reader who allegedly prompted him to write the poem,[10] the poet admired Isaac Penington the younger, with whom he shared a number of convictions. Indeed, Penington was one of the more intellectual and sophisticated early Quaker writers (like Milton he attended Cambridge

University), and he was, at the end of the Interregnum, a passionate defender of that radical republican ideal, the Good Old Cause, as well as "a witness against all false Hirelings."[11] When he wasn't incarcerated in Aylesbury prison during the 1660s, where Ellwood himself was imprisoned, the most prominent Quaker of Buckinghamshire lived near Chalfont St. Giles, where Ellwood found Milton a temporary home during the Great Plague (1665).[12] My discussion of *Paradise Regained*, however, draws not only upon writings by Ellwood and Penington, but upon a wide range of Quaker prophetic writers and texts in order to situate Milton's unusual spiritual epic more richly and concretely in the radical religious milieu of the Interregnum and the Restoration. The emphasis in early Quaker writings on the interiorization of power and kingship, on exhortation and the denunciation of temporal authorities, on unadorned prophetic speech, on great perseverance in the midst of spiritual trials, temptations, and warfare – these and other issues can illuminate the radical religious politics of a poem whose inward-oriented Jesus, led into "the wide Wilderness" (2.232) by the Spirit, remains unmoved and sharply polemical, demonstrating "firm obedience" (1.4) after every kind of temptation the guileful Satan devises or assault he attempts, as he applies "All his vast force" (1.153).

Yet my aim in this chapter is not to claim that the religious politics and language of Milton's radical Puritan epic can be illuminated exclusively in terms of a single sectarian movement or set of beliefs, including Quakerism. As Lucy Hutchinson famously said of her godly republican husband, "he never was any man's Sectary, either in religious or civill matters,"[13] and one might observe the same about Milton, particularly when it came to his radical religious alliances. Milton in his later years remained a religious individualist and, after all, never joined a separatist congregation or "gathered church," nor converted to Quakerism, as did Lilburne and Winstanley. Yet several of his late tracts, notably his companion pieces *A Treatise of Civil Power* and *Likeliest Means to Remove Hirelings*, voice radical spiritual concerns (e.g. an emphasis on guidance by the inward persuasive motions of the Spirit, the fierce rejection of tithes to support a parochial clergy, the denial of civil magistrates any authority over matters of religion) that are indeed close to Quaker ones.[14] *Paradise Regained*, as I hope to show, imaginatively reproduces some of the most compelling radical religious beliefs and themes of Milton's age, as he creates his own variations upon them and invests them with his distinctive aesthetic concerns.

TRIED THROUGH ALL TEMPTATION

The religious politics of trial and temptation were particularly urgent when Milton published his spiritual epic in 1671. Among radical religious groups, the Quakers endured especially severe trials and adversities during the Interregnum and the Restoration as their faith was constantly being tested by worldly powers and authorities:[15] their "firm obedience," both as a group and as individual saints, was, in the words of *Paradise Regained*, "fully tried / Through all temptation" (1.4–5). Like Milton's Jesus, God would "exercise [them] in the Wilderness" (1.156) of the world with all its dangers, as well as its enchantments. The sense of enduring "various exercises, trials, and troubles" as strenuous preparation for a godly vocation is pervasive in George Fox's famous *Journal*;[16] and it is central to the writings and life of Isaac Penington (1616–1679), who converted to Quakerism in 1658, after hearing Fox preach, and then spent six periods in prison between 1661 and 1671. "The Lord," wrote Ellwood in his testimony concerning Penington, "had led him through many a strait and difficulty, through many temptations, tryals and exercises (by which he had tryed and proved him)," and Penington himself observed in 1661 that the saint should indeed expect "*Straits, Wants, Tryals, Temptations, inward Weaknesses, buffetings from the Enemy* . . . which God seeth necessary to Exercise the Spirits of his with, that he might fit them for himself."[17] Known for his learning, sharp wit, and retiring spirit – as well as his forceful denunciation of the Cavaliers for their abuses of Friends – Penington himself showed during the Restoration era a "constant perseverance" (1.148) and "Saintly patience" (3.93), phrases applied in *Paradise Regained* to Job (surpassed as a model by Milton's Jesus).[18] Indeed, the quiet heroism of trial, patience, and suffering so central to *Paradise Regained* and its inwardly focused Jesus, who conquers "Satanic strength" by "Humiliation and strong Sufferance" (1.160–61), takes on a more specific spiritual resonance and emotional force when we consider Milton's poem in relation to the politics of Quakerism – that religious and political movement profoundly defined by a sense of trial, suffering, and steadfastness in the 1650s, 1660s, and beyond.[19]

Thus Jesus's description of his own series of trials, adversities and dangers, later repeated by Satan himself (4.386–88, 478–79), would have had a more urgent and pointed resonance in the poem's Restoration context, when the persecution of the Quakers, Baptists, and other dissenters by the religious establishment and civil powers had become increasingly acute – especially during the early and mid-1660s and in 1670–71. Under the repressive Clarendon Code (1661–65) enacted by the Cavalier Parliament and beginning with the Quaker Act and the Act of Uniformity (1662), dissidents rejecting the rites and authority of the Church of England were regularly beaten or abused, fined, prosecuted, and imprisoned; and then they often suffered appalling conditions in gaol. The new and severe Conventicle Act of 1670, issued the year before Milton published *Paradise Regained* and considered by Marvell "the Quintessence of arbitrary Malice," was specifically a political weapon aimed against "the growing and dangerous practices of seditious sectaries and other disloyal persons" operating "under pretence of tender consciences . . . [to] contrive insurrections (as late experience hath shown)." It encouraged a new wave of persecution against the godly, even if the government could not prevent private dissenting worship.[20] Ellwood himself characterized the moment of the 1670 Act as a particularly "stormy time," and observed that this "unjust, unequal, unreasonable and unrighteous law . . . was rigorously prosecuted against the meetings of dissenters in general, though the brunt of the storm fell most sharply on the people called Quakers."[21] Defining his vocation, Milton's Jesus does indeed sound like one of the godly witnesses who, under a state of siege, will endure much suffering and abuse at the hands of hostile authorities:

> What if he hath decreed that I shall first
> Be tried in humble state, and things adverse,
> By tribulations, injuries, insults,
> Contempts, and scorns, and snares, and violence,
> Suffering, abstaining, quietly expecting
> Without distrust or doubt, that he may know
> What I can suffer, how obey?   (3.188–94)

In 1660 Margaret Fell had called the hated and despised Quakers "a *suffering people*, under every *Power & Change*, and under *every profession of Religion* that hath been . . . since we were a People"; and Fox himself, "a person suspected to be a disturber of the peace of the nation, a common enemy to His Majesty . . . the King," stressed the great suffering and cruel persecutions endured by the Quakers during both the Interregnum and the Restoration.[22] Indeed, no other radical Puritan group in the 1650s and 1660s – as they followed the dictates of the Spirit within, resisted all forms of "carnal power," and represented a new apostolic dispensation – would illustrate more poignantly than the Quakers Milton's embittered historical narrative at the end of *Paradise Lost*:

"Whence heavy persecution shall arise / On all who in the worship per-
severe / Of Spirit and Truth; the rest, far greater part, / Will deem in
outward Rites and specious forms / Religion satisfi'd" (12.521, 531–35).

Yet in *Paradise Regained* the poet's emphasis is less on the severity of persecution registered at the end of his first sacred epic and more on the
inner faith and quiet expectation exemplified by the patient messianic
hero who endures constant trials and temptations – and who perseveres,
overcomes, and ultimately regains "lost Paradise" (4.608), while vigorously engaging with his great spiritual and political adversary. Those
saints who have "come through great Tribulations," wrote the Quaker
Edward Burrough, "are refined and purified" by that arduous process;[23]
for the early Quakers inward strength, obedience, and faith were indeed
fully tested and proven by trials and tribulations in the hostile wilderness
of this world. In the wilderness of *Paradise Regained*, the inward and
human Messiah himself undergoes "just trial" (3.196) and thus "by
merit" (1.166) more than anything else proves his right to become the
King of Kings.

Paradise Regained, moreover, was written at a moment when Quaker
testimonies themselves began to assert the need to record these extraordinary "deeds / Above Heroic" (1.14–15) performed by those patient and
obedient saints with "pious Hearts" (1.463) who were under a continual
state of siege, harassment, and tried "Through many a hard assay even
to the death" (264). Ellwood's testimony concerning Penington portrayed a steadfast Quaker saint who esteemed "the reproach of Christ
greater riches then the Treasures of Egypt" and who, in the process of
being led through his many temptations and exercises, had "turned his
back upon . . . all" "the Preferments and Honours of the world."[24] Such
trials and deliverances of saints in the wilderness of the world, furthermore, could be interpreted as a manifestation of God's providential
work in history. So in his memorial of 1662 to the Quaker prophet James
Parnell, Stephen Crisp observed that "if ever any age had cause" to keep
in "Remembrance the words and sayings, great deliverances and spiritual battles, and mighty and noble acts of God," it was surely this one.
Here was the kind of heroic material that was worthy of remembrance:
great spiritual deeds of obedience done in an age of religious turmoil,
characterized by suffering, trial, and perseverance, in which the Quakers
themselves, as God's inward people, played a central role; for through
them God might perform remarkable acts and "mighty works of
wonder."[25] In its own quiet way, too, *Paradise Regained* announces itself as
a new kind of radical Puritan epic, one suited for this unprecedented age

of spiritual inwardness, trials, and exercises. Its prophetic poet will tell
of spiritual struggles, temptations, and perseverance – how the austere
Son of God, armed with the spirit of meekness, performed alone in "his
Victorious Field / Against the Spiritual Foe" (1.9–10) "mighty work"
(186) "unrecorded left through many an Age" (16).

REGAL TEMPTATIONS

Milton's radical Puritan epic records for his own age the deeds of an
austere and inward Jesus tried by a full range of temptations – sensual,
active, and contemplative – indicating that he could have been exercised
no more in the wilderness of this world. As Isaac Penington himself
noted, "in the Wilderness" the saint who endures "many straits" and
"exercises" can expect to be tried not only by physical adversities and
"open force," but "also with enchantments" and more beguiling kinds of
temptations.[26] In *Paradise Regained*, the luxurious and sensual temptations
themselves display Satan's skill "in regal Arts, / And regal Mysteries"
(3.248–49), and thus deserve some attention before we consider other
aspects of the spiritual epic and its polemical politics in relation to
radical religious culture of the 1650s and 1660s. In Book 2 Milton's Jesus
refuses the very temptation – much more enchanting this time around –
to which Adam and Eve succumbed in Paradise: "Alas how simple, to
these Cates compar'd, / Was the crude Apple that diverted *Eve!*"
(2.348–49), the poet proclaims as he describes the lavish banquet Satan
offers the Son of God. Milton's brilliant addition to the Gospel accounts
is presented in a particularly alluring manner, conveyed through the
texture and detail of his poetic description:

> Our Savior lifting up his eyes beheld
> In ample space under the broadest shade
> A Table richly spread, in regal mode,
> With dishes pil'd, and meats of noblest sort
> And savor, Beasts of chase, or Fowl of game,
> In pastry built, or from the spit, or boil'd,
> Grisamber steam'd . . .   (2.338–44)

Besides suggesting that the world itself is a great feast for the eyes, this
spectacular temptation conveys – and is reinforced by the series of con-
junctions "or" – a sense of the power of the illusion Satan has staged
and the range of sensual choices he has made available. Indeed, the
poem's depiction of the hungry and pious Jesus refusing this Satanic
banquet – a temptation which highlights his long period of fasting "in

the wide Wilderness" (2.232) of the world – might well have evoked a historically more specific form of spiritual austerity and endurance in an age of radical sectarian culture such as Milton's. Because Jesus had fasted during his temptation in the wilderness (Matt. 4:2; Luke 4:2), and because fastings were among the trials of a true apostle (see e.g. 2 Cor. 6:5, 11:27), many early Quakers and their leaders (including Nayler, Fox, Richard Hubberthorne, and others) had fasted seven, twelve, fourteen, and even twenty days or more in the world's wilderness to demonstrate divine approval and the Lord's power in them.[27]

Milton, moreover, gives this Satanic banqueting scene political implications. Spread out attractively "in regal mode," the banquet resembles the feast of an extravagant Cavalier or a French court – its alluring dishes are all symbolic of wealth and privilege – and thus it anticipates the poem's subsequent temptations of riches, regal power, and Roman luxury. In April 1660 Milton, who dared even that late to speak out against "sumptuous courts" with their "vast expence and luxurie," was already beginning to notice the "enticements and preferments" offered by the court of Louis XIV which "daily draw away and pervert the Protestant Nobilitie." Such courtly enticements included "the eating and drinking of excessive dainties" (*The Readie and Easie Way*, 2nd edn., *CPW* 7:425–26) or what Jesus dismisses in *Paradise Regained*, in response to the temptation of Satan's great banquet, as "pompous Delicacies" (2.390). Even the suggestion of Belial, that Cavalier spirit associated with "Courts and Regal Chambers" (2.183), is not lost on Satan, who earlier seemed to reject his advice. Belial suggests that Jesus should be enticed with "amorous Arts" and "enchanting tongues" (158), and the enchanting romance temptation offers "Ladies of th' *Hesperides*, that seem'd / Fairer than feign'd of old" (357–58). But for the poet of *Paradise Regained*, more than for his austere Quaker contemporaries (who preferred a plain culture without ornamentation in language, dress, the arts, and so on), such an enchanting and sensual temptation would have had a distinctly aesthetic appeal. It evokes, after all, Milton's own earlier poetic ideals which had once included his intense attraction – still evinced in this luxurious description – to the language of romance and its world of sensuous enchantment.

Satan's imperial Rome likewise conveys a sense of decadent, luxurious power as Satan shows Jesus, from the "specular Mount" (4.236), the most glorious of "all / The Kingdoms of the world" (4.88–89). With its "sumptuous gluttonies, and gorgeous feasts" lavishly displayed and served, the Rome temptation resembles in culinary details the earlier

Satanic banquet with all its regal temptations, as the poor and hungry Jesus reminds his tempter that he still feels "thirst / And hunger" (4.113–21). The sumptuous architecture of "great and glorious *Rome*," created by the "skill of noblest Architects" and "the hand of fam'd Artificers" (4.33–37, 44–60) and recalling the baroque city of Milton's Italian journey, contributes to the sense of visual magnificence, while evoking a temporal power who, in the words of Milton's *Readie and Easie Way*, "can display with such vanitie and ostentation his regal splendor so supereminently" (*CPW* 7:429). Resemblances between that late tract, with its critique of regal display, and *Paradise Regained*, with its emphasis on the alluring "grandeur and majestic show / Of luxury" (4.110–11), suggest that Satan's imperial Rome is indeed meant to represent the extravagance of regal power in Restoration culture. Roman and Stuart ostentation hardly seem remote from each other, this radical Puritan epic suggests. And when we consider that during the 1660s Milton had been exposed to the plain culture and aesthetic of Quakerism (which, besides emphasizing plain speech, extended to architecture),[28] the austere Jesus's firm dismissal of Satan's lavish display becomes even more pointed. Indeed, Jesus makes no conciliatory gesture of any kind when offered the kingdoms of the world. In this respect, he differs from some Quakers in post-revolutionary England who, though not support-ers of hereditary monarchy, were willing to accept regal dominion if it respected religious freedom and who therefore sought the returned Stuart king's protection; some even thought Charles II a man "of sober countenance."[29]

Thus during the temptation to a luxurious Rome, Jesus altogether dis-misses Satan's "politic maxims" (3.400), without giving a more accom-modating political response, like this one made by one of Milton's more moderate Quaker contemporaries in the Restoration: "though after outward power, authority, rule, government or dominion we seek not, nor do desire it, yet we despise it not, but do own it in its place."[30] As Satan represents the decadent Tiberius as old and engaging in "horrid lusts" (4.94), he attempts to persuade Jesus that "with Regal Virtues" (98) he can ascend the worldly Roman throne with ease, thereby freeing his servile people. But Jesus's utter rejection of Satan's offer of Rome in the age of Tiberius actually places *Paradise Regained* in a radical antimonar-chical tradition even less compromising with regard to temporal monar-chy than Milton's contemporary Quakers could sometimes be. Indeed, a highly provocative radical text of the Restoration written in the tradi-tion of political resistance associated with John Knox, Christopher

Goodman, and the revolutionary Milton himself, singled out Tiberius as one of those cunning rulers from antiquity who rose to power and then oppressed his people and "committed all manner of outrages"; *Mene Tekel; or, The Downfal of Tyranny* (1663) proclaimed that though such Antichristian rulers "spend [their] time in wantonness, luxury, prodigality and tyranny," and though "they [might] endure long, they will not endure alwayes."[31] Jesus's ultimate target, however, is not primarily the monstrous Tiberius, but the "Devil who first made him such" (4.129), as well as other ostentatious earthly monarchies. Conceding nothing to Satan's regal offers, the Son of God will strike at the very origins of temporal power in order to uproot it. Seen in relation to the ongoing radical religious culture in the Restoration, the disdainful responses of Milton's Jesus towards Satan's temptations of regal power and luxury can give this spiritual epic a sharp polemical edge missed by those of its commentators who suggest that the great poems reveal a Milton who has largely withdrawn from politics into faith.

THE OBSCURITY OF JESUS

Indeed, among the more provocative sociopolitical aspects of Milton's Puritan epic is the way it keeps representing the future King of Kings as obscure, private, and poor – particularly in the context of Satan's regal temptations and in the context of seventeenth-century radical religious culture where the representation of mighty weakness could have unorthodox social and political implications. Being "unknown," as Satan observes, as well as "low of birth" (2.413) and "Bred up in poverty and straits at home" (415), the hungry and solitary Jesus, depicted in the process of discovering his ministry, hardly qualifies as an aristocratic epic hero, let alone a traditional monarch surrounded by regal splendor, power, and riches, all signs of what Milton on the eve of the Restoration had called "regal prodigalitie" (*CPW* 7:460). The retiring carpenter's son, after all, has experienced nothing of the world's "glory, / Empires, and Monarchs, and their radiant Courts" (3.236–37), and he seems unlikely to rise to the highest position of political power. The poem thus presents Milton's "Unmarkt" (1.25) and inward Messiah – "our Savior meek" (4.401, 636) – as a striking contrast to figures of aristocratic wealth and epic status. In terms of his humble background, moreover, he is further linked to his humble disciples, Andrew, Simon Peter, and others, the gathering we see at the beginning of Book 2 of "Plain Fisherman, (no greater men them call) / Close in a Cottage low together" (2.27–28).

These lowly pastoral figures contribute to the poem's georgic themes,[32] while highlighting its sense of political and historical urgency. Perplexed by the faithful Jesus's retirement into the desert, they anxiously pray for deliverance from earthly monarchies and yearn for the coming of the Messiah and his kingdom – "Send the Messiah forth, the time is come" – in lines that simultaneously evoke mid-seventeenth-century radical religious millenarian yearnings and the crisis of the godly in the Restoration: "Behold the Kings of th'Earth how they oppress / Thy chosen, to what height thir pow'r unjust / They have exalted" (2.43–46).

The poem's emphasis on the Messiah's own poor and obscure status – and on his being "tried in humble state" (3.189) – in effect contributes to Milton's redefinition of Jesus's political ministry as a manifestation of mighty weakness able to unsettle "the kings of the earth": "the mystery of his comming," Milton writes in his prose, was "by meane things and persons to subdue mighty ones" (*An Apology, CPW* 1:951). In *The Tenure of Kings and Magistrates*, Milton recalls the sharpness with which the humble yet prophetic Jesus, perceived as a potential threat by Herod, addressed the Pharisees, dismissing the tyrannical "fox" by saying "I cast out devils" (Luke 13:32): and so "although hee himself were the meekest, and came on earth to be so," Milton observes, "yet to a Tyrant we hear him not voutsafe an humble word" (*CPW* 3:217). Milton's radical spiritual epic itself reveals "that misterious work of Christ" who "by lowlines" is able "to confound height" as it dramatizes through the trials and temptations of Jesus "the mighty operation of the spirit" (*Reason of Church-Government, CPW* 1:829–30, 833).[33]

This depiction of mighty weakness would have had considerable cultural and symbolic resonance in mid-seventeenth-century England, when radical religious prophets, leaders, and writers were especially conscious of their vocational histories and social status, and when they depicted the saints, upon whom God would pour out his Spirit, as both mighty and humble, meek and forceful. Such meekness, the visionary Mary Cary observed, "shall be consistent with courage, stoutness, and valour also, when God calls them to exercise it."[34] Radical religious writers and saints often gave their own humble backgrounds and vocations, as well as the lowly background of King Jesus, a highly politicized meaning which challenged usual assumptions about social hierarchy, nobility, and government. Thus they represented themselves and their followers as "poor, despised, and rejected," in the words of Edward Burrough, "yet Dreadful and Mighty, because the Majesty and Presence of the Lord God is with us, who hath called us, and chosen us."[35] God might thus choose contemptible ones of the world who are rich in faith and piety to effect his greatest designs, including unthroning the powers of the earth.[36] Since God "*delights* to bring about *great* and *mighty* things to pass, by very *unworthy*, and very *unlikely* Instruments," one radical preacher told Parliament the day after the regicide, then the humblest individual could have immeasurable value in the eyes of God, thereby acting as a channel of divine revelation.[37] In this age, even those from modest or poor backgrounds and livelihoods had been called to perform godly deeds "Above heroic," though these prophets and leaders themselves might paradoxically be from below in terms of social rank and appearance.

And so when Satan tempts the poor, unknown Jesus with riches as the means to obtain political influence and kingly power – "Get Riches first, get Wealth, and Treasure heap" (2.427) – Jesus responds by highlighting the spectacular careers of those biblical leaders, including David, risen up from "lowest poverty" and humble stations to achieve "highest deeds" and charismatic roles:

> *Gideon* and *Jephtha*, and the Shepherd lad,
> Whose offspring on the Throne of *Judah* sat
> So many Ages, and shall yet regain
> That seat, and reign in *Israel* without end. (2.438–42)

Gideon of course was engaged in threshing wheat when called by the Lord, while Jephthah, who becomes leader of the people of Gilead in Judges II, was the son of a harlot and an outcast. Jesus augments this provocative response by adding Roman republican heroes who had led a poor, simple life but "Who could do mighty things, and could contemn / Riches though offer'd from the hand of Kings" (2.448–49). His challenging speech subverts the traditional epic assumption of the heroic political leader as aristocratic, not to mention the idea that kingship and its power are necessarily associated with honor, riches, and aristocracy: even the obscure Messiah "in this poverty" might "as soon / Accomplish" the same kinds of extraordinary deeds and leadership – "perhaps and more" (2.451–52).

As the Quaker prophet George Fox the younger had dared to warn Charles II at the Restoration, "many times [God's] instruments, when they begin his . . . work, appear very contemptible," especially in terms of outward appearance and vocation, though "the Lord God appeare[s] mightily in those his instruments."[38] In response to Satan's offer of riches as the means to power, Jesus's challenging speech thus gains an even sharper polemical edge when situated in the social context of mid-seventeenth-century radical religious culture, with its highly inward and unconventional conceptions of authority, calling, and prophecy. Winstanley the Digger, for example, had stressed that "Fishermen, Shepherds, Husbandmen, and the Carpenters son . . . spake and writ as the Spirit gave them utterance, from an inward testimony" and that Christ "is now rising in Husbandmen, Shepherds, Fishermen," while Isaac Penington asked how God in "former ages" reproved "the Kings and Princes of *Israel*": "Not by the eminent Priests and Prophets, whom they expected to be taught by," he concluded, "but by Herdsmen, by Plowmen, by Prophets which they despised."[39] Moreover, the Quaker Richard Hubberthorne, in an autobiographical testimony of his ministry as one of the prophets and dynamic leaders of God's people in the 1650s, cited the examples of Elisha, who "was a plough-man . . . when the Word of the Lord came to him," and Amos, who was a herdsman: "and I do witness the same Call," added Hubberthorne, "who was a Husbandman . . . till the Word of the Lord came and called me from it, and he turned my mind within."[40] In this world of radical spiritual culture, then, the idea of the prophetic leader as a pastoral or georgic figure – humble in appearance and vocation but mighty in the power of the Lord – could possess significant political and social symbolism. Of all the charismatic Quaker leaders to emerge in the 1650s, James Nayler particularly impressed the young Thomas Ellwood (who was himself a gentleman); that sectarian prophet's words "had the greater force" upon Ellwood "because he looked but like a plain simple countryman, having the appearance of a husbandman or a shepherd."[41] Such prophetic leaders, like the obscure and inward-looking hero of Milton's radical spiritual epic, might indeed seem "Little suspicious to any King" (2.82). Yet they represented a spiritually unconventional and socially subversive religious culture, both during the Interregnum and the Restoration, that could sharply challenge and revise – as does *Paradise Regained* and its humble yet prophetic Jesus – the received notions, symbols, and language of secular power, hegemony, and kingship.[42]

THE POLITICS OF INTERIORITY

The unusual emphasis on interiority in *Paradise Regained* – even when it comes to issues of political authority, rule, and kingship – especially reinforces the poem's close connections with contemporary radical religious culture. Its Jesus is private, introspective, and solitary, as he relies on the

Spirit to guide and lead him in the wilderness of the world. Indeed, in the manner of religious radicals like the Quakers, who associated the inward Spirit with direct "leadings" and individual guidance,[43] "this glorious Eremite" (1.8) is led by "the Spirit" as he walks "alone" into the hostile wilderness where he muses inwardly on the meaning of his prophetic ministry as Messiah: there he finds himself absorbed in "holy Meditations," "the Spirit leading / And his deep thoughts, the better to converse / With solitude," until he is "far from track of men, / Thought following thought, and step by step led on" (1.195, 189–92). The Jesus of Milton's poem who undergoes this private ritual – and who descends into himself and is led "by some strong motion" (1.290) into the wilderness – manifests the concern with spiritual inwardness and vocation characteristic of radical religious culture of the 1650s and 1660s, including the later Milton's own concern with "the inward perswasive motions of [God's] spirit" (*Civil Power*, *CPW* 7:261) as the truest guide. Even the earnest and inward qualities of Milton's young Jesus, rehearsed in his first holy meditation, evoke striking connections here. Thus as a child, the Quaker prophet Francis Howgill describes how he set his heart to know "God which the world professed and which [he] had read of in the Scripture . . . and [he] attended to much reading and meditation," so that he was "sober, and serious alone," taking no delight in childish sports and pastimes.[44] And Fox himself as a child, "being more religious, inward, . . . and observing beyond his years," refused, in the words of William Penn, "childish and vain sports and company" as he manifested a "singular temper."[45] In a similar manner we find the precocious Jesus of *Paradise Regained* meditating on his messianic office, while recalling that in his early years he took no pleasure in "childish play," for instead his "mind was set / Serious to learn and know" the "Law of God" as he prepared himself "to promote all truth, / All righteous things" (1.201–7).

The unknown Jesus's mighty deeds are themselves "in secret done" (1.15) – done in solitude, in retirement, in private.[46] By choosing to dramatize deeds "Above heroic" done in secret by a deeply introspective Jesus, Milton not only drastically revises the epic heroic ethos: he also signals his poem's relation to radical religious culture during the Interregnum and the Restoration. Guided by the Holy Spirit, the early Quakers themselves, writes Penington, particularly "turned [their] minds inwardly towards [their] Lord and Saviour, to mind his inward appearance, his inward shinings, his inward quicknings"; Penington himself was noted for being "frequent in retirements, and very inward with the Lord."[47] But being "retiring in spirit to the Lord," as Ellwood himself often was,[48] might seem to make the godly individual either ineffective or disengaged politically; in urging the reclusive Jesus to establish his kingdom on earth through heroic and revolutionary actions, Satan reproaches the Son for "thus retiring" (3.164) inwardly. Satan, however, misconstrues the highly unconventional nature of the prophetic office and power of that "inward Oracle" dwelling in "pious Hearts" (1.463). As this radical Puritan poem reveals, deep spiritual inwardness and vigorous polemical engagement with temporal powers can indeed coexist. Even the saintly Penington, who grew intensely inward during his trials and exercises of the Restoration, nevertheless remained, like Milton's firm and inward-looking Jesus, "very zealous . . . for the Truth, unwearied in promoting it, bold and undaunted in the defence of it."[49]

During his first soliloquy we see the inward-oriented Son of God, without full knowledge of his ministry, meditating on the nature and means of achieving his "mighty work," which involves his political role: "To rescue *Israel* from the *Roman* yoke, / Then to subdue and quell o'er all the earth / Brute violence and proud Tyrannic pow'r, / Till truth were freed, and equity restor'd" (1.217–20). But rather than choosing revolution by arms to effect political liberation, the young Jesus decided it was "more humane, more heavenly" to use "winning words to conquer willing hearts, / And make persuasion do the work of fear" (1.221–23). In this sense Jesus, who fights his own "great duel" (1.174) in the poem, differs not only from the usual epic warrior who aspires to achieve "victorious deeds" and "heroic acts" (215–16). Given the immediate cultural context of *Paradise Regained* – particularly radical religion – he also differs as a revolutionary from extreme militant radicals like the zealous Fifth Monarchists with their chiliastic ideology which Milton had briefly dismissed in the first edition of *The Readie and Easie Way*; during the 1650s and 1660s they taught that the Second Coming of King Jesus would be precipitated by a violent remodelling of society, with the saints seizing civil and military power.[50] Temporal kings, for whom Milton's Jesus has only scorn, would then be bound in chains and dashed to pieces. And yet their most famous armed insurrection during the Restoration – Thomas Venner's bloody rising in London (January 1661) – had failed, fueling fears of religious radicals and rebellion and resulting in the widespread arrest and persecution of Quakers and other sectaries, including Thomas Ellwood. Indeed, from Ellwood's perspective, these militant millenarians "little understood . . . the nature of His kingdom, though He Himself had declared it was not of this world."[51] While the early

Quakers were by no means consistent pacifists, even during the Restoration,[52] they often proclaimed, stressing the spiritual inwardness and power of the kingdom of Jesus, that Christ's weapons in the war against the world are spiritual weapons: his "Weapons are not carnal, yet are they mighty through God to . . . overturning the foundation of Satans kingdom."[53] The introspective Jesus of Milton's poem likewise discovers that there are other kinds of mighty weapons besides those of armed revolt – the sharp, quelling power of the prophetic Word itself, for instance – with which to maintain "great warfare" (1.158) against the Prince of this world and overturn his temporal kingdoms and strongholds. And yet when Jesus adds "the stubborn only to subdue" (1.226) to his speech advocating "winning words," he acknowledges, in a line too readily overlooked by commentators who wish to insist on this spiritual poem's pacifism, that verbal persuasion alone will *not always* do the hard work of deliverance.

In giving his brief epic such a notably spiritual and interior dimension, Milton drastically redefines the very nature of politics and kingship. But this poem does not simply repudiate worldly kingship; it also makes kingship and power inward, just as it later makes learning and wisdom inward matters (4.322–30), redefining them in terms of a spiritual kingdom of the mind.[54] The passage in *Paradise Regained* that gives greatest interiority to politics is immediately preceded by lines in which Jesus, having just demonstrated his spiritual might by rejecting riches, rejects the earthly crown "Golden in show," noting that it "Brings dangers, troubles, cares, and sleepless nights" (2.459–60). His condemnation recalls Milton's description of worldly kingship, with its Macbeth-like anxieties and burdens, in *The Readie and Easie Way*: "though looking big, yet [it is] . . . full of fears, full of jealousies, startl'd at every ombrage" (*CPW* 7:457). Jesus's concern lies ultimately with an entirely different kind of kingship – an inward rule whose power and discipline over "the inner man" is not dependent on any worldly "force" (2.477, 479) or external authority but is nevertheless necessary for the righteous godly leader who seeks to guide nations by an active faith. Indeed, rather than simply repudiating politics, his lines resonate with the political language of radical religious discourse, including Milton's own late pre-Restoration polemics, where interiority and politics are realigned:

> Yet he who reigns within himself, and rules
> Passions, Desires, and Fears, is more a King;
> Which every wise and virtuous man attains:
> And who attains not, ill aspires to rule

Cities of men, or headstrong Multitudes,
Subject himself to Anarchy within,
Or lawless passions in him, which he serves.
But to guide Nations in the way of truth
By saving Doctrine, and from error lead
To know, and knowing worship God aright,
Is yet more Kingly . . .   (2.466–76)

This forceful rejoinder to Satan is remarkably close in vision to the
inward politics and teaching of Milton's *Treatise of Civil Power* (1659),
which I quoted from at the opening of this chapter: "Christ hath a
government of his own . . . it governs not by outward force . . . it deals
only with the inward man and his actions." The vision of that late tract
– with its unusual emphasis on "the spirit . . . of God within us," on "the
inward man" and the private, individual conscience, and on God's
"inward power" and kingdom (*CPW* 7:244, 257, 261) – is itself close to
the radical Quaker notion that the kingdom of Jesus would come "not
by an outward visible shining body, quelling and over-awing the enemies
of his Kingdom, but by his inward and invisible Power in the hearts of
his People," for, as Isaac Penington stressed, "that which we sought
without, was to be found within . . . there was the Kingdom."[55] The
Spirit Jesus refers to in *Paradise Regained* – that "inward Oracle" sent to
"teach [God's] final will" (1.461–63) – is mankind's "teacher and
ruler . . . within him," to quote Winstanley, another radical religious
writer who perceived acutely how those who pursue the deceptive
"Kingdome without," with its "outward objects," are subject to "inward
trouble" and "slavish feare within," since "they know not how to governe
themselves."[56] Secular kingship, along with its riches, is thus "oftest
better miss't" (2.486), Jesus concludes. His polemical response redefines
kingship in a way that severs its politics altogether from temporal authorities and outward forms: the authority he promotes, since he relies
wholly on the direct operations of the Spirit within, is completely internalized and yet paradoxically "more kingly."

In a millennial work prophesying "the total . . . Ruin of the MON-
ARCHIES of this World," Sir Henry Vane defined during the
Restoration "*A Kingdom inward*": "the commanding, ruling Principle of
Life in the true Saint, as a Law written in his inward parts" which prepares saints to retreat "into the Wilderness, and to continue in such a solitary . . . desolate condition, till God calls them out of it."[57] Indeed, both
in his retirement into the wilderness and in his polemical engagements
with Satan, the solitary Jesus of *Paradise Regained* exemplifies this radical

religious sentiment as it continued to exist after the restoration of the Stuart monarchy and state church: "where the Word of God rules in the heart," observed George Fox in reference to Luke 4 and the temptations of Jesus in the desert, "the Devil hath no power."[58] Nevertheless, the saints had to be particularly vigilant about the interior kingdom since, as Burrough warned them during the Restoration, Antichrist's government is "set up . . . not only in all Nations at large," but "his Authority, Power and Dominion" is also interior and "in the Hearts of the Ungodly."[59] In *Paradise Regained*, Jesus demonstrates the power and conviction of that inner spiritual kingdom – a kingdom enabling him to endure the trials of a hostile world and the temptations of a subtle foe as he waits patiently to fulfill his eschatological role.

In his polemical speech concluding Book 2, then, Jesus thoroughly revises kingly politics and its language, based upon an internal sense of authority unconstrained by external power, rituals, and kingship. He still speaks of guiding "Nations in the way of truth / By saving Doctrine," suggesting that this more internal, spiritual kingship does not result in his complete retreat from the world: there the inward-oriented saint remains a prophetic figure who guides "nations in the way of truth" by challenging temporal kingship and human authorities, as well as the political language and symbolism which sustains them. Just how provocative his response might sound in an age of royalist ascendancy, when dissenters were regularly harassed and tried by state and church authorities, is suggested by the opposition a confrontational Margaret Fell set up between the external authority of King Charles and the inner spiritual authority of the King of Kings. On trial in 1664 over the issue of taking the Oath of Allegiance, the Quaker Fell highlighted the great "controversie" existing "betwixt Christ Jesus and King *Charles*": even if she owned allegiance to the King of England, she asserted, "Christ Jesus is King of my Conscience."[60] In his own quiet way, the inward Jesus of Milton's poem is himself engaged polemically in turning the world upside down by drastically reconceiving the very terms and authority of kingly government. "This Monarchical Government of Christ," asserted William Erbery the Seeker, "*shall confound . . . all Worldly Government*";[61] indeed, the vision of the power of Christ's inner spiritual kingdom begins to have something of this unsettling effect during the dramatic confrontation between Jesus and Satan in *Paradise Regained*: startled by the force of the Son of God's polemical rejoinder at the end of Book 2, Satan "stood / A while as mute confounded what to say, / What to reply" (3.1–3).

WAITING UPON GOD: JESUS AS RADICAL PURITAN SAINT AND PROPHET

Paradise Regained, moreover, dramatizes that the Kingdom of God, to use the words of James Nayler, "cannot be moved, but . . . is able to keep you against all assaults of the enemy."[62] Radical religious discourse, particularly Quaker writing, often envisioned the inward-looking saint enduring great opposition and trials and yet remaining, almost in a superhuman fashion, firm and unmoved – in the manner indeed of Milton's own unflinching Jesus. Throughout Satan's many kinds of "fresh assaults" (4.570), Jesus remains unmoved: he is "not mov'd" (2.407) by the lavish banquet temptation; he remains "unmov'd" (3.386, 4.109) by the ostentatious display of Parthian military might and the "majestic show" (4.110) of Roman imperial power and luxury; and, though all alone and hungry in a "wild solitude" (2.304), he is "Unshaken" (4.421) by Satan's powerful storm and sits "unappall'd in calm and sinless peace" (425), even as Satan has raised hellish furies and ghosts to terrorize and tempt him. The brow of Jesus, moreover, remains "unalter'd" (1.493) when Satan desires access to him so that he can hear the Son of God's aesthetically appealing "ways of truth" (1.478). Satan attempts to move the austere Jesus at that moment by praising the poetic qualities of his "winning words" – qualities central to Milton's own aesthetic sensibility as a prophetic writer: though the ways of truth may be hard, they are "Smooth on the tongue discourst, pleasing to th' ear, / And tunable as Silvan Pipe or Song" (1.479–80). As Satan recognizes, Jesus combines religious prophecy with aesthetic expression. Indeed, Satan provocatively suggests, since God "Suffers the Hypocrite or Atheous Priest" to "minister / About his Altar" (1.487–89) – an unmistakable reference to the Restoration church – why should the Son himself spurn Satan's access to him and his attractive discourse? Yet even this shrewd appeal on Satan's part fails to move the Son of God.

One of the similes at the opening of Book 4, where Satan is compared to the froth of waves dashing against a rock, underscores the poem's depiction of the unmoved Son of God whose mighty Christian weakness triumphs over the power of Satanic strength:

> Or [as] surging waves against a solid rock,
> Though all to shivers dash't, th'assault renew,
> Vain batt'ry, and in froth or bubbles end;
> So Satan, whom repulse upon repulse
> Met ever . . .   (4.18–22)

Commentators usually note classical analogues in Homer and Virgil to illuminate these lines; but equally pertinent, especially given Milton's contemporary cultural context, is the biblical image of the "solid rock" representing the firm foundation of the Christian faith which cannot be moved by storms or tempests (as in, for instance, Matthew 7:24–25). The image of a great solid rock in the midst of surging waves had been exploited in the iconography of that most famous of "dangerous Frontispices" (in the words of *Areopagitica*, *CPW* 2:524), the one to that "shrewd" popular book *Eikon Basilike* (1649) which Milton had strenuously tried to demolish in *Eikonoklastes*. In the king's book, the image had evoked an unmoved and constant saintly Charles I in the midst of great political and religious turbulence; in Milton's spiritual epic the biblical rock instead evokes the firmness of the saintly, austere Jesus throughout Satan's repeated assaults and his temptations to acquire various forms of alluring and aggrandizing worldly power.

Indeed, this biblical image had particular resonance for a wide range of religious radicals in the turbulent decades of the mid-seventeenth century: in *The New Law of Righteousnes* (1649) Winstanley envisioned Christ as "the one power of Righteousnesse" which "shall not be shaken nor moved, but stand firm forever"; while "the kingdom of the flesh and devil . . . must be shaken to pieces and fall," "the kingdom of heaven or of God . . . is that Rock that cannot be moved."[63] Near the end of the Interregnum, the Fifth Monarchist Christopher Feake would write similarly about the kingdom of Christ "built upon a Rock, the Rock of ages; the Windes and Waves cannot undermine it, or overthrow it."[64] And George Fox, who suffered repeated assaults from both spiritual and physical foes, referred to "the living unmovable word of the Lord God" and envisioned Christ as the rock which "will stand when the World is gone, over all the storms and tempests, they cannot move the Rock."[65] The image continued to have resonance in the year Milton published his spiritual epic: in verses written upon his death, the Fifth Monarchist preacher Vavasor Powell was compared to "a Rock that is assaulted by / Impetuous waves," and yet despite repeated tribulations throughout his life, which included numerous imprisonments and cross-examinations during the Restoration, he "unmov'd did stand / In the Lords work."[66]

In *Paradise Regained* Milton therefore appropriates the biblical symbol of the impregnable rock – giving it an interpretation more consonant with contemporary radical religious and political culture – as he represents "*Israel's* true King" (3.441) fully tried through all temptation. Jesus remains undaunted before worldly powers just as the Quakers or John

Lilburne himself did. When royalist captors in the early 1640s tried to win Lilburne over with "many proffers of worldly honours and prefer-ments, which came even from the King himselfe . . . [Lilburne] remained unmoveable as a rock," noting in the margin of one of his tracts that the rock was an image of his "strong faith" in the face of all royalist "conju-rations or imprecations."[67] In the case of dissenters like the Quakers, remaining unmoved like a "rock / Of Adamant" (4.533–34), while enduring repeated temptations and assaults, reinforced a sense that these radical Puritan saints were indomitable in spirit, rectitude, and steadfast-ness. More than any other persecuted dissenters in Restoration England, Richard Greaves observes, they "did not flee when magistrates appeared but stood their ground as witness to their faith" and, in the words of Thomas Ellwood, would not "dodge and shift" when Satan raised a "storm of persecution" against them.[68] But remaining steadfast as a rock was not necessarily construed by religious radicals as simply a defensive stance: alluding to Psalm 62, Winstanley described "the Kingdome of heaven within" as "the Rock of defence and offence," for it is "the power that makes a man bold as a Lion."[69] The fervent responses of Milton's inward Messiah in this spiritual epic suggest that remaining unmoved is anything but a simple posture of political quietism.

Nor is the steadfast hero of faith in *Paradise Regained* moved by Satan criticizing his slowness to assume the role of a martial leader who has the opportunity to win glory, fame, and national conquests – all of which Satan, who tries to advise Jesus on political matters, invokes to measure heroic actions and epic-scale achievements. "Thy years are ripe, and over-ripe" (3.31), Satan tells him as he renews his temptations, so "Why move thy feet so slow to what is best" (3.224) having reached "full age" and "fulness of time" (4.380)? Yet Jesus's sense of his messianic vocation and its fulfillment in the fulness of time is hardly defined by the pressures associated with martial prowess or traditional heroic values. He intends instead to wait since "All things are best fulfill'd in their due time" (3.182; cf. 3.440), as he shifts the debate to another register altogether, refuting with his Puritan-style responses Satan's pagan conceptions of time and heroism.[70] "The time prefixt I waited" (1.269), observes Jesus, as he rehearses his past attempts to search out the meaning of his prophetic identity as the promised Messiah. This notion of "due time," of waiting and "quietly expecting" (3.192) in the face of temptation and in the midst of strenuous trials, itself had crucial implications within radical Puritan culture and politics during the Revolution and the Restoration.[71] It suggested a more inward notion of time and providential fulfillment, one defined by an internal sense of faith, strength, and godly patience rather than by any external form of power, glory, or temporal authority. "God's time is best," observes the godly Commonwealthsman in Algernon Sidney's *Court Maxims* (1664–65): "They that depend upon him fall not into impatience for the delay of his coming, nor are frightened at the boasting of his and their enemies."[72]

And yet as the Restoration rapidly neared, Milton's countrymen had indeed fallen into such "impatience for the delay of his coming." Evoking the alarming language and imagery of impatience, the visionary Milton had concluded the second edition of his *Readie and Easie Way* by warning his countrymen who were deserting the Good Old Cause for the house of Stuart, especially "after all this light among us." There he had urged them "to bethink themselves a little and consider whether they are rushing," as he exhorted "this torrent . . . of the people, not to be so impetuos, but to keep thir due channell," lest they are hurried to "a precipice of destruction" as a result of "the deluge of this epidemic madness." In the mad rush towards the Restoration, that sense of "due time" and saintly patience, crucial to radical Puritans of the Interregnum who acted according to the divine light, had been dangerously abandoned by "a misguided and abus'd multitude" (*CPW* 7:462–63).

The sense of "due time" might, furthermore, entail uncertainty or limited knowledge about God's ways, leadings, and plans as Puritan saints encountered trials and crises in the process of waiting. The solitary and human Jesus of Milton's poem wonders in the midst of the mazelike wilderness, "Where will this end?" (2.245), for "to what intent" he is led into this desert he learns "not yet" (1.291–92). So too Jesus's perplexed followers, fearing that they have lost their Messiah, express their anxious thoughts, but then decide to "wait" (2.49) upon God, as does Mary herself ("But I to wait with patience am inur'd," 2.102). As Thomas Young the Smectymnuan wrote, "Though the faithfulnesse of Gods promise is knowne" to the saints, "yet the particular period or set time, wherein this promise shall take effect, is unknowne to them," and "because they [know] not when it should bee, God requires of them to waite."[73] Likewise, echoing the Psalms (e.g. 37:7, 40:1), Joshua Sprigge observed in the Army Debates at Whitehall (1648) that "if we could have but patience to wait upon [God], we should see he would bring us out of this labyrinth wherein we are."[74] And in the Restoration, the poet-prophet George

Wither offered his own version of such saintly advice: "Let not then the length or sharpness of any Persecution discourage from a Constant waiting upon GOD, whose Grace will be a sufficient Assistance in all *Probations*."[75] This Puritan-style state of "Constant waiting" is the experience of Milton's Jesus, who waits patiently and without full knowledge in the wilderness for the occasion to fulfill his messianic role – and then, unshaken even by his final temptation, makes a dramatic stand on the pinnacle, demonstrating perfect obedience. "Truly, there is as real deliverance witnessed inwardly," wrote the Quaker Penington, "by those that wait upon the Lord and are faithful to the leadings of his holy Spirit."[76]

Still, the most effective strategy Satan uses to prompt the reclusive Jesus to move more decisively in establishing his kingdom is to remind him of the career of the revolutionary martial leader Judas Maccabeus. In Book 3 (lines 165ff.) Satan urges the slow-moving Jesus to seize the historical moment and become a political activist like Maccabeus in order to free a Judaea in bondage under the tyrant Tiberius's power and assume David's throne. One of the striking features of this late poem is the way it imaginatively reengages issues of Milton's revolutionary writings and experiences: not only his profound suspicion of temporal forms of regal power (as opposed to a more spiritual kind of inward power), but also his own temptation in the 1640s and 1650s to become a political activist and zealous radical who might heroically free his countrymen from bondage by means of violent rebellion. Jesus, however, remains "unmoved" even by political temptations that most clearly recall some of Milton's deepest revolutionary yearnings. Yet as this interior epic dramatizes, there may be more than one way to respond as a revolutionary: waiting for things to be "fulfilled in their due time" suggests, rather than political resignation, a prophetic sense of expectation particularly resonant in the culture of radical Puritanism which emphasized "a time coming when Jesus Christ shall have the Kingdomes of the world subjected to him."[77]

Indeed, tempted by great spectacles of power, empire, and kingship, the Jesus who waits patiently like some Puritan saint can firmly insist that his time "is not yet come" (3.397), while also responding in a manner that is ominously prophetic. Referring to the fulfillment of his kingdom in due time, Jesus, who has searched the Old Testament prophets in order to discover his messianic identity (1.259–63), envisions his apocalyptic role in history when he will dash "to pieces" all the kingdoms of the world; then he will not be found "slack" (3.398):

> Know therefore when my season comes to sit
> On *David's* Throne, it shall be like a tree
> Spreading and overshadowing all the Earth,
> Or as a stone that shall to pieces dash
> All Monarchies besides throughout the world,
> And of my Kingdom there shall be no end.   (4.146–51)

Humble and obscure Jesus may be, but his role in world history will be truly apocalyptic.[78] Biblical prophecies like the one quoted above were put to threatening political uses during the Revolution and the Interregnum: Jesus's reference to Daniel 2:31–35 recalls Milton's own polemical use of this prophetic text in his early apocalyptic prose, where he had envisioned using the "weapon" of Scriptures to "throw down" and "batter" to pieces the "*Nebuchadnezzars* Image" of Laudian episcopacy (*Animadversions, CPW* 1:700). In his late poem the coming messianic kingdom – an eternal one and, as the lines above suggest, the only kingdom of genuine divine origin and power – is likened to the supernatural stone of Daniel which destroys temporal kingdoms. During the Interregnum, the Quaker William Dewsbury, in his *True Prophecie of the Mighty Day of the Lord*, had not only urged the saints to "wait upon [the Lord] to be guided by His Power," but, alluding to Daniel 2:35, had warned the rulers of the Protectorate against setting up the great image of Nebuchadnezzar since "the Kingdom of the Lord Jesus . . . shall break down all the Kingdoms of world and shall fill the whole Earth."[79] Jesus's prophecy in *Paradise Regained*, with its millenarian implications, would have had an ominous resonance after the Restoration, when nonconformist religious writers could still express a similar kind of unsettling vision with regard to temporal monarchy. "The Kings of the earth are afraid lest Christs Government should un-king them," wrote the radical Puritan minister William Dyer in a tract proclaiming the power of Christ's eternal kingdom to break mighty kings in pieces and "*put all his enemies under his feet*" (echoing I Cor. 15:25): "Alas, what are all the Crowns and Kingdomes of the world, all the Thrones and Scepters of Kings to Christ?"[80] As a prophetic text whose charged tone is sometimes far from moderate, *Paradise Regained* itself can assume a political dimension that is more polemically engaged – and surely less quietist and passively resigned – than the inward and politically withdrawn Restoration poem it is often assumed to be. However retiring the inward-looking Jesus may be, he hardly expiates "himself in a retired silence" – words Marvell used in 1673 to describe Milton since "His Majesties happy Return."[81]

Jesus's increasingly sharp responses dramatize his vigorous polemical engagement rather than withdrawal or quiescence. This is a radical spiritual poem full of dispute and verbal duelling; indeed, it illustrates the power of verbal weapons to unsettle and vex. The Son of God's righteous vehemence is a crucial dimension of his contentious responses to Satan's later temptations, including the immensely attractive temptation to knowledge. Here Satan appeals to a Jesus whose meditative mind focuses inwardly, as Satan describes Athens as a place of "sweet recess," "studious walks," "studious musing," and "retirement" (4.242–49): all this learning, eloquence, and philosophy will make Jesus "a King complete / Within [himself]" (283–84). To be sure, Satan's evocation of Greek poetic arts, political rhetoric, and the wisdom of Socrates recalls some of Milton's own deepest intellectual and aesthetic yearnings, thereby creating an uneasy tension at this point in the poem. Satan's inclusion of Socrates and his philosophy is particularly shrewd, since Jesus had earlier singled out the poor Socrates for praise because of his suffering unjustly for "truth's sake" (3.96–99). But for the Son of God, as for the cultured Quaker William Penn in 1669, the austere Socrates is to be singled out less for his doctrine and more for his "divine, severe, just, and self-denying life": he is the just man among pagans who most nearly resembles Milton's Jesus or the austere Quakers themselves.[82] Moreover, when Jesus here administers "a sharp & corrosive sentence," as he dismisses Satan's appealing temptation (pagan culture and learning he calls "false, or little else but dreams, / Conjectures, fancies, built on nothing firm" (4.291–92)), he does not necessarily express Milton's own austere rejection of classical culture, since *Paradise Regained*, after all, was published along with a dramatic poem closely based upon classical tragedy. Rather, he dramatizes that fierce Miltonic stance of polemical engagement and vehement response: an instance of countering rhetorical extreme with rhetorical extreme and an example of "the high and vehement speeches of our Saviour" which the controversialist admired in his prose (and considered an "art of powerful reclaiming"), such as when Christ gives "a sharp and vehement answer to a tempting question."[83] Thus Christ, though "himselfe the fountaine of meeknesse," "found acrimony anough to be still galling and vexing the Prelaticall Pharisees" (*CPW* 1:900–1). This is no less true of the meek, calm yet sharply polemical Jesus of *Paradise Regained*.[84]

In emphasizing that "he who receives / Light from above, from the fountain of light, / No other doctrine needs" (4.288–90), Jesus resembles in his polemical response Milton's Quaker contemporaries who, though thoroughly steeped in the Bible and capable of quoting it to devastating effect, tended to emphasize the Spirit's inner illumination (and the Light within) above the letter of Scripture, as Milton himself does in *De Doctrina Christiana*.[85] Human learning from this radical religious perspective was in any case unnecessary, the prophetess Anna Trapnel proclaimed, since "Christs Scholars . . . are perfected / with learning from above"; moreover "the *teaching of God*," another radical spiritual writer observed, "is an inward *Spiritual* kinde of *teaching*."[86] Jesus's polemical response accords with Milton's radical religious contemporaries, moreover, in scorning verbal ornament ("swelling Epithets thick laid / As varnish on a Harlot's cheek," 4.343–44) or what George Fox called "great swelling words of vanity," while praising the "majestic unaffected style" of the Hebrew prophets over classical oratory: "In them is plainest taught, and easiest learnt, / What makes a Nation happy, and keeps it so, / What ruins Kingdoms, and lays Cities flat" (359, 361–63).[87] Plain prophetic discourse was itself a rhetorical weapon exploited in radical religious writing and speaking during the Interregnum and the Restoration, since it evoked the practice of the ancient prophets fearlessly admonishing those in authority.[88] Thus George Fox the younger, who did not hesitate to admonish and instruct temporal authorities, including the restored monarch, wrote in 1660 that "as the Lord shall move us, we shall be willing to show the governors in plainness, what is wrong with them, and in the government."[89] It is in relation to this contemporary milieu – where we see evidence of continued polemical engagement among radical religious writers during the Restoration – that we need to consider the political claims the austere Jesus makes for the unaffected style and power of prophetic discourse, which his own "sharp, but saving words" (*The Reason of Church-Government*, *CPW* 1:804) in *Paradise Regained* exemplify.

In his "*Day* of *Temptations* and *Tryals*," to recall the words of Edward Burrough, the meek, inward-looking Messiah of *Paradise Regained* does indeed "put on *strength*, that he [might] stand, and never *be moved*," thus demonstrating that his mighty weakness has a "Godlike force" (4.602) capable of overcoming the strength of Satanic power. The eschatological thrust of the poem's ending – as Satan falls stunned "with amazement" (4.562) at the wondrous revelation of Jesus on the pinnacle as both perfect man and God – highlights this dramatic apocalyptic victory, while looking forward to other battles at the end of time. The spiritual kingdom of Jesus is here, *Paradise Regained* suggests, and yet it is also to come at that point in the future when Satan, who "shalt not long / Rule in the Clouds," "shalt fall from Heav'n trod down / Under his feet" (4.618–21). Both deeply inward and mighty in the power of the Lord, Jesus has vanquished all worldly temptations and assaults. In his unusual spiritual epic, Milton thus offered his dissenting countrymen in Restoration England a provocative representation of the faithful, unmoved saint following the dictates of the Spirit. Indeed, he created a compelling model for radical religious saints who found themselves exercised in an age of acute trials and uncertainty, but who nevertheless chose to wait upon God in the wilderness, even as they may have anxiously wondered: "Where will this end?"[90]

CHAPTER NINE

The saint's revenge: radical religion and politics in Samson Agonistes

Just a year after Milton published his dramatic poem based on Judges, the Quaker Francis Howgill compared one of the most fiery revolutionary Quakers, Edward Burrough, to Samson. Burrough was "very dreadful to the Enemies of the Lord," Howgill observed in his testimony concerning the life, trials, and labors of "That True Prophet" and "Faithful Servant of God"; and he went on to marvel: "how great an Alarum didst thou give in thy day, that made the Host of the Uncircumcised greatly distressed!" Howgill paid testimony to the powerful Quaker writer and charismatic political leader by representing him in militant biblical terms and as one who "shalt be recorded among the Valiants of *Israel*, who attained to the first Degree through the Power of the Lord, that wrought mightily in thee in thy day." Burrough had resembled not only the champion David – "how have I seen thee with thy Sling and thy Stone . . . wound the Mighty!" – but the mighty combatant from Judges who slew the uncircumcised and carried out other "great exploits" (*SA*, line 32) and "wrought such wonders with an Ass's Jaw" (1095): "with [the Jaw-bone of an Ass] thou hast slain the *Philistines* Heaps upon Heaps, as *Sampson*."[1] As Howgill's testimony suggests, the militant and faithful Samson who represents the godly saint actively at war with the world could have great potency for radical religious culture and writing – even after the Restoration.

As a biblical model intended to represent a version of the radical saint in a state of anguish and crisis, the Miltonic Samson is intensely inward looking, suffers acutely from a sense of failed vocation, and yet rouses himself once more as he is prompted by "the inward perswasive motions of [the] spirit" to engage in decisive violent action.[2] Although it is difficult to date *Samson Agonistes* precisely,[3] its publication in 1671 does indeed invite us to construe its implications in relation to the Restoration, as well as the turbulent years of the Revolution: it is a work that looks painfully back to the past, registers the sharp disruption between the glorious past and the tragic present, and depicts a militant saint who, moved by the Spirit, acts "of [his] own accord" (1643) in response to the present moment of political bondage and idolatry. My aim in this chapter is to consider its radical spiritual dimensions, apocalypticism, and politics in relation to a wide range of radical religious writings from the 1640s, 1650s, and thereafter – the kinds of writings often discussed in previous sections of this book.[4] Such works from the Revolution and its aftermath help to illuminate the radical spiritual and political implications of Milton's *Samson Agonistes*, the texture of its dramatic writing and its raw emotional power, as well as the poet's distinctive handling of the Samson story from Judges. And they remind us that the written discourse of radical religion, in its more assertive and aggressively apocalyptic man-ifestations, spilled over into the Restoration when it was by no means simply contained or muted.[5] Nevertheless, my aim is not to align *Samson Agonistes* with any one particular group of radical separatist writers – since Milton himself, after all, cannot be thoroughly identified with any one radical religious movement or sect[6] – or even with one contempo-rary historical event; readers of Milton's Old Testament drama, I believe, need not make such connections too literally or narrowly. Rather, the drama remains, in terms of its historical associations, highly suggestive: its radical spiritual and political themes evoke the religious politics of the Revolution as well as of the Restoration – a critical moment when God's saints, many of them "Prisoner[s] chain'd" (7), were subject to "th'unjust tribunals, under change of times" (695) and yet still might be represented in a radical Protestant poem as "very dreadful to the Enemies of the Lord," to use the words of the Quaker prophet Francis Howgill.[7]

Milton's is an unsettling drama, I will argue, about the mightiness of the Spirit of God which comes upon the militant saint yet once more and prompts him to commit a spectacular act of "horrid" destruction (1542). The apocalyptic and dreadful character of Samson's horrid act can be closely aligned with the fiery radical religious discourse of the revo-lutionary years and their aftermath. As we shall see, Milton's daring treatment of the Samson story enabled him to dramatize – and at times complicate – some of the major concerns of religious radicalism and its politics.[8] His drama registers the intense inwardness of radical religious culture, its emphasis on the potency of the Spirit's motions and the saint's waiting upon God, its concern with the inscrutable actings of providence, and, among more militant visionaries, its concern with terrifying apocalyptic vengeance. In its own way, then, *Samson Agonistes* powerfully dramatizes again the interaction of politics and radical religion in Milton's age – an age when religious ferment, as we have seen, had often fueled revolution and stimulated new expressions of literary creativity.[9]

RADICAL RELIGION AND THE SPIRIT OF THE LORD

The Samson story allowed Milton to write a drama of the inward Spirit of God which, one last time, comes mightily upon the militant saint (the Spirit of the Lord moving Samson is emphasized in Judges 13:25, 14:6, 19; 15:14). Milton's radical Protestant drama of the Spirit's workings is of course much more interior than the story narrated in the Book of Judges, and his imaginative handling of the motif owes much to radical religious ideology which flourished during the English Revolution and continued, despite fierce persecution of the saints, into the Restoration. Like other religious radicals, Milton had stressed in his controversial and theological prose that one should follow the guidance of the Spirit within rather than any law of humankind (see e.g. *Civil Power*, *CPW* 7:242; *De Doctrina Christiana*, *CPW* 6:527, 531); moved by the rousing motions of the Spirit, the saintly Samson, to use the words of *The Tenure of Kings and Magistrates*, undertakes one of those "great actions, above the form of [human] Law or Custom" (*CPW* 3:194). A wide spectrum of revolutionary Puritans, from Oliver Cromwell to the Seeker William Erbery to the early Quakers, waited for the Spirit to take them out of Babylon and to lead them in the wilderness of the world.[10] Milton's former tutor, the Smectymnuan Thomas Young, while never as spiritually radical as Milton became during the Revolution, observed, moreover, that *"Gods Spirit strengthens* all such as waite upon the Lord."[11] *Samson Agonistes* illustrates this observation in a particularly daring fashion, as his intensely inward-looking and anguished Samson, prompted by the Spirit's inward persuasive motions, finds the "Heav'n-gifted strength" (36) at the end to commit his final act of catastrophic devastation against the lordly idolaters of Dagon.

But while encouraging saints to wait upon the Lord for an "intimate impulse" and to be guided by his power (as we saw in the chapter on *Paradise Regained*), revolutionary Puritan writers stressed that saints should not be impatient and murmur against God, despite their acute sufferings, persecutions, anxieties, and feelings of rage. "Whatsoever your condition is, murmur not at it, but waite" for "the powerfull day of the Lord," Gerrard Winstanley observed to the oppressed saints in the

midst of one of his most potent visions of apocalyptic crisis.[12] "Why,"
asked Edward Burrough as he addressed the anxious saints in the year
of the Restoration, "should *we murmure* against God? or say, Why hast
thou *done it*? But let *us* travel in *Patience* through all the *Oppressions*, and in
the *Power* of the Lord, *we* shall work through *them*."[13] Furthermore,
Thomas Young, who in the 1640s singled out Samson as a saint for his
valiance in waiting upon the Lord, also warned the faithful in Parliament
of the dangers of murmuring against God in moments of great spiritual
crisis and affliction: "If it bee one propertie of Gods people to waite on
the Lord in all their troubles, then such as are so farre from waiting on
God in the day of their troubles that they dare murmure, fret and rage
against the Lord."[14]

Samson Agonistes, however, was written by a poet who at moments of
spiritual crisis could indeed record his own "restless thoughts" (19) and
feel the powerful temptation to murmur against God (as in the famous
sonnet on his blindness, where Patience checks his "murmur"); his poem
thus dramatizes the urge to murmur against providence rather than
quietly wait for the Lord's next command. Milton's daring drama, in
other words, offers a more probing treatment of this issue than the
Puritan sermon by Young, who had singled out Samson as one of the
faithful saints: the dramatic poet does not retreat from representing the
disturbing implications of an anguished saint who feels such a profound
sense of "shame and sorrow" (457) and thus passionately murmurs
against God.[15] Rather, Milton dares to highlight that anxious murmuring – the urge to "quarrel with the will / Of highest dispensation"
(60–61) – in his radical Protestant work about the apparently failed
career of God's valiant saint who, plagued by a sense of his uselessness
and "Heav'n's desertion," has become "the scorn and gaze" of ungodly
"cruel enemies" who despise him and "who come to stare / At [his]
affliction" (632, 34, 642, 112–13). "Ask for this great Deliverer now, and
find him / Eyeless in *Gaza* at the Mill with slaves, / Himself in bonds
under *Philistian* yoke," murmurs the blind, embittered Samson in the
"day of his troubles" before checking this powerful urge to complain and
sharply blaming himself: "Yet stay, let me not rashly call in doubt /
Divine Prediction" (40–44; cf. 373–80). The mentally restless and tormented Samson, who is nearly ready to mutiny against providence, wres-
tles with his own powerful urge to murmur against God – an urge
augmented by the profound humiliation of his blindness and slavish
imprisonment which expose him "To daily fraud, contempt, abuse and
wrong" (76). By dramatizing at first a despairing Samson who must

restrain his urge to "fret and rage against the Lord" and who finds that he is far from waiting patiently upon God in the midst of all his troubles and oppressions, Milton represents the acute agony of an inward-looking radical Puritan saint who truly believes that the days of his divine impulses are over.

Samson Agonistes, as some of its most provocative commentators have recently shown, is a drama that raises profound questions and doubts in the troubled minds of its characters and readers struggling to interpret the meaning of Samson's shocking tragedy.[16] Nevertheless, there is no need to turn *Samson Agonistes* into a drama of indeterminacy where all meanings – especially in relation to Samson's ruptured and painful career, as well as his last divine prompting – are simply ambiguous and doubtful. The context of radical Puritanism enables us to recognize the disturbing features of Milton's drama as essential to its daring treatment of radical religious concerns. But we need not adopt a position of extreme skepticism that prompts us to doubt the profound source of Samson's "rousing motions" – the inward persuasive motions of the Spirit which guide this Hebrew champion in matters of war and politics and which identify Samson with the saints of radical religion in Milton's England. As the Samson-like Edward Burrough himself put it, "the Saints in former generations . . . were led . . . by the Spirit of God, as all the servants of God are."[17] In his *De Doctrina Christiana* the heretical Milton had considered the Spirit "the pre-eminent and supreme authority," even in relation to scriptural authority (though other religious radicals, including the Quakers, went even further in elevating the Spirit above the Scriptures), stressing as well how it superseded all human laws and should therefore be followed by faithful saints before them – no matter how inscrutable the workings of the inward Spirit and God's providence might appear to human commentators and understanding.[18] In this sense, Milton was considerably more radical than the Presbyterians or conservative Puritans whose politics, orthodox religious convictions, and "acted zeale" (*CPW* 3:236) he sharply countered in *The Tenure*. Alarmed by sectarianism and dismayed by the violent political events of 1648–49, which Milton ardently supported, these cautious scripturalists had warned the Army and its council against the revolutionary and radical antinomian implications of following the impromptu motions of God's Spirit: "Nor is it safe to be guided by Impulses of Spirit . . . without or against the rule of Gods written Word."[19] Indeed, when in the 1660s the godly republican Edmund Ludlow recalled Thomas Harrison's activism in pursuing "the justice of the putting of the late King to death," he noted that the zealous regicide and Army officer "had a more then ordinary impulse of spirit."[20]

In *An Apology against a Pamphlet,* moreover, Milton himself stressed the importance of "obedience to the Spirit of God, rather then to the faire seeming pretences of men" (*CPW* 1:937) – or one might add, in the case of *Samson Agonistes,* "the faire pretences" of a woman like the alluring "sorceress" (819) Dalila, whose "false pretexts and varnish'd colors" (901), as well as her "feign'd Religion" (872), Samson fiercely resists. In terms of the drama's concern with the power and impulses of the Spirit, this episode is indeed suggestive. Dalila's own internalized agon is a caricature of Samson's "hard contest" (864–65) as she describes the "assaults," "snares," and "sieges" (845–46) she endured from the Philistine magistrates and priests who repeatedly pressured her to ensnare the mighty Hebrew warrior. Ultimately, readers alert to the radical religious concerns of Milton's drama are meant discern how her "motions" differ significantly from those internalized ones of the radical saint: glory and patriotism, the desire for wealth and particularly fame (830–31, 971–94), and her service to the god Dagon are what moved her to act treacherously – "zeal mov'd thee," Samson lashes out at her, "To please thy gods thou didst it" (895–96).

The scene where Samson follows the leadings and "motions" of the Spirit as he is commanded to appear before the Philistine spectacle thus especially evokes the concerns of radical religion and its saints with the inner work of the Spirit and its impulses to act and engage with worldly powers. The Quaker prophet and leader George Fox, for example, recounts in his famous *Journal* how "several times" while suffering imprisonment he "had motions from the Lord" to go out and confront the priests, justices, and people committed to the world who were often "in great rage" against him.[21] Physical imprisonment of the sort Samson suffers or Fox frequently endured could not stop the inward motions of the Spirit. Fervently rejecting fixed forms in matters of religion, Milton considered one of the "two most unimprisonable things" "that Divine Spirit of utterance that moves" our prayers (*CPW* 3:505), and *Samson Agonistes* dramatizes how "the quickning power of the *Spirit*" (*Of Reformation, CPW* 1:522) has its own secret motions not stifled by outward prison chains any more than it could be by carnal forms in religion or by an oppressing civil power. Furthermore, in radical religious culture, as one of its major historians has shown, this emphasis on the immediate movings of the Lord's Spirit within the saint had little to do with human reason ("the weak mightines of mans reasoning," as Milton could call it (*CPW* 1:827)) or rational faith.[22] Milton's radical Protestant drama, much more than the original story in Judges, highlights the impromptu workings of the Spirit in the tense episode where a scornful Samson, recalling his holy commitments as a Nazarite, at first adamantly refuses to perform in Dagon's idolatrous temple ("I will not come," he insists twice) and submit himself to the contempt of his foes ("to be thir fool or jester") and then concedes finally to go along with the Philistine officer when he begins "to feel / Some rousing motions in [him]" (see 1319–89). Milton's imaginative and free treatment of Judges here enables him to dramatize the disparity between the constraints of "outward force" and what he called in *Civil Power* "the inward perswasive motions of [the] spirit." It is "that Spirit that first rusht on [him] / In the camp of *Dan*" (1435–36) that returns yet once more to the warrior saint, inwardly prompting him to go off to the heathen temple – a "place abominable" – and act.

We have seen already how Milton's drama of the anguished saint complicates the radical Puritan emphasis on the virtue of waiting patiently and obediently upon the Lord for the divine impulse – an issue, as we saw in the last chapter, which Milton richly explores in *Paradise Regained*, where the inward-looking Jesus embodies the perfect saint of radical religious culture who waits with a spirit of meekness and patience. Thus the Quakers, who were constantly warring against worldly institutions and Antichristian powers, particularly emphasized how their saints waited patiently while suffering great reproaches and persecution during the Interregnum and the Restoration.[23] In *Samson Agonistes* the Chorus extols "patience" as "more oft the exercise / Of Saints" (1287–88) and it is towards the end of Milton's radical Puritan drama that the blind Samson finally does demonstrate his own particular kind of saintly patience when, having responded to the promptings of the rousing motions within, he is first displayed in the great Philistine spectacle: as the messenger relates, Milton's saintly Samson was "patient but undaunted where they led him" (1623). In *Samson Agonistes* Milton has presented an anguished saint who is afflicted by his enemies, and then, during the last hour of his career, waits patiently in a fearless manner; like a radical saint who remains firm in the midst of worldly adversaries, he waits for the Spirit of the Lord to move him to commit one final, terrifying act of apocalyptic force. "Patient but undaunted" at the very end of his spiritual and physical trials, the Miltonic Samson illustrates dramatically what that fierce godly republican, Edmund Ludlow, called "the howre of the Saints' patience" as they wait for the moment when the "Lord's wrath" will strike, thereby resulting in "the vindicating of his honour and great name, so much reproached"; his stance likewise illustrates what the visionary Digger Winstanley, addressing the saints as both priestly and kingly powers oppressed them, called "wait[ing] for the breakings forth of the powerfull day of the Lord."[24]

For radical religious writers, Samson being moved inwardly by the Lord's Spirit could signal the operation of an awesome conquering power of divine origin, as it did for the Independent minister and Fifth Monarchist preacher John Canne, a writer whose own justification of the Revolution was influenced by Milton's *Tenure of Kings and Magistrates*. Milton's Old Testament champion roused by the Spirit becomes, in Canne's words, one of God's mighty warrior saints who "shall have Gods presence so . . . powerfully with them, that the enemies, through a dreadful fear, shall not know what to do for their own safety, nor how to oppose the work of God in the hands of his mighty ones. As it is said of *Barak, Gideon, Samson* . . . that *the Spirit of the Lord came upon them*, and in that Spirit they went forth, conquering and to conquer."[25] And so once its militant saint feels the urging of his inward rousing motions, *Samson Agonistes* becomes a drama about the work of the Spirit and its conquering power; Milton gives dramatic expression to the notion voiced by the regicide and Anabaptist William Goffe during the famous Putney Debates of 1647: "Now the work of the Spirit is, that we do pull down all works [that are not] of the Spirit whatsoever."[26]

"UNSEARCHABLE" PROVIDENCE

Samson Agonistes is nevertheless a radical religious drama that suggests that the Spirit's power and providence can operate in mysterious and profoundly unsettling ways. The issue of providentialism, which I want to address in this section, was crucial to radical Puritan culture. But while providence was often invoked by Milton's revolutionary Puritan contemporaries to explain extraordinary political and military events – including Cromwell's great military successes in the 1640s and early 1650s – and to explain divine blessing or rebuke, "the secret and unsearchable Mysteries of high Providence," to use Milton's words (*CPW* 3:564), could indeed seem inscrutable or severe, while its actings could seem unexpected.[27] Cromwell, who himself believed in the power of the Spirit, likewise fervently believed with many other revolutionary Puritans (including Milton) in a wondrous providential design at work in the Civil

Wars and the traumatic political events of the Revolution: "a Divine Presence hath gone along with us in the late great transactions in this nation" which swept away the bishops, the monarchy, and the House of Lords, he observed in a letter to John Sadler, one of Milton's Commonwealth friends and later a member of the Council of State; but Cromwell also observed "those strange windings and turnings of Providence; those very great appearances of God, in crossing and thwarting the purposes of men."[28] In its own way *Samson Agonistes*, a work deeply concerned with "The mystery of God" (378), dramatizes how truly unexpected and confounding the "windings and turnings" of providence can be with its great alterations.

In the past, Samson's glorious career as an "invincible" militant deliverer under God's "special eye" seemed to confirm a sense of marvelous providential triumphs, as though Samson were the Cromwell of his age: thus we hear about those "wond'rous actions" and "high exploits by him achiev'd" against the uncircumcised, when his locks contained the strength "of a Nation arm'd" and Israel's Lord "wrought things . . . incredible / For his people of old" (341, 636, 1440, 1492–94, 1532–33). In those days, the "strange windings" of providence included prompting the saintly deliverer, by means of an "intimate impulse" (223; cf. 421–22), to marry women of the enemy tribe. To the Israelites who visit the dejected Samson of the present, however, God's providential ways – "th' unsearchable dispose / Of highest wisdom" (1746–47) – remain not only mysterious, but seem, as the deeply perplexed Chorus reveals in its agonized responses, utterly confounding and contradictory, especially towards one of his "solemnly elected" champions (678):

> God of our Fathers, what is man!
> That thou towards him with hand so various,
> Or I might say contrarious,
> Temper'st thy providence through his short course,
> Not evenly . . .   (667–71)

Having just heard Samson's highly graphic lament over his acute mental torment, "swoonings of despair," and "sense of Heav'n's desertion" (631–32), the Chorus gropes, much like bewildered characters out of a Greek tragedy, for some comprehensible meaning to what appears as God's unfathomable and mutable providence, which has brought about this "change beyond report, thought, or belief" (117). The Danites remain confounded too at the crucial moment in the drama when

Samson, prompted by the inward motions of faith, agrees to accompany the Philistine officer to the temple of Dagon: "How thou wilt here come off surmounts my reach" (1380).

As revolutionary Puritan writers noted, that sense of uncertainty or the unknown was itself part of the saint's trials as he was guided by the Spirit and served as an instrument of providence. Thus John Owen, the apocalyptic Independent preacher of the Commonwealth, stressed the inscrutability of God's providences, noting that God keeps men in

darknesse and obscurity, whereby he holds the minds of men in uncertainty, and suspence, for his own glorious ends. . . . he brings not forth his work all at once, but by degrees, and sometimes sets it backward, and leads it up and down, as he did his people of old in the wildernesse. . . . When God is doing great things, he delights . . . to keep the minds of men in uncertainties, that he may . . . try them to the utmost.[29]

In Owen's terms, Milton's Samson as an instrument of God's providence has indeed been set "backward" as God keeps both his saint, who is tried to the utmost in this drama, and his Hebrew compatriots in a state of profound "uncertainty," as well as "suspence." The "actings of God's providence," as Owen stressed elsewhere, are "exceedingly unsuited to the Reasonings and Expectations of the most of the Sonnes of men".[30] Milton's dramatization of the Chorus' baffled responses to the torment and inward griefs of God's former champion would seem to confirm such a view of mysterious providential workings which altogether defy human "Reasonings and Expectations." Owen's comments about the enigmatic providence by which the Lord works his "glorious ends" and does "great things" also convey in contemporary terms something of the Chorus' final sense, expressed after Samson has desolated the Philistine temple and lords, that

> Oft [God] seems to hide his face,
> But unexpectedly returns
> And to his faithful Champion hath in place
> Bore witness gloriously.   (1749–52)

But Owen's statements attempting to explain the inscrutability of providence do not fully convey, as Milton's drama so powerfully does, the sense of profound spiritual and mental agony felt by the suffering, humiliated, and imprisoned saint whose unassuaged griefs "ferment and rage" internally as "a ling'ring disease" "finding no redress" (617–19). Nor do they fully convey the agony felt by those anxious Israelites who desperately attempt to comprehend the mysterious – and seemingly contradictory – turnings of providence after having observed the depth of Samson's suffering and tragic condition. *Samson Agonistes* dramatizes, as one revolutionary commentator on the paradoxes of providence observed, how the "Saints extremities are Gods opportunities."[31] Milton's drama of this blind and tormented saint, whose shattered career seems like a painful enigma, is thus among the most daring and disturbing literary treatments of the paradoxes and ambiguities of Puritan providentialism that we have.

In *Samson Agonistes* the obscure workings of providence and the Spirit are conveyed through Samson's own tentative, unspecific language as he prepares himself for and begins to speak about his last (but in his mind uncertain) performance before the Philistines: in response to the Chorus, Samson refers to God dispensing with him "in Temples at Idolatrous Rites / For *some* important cause" as he feels "*Some* rousing motions in [him] which dispose / To *something* extraordinary [his] thoughts" (1378–79, 1382–83; emphasis added). And as he leaves with the public officer, there remains a sense of mystery about Samson's assertion that "this day will be remarkable in [his] life / By *some* great act" (1388–89; emphasis added). Nor is that sense of mystery dispelled when the messenger describes Samson, situated between the pillars, revolving in his mind "*some* great matter" (1638; emphasis added). As the drama suggests, the Spirit or the "motions" Samson feels inwardly may lead towards an unknown or uncertain end, though not necessarily a disreputable one: "Happ'n what may, of me expect to hear / Nothing dishonorable, impure, unworthy / Our God, our Law, my Nation, or myself; / The last of me or no I cannot warrant" (1423–26). In effect, when Samson agrees to enter the temple of Dagon, a "place abominable" (1359) to a Nazarite, he submits to the providence of God, much as a godly and religious soldier like Cromwell often claimed to be doing; and Samson does so even when it appears to be an inscrutable authority.[32] Thomas Young wrote, in a work that emphasizes the Spirit guiding the saints (including Samson), that "*Hee* can bring [the saints'] wayes to passe though *they* see not how" – a perspective that applies to Milton's Samson, especially when Young adds that such saints "grow couragious, because *Gods Spirit strengthens* all such as waite upon the Lord."[33] That is indeed what happens to Milton's Samson, who finds new resolve as he follows the impromptu motions of the Spirit, even as an element of uncertainty remains about what will transpire in Dagon's temple. Towards the end of the Interregnum, the Quaker prophet Francis Howgill wrote that "as the day of the Lord is a mysterie, the spirit of the Lord is the onely discoverer of it":[34] the unexpected cataclysmic destruction at the end of *Samson Agonistes* – that "some great act" Samson commits after he has felt his rousing motions within – does indeed suggest that the mighty day of the Lord is a mystery and that the Spirit is the "discoverer of it."

Some radical Puritans, moreover, highlighted the relation between God's mysterious providences and unsettling acts of apocalyptic destruction and overturning in their age. Revolutionary Puritans did not see terrifying shakings and unexpected acts of destruction as arbitrary or capricious events; rather, they saw them as acts designed by providence itself. The radical preacher John Canne, for example, registered that sense of a surprising, disorienting providence when he wrote in an apocalyptic tract addressed to Cromwell and Milton's friend Robert Overton (the radical godly Parliamentary officer warmly praised in the *Defensio Secunda*) that "these latter times will be accompanied with such great destractions, confusions, divisions, as people will be at a losse, and so in darknesse, that they will not know what to doe, which way to take, nor how to dispose of themselves. . . . Gods marvelous work now in the world, will move so contrary to mens expectations and self interest."[35] Similarly, another commentator on the inscrutable and mighty ways of God's providence observed that when God "shall come" and "overturn" and "throw down the mighty, lay waste and make desolate strong Cities, fortified Nations, and the greatest Monarchies," this may be "unexpected by us" and "unlooked for."[36] Indeed, by operating mysteriously or secretively, God would confound his enemies all the more effectively. The radical minister Thomas Brooks, exulting in the Revolution just after Pride's Purge and commenting on "strange providences," observed that "God . . . will save his people, and ruine their enemies by very darke, and mysterious wayes . . . and unlikely meanes" so "that their enemies may be the more dreadfully ashamed, and confounded."[37] And so it happens in the horrid catastrophe of *Samson Agonistes*. Like these revolutionary Puritan writers, Milton himself powerfully conveys a sense of mysterious, "unlooked for" destruction and God's participation in it as providence "unexpectedly returns" at the end of the drama: thus the Philistine lords and nobility are "distracted" and struck "with amaze" (1286, 1645) by Samson's great act and the power of "Gods marvelous work in the world." To quote from Milton's *De Doctrina Christiana*, the catastrophic devastation wrought by Samson the militant saint and the wonder it evokes dramatically illustrate that "the extraordinary providence of God is that by which he produces some effect outside the normal order of nature or gives to some chosen person the power of producing this effect" (*CPW* 6:341).

"DEARLY-BOUGHT REVENGE"

Radical religious writers who violently denounced ungodly earthly powers and authorities during the revolutionary years and the Restoration could emphasize a powerful ethic of apocalyptic and Old Testament vengeance wrought by a mighty God of hatred and fury against his idolatrous and profane enemies. This is an important contemporary context that illuminates the apocalyptic fury of Milton's own terrifying God in *Samson Agonistes*, as well as the "dreadful way" (1591) that the militant Samson, capable of "sudden rage" (953), takes his revenge on the idolatrous and uncircumcised Philistines. Milton's work, in other words, is a poetic dramatization of divine vengeance potently expressed in the more vehement and apocalyptically threatening radical religious discourse of the Interregnum and its aftermath. "A day of vengeance is coming upon you all; that the Lord will be recompensed upon you all his adversaries," George Fox prophesied to the ungodly ones of his age (echoing Isaiah 34:8 and 35:4), as he evoked a sense of terror and warned that the dreadful day of the Lord's wrath was near at hand.[38] And in the year of the Restoration, Milton's student and Quaker friend Thomas Ellwood prophesied that God's "indignation and fury [would] break out upon" the priests of the nation and "utterly consume [them] from off the earth," while another Quaker prophet in 1666 envisioned "times of horror and amazement . . . amongst those that have withstood him," since God's appearance would "be fierce and terrible; even so terrible, as who shall abide his coming? for the Lord will work both secretly and openly."[39] In a similar fashion, Milton's Old Testament drama shows the awesomeness of Israel's God of power who works "both secretly and openly" to destroy his enemies, the aristocracy and priesthood of the Philistines, thereby creating a scene of "horror and amazement."

Revolutionary Puritans could compare Samson's act of destruction against the Philistines to the Lord's desolation of worldly powers in their own age. As John Owen observed in a sermon preached before the House of Commons during the new Commonwealth:

Now as *Sampson*, intending the destruction of the Princes, Lords, and residue of the Philistines, who were gathered together in their Idoll temple, he effected it by pulling away the pillars whereby the building was supported; whereupon the whole frame topled to the ground: So the Lord intending the ruine of that mighty power, whose top seems to reach to heaven, will do it by pulling away the pillars and supporters of it, after which it cannot stand one moment. Now what are the Pillars of that fatall Building? are they not the powers of the world as presently stated and framed?[40]

The "Idoll temple" of Dagon in *Samson Agonistes* – with its "great Feast" and "Great Pomp," its "illustrious Lords," its "Idolatrous Rites" (1315, 436, 1318, 1378) and superstitious ceremonies – does indeed represent such worldly powers; and its destruction "with burst of thunder" (1651) enables Milton to imagine a horrid scene in which the powers of the world "cannot stand one moment," as the Lord demonstrates his dreadful power and (to borrow words from the wrathful Son in *Paradise Lost*) pours out "indignation on [the] Godless" (6.811). The last great act of Milton's Samson thus embodies the impulse of apocalyptic revolutionaries to pull down mighty worldly powers so that only the Lord himself is exalted: militant Puritan revolutionaries in Parliament's Army had considered that one of the chief aims of the Civil Wars was "the pulling down of Babylon," and Cromwell himself observed after one of his great military victories that "wherever anything in this world is exalted, or exalts itself, God will pull it down, for this is the day wherein He alone will be exalted."[41]

Radical religious writers in the Revolution and Restoration frequently envisioned that the mighty day of the Lord's wrath and desolation would come unexpectedly and suddenly upon the ungodly. Gerrard Winstanley suggested that the destruction of Babylon, when it came, would indeed be quick – "The Lord will do this work speedily, *Babylon* shall fall in one hour" – while Francis Howgill envisioned desolation and "great slaughter" coming upon the ungodly when they are unaware.[42] Moreover, the Quaker Dorothy White, claiming that the Spirit of the Lord was upon her and warning the nation with fierce prophecies just before the Restoration, envisioned "that the Approach of the *Great* and *Terrible Day* cometh, and that very swiftly."[43] And in verses dating from 1662, Thomas Ellwood prophesied "that speedy vengeance He will take on all / Who persecute His saints and them enthrall," while elsewhere he envisioned that "day of sad calamity" and "utter desolation" which would "speedily overtake" the ungodly priests of his nation and the sons of Belial.[44] Such swift, unexpected vengeance against those Philistine lords and priests who persecute and enthrall God's saint does indeed occur in *Samson Agonistes*; as the Chorus observes about the mighty deliverer, anticipating the final catastrophe: "Swift as the lightning glance he executes / His errand on the wicked, who surpris'd / Lose thir defense" and are "amazed" (1284–86). Milton the controversialist himself admired "the sudden assault" with which God's "reforming Spirit" could strike down carnal powers, frustrating ungodly persecutors and false prophets "with sudden confusion and amazement" (*Animadversions*, *CPW* 1:704–5). And so in *Samson Agonistes* God assists the apocalyptic catastrophe by sending "a spirit of frenzy" among the idolatrous and drunken Philistines, urging "them on with mad desire / To call in haste for thir destroyer"; thus "Insensate left" and struck "with blindness internal," they "Unwittingly importun'd / Thir own destruction to come speedy upon them" (1675–78, 1685–86, 1680–81).[45] In Milton's drama, the destruction and slaughter suffered by the Philistines who have "Fall'n into wrath divine" is both great and sudden: "*Gaza* yet stands," reports the messenger, "but all her Sons are fall'n, / All in a moment overwhelm'd and fall'n" (1683, 1558–59).

Milton himself had urged the speedy destruction of Babylonish powers in his own fiery polemical writings. Recognizing that reformation was often slow-moving and long work in his tumultuous age, he nevertheless reminded his fellow citizens that such good kings of Judah as Asa, Hezekiah, and Josiah had effected reformations, including the destruction of idols and idolatrous priests, which were "speedy and vehement" (*Of Reformation*, *CPW* 1:602). And as early as *The Reason of Church-Government* he was warning that the miseries of papist Ireland, where he believed that his Protestant countrymen had been recently slaughtered and martyred, were "urgent of a speedy redresse" (*CPW* 1:799). Consequently the long work of reformation, he suggested, needed to be pushed forward "with all possible diligence and speed" (*CPW* 1:800). Later, writing on behalf of the English Republic, Milton himself would promote Cromwell and the New Model Army's speedy vengeance and ruthless reconquest of Ireland (see Chapter 6), which included the "desolation" of "Hostile Cit[ies]" (*SA*, line 1561); helping to fabricate the image of Cromwell as the conquering hero, Milton would recall how "in one battle [Cromwell] instantly broke the power of Hibernia" (*CPW* 4:670).[46] Indeed, when it came to justifying the violent revolution of 1648–49, and especially the purging of Parliament's "rott'n Members" who opposed it, Milton praised "their speedy seisure and exclusion" by the Army (*Observations upon the Articles of Peace*, *CPW* 3:328). In its own way,

Milton's drama envisions such a "speedy redresse," as God and his militant saint speedily enact a terrifying vengeance against the ungodly Philistines who have "Fall'n into wrath divine."

In 1660 the Quaker Ellwood prophesied, moreover, that "the Lord is arisen to fight for Sion" and that the fall of "Babilon the great . . . shall make a great noise" (as in Jeremiah 50:46) and that "the sound thereof . . . shal strike terror to all those who admire and love her beauty: fear, amazement, [and] astonishment" would seize upon all who worship or traffic with her.[47] Though it is not mentioned in Judges, such a "great noise" of desolation and ruin capable of striking terror and amazement is indeed heard in *Samson Agonistes*: there the fall of Dagon is described as a "hideous noise . . . / Horribly loud," a universal groan

> As if the whole inhabitation perish'd[.]
> Blood, death, and deathful deeds are in that noise,
> Ruin, destruction at the utmost point.   (1509–14)

As Samson is about to wreak his act of terrible destruction, he prophesies that the spectacular performance of his strength "with amaze shall strike all who behold" (1645), a line evoking a sense of wonder at the great power of this God of terror and his militant saint, and a line recalling the Chorus' earlier observation that those ungodly who are struck swiftly "Lose thir defense, distracted and amaz'd" (1286): so God confounds and destroys idol worshippers whose temple collapses "with burst of thunder." Milton's *Samson Agonistes* is thus the product of a turbulent age when radical spiritualist writers still believed, as the prophet George Fox did for example, that "the power of the Lord was so strong as it struck a mighty dread amongst the people" so that "they were in an amazement."[48] Even in a Restoration Puritan text like *The Pilgrim's Progress*, we may recall, Christian learns about "the dread and amazement of enemies" of the Lord as he is shown "some of the engines with which some of [the Lord's] servants had done wonderful things"; those servants include Samson and Gideon, as well as the "renown'd" Jael who slew Sisera with hammer and nail (see *SA*, lines 988–90).[49]

Like Fox's dreadful God who threatened to execute vengeance during the years of revolutionary Quakerism, Milton's in *Samson Agonistes* is also a God of "living Dread" (1673) and terror – a God who is awesome in his power and who will prove terrifying to his idolatrous, heathenish enemies.[50] "Dreadful is the Lord . . . and terrible to the wicked," Fox announced in one of his most fiery prophetic tracts from the Interregnum, *Newes Coming up out of the North*, where he envisioned that "the terrible One is coming with his power, to shake terribly the earth" and astonish the heathen and profane.[51] "Fear the living God of heaven and earth, who is dreadful," Fox thundered as he threatened earthly powers during the 1650s.[52] And the Quaker prophet Edward Burrough who could make "the Host of the Uncircumcised greatly distressed," as Howgill put it, had himself warned that "the day of the Lord is powerful and dreadful, that shall come upon the Heathen" and he "will be avenged of his enemies."[53] Radical religious writers envisioned their own tumultuous age of revolution and upheaval in terms of an apocalyptic theomachia, a mighty "contest . . . / 'Twixt God and *Dagon*" (461–62); yet the "power of *Israel's* God" (1150) was so great and dreadful that it could not be resisted by the uncircumcised: "who is there amongst all the mighty Host of the Uncircumcised," asked one bellicose Quaker prophet at the time of the Restoration, "that shall lift a hand *against the Sword of the Lord, and of Gideon, and prosper?*"[54] And so when Samson, that "dreadful enemy" of "th'uncircumcis'd," goes off to perform in the temple of Dagon, he serves God's "glory best, and spread[s] his name / Great among the Heathen round" by showing "whose God is strongest" (1622, 640, 1429–30, 1155) and astonishing them with his final, terrifying performance of the Lord's vengeance.

Like the threatening, overturning God of religious radical writing, Milton's God of awesome power in *Samson Agonistes* is likewise a mighty leveller – levelling in a moment Dagon's theater and temple and decimating the "choice nobility and flower" (1654) of the Philistines. To be sure, Milton's God of power differs in one sense from the levelling God of such mid-seventeenth-century radical spiritual writers as Abiezer Coppe, George Foster, Winstanley, or Fox himself: unlike them, Milton does not depict a mighty Lord who, in the day of his dreadful appearance, will furiously level or overturn the economic and social order.[55] Nevertheless, *Samson Agonistes* gave Milton one last opportunity to represent in a poetic drama the Lord as an apocalyptic leveller – a depiction that resonates with enthusiastic visions of revolutionary levelling in the 1640s and 1650s, while highlighting the horrid consequences of the destruction and slaughter. Inspired by the powerful God of Isaiah and Ezekiel, Coppe, for example, depicted the Lord of Hosts as "a mighty Leveller" who would rise "to shake terribly the earth" and "utterly abolish" the idols, while one chaplain of the radicalized New Model Army, the Seeker William Erbery, observed that when "the Spirit and power of the Lord appear[s] in [the saints], all the powers of men, and mighty things, Kingdomes and Cities shall fall down before them, and be levelled at their feet."[56] Moreover, in his apocalyptic moments, Cromwell, who emphasized waiting on the Spirit and the Lord, could envision a terrifying God who "breaks the enemies of His Church in pieces."[57] This was an awesome God "who is not to be mocked or deceived," Cromwell observed, "and is very jealous when His Name and religion are made use of to carry on impious designs, [so that He] hath taken vengeance of such profanity, even to astonishment and admiration."[58] In the turbulent Old Testament world of *Samson Agonistes*, we find such a powerful God of levelling and desolation – a Lord who arouses "astonishment" in earthly powers as he brings them to nothing and transforms an idolatrous place of worship into a "place of horror" (1550).

The language of militant religious radicalism could stress as well that the warrior Lord of awesome power would manifest himself in the saint who battles against the ungodly and profane world.[59] As the Quaker prophet Edward Burrough told the saints, "the Lord is with you as a mighty terrible one, and therefore shall all your persecuters be ashamed and confounded." So the "terrible" Lord is with Milton's Samson during the final catastrophe – we have seen how he contributes to it by sending a "spirit of frenzy" among the Philistines. Moreover, the radical religious saint – a "single combatant" (344) accompanied by this "mighty terrible one" – could assume a Samson-like power, reminding us of the Old Testament warrior capable of conquering a thousand Philistines. "In the battle," Burrough went on to envision, "shall you obtain the conquest, and all your enemies shall be put to flight, and one of you shall chase a thousand, for he is with you who hath all power in his hand . . . therefore be not discouraged at the raging and swelling words of your Adversaries, but be bold and valiant and faithful to him . . . Ye are my fellow Souldiers."[60] Nor is the Miltonic Samson, when he aligns himself yet once more with "the power of *Israel's* God" (1150), discouraged by "the raging and swelling words" of his adversaries: in his confrontation with Harapha, a trial scene Milton has added to the Judges story, Samson himself is not discouraged by the verbal "indignities" of his giant adversary who calls him "A Murderer, a Revolter, and a Robber" (1168, 1180). Milton's saint not only mocks this adversary and his "glorious arms," as well as the "honorable Lords" of the Philistines, but no longer despairing of the Lord's "final pardon" and faithfully trusting "in the living God" (1130, 1108, 1171, 1140), he is soon moved inwardly by the Spirit to go off and commit another hostile act against the Lord's enemies as his ready instrument.[61] "Nothing but . . . the mighty power of God in men," William Erbery wrote using scriptural and militant language in the midst of the traumatic overturnings of the Revolution, "could in so short a time cast down so many strong Holds, conquer so many . . . Armies": this "appearance of God in the saints" had brought about "the greatest destruction in the Land."[62] When Milton's Samson casts down the stronghold of the Philistine temple, bringing desolation to a hostile city, he too has become a warrior saint who, "With inward eyes illuminated" (1689) and accompanied by the Lord's Spirit, has once again internalized and manifested the power of "the mighty terrible one" to become "[t]he dread of *Israel's* foes" (342).[63]

Moreover, it is notable that in his portrait of Samson as radical saint moved by the Spirit to enact dreadful holy vengeance, Milton has significantly suppressed the implications of Judges 16:30: "And Samson said, Let me die with the Philistines." Milton, in other words, has carefully chosen not to portray Samson as a radical saint on a suicide mission of destruction. In the argument to his drama, Milton himself notes that the destruction Samson brought to the Philistines he did "by accident to himself"; and subsequent passages in the drama make it clear just how much Milton wishes to dissociate his inward-looking saintly hero from the traditional accusation of suicide and "Self-violence": Samson with the Philistines "immixt, inevitably / Pull'd down the same destruction on himself" (1584, 1657–58; cf. 1587–88), the messenger reports, and he was "self-kill'd / Not willingly, but tangl'd in the fold / Of dire necessity" (1664–66), the Chorus observe. Manoa, moreover, describes Samson's violent death as "noble" (1724) – a characterization with which modern critics may feel uncomfortable because of the militant nature of Samson's life and final act, though one that corresponds with Milton's suppression of the issue of suicide.[64] Imbued with a holy ruthlessness at the end of the drama, the Miltonic Samson is a saint moved one last time by the Spirit to commit an act of revenge and destruction, but willful self-destruction is not part of that horrid act in which he fulfills his vocation "gloriously."[65] The Protestant commentator Peter Martyr, who Milton considered "a Divine of formost rank" and whose commentary on Judges he admired, observed about Samson: "Neyther can it be properlye sayde that Samson kylled himselfe. He dyed in deede, but he prescribed not unto hymself this ende, namely to dye. [He] sought vengeaunce of hys enemies, whych he understoode woulde by this meanes ensue."[66] By suppressing the implications of suicide in his drama, Milton has by no means lessened the horrifying nature of

Samson's great act – a revenge "dearly bought" which results in "heaps of slaughter'd" enemies whose blood soaks his own dead body and covers it with "clotted gore" (1660, 1530, 1725–26, 1728). But Milton also makes it more possible for the radical godly reader – a reader less likely to be morally repulsed by the drama's holy violence – to perceive the vengeful Samson as a valiant saint moved by the Spirit to carry out God's militant will and work against idolatrous, uncircumcised enemies who are, in the words of the fiery Quaker Francis Howgill, "to be slain heaps upon heaps."[67]

Milton's drama does indeed highlight the motivation of dreadful revenge: in his act of terrifying destruction, Samson "hath quit himself / Like *Samson*" and "Fully reveng'd" himself upon Israel's enemies, leaving "them years of mourning, / And lamentation" (1709–13). The authority of the Biblical story itself lies behind an emphasis on vengeance when Samson prays, just before destroying the Philistine temple, "O God, that I may be at once avenged of the Philistines for my two eyes" (Judges 16:28). But the crucial difference is that *Samson Agonistes* presents the spectacular vengeance as more cosmic and apocalyptic – not as Samson's private revenge taken on the Philistines for the loss of his two eyes.[68] Milton's handling of the motif of divine vengeance, furthermore, is consistent with his political and theological writings where this author of the chilling cry "Avenge, O Lord, thy slaughter'd Saints" could justify it as fervently as some radical Puritan contemporaries did, especially upon the enemies of God or of the church.[69] But in *The Tenure of Kings and Magistrates* Milton was also at pains to distinguish between private acts of revenge and enmity – the sort that would have characterized David lifting his hand against Saul – and revenge as a godly and political act: "And if *David* refus'd to lift his hand against the Lords anointed, the matter between them was not tyranny, but privat enmity, and *David* as a privat person had bin his own revenger, not so much the peoples" (*CPW* 3:216).

Indeed, Milton's vision of holy vengeance evokes comparisons, as I have been arguing in this chapter, with revolutionary Puritan writers who either encouraged militant activism or used bellicose language to further what they perceived to be the will of the Lord and to highlight their warfare with an ungodly world. Preaching to the Commons after the destruction of the royalist forces at Worcester, for example, an exhilarated John Owen justified the wrathful Lord of power taking "great revenges" on his enemies by referring to Psalm 110:6, a militant passage close to the vengeful spirit dramatized in *Samson Agonistes* and one Milton cited in *De Doctrina Christiana* to emphasize God's judgment upon the Gentiles: the Lord "shall judge among the heathen, he shall fill the places with the dead bodies."[70] Moreover, Milton's immediate contemporary, the radical poet-prophet and pamphleteer George Wither, in 1660 described the *"LORD of Hosts"* as a "General of a two-fold *Militia*, furnished with distinct weapons according to the several services whereby they are to glorifie him; the one *Natural*, and the other *Spiritual*; and that he makes use of both to . . . destroy the *Enemies* of his *Kingdom*." Milton's Samson could well be aligned with the first group of Wither's radical saints who, moved by divine impulse to serve as executioners of God's judgments, resort to more militant actions: they are employed by the Lord "in shedding the blood of his *malicious opposers* . . . sometime, with hazzard or loss of their own."[71] In another text, written close to the Restoration, Wither compared himself to the saintly Samson who is roused up to execute divine vengeance: "as heretofore befel *Sampson*, (and hath oft befallen many of *Gods* servants in their *Frailties*) with the *Philistines*, he must first have occasion given, by an outward injury, before he could be rowzed up to execute *GOD's* Vengeance upon the Enemies of his *Country*."[72] Milton's radical Protestant drama does indeed highlight Samson's frailties – he is not the "perfect man" of *Paradise Regained* – as well as his inward griefs and "outward injury"; but it also presents his horrid act of revenge as an act of God's apocalyptic vengeance appropriate for one of God's saints roused by the motions of the Spirit within. *"Such honour have all his Saints,"* observed Henry Vane, "authorized and enabled to administer . . . the revenging justice of God."[73]

As Samson executes divine vengeance and pulls down the temple and theater of Dagon "With horrible convulsion to and fro" (1649), he acts with the power of a tempest that has been internalized and unleashed: thus, when situated between the temple's "two massy Pillars," he strains "all his nerves" and bows "As with the force of winds and waters pent, / When Mountains tremble" (1633, 1646–48; cf. 963–64). The messenger's description highlights the awesome power contained and released, as though pent-up spiritual forces were being violently released through Samson's horrid act bringing down the temple pillars "with burst of thunder." In his revolutionary apocalyptic writing, the Independent minister Peter Sterry envisioned that the Lord of awesome power would manifest himself "in a *tempest* of a *whirle-wind*" as he comes "to shake dreadfully the whole Earth."[74] The tempestuous winds and waters highlight the elemental force of Samson's act and his wrathful power.[75] Moreover, the vision of trembling mountains itself had apocalyptic resonance in the revolutionary years, especially for radical prophetic writers warning of the Lord's wrath and judgment; thus in *The Trumpet of the Lord Sounded* (1654), George Fox warned with prophetic fervor (echoing such scriptural passages as Isaiah 5:25, Jeremiah 5:24, and Habakkuk 3:10), "Tremble, ye mountains and hills, before the Lord: for out of Sion doth the Lord utter his voice. Wo, wo to all you who inhabit the earth: you will be scattered as the wind scatters the chaff; you will be consumed as the fire consumes the stubble: for the mighty day of the Lord is coming."[76] The sense of cataclysmic destruction that accompanies the coming of the mighty day of the Lord and consumes the ungodly is likewise conveyed through the forceful language of *Samson Agonistes* and its vision of horrifying destruction meted out to the heathenish worshippers of Dagon.

Milton, furthermore, dramatizes at the end of *Samson Agonistes* the crucial activism of the vengeful godly saint whose destructive agency is interwoven with powerful divine forces. Providentialism itself could encourage a distrust of human agency and a dependence upon the divine; one revolutionary Puritan, for example, suggested that providence was responsible for all human actions and that men were nothing but "secondary causes" in the process and instruments of its work: "all men good and bad are but Instruments in Gods hand, secondary causes, and can do nothing but what God by Providence leads them to do, or permits to be done to effect his own purpose and secret decree, ordering all and every Action thereunto."[77] But in *Samson Agonistes* Milton has complicated this view by dramatizing the mutual interaction of providence's mysterious designs and Samson's own agency as a warrior saint – he is by no means simply a passive instrument in the hands of the Almighty. Retribution is to be at divine and human hands. As Samson asserts towards the drama's end, when he chooses to obey the Philistine order and go to the temple of Dagon, "Commands are no constraints. If I obey them, / I do it freely" (1372–73). The conscience and faith of this radical Old Testament saint are neither constrained nor compelled, so that he remains a free agent to respond to providential promptings and the leadings of the Spirit.

Moreover, when Samson observes that "Masters' commands come with a power resistless / To such as owe them absolute subjection" (1404–5), his ambiguous lines, addressed to the public officer, refer to two "masters" – the Philistines, who command that he appear before their popular feast in honor of Dagon, and the Lord himself, to whose will Samson is in the process of submitting. Much like a revolutionary

Puritan saint, then, Samson shows disciplined submission in service of his demanding God, while also exercising his own agency.[78] In the midst of civil war, Thomas Young had urged the saints to wait upon the Lord – as Samson had – and yet to be active: "let . . . your hands [be] active with all faithfulnesse to fulfill what is required of you in your Sphere."[79] In Milton's radical spiritual drama such faithful activeness is given especially daring exploration. Samson, having obeyed the Philistine commands, "hast fulfilled / The work" (1661–63) required of him in his sphere when at the end he performs of "[his] own accord" and displays another act of his awesome strength and God's awesome power: the horrid retribution in which he slaughters more foes in number "Than all [his] life had slain before" (1668) is an expression of both divine and human agency. Exercising his own agency one last time "with eyes inward illuminated," Samson the militant, faithful champion of God embodies Milton's unsettling dramatic vision of a radical saint who, having followed the impromptu motions of the Spirit, proves "dreadful to the Enemies of the Lord."

Afterword

TWO-HANDED ENGINE: POLITICS AND SPIRITUAL WARFARE IN THE 1671 POEMS

Milton's publication of his 1671 poems together was a provocative gesture. The visionary Puritan poet boldly printed his name on the title page of his volume to which he added *Samson Agonistes*, yet he offered no commentary that might aid a fit or dissenting audience to interpret the political and radical religious implications of juxtaposing his spiritual epic about the saintly, introspective Jesus who rejects all worldly temptations with his drama about the anguished, inward-looking Samson who resorts to a dreadful act of holy violence. In 1671 Milton was able to present dissenting readers with two representations of radical sainthood and two different kinds of literary responses to the political and spiritual crises of the Revolution and Restoration. Published together, these two radical religious poems give the volume of 1671 an open-ended dimension. Both poems imaginatively explore political options in apocalyptic or eschatological contexts as they present their two godly witnesses following the guidance of the Spirit's inward persuasive motions at moments of national and religious crisis. Yet the shattering apocalyptic violence of the second poem is not altogether reconciled with the verbal combat of the other.

The spiritual politics of Milton's *Paradise Regained*, we have seen, by no means suggest that Milton withdrew from vigorous polemical engagement after the Restoration or that he was even unequivocally a pacifist.[1] *Paradise Regained* is unorthodox in its spiritual implications, as well as challenging and polemical in its revisions of conventional political discourse. This brief Puritan epic – intensely inward yet sharply engaged with temporal powers – is more deeply indebted than is usually recognized to the radical religious culture of both the Interregnum and the Restoration years, where we surely need to emphasize important continuities and not only differences. *Paradise Regained* redefines and dramatizes a model of radical Puritan response – one more verbal in its combative nature – that complements but by no means clearly repudiates or supersedes, as some recent commentators insist, the apocalyptic vengeance and militant heroism dramatized in its companion poem.[2] The publication of the poems together therefore enabled Milton to juxtapose two distinctive representations of radical religious and political sainthood without necessarily suggesting that one model is altogether preferable to the other. In the case of *Samson Agonistes*, Milton was able to explore radical religious concerns in a dramatic poem that evokes the tragic heroism of militant Puritanism. Indeed, Milton's publishing the poems in a single volume seems to me a double-edged political gesture, one more ambiguous than those critics uneasy with the deadly apocalyptic violence of his drama wish to acknowledge.

Because this point has implications for interpreting the poet's political alignments at the end of his literary career, I wish to address it briefly – and more speculatively – by way of concluding the preceding chapters on radical religion and politics in the 1671 poems. Can we be certain, after all, that Milton wanted his fit readers to see Jesus's sharp rhetoric and "winning words" (1.222) in *Paradise Regained* as superseding Samson's "horrid spectacle" (*SA*, line 1542) and militant act of godly vengeance? *Samson Agonistes* follows the spiritual epic, rather than the other way around, so that in terms of the poetical volume as a whole we cannot argue that we move from the violent Old Testament ethos of the tragic drama to the more enlightened, New Testament ethos of *Paradise Regained*, whose godly witness demonstrates retrospectively the flaws of the militant hero of faith and his terrible code of apocalyptic revenge. In considering this issue, we might elaborate further on George Wither's observation from *Fides-Anglicana* (1660) quoted in Chapter 9: "Know . . . that the *LORD of Hosts* . . . is General of a two-fold *Militia*, furnished with distinct weapons according to the several services whereby they are to glorifie him; the one *Natural*, and the other *Spiritual*; and . . . he makes use of both to . . . destroy the *Enemies* of his *Kingdom*, as occasion is given. The first he employeth in shedding the blood of his *malicious opposers*, . . . sometime, with hazard or loss of their own; and the other, (if need be) he engageth in *sufferings*." Wither was describing, soon after the Restoration, two kinds of weapons employed by God and his saints, who follow divine impulses: both are "proper to a *spiritual warfare*." Those faithful servants of God who do not resort to violent means to destroy his enemies may be considered "*Saints* and *Souldiers*, in the most super-eminent degree"; but "many of the former," Wither adds, "may be *Saints* also, who when their *natural corruptions* have been soaked in their own *blood*, or *sufferings* and the stains washed out . . . shall have a share both in his *Victories* and *Triumphs*."[3] In other words, those saints also serve who follow the Spirit's impromptu motions to perform acts of "dearly bought revenge, yet glorious" (*SA*, line 1660). Wither's two kinds of saints, representing God's "two-fold *Militia*" destroying "the *Enemies* of his *Kingdom*," receive their greatest imaginative embodiment in Milton's poetic volume, where he portrays alternative models of radical saint-hood through the strenuous trials, sufferings, and triumphs of Jesus and Samson.

The publication of *Paradise Regained* and *Samson Agonistes* in one volume could therefore be construed as a deeply ambivalent or double-edged response to the worldly politics and "carnal power" (*Paradise Lost*, 12.521) of the Restoration. When it comes to matters of religion, Milton writes in *Civil Power*, God "commands us . . . to search, to try, to judge of these things our selves" (*CPW* 7:243); we might say the same about the radical religious poems Milton juxtaposed in 1671. Milton left it up to fit, dissenting readers of his volume "to search, to try, to judge of these things" for themselves, and to decide which means of spiritual warfare – the verbal duelling of Jesus or the holy violence of Samson – is a more appropriate response in an age of royalist ascendancy. Indeed, the suggestiveness of his volume emerges from Milton's enabling two radical religious perspectives to appear side by side. Miltonic ideology has recently been well described in terms of its plurality;[4] in case of the religious politics of the 1671 volume, I would emphasize Milton's calculated indeterminacy.

By publishing these two poems together, Milton seems to have embraced more divergent political and religious responses than did his Quaker contemporaries, especially in Restoration England. Yet it is worth stressing that the professed pacifism and political moderation of the Quakers after 1660 was often at odds with the militancy and fervor of their apocalyptic rhetoric and visions, which by no means disappeared after the Interregnum, as we saw in the preceding two previous chapters; there was in any case ambiguity among Milton's Quaker contemporaries regarding the issue of pacifism. Not only was the prophetic Quaker writer and leader Edward Burrough depicted in 1672 as a valiant warrior and a mighty Samson destroying the Philistines "Heaps upon Heaps," but William Dewsbury could warn his persecuting coun-trymen in 1666 of the fierceness of the Lord's wrath and the "terrible vengeance" with which he will manifest himself and his dreadful power: "then will he come upon you in the fearceness of his wrath, and break you to peeces, like potsherds," wrote Dewsbury of all those who delight "in pride, pleasures, pomp, riches, and glory, in this present World."[5] The persecution of the saints during the Restoration likewise stimulated Thomas Ellwood's apocalyptic vengeance fantasies against worldly power. Refusing to take the Oath of Allegiance and imprisoned with fellow Quakers in 1662 (after being employed by Milton), and therefore feeling acutely "the prophaneness, debaucheries, cruelties, and other horrid impieties of the age," he envisioned in verses written to console himself, "that dreadful day" wherein a provoked God will strike sad England with "Wrath, fury, vengeance and destruction / The just reward of persecution."[6] Even after the Restoration, the zeal of Quaker language and exhortation, aimed at engaging an ungodly state and world, was often fueled by a vision of divine power, apocalyptic judg-ment, and holy vengeance close to the cataclysmic vision and language of Milton's tragedy dramatizing the destruction which has "come speedy" upon ungodly "mortal men / Fall'n into wrath divine" (1681–83).

There is, then, a profound indeterminacy about the 1671 volume in terms of its radical spiritual politics and Milton's imaginative responses. This indeterminacy we should resist resolving by insisting that the poet's political and religious radicalism after the Restoration can be firmly aligned with one prophetic poem and its heroic vision more closely than with the other. By publishing *Paradise Regained* together with *Samson Agonistes*, Milton created a provocative volume that could itself function like a two-edged sword or even like a two-handed engine. In one poem he envisioned what it might be like to repudiate all temporal kingdoms and powers and establish the inward kingdom of Jesus through humble actions, the power of the Spirit, and "winning words"; in the other he envisioned what it might be like, in a spectacular act of holy violence and revenge, to destroy the idols and theater of Dagon and his worshippers. Years after the Restoration, this radical Puritan prophet and poet was indeed able to smite once and smite no more.

Notes

INTRODUCTION

1 *The True Levellers Standard Advanced* (April 1649), in Winstanley, *Works*, p. 252.
2 I quote, respectively, from Michael Wilding, *Dragons Teeth: Literature in the English Revolution* (Oxford, 1987), p. 2, and Corns, *Uncloistered Virtue*, p. 1. Other notable studies include *Freedom and the English Revolution: Essays in History and Literature*, ed. R. C. Richardson and G. M. Ridden (Manchester, 1986); Derek Hirst, "The Politics of Literature in the English Republic," *SC*, 5, 2 (1990), 133–55; Christopher Hill, *A Nation of Change and Novelty: Radical Politics, Religion, and Literature in Seventeenth-Century England* (London, 1990); Elizabeth Skerpan, *The Rhetoric of Politics in the English Revolution, 1642–1660* (Columbia, 1992); *Pamphlet Wars: Prose in the English Revolution*, ed. James Holstun (London, 1992); Steven N. Zwicker, *Lines of Authority: Politics and English Culture, 1649–1689* (Ithaca, NY, 1993); Sharon Achinstein, *Milton and the Revolutionary Reader* (Princeton, 1994); Nigel Smith, *Literature and Revolution in England, 1640–1660* (New Haven, 1994); Joad Raymond, *The Invention of the English Newspaper: English Newbooks, 1641–1649* (Oxford, 1996). Also see John Rogers, *The Matter of Revolution: Science, Poetry, and Politics in the Age of Milton* (Ithaca, NY, 1996), on interactions between the English and the Scientific Revolutions and their impact on literary culture. See also the studies of republicanism and seventeenth-century literature cited in note 12.
3 On interconnections between aesthetics and politics in the English Revolution (and beyond), though with little reference to religion, see the introduction, "Refiguring Revolutions," by Kevin Sharpe and Steven N. Zwicker to their edited collection, *Refiguring Revolutions: Aesthetics and Politics from the English Revolution to the Romantic Revolution* (Berkeley, 1998), pp. 1–29; Zwicker, *Lines of Authority*, chs. 2–3.
4 I use the term "ideology" in the broader, more neutral sense of "any kind of intersection between belief systems and political power," irrespective of whether the ideas and political action aim to preserve, amend, or uproot a given social order: see Terry Eagleton, *Ideology: An Introduction* (London, 1991), pp. 6–7.
5 As a recent challenge to this tendency, see *Religion, Literature, and Politics in Post-Reformation England, 1540–1688*, ed. Donna Hamilton and Richard

Strier (Cambridge, 1995); and Debora Shuger, *Habits of Thought in the English Renaissance: Religion, Politics, and Dominant Culture* (Berkeley, 1990). On the intersection between religion and politics during the early Stuart period, see Ann Hughes, *The Causes of the English Civil War* (London, 1991), ch. 2; Christopher Hill, "The Necessity of Religion," in *The Collected Essays of Christopher Hill, Volume II: Religion and Politics in 17th-Century England* (Brighton, 1986), pp. 11–18. On the intersection during the Civil War and the Interregnum, see A. L. Morton, *The World of the Ranters: Religious Radicalism in the English Revolution* (London, 1970), ch. 1; B. Reay, "Radicalism and Religion in the English Revolution: an Introduction," in *Radical Religion*; Blair Worden, "Toleration and the Cromwellian Protectorate," in *Persecution and Toleration: Studies in Church History* 21, ed. W. J. Sheils (Oxford, 1984), p. 214. See also William M. Lamont, *Godly Rule: Politics and Religion, 1603–1660* (London, 1969); *Politics, Religion, and The English Civil War*, ed. Brian Manning (London, 1973); Michael Finlayson, *Historians, Puritanism, and the English Revolution: The Religious Factor in English Politics before and after the Interregnum* (Toronto, 1983).

6 The phrase is John Morrill's in *The Nature of the English Revolution* (London, 1993): see Part I. For religious tensions and the origins of the Civil War, see also Anthony Fletcher, *The Outbreak of the English Civil War* (London, 1981), esp. pp. xxx, 405–6, 417–18; Conrad Russell, *The Causes of the English Civil War* (Oxford, 1990), pp. 58–62; Patrick Collinson, *The Birthpangs of Protestant England: Religion and Cultural Change in the Sixteenth and Seventeenth Centuries* (New York, 1988), ch. 5 ("Wars of Religion"); Michael R. Watts, *The Dissenters: From the Reformation to the French Revolution* (Oxford, 1978), p. 77; Barbara Donagan, "Did Ministers Matter? War and Religion in England, 1642–1649," *JBS*, 33 (1994), 119–156. See Glenn Burgess, "Was the English Civil War a War of Religion? The Evidence of Political Propaganda," *HLQ*, 61, 2 (2000), 173–201, on the intersection of law and religion.

7 See Achsah Guibbory, *Ceremony and Community from Herbert to Milton: Literature, Religion, and Cultural Conflict in Seventeenth-Century England* (Cambridge, 1998). I quote from *Religio Medici*, I.5, in *Sir Thomas Browne: Selected Writings*, ed. Sir Geoffrey Keynes (Chicago, 1968). See also Leah S. Marcus, *The Politics of Mirth: Jonson, Herrick, Milton, Marvell, and the Defense of Old Holiday Pastimes* (Chicago, 1986), esp. chs. 5–7.

8 See Hobbes, *Behemoth: The History of the Causes of the Civil Wars of England*, in *The English Works*, ed. William Molesworth, 11 vols. (London, 1839–45), 6:343 ("our rebels were publicly taught rebellion in the pulpits"). For Clarendon, see *History*, 1:385–87, 496, 2:277–78, 319–22, on factious, incendiary ministers. For Baxter on the stimulus of sectarian religion and preaching, see *Reliquiae Baxterianae*, ed. Matthew Sylvester (London, 1696), Part I, pp. 56, 76–78, 102–3, 116, 133, 146, 180. See also Barry Coward, "Was there an English Revolution in the Middle of the Seventeenth Century?" in *Politics and People in Revolutionary England: Essays in Honour of Ivan Roots*, ed. Colin Jones, Malyn Newitt, and Stephen Roberts (Oxford, 1986), pp. 29–30.

9 *Behemoth*, in *English Works*, 6:191; see also 6:167.

10 *Puritanism and Liberty*, p. 138; John Cardell, *Gods Soveraign Power over Nations* (London, 1648), epistle dedicatory.

11 *Religio Medici*, I.8.

12 David Norbrook's *English Republic*, the most wide-ranging account to date, makes a splendid contribution here. Other notable studies (especially of Milton) include *Milton and Republicanism*, ed. David Armitage, Armand Himy, and Quentin Skinner (Cambridge, 1995); Smith, *Literature and Revolution*, ch. 6; Nicholas von Maltzahn, *Milton's History of Britain: Republican Historiography in the English Revolution* (Oxford, 1991); Blair Worden, "Milton's Republicanism and the Tyranny of Heaven," in *Machiavelli and Republicanism*, ed. Gisela Bock, Quentin Skinner, and Maurizio Viroli (Cambridge, 1990), ch. 11; Annabel Patterson, *Reading between the Lines* (Madison, 1993), pp. 211–75; Janel Mueller, "Contextualizing Milton's Nascent Republicanism," in *Of Poetry and Politics: New Essays on Milton and His World*, ed. P. G. Stanwood (Binghamton, 1995), pp. 263–82. On the Republic's visual and verbal discursive strategies, see now Sean Kelsey, *Inventing a Republic: The Political Culture of the English Commonwealth, 1649–1653* (Manchester, 1997). See also Quentin Skinner, *Liberty Before Liberalism* (Cambridge, 1998).

13 *The Early Lives of Milton*, ed. Helen Darbishire (London, 1932), p. 14.

14 Cf. William Kolbrener, *Milton's Warring Angels: A Study of Critical Engagements* (Cambridge, 1997), a recent study that addresses Milton's republicanism but also warns against a bifurcation between Milton the "politician" and Milton the "poet" and "theologian": pp. 4, 32–33.

15 For the seminal work on these radical groups and their ideas, see Hill, *WTUD*. See also Michael A. Mullett, *Radical Religious Movements in Early Modern Europe* (London, 1980); *Radical Religion*; R. J. Acheson, *Radical Puritans in England, 1550–1660* (London and New York, 1990). For recent literary studies of these movements, see Smith, *Perfection Proclaimed*; Corns, *Uncloistered Virtue*, ch. 5; Hill, *A Nation of Change of Novelty*, esp. chs. 7–10.

16 On radical ideas and the "middle sort of people," see Brian Manning, *The English People and the English Revolution* (London, 1976). For a recent account of religion, politics, and dominant culture in the English Renaissance, see Shuger, *Habits of Thought*.

17 I quote Captain John Clarke in the Putney Debates: *Puritanism and Liberty*, p. 39.

18 *Gangraena* (London, 1646), Part III, The Preface. For Edwards and the Levellers, see Chapter 1 of this study. Lilburne considered this an "ulcerous book": *The Oppressed Mans Oppressions declared* ([London, 1646/47]), p. 21. On radical preaching blowing "the Bellows of Rebellion" and ruining "the stately Fabrick of an incomperable Monarchy," see the sneering portrait of Hugh Peter in *Rebels no Saints: or, A Collection of the Speeches, Private Passages, Letter and Prayers of those Persons lately Executed* (London, 1661), p. 94. See also Roger L'Estrange, *The Dissenters Sayings* (London, 1681).

19 Recent accounts include Paul Christianson, *Reformers in Babylon: English Apocalyptic Visions from the Reformation to the Eve of the Civil War* (Toronto, 1978); William M. Lamont, *Richard Baxter and the Millennium* (London, 1979); Bernard Capp, "The Fifth Monarchists and Popular Millenarianism," in *Radical Religion*, pp. 165–89.

20 *Reliquiae Baxterianae*, Part I, p. 279; on sectarianism and rebellion, see esp. pp. 102–3. On fears of sectarian excesses, see Robert Ashton, *Counter-Revolution: The Second Civil War and its Origins, 1646–8* (New Haven, 1994), pp. 241–45.

21 *Writings and Speeches*, 3:226–28. Chapter 5 of this study discusses Cromwell and the sectarian threat.

22 See e.g. *Rebels no Saints*, p. 154; see also Thomas Marriot, *Rebellion Unmasked* (London, 1661), p. 23.

23 See e.g. John Bramhall, *The Serpent-Salve* (1643), in Andrew Sharp, *Political Ideas of the English Civil Wars, 1641–1649* (London, 1983), pp. 27–29, 54–55. See also the selections from Griffith Williams (pp. 30–31), as well as Williams's *Vindiciae Regum; or, The Grand Rebellion* (Oxford, 1643), pp. 29–30, 46, 53, 79 (on these last two pages he quotes the Homily of the Church of England against willful rebellion), and Williams's *Jura Majestatis* (Oxford, 1644), pp. 7, 174; and Peter Heylyn, *The Rebells Catechisme* ([Oxford], 1643). The appeal to Romans 13 was reiterated in the Restoration at the time of the Fifth Monarchist insurrections in London: Marriot, *Rebellion Unmasked*, p. 26.

24 Prynne, *A Plea for the Lords* (1648), in *Political Ideas of the English Civil Wars*, p. 33.

25 See also *Brief Notes Upon a Late Sermon*, *CPW* 7:475, 482–83.

26 Cf. Ann Hughes, "The Frustrations of the Godly," in *Revolution and Restoration: England in the 1650s*, ed. John Morrill (London, 1992), p. 77.

27 See John Morrill's introduction to *Revolution and Restoration: England in the 1650s*, p. 13.

28 *Stuart Constitution*, p. 292; *Constitutional Documents*, p. 388.

29 See Anthony Ascham, *Of the Confusions and Revolutions of Government* (London, 1649).

30 Christopher Hill, "The Word 'Revolution' in Seventeenth-Century England," in *For Veronica Wedgwood: These Studies in Seventeenth-Century History*, ed. Richard Ollard and Pamela Tudor-Craig (London, 1986), pp. 134–51; Ilan Rachum, "The Meaning of 'Revolution' in the English Revolution (1648–1660)," *JHI*, 56 (1995), 195–215. See also Vernon Snow, "The Concept of Revolution in Seventeenth-Century England," *HJ*, 5, 2 (1962), 167–190. For other valuable accounts of the concept and terminology, see Perez Zagorin, *Rebels and Rulers, 1500–1660*, 2 vols. (Cambridge, 1982), vol. 1, ch. 1; Raymond Williams, *Keywords: A Vocabulary of Culture and Society*, rev. edn. (New York, 1983), pp. 270–74.

31 *A Christian Standing & Moving Upon the true Foundation* (London, 1648), p. 49.

32 *The Little Horns Doom & Downfall: or a Scripture-Prophesie of King James, and King Charles, and of this present Parliament, unfolded* (London, 1651), sig. A5r.

33 *Writings and Speeches*, 3:53–54; cf. 3:590–92.

34 *The Crying Sinnes Reproved. Whereof The Rulers and People of England, are highly guilty* (London, 1656), p. 13.

35 I quote from Cardell, *Gods Soveraign Power*, p. 3; John Owen, *The Advantage of the Kingdome of Christ in the Shaking of the Kingdoms of the World* (Oxford, 1651), pp. 10–11; Owen, *A Sermon Preached to the Parliament* (Oxford, 1652), p. 15; Barker, *A Christian Standing*, p. 45. Cf. *The Diary of Ralph Josselin*, ed. Alan Macfarlane (Oxford, 1976), p. 227 (31 Dec. 1650). Even Cromwell himself thought "the Lord hath done such things amongst us as have not been known in the world these 1000 years": *Writings and Speeches*, 3:592–93.

36 On the range of radical thought in the period, see G. E. Aylmer, "Collective Mentalities in Mid-Seventeenth-Century England," in *Transactions of the Royal Historical Society*, 5th series, 38 (1988), 1–25.

37 One of course compares Hill's controversial major study of Milton's dialogue with lower class radicals and fringe groups: *Milton and the English Revolution* (repr. Harmondsworth, 1979 [1977]).

38 The argument in this paragraph was elaborated in a lecture I delivered at the Sixth International Milton Symposium at the University of York (July 1999): "Milton and Marvell among the Religious Radicals and Sects: Polemical Engagements and Silences." A version of this essay is forthcoming in *MS*, 40 (2001).

39 Milton never responded when the Rump ordered him "to make observations" upon the two parts of Lilburne's *England's New Chains Discovered*: *Life Records*, 2:239–40.

40 Here I differ from Hill, who sees Milton "in permanent dialogue with the plebeian radical thinkers of the English Revolution" (*Milton and the English Revolution*, p. 5).

41 Cf. Milton's *Likeliest Means*: "I have thus at large examind the usual pretences of hirelings, colour'd over most commonly with the cause of learning and universities: as if with divines learning stood and fell" (*CPW* 7:317).

42 See Fox, *Journal*, p. 350; *The History of the Life of Thomas Ellwood*, ed. C. G. Crump (London, 1900), pp. 13, 23, 30–31, 87, 126, 130–31, 196. Ellwood of course would later edit the manuscript of Fox's *Journal*.

43 *The Experience of Defeat: Milton and the Some Contemporaries* (Harmondsworth, 1984), p. 17. Hill's *WTUD* likewise focuses on radical ideas.

44 For the new historicist tendency "to discover limits or constraints upon individual intervention," see Stephen J. Greenblatt, *Learning to Curse: Essays in Early Modern Culture* (London, 1990), pp. 164–65.

45 Cf. Ernest Sirluck's assertion that in "his general tendency" and "in his particular ideas" Milton in 1643–45 "*reflected* the revolutionary context" (*CPW* 2:2; emphasis added).

46 *Catalogue of the Pamphlets, Books, . . . Collected by George Thomason 1640–1661*, ed. G. K. Fortesque, 2 vols. (London, 1908), I, p. xxi; II, p. 590.

47 See the Acts of 1647, 1649, and 1653 intended to punish authors, printers,

sellers and buyers of unlicensed pamphlets: *Acts and Ordinances*, 1:1021–23, 2:245–54, 696–99.

48 Underdown, *Pride's Purge*; Worden, *Rump Parliament*; Woolrych, *Commonwealth*; G. E. Aylmer, *Rebellion or Revolution? England, 1640–1660* (Oxford, 1986), ch. 6; Morrill, *The Nature of the English Revolution*; Toby Barnard, *The English Republic, 1649–1660*, 2nd edn. (London, 1997), ch. 3

49 Quoted in Christopher Hill, Barry Reay, and William Lamont, *The World of the Muggletonians* (London, 1983), p. 25.

50 Richard Overton with William Walwyn's collaboration, *A Remonstrance of Many Thousand Citizens, and other Free-born People of England* (London, 1646), p. 6.

51 Jack A. Goldstone, *Revolution and Rebellion in the Early Modern World* (Berkeley 1991), p. xxiv.

1 LILBURNE, LEVELLER POLEMIC, AND THE AMBIGUITIES OF THE REVOLUTION

1 See e.g. *The Grand Plea of Lieut. Col. John Lilburne* ([London, 1647]), p. 19 (in part 2) where Lilburne complains of being branded "the head and chiefe of a generation or faction of men that are altogether for Anarchy and confusion, and would have no government at all in the Kingdome, . . . and so distroy all law and property." See also John Lilburne, Thomas Prince, and Richard Overton, *The Picture of the Councel of State* (1649), in *The Leveller Tracts, 1647–1653*, ed. William Haller and Godfrey Davies (New York, 1944), p. 193, and [Clement Walker], *The Triall of Lieut. Collonell John Lilburne . . . at the Guild-Hall of London* ([London, 1649]). The term "Leveller," first used to characterize Lilburne and his colleagues in November 1647 (the same month in which their first *Agreement of the People* appeared), was of course one of opprobrium; the movement was clearly recognizable to contemporaries well before this as Thomas Edwards' full-scale assault on the Levellers at the end of 1646 suggests (see below).

2 Lilburne, *Rash Oaths unwarrantable* ([London,1647]), p. 32. See also *The Triall of Lieut. Collonell John Lilburne*, p. 56. On the Levellers called heretics and seditious sectaries, see Lilburne, *The Second Part of Englands New-Chaines Discovered*, in *The Leveller Tracts*, p. 173; on their pamphlets as seditious against the infant Commonwealth, see *A Declaration of the Parliament . . . Discovering the Dangerous Practices of several Interests, against the Present Government, and Peace of the Commonwealth* (London, 1649), p. 25, and [John Canne], *The Discoverer* (London, 1649), First Part, title page. See also Lilburne, *An Impeachment of High Treason against Oliver Cromwell, and his Son in Law Henry Ireton* (London, 1649), pp. 63–64.

3 The prolix, undisciplined character of his polemical writing has made it a challenge for literary historians to analyze; however, see the recent valuable accounts of Leveller writing and its political contexts in Corns, *Uncloistered Virtue*, pp. 130–32, 134–46; Sharon Achinstein, *Milton and the Revolutionary Reader* (Princeton, 1994), ch. 1; Nigel Smith, *Literature and Revolution in England, 1640–1660* (New Haven, 1994), ch. 4. On issues of gender and

narrative in Leveller writing, see Ann Hughes, "Gender and Politics in Leveller Literature," in *Political Culture and Cultural Politics in Early Modern England*, ed. Susan D. Amussen and Mark A. Kishlansky (Manchester, 1995), pp. 162–88. Still valuable for its attention to literary qualities in Lilburne's popular prose style and self-presentation is Joan Webber, *The Eloquent "I": Style and Self in Seventeenth-Century Prose* (Madison, 1968), ch. 3; on Lilburne's style and politics, see also A. L. Morton, "The Place of Lilburne, Overton, and Walwyn in the Tradition of English Prose," *Zeitschrift für Anglistik und Amerikanistik*, 6 (1958), 5–13.

4 The bibliography on the Levellers and their political activities is extensive. Notable studies include Don M. Wolfe's introduction to his *Leveller Manifestoes of the Puritan Revolution* (1944; repr. New York, 1967); Perez Zagorin, *A History of Political Thought in the English Revolution* (London, 1954), ch. 2; William Haller, *Liberty and Reformation in the Puritan Revolution* (New York, 1955), chs. 8–10; Joseph Frank, *The Levellers: A History of the Writings of Three Seventeenth-Century Social Democrats: John Lilburne, Richard Overton, William Walwyn* (Cambridge, MA, 1955); Henry Noel Brailsford, *The Levellers and the English Revolution*, ed. Christopher Hill (London, 1961); C. B. MacPherson, *The Political Theory of Possessive Individualism: Hobbes to Locke* (Oxford, 1962), ch. 3; B. Manning, "The Levellers," in *The English Revolution, 1600–1660: Essays*, ed. Eric William Ives (London, 1968), pp. 144–58; Hill, *WTUD*, chs. 4, 7; G. E. Aylmer's introduction to his edition, *The Levellers in the English Revolution* (Ithaca, NY, 1975); Murray Tolmie, *The Triumph of the Saints: The Separate Churches of London, 1616–1649* (Cambridge, 1977), ch. 7; Michael R. Watts, *The Dissenters: From the Reformation to the French Revolution* (Oxford, 1978), pp. 117–29; Austin Woolrych, *Soldiers and Statesmen: The General Council of the Army and Its Debates, 1647–1648* (Oxford, 1987), passim; F. D. Dow, *Radicalism in the English Revolution, 1640–1660* (Oxford, 1985), ch. 3; David Wootton, "Leveller Democracy and the Puritan Revolution," in *The Cambridge History of Political Thought, 1450–1700*, ed. J. H. Burns (Cambridge, 1991), 412–44. Still worth consulting are W. Schenk, *The Concern for Social Justice in the Puritan Revolution* (London, 1948); D. B. Robertson, *The Religious Foundations of Leveller Democracy* (New York, 1951). On Lilburne's career, see M. A. Gibb, *John Lilburne the Leveller* (London, 1947); Pauline Gregg, *Free-born John: A Biography of John Lilburne* (London, 1961).

5 Lilburne, *Englands New Chains Discovered*, in *The Leveller Tracts*, p. 157. The resolution of the Commons passed on 4 January 1649 are close to these words: "the people are, under God, the original of all just power" (*Stuart Constitution*, p. 292); see also Brailsford, *The Levellers and the English Revolution*, p. 98.

6 See e.g. Lilburne's *An Anatomy of the Lords Tyranny and Injustice exercised upon Lieu. Col. John Lilburne* ([London, 1646]), p. 3; *Londons Liberty in Chains discovered* ([London, 1646]), p. 24; *Regall Tyrannie Discovered* (London, 1647), p. 64.

7 Vividly described in Lilburne, *A Worke of the Beast* (1638), in *Tracts on Liberty*, vol. 2. See also Lilburne, *The Christian Mans Triall*, 2nd edn. (London, 1641);

and *Englands Weeping Spectacle: Or, The sad condition of . . . Lilburne* ([London], 1648), pp. 2–3. For Lilburne as disperser of libelous books, see *Christian Mans Triall*, p. 8.

8 *A Worke of the Beast*, in *Tracts on Liberty*, 2:20. See also pp. 22, 24, 32, 33 (Lilburne's verses). For Lilburne and the Book of Revelation, see as well *The Christian Mans Triall* and *Innocency and Truth Justified* (London, 1645), esp. pt. 2, where Lilburne also describes himself as "a young Souldier of Jesus Christ" (p. 3). On Lilburne and martyrdom, see Clarendon, *History*, 5:305; Frank, *The Levellers*, pp. 16–25; Webber, *The Eloquent "I"*, pp. 72–73; Corns, *Uncloistered Virtue*, pp. 138–43 (for his complex debt to Foxe); John R. Knott, *Discourses of Martyrdom in English Literature, 1563–1694* (Cambridge, 1993), pp. 144–50.

9 See *A Worke of the Beast*, in *Tracts on Liberty*, 2:19 (citing Rev. 3:16); cf. Milton, *CPW* 1:537, 1:690, 1:868, 3:245.

10 For details of Lilburne's biography, see Gregg, *Free-born John*. For his dramatic acquittal in the summer of 1653, see *A Collection of the State Papers of John Thurloe*, ed. Thomas Birch, 7 vols. (London, 1742), 1:442; Bodleian Library, MS. Clarendon 46, fol. 208v.

11 *An Impeachment of High Treason*, p. 24. See also Brian Manning, "The Levellers and Religion," in *Radical Religion*, p. 70.

12 *An Anatomy of the Lords Tyranny*, p. 3; *Regall Tyrannie*, p. 68; *As You Were* ([Amsterdam?], 1652), p. 7; *Strength out of Weaknesse* (London, 1649), p. 21; *L. Colonel John Lilburne Revived* ([London], 1653), p. 3.

13 *Memoirs of the Life of Colonel Hutchinson*, ed. James Sutherland (London, 1973), p. 191. Lilburne attempted to counter this image of himself in *The Just Defence* (1653).

14 *The Just Defence*, in *The Leveller Tracts*, p. 450; cf. *Rash Oaths*, p. 31; *As You Were*, p. 7; *A Copie of a Letter to Mr. William Prinne* (1645), in *Tracts on Liberty*, 3:183. On Lilburne as "turbulent," see also the Presbyterian tract *Hinc Illae Lacrymae: Or the Impietie of Impunitie* (London, 1648), p. 16; Bodleian Library, MS. Clarendon 46, fol. 207v (letter dated 19 Aug. 1653); and the satirical song in *Rump: or an Exact Collection of the Choycest Poems and Songs Relating to the Late Times* (London, 1662), p. 325.

15 *A Manifestation* (1649), in *The Leveller Tracts*, p. 278. Eager to refute these charges (see pp. 278–80), the Levellers stressed their desire to retain property and hierarchy, as they did in the second *Agreement of the People*, where the Representative was forbidden to "levell mens Estates, destroy Propriety, or make all things common": *Leveller Manifestoes of the Puritan Revolution*, p. 301; cf. Lilburne's *Whip for the present House of Lords* ([London, 1647/48]), p. 2, and Hutchinson, *Memoirs of the Life of Colonel Hutchinson*, p. 171. The reference to "Chaos" occurs in *The Triall of . . . John Lilburne*, p. 99. See also Overton's *An Alarum to the House of Lords* ([London], 1646), which describes Lilburne as having been accused of subverting the "fundamentall Lawes and Government of this Kingdome" (p. 6); and *Walwyns Just Defence*, where that Leveller refutes the notion that he aims "at the destroying of Religion, and

at the subversion of all Government" (*Walwyn*, p. 409; cf. pp. 415, 417, 419). For the association of Levellers with civil anarchy, see as well *An Agreement of the People*, in *Leveller Manifestoes*, p. 231; Overton, *An Appeale From the Degenerate Representative Body . . . to . . . The free People . . . of England* (1647), *ibid.*, p. 158; T. B., *The Engagement Vindicated* (London, 1650), p. 11; *Hinc Illae Lacrymae*, p. 13; *The State Papers of John Thurloe*, 1:435, 449.

16 *Gangraena* (London, 1646), Part III, pp. 153–61; see also pp. 148–52, 197–204, 208–9, 211–12, 214, 217, 229, 230, 232, 262, as well as Part I, dedicatory epistle, and pp. 33, 52–53, 96; and Part II, pp. 25–30. On the Levellers in relation to sectarianism, see Tolmie, *The Triumph of the Saints*, ch. 7; and Keith Lindley, *Popular Politics and Religion in Civil War London* (Aldershot, 1997), pp. 397–98, 414. On the subversiveness of the Levellers and the danger of their "Anarchicall levelling," see also *A Declaration of Some Proceedings of Lt. Col. John Lilburn* (1648) by Walter Frost (*The Leveller Tracts*, p. 93), and Cromwell's fears in the Putney Debates: *Puritanism and Liberty*, p. 59.

17 *The Triall of . . . John Lilburne*, p. 68; see also p. 56. On Lilburne being falsely accused of "all the erronious tenents of the poor Diggers at George hill in Surrey," see Lilburne, *The Legall Fundamentall Liberties of the People of England Revived, Asserted, and Vindicated* (London, 1649), p. 75, and Canne, *The Discoverer*, passim. Lilburne mentions two key Digger texts: *The True Levellers Standard* and *The New Law of Righteousnes*.

18 See the Army chaplain Hugh Peter's condemnation of Lilburne recorded in *A Discourse Betwixt Lieutenant Colonel John Lilburn . . . and Mr Hugh Peter* (London, 1649), pp. 5–6, and Canne in *The Discoverer*, p. 5; cf. the indictment against Lilburne recorded in *The Triall*, p. 69 (referring to his "bitter language"). Baxter recalled the fervency of Leveller discourse: "they drowned all Reason in fierceness, and vehemency, and multitude of words" (*Reliquiae Baxterianae*, ed. Matthew Sylvester (London, 1696), Part I, p. 54). See also Clarendon on Lilburne's virulent writing in *History*, 5:305.

19 *An Anatomy of the Lords Tyranny*, p. 4; *Vox Plebis, or The Peoples Out-cry* (London, 1646), p. 32; *A Declaration of Some Proceedings*, in *The Leveller Tracts*, pp. 95–96.

20 See *Liberty Vindicated against Slavery* ([London], 1646), *The Oppressed Mans Oppressions declared* ([London, 1646/47]), and *Strength out of Weaknesse*.

21 *The Just Man in Bonds* (1646), in *Walwyn*, p. 217. The tract was published anonymously but was very likely the work of Walwyn: see Gregg, *Free-born John*, p. 144. Cf. Lilburne's *Just Defence* where he refers to resisting "an inlet of the sea of will and power" (*The Leveller Tracts*, p. 455).

22 *A Whip for the present House of Lords*, p. 3.

23 The phrase comes from *A Declaration of Some Proceedings*: *The Leveller Tracts*, p. 93.

24 See e.g. Cuthbert Sydenham, *An Anatomy of Lieut. Col. John Lilburn's Spirit and Pamphlets* (London, 1649), esp. p. 1; and *A Declaration of Some Proceedings*, in *The Leveller Tracts*, pp. 93–94, on Lilburne's "heaps of scandalous Books and Papers." For the second quotation in my text, see the Rump's Attorney

General Edmund Prideaux in *Strength out of Weaknesse*, p. 23; Lilburne responded that he could make a book "upon any subject in 3 or 4 daies space."

25 *The Resolved Mans Resolution* ([London, 1647]), p. 1.
26 *The Triall of . . . John Lilburne*, pp. 56–57, 61, 64, 68. See also Canne's *The Discoverer* for the Levellers' "spreading seditious and scandalous Bookes" against the Commonwealth (sig. A2r); and William Prynne's association of Lilburne and his flamboyantly printed texts with a "monstrous Generation of New TYRANNICAL STATE-HERETICKS": *A Seasonable, Legall, and Historicall Vindication* (London, 1654), p. 3 (cf. p. 48).
27 *A Worke of the Beast*, in *Tracts on Liberty*, 2:25; [John Lilburne], *Plaine Truth without Feare or Flattery* ([London], 1647), p. [20]. Cf. *A Worke of the Beast*, in *ibid.*, 2:22, where he dares not hold his peace, but speaks to his brethren "with boldnes in the might and strength of [his] God."
28 *A Worke of the Beast*, in *Tracts on Liberty*, 2:22. See also Corns, *Uncloistered Virtue*, p. 139, on Lilburne's dramatic impulse.
29 *An Anatomy of the Lords Tyranny*, p. 4. Lilburne was gagged because of the "boldnes and courage in [his] speech": *A Worke of the Beast*, in *Tracts on Liberty*, 2:25.
30 *The Triall of . . . John Lilburne*, p. 64; cf. p. 65.
31 Worden, *Rump Parliament*, p. 76.
32 *Englands Weeping Spectacle*, p. 2. On the Levellers and the creation of a new public readership in the Revolution, see Morton, "The Place of Lilburne, Overton, and Walwyn"; Achinstein, *Milton and the Revolutionary Reader*, ch. 1; Smith, *Literature and Revolution*, chs. 1, 4; Wootton, "Leveller Democracy and the Puritan Revolution," pp. 414–15.
33 *To the Supream Authority of this Nation, the Commons assembled in Parliament: The humble Petition of divers wel-affected Women* (London, [April] 1649), pp. 4, 7; *To the Supreme Authority of England, The Commons Assembled in Parliament. The Humble Petition of divers well-affected Women, of the Citie of London and Westminister* ([London, May] 1649); *Perfect Occurrences*, no. 121, 20–27 April 1649, pp. 997–98. See also the vivid account of women petitioning the Barebone's Parliament on Lilburne's behalf in July 1653: Bodleian Library, MS. Clarendon 46, fols. 131v–132v. Already by December 1646 Thomas Edwards was complaining of the "many reproachfull words" of Leveller petitions, including Elizabeth Lilburne's: *Gangraena*, Part III, p. 197. The subject of women Leveller petitioners unfortunately remains beyond the scope of this chapter; see, however, Patricia Higgins, "The Reactions of Women, with Special Reference to Women Petitioners," in *Politics, Religion and the English Civil War*, ed. Brian Manning (London, 1973), pp. 179–222, and Stevie Davies, *Unbridled Spirits: Women of the English Revolution, 1640–1660* (London, 1998), pp. 61–87.
34 *An Anatomy of the Lords Tyranny*, p. 16.
35 *Plaine Truth*, p. 20.
36 *The Resolved Mans Resolution*, p. 11. Cf. Webber, *The Eloquent "I"*, p. 65.

37 *Strength out of Weaknesse*, p. 15.
38 *The Picture of the Councel of State*, in *The Leveller Tracts*, p. 215.
39 *An Appeale*, in *Leveller Manifestoes*, p. 187.
40 *The Resolved Mans Resolution*, p, 13.
41 See *Regall Tyrannie Discovered*, p. 65. Cf. *A Worke of the Beast*, in *Tracts on Liberty*, 2:27; *The Oppressed Mans Oppressions declared*, p. 18; *An Anatomy of the Lords Tyranny*, p. 5; Overton, *An Alarum to the House of Lords*, p. 5; *The Resolved Mans Resolution*, p. 4; *Legall Fundamentall Liberties*, pp. 1, 14, 26; *The Triall of . . . John Lilburne*, p. 38.
42 See *An Appeale*, in *Leveller Manifestoes*, p. 194.
43 *An Anatomy of the Lords Tyranny*, p. 6.
44 *Londons Liberty*, p. 10; title page to Overton, *An Alarum to the House of Lords*. Cf. Lilburne, *Jonahs Cry out of the Whales belly* ([London, 1647]), p. 2; *The Recantation of Lieutenant Collonel John Lilburne* (London, 1647), p. 3.
45 See e.g. the account of his undauntedness on the battlefield in *The Triall of . . . John Lilburne*, p. 3. See also *Innocency and Truth Justified*, pt. 2, p. 65, *Strength out of Weaknesse*, p. 10, *Vox Plebis*, p. 58, *The Upright Mans Vindication* (London, 1653), p. 4.
46 See Overton's defense of Lilburne: *An Alarum to the House of Lords*, p. 3. On Lilburne as "a man of gallantry," see *L. Colonel John Lilburne Revived*, p. 1, and *The Upright Mans Vindication*, p. 4.
47 *An Anatomy of the Lords Tyranny*, p. 15.
48 *As You Were*, p. 3.
49 *As You Were*, p. 4.
50 *Mercurius Pragmaticus*, no. 19, 18–25 Jan. 1647/48; for a full account of the story, see Gregg, *Free-born John*, pp. 226–36.
51 Lilburne, *The Charters of London* (London, 1646), p. 2. Gregg, *Free-born John*, pp. 148, 164, 269. The third *Agreement* was smuggled out of the Tower.
52 *Englands Weeping Spectacle*, pp. 10–11. Frank, *The Levellers*, suggests that the tract may be by Walwyn: pp. 162, 314 n.82.
53 *Londons Liberty*, p. 34; *The Prisoners Plea for a Habeas Corpus* ([London, 1648]), sig. B2r. See also *The Oppressed Mans Oppressions declared*, p. 37; *The Resolved Mans Resolution*, pp. 1, 26–27; *The Juglers Discovered* ([London, 1647]), p. 6; *Jonahs Cry*. p. 4; *L. Colonel John Lilburne Revived*, p. 7 (of the letter dated 18 Jan. 1653).
54 *Londons Liberty*, p. 59. See also Lilburne, Walwyn, Prince, and Overton, *A Manifestation*, in *The Leveller Tracts*, pp. 277–78; and Lilburne, *The Resolved Mans Resolution*, p. 7.
55 *Regall Tyranny Discovered*, p. 66.
56 *Legall Fundamentall Liberties*, p. 21; *L. Colonel John Lilburne Revived*, p. 3. In the latter text, Lilburne observes that he has "read the Scripture . . . diligently" (p. 8). On the Bible and religion in Leveller writing, see also Iwan Russell-Jones, "The Relationship Between Theology and Politics in the Writings of John Lilburne, Richard Overton, and William Walwyn" (Oxford Univ. D.Phil, 1987); Manning, "The Levellers and Religion";

Elizabeth Tuttle, "Biblical Reference in the Political Pamphlets of the Levellers and Milton, 1638–1654," in *Milton and Republicanism*, ed. David Armitage, Armand Himy, and Quentin Skinner (Cambridge, 1995), pp. 63–81.

57 For Lilburne's opinion of the *Book of Declarations* cited here, see *A Discourse Betwixt Lieutenant Colonel John Lilburn . . . and Mr Hugh Peter*, p. 4; for Coke as the "great Oracle," see *The Triall of . . . John Lilburne*, p. 4; and for Magna Carta, see *An Alarum*, p. 6. On his use of "his old buckler, *magna carta*" in his dramatic trial of 1653, see *State Papers of John Thurloe*, 1:367. See also Andrew Sharp, "John Lilburne and the Long Parliament's *Book of Declarations*: A Radical's Exploitation of the Words of Authorities," *History of Political Thought*, 9, 1 (1988), 19–44; Glenn Burgess, "Protestant Polemic: the Leveller Pamphlets," *Parergon*, 11, 2 (1993), 55–56.

58 *Regall Tyranny Discovered*, p. 25. On radical uses of the Confessor's laws, see Janelle Greenberg, "The Confessor's Laws and the Radical Face of the Ancient Constitution," *EHR*, 104 (1989), 611–37.

59 See *A Discourse Betwixt Lieutenant Colonel John Lilburn . . . and Mr Hugh Peter*.

60 See e.g. (among many references) *Londons Liberty in Chains*, p. 22; *The Charters of London*, p. 2; *The Oppressed Mans Oppressions declared*, pp. 2, 18; Overton, *An Alarum to the House of Lords*, p. 6; *The Resolved Mans Resolution*, pp. 5, 7, 13, 20, 23, 24, 30, 31, 33, 38, 39–40; *Rash Oaths*, p. 3; *The Juglers Discovered*, p. 6; *The Prisoners Plea for a Habeas Corpus*, sigs. Ar, Br, [B3r]; *Legall Fundamentall Liberties*, pp. 22, 24–25, 26, 27, 60; *A Salva Libertate* ([London, 1649]) which he concludes by citing *Legall Fundamentall Liberties*; *Strength out of Weaknesse*, p. 7; *L. Colonel John Lilburne Revived*, p. 2.

61 *A Pearle in a Dounghill. Or Lieu. Col. John Lilburne in New-gate* ([London, 1646]); *A Whip for the Present House of Lords*, p. 6. See also Walwyn, *The Just Man in Bonds*, in *Walwyn*, p. 221, and *Englands Weeping Spectacle*, p. 8. For Overton as the likely editor of *A Pearle*, see *Walwyn*, p. 529.

62 *An Anatomy*, p. 12. The Quakers were not alone in resorting to such symbolic gestures: John Saltmarsh kept on his hat in the presence of Fairfax in 1647: Watts, *The Dissenters*, p. 192; Geoffrey Nuttall, *The Holy Spirit in Puritan Faith and Experience* (Oxford, 1947), p. 83 n.7. The Diggers Everard and Winstanley stood before Lord General Fairfax with their hats on: *The Perfect Weekly Account*, 18–25 April 1649, p. 455; *Perfect Occurrences*, no. 121, 20–27 April 1649, p. 988. The Fifth Monarchist Venner also refused to put off his hat to Cromwell (Brailsford, *The Levellers and the English Revolution*, p. 46), and the Ranter Coppe refused before a parliamentary committee: *The Weekly Intelligencer*, no. 2, 1–8 Oct. 1650, p. 16.

63 Baxter noted that the Levellers were against the doctrine of election and for "the power of Free-will": *Reliquiae Baxterianae*, Part I, pp. 53–54. See also J. C. Davis, "The Levellers and Christianity," in *Politics, Religion and the English Civil War*, ed. B. Manning (London, 1973), pp. 231–33.

64 *Strength out of Weaknesse*, p. 2. In *A Worke of the Beast* the martyred Lilburne was already asserting that the Lord would carry him through his sufferings

"with an undaunted Spirit" (*Tracts on Liberty*, 2:6); cf. *Legall Fundamentall Liberties*, p. 23. On Lilburne appearing "undaunted" during his 1653 trial when he was indicted for high treason, see Clarendon, *History*, 5:307–8.

65 *The Triall of . . . John Lilburne*, p. 119 (mispaginated p. 103). Cf. "To the Reader" in *The Christian Mans Triall*. See also *The Recantation* where he refers to his "undaunted courage" in the midst of affliction (p. 5); and also *Englands Weeping Spectacle*, p. 3.

66 *A Remonstrance of Lieut. Col. John Lilburn* (London, 1652), p. 7. For Lilburne's conversion to Quakerism, see *The Resurrection of John Lilburne* (London, 1656); for his "serious reading" of texts by such Quaker prophets as James Nayler, William Dewsbury, and others, see esp. p. 5. The main connection between Quakers and Levellers was Lilburne, described by one Quaker prophet as "zealous & forward for the truth" (Richard Hubberthorne to George Fox, Swarthmore MSS. 4:14, Friends House Library, London; see also 3:96). Cf. Geoffrey F. Nuttall, "Overcoming the World: The Early Quaker Programme," in *Sanctity and Secularity: The Church and the World*, ed. Derek Baker (Oxford, 1973), pp. 155–61.

67 See, however, his urgent expression of the coming of Christ in *A Copie of a Letter* in *Tracts on Liberty*, 3:184–85. Cf. Burgess, "Protestant Polemic," who asserts "that Leveller writing shows a remarkable absence of millenarian ideas" (p. 65).

68 *A Worke of the Beast*, in *Tracts on Liberty*, 2:6, 20. The myth of the Lamb also inspired his notion of martyrdom in *Innocency and Truth Justified*, pt. 2, p. 14.

69 *Tracts on Liberty*, 3:271, 305.

70 *A Copie of a Letter* in *Tracts on Liberty*, 3:184–85. Cf. *Innocency and Truth Justified*, pt. 2, p. 16; *Vox Plebis*, p. 2; *The Resolved Mans Resolution*, p. 9; *Plaine Truth*, p. 12.

71 *An Impeachment*, p. 18.

72 *As You Were*, pp. 26–27. See also Lilburne's references to the Lord as "a MIGHTY TERRIBLE ONE" (as in Jer. 20:11) who threatens Cromwell (p. 28); and Lilburne's prophesy that "the day of the Lord is neare upon all the heathen": *L. Colonel John Lilburne Revived*, p. 8.

73 *Strength out of Weaknesse*, pp. 2, 1.

74 *Strength out of Weaknesse*, p. 12. Cf. his defiant response to "the pretended Atturney General" in *A Salva Libertate*. On the problem of consent and the constitutional experiments of the 1650s, see also John Morrill, *The Nature of the English Revolution* (London, 1993), p. 24.

75 For the official proclamation, see *Constitutional Documents*, p. 388.

76 *Jonahs Cry*, p. 11; cf. *Rash Oaths unwarrantable*, p. 22.

77 On the meanings of the word "tyranny," see Derek M. Hirst, "Freedom, Revolution, and Beyond," in *Parliament and Liberty from the Reign of Elizabeth to the English Civil War*, ed. J. H. Hexter (Stanford, 1992), pp. 252–74, esp. p. 265.

78 His concern with interconnections between dissimulation and new kinds of tyranny is suggested already in the full title of his major pamphlet, *Englands*

Birth-right Justified against all Arbitrary Usurpation, whether REGALL or PAR-LIAMENTARY, or under what Vizor soever ([London, 1645]). On the Merchant Adventurers, see Robert Brenner, *Merchants and Revolution: Commercial Change, Political Conflicts, and London's Overseas Traders, 1550–1653* (Princeton, 1993), pp. 381–87.

79 *Tracts on Liberty*, 3:258.

80 *Londons Liberty*, p. 41.

81 Overton, *An Alarum to the House of Lords*, p. 7; *Londons Liberty*, p. 37; cf. *Regall Tyrannie*, 90, and Overton (with Walwyn), *A Remonstrance of Many Thousand Citizens, and other Free-born People of England* ([London], 1646), p. 8.

82 *An Alarum*, p. 8; *Londons Liberty in Chains*, p. 6; cf. *Charters of London*, p. 5.

83 On Lilburne's reference to England's Nimrods, see *Londons Liberty in Chains discovered*, pp. 19, 21. On the London and liberty in the Revolution, see Lawrence Manley, *Literature and Culture in Early Modern London* (Cambridge, 1995), ch. 10.

84 *A Whip for the Present House of Lords*, p. 2: liberty and property are, Lilburne adds, "quite opposite to communitie and Levelling."

85 See e.g. *The Recantation*, pp. 2–3.

86 *Rash Oaths*, p. 27.

87 *Plaine Truth*, p. 20; *Jonahs Cry*, p. 4.

88 *Plaine Truth*, p. 4; cf. p. 13 where he uses the word "snare"; and see his depiction of them as "pretended reformed presbyter-Ministers" in *The Oppressed Mans Oppressions declared*, p. 19. By the summer of 1646 Parliament was by a majority Presbyterian. See also Overton's attack on Presbyterian power and influence: *An Arrow Against All Tyrants* ([London], 1646).

89 *Plaine Truth*, pp. 13, 19. Cf. Lilburne's depiction of Lords themselves as "the sons of pride and tyranny" (*Regall Tyrannie*, p. 65), recalling the oppression and tyranny perpetuated by Laud and Strafford in the 1630s. See also Overton's attack on the devilish, Antichristian Presbyterian clergy in *An Arrow Against All Tyrants*.

90 *Plaine Truth*, p. 5.

91 On Milton and Circean themes in *Eikonoklastes*, see *CPW* 3:488, 582, 601; *Regall Tyrannie*, p. 50. Cf. Overton, *A Remonstrance of Many Thousand Citizens*, p. 5; and James Freize, *The Levellers Vindication* (London, [1649]), on "the Syrene inchantments of the sons of *Beliall*" (p. 4), referring to the lawyers in the new Commonwealth.

92 *Plaine Truth*, p. 5; *Englands Birth-right Justified* (1645) in *Tracts on Liberty*, 3:266.

93 *Regall Tyranny*, p. 25.

94 *The Triall . . . of Lilburne*, p. 114 (mispaginated p. 98). On Lilburne's fear that he will be ensnared by such laws, see pp. 27, 31, 41, 44, 117, 147.

95 *The Charters of London*, pp. 4, 5. The author of *Englands Weeping Spectacle*, an account of Lilburne's sufferings and struggles, likewise notes Lilburne's concern with the juggling and dissimulating behavior of legal and political authorities: see pp. 8–10.

96 *Tracts on Liberty*, 3:292–94, 284.

97 *A Remonstrance of Many Thousand Citizens*, p. 4.

98 Overton, *A Remonstrance*, p. 19.

99 *The Just Defence*, in *The Leveller Tracts*, pp. 451, 460. Because the accusation of pretence in matters of political liberty and its rhetoric had great potency in this unstable period, it could also be turned against the Levellers: one hostile response to Lilburne's *Second Part of Englands New-Chaines Discovered*, written by a defender of the Republic, accused the Levellers of their "seditious wayes and wyles" operating against the new Commonwealth "under the pretence and colour of *Libertie*": see *The Discoverer*, p. 1. On "their pretended principle of libertie," see also *The Diary of Ralph Josselin, 1618–1683*, ed. Alan Macfarlane (Oxford, 1976), p. 161; and Clarendon, *History*, 4:241.

100 *Jonahs Cry out of the Whales belly*, p. 12. See also *As You Were*, p. 10; cf. Overton, *An Alarum to the House of Lords*, p. 8.

101 *A Manifestation*, in *The Leveller Tracts*, p. 281. See also Lilburne's marginal comment on Colonel Thomas Rainsborough who "daubed & jugled not as the others did, but spoke his mind freely" (*An Impeachment*, p. 57).

102 *Englands New Chains Discovered*, in *The Leveller Tracts*, p. 167; see also *Englands Birth-Right Justified*, in *Tracts on Liberty*, 3:268–69. Cf. John Saltmarsh's concern that the health of a state is maintained by liberty of the press and "free debates and open conferences": *The Smoke in the Temple* (London, 1646), p. 3.

103 The phrase is from Lilburne's interview with the Rump's Attorney General in *Strength out of Weaknesse*, p. 15.

104 See e.g. *Jonahs Cry*, p. 8.

105 *The Grand Plea*, p. 23.

106 *An Impeachment*, pp. 8, 45; on Cromwell's juggling with the king, see p. 4.

107 *As You Were*, title page, pp. 14, 15; cf. *The Upright Mans Vindication*, pp. 2, 23, and *Englands Weeping Spectacle*, p. 10. On Cromwell's "pretended friendship" to Englishmen, see also *An Impeachment*, p. 32.

108 *As You Were*, p. 15.

109 For the passage Lilburne cites, see *CPW* 4:535–36. Lilburne's citation of Milton was first noted by Don M. Wolfe, "Lilburne's Note on Milton," *Modern Language Notes*, 56 (1941), 362–63.

110 Lilburne could have found evidence for Milton's chivalric self-presentation in relation to the Commonwealth in the frontispiece to *A Defence* (which displays a shield): *CPW*, 4:298.

111 *As You Were*, pp. 15–16. How the republican Milton regarded Lilburne's seditious writings against the Republic remains a matter of conjecture; in March 1649 the Council of State requested him to reply to Lilburne's recent polemical onslaught, *Englands New Chains Discovered* and *The Second Part of Englands New-Chaines Discovered*, but Milton, significantly, chose to remain silent: see *Life Records*, 2:239–40.

112 *As You Were*, pp. 28, 22–23.

113 Gregg, *Free-born John*, pp. 268, 285–86; Aylmer, *The Levellers in the English Revolution*, p. 149; Marie Gimelfarb-Brack, *Liberté, Egalité, Fraternité, Justice! La Vie et l'oeuvre de Richard Overton, Niveleur* (Berne, 1979), pp. 379–80.

114 *The Hunting of the Foxes* ([London], 1649), p. 114. Cf. e.g. Milton, *CPW* 1:614, 1:755, 1:856, 3:322, 3:241, 3:257, 4:650, 7:280; and see also Walwyn, *A Word in Season*, in *Walwyn*, p. 199.

115 *The Hunting of the Foxes*, p. 7.

116 *The Hunting of the Foxes*, pp. 7–8. The Leveller John Wildman had himself described the Grandees in similar terms: *Putney Projects. Or the Old Serpent in a new Forme* ([London], 1647). On the dissimulating politician shrouding himself under "the finest cloak of Religion," see Walwyn, *Walwyn*, p. 381. Also see Lilburne, *As You Were*, pp. 5, 32 (referring to Cromwell), *The Legall Fundamentall Liberties*, p. 59, *Second Part of Englands New-Chaines*, in *The Leveller Tracts*, pp. 175–76, 180, and *The Upright Mans Vindication* ([London], 1653), pp. 2, 23; and Overton, *A Remonstrance of Many Thousand Citizens*, p. 8, and *An Arrow Against All Tyrants*, p. 12 (with reference to the clergy).

117 *The Hunting of the Foxes*, p. 12.

118 *Second Part of Englands New-Chaines*, in *The Leveller Tracts*, pp. 175–76; cf. p. 180.

119 *The Hunting of the Foxes*, pp. 9, 14. Cf. *Legall Fundamentall Liberties* where Lilburne observes that Cromwell is "absolute king" and that Ireton "shewed himself an absolute King, if not an Emperor, against whose will no man must dispute" (pp. 27, 35), and *An Appeale*, where Overton writes that "we would not indure in the King, to pluck off the *Garments of Royalty* from oppression and tyranny, to dresse up the same in *Parlament Robes*" (*Leveller Manifestoes*, p. 177).

120 *The Hunting of the Foxes*, p. 9. See also Lilburne, *The Prisoners Plea for a Habeas Corpus*, sig. [B3r].

121 *The Hunting of the Foxes*, p. 14. Cf. Lilburne's *Legall Fundamentall Liberties*, sig. A2v.

122 See e.g. *Legall Fundamentall Liberties*, pp. 32–34, 39, 59, 64, 67–68. On the Rump as a "Mock power" "most tyrannically erected and set up, and imposed upon the free people of this Nation," see also Lilburne, *A Salva Libertate*; and *An Outcry of the Youngmen and Apprentices of London* [London, 1649], p. 2.

123 *Strength out of Weaknesse*, p. 4 (where Lilburne also refers to "a mock Parliament" under "the fiction or shaddow of Majestrates"). See also p. 17 for his use of the word "fiction" in relation to the Rump Parliament and the Attorney General's authority.

124 *An Impeachment*, p. 15 (second page with this numbering).

125 *Samson Agonistes*, line 194; *An Impeachment*, p. 8.

126 On Cromwell's determination "to break [the Levellers] in pieces" in the spring of 1649, see *The Picture of the Councel of State*, in *The Leveller Tracts*, p. 204. On Lilburne's bitter recollection, in August 1649, of the Burford defeat, see *An Outcry of the Youngmen and Apprentices of London*.

127 *An Impeachment*, pp. 15–16.

128 *Paradise Lost*, 7.24–25; cf. *Englands Weeping Spectacle*, p. 3 ("he is not a changer with the times"); and Andrew Sharp, "John Lilburne's Discourse of Law," *Political Science*, 40, 1 (1988), 19.

129 *Englands New Chains Discovered*, in *The Leveller Tracts*, p. 157.

130 *Englands New Chains Discovered*, in *The Leveller Tracts*, pp. 160–62.
131 *Englands New Chains Discovered* and *Second Part* (March 1649), in *The Leveller Tracts*, pp. 165, 172; cf. 182, 188 (on the Rumpers' "dissembled repentances"). On Cromwell's "often dissembled Repentances," see *The Picture of the Councel of State*, in *The Leveller Tracts*, p. 210.
132 For the response of the House of Commons to Lilburne's "seditious" book, see *CJ*, 6, 174 (27 March 1649); *Writings and Speeches of Oliver Cromwell*, 2:41; *Walwyn*, pp. 364 (where Walwyn reports that it is called "a very dangerous Book, full of sedition and treason"), 372. On mounting tensions, see also Bodleian Library, MS. Clarendon 37, fol. 32.
133 *Second Part*, in *The Leveller Tracts*, pp. 188, 179; cf. p. 181. See also *A Discourse Betwixt Lieutenant Colonel John Lilburn . . . and Mr Hugh Peter*, where Lilburne, visited by Peter in the Tower, even accused the Army preacher of being one of the "stalking horses of the great men of the Army, with fair and plausible pretences to insinuate into men" (p. 2).
134 *Second Part*, in *The Leveller Tracts*, pp. 185, 183.
135 *Second Part*, in *The Leveller Tracts*, p. 180.
136 *Second Part*, in *The Leveller Tracts*, p. 184. For a view, however, of Lilburne's inconsistency after the dissolution of the Rump, see Woolrych, *Commonwealth*, pp. 129–30, 250–61; as Woolrych points out, his addresses to the interim government vacillated "between invective and pleading" (p. 251).
137 As David Norbrook notes, Marvell's lines, while sounding an affirmative note, are "not unequivocally triumphal": "Marvell's 'Horatian Ode' and the Politics of Genre," in *Literature and the English Civil War*, ed. Thomas Healy and Jonathan Sawday (Cambridge, 1990), p. 164.

2 GERRARD WINSTANLEY AND THE CRISIS OF THE REVOLUTION

1 Studies of the Rump's shortcomings as a revolutionary regime include Underdown, *Pride's Purge*, ch. 9; Worden, *Rump Parliament*; Woolrych, *Commonwealth*; Toby Barnard, *The English Republic, 1649–1660*, 2nd edn. (London and New York, 1997), ch. 3. For a more positive account of the Rump (though without denying its political ambiguities), see Sean Kelsey, *Inventing a Republic: The Political Culture of the English Commonwealth, 1649–1653* (Manchester, 1997).
2 For a list of Winstanley's writings, along with other known Digger texts, see Christopher Hill's edition, *Winstanley: The Law of Freedom and Other Writings* (Cambridge, 1983), pp. 72–74.
3 *Works*, pp. 472, 477, 507. Quotations from Winstanley's works are taken from the Sabine edition and noted parenthetically in my text, except for those early works of 1648 not printed by Sabine, as well as more recently discovered Winstanley texts.
4 See Underdown, *Pride's Purge*, pp. 174, 281, 298; J. P. Cooper, "Social and Economic Policies under the Commonwealth," in *The Interregnum: The Quest for Settlement, 1646–1660*, ed. G. E. Aylmer (London, 1972), p. 123; C. G. A. Clay, *Economic Expansion and Social Change: England 1500–1700*, 2 vols.

(Cambridge, 1984), 1:230; Brian Manning, *1649: The Crisis of the English Revolution* (London, 1992), pp. 79–89, 111. The winter of 1648–49 was particularly severe.

5 As Brian Manning notes, "the main agrarian issue of the 1640s was the enclosure of commons and waste grounds" (*The English People and the English Revolution, 1640–1660* (London, 1976), p. 292).

6 Cf. Underdown, *Pride's Purge*: "Social reform . . . produced much talk but little action" during the years of the Rump (p. 280).

7 See also *Works*, p. 395: "I have Writ, I have Acted, I have Peace: and now I must wait to see the Spirit do his own work in the hearts of others."

8 On the extent of the Digger movement, including Digger evangelizing, see Keith Thomas, "Another Digger Broadside," *P&P*, 42 (1969), 59, 65; *Works*, pp. 439–41, 649–51.

9 See e.g. *Works*, p. 388, for Winstanley's hope that "the poor and the meek shall inherit the earth" (echoing Ps. 37:11 and Matt. 5:5); and Thomas, "Another Digger Broadside," 63.

10 See *Works*, pp. 284–85, 295–96, 346, as well as the account of their sufferings at the end of *A New-Yeers Gift*: pp. 392–93; for the burning of Digger houses, see *Works*, p. 434. On contemporary hostility toward the Diggers, see also D. W. Petegorsky, *Left-Wing Democracy in the English Civil War: A Study of the Social Philosophy of Gerrard Winstanley* (London, 1940), pp. 161, 164, 169, 171, 173–75; and especially John Gurney, "Gerrard Winstanley and the Digger Movement in Walton and Cobham," *HJ*, 37, 4 (1994), 775–802.

11 The incident occurred on 11 June 1649: *Works*, pp. 295–96. See also the account in Manning, *1649*, pp. 124–25.

12 On Winstanley's likely conversion to Quakerism, see Richard T. Vann, "From Radicalism to Quakerism: Gerrard Winstanley and Friends," *JFHS*, 49 (1959–61), 41–46; Vann, "The Later life of Gerrard Winstanley," *JHI*, 26 (1965), 133–36; James Alsop, "Gerrard Winstanley's Later Life," *P&P*, 83 (1979), 73–81. See also Barry Reay, "Quakerism and Society," in *Radical Religion*, p. 149, for a letter from the Quaker Edward Burrough reporting Winstanley's belief that the Quakers were carrying on the Diggers' work. For fragmentary evidence concerning his career after 1652, including evidence of a moderately prosperous existence, see J. Alsop, "Gerrard Winstanley: Religion and Respectability," *HJ*, 28, 3 (1985), 705–9.

13 On this matter, see G. E. Aylmer, "The Religion of Gerrard Winstanley," in *Radical Religion*, pp. 92–93, who, in my view, rightly emphasizes interconnections between Winstanley's communism and his theology, though he notes that "the emphasis varies in different pamphlets." Cf. Fenner Brockway, *Britain's First Socialists* (London, 1980), who asserts that "Two hundred years before Karl Marx's *Das Kapital*, Gerrard Winstanley defined the fundamental principles of socialism" (p. 127).

14 For a contrary view stressing the rapid development of Winstanley's secularized thought, see George Juretic, "Digger no Millenarian: The Revolutionizing of Gerrard Winstanley," *JHI*, 36 (1975), 263–80. On his secular rationalism, see also C. H. George, "Gerrard Winstanley: A Critical

Retrospect," in *The Dissenting Tradition*, ed. C. Robert Cole and Michael E. Moody (Athens, OH, 1975), pp. 191–225. Yet even the title page of *The Law of Freedom* directed Winstanley's readers to two key apocalyptic texts: Rev. 11:15 and Dan. 7:27.

15 See e.g. Lewis H. Berens, *The Digger Movement in the Days of the Commonwealth* (London, 1961 [1906]); Petegorsky, *Left-Wing Democracy in the English Civil War*; W. S. Hudson, "The Economic and Social Thought of Gerrard Winstanley," *Journal of Modern History*, 18, 1 (1946), 1–21; Perez Zagorin, *A History of Political Thought in the English Revolution* (London: 1954), ch. 4; Christopher Hill, *WTUD*, ch. 7; Hill, "The Religion of Gerrard Winstanley," *Past and Present Supplement*, no. 5 (1978); Hill, "Winstanley and Freedom," in *Freedom and the English Revolution: Essays in History and Literature*, ed. R. C. Richardson and G. M. Ridden (Manchester, 1986), pp. 151–68; Juretic, "Digger no Millenarian"; George, "Gerrard Winstanley: A Critical Retrospect"; Olivier Lutaud, *Winstanley: Socialisme et Christianisme sous Cromwell* (Paris, 1976); Lotte Mulligan, John K. Graham, and Judith Richards, "Winstanley: A Case for the Man as He Said He Was," *JEH*, 28 (1977), 57–75; J. C. Davis, *Utopia and the Ideal Society: A Study of English Utopian Writing, 1516–1700* (Cambridge, 1981), ch. 7; Aylmer, "The Religion of Gerrard Winstanley," in *Radical Religion*, pp. 91–119; F. D. Dow, *Radicalism in the English Revolution, 1640–1660* (Oxford, 1985), pp. 74–80. I have not noted important differences of opinion among these scholars, but I agree with those (e.g. Aylmer and Hill) who stress interconnections between Winstanley's radical theology and politics. See also Andrew Bradstock, "Sowing in Hope: the Relevance of Theology to Gerrard Winstanley's Political Programme," *SC*, 6, 2 (1991), 189–204.

16 Studies which have begun to explore literary or rhetorical dimensions of Winstanley's writings include Corns, *Uncloistered Virtue*, pp. 146–74; and T. Wilson Hayes, *Winstanley the Digger: A Literary Analysis of Radical Ideas in the English Revolution* (Cambridge, MA, 1979), a study which stresses (more than I) the typological method of biblical analysis in Winstanley's works, as well as his alchemical metaphors. See also Nigel Smith, *Literature and Revolution in England, 1640–1660* (New Haven, 1994), pp. 172–76; and, for Winstanley's idiosyncratic use of the Bible, John R. Knott, *The Sword of the Spirit: Puritan Responses to the Bible* (Chicago, 1980), ch. 4. John Rogers, *The Matter of Revolution: Science, Poetry, and Politics in the Age of Milton* (Ithaca, NY, 1996), pp. 40–51, argues, more strongly than I would, for an unresolved conflict between Winstanley's activist rhetoric and his pacifist theology.

17 On the politics of apocalypticism and millenarianism during Winstanley's age, see John P. Laydon, "The Kingdom of Christ and the Powers of the Earth: The Political Uses of Apocalyptic and Millenarian Ideas in England, 1648–1653" (Ph. D. dissertation, Cambridge University, 1977). See also Bernard Capp, "The Political Dimension of Apocalyptic Thought," in *The Apocalypse in English Renaissance Thought and Literature*, ed. C. A. Patrides and Joseph Wittreich (Ithaca, NY, 1984), pp. 109–18; and P. G. Rogers, *The Fifth Monarchy Men* (London, 1966), ch. 1.

18 *Several Pieces Gathered into one Volume*, title page and sig. A3v. This is the second edition of five of Winstanley's works, a collection published in 1649 and printed for Giles Calvert, printer for nearly all the Digger writings; I quote from the copy in the Manchester public library.

19 From his early works, Winstanley is critical of "whosoever preaches from his book, and not from the anointing" (*The Mysterie of God* (1648), p. 37); he himself claims to "have writ nothing but what was given me of my Father" (sig. A2v). See also his address "To the Reader" in *Several Pieces*.

20 See also Smith, *Perfection Proclaimed*, p. 383, who notes the importance of this scriptural text for radical religious writers.

21 On the regime's failure to address the grievances of hardships of the lower orders, see Underdown, *Pride's Purge*, pp. 261, 281–2, 284, 329; Woolrych, *Commonwealth*, p. 7.

22 For a different approach to the early writings, but one which notes their intimations of later Digger doctrines, see J. Sanderson, "The Digger's Apprenticeship: Winstanley's Early Writings," *Political Studies*, 22, 4 (1974), 453–62. See also Timothy Kenyon, *Utopian Communism and Political Thought in Early Modern England* (London, 1989), pp. 154–62.

23 I quote from the first edition, which appears in the British Library and which was printed for Giles Calvert. This text, and the two subsequent ones by Winstanley which I discuss, are only summarized in Sabine.

24 In resorting to biblical arithmetic, Winstanley was not alone in this age of apocalyptic writing: see e.g. Mary Cary, *The Little Horns Doom & Downfall* (London, 1651); John Canne, *A Voice From the Temple to the Higher Powers* (London, 1653), pp. 13–14; Canne, *The Time of the End* (London, 1657).

25 This near-Digger tract refers to Rev. 13, where mention is made "of an ugly beast with seven heads and ten horns, which horns did persecute the Saints: now in *Revel.* 17. horns are there declared to be Kings, so that Kings are of the Beast" (*Works*, p. 613).

26 On the antitheatrical prejudice in Puritan discourse, see Jonas Barish, *The Anti-Theatrical Prejudice* (Berkeley, 1981), ch. 6.

27 On the theatricalism and subtle forms of Antichrist, see the verses concluding *The Breaking of the Day of God*, p. 128; cf. [William Dell], *The City-Ministers unmasked* (London, 1649), p. 22, and *The Tryal of Spirits* (London, 1653), pp. 13, 59, 63.

28 I quote from the first edition in the Thomason collection; Thomason received his copy in July 1648.

29 On uses of alchemical language in seventeenth-century politics and religion, see J. Mendelsohn, "Alchemy and Politics in England," *P&P*, 135 (1992), 30–78.

30 Cf. the antinomian Ranter Joseph Salmon who portrays himself as a fool in *A Rout, A Rout* (London, 1649).

31 See *Acts and Ordinances*, 1:1133–36. Everard himself had been arrested for alleged blasphemy. See also *Truth Lifting up Its Head*, in *Works*, pp. 130–31.

32 See also *The Saints Paradise*, pp. 93, 122–25.

33 *Puritanism and Liberty*, p. 178. See also John Morrill, *The Nature of the English*

Revolution (London and New York, 1993), pp. 18–19; B. S. Capp, *Fifth Monarchy Men* (London, 1972), pp. 50, 53, 56.

34 See esp. Capp, *Fifth Monarchy Men*, p. 56; Underdown, *Pride's Purge*, ch. 9; and Worden, *Rump Parliament*, passim, for the most thorough study. See also Morrill, *The Nature of the English Revolution*, pp. 24–25.

35 John Lilburne, *Englands New Chains Discovered* (London, 1649), sig. Br.

36 Isaac Penington, *A Word for the Commonweale* (London, February 1649/50), p. 1.

37 See the Commons' resolution of 4 January 1649, where it is declared "That the people are, under God, the original of all just power": *Stuart Constitution*, p. 292.

38 So too Joseph Salmon, later the Ranter writer, insisted that there was no need to go to Rome or Canterbury to discover Antichrist since it was "in thee." See *Anti-christ in Man* (London, 1647), p. 34; cf. James Nayler, *Antichrist in Man* (London, 1656), p. 2.

39 See Bauthumley's *The Light and Dark Sides of God* (1650), in *Ranter Writings*, p. 260: "if men were acted & guided by that inward law of righteousnesse within, there need be no laws of men, to compel or restrain men, and I could wish that such a spirit of righteousnesse would appear, that men did not act or do things from externall rules, but from an internall law within." See also George Foster, *Sounding of the Last Trumpet* ([London], 1650), p. 52.

40 See Keith Thomas, *Religion and the Decline of Magic* (New York, 1971), pp. 469–92; and Christopher Hill, Barry Reay, and William Lamont, *The World of the Muggletonians* (London, 1983), p. 31.

41 See *De Doctrina Christiana*, where Milton emphasizes the internal law of the Spirit above all other authorities: *CPW* 6:532, 534, 535–36, 537.

42 See *The Likeliest Means to Remove Hirelings out of the Church* (1659), in *CPW* 7:315–17. Cf. *The Mysterie of God*, p. 37.

43 *Works*, p. 281; *The Perfect Weekly Account*, 18–25 April 1649, pp. 454–55; Manning, *1649*, pp. 121–22.

44 Cf. *A New-Yeers Gift*, p. 376, for a similar formulation.

45 Cf. Peter Chamberlen's *The Poore Mans Advocate, or, Englands Samaritan* (London, [1649]), which likewise appeared in April, and which warned the "unsettled" government, which "hath many enemies," to provide for the poor when "many [are] starving dayly for want of bread" (p. 2). The Digger tract, however, has a more visionary and mythopoeic dimension; its communist message is likewise distinctive.

46 See e.g. *A New-Yeers Gift*: "this power of darknes is mans fall, or the night time of mankind" (p. 380). On Winstanley's preoccupation with the Fall, see Kenyon, *Utopian Communism and Political Thought*, pp. 131–45.

47 On the mounting sectarian stridency of the early 1650s, see Derek Hirst, "The Failure of Godly Rule in the English Republic," *P&P*, 132 (1991), 36, 38; Woolrych, *Commonwealth*, p. 58.

48 Although Winstanley and the Diggers were realistic enough to appeal at times to powerful leaders such as Fairfax and Cromwell, one hardly needs

to conclude, as J. C. Davis does, that "Winstanley always had a respect for power. . . . He never was an anti-authoritarian" (*Utopia*, p. 182; cf. pp. 183, 190).

49 See his 1650 pamphlet (written in dialogue form), *"England's Spirit Unfoulded: or, An Incouragement to Take the Engagement*: A Newly Discovered Pamphlet by Gerrard Winstanley," ed. G. E. Aylmer, *P&P*, 40 (July 1968), 3–15.

50 See *Constitutional Documents*, pp. 137–44. In 1649 Milton himself recalled the famous phrase in *Eikonoklastes*: see *CPW* 3:441.

51 See e.g. his sharp warning that if they do not act to "set Christ upon his throne in *England*," the lamb will "shew himself a Lion, and tear [them] in pieces for [their] most abominable dissembling Hypocrisie" (p. 386).

52 On the aroused hopes among commoners that they might also benefit from the new freedom after Parliament's victory over the king, see Joan Thirsk, "Agrarian Problems and the English Revolution," in *Town and Countryside in the English Revolution*, ed. R. C. Richardson (Manchester, 1992), pp. 182–83.

53 As Underdown notes, after the 1648–49 Revolution the Presbyterians still dominated the pulpits over most of England (*Pride's Purge*, p. 330).

54 Keith Thomas has accurately established the date for this tract in "The Date of Gerrard Winstanley's *Fire in the Bush*," *P&P*, 42 (1969), 160–62. Winstanley published only seven of the thirteen chapters he intended to write for this apocalyptic tract: see *Works*, p. 449.

55 Since Winstanley wrote and published *Fire in the Bush* nearly a year after he began the Digger experiment, it is hard to agree with Juretic's thesis that "once he began his Digging cooperative Winstanley's ideas became rapidly secularized" ("The Revolutionizing of Gerrard Winstanley," 269). For connections between theological and political modes of thought in Winstanley, cf. Corns, *Uncloistered Virtue*, pp. 170, 172.

56 Winstanley's first reference in his Digger writings to the war in Heaven between Michael and the Dragon (Rev. 12:3, 7) occurs in *A New-Yeers Gift* (p. 33); the myth becomes important in subsequent writings, especially in *Fire in the Bush*. Cf. *The Mystery of God*, p. 29.

57 See e.g. the Fifth Monarchy prophetess Mary Cary's political interpretation of this scriptural text in *The Little Horns Doom & Downfall*, pp. 2–8. For Cary the vision becomes a means of interpreting the late king's power in relation to the Roman Beast to which England was subjected; Winstanley's visionary rendering has a greater socioeconomic dimension. See also the near-Digger text, *More Light Shining in Buckinghamshire* (1649), in *Works*, pp. 635–36.

58 On "Prisons, Whips, and Gallows" as "the torments of this Hell" under kingly power and the government of darkness, see Winstanley's *Watch-Word to the City of London* (1649), p. 324; *A New-Yeers Gift*, p. 388; and *The Law of Freedom*, pp. 522–23.

59 Cf. Abiezer Coppe's reference to the "unspotted beauty and majesty" of "even base things" in the title page to *A Second Fiery Flying Roule* (London, 1649).

60 Cf. *The Breaking of the Day of God*, p. 106, where Winstanley's allegorical

imagination begins to work in a similar fashion and is no less intensely anti-ecclesiastical: the Dragon and the Leopard, he writes, "committed fornication together; then they begat this Beast (or Ecclesiasticall power) to kill and suppresse, not men and women simply, but the manifest appearance of God in them."

61 See also Fifth Monarchist discourse where the little horn represents the persecuting powers of Charles I: e.g. Cary, *The Little Horns Doom.*

62 For responses by radical writers to the social, ecclesiastical, economic, and legal order which contributed to class conflict and oppression of the poor, see Manning, *The English People and the English Revolution*, esp. ch. 9.

63 John Owen, *The Shaking and Translating of Heaven and Earth* (London, 1649), p. 35.

64 On the Dragon's power behind tithes, see George Fox, *The Law of God, the Rule for Law-Makers* (London, 1658), p. 8, and Winstanley's *A New-Yeers Gift*, where he cites tithes as a manifestation of the "confederacie between the Clergy and the great red Dragon" (p. 387). Cf. Milton's connection between the national church and the Beast of Revelation in his attack on hirelings: *Likeliest Means, CPW* 7:306, 308, 320. On the Beast and its connection with dissimulation in religion, see also Canne, *The Time of the End*, p. 224. On class issues in relation to tithes, see A. L. Morton, *The World of the Ranters: Religious Radicalism in the English Revolution* (London, 1970), p. 11; on radical Puritan grounds for objecting to them, see Woolrych, *Commonwealth*, p. 236.

65 Cf. *A New-Yeers Gift*, where Winstanley observes that some priests make "Religion and Gospel" "a Cloke for their Knavery" (p. 373); and *The Law of Freedom*, where kingly power pretends to godliness by praying and preaching and keeping "Fasts and Thanksgiving-days to God," all as "a cloak to hide his Oppression from the people" (p. 530).

66 Dell, *The Tryal of Spirits*, p. 21.

67 See also *The Law of Freedom*: "likewise hath the Scriptures of *Moses*, the Prophets, Christ, and his Apostles, been darkened and confounded by suffering Ministers to put their Inferences and Interpretations upon them" (p. 555). For similar Leveller objections, see Brian Manning, "The Levellers and Religion," in *Radical Religion*, p. 66.

68 *The Vanitie of the Present Churches* (1649), in *Walwyn*, p. 327. Cf. Milton's *Areopagitica, CPW* 2:548.

69 On illiteracy and the poor in early modern England, see David Cressy, *Literacy and the Social Order: Reading and Writing in Tudor and Stuart England* (Cambridge, 1980), chs. 6 and 7, who stresses the correlation between social structure and illiteracy; on the illiteracy of poor husbandmen especially, see pp. 106, 125, 127, 156–57. See also Keith Wrightson, *English Society, 1580–1680* (London, 1982), pp. 220–21. On the clergy making religion obscure to the people, see Manning, *English People and the English Revolution*, p. 275.

70 I cite, respectively, from Milton, *CPW* 3:347, and from Winstanley's *Breaking of the Day of God*, p. 57.

71 See John Saltmarsh, *Groanes for Liberty* (London, 1646), on the prelates "that

dazle the eyes, and astonish the senses of poor people with the glorious name of the church . . . this is the Gorgons Head that hath enchaunted them and held them in bondage to their errors" (p. 13). And for the rich and the mighty as sorcerers who have made the common people miserable, see *Englands Troublers Troubled, Or the just Resolutions of the plaine-men of England Against the Rich and Mightie* ([London], 1648), a text which condemns "the cup of [their] owne sorceries and abominations" (p. 14). See also the near-Digger text, *Light Shining in Buckinghamshire*, in *Works*, p. 619; and *The New Law of Righteousnes*, p. 242.

72 See also Winstanley's observation that "by this multitude of waste discourse, people are blinded" (pp. 242–43). Cf. the Digger criticism of landlords who employ "words of flattery to the plain-hearted people, whom they deceive, and that lies under confusion and blindness" (p. 259); and Winstanley's mistrust of "the fair words of a Parliament" (p. 306).

73 Cf. Winstanley's description of "reason the spirit of burning" casting out "that enslaving covetous Kingly power" which is within: *England's Spirit Unfoulded*, ed. Aylmer, p. 13.

74 Foster, *The Sounding of the Last Trumpet*, p. 15. Foster's work was published in April 1650, soon after the appearance of *Fire in the Bush*. See Coppe, *A Fiery Flying Roll* (1649), for the Lord as "that mighty Leveller" (*Ranter Writings*, pp. 87, 90), though Coppe distinguishes himself from the Diggers by not engaging in "digging-levelling" (p. 86). See also the Digger poet Robert Coster's *A Mite Cast into the Common Treasury*, in *Works*, p. 659. For other examples from this period of God depicted as the great leveller, see Christopher Hill, *The English Bible and the Seventeenth-Century Revolution* (Harmondsworth, 1993), pp. 120–21. On the rhetoric of mighty levelling in Ranter writing, see Chapter 3 of this study.

75 Winstanley's language of levelling revises (in Digger terms) Isaiah 40:4; on hills and valleys as class symbols, see Morton, *World of the Ranters*, p. 18. See also *Works*, pp. 153, 428, and 575–76 (where he envisions the commonwealth army in his utopian platform levelling "Mountains to the Valleys").

76 Winstanley also indicates that he had heard about Hugh Peter's preparation of *Good Work for a Good Magistrate* (1651), a text he waited to see since it argued "That the Word of God might be consulted with to finde out a healing Government" (p. 509); Peter's text looks at religion, the poor, justice, the law, among other topics, in relation to the well-being of the new Commonwealth.

77 Cf. *A Watch-Word to the City of London* (1649) where Winstanley observes that "in all the passages of these eight yeers troubles I have been willing to lay out what my Talent was, to procure Englands peace inward and outward" (p. 315).

78 See e.g. John Spittlehouse, *The first Addresses to His Excellencie the Lord General* (London, 1653), "To his Excellency the Lord General *Cromwel*." On representations of Cromwell as Moses delivering the Israelites from bondage, see also Barry Coward, *Cromwell* (London, 1991), pp. 43, 113; Worden, *Rump*

Parliament, p. 274; Capp, "The Political Dimension of Apocalyptic Thought," pp. 114–15. On whether or not Cromwell accepted his role as God's instrument as a test applied by radical Puritans to his authority, see J. C. Davis, "Religion and the Struggle for Freedom in the English Revolution," *HJ*, 35, 3 (1992), 521–22.

79 See lines 5–9; cf. *Second Defence*, *CPW* 4:670–71. See also Christopher Feake's retrospective account of the victory in *A Beam of Light, Shining in the Midst of Much Darkness and Confusion* (London, 1659): "It may easily be conceived, how the hearts and mouths of the *Dissenting Brethren*, and all their *fellow Sectaries* were fil'd with joy" (p. 37). For Cromwell's own recollection, see *Writings and Speeches*, 3:54, as well as 2:463 and 3:5.

80 Dell, *The Crucified and Quickened Christian* (London, [1652]), "The Epistle Dedicatory," addressed to Cromwell. Dell went on to tell Cromwell: "your greatest praise, above the rest, is this, That *the spirit of the Lord is upon you, and his word is in your mouth.*"

81 On Cromwell and godly reformation, see Coward, *Cromwell*, passim; Worden, *Rump Parliament*, pp. 201, 278, 381; Woolrych, *Commonwealth*, p. 395. On Cromwell as reluctant revolutionary, see Underdown, *Pride's Purge*, pp. 148, 184. On "the conflict between radical Puritanism and conservative constitutionalism within the breast of Cromwell," see Woolrych, *ibid.*, pp. 396–97; G. E. Aylmer, *Rebellion or Revolution?: England 1640–1660* (Oxford, 1986), pp. 97, 204; Worden, *ibid.*, p. 274.

82 *Writings and Speeches*, 2:325; cf. 2:463, where, after the battle of Worcester, he warned Parliament not to permit "the fatness of these continued mercies" to "occasion pride and wantonness, as formerly the like hath done to a chosen nation." See also Coward, *Cromwell*, pp. 80, 107; Worden, *Rump Parliament*, p. 237.

83 See esp. Cromwell's telling assertion about "the ranks and orders of men": "A noblemen, a gentleman, a yeoman . . . That is a good interest of a nation and a great one" (*Writings and Speeches*, 3:435; cf. 3:452). See also Coward, *Cromwell*, 107; John Morrill, "Introduction" to *Oliver Cromwell and the English Revolution*, ed. Morrill (London and New York, 1990), p. 16.

84 For Trapnel's prophetic warning that Cromwell do justice to the poor, see *The Cry of the Stone: or a Relation of Something spoken in Whitehall, by Anna Trapnel, being the Visions of God* (London, 1654), esp. pp. 52, 54–55. For George Wither, see *Vaticinium Casuale* (London, 1655), pp. 12–14; and for Milton's warnings about the dangers of regal forms in the Protectorate, see *Second Defence*, *CPW* 4:673–74, 681–82. See also George Fox and James Nayler, *To Thee Oliver Cromwell* (London, 1655); and Spittlehouse, *The first Addresses*, pp. 5, 24–25.

85 See Underdown, *Pride's Purge*, pp. 280–81, 282–84; Woolrych, *Commonwealth*, p. 7; Margaret James, *Social Problems and Policy during the Puritan Revolution: 1640–1660* (London, 1930), ch. 6.

86 Cf. John Spittlehouse, who warns Cromwell and the rulers of the Commonwealth in 1653 not to halt "betwixt light and darkness, Christ and Antichrist, God and Mammon" (*The first Addresses*, p. 24).

87 See *The Readie and Easie Way*, *CPW* 7:435–36, 437.

88 On the association of lawyers with the Beast of Revelation, see *Light Shining in Buckinghamshire*, in *Works*, p. 618. On abbreviating and simplifying the Commonwealth laws, see also John Streater, *A Glympse of That Jewel, Judicial, Just, Preserving Libertie* (London, 1653), p. 5. On anti-lawyer sentiment, see Capp, *Fifth Monarchy Men*, pp. 89, 159, 167; Manning, *The English People and the English Revolution*, pp. 269–74, 302–3; James Sharpe, "The People and the Law," in *Popular Culture in Seventeenth-Century England*, ed. Barry Reay (London, 1985), pp. 258–59.

89 On law reform as "a live issue" at the end of 1651, see Underdown, *Pride's Purge*, p. 278; on law as symbolic of social slavery, see Worden, *Rump Parliament*, p. 114. See also Donald Veall, *The Popular Movement for Law Reform, 1640–1660* (Oxford, 1970).

90 For a comparable view of the laws as snares which may be used by the crafty to crush the simple and plain-hearted, see Penington, *A Word for the Commonweale*, p. 8.

91 On the lack of educational reform under the Rump, see Underdown, *Pride's Purge*, pp. 280–81; Woolrych, *Commonwealth*, p. 7.

92 See the postscript to *Englands Spirit Unfoulded*, p. 14, and *Works*, p. 401, where he stresses that ranting breeds idleness.

93 Winstanley no doubt has Ranter practices in mind when he refers, at the beginning of *The Law of Freedom*, to the "Freedom to have Community with all Women" as "the *Freedom* of wanton unreasonable Beasts" which "tends to Destruction" (p. 519); see also pp. 366–67, 526. On interconnections between religious and sexual rebellion in the Revolution, see James Grantham Turner, *Libertines and Radicals in Early Modern London: Sexuality, Politics and Literary Culture, 1630–1685* (Cambridge, forthcoming).

94 On georgic elements in Winstanley's writing, see Anthony Low, *The Georgic Revolution* (Princeton, 1985), pp. 215–20. On the history and literature of the land in the early modern period, see now Andrew McRae, *God Speed the Plough: The Representation of Agrarian England, 1500–1660* (Cambridge, 1996).

95 See e.g. Phyllis Mack, *Visionary Women: Ecstatic Prophecy in Seventeenth-Century England* (Berkeley and Los Angeles, 1992), p. 73, for recent comment on this. See also George Shulman, *Radicalism and Reverence: The Political Thought of Gerrard Winstanley* (Berkeley and Los Angeles, 1989), pp. 209–58; Aylmer, "The Religion of Gerrard Winstanley," pp. 111, 113. Hill's suggestion that the severe regulations and penalties proposed by Winstanley were intended for a transitional period in the progress towards his ideal society is not wholly convincing ("Winstanley and Freedom," p. 159).

96 E.g. one who inflicts bodily injury on another "shall be struck himself by the Executioner blow for blow, and shall lose eye for eye, tooth for tooth, limb for limb, life for life" (pp. 591–92); cf. p. 554. In terms of Winstanley's preparedness to countenance the death penalty for counter-revolutionary activity, cf. the compromises of the third Leveller *Agreement of the [Free] People* (1 May 1649) in *The Levellers in the English Revolution*, ed. G. E. Aylmer (Ithaca, NY, 1975), pp. 159–68.

97 Corns, *Uncloistered Virtue*, p. 174, has most recently stressed Winstanley's awareness of his audience.

98 See e.g. his description of the army in the commonwealth: it "is to be made use of to resist and destroy all who endeavor to keep up or bring in Kingly Bondage again" (p. 573); or see his section on laws against buying and selling: "If any do buy and sell the Earth or fruits thereof, unless it be to, or with strangers of another nation, . . . they shall be put to death as traytors to the peace of the *Common-wealth*; because it brings in Kingly bondage again" (pp. 594–95). Davis, however, exaggerates when he refers to "an apparatus of totalitarian discipline" in Winstanley's platform: *Utopia*, p. 182; cf. p. 193, and see Davis's *Fear, Myth, and History: The Ranters and the Historians* (Cambridge, 1986), p. 24.

99 I quote from the title page of the original edition of *The Law of Freedom* (London, 1652) since Sabine does not print these verses in his modern edition.

100 *The British Republic, 1649–1660* (London, 1990), p. 32. Cf. Zagorin's view of Winstanley as "one of the pre-eminent political thinkers of his time" (*A History of Political Thought in the English Revolution*, p. 56), a view emphasized by Petegorsky, *Left-Wing Democracy*, pp. 122, 128, and confirmed by Hill in "Winstanley and Freedom," pp. 164–65. See also Kenyon, *Utopian Communism and Political Thought*, chs. 4–6.

101 *Tyranipocrit, Discovered with his Wiles* (Rotterdam, 1649), pp. 35, 36. Yet even this remarkable anonymous author, though similar to Winstanley in his perceptions of hypocrisy and tyranny, did not argue for common ownership: see Aylmer, "Gerrard Winstanley," p. 115. On the Rump having effected corruption "in a new guise," see also Isaac Penington, *The Fundamental Right, Safety and Liberty of the People* (London, 1651), p. 22. Cf. Derek Hirst's observation, which Winstanley's acute analyses confirm, that "The History of the 1640s and 1650s . . . taught Englishmen the many meanings of the word 'tyranny'": "Freedom, Revolution, and Beyond," in *Parliament and Liberty from the Reign of Elizabeth to the English Civil War*, ed. J. H. Hexter (Stanford, 1992), p. 265.

3 RANTER AND FIFTH MONARCHIST PROPHECIES: THE REVOLUTIONARY VISIONS OF ABIEZER COPPE AND ANNA TRAPNEL

1 *CJ*, 6:354.

2 I quote from "An Act against several Atheistical, Blasphemous and Execrable Opinions, derogatory to the honor of God, and destructive to humane Society" (9 Aug. 1650), in *Acts and Ordinances*, 2:409–12 (p. 409).

3 For Coppe's assertion, see *A Fiery Flying Roll* (1649), in *Ranter Writings*, pp. 81, 91; subsequent quotations from Coppe are taken from this edition. Clarkson's assertion is from *A Single Eye All Light, no Darkness* (1650), in *Ranter Writings*, p. 169; Clarkson's heretical text was likewise investigated by Parliament: *CJ*, 6:427, 444. For an echo of Coppe's assertion, see George

Foster, *The Sounding of the Last Trumpet: or, Severall Visions, declaring the Universall overturning and rooting up of all Earthly Powers in England* ([London], 1650), p. 28.

4 See the letter from Coppe to Salmon and Wyke, in which Coppe observes that he is imprisoned at Coventry and in Newgate "for suspition of Blasphemie and Treason agt the State": reprinted from the Clarke Papers, Vol. 18, Worcester College, Oxford, in *Ranter Writings*, p. 117. For the history of blasphemy, see Leonard W. Levy, *Treason against God: A History of the Offense of Blasphemy* (New York, 1981). On orthodox Puritan notions of the offense (and Milton's response to them), see my essay "Treason against God and State: Blasphemy in Milton's Culture and *Paradise Lost*," in *Milton and Heresy*, ed. Stephen Dobranski and John Rumrich (Cambridge, 1998), pp. 176–98.

5 Walter Rosewell, *The Serpents Subtilty Disarmed* (London, 1656), p. 16; like many of the contemporary polemical responses to the Ranters, this one tended to exaggerate their real danger to the ecclesiastical and political order. Cf. Ephraim Pagitt, *Heresiography*, 5th edn. (London, 1654), pp. 143–44, on Ranters condemning authority and denying all obedience.

6 See *CJ*, 6:357 for 4 Feb. 1649/50; Worden, *Rump Parliament*, p. 233.

7 *Acts and Ordinances*, 2:410. Although the Act does not specifically mention the Ranters, it was drafted by a committee established in June 1650 to report on Laurence Clarkson's *A Single Eye All Light* and "the several abominable Practices of a Sect called Ranters" (*CJ*, 6:427). The entry for 8 Nov. 1650 likewise suggests that the Act was intended to suppress the Ranters: "*Ordered*, That the Committee, formerly appointed to bring a Bill against the Ranters, be revived" (*CJ*, 6:493). See also John Tickell, *The Bottomles Pit Smoaking in Familisme* (Oxford, 1651), "To the Reader."

8 See *A Remonstrance of The sincere and Zealous Protestation of Abiezer Coppe* (1651), in *Ranter Writings*, p. 121.

9 The Blasphemy Act exempted those "distracted in brain" (*Acts and Ordinances*, 2:410); hence Coppe's behavior: see *The Weekly Intelligencer of the Commonwealth*, no. 2, 1–8 Oct. 1650, p. 16; *Severall Proceedings in Parliament*, no. 53, 26 Sept.–3 Oct. 1650, p. 794; *Perfect Passages of Every Daies intelligence*, no. 13, 27 Sept.–4 Oct. 1650, p. 102. For Coppe's imprisonments, see *Severall Proceedings*, no. 16, 11–18 Jan. 1649/50, p. 213; *A Perfect Diurnall of some Passages*, no. 6, 14–21 Jan. 1649/50, p. 42; *A Perfect Diurnall*, no. 15, 18–25 March 1649/50, p. 141; Anne Laurence, *Parliamentary Army Chaplains, 1642–1651* (Woodbridge, 1990), pp. 115–16.

10 On fears of sectarian license in the new Republic and the responses to it by the Rump, see Keith Thomas, "The Puritans and Adultery: The Act of 1650 Reconsidered," in *Puritans and Revolutionaries: Essays in Seventeenth-Century History presented to Christopher Hill*, ed. Donald Pennington and K. Thomas (Oxford, 1978), pp. 257–82. On the Ranters and Quakers as threats to the social order, see also Underdown, *Pride's Purge*, p. 330.

11 See A. L. Morton, *The World of the Ranters: Religious Radicalism in the English Revolution* (London, 1970), pp. 17, 92; J. F. McGregor, "The Ranters: A Study in the Free Spirit in English Sectarian Religion, 1649–1660" (unpublished

B.Litt thesis, Oxford University, 1968); McGregor, "Seekers and Ranters," in *Radical Religion*, pp. 122, 131; Bernard Capp, in "Debate: Fear, Myth and Furore: Reappraising the Ranters," *P&P*, 140 (1993), 165 (for the full debate, see 155–210).

12 *Plain Scripture Proof of Infants Church-membership and Baptism* (London, 1651), pp. 147–48. On the horrors of religious divisions, see p. 149.

13 For the recent debate about the Ranters as a movement and threat in the English Revolution, see "Fear, Myth and Furore: Reappraising the Ranters" cited in note 11, a series of responses stimulated by the controversial work of J. C. Davis in *Fear, Myth, and History: The Ranters and the Historians* (Cambridge, 1986), who argued that the Ranters were largely a fabrication of the yellow-press pamphleteers and who challenged the work of Christopher Hill, A. L. Morton, and J. F. McGregor. Davis's initial response to those unpersuaded by his book appeared in his "Fear, Myth and Furore," *P&P*, 129 (1990), 79–103. Other critical responses to Davis's work include G. E. Aylmer, "Did the Ranters Exist?" *P&P*, 117 (1987), 208–19; E. P. Thompson, "On the Rant," in *Reviving the English Revolution: Reflections and Elaborations on the Work of Christopher Hill*, ed. G. Eley and W. Hunt (London, 1988), pp. 153–60; Christopher Hill, "Abolishing the Ranters," in *A Nation of Change and Novelty: Radical Politics, Religion and Literature in Seventeenth-Century England* (London, 1990), pp. 152–94; William M. Lamont, "The Puritan Revolution: A Historiographical Essay," *The Varieties of British Political Thought*, ed. J. G. A. Pocock (Cambridge, 1993), pp. 138–41; Nicholas McDowell, "A Ranter Reconsidered: Abiezer Coppe and Civil War Stereotypes," *SC*, 12, 2 (1997), 173–205.

14 Some connections between the Ranters and Winstanley are noted by B. J. Gibbons in "Fear, Myth and Furore," 178–94, passim. My focus on Winstanley and Coppe develops from the analysis in Chapter 2 of this study.

15 *Some Sweet Sips, of some Spirituall Wine* (1649), in *Ranter Writings*, p. 49.

16 For Winstanley's principal attacks, both dated 1650, see "A Vindication of Those . . . Called Diggers," in *Works*, pp. 399–403; and *England's Spirit Unfoulded: or, An Incouragement to Take the Engagement* (1650), ed. G. E. Aylmer, *P&P*, 40 (1968), 14–15. For Winstanley's reference to the Ranter Laurence Clarkson, see *Fire in the Bush*, in *Works*, p. 477; and for Clarkson's criticism of Winstanley's "self-love and vain-glory," see *Lost Sheep Found* (London, 1660), p. 27. Winstanley never specifically refers to Coppe.

17 *Civil Power*, *CPW* 7:246–47. See also my essay, "Treason against God and State."

18 The Act partly aimed to conciliate moderate Presbyterians; on the strength of the Rump Presbyterians, see Underdown, *Pride's Purge*, p. 270. On the Rump's general antipathy towards sectarian doctrines and enthusiasm, see Woolrych, *Commonwealth*, p. 8. On the Puritan campaign for moral reform, see Christopher Durston, "Puritan Rule and the Failure of Cultural Revolution, 1645–1660," in *The Culture of English Puritanism, 1560–1700*, ed. Durston and Jacqueline Eales (London, 1996), pp. 218–19.

19 *Acts and Ordinances*, 2:383–89, 393–97. See also Underdown, *Pride's Purge*, p. 275; Thomas, "The Puritans and Adultery: The Act of 1650 Reconsidered"; McGregor, "Fear, Myth and Furore," 158.

20 *A Remonstrance of The sincere and Zealous Protestation of Abiezer Coppe*, in *Ranter Writings*, p. 119. On Coppe's notorious reputation for blasphemy, see Christopher Fowler, *Daemonium Meridianum. Satan at Noon. Or, Antichristian Blasphemies* (London, 1655), pp. 60–61.

21 Fox, *Journal*, p. 47; also pp. 181–83, 212, 419. On Fox and Coppe, see p. 195; and also Norman Cohn, *The Pursuit of the Millennium*, rev. edn. (New York, 1970), p. 289. Fox accused the Ranters of wantonness and indulgence in tobacco and ale: *Journal*, p. 79. See also J. F. McGregor, "Ranterism and the development of early Quakerism," *JRH*, 9, 4 (1977), 349–63.

22 Ranter writing has largely been the subject of debate among historians arguing over the significance of Ranterism. Only recently has it become the subject of sustained treatment by literary scholars: see e.g. Smith, *Perfection Proclaimed*, passim; Corns, *Uncloistered Virtue*, pp. 174–93; Clement Hawes, *Mania and Literary Style: The Rhetoric of Enthusiasm from the Ranters to Christopher Smart* (Cambridge, 1996), chs. 1–3, for a stylistic and rhetorical analysis of Coppe's writing and "manic" persona. See also James Holstun, "Ranting at the New Historicism," *ELR*, 19, 2 (1989), 189–225; and, for the ways in which Coppe draws upon his early linguistic training to parody and subvert intellectual forms, see McDowell, "A Ranter Reconsidered."

23 See Valerie Pearl, *London and the Outbreak of the Puritan Revolution* (London, 1961); Keith Lindley, "London's Citizenry in the English Revolution," in *Town and Country in the English Revolution*, ed. R. C. Richardson (Manchester, 1992), pp. 19–45. In his rich study, *Literature and Culture in Early Modern London* (Cambridge, 1995), Lawrence Manley does not mention Coppe and the Ranters; see ch. 10 on the Revolution.

24 The frustration of such revolutionary hopes is, of course, one of the themes of Underdown's *Pride's Purge*.

25 See the revealing account of Coppe's early life in *Copp's Return to the wayes of Truth* (1651), Error I, in *Ranter Writings*, pp. 134–35. For other details of Coppe's biography, see the *DNB*, and *Biographical Dictionary of British Radicals in the Seventeenth Century*, ed. Richard Greaves and Robert Zaller, 3 vols. (Brighton, 1982–84), s.v. Coppe; McDowell, "A Ranter Reconsidered," 174–79 (on Coppe's humanist education); Robert Kenny, "'In These Last Dayes': The Strange Work of Abiezer Coppe," *SC*, 13, 2 (1998), 158–60 (on "the moderate Calvinist Coppe"). For a biased account, see Anthony Wood, *Athenae Oxonienses*, 2nd edn., 2 vols. (Oxford, 1721), 2:500–2.

26 See Baxter, *Plaine Scripture Proof*, p. 148: Coppe "re-baptized more then any one man that ever I heard of in the Countrey, witnesse *Warwickshire*, *Oxfordshire*, part of *Worcestershire*, &c." See also Wood, *Athenae Oxonienses*, 2:501; Kenny, "The Strange Work of Abiezer Coppe," 160–62.

27 On this aspect of Ezekiel, see Joel Rosenberg, "Jeremiah and Ezekiel," in *The Literary Guide to the Bible*, ed. Robert Alter and Frank Kermode (Cambridge, MA, 1987), p. 195.

28 *An Apology against a Pamphlet, CPW* 1:901; cf. 1:803.

29 See *Some Sweet Sips*, in *Ranter Writings*, p. 60; cf. *A Fiery Flying Roll*, where Coppe in the streets of London brandishes "the Sword of the Spirit" (p. 87).

30 For Warr, see *The Privileges of the People* (London, 1649), title page.

31 This theme of "universall peace and freedome," created by the mighty levelling God, was likewise stressed in 1650 by the millenarian George Foster who was influenced by the visionary writing of Coppe: see *The Sounding of the Last Trumpet*, p. 14.

32 Cf. George Foster, who urges his reader to "let these times move thee to pitty, and softness and tenderness of heart, with a yearning bowels of pitty and compassion to thy poor fellow-creatures": *The Pouring Forth of the Seventh and Last Viall* (London, 1650), "The Epistle to the Reader."

33 See e.g. such studies as Underdown, *Pride's Purge*, Worden, *Rump Parliament*, Woolrych, *Commonwealth*; John Morrill, *The Nature of the English Revolution* (London, 1993), pp. 24–25, ch. 18 (with John Walter).

34 *Pride's Purge*, p. 284. See also Joan Thirsk, "Agrarian Problems and the English Revolution," in *Town and Countryside in the English Revolution*, ed. R. C. Richardson (Manchester, 1992), p. 174; Woolrych, *Commonwealth*, p. 7.

35 *Some Sweet Sips*, in *Ranter Writings*, p. 55; cf. the voice from heaven he hears saying "Thrice happy they, who die to *Formes*, and live in *Power*" (p. 67), and Coppe on his having "thundered" against "*Idolatrous Formality*": *A Remonstrance*, in *Ranter Writings*, p. 120. See also his preface to Richard Coppin's *Divine Teachings*: *Ranter Writings*, p. 76. On revolutionary discourse challenging formality, see J. C. Davis, "Against Formality: One Aspect of the English Revolution," in *Royal Historical Society Transactions*, 6th series, vol. 3 (London, 1993), pp. 265–88.

36 *A Remonstrance*, in *Ranter Writings*, p. 121.

37 See Baxter, *Plain Scripture Proof*, p. 148; McGregor, "Seekers and Ranters," in *Radical Religion*, p. 130. On Coppe's skills as orator and preacher, see also *Severall Proceedings*, no. 16, 11–18 Jan. 1649/50, p. 213.

38 *The Sounding of the Last Trumpet*, sig. A2v, p. 14; see also pp. 19 and 42, and Foster's sequel, *The Pouring Forth of the Seventh and Last Viall*, "The Epistle to the Reader." See too the Digger poet Robert Coster, *A Mite Cast into the Common Treasury* (December 1649), in *The Works of Gerrard Winstanley*, p. 659. On Winstanley's levelling rhetoric, see Chapter 2 of this study.

39 *A Rout, A Rout* (1649), in *Ranter Writings*, p. 190.

40 Cf. *Some Sweet Sips*, where the Lord proclaims that "my people shall know no Arch-Bishop, Bishop, &c. but my Self. . . . they shall know no Pastor (neither) *Teacher, Elder*, or *Presbyter*, but the Lord, that Spirit" (*Ranter Writings*, p. 56).

41 *CPW* 3:509.

42 George Foster's God would also make "great and mighty men run into the holes of the rocks, and throw away *their Idols of gold and silver* . . . that there may be universal love and freedome" and equality (*The Sounding of the Last*

Trumpet, p. 17; see also p. 27). For the threat of judgment and the Lord shaking "horribly the Earth," see also the letter by Andrew Wyke (April 1650) in Clarke MS 18 (Worcester College, Oxford), fols. 25–27.

43 See *Some Sweet Sips* and *Second Fiery Flying Roule* in *Ranter Writings*, pp. 53, 100. In the former text, Coppe prays "O come! come Lord Jesus, come quickly, as a thiefe in the night." Cf. George Foster on the mighty God of Jacob who "will break in like a mighty man, and confound you of a sudden" (*The Pouring Forth of the Seventh and Last Viall*, "The Epistle").

44 McGregor, "The Ranters, 1649–1660," appropriately compares Coppe's God to "an urban Robin Hood" (p. 51).

45 Cf. Coppe: "For the day of the Lord of Hoasts, shall be upon every one that is proud, and lofty, and upon every one that is lifted up, and he shall be brought low" (p. 87).

46 On this interaction, see Barry Reay's introduction to *Popular Culture in Seventeenth-Century England*, ed. Reay (London, 1985), pp. 1–30.

47 See George Fox, *A Warning to All in this proud City called London to call them to Repentance* ([London, 1655]): "Plagues, plagues, plagues, is to be poured upon thee," Fox warns the city abounding in pride, hypocrisy, and oppression and "full of Inventions, and full of Images and Image-makers." See also Margaret Fell, *The Citie of London Reproved for its Abominations* (London, 1660), which fiercely reproves London on the eve of the Restoration.

48 On signs in Quaker culture, see Richard Bauman, *Let Your Words be Few: Symbolism of Speaking and Silence among Seventeenth-Century Quakers* (Cambridge, 1983), pp. 84–94. Coppe is echoing Isaiah 8:18 (see also his *Remonstrance*, in *Ranter Writings*, p. 120); but also relevant are such passages as Ezekiel 12:6, Acts 2:43, 5:12, 14:3, Heb. 2:4, 2 Cor. 12:12.

49 *The Sounding of the Last Trumpet*, sig. A2v (echoing 1 Cor. 1:27–28). See also Foster's *The Pouring Forth of the Seventh and Last Viall*, "The Epistle"; and cf. John Spittlehouse, *An Answer to one Part of the Lord Protector's Speech* (London, 1654), sig. A2v.

50 *Divine Teachings* (London, 1649), p. 3.

51 Furthermore, as Coppe later observes, the Seeker William Sedgwick embodies for him the radical spirit of communal giving dramatized by Coppe's strange story: "*Wil.Sedgwick* (in me) bowed to that poor deformed ragged wretch, that he might inrich him, in impoverishing himself" (p. 109).

52 "An Additional and Preambular Hint" to Richard Coppin's *Divine Teachings*, in *Ranter Writings*, p. 78.

53 *A Watch-Word to the City of London and The Armie* (1649), in *Works*, p. 315.

54 Cf. also Coppe's admiration for Hosea "who went in to a whore" (p. 104).

55 On the theatrical virtuousity of Coppe's writing from a different perspective (that draws upon Wittgenstein to explore the limits of Coppe's vision), see also Byron Nelson, "The Ranters and the Limits of Language," in *Pamphlet Wars: Prose in the English Revolution*, ed. James Holstun (London, 1992), pp. 60–75 (esp. 60–61, 69–70)

56 Keith Thomas, *Religion and the Decline of Magic* (New York, 1971), pp. 502–12;

Brian Manning, *1649: The Crisis of the English Revolution* (London, 1992), pp. 116–18.

57 *Plain Scripture Proof*, p. 148.

58 On the subversiveness of parody in early modern popular culture, see Peter Burke, *Popular Culture in Early Modern Europe* (New York, 1978), pp. 122–23.

59 See Salmon's postscript to *A Rout, A Rout*, in *Ranter Writings*, p. 200.

60 For a perceptive discussion of Coppe's sexual behavior in relation to his rapturous Biblical rhetoric, see James Grantham Turner, *One Flesh: Paradise Marriage and Sexual Relations in the Age of Milton* (Oxford, 1987), pp. 88–94.

61 The proverb comes of course from *The Marriage of Heaven and Hell*, a prophetic poem inspired (like Coppe's poetic prose) by Isaiah and Ezekiel. See also A. D. Nuttall, *The Alternative Trinity: Gnostic Heresy in Marlowe, Milton, and Blake* (Oxford, 1998), p. 211.

62 *Ranter Writings*, p. 119; further references to these works are cited parenthetically in my text.

63 On radical spiritualists in the Interregnum and the indwelling God, see Gibbons, "Fear, Myth and Furore," pp. 188–89.

64 Tickell, *The Bottomles Pit*, p. 32, and passim. *Copp's Return* has been called a wholly sincere recantation (Kenny, "The Strange Work of Abiezer Coppe," 170–71), but Tickell's skeptical account suggests a more complex perspective and that Coppe, who could ironically refer to himself as "the (supposed) Author of the Fiery flying Roll," had not altogether disowned the error *"That Swearing and Cursing is no Sin"* (*Ranter Writings*, pp. 124, 142), See also Hill's discussion in *A Nation of Change and Novelty*, pp. 179–80.

65 The religious beliefs and political visions of women prophets in the Revolution are now receiving more thorough study: see e.g. Elaine Hobby, *Virtue of Necessity: English Women's Writing, 1649–88* (Ann Arbor, 1989), ch. 1; Phyllis Mack, "Women as Prophets During the English Civil War," *Feminist Studies*, 8, 1 (1982), 19–45; Mack, *Visionary Women: Ecstatic Prophecy in Seventeenth-Century England* (Berkeley, 1992); Patricia Crawford, "The Challenges to Patriarchalism: How did the Revolution affect Women?" in *Revolution and Restoration: England in the 1650s*, ed. John Morrill (London, 1992), pp. 119–28; Manning, *1649*, pp. 138–42; Megan Matchinske, "Holy Hatred: Formations of the Gendered Subject in English Apocalyptic Writing, 1625–1651," *ELH*, 60 (1993), 349–77; Stevie Davies, *Unbridled Spirits: Women of the English Revolution, 1640–1660* (London, 1998). On radical female political initiatives in the Revolution, see Sara Mendelson and Patricia Crawford, *Women in Early Modern England* (Oxford, 1998), pp. 394–418.

66 *Strange and Wonderful Newes from White-hall: Or, The Mighty Visions Proceeding from Mistris Anna Trapnel* (London, 1654), title page.

67 See *The Cry of a Stone. Or a Relation of Something Spoken in Whitehall, by Anna Trapnel, being the Visions of God* (London, 1654), pp. 2, 7, which lists some "of very many persons of all sorts and degrees" who came to hear her prophecies, including Col. Sydenham of the Council of State (praised by Milton

in *A Second Defence*), Cols. West, Bennett, and Bingham (members of the late Barebone's Parliament), and several ladies; one spectator, Thomas Allen, was later Lord Mayor of London; see B. S. Capp, *The Fifth Monarchy Men* (London, 1972), p. 41, and Woolrych, *Commonwealth*, p. 388. Subsequent page references to Trapnel's work appear parenthetically in my text; I cite from the copy in the Thomason Collection. See also *Strange and Wonderful Newes from White-hall*, pp. 3–4.

68 On Fifth Monarchists and "Overturning dayes," see John Spittlehouse, *The first Addresses to his Excellencie the Lord General* (London, 1653), "To his Excellency"; Capp, *Fifth Monarchy Men*, p. 67; and Trapnel's *Cry of a Stone*, p. 63.

69 On Cromwell as a second Moses, see e.g. Spittlehouse, *The first Addresses*, "To his Excellency"; Spittlehouse, *A Warning-Piece Discharged* (London, 1653), esp. pp. 6–25; John Rogers, *A Few Proposals, relating to Civil Government* (London, 1653). On Cromwell as a happy instrument for the dissolving of the Rump, see John Canne, *A Voice from the Temple* (London, 1653), epistle dedicatory.

70 For Fifth Monarchists on Cromwell as "the dissembleingst perjured villaine in the world," see *A Collection of the State Papers of John Thurloe*, ed. Thomas Birch, 7 vols. (London, 1742), 1:641; and see *Calendar of State Papers, Domestic Series, 1653–1654*, p. 306 (20 Dec. 1653) for Vavasor Powell's inflammatory preaching at Blackfriars. See also Christopher Feake, *A Beam of Light, Shining in the Midst of much Darkness and Confusion* (London, 1659), pp. 51–52; Woolrych, *Commonwealth*, pp. 363–64. Chapter 5 of this study discusses seditious Fifth Monarchist rhetoric in relation to the Protectorate and Marvell's *First Anniversary*.

71 See also the 1654 letter by B. T. on Trapnel's prophesyings in which the author is "perswaded she hath communion with God": Bodleian Library, MS Rawlinson A.21, fols. 324–25.

72 For details of Trapnel's biography during the revolutionary years, see A. Cohen's entry on her in *Biographical Dictionary of British Radicals in the Seventeenth Century*. For the reference to her "Mighty Visions," see *Strange and Wonderful Newes from White-hall*, title page. On Powell at Whitehall, see *The Life and Death of Mr. Vavasor Powell* (London, 1671), p. 128.

73 *Severall Proceedings of State Affaires*, no. 225, 12–19 Jan. 1653/54, pp. 3562–64; *Strange and Wonderful Newes*. For Nedham's report to Cromwell, see *Calendar of State Papers, Domestic Series, 1653–1654*, p. 393.

74 See *Anna Trapnel's Report and Plea, Or, A Narrative of her Journey from London into Cornwal* (London, 1654), pp. 49, 52; and "To the Reader." Cf. *The Cry of a Stone*, p. 67. See also *The Weekly Intelligencer*, no. 328, 18–25 April 1654, pp. 229–30; no. 243, 30 May–6 June 1654, p. 280.

75 Untitled volume (1658), Bodleian Library S.1.42 Th; p. 273; cf. pp. 247, 250.

76 See the title page to *The Cry of a Stone*. Cf. Trapnel's *A Legacy for Saints* (London, 1654), p. 21.

77 See 1 Timothy 2:11–12 as well as 1 Cor. 14:34. For sectarian women challenging traditional gender roles, see Patricia Crawford, *Women and Religion*

in England, 1500–1700 (New York and London, 1993), pp. 119–82; Sharon Achinstein, "Women on Top in the Pamphlet Literature of the English Revolution," *Women's Studies*, 24, 1–2 (1994), 131–63 (esp. 143–48); and the scholarship cited above in note 65. For questions of gender in relation to Trapnel and female prophecy, see also Kate Chedgzoy, "Female Prophecy in the Seventeenth Century: The Instance of Anna Trapnel," in *Writing and the English Renaissance*, ed. William Zunder and Suzanne Trill (London and New York, 1996), pp. 239–54.

78 On her trance-like state, see also *Severall Proceedings*, p. 3563; she took to bed in the lodging of Mr. Robert, the warden of Whitehall. Large portions, though not all, of Trapnel's prayers and songs were recorded in *The Cry of a Stone*; they do not, however, appear in the briefer account, *Strange and Wonderful Newes*.

79 See *The Cry of a Stone*, pp. 3, 10; on the Ranters cf. Trapnel's untitled book of verse, pp. 273–74. See also the brief account of Trapnel in Owen C. Watkins, *The Puritan Experience* (London, 1972), pp. 91–93.

80 For a similar Fifth Monarchist use of this prophetic passage from Joel, see Mary Cary, *The Little Horns Doom & Downfall* (London, 1651), pp. 236–39. See also Crawford, *Women and Religion in England*, pp. 133, 145–46.

81 See the preface to *The Cry of a Stone*, "To all the wise Virgins in Sion, who . . . wait for the Bride-grooms coming"; and *A Legacy for Saints*, p. 49. See also Mendelson and Crawford, *Women in Early Modern England*, p. 411.

82 On Trapnel and Bingham, see Woolrych, *Commonwealth*, p. 275.

83 Cf. Trapnel's vision of four horns, the last representing Cromwell, in *Strange and Wonderful Newes from White-hall*, pp. 4–6. Nigel Smith notes how the vision of Cromwell and the bulls is repeated and reworked elsewhere in Trapnel's writings: *Perfection Proclaimed*, p. 94.

84 For a different and stimulating perspective on Trapnel's symbolic imagination, especially in relation to the power of written language, see Hilary Hinds, *God's Englishwomen: Seventeenth-Century Radical Sectarian Writing and Feminist Criticism* (Manchester, 1996), pp. 122–28. See also Diane Purkiss, "Producing the Voice, Consuming the Body: Women Prophets of the Seventeenth Century," in *Women, Writing, History, 1640–1740*, ed. Isobel Grundy and Susan Wiseman (Athens, GA, 1992), pp. 139–58, passim.

85 See the title page to *Strange and Wonderful Newes*.

86 *Severall Proceedings*, p. 3563.

87 *Severall Proceedings*, pp. 3563–64.

88 On the Fifth Monarchist view of the Dutch war as a means of hastening the overthrow of Antichrist and the millennium, see Capp, *Fifth Monarchy Men*, pp. 53–54, 59, 72, 80–81, 152–54; Capp, "The Fifth Monarchists and Popular Millenarianism," in *Radical Religion*, pp. 180, 188; Woolrych, *Commonwealth*, pp. 286–87.

89 See Milton's *Second Defence*, *CPW* 4:681.

90 Cf. the antimonarchic sentiment in 1 Samuel 8:7, 10:19, 12:12.

91 Woolrych, *Commonwealth*, p. 365.

92 Cf. her warning to all those who have given their strength "to the *Delilahs* of the earth; every thing shall overcome you; every thread shall bind you" (p. 52).

93 Visiting Whitehall in January 1656, Evelyn "found it very glorious and well furnish'd": *The Diary of John Evelyn*, selected and ed. John Bowle (Oxford and New York, 1985), p. 167.

94 *Writings and Speeches of Oliver Cromwell*, 3:437–38, 435. For discussion of this speech in relation to the radical saints and Marvell, see Chapter 5 of this study. See also John Spittlehouse, *An Answer to one Part of the Lord's Protector's Speech* (London, 1654).

95 On elitist tendencies in Fifth Monarchist discourse, see Capp, *Fifth Monarchy Men*, pp. 63, 82, 90, 138, 144; Capp, "The Fifth Monarchists and Popular Millenarianism," in *Radical Religion*, p. 187. Mary Cary thought the saints would enjoy "rich apparel": *Little Horns Doom & Downfall*, p. 270.

4 THE WAR OF THE LAMB: THE REVOLUTIONARY DISCOURSE OF
GEORGE FOX AND EARLY QUAKERISM

1 This and the previous quotation are from the Oxfordshire Friends Testimony in *Gospel-Truth Demonstrated, in A Collection of Doctrinal Books, Given forth by that Faithful Minister of Jesus Christ, George Fox* (London, 1706).

2 James Nayler referred to this apocalyptic text in a key tract, *The Lambs Warre against the Man of Sinne* (London, 1658). See also Hugh Barbour, *The Quakers in Puritan England* (New Haven, 1964), pp. 1, 40, who notes the frequency of the phrase in Quaker texts; and Geoffrey F. Nuttall, *Christianity and Violence* (Royston, 1972), pp. 14–15, 38. References to the Bible are to the King James version, since Fox seems to have quoted from it. On the development and impact of early Quaker writing, see the studies in *The Emergence of Quaker Writing: Dissenting Literature in Seventeenth-Century England*, ed. Thomas N. Corns and David Loewenstein (London, 1995).

3 The conquering Lamb derived from Revelation, while the Lamb of meekness derived from Isaiah: see Geoffrey F. Nuttall, "Overcoming the World: The Early Quaker Programme," in *Sanctity and Secularity: The Church and the World*, ed. Derek Baker (Oxford, 1973), p. 162.

4 Barry Reay, *The Quakers and the English Revolution* (London, 1985), p. 27; Reay suggests the numbers may have reached 60,000.

5 Thus one large gathering of the new sect elicited the following comment (dated 9 Jan. 1654/55): "They have a printer with them, and sixe are constantly writing." See *A Collection of the State Papers of John Thurloe*, ed. Thomas Birch, 7 vols. (London, 1742), 3:94. For a full account of the role of writing in their early definition as a movement, see Kate Peters, "Patterns of Quaker Authorship, 1652–1656," in Corns and Loewenstein, *The Emergence of Quaker Writing*, pp. 6–24; see also Thomas O'Malley, "The Press and Quakerism, 1653–59," *JFHS*, 54, 4 (1979), 169–84.

6 Edward Burrough, *A Warning from the Lord to the Inhabitants of Underbarrow*

(1654), in *The Memorable Works of a Son of Thunder and Consolation: Namely, That True Prophet, and Faithful Servant of God* (London, 1672), pp. 16, 17.

7 See the Oxfordshire Friends Testimony, in *Gospel-Truth Demonstrated*.

8 I allude to Fox's powerful tract of 1659, *The Lambs Officer*, discussed below.

9 The quotation from Fox is from William Dewsbury, James Nayler, George Fox, and John Whitehead, *Several Letters Written to the Saints of the Most High* (London, 1654), p. 13. On the sectarian challenge in the Interregnum, see Derek Hirst, "The Failure of National Reformation in the 1650s," in *Religion, Resistance, and Civil War*, ed. Gordon J. Schochet (Washington, DC, 1990), pp. 53–54. On the Quakers during the revolutionary years, see esp. Reay, *The Quakers and the English Revolution*; and Christopher Hill, "Quakers and the English Revolution," *JFHS*, 56, 3 (1992), 165–79. On Fox during the revolutionary decades, see now H. Larry Ingle, *First Among Friends: George Fox and the Creation of Quakerism* (New York and Oxford, 1994), chs. 1–12.

10 On interconnections between politics and radical religion in this period, see esp. the studies in *Radical Religion*. On sectarian religious literature during the period of early Quakerism, see Smith, *Perfection Proclaimed*.

11 For a different view of the Lamb's War, cf. Leonard W. Levy, who suggests that "the war was not directed against the government or the social order" (*Treason against God: A History of the Offense of Blasphemy* (New York, 1981), p. 260).

12 On the connection between the Quakers, militant Puritan politics, and the Army, see Alan Cole, "The Quakers and the English Revolution," *P&P*, 10 (1956), 39–54; Reay, *The Quakers and the English Revolution*, pp. 18–19, 41–42, 83, 88–90, 107–8; Reay, "The Quakers, 1659, and the Restoration of the Monarchy," *History*, 63 (1978), 195–96, 201–3 (on Quakers in the Army and militia in 1659); Hill, *WTUD*, pp. 241–48; Hill, "Quakers and the English Revolution"; Ian Gentles, *The New Model Army in England, Ireland and Scotland, 1645–1653* (Oxford, 1992), pp. 91, 113–14.

13 Fear of the Quaker menace has been thoroughly documented by Barry Reay, "Popular Hostility towards Quakers in mid-seventeenth-century England," *Social History*, 5, 3 (1980), 387–407. See also David Underdown, *Revel, Riot, and Rebellion: Popular Politics and Culture in England, 1603–1660* (Oxford, 1985), pp. 250–55; Leo Damrosch, *The Sorrows of the Quaker Jesus: James Nayler and the Puritan Crackdown on the Free Spirit* (Cambridge, MA, 1996), ch. 1.

14 *One Sheet against the Quakers* (London, 1657), pp. 8–9, 4; see also p. 5. Cf. *Reliquiae Baxterianae*, ed. Matthew Sylvester (London, 1696), Part I, p. 77; Part II, p. 180.

15 See William Penn's preface to George Fox's *Journal*, p. xliii.

16 George Fox and James Nayler, *A Word from the Lord, unto all the faithlesse Generation of the World* ([London], 1654), p. 9; cf. *Journal*, p. 280. Geoffrey Nuttall observed that "Fox's adoption and application of Scripture imagery still awaits the systematic investigator" (*Christianity and Violence*, p. 15). Without claiming to be comprehensive, this chapter investigates the striking application of apocalyptic imagery and language in Fox's revolutionary

writings. On apocalyptic ideas during the emergence of Quakerism, see John Patrick Laydon, "The Kingdom of Christ and the Powers of the Earth: The Political Uses of Apocalyptic and Millenarian Ideas in England, 1648–1653" (Ph.D. dissertation, Cambridge University, 1977); Bernard Capp, "The Political Dimension of Apocalyptic Thought," in *The Apocalypse in English Renaissance Thought and Literature*, ed. C. A. Patrides and Joseph Wittreich (Ithaca, NY, 1984), pp. 109–18; Barbour, *The Quakers in Puritan England*, 182–88; H. Larry Ingle, "George Fox, Millenarian," *Albion*, 24, 2 (1992), 261–78.

17 On the *Journal*, see Thomas N. Corns, "'No Man's Copy': The Critical Problem of Fox's *Journal*," in Corns and Loewenstein, *The Emergence of Quaker Writing*, pp. 99–111.

18 *To all that would know the Way to the Kingdom* ([London, 1654]), p. 4: "the Word cuts asunder, hews down all wickedness, corruption, pride and honour of man . . . and the Word of the Lord is a fire." I quote from the edition of the tract dated 27 June by George Thomason.

19 *To all that would know the Way*, p. 5.

20 See p. 10 where Fox announces that "The Lord is rising, and surely he will be avenged of all his Adversaries."

21 For another powerful example of Fox's threatening use of Ezekiel's glittering sword, see *A Voice of the Lord to the Heathen* (London, 1656), p. 7.

22 *To all that would know the Way*, pp. 11–12. As Fox wrote elsewhere in 1654, "the true Prophets, Apostles, and Christ, these had all favour and discerning, to Judge between light and darkness, truth from evil": *True Judgement, or, The Spiritual-Man, Judging all Things* (London, 1654), p. 4.

23 Fox's phrases are from *To all that would know the Way*, p. 13. On prophets, including Isaiah, Jeremiah, Ezekiel, and Micah, who spoke forth freely, see also Fox's *Newes Coming up out of the North, Sounding towards the South* (London, 1654), p. 44.

24 *To all that would know the Way*, p. 9.

25 *A Fiery Flying Roll*, in *Ranter Writings*, pp. 80, 94, 98, 100, 103.

26 On the southward movement of Quaker preachers led by the inward Spirit, see Barbour, *Quakers in Puritan England*, pp. 50–51, 55, 59; William C. Braithwaite, *The Beginnings of Quakerism*, 2nd edn. (Cambridge, 1955), ch. 8; Reay, *The Quakers and the English Revolution*, p. 10. On the contribution of Quaker publishing to the growing sect, see Peters, "Patterns of Quaker Authorship, 1652–1656."

27 *Newes Coming up out of the North*, title page; p. 5 (echoing Zephaniah 1:16).

28 *Newes Coming up out of the North*, title page. Cf. James Nayler, *A Lamentation (By one of Englands Prophets) Over the Ruines of this Oppressed Nacion* (York, 1654), title page and passim.

29 Oxfordshire Friends Testimony, in *Gospel-Truth Demonstrated*.

30 *Newes Coming up out of the North*, p. 8.

31 On the dominant theme of victory in Fox's writing and life, see Nuttall, "Overcoming the World," p. 148.

32 *Newes Coming up out of the North*, p. 31; cf. p. 37.

33 *Newes Coming up out of the North*, p. 18.

34 *Newes Coming up out of the North*, pp. 18–19.

35 On the gap between ideals and performance in the Republic, see Underdown, *Pride's Purge*, pp. 258, 335.

36 *Newes Coming up out of the North*, pp. 19, 35–36, 37–38; cf. Fox, *A Message from the Lord, to the Parliament of England* (London, 1654). Quaker agitation against tithes was particularly intense: see Barry Reay, "Quaker Opposition to Tithes, 1652–1660," *P&P*, 86 (1980), 98–120.

37 *Newes Coming up out of the North*, p. 19. For the Lord's promise in Joel 2, see also the discussion of Trapnel in Chapter 3 of this study, esp. p. 118.

38 For the two phrases from Fox, see *Newes Coming up out of the North*, pp. 13, 20.

39 For the quotation, see Fox's section in *A Word from the Lord*, p. 12.

40 *Newes Coming up out of the North*, pp. 20–21. On the day of the Lord "grown very terrible," see also Fox's *The Vials of the Wrath of God* (London, 1654), p. 8. See also *The Glorie of the Lord Arising, Shaking terribly the Earth, and Overturning All* (London, 1654), a Quaker text attributed to Fox by Ingle (*First Among Friends*, p. 363), though published anonymously.

41 See *A Warning from the Lord to the Pope: And to all His Train of Idolatries* (London, 1656), p. 13; and *To those that have been formerly in Authority, and have broken Covenant with God & Man* (London, [1660]), p. 8.

42 George Fox, *The Vials of the Wrath of God*, p. 8 (alluding to Jer. 23:19, 30:23 and Ps. 1:4); *The Trumpet of the Lord Sounded* (London, 1654), p. 9.

43 *Newes Coming up out of the North*, pp. 12, 34; cf. 9. See also *The Trumpet of the Lord Sounded*, p. 9, for the mighty day of the Lord burning as an oven. For a rich account of the *odium Dei*, especially in relation to Milton, see Michael Lieb, "'Hate in Heav'n': Milton and the *Odium Dei*," *ELH*, 53 (1986), 519–39.

44 George Fox, *A Cry for Repentance, unto the Inhabitants of London chieflie* (London, 1656), pp. 1–4. See also *The Wrath of the Lamb* (1658), in *Gospel-Truth Demonstrated*, pp. 143–44.

45 *Newes Coming up out of the North*, p. 30.

46 *Newes Coming up out of the North*, p. 32.

47 This text was first published in 1654 by Giles Calvert, and then followed by a second edition in 1655.

48 *The Vials of the Wrath of God*, pp. 1, 9.

49 See *Newes Coming up out of the North*, p. 13.

50 Baxter's complaints about the Quakers suggest that they could be as vicious as the ungodly they condemned: shocked by their "railing language," he observed that the Quakers "bark and bawl at our Religion, Ministry and Church" (*One Sheet*, pp. 4, 3).

51 *The Vials of the Wrath of God*, p. 1.

52 *The Vials of the Wrath of God*, p. 9.

53 See e.g. *A New-Yeers Gift* where Winstanley writes of the powers, especially the power of lawyers, who are "devourer[s] and tearer[s] of the creation" (*Works*, p. 381).

54 See *The Vials of the Wrath of God*, pp. 7–9, for the pages from Fox cited in this paragraph.

55 Fox's name does not appear on the title page of the text, though his initials appear on p. 10; the tract was printed for Giles Calvert.

56 *The Trumpet of the Lord Sounded*, pp. 1–3; cf. *News Coming up out of the North*, p. 36. For Coppe and the harlot, see e.g. *Ranter Writings*, p. 114, and Chapter 3 of this study.

57 *The Trumpet of the Lord Sounded*, p. 15.

58 *The Trumpet of the Lord Sounded*, pp. 4, 5.

59 *The Trumpet of the Lord Sounded*, pp. 16–17.

60 *The Great Mistery of the Great Whore Unfolded* (London, 1659), "To the Reader," sig. (b2)r.

61 *The Great Mistery*, pp. 67, 93, 219; cf. pp. 227, 266. Fox's huge tract runs to 375 pages.

62 Barry Reay has plausibly suggested that since the copy of *The Lambs Officer* in the Bodleian Library was bound with tracts printed during the restoration of the Rump, it was likely that it appeared then: "The Quakers, 1659, and the Restoration of the Monarchy," 194 n. 3. On millenarian writing and exhortation during this period of 1659, see Austin Woolrych, "Last Quests for a Settlement, 1657–1660," in *The Interregnum: The Quest for Settlement*, ed. G. E. Aylmer (London, 1972), pp. 190–91, 195; on widespread Quaker writing in particular during 1659, see Nuttall, "Overcoming the World," p. 152, and Ronald Hutton, *The Restoration: A Political and Religious History of England and Wales, 1658–1667* (Oxford, 1985), pp. 121–22.

63 Reay, *The Quakers and the English Revolution*, p. 90, and "The Quakers, 1659, and the Restoration of the Monarchy," 203.

64 Among many tracts, see e.g. Isaac Penington the younger, *To the Parliament, the Army, and all the Wel-affected in the Nation* (London, 1659); James Freeze, *The Out-cry! and Just Appeale of the Inslaved People of England* (n.p., 1659); J. Hodgson, *Love, Kindness, and due Respect, By Way of Warning to the Parliament of the Common-wealth* (London, 1659); William Cole, *A Rod for the Lawyers . . . To which is added, A word to the Parliament* (London, 1659); Edward Burrough, *To the Parliament of the Common-wealth of England* (London, 1659); Burrough, *Satan's Design Defeated* (1659), in *The Memorable Works of a Son of Thunder and Consolation* (London, 1672), esp. p. 524. See also A. H. Woolrych, "The Good Old Cause and the Fall of the Protectorate," *The Cambridge Historical Journal*, 13, 2 (1957), 155–56, 158–59 (for the revival of Leveller demands); Toby Barnard, *The English Republic, 1649–1660*, 2nd edn. (London, 1997), p. 68; Reay, "The Quakers, 1659, and the Restoration," 194–95.

65 Underdown, *Pride's Purge*, pp. 349–50; and Reay, "The Quakers, 1659, and the Restoration of the Monarchy," 193–213, for the fullest account of threatening sectarian activity during this year, as well as anti-Quaker sentiment.

66 See e.g. Bodleian Library, MS. Clarendon 63, fol. 263r: "3 or 4 thousand men of Congregation[al] Churches are armed: they are called anabaptists and Quakers." On the danger to religion and the godly ministry, see fol. 339v. See also fols. 153r, 264r. Cf. William Prynne, *A true and perfect Narrative of what was done* ([London], 1659), p. 88.

67 *Sir George Booth's Letter of the 2nd of August, 1659* (London, 1659), pp. 5–6.
68 *The Lambs Officer* (London, 1659), pp. 21, 1.
69 See the title page.
70 *The Lambs Officer*, p. 4 and passim.
71 *The Lambs Officer*, pp. 2–3.
72 *The Lambs Officer*, pp. 19, 8, 9–10.
73 *The Lambs Officer*, pp. 16–17; cf. pp. 13–14, 21, and *The Great Mistery*, p. 97.
74 *The Lambs Officer*, p. 21.

5 MARVELL, THE SAINTS, AND THE PROTECTORATE

1 That tension is a main theme of Woolrych's *Commonwealth*; see also Barry Coward, "Was there an English Revolution in the Middle of the Seventeenth Century?" in *Politics and People in Revolutionary England: Essays in on Honour of Ivan Roots*, ed. Colin Jones, Malyn Newitt, and Stephen Roberts (Oxford, 1986), pp. 30–31.
2 *Mercurius Politicus*, no. 240, 11–18 January 1654/55, p. 5066.
3 George Smith, *Gods Unchangeableness: or Gods Continued Providence* (London, 1654/55), p. 41; John Morrill, "Cromwell and His Contemporaries," in *Oliver Cromwell and the English Revolution*, ed. Morrill (London and New York, 1990), p. 268; Cromwell, *Writings and Speeches*, 3:466.
4 As J. C. Davis observes, "The high years of the protectorate – 1654 to 1656 – should be seen as years of profound religious/political crisis": "Cromwell's Religion," in Morrill, *Cromwell and the English Revolution*, p. 187. For the broader political context of Marvell's poem, see Derek Hirst, "'That Sober Liberty': Marvell's Cromwell in 1654," in *The Golden and Brazen Wold: Papers in Literature and History*, ed. John M. Wallace (Berkeley, 1985), pp. 17–53.
5 *A True State of the Case of the Commonwealth* (London, 1654), p. 34. Its attribution to Nedham has now been convincingly established: Woolrych, *Commonwealth*, p. 96 nn.65, 68.
6 *Writings and Speeches*, 3:64, 435 (cf. 3:437–38, 4:417); Woolrych, *Commonwealth*, pp. 395, 397.
7 *Writings and Speeches*, 3:225–26; *Mercurius Politicus*, no. 197, 16–23 March 1654, pp. 3353–56. Cf. Cromwell's speech to the Barebone's Parliament: "we have rather desired healing and prospiciency" (3:55).
8 *Writings and Speeches*, 3:434–38; cf. 3:584 on the dangers of levelling. See also Smith, *Gods Unchangeableness*, p. 41.
9 *Constitutional Documents*, p. 416; cf. *Writings and Speeches*, 3:227–28, 459 (on liberty of conscience). On the extent of and limits to Cromwell's "toleration" in the 1650s, see Blair Worden, "Toleration and the Cromwellian Protectorate," in *Persecution and Toleration: Studies in Church History* 21, ed. W. J. Sheils (Oxford, 1984), pp. 199–233; and Barry Coward, *Oliver Cromwell* (London and New York, 1991), pp. 110–12, 122–23, 148, 150, 163–64.
10 Indeed, John Hall had recently likened the diseased and stagnant Rump

itself to "a standing water growing corrupt": *Confusion Confounded* (London, 1654), p. 2. The political and Christic significance of these lines are perceptively discussed in Hirst, "Marvell's Cromwell," pp. 40–41.

11 *A Second Beacon Fired. Humbly Presented to the Lord Protector and the Parliament* (London, 1654), p. 10; Francis Howgill, *The Fiery darts of the Devil quenched* (London, 1654), pp. 2, 10; *Mercurius Politicus*, no. 227, 12–19 Oct. 1654, p. 3846; Barry Reay, *The Quakers and the English Revolution* (London, 1985), p. 10; Ann Hughes, "The Frustrations of the Godly," in *Revolution and Restoration: England in the 1650s*, ed. John Morrill (London, 1992), ch. 4.

12 See the broadsheet by Edward Burrough: *For the Souldiers, and all the Officers of England, Scotland, a warning from the Lord* (London, 1654).

13 Dewsbury, *A True Prophecy*, p. 6. See also James Nayler, *A Few Words occasioned by a Paper lately Printed, Stiled, A Discourse concerning the Quakers* ([London?], 1654), p. 21; George Fox, *To all that would know the Way* (London, 1654); Fox *A Message from the Lord to the Parliament of England* ([London, 1654]).

14 *A Warning from the Lord . . . Occasioned by a late Declaration; stiled A Declaration of His Highness the Lord Protector* (London, 1654), p. 1 and passim.

15 John Spittlehouse, *Certaine Queries Propounded* (London, 1654), p. 4; John Rogers, *Mene, Tekel, Perez, or A little Appearance of the Hand-Writing . . . Against the Powers and Apostates of the Times* ([London, 1654]), p. 2; *A Declaration of Several of the Churches of Christ and Godly People* (London, 1654), pp. 3–4; *Writings and Speeches*, 3:614; Christopher Feake, *A Beam of Light, Shining in the Midst of much Darkness and Confusion* (London, 1659), pp. 51–52. For the declaration, see *Stuart Constitution*, pp. 263–68.

16 The Protector was allowed, however, to legislate by ordinance until his first triennial parliament in September. On Cromwell bound by council and parliament, see *Writings and Speeches*, 3:455; Woolrych, *Commonwealth*, pp. 365–69, 376; Hirst, "The Lord Protector, 1653–1658," in *Oliver Cromwell and the English Revolution*, pp. 136–37.

17 Woolrych, *Commonwealth*, p. 12, quoting from the first Fifth Monarchist manifesto, *Certain Queries Humbly presented . . . to the Lord General and Council of War* (1649), in *Puritanism and Liberty*, pp. 241–47. See also Hall, *Confusion Confounded*, p. 7.

18 See *A Collection of the State Papers of John Thurloe*, ed. Thomas Birch, 7 vols. (London, 1742), 1:621, 641; 2:67, 163, 174. On Charles and Cromwell as the little horn, see e.g. William Aspinwall, *An Explication and Application of the Seventh Chapter of Daniel* (London, 1654); John More, *A Trumpet Sounded: Or, The Great MYSTERY of the Two Little Horns Unfolded* ([London], 1654); and Chapter 5 of this study.

19 E.g. John Rogers, *To His Highnesse Lord General Cromwel, Lord Protector, &c.* ([London] 21 Dec. 1653): "Antichrist works (now) more in a mystery of Iniquity then ever."

20 A sermon preached on 5 January 1656/57: Thurloe, *State Papers*, 5:756; see also 2:128; Christopher Feake, *The Oppressed Close Prisoner in Windsor-Castle, His Defiance to the Father of Lyes* (London, 1654), p. 105; B. S. Capp, *The Fifth*

Monarchy Men (London, 1972), p. 184; Capp, "The Fifth Monarchists and Popular Millenarianism," in *Radical Religion*, pp. 174–75.

21 *Calendar of State Papers, Domestic Series, 1653–1654*, p. 306.

22 *The Old Leaven Purged Out. Or, the Apostasy of this Day* ([London], 1658), 2nd pagination, pp. 19–20.

23 *A Declaration of several the Churches of Christ*, p. 5; Spittlehouse, *An Answer to one Part of the Lord Protector's Speech: or, A Vindication of the Fifth Monarchy-men* (London, 1654), p. 17; *The Protector (so called) In Part Unvailed* (London, 1655), pp. 46–49, 59; Thurloe, *State Papers*, 5:756 (cf. 3:484); *The Old Leaven Purged*, p. 11.

24 *Stuart Constitution*, pp. 313–16. See also *Writings and Speeches* on endeavoring "to put a stop to that heady way . . . of every man making himself a Minister and a preacher" (3:440).

25 *The Oppressed Close Prisoner in Windsor-Castle*, title page; p. 4; *Writings and Speeches*, 3:545–46.

26 *The New Non-Conformist* (London, 1654), sig. A3r.

27 See the vivid account of Feake and Rogers at Windsor Castle, 18 May 1655, in MS Rawlinson A.26 (Bodleian Library), fol. 248; for the full account, see fols. 239–51.

28 *Confusion Confounded*, pp. 8, 18. On Hall's republicanism, see Norbrook, *English Republic*, pp. 169–80, 212–21, 343.

29 *Confusion Confounded*, pp. 8, 7.

30 *A True State*, p. 19; see also pp. 43, 51. For recent perspectives on Marvell's concept of liberty in the context of the Interregnum and Restoration, see *Marvell and Liberty*, ed. Warren Chernaik and Martin Dzelzainis (Basingstoke, 1999); on the *First Anniversary* and the coexistence of order and liberty, see Warren Chernaik, *The Poet's Time: Politics and Religion in the Work of Marvell* (Cambridge, 1983), pp. 42–55, 56–59, 115–16. On Nedham and the experimental Protectorate, see also Norbrook, *English Republic*, pp. 326–30; Joad Raymond, "Framing Liberty: Marvell's *First Anniversary* and the Instrument of Government," *HLQ*, 63, 3 (2000). I thank Joad Raymond for allowing me to read this article in typescript.

31 *A True State*, pp. 42 (where Nedham's attack on radical sectarian opinions anticipates Cromwell's in the speech of 4 Sept.), 43; *Calendar of State Papers, Domestic Series, 1653–1654*, pp. 304–8, 393 (on Trapnel's visions).

32 *A True State*, pp. 14–15, 17, 18.

33 See esp. *Writings and Speeches*, 3:587.

34 *Writings and Speeches*, 3:437; see also 4:717.

35 *Writings and Speeches*, 3:459.

36 *A Declaration of Several of the Churches of Christ* (2 Sept. 1654), pp. 1, 4–5; Spittlehouse, *Certain Queries* (dated 1 Sept.), p. 4; Capp, *Fifth Monarchy Men*, p. 105. Cromwell's attack on "the mistaken notion of the Fifth Monarchy" was then quickly countered by Spittlehouse: *An Answer to one Part of the Lord Protector's Speech.*

37 *A Seasonable, Legall, and Historicall Vindication* (London, 1654), pp. 3, 48.

38 Lionel Gatford, *A Petition for the Vindication of the Publique use of the Book of Common Prayer*, along with *Certain Quaeries Concerning the Ordinance for ejecting Scandalous, Ignorant, and Insufficient Ministers and Schoolmasters* (London, 1654), p. 34.

39 Michael Wilding, *Dragons Teeth: Literature in the English Revolution* (Oxford, 1987), pp. 114–37, 150–56; John Rogers, *The Matter of Revolution: Science, Poetry, and Politics in the Age of Milton* (Ithaca, NY, 1996), p. 41. See also Corns, *Uncloistered Virtue*, p. 229.

40 Thus Quaker prophets had recently warned the Protector that "all the tall Cedars shall bow": *This was the word of the Lord which John Camm and Francis Howgil was moved to declare and write to Oliver Cromwell* (London, 1654), sig. A2r–v. On creating the godly nation, see Anthony Fletcher, "Oliver Cromwell and the Godly Nation," in *Oliver Cromwell and the English Revolution*, ch. 8.

41 *Writings and Speeches*, 3:62; Fletcher, "Oliver Cromwell and the Godly Nation," p. 211.

42 *Writings and Speeches*, 3:372–73, 504, 546–47, 607–16, 619, 639; 4:309, 440, 867–68; Fox, *Journal*, pp. 274, 289, 350; Swarthmore MSS. 3:34 (Friends House Library, London), Anthony Pearson to George Fox; Austin Woolrych, "The Cromwellian Protectorate: A Military Dictatorship?" *History*, 75 (1990), 212.

43 Chernaik, *The Poet's Time*, pp. 49, 128–29, 138; N. H. Keeble, "Why Transprose *The Rehearsal?*" in *Marvell and Liberty*, pp. 249–53. On the late Marvell's defence of nonconformity, see also William Lamont, "The Religion of Andrew Marvell: Locating the 'Bloody Horse'," in *The Political Identity of Andrew Marvell*, ed. Conal Condren and A. D. Cousins (Aldershot, 1990), pp. 135–56.

44 The point is well illustrated in Woolrych, *Commonwealth*, pp. 389–90.

45 Wither, *Vaticinium Causuale: A Rapture Occasioned By the late Miraculous Deliverance of His Highnesse the Lord Protector* (London, 1654); Milton, *A Second Defence of the English People, CPW* 4:666–80. See also Wither, *The Protector. A Poem* (London, 1655). On Wither's Protectoral poems, see Norbrook, *English Republic*, pp. 351–57.

46 *Writings and Speeches*, 3:587; Woolrych, *Commonwealth*, p. 366 n.40, observes that "democracy" probably refers to the unbounded rule of the Rump, though it may "conceivably refer to the Levellers." See also Smith, *Gods Unchangeableness*, p. 53.

47 E. M., *Protection Perswading Subjection* (London, 1654), pp. 27, 26. See also the anti-sectarian passages from Nedham and Hall quoted above. And see Nedham's *The Observator, with A Summary of Intelligence*, no. 1, 24–31 Oct., pp. 4, 7, 9–10; *The Observator*, no. 2, 31 Oct.–7 Nov. 1654, pp. 27, 30; T. W., *The Prime Work of the First Tripple Parliament* (London, 1654), pp. 3–4. For other examples of press caricatures and attacks on sectarians, see Worden, "Toleration and the Cromwellian Protectorate," p. 212. Cf. Marvell's satirical treatment of sectarianism, disorder, and the Dutch: "The Character of Holland" (1653), lines 67–72.

48 *Mercurius Politicus*, no. 236, 14–21 Dec. 1654, p. 5002; *A Perfect Account*, no. 206, 12–19 Dec. 1654, p. 1647; *CJ*, 7:400, 416. On Biddle, see also Worden, "Toleration and the Cromwellian Protectorate," pp. 203–5, 218, 220–22.

49 On sects, heresies, and the plague, see e.g. Pagitt, *Heresiography: Or a Description of the Heretickes and Sectaries*, 5th edn. (London, 1654), "The Epistle Dedicatory"; Jonathan Clapham, *A Full Discovery and Confutation of . . . the Quakers* (London, 1656), p. 76; *A Second Beacon Fired*; [Alexander Griffith], *Strena Vavasoriensis . . . Or a Hue and Cry after Mr. Vavasor Powell* (London, 1654), p. 26. For Cromwell, see *Writings and Speeches*, 3:461.

50 See the account of the Hyde Park accident in *Writings and Speeches*, 3:474.

51 *The City of God against the Pagans*, trans. Eva M. Sanford and William M. Green, 7 vols. (Cambridge, MA, 1965), Book 16:2, vol. 5, p. 7.

52 Pagitt, *Heresiography*, p. 55.

53 See Pagitt, *Heresiography*, title page, and pp. 136–37; William Prynne, *The Quakers Unmasked* (London, 1655), p. 3.

54 See e.g. the attack on Vavasor Powell in *Strena Vavasoriensis*, pp. 22–23.

55 See e.g. Edward Phillips, *The New World of Words*, 6th edn. (London, 1706), s.v. "Alcoran" and "Mahomet or Muhammed." On the connection between the spread of Islam and new heresies, see e.g. Clapham, *Discovery . . . of . . . the Quakers*, dedicatory epistle, pp. 62, 73. See also Juan Andres, *The Confusion of Muhamed's Sect, or Confutation of the Turkish Alcoran*, trans. I.N. (London, 1652).

56 *An Account of the Rise and Progress of Mahometism*, ed. Hafiz Mahmud Khan Shairani (Lahore, 1954), p. 158; see also p. 86. For an illuminating account of the book's importance (it remained unpublished in Stubbe's lifetime), see Christopher Hill, *The Experience of Defeat: Milton and Some Contemporaries* (Harmondsworth, 1984), pp. 259–64.

57 Pagitt had recently linked the Ranters and Quakers together as "contemners of authority," and had claimed that the Ranters were more blasphemous than the Mahometans: *Heresiography*, pp. 143–44. Cf. Bunyan who linked the Quakers with Ranters: Edward Burrough, *The True Faith of the Gospel Peace* (1656), in *The Memorable Works of a Son of Thunder* (London, 1672), p. 138. For a Quaker who kept his hat on during a meeting with the Protector, see *Writings and Speeches*, 3:373.

58 Pagitt, *Heresiography*, "The Epistle Dedicatory." Cf. Prynne, *The Quakers Unmasked*, pp. 1, 3; Griffith, *Strena Vavasoriensis*, p. 25. In his forthcoming Longman edition of Marvell's poetry, Nigel Smith cites John Tickell, *The Bottomles Pit Smoaking in Familisme* (Oxford, 1651). For the apocalyptic resonances of Marvell's catalogue, see also Margarita Stocker, *Apocalyptic Marvell: The Second Coming in Seventeenth-Century Poetry* (Brighton, 1986), pp. 23–24.

59 Mary Penington, *Experiences in the Life of Mary Penington*, ed. Norman Penny (1911; repr. London, 1992), p. 52; Prynne, *The Quakers Unmasked*, pp. 5, 6, 7; [Donald Lupton], *The Quacking Mountebanck or The Jesuite turn'd Quaker* (London, 1655); Richard Baxter, *One Sheet against the Quakers* (London, 1657), p. 8; Fox, *Journal*, p. 142; Reay, *The Quakers and the English Revolution*, pp. 59, 71, 81.

60 Pagitt, *Heresiography*, pp. 121–25; *Speeches and Writings*, 3:438.
61 See e.g. Tickell, *The Bottomless Pit*, p. 86; Richard Baxter, *Reliquiae Baxterianae*, ed. Matthew Sylvester (London, 1696), Part I, p. 76.
62 See e.g. Baxter, *Reliquiae Baxterianae*, Part I, pp. 76–77; Pagitt, *Heresiography*, p. 128, on "Antiscripturians." See also Nedham, *A True State*, p. 42.
63 *CJ*, 7:410 (30 Dec. 1654); *Mercurius Politicus*, no. 238, 28 Dec.–4 Jan. 1654, p. 5034.
64 See e.g. Pagitt, *Heresiography*, pp. 143–44, 145; *Protection Perswading Subjection*, p. 18; Griffith, *Strena Vavasoriensis*, p. 26; *Mercurius Politicus*, no. 236, 14–21 Dec. 1654, p. 5002; *Mercurius Politicus*, no. 238, 28 Dec.–4 Jan. 1654/55, p. 5034; *CJ*, 7:398–99, 401. The 1650 Blasphemy Act, which aimed to curb atheistical and blasphemous opinions, was invoked in the proposed parliamentary constitution of the first Protectorate Parliament (*Constitutional Documents*, p. 436; see also p. 443) and in the August 1654 Ordinance for Ejectors (*Stuart Constitution*, p. 315).
65 Pagitt, *Heresiography*, p. 117. See also William Aspinwall, *The Legislative Power in Christ's Peculiar Prerogative* (London, 1656), p. 37. The Fifth Monarchists were regularly called "Anabaptists."
66 *Mercurius Politicus*, no. 52, 29 May–5 June 1651, p. 841 (report of Cromwell telling a woman Ranter "she was so vile a creature, as he thought her unworthy to live"); Swarthmore MSS. 3:34 (where Cromwell reportedly said that "the light within hadd ledd the Ranters & all that followed it into all manner of wildnesses"); Worden, "Toleration and the Cromwellian Protectorate," pp. 210–12; Davis, "Cromwell's Religion," p. 196.
67 *Writings and Speeches*, 3:438 (with reference to the Fifth Monarchists), 436. See also Nedham, *A True State*, pp. 18, 43; Smith, *Gods Unchangeableness*, p. 15; Woolrych, *Commonwealth*, pp. 365–66, 368. For the Fifth Monarchist view of the present carnal laws, see e.g. Rogers, *To His Highnesse Lord General*. Cromwell feared that the Mosaic laws, open to subjective interpretation, would be "the confusion of all things": *Writings and Speeches*, 4:489; Capp, *The Fifth Monarchy Men*, p. 162.
68 Cf. Pagitt, *Heresiography*, "To the Reader": the sectarians "arrogate to themselves the shadow of austerity and shew of holinesse."
69 *Writings and Speeches*, 3:436, 459, 586; Davis, "Cromwell's Religion," pp. 185–86, 194.
70 See Pagitt, *Heresiography*, "To the Reader"; Edwards, *Gangraena*, Part III, pp. 64–68; Cromwell, *Writings and Speeches*, 4:471. On Quakers going "naked as a sign" of their regenerate nature, see Reay, *The Quakers and the English Revolution*, p. 36.
71 See Smith's forthcoming edition of Marvell's poetry, note to line 264; Trapnel, *The Cry of a Stone* (London, 1654), pp. 12–13.
72 *Strena Vavasoriensis*, p. 18.
73 *Writings and Speeches*, 3:582, 584. Cromwell's phrase "briers and thorns" clearly has biblical resonance: see e.g. Isa. 5:6, 7:24, 25, 27:4, 32:13; Ezek. 2:6. In a scriptural story to which Marvell later alludes (see below), Gideon also uses briers and thorns to tear the flesh of Israelites who betray him:

Judg. 8:7, 16. For the brier as a prickly shrub, formerly including the bramble, see s.v. "brier," *OED* 1; see also s.v. "thorn," *OED* II.4.a.

74 *The Protector . . . Unvailed*, pp. 23, 25, 80; cf. pp. 3, 84. This was a millenarian text published anonymously in October 1655.

75 Cf. Smith, *Gods Unchangeableness*, pp. 29, 41.

76 On Cromwell's yearning to retire to a private life, see *Writings and Speeches*, 3:452–53.

77 E.g. one of Charles's agents, John Gerard, was executed in July 1654 for plotting to assassinate Cromwell: David Underdown, *Royalist Conspiracy in England, 1649–1660* (New Haven, 1960), pp. 100–102. See also *Writings and Speeches*, 4:267, on subversive radicals intriguing with royalists.

78 *Writings and Speeches*, 3:438.

79 *Writings and Speeches*, 3:438; also 436.

80 Woolrych, *Commonwealth*, p. 14.

81 *The Protector . . . Unvailed*, p. 74.

82 The poem's political apocalypticism has only recently received attention: see Stocker, *Apocalyptic Marvell*, pp. 13–27; Gayle S. McGlamery, "The Rhetoric of Apocalypse and Practical Politics in Marvell's 'The First Anniversary of the Government under O.C.'," *South Atlantic Review*, 55, 4 (1990), 19–35; Hirst, "Marvell's Cromwell," pp. 35–36, 41–42 (on the poem's millenialism). My account places greater emphasis on the new political potency Marvell gives millenarian language in relation to tensions within Cromwell and the Revolution. On Marvell's image of Cromwell and the danger of misinterpretation, see also Laura L. Knoppers, *Constructing Cromwell: Ceremony, Portrait, and Print, 1645–1661* (Cambridge, 2000), ch. 3, esp. pp. 98–102.

83 *Writings and Speeches*, 3:61–64; *The Protector . . . Unvailed*, p. 23.

84 See Spittlehouse, *An Answer to one Part of the Lord Protector's Speech*, pp. 2, 6 (quoting from Cromwell's speech of 4 July 1653). Cf. Feake, *A Beam of Light*, p. 48.

85 *The Lord General Cromwel's Speech Delivered in the Council-Chamber* ([London], 1654); Woolrych, *Commonwealth*, pp. 400–1.

86 John Morrill, "Introduction," in *Cromwell and the English Revolution*, p. 16.

87 *Writings and Speeches*, 3:64. The passage is sensitively analyzed by Woolrych in *Commonwealth*, pp. 147–49.

88 On Cromwell's antiformalism, see Davis, "Cromwell's Religion."

89 See also Wither, *The Protector*, who writes that Cromwell "was sent to be / His *Ways preparer*" (p. 28).

90 See e.g. Mary Cary, *The Little Horns Doom & Downfall* (London, 1651), pp. 139–68; Capp, *Fifth Monarchy Men*, pp. 190–91.

91 *Writings and Speeches*, 1:677–78, 3:65, 4:51–55; Fletcher, "Cromwell and the Godly Nation," p. 211–12; David S. Katz, *Philo-Semitism and the Readmission of the Jews to England, 1603–55* (Oxford, 1982), p. 7.

92 MS Rawlinson A.26, fol. 243: Feake and Rogers preaching at Windsor Castle; *Writings and Speeches*, 3:614 (Rogers addressing Cromwell).

93 More, *A Trumpet Sounded*, p. 17.
94 *Writings and Speeches*, 3:442
95 Woolrych, *Commonwealth*, p. 15.
96 See esp. *Writings and Speeches*, 3:461 (cf. 3:225); Davis, "Cromwell's Religion," p. 187.
97 Speech to the Barebone's Parliament: *Writings and Speeches*, 3:64.
98 On the tentative language of that vision, see also Annabel M. Patterson, *Marvell and the Civic Crown* (Princeton, 1978), pp. 68–70.
99 *Writings and Speeches*, 3:461.
100 *Writings and Speeches*, 3:89; see also 3:615.
101 *Stipendariae Lacrymae, or, A Tribute of Teares* (The Hague, 1654), p. 8. Thomason dated his copy 14 July.
102 *Writings and Speeches*, 3:437–38. For Cromwell and the problem of finding "consent," see 4:221. On Cromwell's love of music, see Coward, *Cromwell*, pp. 105–6.
103 *A True State*, p. 43. Cf. Cromwell, *Writings and Speeches*, 3:435. And see also Smith, *Gods Unchangeableness*, sig. A2v, for Cromwell as "a skilfull *Esculapius*" who "heal[s] the distemper of three sick and wounded Nations."
104 See *Writings and Speeches*, 4:717, for Cromwell's use of this phrase with respect to the sects.
105 *A True State*, p. 13; *Confusion Confounded*, pp. 4–5.
106 Rogers, *To High Highnesse Lord General Cromwel*.
107 *The Cry of a Stone*, p. 50.
108 *The Protector . . . Unvailed*, pp. 47, 67–68.
109 *The Oppressed Close Prisoner in Windsor-Castle*, p. 105; dated 19 Dec. by Thomason.
110 Thurloe, *State Papers*, 5:758–59.
111 *A True State*, pp. 2, 18; cf. p. 27.
112 *A True State*, pp. 33–34. A different (Hobbesian) context for Marvell's political image of the state as a building is argued for in R. I. V. Hodge, *Foreshortened Time: Andrew Marvell and Seventeenth-Century Revolutions* (Cambridge and Totowa, NJ, 1978), pp. 106–13. Raymond, "Framing Liberty," provides additional contemporary examples of the political language of building and harmony.
113 *Writings and Speeches*, 3:438, 442.
114 *Writings and Speeches*, 3:439.
115 *A True State*, pp. 32, 50, 46.
116 On the resonant implications of the word "Frame" in relation to the new political constitution, see esp. Raymond, "Framing Liberty."
117 Woolrych, *Commonwealth*, p. 364; *Writings and Speeches*, 4:441.
118 Thus Cromwell described the first Protectoral Parliament: *Writings and Speeches*, 3:440. On Marvell's poem and the challenge of a constitutional settlement, see Warren Chernaik, "'Every conqueror creates a muse': Conquest and Constitutions in Waller and Marvell," in Chernaik and Dzelzainis, *Marvell and Liberty*, pp. 200–11.

119 On the place of resistance and opposition in Marvell's vision of the political order, see Norbrook, *English Republic*, p. 345.

120 *Writings and Speeches*, 3:463; G. E. Aylmer, *Rebellion or Revolution? England, 1640–1660* (Oxford, 1986), p. 170; Woolrych, "The Cromwellian Protectorate," 213.

121 See, e.g., Milton's depiction of "that hero Gideon . . . himself greater than a king" in *A Defence* (1651), *CPW* 4:370; see also 7:473–74.

122 See the Welsh Fifth Monarchist manifesto inspired by Powell: *A Word for God* ([London], 1655), p. 5. See also Capp, *Fifth Monarchy Men*, p. 110

123 See e.g. *Protection Perswading Subjection*, p. 7; Smith, *Gods Unchangeableness*, pp. 8, 29; John Moore, *Protection Proclaimed* (London, 1655), "To the Reader," p. 5. See also Arise Evans, *The Voice of the Iron Rod* (London, 1655), p. 3.

124 On Cromwell and Gideon, see John Morrill and Phil Baker, "Oliver Cromwell and the Sons of Zeruiah," in *A Cruel Necessity? The Regicides and the Execution of Charles I*, ed. Jason Peacey (Basingstoke and London, 2001); *Writings and Speeches*, 1:619, 3:584. For Cromwell and Phineas, see *Writings and Speeches*, 2:186; and George Smith's defence of the Protectorate, *Gods Unchangeableness*, p. 37.

125 *Constitutional Documents*, p. 415; *Writings and Speeches*, 3:589. For the hope that the Protectorate would establish "the quiet and prosperity of this people," see Hall, *Confusion Confounded*, p. 20. On the parallel with biblical judge Gideon and Marvell's argument against kingship, see Steven N. Zwicker, "Models of Governance in Marvell's 'The First Anniversary'," *Criticism*, 16 (1974), 1–12, who persuasively challenged John M. Wallace's suggestion (*Destiny His Choice: The Loyalism of Andrew Marvell* (Cambridge, 1968), pp. 106–40) that the poem aims to persuade Cromwell to accept the crown. See also Annabel Patterson, "Against Polarization: Literature and Politics in Marvell's Cromwell Poems," *ELR*, 5 (1975), 264, 266; *Marvell and the Civic Crown*, pp. 81–87; Hirst, "Marvell's Cromwell," pp. 20–21, 26, 28–29, 31–32.

126 *Writings and Speeches*, 4:270, where Cromwell compares his service to that of a constable, not a king; see also Woolrych, *Commonwealth*, pp. 356, 365, 376. On Cromwell's brutal ambition and hypocrisy, see e.g. the broadsheet *A Declaration of the Free-born People of England, now in Armes against the Tyrannie and Oppression of Oliver Cromwell* (n.p., 1655).

127 "He hath not the title of king, but he doth all the offices and the functions of the king": Thurloe, *State Papers*, 2:656 (the governor of Calais to the French ambassador in England; Oct. 1654). On the Protector's quasi-regal style, see also Coward, *Cromwell*, pp. 99–100; Roy Sherwood, *The Court of Oliver Cromwell* (London, 1977); Hirst, "Marvell's Cromwell," p. 22.

128 *The Protector . . . Unvailed*, p. 42. See also *A Declaration of the Free-born People*. On the lack of popular mandate behind the Instrument of Government, see Aylmer, *Rebellion or Revolution?*, p. 164; cf. Nedham, *A True State*, p. 29, for the claim that the government was "sufficiently popular."

129 Christopher Feake bewailed "the gradual declension and defection since Worcester": *The New Non-Conformist*, "A short Word to the faithful Remnant."

130 *The Protector . . . Unvailed*, p. 64; the author goes on to quote from "a sure hand" who was in France since the Protectorate and notes the French lack of esteem for England's present state. See also Feake, *A Beam of Light*, p. 52.

131 *The Protector . . . Unvailed*, p. 64.

132 *Writings and Speeches*, 3:439, 441. See also Moore, *Protection Proclaimed*, p. 7.

133 *Writings and Speeches*, 3:582, 586. See also a letter of January 1654/55, in which he observes, "so unwilling are men to be healed and atoned" (3:572).

134 *Writings and Speeches*, 3:555–59, 561–62, 567–73, 577–78, 585, 596, 604–5, 619–25, 634–35, 646–54; Smith, *Gods Unchangeableness*, p. 41; Bodleian Library, MS. Clarendon 49, fol. 352r; Ms. Rawlinson A.26, fols. 239–51 (for Feake and Rogers); Capp, *Fifth Monarchy Men*, pp. 106–11; Toby Barnard, *The English Republic, 1649–1660*, 2nd edn. (London and New York, 1997), pp. 47–49.

135 *Writings and Speeches*, 3:626–27 (15 Feb. 1654/55).

6 MILTON, ANTICHRISTIAN REVOLTS, AND THE ENGLISH REVOLUTION

1 [Dudley Digges], *The Unlawfulnesse of Subjects taking up Armes against their Sovereigne* ([Oxford], 1643), p. 125. On the fears of changing monarchy into anarchy, see e.g. Milton's *Observations upon the Articles of Peace*, in *CPW* 3:312, a response to a letter by the Earl of Ormond who considered the Rump Parliament's rebellion "monstrous and unparaleld" (*CPW* 3:292).

2 *Vindiciae Regum; or, The Grand Rebellion* (Oxford, 1643), pp. 1–2; on the monstrousness of rebellion, see also pp. 91–92. In *Jura Majestatis, The Rights of Kings both in Church and State* (Oxford, 1644), Williams describes rebellion as "an unexpressable iniquity" (p. 174).

3 Edward Symmons, *A Loyall Subjects Beliefe . . . a Letter to Master Stephen Marshall* (Oxford, 1643), p. 60.

4 See e.g. *The Rebels Looking-Glasse: or, The Traytors Doome* ([London], 1649), p. 16; Symmons, *A Loyall Subjects Beliefe*, p. 44; John Booker, *A Bloody Irish Almanack, or, Rebellious and Bloody Ireland* (London, 1646), pp. 3, 11; John Cook, *King Charls his Case* (London, 1649), p. 29 (in response to the Irish rebels of the 1640s). The first two texts are by royalist sympathizers, the last two by parliamentarian supporters. For further examples of royalist responses, see the selections by John Bramhall, Joshua Spelman, and Peter Heylyn in Andrew Sharp, *Political Ideas of the English Civil Wars, 1641–1649* (London, 1983), pp. 54–60.

5 Cf. *PL* 1.479, 2.625, 2.675, 10.509–532, 10.596, 10.986.

6 For one of the few recent discussions of Milton and Irish political affairs, see Thomas N. Corns, "Milton's *Observations upon the Articles of Peace*: Ireland under English eyes," in *Politics, Poetics, and Hermeneutics in Milton's Prose*, ed. David Loewenstein and James Grantham Turner (Cambridge, 1990), pp. 123–34. See also Willy Maley, "Rebels and Redshanks: Milton and the British Problem," *Irish Studies Review*, 6 (1994), 7–11.

7 See *Behemoth: The History of the Causes of the Civil Wars of England*, in *The English Works*, ed. William Molesworth, 11 vols. (London, 1839–45), 6:167, 188 (where he links the Presbyterians with "other democratical men"), 191–98, 201, 223–25, 258–59.

8 Edward Symmons, *A Vindication of King Charles: Or, a Loyal Subjects Duty* ([London], 1648), p. 158.

9 For Milton's friendship with Nedham, see *The Early Lives of Milton*, ed. Helen Darbishire (London, 1932), pp. 44, 45, 74; Blair Worden, "Milton and Marchamont Nedham," in *Milton and Republicanism*, ed. David Armitage, Armand Himy, and Quentin Skinner (Cambridge, 1995), ch. 9.

10 *A Short History of the English Rebellion* (1661), in *The Harleian Miscellany: A Collection of Scarce, Curious, and Entertaining Pamphlets and Tracts*, 10 vols. (London, 1808–13), 2:528.

11 See [Joseph Jane], *Salmasius his Dissection and Confutation of the Diabolical Rebel Milton* (London, 1660), a reissue of Jane's 1651 tract (*Eikon Aklastos: The Image Unbroaken*) attacking Milton's *Eikonoklastes*, cited in *Life Records*, 4:294–95. On Charles I and his Arminian advisors as dangerous innovators, see Barry Coward, "Was There an English Revolution in the Middle of the Seventeenth Century?" in *Politics and People in Revolutionary England: Essays in Honour of Ivan Roots*, ed. Colin Jones, Malyn Newitt, and Stephen Roberts (Oxford, 1986), pp. 19–20; John Morrill, "What was the English Revolution?" *History Today*, 34 (1984), 13, 15.

12 See *Life Records*, 2:240, 250, 314–15. Milton was ordered (on June 25, 1650) to "peruse the Examination taken by the Committee of the Armie concerning the insurrection in Essex, and to make extracts" so that the Council of State might "judge what is fit to bee taken into Consideration." On "those dangerous insurrections," see also John Goodwin, *The Obstructours of Justice. Or A Defence of the Honourable Sentence passed upon the late KING* (London, 1649), pp. 2, 55.

13 *Life Records*, 2:315–17.

14 Wither cites *The Tenure* and the right to call a tyrant to account in *Respublica Anglicana* (London, 1650), p. 41; John Goodwin cites *The Tenure* in *The Obstructours of Justice*, pp. 47, 53, 71, 73, 78–80, 94–95, 123.

15 *The Obstructours of Justice*, "The Epistle Dedicatorie," and p. 15. On active citizenship and free states, see also Marchamont Nedham's commentary in *Mercurius Politicus*, no. 82, 25 Dec.–1 Jan. 1651, pp. 1303–4. For Milton and natural law, see Ernest Sirluck, "Milton's Political Thought: The First Cycle," *Modern Philology*, 61 (1964), 209–24; R. S. White, *Natural Law in English Renaissance Literature* (Cambridge, 1996), ch. 9. Cf. Cook, *King Charls his Case*, pp. 16, 27.

16 The phrase here is from Milton's citation of Christopher Goodman's *How Superior Powers Oght to Be Obeyd of Their Subjects: and Wherin They May Lawfully by Gods Worde Be Disobeyed and Resisted* (Geneva, 1558), p. 190; see also p. 84: "Obedience is to heare God rather then man, and to resiste man rather then God."

17 For Milton's citation and use of Knox, see *CPW* 2:534, 3:223–25, 3:248, 3:329; cf. 4:661–62. See also Goodwin, *The Obstructours of Justice*, pp. 46–47, 71–72, 82.

18 See "London's Counter-Revolution," in *The Interregnum: The Quest for Settlement, 1646–1660*, ed. G. E. Aylmer (London, 1972), p. 30. For a study questioning clear-cut divisions between Presbyterians and Independents during the early 1640s, see also Avihu Zakai, "Religious Toleration and Its Enemies: The Independent Divines and the Issue of Toleration during the English Civil War," *Albion*, 21, 1 (1989), 1–33, esp. 6, 10, 12, 19.

19 [John Lilburne], *Plaine Truth without Feare or Flattery: or a True Discovery of the Unlawfulnesse of the Presbyterian Government* ([London], 1647), p. 5.

20 Thus in one text the Presbyterians railed against "blasphemous *Antiscripturisme, Antitrinitarianisme, Antinomianisme, Socinianisme*, and many other such like heterodox *opinions*": *An Apologeticall Declaration of the Conscientious Presbyters of the Province of London* (London, 1649), p. 3; see also *A Vindication of the Presbyteriall-Government, and Ministry* (London, 1650), pp. 101–4, which mentions free will, mortalism, anti-Sabbatarianism, and other heretical beliefs and practices. Even the moderate Richard Baxter disliked some of the Presbyterians who were not tender enough to dissenting brethren: *Reliquiae Baxterianae*, ed. Matthew Sylvester (London, 1696), Part I, p. 143.

21 Pearl, "London's Counter-Revolution," pp. 29–56; Keith Lindley, "London's Citizenry in the English Revolution," in *Town and Countryside in the English Revolution*, ed. R. C. Richardson (Manchester, 1992), p. 37; Robert Ashton, *Counter-Revolution: The Second Civil War and its Origins, 1646–8* (New Haven, 1994), ch. 8.

22 See *A Serious and Faithfull Representation of the Judgements of Ministers of the Gospell within the Province of London* (London, 1649), p. 7. See also David Underdown, *Royalist Conspiracy in England, 1649–1660* (New Haven and London, 1960), pp. 3–4.

23 G. E. Aylmer, "Introduction: The Quest for Settlement," in *The Interregnum*, pp. 4–5.

24 [William Dell], *The City-Ministers unmasked* (London, 1649), p. 15; see also John Price, *Clerico-Classicum, or, The Clergi-allarum to a third war* (London, 1648/49), p. 53, and *A Parallell between the Ministerial Ingenuity of the Forty seven London Ministers* (London, 1649), p. 7. On Marshall's *Meroz Cursed* and other militant Puritan sermons, see Anthony Fletcher, *The Outbreak of the English Civil War* (London, 1981), pp. 344–45; John F. Wilson, *Pulpit in Parliament: Puritanism during the English Civil Wars, 1640–1648* (Princeton, 1969); Paul Christianson, "From Expectation to Militance: Reformers and Babylon in the First Two Years of the Long Parliament," *JEH*, 24 (1973), 225–44. On ministers justifying and promoting war, see also Barbara Donagan, "Did Ministers Matter? War and Religion in England, 1642–1649," *JBS*, 33 (1994), 119–56.

25 *City-Ministers unmasked*, pp. 13, 10; John Goodwin, *Sion-Colledge visited*

(London, 1648), p. 11; see also George Wither, *The British Appeals, With Gods Mercifull Replies* (London, 1651), pp. 24–26. For a Presbyterian response to the accusation that they had changed their consciences with the times, see *A Vindication of the Presbyteriall-Government*, p. 67.

26 See also *The Tenure*, *CPW* 3:242–43, and *A Defence*, *CPW* 4:334–35 (where Milton essentially recapitulates the argument of *The Tenure*).

27 In *A Second Defence* Milton recalls that he "attacked, almost as if [he] were haranguing an assembly, the pre-eminent ignorance or insolence of these ministers" (*CPW* 4:626). See also the Fifth Monarchist Christopher Feake on the famous Presbyterian text being turned upon the them: *A Beam of Light, Shining in the Midst of much Darkness and Confusion* (London, 1659), p. 22.

28 See e.g. *A Serious and Faithfull Representation of the Judgements of Ministers of the Gospell* (dated 18 Jan.); and *An Apologeticall Declaration of the Conscientious Presbyterians*. On Presbyterians using the pulpit and press to disparage the new government, see *Mercurius Politicus*, no. 54, 12–19 June 1651, p. 865, and [Thomas Pride], *The Beacon Quenched* (London, 1652), esp. p. 9. For Presbyterian opposition to the Rump's republican politics, see Worden, *Rump Parliament*, pp. 81–85; Leland H. Carlson, "A History of the Presbyterian Party from Pride's Purge to the Dissolution of the Long Parliament," *Church History*, 11 (1942), 83–122. See also the summary of the Presbyterian position by Merritt Hughes in *CPW* 3:2–4; and, for the emergence of their views in the 1640s, see Noel H. Mayfield, *Puritans and Regicide: Presbyterian-Independent Differences over the Trial and Execution of Charles (I) Stuart* (Lanham, MD, and London, 1988), ch. 4.

29 *Constitutional Documents*, pp. 267–71.

30 Goodwin, *The Obstructours of Justice*, p. 48 (cf. pp. 49–57); Price, *Clerico-Classicum*, pp. 26, 41. For typical Presbyterian appeals to the Solemn League and Covenant, see *A Serious and Faithfull Representation*, p. 6; *An Apologeticall Declaration of the Conscientious Presbyterians*, pp. 2, 6–8; *A Necessary Representation* (1649) by the Belfast Presbyterians, in *CPW* 3:296–99; and cf. Milton's other critical responses in *Observations*, *CPW* 3:324, 330–31. On Milton's polemical response to the Presbyterian language of covenant and contract, see Victoria Kahn, "The Metaphorical Contract in Milton's *Tenure of Kings and Magistrates*," in *Milton and Republicanism*, pp. 82–105.

31 Goodwin criticizes "the mouths and pens" of the Presbyterian ministers in *The Obstructours of Justice*: see e.g. pp. 1–2 (where he accuses them of begetting "in their own likenesse, children of seditious, turbulent, and most inveterate spirits"), 48–53, 55–57, 67–72, 73 (where he urges them to peruse Milton's text), 94–95, 97. See also the Independent pamphleteer Price's *Clerico-Classicum*, and *Mercurius Politicus*, no. 16, 19–26 Sept. 1650, pp. 262–63. For a Presbyterian response to the accusation (including Goodwin's) that they are "movers of sedition among the people," "Pulpit Incendiaries," and are "Apostatized from [their] principles," see *A Vindication of the Presbyteriall-Government*, pp. 13, 67–69.

32 In *A Second Defence* Milton compares the shifty ministers to hucksters selling "to the rabble whatever merchandise they wish, whatever trash they please"

(*CPW* 4:640); see also 4:626. On complaints against London Presbyterian ministers stirring up seditious tumults (esp. in the late 1640s), see Ashton, *Counter-Revolution*, pp. 285–86.

33 On the Presbyterians in the late 1640s, cf. Feake, *A Beam of Light*, p. 22.

34 *A Serious and Faithfull Representation*, p. 5. See also *An Apologeticall Declaration of the Conscientious Presbyterians*, pp. 4, 6.

35 On the heroic depiction of Parliament and the Army Council, see also Annabel Patterson, "The Civic Hero in Milton's Prose," *Milton Studies*, 8 (1975), 87. On the ways Milton challenges his readers in *The Tenure*, see Elizabeth Skerpan, *The Rhetoric of Politics in the English Revolution, 1642–1660* (Columbia, 1992), pp. 137–44, 151–52.

36 And perhaps because Milton was so close to Lilburne on this point, he remained silent when ordered by the Rump to refute Lilburne's fierce attack on the Republic: *Life Records*, 2:239–40. Cf. *CJ*, 6:110–111, which asserts the Commons' resolution that the people are "the original of all just power."

37 See *A Defence of the English People*, where Milton praises Pride's Purge, an event inspired by God, and notes that the troops were wiser than the legislators on this crucial political occasion; the soldiers were citizens acting on behalf of the people: *CPW* 4:330, 332–33, 457, 458. See also *Observations*, *CPW* 3:328.

38 For Milton's subsequent critical view of those in power in the Rump, see his remarks to Hermann Mylius (9 February 1651/52) in Leo Miller, *John Milton and the Oldenburg Safeguard* (New York, 1985), pp. 171–72; and the Digression to *The History of Britain*. See also *Second Defence*, *CPW* 4:671.

39 Woolrych, *Commonwealth*, pp. 6, 392–93; Toby Barnard, *The English Republic, 1649–1660*, 2nd edn. (London and New York, 1997), p. 10.

40 Cited from *Macbeth*, ed. Kenneth Muir, The Arden Shakespeare (1962; repr. London, 1976). For the allusion, see the edition of *The Tenure* by W. T. Allison, *Yale Studies in English*, 40 (New York, 1911), p. 59; and Martin Dzelzainis' introduction to his edition, *John Milton: Political Writings* (Cambridge, 1991), p. xi. See also Martin Dzelzainis, "Milton, Macbeth, and Buchanan," *SC*, 4 (1989), 56–58, where he catches echoes of the play and makes connections with Buchanan; my emphasis is more on connections between verbal equivocation and the politics of rebellion.

41 *Stuart Constitution*, p. 288; *The Obstructours of Justice*, p. 63. On Charles as "a Man of Blood," see Patricia Crawford, "'Charles Stuart, That Man of Blood'," *JBS*, 16, 2 (1977), 41–61; Stephen Baskerville, "Blood Guilt in the English Revolution," *SC*, 8, 2 (1993), 181–202; Sarah Barber, *Regicide and Republicanism: Politics and Ethics in the English Revolution, 1646–1659* (Edinburgh, 1998), ch. 4.

42 *An Apologeticall Declaration of the Conscientious Presbyterians*, pp. 8, 9. See also [Zacheus Breedon] *The Humble Advice and Earnest Desires of certain well-affected Ministers . . . To his Excellency Thomas Lord Fairfax* (London, 1649), pp. 8–9, 10.

43 See Goodwin, *The Obstructours of Justice*, p. 53, for a similar argument (though without alluding to Lady Macbeth).

44 Cf. Dell, *City-Ministers unmasked*, pp. 12, 13. See also Price, *Clerico-Classicum*,

p. 26, though Milton makes the point about their contradictory hermeneutics more memorably.

45 Dzelzainis suggests an echo here with *Macbeth* 3.5.4–5: "Milton, *Macbeth*, and Buchanan," 56.

46 See *Mercurius Politicus*, no. 55, 19–26 June 1651, pp. 880–81. Milton's reference to "those two Oaths of Allegeance and Supremacy observ'd *without equivocating, or any mental reservation*" (3:228) also evokes the issue of equivocation associated with the Jesuits. Cf. *CPW* 1:573, 582, 896. On Jesuit equivocation, see Perez Zagorin, *Ways of Lying: Dissimulation, Persecution, and Conformity in Early Modern Europe* (Cambridge, MA, 1990), esp. pp. 155, 163, 187, 191, 204–5, 208–9, 211, 212–13.

47 The revision in the *Character* to "the counterfeit zeal" (*CPW* 5:448) likewise conveys the theatrical sense. Cf. *CPW* 5:447 where he refers to their "great shew of zeal" and *The Likeliest Means* on "thir pretended reformation" (7:295); also *A Defence*, *CPW* 4:512–13, and *Readie and Easie Way*, *CPW* 7:453–54. See also *A Parallell between the Ministerial Ingenuity of the Forty seven London Ministers* on the Presbyterians' "faire pretences" as they operate from their pulpits (sig. A2r). Nicholas von Maltzahn has recently dated the Digression to late February 1648/49, thereby connecting it with *The Tenure*: *Milton's History of Britain: Republican Historiography in the English Revolution* (Oxford, 1991), ch. 2.

48 Cf. Lucy Hutchinson on her husband's abhorrence of "that mallitious zeale" of the Presbyterians: *Memoirs of the Life of Colonel Hutchinson*, ed. James Sutherland (London, 1973), p. 166; and William Walwyn on "artificiall Clergie men" who are "the grand incendiaries of our present miseries" (*The Compassionate Samaritane* (1644), in *Walwyn*, p. 111).

49 Milton refers here to Prynne's attack on the Rump and Army in *A Briefe Memento to the Present Unparliamentary Junto* (London, 1648), published on 4 Jan. 1649.

50 *City-Ministers unmasked*, p. 22. From his different political perspective, Hobbes too stressed Presbyterian artifice and sedition: *Behemoth*, in *English Works*, 6:193–96.

51 Cf. *A Defence*: "restless for power . . . they never cease their seditious attacks against the present government as formerly against the king" (*CPW* 4:335). On Presbyterian dissembling, see also Goodwin, *Sion-Colledge*, p. 11.

52 See Lana Cable, "Milton's Iconoclastic Truth," in *Politics, Poetics, and Hermeneutics in Milton's Prose*, pp. 135–51; David Loewenstein, *Milton and the Drama of History: Historical Vision, Iconoclasm, and the Literary Imagination* (Cambridge, 1990), ch. 3; Skerpan, *The Rhetoric of Politics in the English Revolution*, pp. 117–25; Sharon Achinstein, "Milton and King Charles," in *The Royal Image: Representations of Charles I*, ed. Thomas N. Corns (Cambridge, 1999), pp. 153–57.

53 On the king as rebel to the kingdom, see also Goodwin, *The Obstructours of Justice*, p. 53; cf. pp. 71, 73, 78–80. Charles was accused of raising new commotions and rebellions and "of revolting from the Parliament": Act of 6

Jan. 1648/49 in *Acts and Ordinances*, 1:1253; "The Charge against the King" (20 Jan. 1648/49), in *Constitutional Documents*, p. 373.

54 On the subversion of Parliament's laws, liberties, and power by the king and his counsellors, cf. John Pym's reply to the Earl of Strafford on the occasion of his impeachment in *Stuart Constitution*, pp. 195–97; Joshua Sprigge, *Anglia Rediviva; Englands Recovery* (London, 1647), pp. 3–5.

55 See Milton's Commonplace Book, *CPW* 1:465; cf. *Eikonoklastes*, *CPW* 3:390, for Milton on Spenser and justice. On Milton's reading of Spenser's work, see Willy Maley, "How Milton and Some Contemporaries Read Spenser's *View*," in *Representing Ireland: Literature and the Origins of Conflict, 1534–1660*, ed. Brendan Bradshaw, Andrew Hadfield, and Willy Maley (Cambridge, 1993), pp. 191–208; Paul Stevens, "Spenser and Milton on Ireland: Civility, Exclusion, and the Politics of Wisdom," *Ariel*, 26 (1995), 151–67.

56 On the rebellion in its wider seventeenth-century context, see T. C. Barnard, *Cromwellian Ireland: English Government and Reform in Ireland, 1649–1660* (Oxford, 1975), ch. 1.

57 Henry Jones, *A Remonstrance of Divers Remarkable Passages concerning the Church and Kingdome of Ireland* (London, 1642), p. 1; *The Speech of Bulstrode Whitelocke . . . Concerning the Propositions . . . made by divers Gentlemen, Citizens, and others, for the speedy reducing of the Kingdom of Ireland* (London, 1642), p. 4. Cf. Sir John Temple's authorized history, *The Irish Rebellion* (London, 1646), p. 16. On the revolt posing the danger of the subversion of the Protestant religion, see also *Mercurius Hibernicus* (Bristol, 1644), p. 22; [Thomas Grant], *The Plott and Progresse of the Irish Rebellion* (London, 1644), "A Postscript." On the fear of popish plots in the 1640s, see Brian Manning, *The English People and the English Revolution, 1640–1649* (London, 1976), ch. 2

58 Milton's *Observations* responds in detail to this Belfast Presbyterian text reprinted by Hughes; the Presbyterians' phrase "lawlesse Anarchie" appears in *CPW* 3:298.

59 The *Observations*, perhaps because of its disturbing ideological implications, has received relatively little attention from scholars: see note 6 above. Sirluck touches on it only briefly in "Milton's Political Thought" (see p. 213). See also Hughes' discussion of its background in *CPW* 3:168–83.

60 See *Articles of Peace Made and Concluded with the Irish Rebels, and Papists, by James Earle of Ormond, For and in behalfe of the late King* (May 1649), in *CPW* 3:259–91; see also the related correspondence to which Milton also responds: 3:291–95.

61 *Life Records*, 2:240.

62 Though, as John Morrill reminds us, we should perhaps also remember that the brutal episodes "which have caused most controversy in the last century or so" – Cromwell's massacres at Drogheda and Wexford – were not the subject of debate or denunciation in the mid-seventeenth century: "Cromwell and His Contemporaries," in *Oliver Cromwell and the English Revolution*, ed. Morrill (London and New York, 1990), p. 267. See also Toby Barnard, "Irish Images of Cromwell," in *Images of Oliver Cromwell: Essays for*

and by Roger Howell, Jr., ed. R. C. Richardson (Manchester and New York, 1993). pp. 182–83.

63 For a recent account of Cromwell's conquest, see Ian Gentles, *The New Model Army in England, Ireland, and Scotland, 1645–1653* (Oxford, 1992), ch. 11.

64 On the Irish Rebellion as monstrous and satanic, see Cook's *King Charls his Case*, p. 28 (Cook was the lawyer who prosecuted the king at his trial). See also John Canne, *The Improvement of Mercy* (London, 1649), p. 19; Audley Mervyn, *An Exact Relation of all such occurrences as have happened . . . in the North of Ireland since the beginning of this horrid . . . Rebellion* (London, 1642), p. 1; Edward Bowles, *The Mysterie of Iniquity* (1643), p. 44; *The Kingdomes Monster Uncloaked from Heaven* ([London], 1643), verses about the monstrousness of popery and Irish rebellion. For recent accounts of the Irish Rebellion and its origins, especially in the context of English hostility to popery, see Conrad Russell, *The Fall of the British Monarchies, 1637–1642* (Oxford, 1991), ch. 10; Caroline M. Hibbard, *Charles I and the Polish Plot* (Chapel Hill, 1983), ch. 9. See also Aidan Clarke, "Ireland and the General Crisis," *P&P*, 48 (1970), 79–99; *Ireland: From Independence to Occupation, 1641–1660*, ed. Jane Ohlmeyer (Cambridge, 1995).

65 See Henry Parker's unfinished tract, *The Irish Massacre* (1646), pp. 2–3; and Parker's *The Manifold Miseries of Civil Warre and Discord in a Kingdome* (London, 1642), pp. 6–8. On the rebellion as hellish and savage, see also John Whincop's parliamentary sermon, *Israel's Tears or Distressed Zion* (London, 1645), p. 22; *The Plott and Progresse of the Irish Rebellion*, p. 10; Cook, *King Charls his Case*, pp. 29–30.

66 Richard Baxter, *Reliquiae Baxterianae*, ed. Matthew Sylvester (London, 1696), Part I, pp. 26, 28–29, 37; cf. *The Kingdomes Monster*. On the Irish Rebellion generating a national mood of fear and anxiety, see also Manning, *The English People and the English Revolution*, pp. 23–28; David Underdown, *Fire from Heaven: Life in an English Town in the Seventeenth Century* (New Haven, 1992), pp. 194–95; Russell, *The Fall of the English Monarchies*, ch. 10.

67 *Writings and Speeches*, 2:198–99; Barry Coward, *Oliver Cromwell* (London, 1991), pp. 19, 73; Worden, *Rump Parliament*, p. 216. See also Barnard, *Cromwellian Ireland*.

68 Fletcher, *The Outbreak of the English Civil War*, p. 136.

69 [Thomas Waring], *A Brief Narration of the Plotting, Beginning & Carrying on of the Execrable Rebellion and Butcherie in Ireland* (London, 1649/50), title page, pp. 1, 23–29; *Life Records*, 2:286. Attempting to link Waring's portrait of the devilish Irish with Milton's devils, Catherine Canino identifies the work Milton was assigned to print with Waring's *An Answer to certain seditious and Jesuitical Queres* (1651): "The Discourse of Hell: *Paradise Lost* and the Irish Rebellion," *MQ*, 32, 1 (1998), 15–23. Canino suggests that "it is not clear which book Milton took to be printed" (22 n. 6); I disagree. Waring's *Narration* was published closer to the date of the Rump's request (Thomason's copy is dated 19 March 1649/50) and includes more extensive material on "the Bloody Massacre in Ireland"; Waring's later text provides

more on the longer history of Ireland. Though the second text is addressed to Cromwell, the *Narration* refers to Cromwell's recent military victories and his "prosperous" role as Lord Governor of Ireland (pp. 32–33, 63) and is better suited to the historical moment; the *Narration* also refers to the Articles of Peace between Ormond and the devilish Irish (p. 35; misnumbered 27).

70 In *A Defence* Milton suggests that "some 200,000 English were slain . . . in the single province of Ulster" (*CPW* 4:431). Cf. the figures of some of Milton's contemporaries: John Cook suggests that 152,000 Protestants were "most barbarously and satanically murthered" (*King Charls his Case* (London, 1649), p. 28); commenting on "that cursed rebellion in Ireland" Lucy Hutchinson suggested that more than 200,000 were massacred in two months (*Memoirs of the Life of Colonel Hutchinson*, p. 51); John Canne gave a similar figure in *The Golden Rule*, p. 17, as did Baxter (*Reliquiae*, Part I, pp. 28, 37). A more likely estimate is that 4,000 Protestants died immediately. For contemporary historical accounts of the revolt and its reputed atrocities, see Jones, *A Remonstrance*; Temple, *The Irish Rebellion*.

71 On the rhetoric of Foxean antipopery in relation to the Irish Rebellion, see Ethan Howard Shagan, "Constructing Discord: Ideology, Propaganda, and English Responses to the Irish Rebellion of 1641," *JBS*, 36 (1997), 9–17.

72 *The Kings Cabinet Opened* (London, 1645), p. 44; cf. p. 55. For Milton's familiarity with the king's "cabinet," see e.g. *CPW* 3:397, 484, 523, 525, 526, 537–43, 544, 594. On Charles's apparent willingness to negotiate with the Confederate Catholics, offering them toleration for their religion in return for troops, see Barnard, *Cromwellian Ireland*, p. 6.

73 See Barnard, *Cromwellian Ireland*, p. 6, on the king's willingness to negotiate in the early 1640s. On plans to use the largely Catholic Irish army to subdue Scotland in 1640, see Russell, *The Fall of the British Monarchies*, pp. 127–29.

74 See Cook, *King Charls his Case*, on Charles and the Irish rebels: "he hath since above forty times called them his Subjects, and his good Subjects" (p. 28). For Lilly, see *Monarchy or no Monarchy in England* (London, 1651), p. 105; for his praise of Milton, see p. 81. During his trial by the Rump, Charles was also linked with "the Irish rebels and revolters": see selections in Sharp, *Political Ideas of the English Civil Wars*, p. 48. Conrad Russell has indeed suggested because Charles could tolerate Catholics more than Puritans, he "might have been happier as . . . a King of Ireland than he ever was as King of England" (*The Fall of the British Monarchies*, p. 397). On Charles and the Irish, see also S. R. Gardiner, *History of the Great Civil War*, 4 vols. (1893; repr. New York, 1965), 1:110–27.

75 *Memoirs of the Life of Colonel Hutchinson*, pp. 51–52, 127, 160.

76 *Eikon Basilike: The Portraiture of His Sacred Majesty in His Solitudes and Sufferings*, ed. Philip A. Knachel (Ithaca, NY, 1966), p. 63.

77 Lilly, *Monarchy or no Monarchy*, p. 78; also p. 79.

78 See Waring, *A Brief Narration*, pp. 56, 58, 61, 62.

79 For other early references, see *Church-Government*, *CPW* 1:798–800. The

Cessation Treaty of September 1643, when Charles arranged a cease-fire with the Irish rebels, only fueled suspicions that the devious king was behind the rebellion: see *Eikonoklastes*, *CPW* 3:483–84, 525; Hibbard, *Charles I and the Popish Plot*, pp. 213–16, 225.

80 On Milton's contribution in June 1642 of £4 to a collection for Ireland, see *Life Records*, 2:66–67. Gordon Campbell notes, however, that the manuscript in the Public Record Office is badly damaged and "the evidence strongly circumstantial rather than conclusive" (*A Milton Chronology* (London, 1997), p. 75).

81 [John Lilburne], *Regall Tyrannie Discovered* (London, 1647), p. 51. For Cook see *King Charls*, p. 28. Cf. Lilly, *Monarchy or no Monarchy*, p. 104. See also John Morrill, *The Nature of the English Revolution* (London, 1993), p. 64; William Lamont, *Richard Baxter and the Millennium* (London, 1979), pp. 88–98.

82 See, besides *CPW* 3:473 already cited in my text, 3:474, 475, 478, 481, 482, 483, 537, 580, 596; *A Defence*, *CPW* 4:522, 524. On secrecy as a hallmark of Charles's political style, see Ann Hughes, *The Causes of the English Civil War* (London, 1991), p. 157.

83 Ludlow, *A Voyce from the Watch Tower, Part Five: 1660–1662*, ed. A. B. Worden, (London, 1978), pp. 206, 274; cf. p. 300.

84 See also Milton's *A Defence* for a similar claim: *CPW* 4:430–31, 522. Cf. Price, *Clerico-Classicum*, p. 9; Goodwin, *The Obstructours of Justice*, p. 97; Cook, *King Charls his Case*, pp. 5, 36. See also "The Charge against the King" which called Charles "the occasioner, author, and continuer of the said unnatural, cruel and bloody wars": *Constitutional Documents*, p. 374; and the Remonstrance of the Army, November 1648, in *Stuart Constitution*, p. 288.

85 See *Certaine Sermons or Homilies appointed to be read in Churches* (London, 1623), pp. 276, 304.

86 On attempts to link the king and his court with the Irish Rebellion for purposes of propaganda, see Clarendon, *History*, 1:399–400, 480, 558–59, 2:6; see also Keith J. Lindley, "The Impact of the 1641 Rebellion upon England and Wales, 1641–5," *Irish Historical Studies*, 18 (1972), 164, 166, 176.

87 *Walwyn*, pp. 38, 40, 41, 372, 373; [William Kiffin et al.], *Walwins Wiles* (London, 1649), sig. A3, p. 21; *Tyranipocrit, Discovered* (Rotterdam, 1649), p. 35. See also Norah Carlin, "Irish and Natural Man in 1649, in *Europe and Its Others*, ed. Francis Barker et al. (Colchester, 1984), p. 91; Carlin, "The Levellers and the Conquest of Ireland," *HJ*, 30 (1987), 269–88; Patricia Coughlan, "'Cheap and Common Animals': The English Anatomy of Ireland in the Seventeenth Century," in *Literature and the English Civil War*, ed. Thomas Healy and Jonathan Sawday (Cambridge, 1990), p. 209; Christopher Hill, "Seventeenth-Century English Radicals and Ireland," in *A Nation of Change and Novelty: Radical Politics, Religion and Literature in Seventeenth-Century England* (London, 1990), ch. 8. For Marten and the Irish Rebellion, see C. M. Williams, "The Anatomy of a Radical Gentleman: Henry Marten," in *Puritans and Revolutionaries*, ed. D. Pennington and Keith Thomas (Oxford, 1978), p. 126. On Leveller sympathies for the Irish, see also Gentles, *New Model Army*, pp. 330–31.

88 *Writings and Speeches*, 2:124, 127.
89 *British Appeals*, pp. 12–13, 39. Cf. Waring, *A Brief Narration*, pp. 13, 41–64; and on the prosecution of revenge, see sig. A3r. The apocalyptic fervor stimulated by the Irish crisis was by no means quelled later during the Interregnum: in *The Visitation of the Rebellious Nation of Ireland* (1656), the Quakers Francis Howgill and Edward Burrough represented the rebellious Irish as savage, ungodly, and sunk in Antichristian idolatry.
90 Feake, *A Beam of Light*, p. 36; *A Defence, CPW* 4:458. See also Waring, *A Brief Narration*, pp. 32–33, 63. Cf. the response of the moderate Puritan divine Ralph Josselin who hears "the great newes of the taking of Wexford" and putting the garrison and some of the inhabitants to the sword: *The Diary of Ralph Josselin, 1616–1683*, ed. Alan MacFarlane (London, 1976), p. 183. See also *Writings and Speeches*, 2:127.
91 See *CPW* 4:670: "The greatest events I shall relate, if I can, with the brevity comparable to the speed with which you are wont to achieve them. When all Ireland was lost, but for a single city, you transported the army and in one battle instantly broke the power of Hibernia." See also the *Observations, CPW* 3:312.
92 See Cromwell, *Writings and Speeches*, 2:124, who described the enemy at Drogheda "filled . . . with much terror." See also Gentles, *New Model Army*, pp. 107–8, 115, 350–57; Barnard, *The English Republic*, p. 15.
93 See also Algernon Sidney's Eunomius, who argues that commonwealths "better employ their power in war than kings" by citing the English Commonwealth "which in five years conquered absolutely Scotland and Ireland": *Court Maxims*, ed. Hans W. Blom, Eco Haitsma Mulier, and Ronald Janse (Cambridge, 1996), p. 18.
94 See also Waring, *A Brief Narration*, p. 30.

7 RADICAL PURITAN POLITICS AND SATAN'S REVOLUTION IN
PARADISE LOST

1 Vane, *A Healing Question Propounded* ([London, 1656]), p. 7. See also Vane's *The Retired Mans Meditations* (London, 1655), a work devoted "to the unmasking the Mysterie of Iniquity in the most Refined and Purest Forms" (title page); *Tyranipocrit, Discovered with his wiles* (Rotterdam, 1649), p. 35; and Christopher Feake, John Simpson, and George Cokayne, *A Faithful Discovery of a Treacherous Design of Mystical Antichrist Displaying Christs Banners* (London, 1654), sig. A2r.
2 *The Memorable Works of a Son of Thunder and Consolation: Namely, That True Prophet, and Faithful Servant of God* (London, 1672), pp. 871, 874–75; see also p. 873. Cf. William Dell, *The Tryal of Spirits* (London, 1653), pp. 52, 59, 63; and Vane, *The Retired Mans Meditations*, pp. 349–50 (the "false seducing spirit is capable of putting forth it self in a greater or lesser degree, in and under all formes, through counterfeit resemblances unto TRUTH").
3 *The History of the Life of Thomas Ellwood*, ed. C. G. Crump (London, 1900), pp. 171–73.

4 Herbert Zarov, "Milton and the Rhetoric of Rebellion," *MQ* 7 (1973), 47–50, Stevie Davies, *Images of Kingship in Paradise Lost: Milton's Politics and Christian Liberty* (Columbia, 1983), and Joan S. Bennett, *Reviving Liberty: Radical Christian Humanism in Milton's Great Poems* (Cambridge, MA, 1989), ch. 3, explore connections with Charles I and royal tyranny; Christopher Hill suggests connections between Satan, his rebel angels, and the military leaders of the Revolution, as well as the royalists: *Milton and the English Revolution* (Harmondsworth, 1979 [1977]), pp. 366–68, 371–72. See also Northrop Frye, *The Return of Eden: Five Essays on Milton's Epics* (Toronto, 1965), p. 28; and for the suggestion that Satan embodies "some of the ways in which the Good Old Cause had gone wrong," see Hill, *Milton and the English Revolution*, p. 366. Sharon Achinstein likewise suggests that the late Milton finds Interregnum leaders "satanic": *Milton and the Revolutionary Reader* (Princeton, 1994), p. 204. Support from the prose of 1659–60 for Milton's views of ambitious Army leaders can be found in *CPW* 7:328–29, 422, 430; but connections with Satan and the rebel angels remain tenuous. On Satan and Cromwell, see below.

5 Likewise, excessively specific historical interpretations of the poem's events can seem strained: see e.g. Hill's attempt to liken Satan's rebellion to Charles I raising his standard in the north and the celestial war to specific battles in the English Civil War: *Milton and the English Revolution*, pp. 371–72.

6 For a different perspective, emphasizing contradictions in Milton's own ideology, see Bob Hodge, "Satan and the Revolution of the Saints," in *Literature, Language, and Society in England, 1580–1680*, ed. David Aers, Bob Hodge, and Gunther Kress (Dublin, 1981), pp. 184–99.

7 In *Machiavelli and Republicanism*, ed. Gisela Bock, Quentin Skinner, and Maurizio Viroli (Cambridge, 1990), pp. 225–45; Worden of course recognizes Satan's false uses of republican discourses, but comes to some different conclusions about them and Milton's politics. On republican values and liberty in *Paradise Lost*, see also Thomas N. Corns, *Regaining Paradise Lost* (London, 1994), pp. 137–39; Mary Ann Radzinowicz, "The Politics of *Paradise Lost*," in *Politics of Discourse: The Literature and History of Seventeenth-Century England*, ed. Kevin Sharpe and Steven N. Zwicker (Berkeley, 1987), pp. 204–29; David Quint, *Epic and Empire: Politics and Generic Form from Virgil to Milton* (Princeton, 1993), pp. 268–69, 300–2, 305–7; and especially Norbrook, *English Republic*, ch. 10, who situates the poem's republicanism in relation to Lucan's *Pharsalia*.

8 See e.g. Lilburne, *The Just Mans Justification* ([London, 1646]), p. 15; *A Whip for the present House of Lords* ([London, 1647/48]), p. 13; *Regall Tyrannie Discovered* (London, 1647), p. 16; *Rash Oaths Unwarrantable* ([London, 1647]), p. 49; *An Impeachment of High Treason against Oliver Cromwell* (London, 1649), p. 48. See also James Sharpe, "The People and the Law," in *Popular Culture in Seventeenth-Century England*, ed. Barry Reay (London and Sydney, 1985), pp. 244–70; Brian Manning, *The English People and the English Revolution, 1640–1649* (London, 1976), pp. 269–74; and, for Milton and Cromwell,

Roger Lejosne, "Milton, Satan, Salmasius and Abdiel," in *Milton and Republicanism*, ed. David Armitage, Armand Himy, and Quentin Skinner (Cambridge, 1995), p. 107.

9 *England's Deliverance from the Northern Presbytery, Compared with its Deliverance from the Roman Papacy* (London, 1652), pp. 5, 7–8.

10 *The Fountain of Slaunder Discovered* (1649), in *Walwyn*, pp. 381–82.

11 *Tyranipocrit*, p. 14, cf. Walwyn, *The Fountain of Slaunder*, in *Walwyn*, p. 381, on the agent of Satan who "shrouds himself under the finest cloak of Religion," and Winstanley, *Works*, p. 446. The Ranter Coppe had attempted "the discovery, and uncovering of the wel-favoured Harlot" in his age of hypocritical Puritan godliness and moral zeal: *Ranter Writings*, p. 113.

12 *Rebels no Saints: or, A Collection of the Speeches, Private Passages, Letters and Prayers of those Persons lately Executed* (London, 1661), sig. A3v; see also p. 154. See as well Thomas Marriot, *Rebellion Unmasked* (London, 1661), pp. 16, 22, 23, 24.

13 *Rebellion Unmasked*, p. 22; also p. 16. Marriot preached this sermon on the occasion of Venner's Rising.

14 *An Impeachment of High Treason against Oliver Cromwell*, p. 8.

15 *The Hunting of the Foxes* ([London], 1649), p. 12. Chapter 1 of this study discusses other examples from Lilburne. On Cromwell's "religious pretences," see especially Lilburne's *As You Were* ([Amsterdam?], 1652). Also see *The Protector (so called) In Part Unvailed* (London, 1655), "To the Reader"; *A Declaration of the Free-born People of England, now in Armes against the Tyrannie and Oppression of Oliver Cromwell* (n.p., 1655).

16 *Memoirs of the Life of Colonel Hutchinson*, ed. James Sutherland (London, 1973), pp. 179–80, 191, 193, 208–9, 211–12. Lucy Hutchinson's dissimulating Cromwell with his "mock Parliaments" closely resembles Leveller depictions. Other critical depictions of Cromwell are surveyed by John Morrill in "Cromwell and His Contemporaries," in *Oliver Cromwell and the English Revolution*, ed. Morrill (London and New York, 1990), pp. 259–81. For the suggestion that there "is something of" Cromwell's major-generals (referred to as Turkish bashaws) in Milton's fallen angels, see Hill, *Milton and the English Revolution*, p. 366.

17 On Satan as "at some level, a portrait of Cromwellian . . . hypocrisy," see Worden, "Milton's Republicanism," in *Machiavelli and Republicanism*, pp. 241–42. On links between Milton's Satan and Cromwellian imperialism or opportunism, see also David Armitage, "John Milton: Poet Against Empire," in *Milton and Republicanism*, pp. 206–25 (esp. pp. 220–21); Hill, *Milton and the English Revolution*, p. 368; J. B. Broadbent, *Some Graver Subject* (New York, 1960), pp. 113–18; Howard Erskine-Hill, *Poetry and the Realm of Politics: Shakespeare to Dryden* (Oxford, 1996), pp. 199–201. The attempt to link a hypocritical Cromwell with Satan can be found at least as early as William Hayley, *The Life of Milton*, 2nd edn. (London, 1796), pp. 131–32, commenting on *PL* 3.682–89; but Hayley's tentative formulation suggests how uncertain such an identification is: "and, perhaps, the recollection of his having

been thus deluded inspired the poet with his admirable apology for Uriel deceived by Satan." Worden himself acknowledges that "the evidence for the development and the depth of Milton's personal hostility is thin" (p. 241). Milton's brief references to Cromwell in *Pro Se Defensio* (Aug. 1655) are by no means negative (*CPW* 4:703, 720); and in *Defensio Secunda* he attacks Presbyterians and other enemies who readily ascribe their mistakes to Cromwell's "trickery and deceit" (4:663). Milton would subsequently participate in Cromwell's funeral: *Life Records*, 4:244–45. Cf. Perez Zagorin, *Milton, Aristocrat and Rebel: The Poet and His Politics* (Woodbridge, Suffolk, 1992), p. 128 n. 9; and see Martin Dzelzainis, "Milton and the Protectorate in 1658," in *Milton and Republicanism*, pp. 183–85, for a succinct summary of the critical debate about Milton's ongoing allegiances to Cromwell.

18 See e.g. *Areopagitica*, *CPW* 2:539; *A Defence*, *CPW* 4:343, 350–51, 352, 383, 388, 466, 469, 485–86, 501, 504, 536; and more humorously, *Second Defence*, *CPW* 4:581. Cf. *Paradise Regained* 4.267–71. On Satan's use of Ciceronian rhetoric, see Barbara K. Lewalski, *Paradise Lost and the Rhetoric of Literary Forms* (Princeton, 1986), pp. 84–85, 94–95.

19 Here I would qualify Worden's claim that "it is the archfiend's false application of political vocabulary, not of religious vocabulary, that the poet exposes" ("Milton's Republicanism," p. 243).

20 Overton with William Walwyn's collaboration, *A Remonstrance of Many Thousand Citizens, and other Free-born People of England* ([London], 1646), pp. 5, 13. See also the Putney Debates in *Puritanism and Liberty*, p. 35 (comments by Captain [John] Merriman), and *The Hunting of the Fox or the Sectaries Dissected* (London, 1648), p. 48, for sectaries as "sons of Belial" casting off the yoke of God and king. For a different (and perceptive) account of Satan's rebellion, emphasizing his political response to a feudal God, see Stevie Davies, *Images of Kingship in Paradise Lost*, pp. 143–48.

21 E.g. where Milton praises "the Parlament and Military Councel [for doing] what they doe without precedent" (*CPW* 3:237).

22 See e.g. *Mercurius Politicus*, no. 103, 20–27 May 1652, pp. 1609–13.

23 See the retrospective statement about the Commonwealth's military power and conquests by the commonwealthsman in Sidney's analysis of Restoration statecraft in *Court Maxims*, ed. Hans W. Blom, Eco Haitsma Mulier, and Ronald Janse (Cambridge, 1996), p. 18; cf. Milton in April 1660 in *CPW* 7:480, where he recalls "a Parlament that conquerd both *Ireland*, *Scotland*, & all thir enemies in *England*, [and] defended thir friends." See also Worden, *Rump Parliament*, p. 86; Jonathan Scott, "The Rapture of Motion: James Harrington's Republicanism," in *Political Discourse in Early Modern England*, ed. Nicholas Phillipson and Quentin Skinner (Cambridge, 1993), p. 145.

24 *Mercurius Politicus*, no. 100, 29 April–6 May 1652, p. 1569.

25 [Thomas Waring], *A Brief Narration of the Plotting, Beginning & Carrying on of that Execrable Rebellion and Butcherie in Ireland* (London, 1650), p. 13; this text is discussed in Chapter 6.

26 John Aubrey reporting Milton's widow in *The Early Lives of Milton*, ed. Helen

Darbishire (London, 1932), p. 7; *Leviathan*, ed. C. B. Macpherson (1968; repr. Harmondsworth, 1985), Part 1, ch. 5.

27 Toland, *The Life of John Milton* (1698), in *The Early Lives of Milton*, p. 182.

28 Lilburne, *Englands Birth-Right Justified* ([London], 1645), p. 1; cf. George Foster, *The Sounding of the Last Trumpet* ([London], 1650), p. 38.

29 *The Time of the End* (London, 1657), p. 232; cf. p. 235.

30 On Milton's warning about pretended liberty, see the Digression, *CPW* 5:449; on "pretended reformation," especially of the Presbyterian clergy, see *Hirelings*, *CPW* 7:295.

31 See the helpful discussion of seventeenth-century tyranny in John Morrill, *The Nature of the English Revolution* (London, 1993), p. 288; see also Quentin Skinner on tyranny versus a free state in *Liberty before Liberalism* (Cambridge, 1998), pp. 48–57.

32 See also *Civil Power*, where Milton characterizes error as "slie and shifting" (*CPW* 7:261).

33 See Ludlow on King Charles before the High Court of Justice insisting that "the kingdome was his by inheritance . . . that being the originall of his title": *A Voyce from the Watch Tower, Part Five: 1660–1662*, ed. A. B. Worden (London, 1978), p. 131; Lucy Hutchinson, *Memoirs of the Life of Colonel Hutchinson*, p. 11.

34 Overton, *An Alarum To the House of Lords: Against their insolent Usurpation of Common Liberties and Rights of this Nation* (London, 1646), p. 3 and passim; *The Tenure*, *CPW* 3:202. See also *CPW* 3:220 where Milton observes "that Dukes, Earles, and Marqueses were at first not hereditary, not empty and vain titles," and 3:264 where he quotes Calvin on monarchs pretending "alwayes in thir Titles, to be Kings"; and cf. the Digression, *CPW* 5:451. For contemporary warnings against flattering members of the Commonwealth with "splendid" titles, see *Mercurius Politicus*, no. 89, 12–19 Feb. 1652, pp. 1409–13; [Francis Osborne], *A Perswasive to a Mutuall Compliance under the Present Government* (Oxford, 1652), p. 4; John Streater, *A Glympse of That Jewel, Judicial, Just, Preserving Libertie* (London, 1653), "To the Reader"; George Wither, *The British Appeals . . . On the behalfe of the Common-wealth of England* (London, 1651), p. 15; John Canne, *A Seasonable Word to the Parliament-Men* (London, 1659), p. 2.

35 For a harsher assessment, see Lucy Hutchinson on Cromwell's making of "mock titles": *Memoirs of the Life of Colonel Hutchinson*, p. 209.

36 See *CPW* 3:598.

37 William Prynne, *A Plea for the Lords* (London, 1648), p. 68; see also p. 7. See *The Tenure* (*CPW* 3:194–95) and Chapter 6 of this study.

38 Quotations from Nedham are from *Mercurius Politicus*, no. 96, 1–8 April 1652, pp. 1505, 1509, 1507; see also *A True State of the Case of the Commonwealth* (London, 1654), p. 3. On Satan as calumniator, see also *De Doctrina Christiana*, *CPW* 6:350.

39 On the Son of power, see Michael Lieb, "Milton's 'Chariot of Paternal Deitie' as a Reformation Conceit," *Journal of Religion*, 65 (1985), 359–77.

40 *Leviathan*, Part 1, ch. 11.

41 *Mercurius Politicus*, no. 77, 20–27 Nov. 1651, p. 1222.

42 For other references to Charles's equivocating and ambiguous replies, see *CPW* 3:480, 495, 4:510; and for his "cunning words," see 3:600.

43 *Walwyn*, pp. 381–82; see also p. 358.

44 See also Milton's attack on the potent tongues of the Belfast Presbyterians: *Observations*, *CPW* 3:327. On the English Presbyterians causing tumult, see as well *CPW* 4:626.

45 See Morrill, *Nature of the English Revolution*, ch. 1; Conrad Russell, *The Causes of the English Civil War* (Oxford, 1990), ch. 8; and the studies in *Conflict in Early Stuart England: Studies in Religion and Politics, 1603–42*, ed. Richard Cust and Ann Hughes (London, 1989). Cf. Kevin Sharpe, *The Personal Rule of Charles I* (New Haven, 1992), for the view that the king was neither autocratic nor tyrannical.

46 See e.g. *The Workes of the Most High and Mighty Prince, James* (London, 1616), pp. 500, 529; and (for a statement from the revolutionary years), *Hunting of the Fox*, p. 6.

47 Zagorin, *Aristocrat and Rebel*, p. 127.

48 So Milton's discussion of Christ and vicegerence suggests in *The Readie and Easie Way*: "All Protestants hold that Christ in his church hath left no vicegerent of his power, but himself without deputie, is the only head therof, governing it from heaven: how then can any Christianman derive his kingship from Christ . . . since Christ not only hath not left the least shaddow of command for any such vicegerence from him in the State . . . but hath expressly declar'd, that such regal dominion is from the gentiles, not from him" (*CPW* 7:429).

49 See Morrill, *Nature of the English Revolution*, pp. 14, 26. On Milton's own arguments for godly discipline, see *The Reason of Church-Government*, ch. 1.

50 See also Hobbes's discussion of sedition predicated on hatred and envy: *De Cive: The English Version*, ed. Howard Warrender (Oxford, 1983), p. 87.

51 Dramatizing at length (rather than treating allusively) the long-term origins of Satan's political unhappiness and spiritual fall into sin in this sacred poem would raise dangerous questions about Heaven, so Milton tries to avoid the delicate issue. See Leopold Damrosch, *God's Plots and Man's Stories: Studies in the Fictional Imagination from Milton to Fielding* (Chicago, 1985), pp. 92–93.

52 See e.g. Russell, *Causes of the English Civil War*: "One of the most conspicuous facts of 1642 is the lack of any warmth or enthusiasm for the King among most of those who had the experience of daily doing business with him" (p. 208); and the examples discussed in Morrill, *Nature of the English Revolution*, ch. 15.

53 Griffith Williams, *Vindiciae Regum; or, The Grand Rebellion* (Oxford, 1643), p. 87.

54 *A Voyce from the Watch Tower*, p. 208; on Ludlow writing in the mid-1660s, see Worden's introduction, p. 15. During the Revolution, the Independent minister John Goodwin cited this scriptural text as a reminder of the "Danger

of Fighting against God": *ΘΕΟΜΑΧΙΑ; or The Grand Imprudence of Men Running the Hazard of Fighting against God* (London, 1644), p. 13;

55 See Chapter 1 of this study; I cite phrases from *Plaine Truth without Feare or Flattery* (London, 1647), pp. 5–7.

56 Cf. *Paradise Regained*, where Jesus, like Gabriel, refers to Satan as "a Fawning Parasite" (1.452).

57 On royalist conspiracy and resistance movements in Milton's age, see David Underdown, *Royalist Conspiracy in England, 1649–1660* (New Haven, 1960). See also Stella P. Revard, *The War in Heaven: Paradise Lost and the Tradition of Satan's Rebellion* (Ithaca, NY, 1980), ch. 3, who places the political intrigue in Milton's Heaven in the context of the Gunpowder conspiracy.

58 As when Gloucester addresses Clarence: "We are not safe, Clarence, we are not safe" (I.1.70); see Milton's discussion of the "deep dissembler" Richard in *CPW* 3:361–62.

59 *To the Parliament of the Common-Wealth of England* (1659), in *Memorable Works*, p. 585.

60 *The Kings Cabinet Opened* (London, 1645), p. 45. On radical responses to the king's political style of secrecy, see my essay, "The King among the Radicals: Godly Republicans, Levellers, Diggers, and Fifth Monarchists," in *The Royal Image: Representations of Charles I*, ed. Thomas N. Corns (Cambridge, 1999), ch. 5.

61 Milton responded to the assertion of the Belfast Presbyterians that they "would not be looked upon as sowers of sedition, or broachers of Nationall and divisive motions" (*A Necessary Representation* [Feb. 1649], *CPW* 3:296).

62 Cf. *The Tenure* and Milton's reference to "lawless Kings, and all who so much adore them" (*CPW* 3:237); and *Observations*, *CPW* 3:307–8. On the political implications of idolatry in the polemical prose and final poems, see now Achsah Guibbory, *Ceremony and Community from Herbert to Milton: Literature, Religion, and Cultural Conflict in Seventeenth-Century England* (Cambridge, 1998), chs. 7–8.

63 See his chapter (19) on "Satan's Counter-work to the three-fold government of Christ," in *The Retired Mans Meditations*, p. 314; the millenarian Vane emphasized that Satan assumed "all formes" so as "to hinder and keep out the approaching glory and power of his second coming."

64 Lieutenant-Colonel William Goffe, in *Puritanism and Liberty*, p. 20.

65 *Politics* V.1.4, trans. H. Rackham (London, 1932), p. 373. This is the second kind of revolution defined by Aristotle; the first kind actually aims at changing the form of government, "for instance from democracy to oligarchy, or to democracy from oligarchy, or from these to constitutional government and aristocracy, or from those to these." Among numerous references to Aristotle's *Politics* in Milton's political writings, see e.g. *CPW* 1:572; 3:199, 204, 361; 4:343, 348, 356, 381, 438, 455–56, 477, 504; 7:484–85.

66 See *CPW* 7:458: "our freedom consists in the civil rights and advancements of every person to his merit." For Milton's retrospective complaint that "bold and active ambition rather then merit had commended" some men

to power during the 1640s, see the Digression, *CPW* 5:443, 445. For critical discussion of birth in relation to why men should be exalted in the Restoration, see the republican dialogues of Algernon Sidney in his *Court Maxims*, esp. pp. 201–2; see also pp. 28, 33 on hereditary power.

67 *Anti-Cavalierisme*, in *Tracts on Liberty*, 2:220. Goodwin was later deeply influenced by his reading of Milton's *Tenure*: see Chapter 6 of this study. For a different approach to Abdiel, see Lejosne, "Milton, Satan, Salmasius and Abdiel," who sees the seraph as "orthodox . . . to the point of being positively Salmasian" (*Milton and Republicanism*, p. 109).

68 See his *Appellation from the Sentence Pronounced by the Bishops and Clergy* (1558), in *The Works of John Knox*, ed. David Laing, 6 vols. (Edinburgh, 1846–64), 4:516. For *The Tenure*, see *CPW* 3:248.

69 *The First Blast of the Trumpet against the Monstrous Regiment of Women* (1558), in *Works*, 4:396, 370, 415. Among other revolutionary Calvinists Milton admired, Christopher Goodman likewise agreed with Knox's emphasis on the right of individual citizens to revolt against ungodly magistrates and idolatrous powers; see Quentin Skinner, *The Foundations of Early Modern Political Thought*, 2 vols. (Cambridge, 1978), 2:223–24, 234–37. Goodwin also cited Knox with approval in this regard: *The Obstructours of Justice* (London, 1649), pp. 46–47, 71.

70 *Anti-Cavalierisme*, 2:221, 222.

71 On Quaker constancy in the midst of great adversity, see Baxter, *Reliquiae Baxterianae* (London, 1696), Part II, p. 436; Michael R. Watts, *The Dissenters: From the Reformation to the French Revolution* (Oxford, 1978), pp. 227–28; and Chapter 8 of this study. For Col. Hutchinson, see *Memoirs of the Life of Colonel Hutchinson*, p. 212; cf. p. 272. See also N. H. Keeble, "'The Colonel's Shadow': Lucy Hutchinson, Women's Writing and the Civil War," in *Literature and the English Civil War*, ed. Thomas Healy and Jonathan Sawday (Cambridge, 1990), pp. 227–47, for a fine discussion of the *Memoirs* (including suggestive parallels with Milton's Samson).

72 On this dramatic encounter and the controversial issue of blasphemy, see my essay "Treason against God and State: Blasphemy in Milton's Culture and *Paradise Lost*," in *Milton and Heresy*, ed. Stephen Dobranski and John Rumrich (Cambridge, 1998), pp. 176–98. On Satan's connection with the two beasts of Rev. 13, cf. Vane, *Retired Mans Meditations*, p. 314.

73 See *The Tenure*, *CPW* 3:243; [John Price], *The Pulpit Incendiary* (London, 1648), p. 27 and passim. See also *Mercurius Politicus*, no. 54, 12–19 June 1651, p. 865, for violent Presbyterian rhetoric against the Republic, as well as no. 67, 11–18 Sept. 1651, pp. 1061–62.

74 *Memoirs of the Life of Colonel Hutchinson*, p. 191; cf. pp. 166, 225.

75 *The Pulpit Incendiary*, pp. 59, 47. Worden ("Milton's Republicanism," p. 230) suggests that Milton never uses the term "saints" to refer to a sense of fellow-feeling (as other radical Puritans did): yet the Puritan term is repeatedly and evocatively used during the War in Heaven, such as when God asks Michael to lead forth the "armed Saints" (6.47; cf. 6.767, 801, 882). Cf.

Eikonoklastes where Milton uses the term (as other radical Puritans did) to describe the saints binding kings in chains: *CPW* 3:598; see also *Tenure, CPW* 3:217, as well as 3:265.

76 *Nature of the English Revolution*, p. 19.

77 Notable studies of the politics of the parliament in Hell include Michael Wilding, *Dragons Teeth: Literature and the English Revolution* (Oxford, 1987), ch. 8; Diana Treviño Benet, "Hell, Satan, and the New Politician," in *Literary Milton: Text, Pretext, Context*, ed. Benet and Michael Lieb (Pittsburgh, 1994), pp. 91–113; Achinstein, *Milton and the Revolutionary Reader*, ch. 5.

78 *Court Maxims*, pp. 82–83. See *Vindiciae contra Tyrannos* in *Constitutionalism and Resistance in the Sixteenth Century*, trans. and ed. Julian H. Franklin (New York, 1969), p. 145, and for Milton's citation, *CPW* 4:659; Milton's nephew, John Phillips, also cites the work in his *Response*: *CPW* 4:905.

79 For this suggestion, see Worden, "Milton's Republicanism," p. 238.

80 Cf. Lejosne, "Milton, Satan, Salmasius and Abdiel," who, unpersuasively in my view, suggests that Abdiel repeats "the most common, standard royalist arguments" (p. 109).

81 On perceptions about Charles I's misgovernment, see also Morrill, *Nature of the English Revolution*, ch. 15.

82 *Court Maxims*, p. 96.

83 See also *Of Reformation*, where Milton refers to the early Father Cyprian who "compares those that neglecting *Gods* Word, follow the doctrines of men, to *Coreh, Dathan*, and *Abiram*" (*CPW* 1:564).

84 See *The City-Ministers unmasked* (London, 1649), p. 11. See also *A Parallell between the Ministerial Ingenuity of the Forty seven London Ministers* (London, 1649), pp. 29–30; and Marchamont Nedham on the Presbyterians in *Mercurius Politicus*, no. 2, 13–20 June, 1650, p. 18.

85 For some citations of this scriptural passage by Presbyterian divines, Independent radicals, and Levellers, among others, see Merritt Y. Hughes's discussion in *CPW* 3:56–58; Hughes, however, does not connect Milton's citation of the passage with the rebellion in Heaven. For royalist uses of the sins of Korah to highlight the dangers of rebellion against magistrates and ministers, see e.g. [John Spelman], *Certain considerations upon the duties both of prince and people* (1642), in Andrew Sharp, *Political Ideas of the English Civil Wars, 1641–1649* (London, 1983), p. 83; Griffith Williams, *Vindiciae Regum; or, The Grand Rebellion*, pp. 2, 7, 11–12, 13, 18; T[homas] S[wadlin], *Children of Beliall, Or, The Rebells* ([London?], 1647), p. 22; *Praemonitus, praemunitus* (London, 1648), p. 3; Edward Symmons, *A Vindication of King Charles* ([London], 1648), p. 31. For its use in the Restoration, as an instance of "men of pride and ambition" setting themselves against godly saints, see Algernon Sidney's *Court Maxims*, p. 189; and as a sign of divine judgment, see Bunyan, *The Pilgrim's Progress*, ed. Roger Sharrock (rev. edn., Harmondsworth, 1987), p. 157.

86 *A Serious and Faithfull Representation of the Judgements of Ministers of the Gospell within the Province of London* (London, 1649), pp. 9, 10.

87 *The Legall Fundamentall Liberties of the People of England* (London, 1649), p. 38.

88 E. M., *Protection Perswading Subjection* (London, 1654), p. 27; see also pp. 26, 28, 30. For other examples, see George Smith, *Gods Unchangeableness: or Gods Continued Providence* (London, 1655), pp. 43–44; John Moore, *Protection Proclaimed* (London, 1655), p. 6; MS. Rawlinson A.26 (Bodleian Library, Oxford), fol. 244.

89 For quotations from Marriot, see *Rebellion Unmasked*, pp. 12–14. See also [Thomas Lamb], *A Fresh Suit against Independency* (London, 1677), p. 49, for the connection between Korah and "our Separatists"; and for the condemned regicides compared to Korah, Dathan, and Abiram, see *Rebels no Saints*, p. 38.

90 For Goodwin, see *The Obstructours of Justice*, pp. 69, 53 (for the specific reference to Milton); for Canne's discussion of the scriptural story, see *The Golden Rule, Or Justice Advanced* (London, 1649), pp. 1–2.

91 *City-Ministers unmasked*, pp. 15, 12.

92 As Regina M. Schwartz notes in *Remembering and Repeating: Biblical Creation in Paradise Lost* (Cambridge, 1988), pp. 20–21.

93 See *Brief Notes*, *CPW* 7:469–86; the quotations are taken from p. 485. Griffith had preached his royalist sermon on 25 March and addressed it to the anti-sectarian General George Monck. For his use of the story of Korah and his rebels, see *The Fear of God and the King* (London, 1660), pp. 54–55, 57.

94 See *An Homilie against Disobedience and Wilfull Rebellion*, in *Certaine Sermons or Homilies appointed to be read in Churches* (London, 1623), p. 292; this orthodox text rejected any form of violent resistance.

95 [Roger Jones], *Mene Tekel; Or, The Downfal of Tyranny* (n.p., 1663), p. 41.

96 See Roger B. Manning, "The Origins of the Doctrine of Sedition," *Albion*, 12, 2 (1980), 99–121, esp. 100–1.

97 *An Alarum To the House of Lords*, p. 8.

98 *Walwyn*, p. 175, as well as pp. 180, 281, 282, 285, 289. See also John Saltmarsh on the papists and prelates reproaching Puritans and nonconformists "as factious and tumultuous" (*The Smoke in the Temple* (London, 1646), p. 25); and William Erbery, *The Testimony of William Erbery* (London, 1658), p. 16.

99 *The Just Defence of John Lilburn*, in *The Leveller Tracts, 1647–1653*, ed. William Haller and Godfrey Davis (New York, 1944), p. 452. See also *Englands Birth-Right Justified*, p. 10; and the Leveller petition, *To the right Honourable and Supreme Authority of this Nation, the Commons in Parliament Assembled. The humble Petition of many thousands* ([London, 1648]), pp. 2, 3–4, 7.

100 *Second Part of Englands New-Chaines Discovered* and *Englands New Chains Discovered*, in *The Leveller Tracts*, pp. 173, 165.

101 *Walwyn*, pp. 169, 115. See also pp. 352–53.

102 *Walwyn*, p. 354; see also p. 376.

103 *The Time of the End*, p. 225.

104 *Fides-Anglicana* (London, 1660), p. 26; [Jones], *Mene Tekel*, p. 61; John Goodwin, *Peace Protected, and Discontent Dis-armed* (London, 1654), p. 16; cf.

Burrough, *Memorable Works*, p. 125. See e.g. Acts 24:5 for Paul as "a mover of sedition among all the Jews."

105 Barry Coward, *Social Change and Continuity in Early Modern England* (London, 1988), p. 95; John Spurr, *The Restoration Church of England, 1646–1689* (New Haven, 1991), pp. 48, 51; Manning, "The Doctrine of Sedition," 102. See also Fox and Bunyan's pilgrim saints reproached as disturbers of the nation and causers of division: Fox, *Journal*, p. 379; *The Pilgrim's Progress*, p. 141.

106 On Presbyterians and the hierarchy of synods, see *The Humble Advice of the Assembly of Divines* (London, 1646), pp. 39, 51–52; Keith Lindley, *Popular Politics and Religion in Civil War London* (Aldershot, 1997), p. 357. For a study of polemical uses of contemporary religious satire in *Paradise Lost* itself, see now John N. King, *Milton and Religious Controversy: Satire and Polemic in Paradise Lost* (Cambridge, 2000), a book that appeared after mine was in press.

107 See also *CPW* 7:242, 243, 247–48, 299; Overton (with Walwyn), *A Remonstrance of Many Thousand Citizens*, criticizing the "*Synod* in judgement . . . countenancing only those of the *Presbytry*, and discountenancing all the Separation, *Anabaptists* and *Independents*" (p. 12); Lilburne, *A Copie of a Letter to Mr. William Prinne* (1645), facsimile in William Haller, ed., *Tracts on Liberty*, 3:184. Milton's rejection of synods was sharply countered by Joseph Jane: *Eikon Aklastos: The Image Unbroaken* ([London], 1651), p. 232. Independents, however, did not necessarily oppose the creation of a national synod: see Avihu Zakai, "Religious Toleration and Its Enemies: The Independent Divines and the Issue of Toleration during the English Civil War," *Albion*, 21, 1 (1989), 9–10.

108 See e.g. "The Epistle Dedicatory" to Parliament in Edwards' *Gangraena* (London, 1646).

109 See the epistle to *De Doctrina Christiana*: *CPW* 6:123.

110 See also Milton's engagement with Griffith over sedition portrayed in *Aeneid* 1.148–50: *CPW* 7:477–78.

111 Cf. Milton on such "cunning deceivers" in the first edn. of *The Readie and Easie Way*: *CPW* 7:355.

112 *The Fear of God and the King*, p. 34: "Little do these men understand the *deceitfulness* of their own *hearts*, which like *Africk*, is ever producing *new Monsters*."

113 On the godly persecuted as seditious in the Restoration, see Sidney, *Court Maxims*, pp. 192–93. For the phrases Lucy Hutchinson uses to describe her godly republican husband, see *Memoirs of the Life of Colonel Hutchinson*, p. 272.

114 Worden, "Milton's Republicanism," p. 244; Robert T. Fallon, *Divided Empire: Milton's Political Imagery* (University Park, 1995), p. ix. Worden emphasizes that Milton's "retreat from politics" is completed with *Paradise Regained*: pp. 244–45. See also William R. Parker, *Milton: A Biography*, 2 vols. (Oxford, 1968), 1:588–95; *John Milton*, ed. Stephen Orgel and Jonathan Goldberg (Oxford, 1990), p. xx (*PL* "barely allows its heretical views to be seen; it similarly suppresses its politics"). Cf. Radzinowicz, "The Politics of *Paradise Lost*," esp. pp. 204–5: my views on this matter remain closer to hers. See also Cedric C. Brown, "Great Senates and Godly Education: Politics

and Cultural Renewal in Some Pre- and Post-Revolutionary Texts of Milton," in *Milton and Republicanism*, p. 58.

115 *The Rehearsal Transpros'd: The Second Part*, ed. D. I. B. Smith (Oxford, 1971), p. 312. See also Ellwood on Milton in the Restoration living "a private and retired life": *The Life of Thomas Ellwood*, p. 88.

116 Jerome McGann, *Social Values and Poetic Acts: The Historical Judgment of Literary Work* (Cambridge, MA, 1988), p. 126. See also Kevin Sharpe and Steven N. Zwicker, "Politics of Discourse: Introduction," in *Politics of Discourse*, p. 19.

8 THE KINGDOM WITHIN: RADICAL RELIGION AND POLITICS IN *PARADISE REGAINED*

1 *A Treatise of Civil Power*, in *CPW* 7:255.

2 Edward Burrough, *A General Epistle to all the Saints* (London, 1660), p. 5.

3 Recent attempts to explore the poem's political implications include Christopher Hill, *Milton and the English Revolution* (Harmondsworth, 1979 [1977]), ch. 30; David Quint, "David's Census: Milton's Politics and *Paradise Regained*," in *Re-membering Milton: Essays on the Texts and Traditions*, ed. Mary Nyquist and Margaret W. Ferguson (New York and London, 1987), pp. 128–47, now incorporated in Quint's *Epic and Empire: Politics and Generic Form from Virgil to Milton* (Princeton, 1993), ch. 8; Michael Wilding, *Dragons Teeth: Literature in the English Revolution* (Oxford, 1987), pp. 249–57; Joan S. Bennett, *Reviving Liberty: Radical Christian Humanism in Milton's Great Poems* (Cambridge, MA, 1989), ch. 6; Laura L. Knoppers, "*Paradise Regained* and the Politics of Martyrdom," *Modern Philology*, 90, 2 (1992), 200–19, now revised in her *Historicizing Milton: Spectacle, Power, and Poetry in Restoration England* (Athens, GA, 1994), ch. 1.

4 For an extreme account of the gospel's government as anti-political in *Paradise Regained*, see Herman Rapaport, *Milton and the Postmodern* (Lincoln and London, 1983), p. 197.

5 See esp. Steven Marx, "The Prophet Disarmed: Milton and the Quakers," *SEL*, 32 (1992), 111–28, which aligns Milton with Quaker pacifism. As will become clear from my subsequent discussion, Milton's relation to Quaker radicalism in the poem is deeper and more complex than Marx's article suggests. On the pacifism of *Paradise Regained*, see also Wilding's *Dragons Teeth*, pp. 251–57. On the poem as an expression of political quietism, see Andrew Milner, *John Milton and the English Revolution: A Study in the Sociology of Literature* (London, 1981), pp. 167–70, 174–76, 178, 185–87. On retirement and retreat as Milton's response to the Restoration, see N. H. Keeble, *The Literary Culture of Nonconformity in Later Seventeenth-Century England* (Leicester, 1987), p. 19; and for the view that Milton's "retreat from politics is complete" with *Paradise Regained*, see Blair Worden, "Milton's Republicanism and the Tyranny of Heaven," in *Machiavelli and Republicanism*, ed. Gisela Bock, Quentin Skinner, and Maurizio Viroli (Cambridge, 1990), pp. 244–45.

6 On the resigned political inactivity and quietist attitude of radicals in the

Restoration, see J. R. Jones, *Country and Court: England, 1658–1714* (Cambridge, MA, 1978), pp. 138–39, and J. P. Kenyon, *Stuart England* (Harmondsworth, 1978), p. 185. This view has recently been challenged by Richard L. Greaves in *Deliver Us from Evil: The Radical Underground in Britain, 1660–1663* (Oxford and New York, 1986); idem, *Enemies under his Feet: Radicals and Nonconformists in Britain, 1664–1677* (Stanford, 1990); and idem, "Shattered Expectations? George Fox, the Quakers, and the Restoration State, 1660–1685," *Albion*, 24, 2 (1992), 237–59. On continuities in seventeenth-century radical experience, see also Smith, *Perfection Proclaimed*, p. 346; Tim Harris, "Introduction: Revising the Restoration," in *The Politics of Religion in Restoration England*, ed. Harris, Paul Seaward and Mark Goldie (Oxford, 1990), pp. 2–4; Barry Reay, *The Quakers and the English Revolution* (London, 1985), pp. 107–110; Jonathan Scott, "Radicalism and Restoration: The Shape of the Stuart Experience," *HJ*, 31, 2 (1988), 453–67; Gary S. De Krey, "Rethinking the Restoration: Dissenting Cases for Conscience, 1667–1672," *HJ*, 38, 1 (1995), 53–83.

7 On the interaction between politics, radical religion, and society in Milton's age, see Barry Reay's introduction to *Radical Religion*, esp. pp. 3, 15–16; see also Richard Bauman, *Let Your Words Be Few: Symbolism of Speaking and Silence among Seventeenth-Century Quakers* (Cambridge, 1983), p. 72, and Geoffrey F. Nuttall, *The Holy Spirit in Puritan Faith and Experience* (Oxford, 1947), pp. 119, 122.

8 Christopher Hill, *WTUD*, pp. 399–400, begins to note connections between *Paradise Regained* and its radical religious milieu; but the issue still deserves much more detailed investigation. For rich accounts of nonconformist literature in the Restoration, see Keeble, *The Literary Culture of Nonconformity in Later Seventeenth-Century England*, as well as his "'Till One Greater Man / Restore Us . . .': Restoration Images in Milton and Bunyan," *Bunyan Studies*, 6 (1995/96), 7–33.

9 For evidence that Winstanley himself later became a Quaker, see James Alsop, "Gerrard Winstanley's Later Life," *P&P*, 82 (1979), 73–81.

10 Having asked Ellwood in 1665 to read *Paradise Lost*, Milton asked the Quaker what he thought of it: "'Thou hast said much here of "Paradise Lost"','Ellwood responded, 'but what hast thou to say of "Paradise Found"?' He made me no answer, but sat some time in a muse." When Ellwood later went to visit Milton in London, Milton showed him the poem: "This is owing to you, for you put it into my head by the question you put to me at Chalfont, which before I had not thought of" (*The History of the Life of Thomas Ellwood*, ed. C. G. Crump (London, 1900), p. 145). On Milton's relation with Ellwood, see Elizabeth T. McLaughlin, "Milton and Thomas Ellwood," *Milton Newsletter*, 2 (1967), 17–28; on Ellwood's possible literary influence, see J. Max Patrick, "The Influence of Thomas Ellwood upon Milton's Epics," *Essays in History and Literature*, ed. Heinz Bluhm (Chicago, 1965), pp. 119–32.

11 Ellwood tells us that toward Penington Milton "bore a good respect" (*Life of Thomas Ellwood*, p. 89); Penington indeed helped Ellwood find employ-

ment as Milton's reader. For Penington's defense of the Good Old Cause, see *To the Parliament, the Army, and all the Wel-affected in the Nation, who have been faithful to the Good Old Cause* (London, 1659); on Penington and hirelings, see Ambrose Rigg's testimony in *The Works of the Long-Mournful and Sorely-Distressed Isaac Penington* (London, 1681[-80]), sig. br.

12 On Penington in Buckinghamshire, see Richard T. Vann, *The Social Development of English Quakerism, 1655–1755* (Cambridge, MA, 1969), pp. 15, 21–23; Margaret Spufford, "The Importance of Religion in the Sixteenth and Seventeenth Centuries," in *The World of Rural Dissenters, 1520–1725*, ed. Spufford (Cambridge, 1995), pp. 22, 59–60. For a helpful account of Penington's beliefs (though without reference to *Paradise Regained*), see Christopher Hill, *The Experience of Defeat: Milton and Some Contemporaries* (Harmondsworth, 1984), pp. 118–28.

13 *Memoirs of the Life of Colonel Hutchinson*, ed. James Sutherland (London, 1973), p. 167.

14 Moreover, though this is not the place to pursue the matter, Milton published the two radical religious tracts in a year of considerable sectarian agitation in which the Quakers were prominent: see Barry Reay, "The Quakers, 1659, and the Restoration of the Monarchy," *History*, 63 (1978), 193–213. I discuss the implications of this in a forthcoming essay, "Milton among the Religious Radicals and Sects: Polemical Engagements and Silences," *MS*, 40 (2001).

15 For accounts of the adverse conditions in which the early Quakers emerged, see esp. William C. Braithwaite, *The Beginnings of Quakerism*, 2nd edn., rev. Henry J. Cadbury (Cambridge, 1955) and *The Second Period of Quakerism*, 2nd. edn., rev. Henry J. Cadbury (Cambridge, 1961); Hugh Barbour, *The Quakers in Puritan England* (New Haven, 1964); Reay, *The Quakers and the English Revolution*; Vann, *The Social Development of English Quakerism*.

16 Fox, *Journal*, p. 1.

17 See Ellwood's testimony in Penington, *The Works*, sig. c2r; Penington, *To all such as Complain that they want Power* (London, 1661), pp. 7–8.

18 See the testimonies by George Fox, William Penn, Ellwood, and others preceding Penington's *Works* and the entry on Penington by J. W. Frost in the *Biographical Dictionary of British Radicals in the Seventeenth Century*, ed. Richard L. Greaves and Robert Zaller, 3 vols. (Brighton, 1982–84). Ellwood notes Penington's "great constancy and quietness of mind" during his many tribulations (sig. c4r). For the trials of the early Quakers compared to those of Job, see Fox's *Journal*, p. 311.

19 Cf. Knoppers, "The Politics of Martyrdom," who argues that the poem revises the contemporary politics of martyrdom which can be traced back to John Foxe; she, however, does not consider the importance of Quaker martyrdom.

20 Quoted from *Stuart Constitution*, p. 356: for Marvell, see *Poems and Letters*, 2:314. In addition, there was the Conventicle Act in 1664, the Five Mile Act in 1665 (two of the measures in the Clarendon Code), and proclamations against nonconformist preachers in 1668 and 1669; the Declaration of

Indulgence (1672) was canceled in 1673. On the persecution of Dissenters, see Gerald R. Gragg, *Puritanism in the Period of the Great Persecution, 1660–1688* (Cambridge, 1957); Braithwaite, *The Second Period of Quakerism*, ch. 2; Barbour, *The Quakers in Puritan England*, ch. 8; Vann, *The Social Development of English Quakerism*, ch. 3; Reay, *The Quakers in the English Revolution*, pp. 105–6; Michael R. Watts, *The Dissenters: From the Reformation to the French Revolution* (Oxford, 1978), ch. 3; Mark Goldie, "The Theory of Religious Intolerance in Restoration England," in *From Persecution to Toleration: The Glorious Revolution in England*, ed. Ole P. Gell, Jonathan I. Israel, and Nicholas Tyacke (Oxford, 1991), ch. 13; John Spurr, *The Restoration Church of England, 1646–1689* (New Haven, 1991), ch. 2.

21 *Life of Thomas Ellwood*, pp. 169–70.
22 Fell, *A Declaration and an Information From us the People of God called Quakers* (London, 1660), p. 2; Fox, *Journal*, p. 379, as well as pp. 220–21, 352–54, 392, 405–7, 425, 571–72. See also Richard Hubberthorne to George Fox, 29 March 1660, Swarthmore MSS. 4:18 (Friends House Library, London). During the Protectorate nearly two thousand Quakers suffered imprisonment: Alan Cole, "The Quakers and the English Revolution," *P&P*, 10 (1956), 44.
23 *The Memorable Works of a Son of Thunder and Consolation: Namely, That True Prophet, and Faithful Servant of God. . . Edward Burroughs* (London, 1672), p. 462.
24 Penington, *Works*, sig. c2r.
25 See Crisp's *Testimony Concerning James Parnell* (1662), in *Early Quaker Writings, 1650–1700*, ed. Hugh Barbour and Arthur O. Roberts (Grand Rapids, 1973), p. 164; Crisp notes how "in many travails and trials" the young Parnell "obeyed" "the workings of [God's] power in him" (p. 165).
26 *Works*, I, pp. 453–54.
27 See the entry for 11 April 1656 in *The Diary of Ralph Josselin, 1616–1683*, ed. A. Macfarlane (Oxford, 1991), pp. 366–67, on the Quaker James Parnell undertaking to fast forty days and nights. See also James Nayler, *Milk for Babes: and Meat for Strong Men* (London, 1661), pp. 2, 9; Nayler, *A Discovery of the Man of Sin* (London, 1654), p. 7; Fox, *Journal*, pp. 9, 119, 142, 589; Swarthmore MSS. 1:12, 4:181, 4:267. Also see Reay, *The Quakers and the English Revolution*, p. 36; and Braithwaite, *The Beginnings of Quakerism*, pp. 192, 246, 253, 372. And see Anna Trapnel's description of fasting before having prophetic visions: *The Cry of a Stone . . . being in the Visions of God* (London, 1654), pp. 1, 5.
28 See Reay, *The Quakers and the English Revolution*, p. 119.
29 See Greaves, "George Fox, the Quakers, and the Restoration State," 238–40; Hutton, *The Restoration*, p. 147.
30 Benjamin Furly, *The World's Honour Detected* (London, 1663), p. 54, quoted in Bauman, *Let Your Words Be Few*, p. 57.
31 [Roger Jones], *Mene Tekel; or, The Downfal of Tyranny* (n.p., 1663), pp. 49, 43; see also Greaves, *Deliver Us From Evil*, p. 223.
32 See Anthony Low's discussion of the poem's georgic mode in *The Georgic Revolution* (Princeton, 1985), pp. 322–52.

33 And see also *Civil Power*, *CPW* 7:257–58, where Milton cites and discusses 1 Cor. 1:27.

34 See Cary's *The Little Horns Doom & Downfall* (London, 1651), p. 262; on the saints as both humble and filled with the Spirit, see also pp. 247–48. See also Anna Trapnel, *A Legacy for Saints* (London, 1654), on the "meek spirit" of the saints (p. 40); and Edward Burrough's epistle to the reader in George Fox, *The Great Mistery of the Great Whore Unfolded* (London, 1659), sig. (c3)r, where the persecuted but undaunted Quakers are "meek, and humble, and sober."

35 *Memorable Works*, p. 462; cf. Penington, *Works*, I, p. 344: "We have been a poor oppressed People, from the day that the power of the Lord broke forth upon us." The Quakers tended to come from the middling and lower ranks of society, though the movement drew adherents from a wide social range: it attracted some prominent members from the gentry, including Ellwood, William Penn, and Penington himself.

36 See e.g. Anna Trapnel's untitled book of prophetic verses (1658), Bodleian Library (Oxford) S.1.42 Th, p. 185: "For it is thy design, O Lord, / All Monarchies to confound. / And a poor weak people thou hast chosen, / Instruments for it to be." See also Trapnel's *A Legacy for Saints*, pp. 49, 60.

37 John Cardell, *Gods Wisdom Justified, and Mans Folly Condemned* (London, 1649), p. 13. Cf. Cromwell's zealous speech to the Barebone's Parliament, 4 July 1653: *Writings and Speeches*, 3:53. See the illuminating discussion of power and God's humble servants (especially those in Cromwell's army) in Ian Gentles, *The New Model Army in England, Ireland, and Scotland, 1645–1653* (Oxford, 1992), pp. 99–100, 102–3; and Woolrych, *Commonwealth*, p. 8. See also Chapter 3 of this study.

38 *A Noble Salutation and a Faithful Greeting unto Thee Charles Stuart*, in *Early Quaker Writings*, pp. 391–92.

39 Winstanley, *Works*, pp. 238, 475; Penington, *Works*, I, p. 309.

40 *A True Testimony of Obedience to the Heavenly Call* ([London, 1654]), pp. 4–5; cf. James Nayler, *Love to the Lost*, 2nd edn. (London, 1656), p. 25. In *An Improvement of Imprisonment* (London, 1661), George Wither asserted that God would call his prophets from "the *Plow*, / From *Herds*, . . . *Fishing*, from a Trade / Which, in the World small reputation had" (p. 51). See also George Fox, *A General Epistle to Friends* ([London], 1668), p. 9, who stresses that the Word made many fishermen prophetic preachers; and Swarthmore MSS. 2:106 (6 Nov. 1669), where Fox wonders: "Sheppherds & herdsmen wheer are you: what can you saye for God whose abideing is much in the fields, David, Jacob & Amos your fellowe Shepperds & herdsmen . . . they could saye much for God."

41 *Life of Thomas Ellwood*, p. 13. Nayler himself was at the plow "meditating on the things of God" when he was called in 1652: see Barbour, *Quakers*, p. 115.

42 Thus the fiery Quaker writer, James Parnell, attempting to level and reform traditional notions of honor and nobility, observed that "all the true Prophets of God were Noblemen and Gentlemen . . . though of the Nobles

and great Ones of the Earth" they were disdained "because according to the World they were of low Degree, some of them Ploughmen, some Herdsmen, some Shepherds"; and Christ too was "Noble" though he was "scorned to be the King of the Jews" because "according to the World he was of low Degree": see *A Collection of the Several Writings* (London, 1675), p. 90.

43 On the Spirit's work in terms of leading and guiding radical Puritans, see Barbour, *Quakers*, pp. 25–28, 115–17.

44 Howgill, *The Inheritance of Jacob Discovered* (1656), in *Early Quaker Writings*, p. 169.

45 See William Penn's preface to Fox's *Journal*, p. xxxix; cf. Fox's description of his early "gravity and stayedness of mind and spirit not usual in children" (*Journal*, p. 1). See also Melvin B. Endy, *William Penn and Early Quakerism* (Princeton, 1973), pp. 54, 58.

46 As Louis L. Martz notes, "in secret" conveys the Latin *in secreto*: "in solitude, in a solitary place, in retirement" (*Milton: Poet of Exile* (New Haven, 1980), p. 248).

47 Penington, *Works*, II, p. 188 (cf. II, 322, 391–92); and Ellwood's testimony, sig. c2r.

48 *Life of Thomas Ellwood*, p. 155; cf. pp. 51, 66.

49 Ellwood's testimony: Penington, *Works*, sig. c2v.

50 *CPW* 7:380 ("ther would be . . . no more pretending to a fifth monarchie of the saints"). Though more prevalent in the 1650s (see Chapters 3 and 5 of this study), the Fifth Monarchist movement refused to die in the 1660s: not only did Venner's rising of 1661 make them infamous, but Christopher Feake was still arousing concern in 1664. See Greaves, *Enemies Under His Feet*, p. 123; De Krey, "Dissenting Cases for Conscience, 1667–1672," 71–72; and B. S. Capp, *The Fifth Monarchy Men* (London, 1972). For a contemporary attempt to link Milton with the Fifth Monarchists, see *The Censure of the Rota Upon . . . The Ready and Easie Way* (London, 1660), p. 12. See also Hill, *Milton and the English Revolution*, p. 447; Knoppers, *Historicizing Milton*, ch. 5.

51 *Life of Thomas Ellwood*, p. 55; Ellwood alludes to John 18:36 (cf. Milton's *Hirelings*: *CPW* 7:313). Ellwood called Venner's insurrection "that mad prank of those infatuated fifth-monarchy men." See also Fox, *Journal*, pp. 394, 404, 410, 419–20. On Venner's rising and the subsequent persecution of religious radicals, see *The Diary of Samuel Pepys*, ed. Robert Latham and William Matthews, 11 vols. (Berkeley and Los Angeles, 1970–83), 2:11; Ronald Hutton, *The Restoration: A Political and Religious History of England and Wales, 1658–1667* (Oxford, 1985), pp. 150–52, 169, 171; Greaves, *Deliver Us from Evil*, pp. 50–58.

52 See Cole, "The Quakers and the English Revolution," 39–54; Reay, *The Quakers and the English Revolution*, pp. 41–42; Greaves, *Deliver Us from Evil*, pp. 11, 99, 200–1; Greaves, *Enemies*, p. 136; Greaves, "George Fox, the Quakers, and the Restoration State"; and Christopher Hill, "Quakers and the English Revolution," *JFHS*, 56, 3 (1992), 165–79, esp. pp. 170–71, 175. Isaac Penington himself believed that the sword might be "borne uprightly" to

"suppress violent and evil-doers": H. Larry Ingle, *First Among Friends: George Fox and the Creation of Quakerism* (New York and Oxford, 1994), pp. 195–96 (quoting *Works*, 2nd edn. [1761], 1:449).

53 E[dward] B[urrough], *A Declaration of the present Sufferings . . . of the people of God . . . called Quakers* (London, 1659), p. 29. Cf. George Fox, *The Great Mistery of the Great Whore Unfolded* (London, 1659), p. 122.

54 On the poem's redefinition of wisdom in relation to an inner spiritual kingdom, see Barbara K. Lewalski, *Milton's Brief Epic: The Genre, Meaning, and Art of Paradise Regained* (Providence and London, 1966), ch. 11.

55 J. C., *A Defence of the True Church* (1659), p. 29, cited in Reay, *The Quakers and the English Revolution*, p. 42; Penington, *Works*, II, p. 322. Cf. Burrough, *General Epistle to all the Saints*, p. 15.

56 See *Fire in the Bush* (1650), in *Works*, pp. 470, 458. Cf. the Ranter Jacob Bauthumley: "I could wish that such a spirit of righteousnesse would appear, that men did not act or do things from externall laws, but from an internall law within" (*Ranter Writings*, p. 260). On the Lord as "inward Teacher," see also John Lilburne, *The Resurrection of John Lilburne* (London, 1656), p. 13.

57 *The Face of the Times*, in *Two Treatises* ([London], 1662), pp. 59, 73. Cf. James Nayler, *Behold you Rulers: And hearken proud Men and Women* (London, 1660), p. 4.

58 *The Blood of the Martyrs is the Seed of the Church* ([London], 1669), p. 7; this text by Fox is added to *The Arraignment of Popery*.

59 *Antichrist's Government Justly Detected* (1661), in *Memorable Works*, p. 876.

60 *The Examination and Tryall of Margaret Fell and George Fox* [London], 1664), pp. 14–15, 7.

61 *The Testimony of William Erbery* (London, 1658), p. 189.

62 *A Message from the Spirit of Truth* (London, 1658), p. 4.

63 *Works*, p. 234; cf. his characterization of the inward ruling "spirit of truth" as "the rock that will never fayl" (p. 129).

64 *A Beam of Light, Shining in the Midst of much Darkness and Confusion* (London, 1659), p. 58.

65 *Journal*, p. 340; *A general epistle to Friends* ([London?], 1670), p. 8. Fox described Christ as "the R O C K and F O U N D A T I O N of all the Righteous in their Ages" (*Primitive Ordination and Succession, of Bishops, Deacons, Pastors and Teachers in the Church of Christ* [London?], 1675), p. 49. See also Cary, *The Little Horns Doom & Downfall*, pp. 191–92. Cf. Milton's reference to Christ as the true rock (referring to 1 Cor. 10:4) and the sole foundation in *Christian Doctrine*, *CPW* 6:567.

66 *The Life and Death of Mr. Vavasor Powell* (London, 1671), p. 198 (misnumbered p. 178).

67 Recounted in *The Recantation of Lieutenant Collonel John Lilburne, Prisoner in the Tower* (London, 1647), pp. 3–4; see also [Clement Walker], *The Triall of Lieut. Collonell John Lilburne . . . at the Guild-Hall of London* ([London, 1649]), p. 128. For Lilburne's imprisonment in Oxford during 1642–43, see Pauline Gregg, *Free-born John: A Biography of John Lilburne* (London, 1961), pp. 100–5.

68 *Enemies Under His Feet*, p. 137; Ellwood, *Life*, p. 186. See also Richard Baxter, *Reliquiae Baxterianae*, ed. Matthew Sylvester (London, 1696), Part II, p. 436, on Quaker resoluteness and constancy in the Restoration.

69 *Works*, pp. 231–32.

70 On Satan's pagan sense of time and vocation, see Barbara K. Lewalski, "Time and History in *Paradise Regained*," in *The Prison and the Pinnacle*, ed. B. Rajan (Toronto, 1973), pp. 49–81.

71 For different treatments of "due time" in the poem, see Laurie Zwicky, "Kairos in *Paradise Regained*: The Divine Plan," *ELH*, 31 (1964), 271–77, and Edward W. Tayler, *Milton's Poetry: Its Development in Time* (Pittsburgh, 1979), pp. 148–84. On Puritan providentialism in relation to the waiting of the English saint, see Blair Worden, "Providence and Politics in Cromwellian England," *P&P*, 109 (1985), 65. For the theme of waiting "with patience and quietnesse of spirit under all temptations" in the works of Gerrard Winstanley, see *The New Law of Righteousnes*, in *Works*, pp. 178, 223, 231, 243.

72 *Court Maxims*, ed. Hans W. Blom, Eco Haitsma Mulier, Ronald Janse (Cambridge, 1996), p. 92.

73 *Hopes Incouragement* (London, 1644), p. 9.

74 *Puritanism and Liberty*, p. 136; cf. Cromwell in the Putney debates, p. 101. See also Erbery, *The Testimony*, p. 18: "Wait here a while for that Spirit and Power from on high to appear in us . . . and at last . . . we shall be led forth out of this confusion and *Babylon*."

75 *Paralellogrammaton* ([London], 1662), p. 59; cf. p. 79.

76 *Works*, I, p. 459. Penington, observing in 1659 that the work of the Lord had been set back, passionately urged the whole nation to wait upon the Lord: *To the Parliament*, sig. A2v. On waiting patiently for the Lord's "mighty appearance," cf. George Fox the younger, *A Noble Salutation*, in *Early Quaker Writings*, pp. 403–4, and Burrough, *General Epistle to all the Saints*, p. 16.

77 Cary, *The Little Horns Doom & Downfall*, p. 60.

78 On Milton's brief epic in relation to Revelation in particular, though without emphasis on political issues, see Samuel Smith, "'Christs Victorie over the Dragon': The Apocalypse in *Paradise Regained*," *MS*, 29 (1992), 59–82.

79 *A True Prophecie of the Mighty Day of the Lord* (London, 1655), p. 12; see also p. 4. Cf. Sir Henry Vane, *The Retired Mans Meditations* (London, 1655), p. 147.

80 *Christ's Famous Titles, And A Believers Golden-Chain* (London, 1666), pp. 5, 67, 7; cf. p. 28: "Christ is a King that *lives for ever*, and reigns for ever; other Kings they are but of yesterday." See also *Mene Tekel* and George Wither, *Meditations upon the Lords Prayer* (London, 1665), p. 60, on the coming of Christ's kingdom as the means to freedom from temporal governments.

81 *The Rehearsal Transpros'd: The Second Part*, ed. D. I. B. Smith (Oxford, 1971), p. 312.

82 Penn, *No Cross, No Crown* ([London], 1669), pp. 69–72.

83 See *Tetrachordon* where Milton writes of Christ's harsh response to the Pharisees: "And as the offence was in one extreme, so the rebuke, to bring more efficaciously to a rectitude . . . stands not in the middle way of duty,

but in the other extreme" (*CPW* 2:668); and *Doctrine and Discipline of Divorce* (2:282–83). "A sharp & corrosive sentence" comes from the same passage in *Tetrachordon.* Elsewhere Milton compares Christ to "a wise Physician administring one excess against another . . . [he] hath often us'd *hyperbolies* in his teaching" (2:745).

84 See also Peggy Samuels, "Labor in the Chambers: *Paradise Regained* and the Discourse of Quiet," *MS,* 36 (1998), 153–76 (esp. 168–69), for illuminating comments on the Son's reforming vehemence in relation to the Anglican discourse of quietness in the Restoration.

85 See Barbour, *Quakers,* pp. 158–59. For examples of Milton's emphasis on the Spirit's internal illumination and its "supreme authority," see *CPW* 6:579–80, 587–88, 589–90.

86 *The Cry of a Stone,* p. 42; John Cardell, *The Necessity of Divine Instructions in point of Reformation* (London, 1648), p. 10.

87 George Fox, *Trying of Spirits in our Age now as in the Apostles Days* (London, 1683), p. 21, writing of "the fair speeches" of the ungodly ministers and apostles of Satan. See also Milton's *Civil Power:* "in matters of religion he is learnedest who is planest" (*CPW* 7:272); and *Of True Religion, CPW* 8:434.

88 See e.g. William Penn's preface to the original edition of Fox's *Journal* (London, 1694): sig. F2r-v. On Milton's polemical uses of rhetorical plainness in his last pamphlets, see James Egan, "Milton's Aesthetic of Plainness, 1659–1673," *SC,* 12, 1 (1997), 57–83.

89 *A Noble Salutation,* in *Early Quaker Writings,* p. 402; cf. Fell, *A Declaration and an Information,* p. 8. See also John Canne, *A Seasonable Word to the Parliament-Men* (London, 1649), pp. 5–6, on plain dealing and the Good Old Cause. On plain style in Quaker discourse and prophecy, see Bauman, *Let Your Words Be Few.* Other Quaker prophets, critical of the evils of the new regime, consciously evoked in their writings the admonishing tone and spirit of such Hebrew prophets as Jeremiah and Amos and engaged in apocalyptic exhortations: see Greaves, "George Fox, the Quakers, and the Restoration State," 241, for examples from 1662.

90 See also Wither's *Meditations upon the Lords Prayer* on Jesus as a model for the saints: "God leadeth us into some *temptations,* either to be exemplary, or to prove us both for his honour and our own; as when our *Saviour* was *led into the wilderness to be tempted of the Devil*" (p. 173; cf. pp. 156–57).

9 THE SAINT'S REVENGE: RADICAL RELIGION AND POLITICS IN
SAMSON AGONISTES

1 See Francis Howgill's testimony prefacing Edward Burrough, *The Memorable Works of a Son of Thunder and Consolation: Namely, That True Prophet, and Faithful Servant of God . . . Edward Burroughs* (London, 1672); Howgill echoes Judges 15:16. Cf. Burrough to Margaret Fell in Swarthmore MSS 3:17 (1655), Friends House Library, London: he participates "in the ware before whom many Philistian hath fallen."

2 I quote from *A Treatise of Civil Power*, in *CPW* 7:261.

3 On this matter, see especially the review of evidence in Anthony Low, *The Blaze of Noon: A Reading of Samson Agonistes* (New York, 1974), pp. 222–27 (emphasizing correspondences between *De Doctrina Christiana* and the play); Mary Ann Radzinowicz, *Toward Samson Agonistes* (Princeton, 1978), pp. 387–407; and Christopher Hill, *Milton and the English Revolution* (Harmondsworth, 1979 [1977]), pp. 481–86. I am inclined to agree that the dramatic poem was completed after the Restoration.

4 My references, however, will be to a spectrum of revolutionary Puritan writers, some of whom were more spiritually radical than others: there will be references to the writings of John Owen, the Independent minister, and to Oliver Cromwell (a leader often driven by millenarian passions), as well as to the fiery writings of early Quaker prophets.

5 For further confirmation of this, see also the studies by Richard Greaves cited above in Chapter 8, note 6.

6 Milton is not alone in his age in this respect: on the difficulty of identifying Cromwell and many others with any one sect or "way," see J. C. Davis, "Cromwell's Religion," in *Oliver Cromwell and the English Revolution*, ed. John Morrill (London and New York, 1990), pp. 184–85, 207. See also Arthur E. Barker, *Milton and the Puritan Dilemma, 1641–1660* (Toronto, 1942), p. xxiv.

7 For various discussions of Milton's work in relation to the Restoration, see Sharon Achinstein, "*Samson Agonistes* and the Drama of Dissent," in *MS*, 33 (1996), 133–58, as well as the following studies: Nicholas Jose, *Ideas of the Restoration in English Literature* (Cambridge, MA, 1984), pp. 142–63; Laura L. Knoppers, *Historicizing Milton: Spectacle, Power, and Poetry in Restoration England* (Athens, GA, 1994), chs. 2 and 6; and especially the richly textured study by Blair Worden, who considers the context of the trials of regicides in 1662, in "Milton, *Samson Agonistes*, and the Restoration," in *Culture and Society in the Stuart Restoration: Literature, Drama, and History*, ed. Gerald MacLean (Cambridge, 1994), pp. 111–36.

8 On radical religion in Milton's age, see e.g. Michael A. Mullett, *Radical Religious Movements in Early Modern Europe* (London, 1980); *Radical Religion*; Geoffrey Nuttall, *The Holy Spirit in Puritan Faith and Experience* (Oxford, 1947) and *Visible Saints: The Congregational Way, 1640–1660* (Oxford, 1957); Smith, *Perfection Proclaimed*; Michael R. Watts, *The Dissenters: From the Reformation to the French Revolution* (Oxford, 1978), chs. 1–3.

9 On radical religion and revolution, see esp. B. Reay, "Radicalism and Religion in the English Revolution: an Introduction," in *Radical Religion*, pp. 1–21. See also the radical chaplain Hugh Peter's comments in the Whitehall Debates: *Puritanism and Liberty*, p. 138.

10 Davis, "Cromwell's Religion," pp. 188, 199; Nuttall, *The Holy Spirit*.

11 *Hopes Incouragement* (London, 1644), p. 17. This sermon by Young was delivered before the House of Commons.

12 *Fire in the Bush* (1650), in *Works*, p. 488. Cf. his advice to the saints to wait with "quietnesse of spirit under all temptations" (p. 178).

376 Notes to pages 272–76

13 *General Epistle to all the Saints* (London, 1660), p. 14.

14 *Hopes Incouragement*, p. 20; on Samson as valiant saint who grew strong in waiting upon God, see p. 15. Cf. George Smith, *Gods Unchangeabless: or Gods Continued Providence* (London, 1654/55), p. 44.

15 Cf. *Areopagitica* on the Bible, which "brings in holiest men passionately murmuring against providence" (*CPW* 2:517).

16 See e.g. Stanley Fish, "Spectacle and Evidence in *Samson Agonistes*," *Critical Inquiry*, 15, 3 (1989), 556–86; and especially Joseph Wittreich, *Interpreting Samson Agonistes* (Princeton, 1986).

17 *A Warning from the Lord to the Inhabitants of Underbarrow* (1654), in *Memorable Works*, p. 3.

18 See e.g. *CPW* 6:587, 589, as well as 490–91. For valuable discussion of this topic, see also Norman T. Burns, "'Then Stood up Phinehas': Milton's Antinomianism, and Samson's," *MS*, 33 (1996), 27–46.

19 *A Serious and Faithfull Representation of the Judgements of Ministers of the Gospell within the Province of London* (London, 1649), p. 13.

20 *A Voyce from the Watch Tower, Part Five: 1660–1662*, ed. A. B. Worden (London, 1978), p. 126; also pp. 199–200.

21 Fox, *Journal*, pp. 53, 57, 108, 179. On the Spirit's motions in radical religion, see Hugh Barbour, *The Quakers in Puritan England* (New Haven, 1964), pp. 25–28.

22 See Nuttall, *The Holy Spirit*, ch. 2. See also Captain John Clarke in the Putney Debates, who stresses that human reason should be subservient to submitting to the Spirit of God: *Puritanism and Liberty*, pp. 38–39. Cf. the recent discussion of Milton's drama by Joan S. Bennett, *Reviving Liberty: Radical Christian Humanism in Milton's Great Poems* (Cambridge, MA, 1989), ch. 5, esp. pp. 129, 132, 137, 140, 150; and Radzinowicz, *Toward Samson Agonistes*. For a critique of scholars who have overstressed the role of reason in Milton's drama, see William Kerrigan, "The Irrational Coherence of *Samson Agonistes*," *MS*, 22 (1987), 217–32.

23 See e.g. Fox on Quakers, who for years underwent great sufferings with patience and meekness: *Journal*, pp. 277, 353, 381.

24 Ludlow, *A Voyce from the Watch Tower*, pp. 240, 115; Winstanley, *Works*, p. 391. On Ludlow in relation to Milton and the Restoration, see Worden, "Milton, *Samson Agonistes*, and the Restoration," passim.

25 *The Time of the End* (London, 1657), p. 22. For the influence of *The Tenure* on Canne's revolutionary writing, see *The Golden Rule, Or, Justice Advanced* (London, 1649). See also John Cook on Samson's "valiant exploits" and "the Spirit of the Lord" moving "in *Sampson*": *Monarchy No Creature of Gods making* (London, 1651), p. 23.

26 *Puritanism and Liberty*, p. 41.

27 Cromwell, for example, wrote of "an unexpected providence" in bringing judgment on Drogheda and Wexford: *Writings and Speeches*, 2:142. See also the work of the Fifth Monarchist John Cardell, *Gods Wisdom Justified, and Mans Folly Condemned* (London, 1649), p. 37; and Ian Gentles, *The New Model Army in England, Ireland, and Scotland, 1645–1653* (Oxford, 1992), pp. 116–17.

28 See Cromwell to Sadler (31 Dec. 1649) and his speech of 4 July 1653 to the Nominated (Barebone's) Parliament: *Writings and Speeches*, 2:186, 3:53; see also 3:435 on "the Lord's bringing us through so many changes and turnings, as have passed upon us." Cf. Smith, *Gods Unchangeableness*, p. 40. The theme of God's providence is pervasive in Cromwell's writings: in the Barebone's Parliament speech he observed that "in taking off the King, the House of Peers, the pulling down of the Bishops, changing the government, . . . there is a remarkable print of Providence set upon it" (3:54). The radical minister William Dell agreed: see *The City-Ministers unmasked* (London, 1649), p. 25; cf. Milton's *A Defence*, *CPW* 4:499, on "the wonder-working hand of God," and for providence working in the Revolution, see *The Tenure*, *CPW* 3:193. On providential issues in the age, see Blair Worden, "Providence and Politics in Cromwellian England," *P&P*, 109 (1985), 55–99; Anthony Fletcher, "Oliver Cromwell and the Godly Nation," in *Oliver Cromwell and the English Revolution*, ed. John Morrill (London and New York, 1990), ch. 8; Barbara Donagan, "Providence, Chance, and Explanation: Some Paradoxical Aspects of Puritan Views of Causation," *JRH*, 2, 2 (1980), 385–403. On Milton and Sadler, see William R. Parker, *Milton: A Biography*, 2 vols. (Oxford, 1968), 1:250, 313.

29 *A Sermon Preached to the Parliament* (Oxford, 1652), p. 25 (misnumbered 17).

30 *The Advantage of the Kingdome of Christ in the Shaking of the Kingdoms of the World* (Oxford, 1651), p. 8. Cf. the Chorus of *Samson Agonistes* on "vain reasonings," lines 322–25.

31 Cardell, *Gods Wisdom Justified*, p. 9.

32 On Cromwell submitting to providence, see e.g. *Writings and Speeches*, 2:9. See also Captain John Clarke in the Putney Debates: *Puritanism and Liberty*, p. 39. On submitting to the divine even when it was inscrutable, see J. C. Davis, "Religion and the Struggle for Freedom in the English Revolution," *HJ*, 35, 3 (1992), 523.

33 Young, *Hopes Incouragement*, p. 17; cf. p. 19, where he refers to Isaiah 40:31: "they that waite upon the Lord shall renew their strength."

34 *Some of the Misteries of Gods Kingdome Declared, as they have been revealed by the Spirit through Faith* (London, 1658), p. 10.

35 John Canne, *A Voice from the Temple to the Higher Powers* (London, 1653), p. 10. On Canne and Overton, see Barbara Taft, "'They that pursew perfaction on earth . . .' The Political Progress of Robert Overton," in *Soldiers, Writers and Statesmen*, ed. Ian Gentles, John Morrill, and Blair Worden (Cambridge, 1998), pp. 290–91. On God's "secret Providence" and his permitting "something contrary extraordinarily to be done," see also Theodore Haak's commentary on Judges 14:3 in *The Dutch Annotations upon the whole Bible . . . Now faithfully communicated to the use of Great Britain, in English* (London, 1657).

36 Smith, *Gods Unchangeableness: or Gods Continued Providence*, p. 7. See also Cromwell's reference to "an unexpected providence" in God bringing judgment upon Wexford in October 1649: *Writings and Speeches*, 2:142. Cf. Burrough, *Memorable Works*, pp. 592, 612, on the hand of the Lord in wondrous "Overturnings" and "Overthrowings."

37 *Gods Delight in the Progresse of the Upright* (London, 1649), p. 46. Cf. Thomas Banaster, *An Alarum to the World, of the Appearing of Sions King* (London, 1649), p. 5.

38 *Newes Coming up out of the North, Sounding towards the South* (London, 1654), p. 32; cf. pp. 9, 10, 12, 21, 34. See Chapter 4 of this study for further discussion of Fox's fiery writings of the English Revolution.

39 *An Alarm to the Priests; or, A Message from Heaven* (London, 1660), p. 7; Stephen Crisp, *An Epistle to Friends, Concerning the Present and Succeeding Times* (London, 1666), p. 13. The emphasis on the fierceness of the day of God's wrath and vengeance which threatens the ungodly runs throughout early Quaker discourse: see e.g. James Nayler, *A Discovery of the First Wisdom from Beneath, and the Second Wisdom from Above* (London, 1656), p. 24; and the fiery Interregnum prophecies by William Dewsbury. On the furious language of Restoration Quaker prophetic tracts, see also Ronald Hutton, *The Restoration: A Political and Religious History of England and Wales, 1658–1667* (Oxford, 1985), p. 147.

40 *The Shaking and Translating of Heaven and Earth* (London, 1649), p. 27. Cf. Banaster, *An Alarum to the World*, p. 5. On Owen's apocalypticism and the destruction of earthly monarchy, see Tai Liu, *Discord in Zion: The Puritan Divines and the Puritan Revolution, 1640–1660* (The Hague, 1973), pp. 65–66, 67.

41 See [Robert Ram], *The Souldiers Catechisme* (London, 1644), p. 9, and Cromwell's letter to William Lenthall after the battle of Preston (20 August 1648), in *Writings and Speeches*, 1:638; cf. 2:336. On the destruction of Babylon as God's work, see also John Dury, *Israel's Call to March out of Babylon unto Jerusalem* (London, 1646), p. 5.

42 *The New Law of Righteousnes*, in *Works*, p. 186; Howgill, *A Woe against the Magistrates, Priests, and People of Kendall* (London, 1654), p. 1. See also Mary Cary on the sudden ruin of Antichrist: *A Word in Season to the Kingdom of England* (London, 1647), p. 5; and on the suddenness of the terrible day of the Lord, see her *Little Horns Doom & Downfall* (London, 1651), p. 189 (referring to 2 Peter 3:10). Cf. Edmund Calamy who reminded the House of Commons in a sermon "that God can destroy a Nation in an instant" (*Englands Looking-Glasse* (London, 1642), p. 4), and Robert Everard who told Army leaders during the Putney Debates that "there is great expectation of sudden destruction" and need "to seek out some speedy way for relief of the kingdom": *Puritanism and Liberty*, p. 42.

43 *A Lamentation Unto this Nation* (London, [1661]), p. 5; her prophecy was delivered in March.

44 "Speculum Seculi: or, A Looking-Glass for the Times," in *The History of the Life of Thomas Ellwood*, ed. C. G. Crump (London, 1900), p. 120; *An Alarm to the Priests*, pp. 6, 3. One the day of the Lord as sudden and unexpected, cf. also Abiezer Coppe, *Some Sweet Sips, of some Spirituall Wine* (1649) and *A Fiery Flying Roll*, in *Ranter Writings*, pp. 53, 116.

45 Cf. *De Doctrina Christiana* on the workings of providence: "Even in sin, then, we see God's providence at work, not only in permitting it or withdrawing his grace, but often in inciting sinners to commit sin, hardening their hearts and blinding them" (*CPW* 6:331).

46 The reality of Cromwell's campaign – he did not instantly break the power of Ireland and he suffered setbacks – is discussed in Toby Barnard, "Irish Images of Cromwell," in *Images of Oliver Cromwell: Essays for and by Roger Howell, Jr.*, ed. R. C. Richardson (Manchester and New York, 1993), pp. 181–82.

47 *An Alarm to the Priests*, p. 3. Cf. Burrough, *Memorable Works*, pp. 665–66.

48 Fox, *Journal*, p. 74.

49 These are among the history lessons Christian learns in Palace Beautiful: *The Pilgrim's Progress*, ed. Roger Sharrock, rev. edn. (Harmondsworth, 1987), pp. 99–100.

50 For a full exploration of the God of dread in *Samson Agonistes*, especially from a biblical perspective, see Michael Lieb, "'Our Living Dread': The God of *Samson Agonistes*," *MS*, 33 (1996), 3–25.

51 *Newes Coming up out of the North*, pp. 13, 20; cf. pp. 7, 18, 25. See also Fox's prophetic tract, *A Voice of the Lord to the Heathen* (London, 1656), which warns of a God of dread shaking terribly the earth; and George Fox, the younger, *The Dread of Gods Power* (London, [1660]). But the notion of "the terror of the Lord" confounding "His enemies, as in that day" was by no means confined to the most radical of the period's religious writers: see Cromwell, *Writings and Speeches*, 1:619.

52 *A Warning from the Lord, to all such as hang down the head for a Day* (London, 1654), p. 8.

53 Burrough, *A Warning from the Lord to the Inhabitants of Underbarrow* (1654), in *Memorable Works*, pp. 3, 5.

54 John Anderdon, *Against Babylon and her Merchants in England* (London, 1660), p. 7; cf. Humphry Smith, *The Sounding Voyce*, p. 5. Cf. the "matchless Gideon" of Milton's drama: lines 277–89.

55 See Foster, *The Sounding of the Last Trumpet: Or, Severall Visions, declaring the Universall overturning and rooting up of all Earthly Powers in England* ([London], 1650), and Coppe, *The Fiery Flying Roll*, discussed in Chapter 3 of this book; for the levelling God of Winstanley and Fox, see Chapters 2 and 4. On the subject of economic and social levelling in mid-seventeenth-century revolutionary rhetoric, see also Maurice Goldsmith, "Levelling by Sword, Spade and Word," in *Politics and People in Revolutionary England*, ed. Colin Jones, Malyn Newitt, and Stephen Roberts (Oxford, 1986), pp. 65–80.

56 Coppe, *A Fiery Flying Roll*, in *Ranter Writings*, p. 87; Erbery, *The Armies Defence, or, God guarding the Camp of the Saints* (London, 1648), p. 20.

57 *Writings and Speeches*, 2:174. Cf. Erbery, *The Armies Defence*, p. 15.

58 *Writings and Speeches*, 1:669 (letter to William Lenthall, Speaker of the House of Commons, 9 Oct. 1648). See also Burrough, *Memorable Works*, p. 3; and John Canne, *A Seasonable Word to the Parliament-Men* (London, 1659): "God will not be mocked, and it is a fearful thing to fall into his hands" (p. 5).

59 The background for the notion of God as "a man of war" during the revolutionary years is considered in Barbara Donagan, "Did Ministers Matter? War and Religion in England, 1642–1649," *JBS*, 33 (April 1994), 119–56.

60 Burrough, *A Warning from the Lord*, in *Memorable Works*, p. 13.

61 On the godly saint executing God's wrath, see also Algernon Sidney, *Court Maxims*, ed. Hans W. Blom, Eco Haitsma Mulier, and Ronald Janse (Cambridge, 1996): "all who love him will ever be ready instruments in his hand to execute his wrath upon his . . . enemies" (p. 150).

62 Erbery, *The Armies Defence*, p. 14; see also pp. 8–9. The casting down of worldly strongholds echoes such scriptural passages as Micah 5:11, Isaiah 32:11, 2 Cor. 10:4.

63 Cf. Burrough, *General Epistle to all the Saints*, pp. 4–5.

64 On Milton's suppression of the traditional theme of suicide, see also the valuable comments by John Steadman, "Efficient Causality and Catastrophe in *Samson Agonistes*," *MS*, 28 (1992), 219–20. Cf. Wittreich, *Interpreting Samson Agonistes*, who sees Samson's final action "as a foolhardy embracing of self-destruction" (p. 231). Other scholars have simply taken for granted that the drama climaxes with suicide: e.g. Paul M. Dowling, *Polite Wisdom: Heathen Rhetoric in Milton's Areopagitica* (Lanham, MD, and London, 1995), p. 91.

65 On holy ruthlessness and militant Puritanism in Milton's age, see Gentles, *New Model Army*, pp. 107–8, 115, 119.

66 *A Commentary upon the Booke of Judges*, in *Most fruitfull & learned commentaries of Doctor Peter Martir* (London, 1564), fol. 236r. For Milton's familiarity with Martyr's commentary, see the Commonplace Book in *CPW* 1:455–56. Milton admires Martyr as a divine in *The Tenure of Kings and Magistrates*, *CPW* 3:221, as does John Goodwin who is indebted to *The Tenure* in *The Obstructours of Justice* (London, 1649): see pp. 32, 54, 58.

67 *A Woe against the Magistrates*, p. 5. Some modern readers have clearly been repulsed by Samson's vengeful act: in his first edition of Milton's shorter poems, for example, John Carey considers the catastrophe "morally disgusting" (*Milton: Complete Shorter Poems*, ed. Carey (London, 1971), p. 333). See also Irene Samuel, "*Samson Agonistes* as Tragedy," in *Calm of Mind: Tercentenary Essays on Paradise Regained and Samson Agonistes*, ed. Joseph Wittreich (Cleveland, 1971), pp. 235–57; and Wittreich, *Interpreting Samson Agonistes*, passim. More persuasive in my view is Michael Lieb's discussion of *Samson Agonistes* as a work that extols violence: see his *Milton and the Culture of Violence* (Ithaca, NY, 1994), pp. 226–63.

68 Cf. Wittreich, *Interpreting Samson Agonistes*, for the contrary argument that Samson's horrifying act is one of private revenge, shameful violence, and dubious heroism. But Wittreich also notes, quite rightly, that Miltonists have tended to discount revenge as a motive in the drama (see p. 46).

69 See *De Doctrina Christiana*, *CPW* 6:743, 755–56; cf. 346, 604. One could cite numerous examples from the polemical prose. For Milton's justification of divine revenge or vengeance, especially against haughty prelates and tyrannical kings or rulers, see e.g. *Church-Government*, *CPW* 1:793, 861, and *A Defence*, *CPW* 4:352; on divine vengeance on Salmasius and other false prophets, see e.g. *A Defence*, *CPW* 4:431, 499; on vengeance overdue in

regard to the dismemberment of the tyrant Domitian, see *A Defence, CPW* 4:446; on divine vengeance on Alexander More's unclean head, see *Second Defence, CPW* 4:599, 631.

70 *The Advantage of the Kingdome of Christ*, p. 13; *De Doctrina Christiana, CPW* 6:624. For a recent study of the ideological implications of slaughtering the infidel in the name of God, see Regina M. Schwartz, *The Curse of Cain: The Violent Legacy of Monotheism* (Chicago, 1998).

71 *Fides-Anglicana. Or, A Plea for the Publick-Faith of these Nation, Lately pawned, forfeited and violated by some of their former Trustees* (London, 1660), p. 25; see also p. 21 (where Wither discusses Ehud and other biblical figures moved by a divine impulse). Cf. Erbery, *The Armies Defence*, p. 15.

72 *Epistolium-Vagum-Prosa-Metricum: or, An Epistle at Randome, in PROSE and METRE* (London, 1659), p. 27.

73 After quoting Ps. 149 about binding kings in chains and their nobles in fetters of iron, Vane observed that it was the honor of the saints to administer "the revenging justice of God, so as to be a terrour unto all that presume to offend against the principles of natural good and right": *The Retired Mans Meditations* (London, 1655), p. 411.

74 *England's Deliverance From the Northern Presbytery, Compared with its Deliverance from the Roman Papacy* (London, 1652), p. 32 (misnumbered "16").

75 Here one might also compare Guyon's "tempest of his wrathfulnesse" (*Faerie Queene* II.xii.83) as he destroys the Bower of Bliss: another zealous Protestant response.

76 *The Trumpet of the Lord Sounded, And his Sword drawn* (London, 1654), p. 9.

77 Smith, *Gods Unchangeableness*, p. 11. See also Gentles, *New Model Army*, p. 94.

78 On the issue of submission and liberty in radical religious culture, see Davis, "Religion and the Struggle for Freedom," 518, 521, 523.

79 *Hopes Incouragement*, p. 38.

AFTERWORD TWO-HANDED ENGINE: POLITICS AND SPIRITUAL
WARFARE IN THE 1671 POEMS

1 Studies arguing for Milton's pacifist position include works by Steven Marx and Michael Wilding cited in Chapter 8, note 5. For recent studies challenging the notion of Milton's pacifism, see my book, *Milton and the Drama of History: Historical Vision, Iconoclasm, and the Literary Imagination* (Cambridge, 1990), ch. 6; Christopher Hill, *The Experience of Defeat: Milton and Some Contemporaries* (Harmondsworth, 1984), p. 315; and Michael Lieb, *Milton and the Culture of Violence* (Ithaca, NY, 1994).

2 See esp. Joseph Wittreich, *Interpreting Samson Agonistes* (Princeton, 1986), p. 374; Michael Wilding, *Dragons Teeth: Literature and the English Revolution* (Oxford, 1987), pp. 255–57.

3 *Fides-Anglicana. Or, A Plea for the Publick-Faith of these Nation, Lately pawned, forfeited and violated by some of their former Trustees* (London, 1660), pp. 25–26.

4 Thomas N. Corns, "'Some Rousing Motions': The Plurality of Miltonic

Ideology," in *Literature and the English Civil War*, ed. Thomas Healy and Jonathan Sawday (Cambridge, 1990), 110–26.

5 See Francis Howgill's testimony in Burrough, *The Memorable Works of a Son of Thunder and Consolation: Namely, That True Prophet, and Faithful Servant of God . . . Edward Burroughs* (London, 1672), sig. (e2)r, discussed in Chapter 9; Dewsbury, *The Word of the Lord to all the Inhabitants of England* ([London], 1666), pp. 5–7. See also Stephen Crisp's 1666 prophecy concerning "the mighty overturning Power of the Lord God Almighty . . . against this ungodly Generation": *An Epistle to Friends, Concerning the Present and Succeeding Times* (London, 1666), pp. 14–15.

6 *The History of the Life of Thomas Ellwood*, ed. C. G. Crump (London, 1900), pp. 116, 121. Cf. Ellwood's *Alarm to the Priests; or, A Message from Heaven* (London, 1660).

Index